Essentials of New Jersey Real Estate

Fifteenth Edition

Edith Lank

Joan m. Sobeck

with Contributing Editor Marie S. Spodek, CDEI, CNE, CBR

Dearborn
Real Estate Education

This publication is designed to provide accurate and authoritative information in regard to the subject matter covered. It is sold with the understanding that the publisher is not engaged in rendering legal, accounting, or other professional advice. If legal advice or other expert assistance is required, the services of a competent professional should be sought.

President: Dr. Andrew Temte
Executive Director, Real Estate Education: Toby Schifsky
Development Editor: Adam Bissen

ESSENTIALS OF NEW JERSEY REAL ESTATE FIFTEENTH EDITION
©2021 Kaplan, Inc.
Published by DF Institute, Inc., d/b/a Dearborn Real Estate Education
332 Front St. S., Suite 501
La Crosse, WI 54601

Printed in the United States of America

ISBN: 978-1-07-881175-0

CONTENTS

INTRODUCTION

ABOUT THIS BOOK

Essentials of New Jersey Real Estate, 15th Edition, was developed with input from New Jersey educators and was written by authors with extensive educational and practical real estate experience. The text is a valuable tool to help students prepare for real estate licensing exams, as well as for careers in real estate.

The complete version of the New Jersey License Act is reprinted, along with the state commission's rules and regulations.

Other features of this book include:

- twenty-two units organized so topical coverage parallels the state-mandated number of hours of instruction;

- complicated concepts explained in simple language—a reading level that avoids legal jargon and provides definitions for all technical terms the first time they are used;

- a list of key terms, summary of important concepts, key terms review activity, and set of multiple-choice review questions in each unit;

- a glossary of real estate terms that provides detailed definitions of all the key terms found in the text;

- two 110-question sample salesperson licensing exams; and

- helpful websites for each unit.

Getting Started in Real Estate

Now that you are considering a career in real estate, you want to consider certain practical aspects of the brokerage business.

There is no one profile for the successful real estate agent. Top agents, even in the same company, can be as different as day and night. Some are laid-back and quiet, others are energetic and boisterous. They may dress differently, from casual to business-like. Although it was always thought a successful salesperson should drive an immaculate four-door car, he or she may very well sit behind the wheel of a battered sports model, with multiple listing printouts piled high on the passenger seat and lollipop wrappers on the back floor.

Certain traits, though, help tremendously as you approach the business of brokerage.

You need to be a *self-starter*. You receive direction, training, and guidance from your supervising broker, but in the end, you're working for and largely by yourself. You set your own hours, choose your own goals, and pick your own tasks.

It helps to be *flexible*. Every day is different, and your income can be irregular. Sometimes a transaction in which you have invested weeks of work simply falls apart suddenly. On the other hand, a windfall may come in with little effort.

You have to be prepared for *irregular hours*. Yes, you can set your own hours, even sleep in some mornings. But when you're dealing with out-of-towners who have only two days to locate a house and arrange financing, you'll be lucky to find time to answer your cell phone. And you need to be available weekends and evenings, when most buyers are free for house-hunting.

These days, it is essential that you be *computer-literate*. Old-style hands-on service is still important, but most aspects of the brokerage business require you to continually master new technology. Learning how to use social media to your advantage is also key.

Beyond that, to achieve success, you *must enjoy what you're doing*. People who are in other jobs that they do not like watch the clock or count the years until retirement, but those who don't like real estate simply leave the field.

You may find, as you gain experience, that you are drawn to some other specialty in real estate. Careers may begin in residential or commercial sales. A real estate license is the beginning point of much more: business brokerage, investment, appraising, financing, subdivision and development, consulting, education, and more.

Job Description

Many people think selling real estate consists of finding someone who wants to buy a house or finding the right house for a buyer, but that's only the tip of the iceberg.

Your work may also include finding houses to list on the market or locating buyers who want assistance, estimating value so you can advise sellers or buyers, writing advertising, holding open houses, showing property, and prequalifying buyers to better advise them on what they can afford to look at.

When a match is found between buyer and seller, you negotiate purchase agreements, help buyers arrange financing, and serve as liaison with inspectors, attorneys, lending institutions, and title companies. You monitor paperwork to assure smooth progress to eventual transfer of title.

Only then does your broker receive commission on your transaction, and you receive a share.

Choosing a Broker

The choice of a supervising broker is crucial to your early success. You will be well repaid for time invested in careful selection of the office with which you associate.

You need not limit your search to those offices currently advertising for associates. Most active brokers are interested in talking with ambitious newcomers.

Plan on interviewing at least three offices; six is not too many. You'll learn a lot along the way. You will eliminate one or two and be eliminated as well. The more questions you ask, the more information you will gain on which to make your final decision.

Start by determining which firms are currently active in the areas that interest you, which offices are located near your home, or which companies deal in the type of property that attracts you. Brokers specialize, particularly along geographic lines.

Drive around the neighborhood noting which names appear most on For Sale signs, and read the classified ads and brokers' web pages.

Include in your list large firms and small independents and those belonging to national franchises. Call each office on your list and ask for an interview with the managing broker.

Then keep all the appointments, even if you think you have found the right firm in the first interview. You will pick up valuable viewpoints along the way.

Give less consideration to the broker who promises to furnish you with lots of leads, and more to the one who promises to teach you how to develop your own business. The most critical factor is the amount and type of training you receive. In a small firm, it may be one-on-one guidance; in a large firm, organized classroom instruction.

Questions to Ask

While you are being interviewed, don't hesitate to ask questions of the broker. The interview works both ways, and you are deciding where best to invest your own time and effort. You want to know, not necessarily in order of importance:

- What sort of training will I be offered?
- Is there a formal training program or is training "ad hoc" or as requested?
- Do you hire part-timers? What is your definition of a part-timer?
- What is the firm's presence on the internet?
- Who pays for advertising, postage, long-distance calls, and computer access?
- What are my costs for membership in a REALTOR® association and/or multiple listing service?
- Is part of the commission shared with a franchise?
- What will errors and omissions insurance cost?
- How soon and under what requirements will I have access to floor time? How are referrals handled when I'm on "floor duty" answering telephone calls? (There's no one right answer, but it's interesting to learn about different firms' policies.)
- Do you have a mentoring program? Is the mentor compensated out of my commission or by the firm?
- Is there a "farming" program? If so, how are neighborhoods allocated, especially for a new person?
- On average, what do new salespeople earn?
- Is the manager competing, non-competing, or limited competing with me?
- How often are office meetings held? May I attend one?

Don't hesitate to ask about the split—the division of commission you've earned—between the office and yourself. After all, if you have trouble talking about money, you're going to have a hard time in real estate. Many firms start beginners at 50/50, with a sliding scale or bonuses for experienced associates who require less guidance.

In most offices, you are considered, for IRS purposes, an independent contractor (discussed elsewhere in this book) rather than an employee. Don't expect to hear about employee benefits like paid vacations or health insurance. Once started in real estate, you should arrange for your own health insurance, bank part of your commissions for quarterly estimates of income tax due, and invest some of your rising income through an IRA and/or Self-Employed Retirement Program (SERP). Recognize that these may take up as much as half of every commission check.

Once You've Started

Every transaction is different, posing different challenges. For the real estate agent, negotiating a sale and bringing it to a successful conclusion—with a win/win outcome in which every party is pleased—is a creative achievement.

Good luck to you!

ABOUT THE AUTHORS

Edith Lank is a charter member and former director of the national Real Estate Educators Association (REEA). She taught prelicensing courses at the college level for 15 years, has a syndicated weekly real estate column, and is the author of six real estate books.

Joan m. Sobeck, CRS, GRI, is a REALTOR® from Bergen County, New Jersey and a past president of the New Jersey REALTORS®. During her 50 years as a REALTOR®, she served more than 10 years as a director of NAR and remains a director of both her local and state associations. Ms. Sobeck has either chaired or served on more than 50 committees, including REALTOR® Risk Reduction, Real Estate License Law, Equal Opportunity and Publications. She is a co-author of *Real Estate Brokerage: A Management Guide*.

ABOUT THE CONTRIBUTING AUTHOR

Marie S. Spodek, CDEI, CNE, CBR, is a long-time Dearborn author and editor who participates in the development of many products. Among others, her works include *Environmental Issues in Your Real Estate Practice* and *Sustainable Housing and Building Green*. Marie was the first recipient of the Real Estate Educators Association's Jack Weidemer Distinguished Career Award.

ACKNOWLEDGMENTS

The authors wish to thank those who participated in the preparation of the 15th edition of *Essentials of New Jersey Real Estate*, including:

Philip J. Buonomo, Licensed Real Estate Instructor, Broker/Salesperson, ABR, SRES, SFR, e-Pro

Pat Halligan, Broker Salesperson, American School of Business

Special thanks to all of those who provided valuable contributions to the development of previous editions, including:

W. Thomas Anderson, III	Douglas Davenport, Wells Fargo Home Mortgage
Joyce Andreoli	Charles Davies
Edwin H. Britten	Edward C. Davies
Antonio F. Brown	Thomas D. Demetriades
Evan Butterfield	John R. Dinardo
Eileen Cahill	Solomon Dumitrescu
Patricia Cerrigone	Frank Felice
Stephen A. Chambers	Linda Finkelstein
Jerry Cohen	Joseph R. Fitzpatrick
Steve Daroff	

Patrick J. Fox

Jack Gleason

John Grieder

Wally Grigo

Jeffrey Grossman

Charles E. Haight, Jr., CPCU-CRB

Donald R. Haven

Gerry Hoffman

David Horowitz

John S. Jones

Robert A. Kiamie

Dolores Kovalcik

William J. Lauten

Melvyn Lissner

Rita Magarelli

Joe Marovich

Louise A. Masurat, GRI

Francis McCarthy

Matthew D. Moeller

David L. Moreno

Vincent P. Murphy

Dorothy Nicklus

James F. O'Hagen

Hung Pham

Gerald A. Pocock

Barbara Portman

Pat Renner

Rose Marie Rothrock

Martha Sahin

Bruce Shapiro

Thomas Sheridan

Marlon Temple

Margaret Thomas

Teresa Tilton

Hedda Tischler

David A. Verona

John Viteretti

Lee Wein

We like to hear from our readers. You are our partners in the real estate education process. Comments about this text or any services we provide are always appreciated and should be directed to contentinquiries@dearborn.com.

UNIT 1

Real Estate Licensing

LEARNING OBJECTIVES

When you have completed this unit, you will be able to accomplish the following.

> Describe classes of New Jersey real estate licenses including the qualifications for and exemptions from licensure.
> Explain licensing procedures for New Jersey residents, out-of-state residents, and rental referral companies.

KEY TERMS

broker	Real Estate License Act	salesperson
broker-salesperson	real estate referral	salesperson licensed with
continuing education	company	a real estate referral
Guaranty Fund	REALTOR®	company (SLWRERC)
New Jersey Real Estate	REALTOR-ASSOCIATE®	Title 11, Chapter 5
Commission	referral fee	

WHO MUST BE LICENSED

Anyone who takes part in a real estate transaction in New Jersey for another person for a fee, commission, or other valuable consideration must have a real estate license. The state of New Jersey created real estate licensing regulations to protect the general public from unscrupulous brokers and salespeople.

In New Jersey, licenses have been administered since 1921 by the **New Jersey Real Estate Commission**, operating within the Department of Banking and Insurance. Licenses are governed by

■ the Real Estate License Act, known as Title 45, Chapter 15; and

■ rules and regulations set up by the commission, known as **Title 11, Chapter 5**, Administrative Code.

The statute and rules are reprinted in Appendix A at the end of this book. Additional copies may be obtained by sending a certified or cashier's check, money order, or a broker's business check made out to the State Treasurer for $10, to the New Jersey Real Estate Commission, Education Section, P.O. Box 328, Trenton, NJ 08625-0328.

The commission may be reached by calling 609-292-7272, pressing 0, and asking for Real Estate. Useful information is available at its website, http://www.state.nj.us/dobi/division_rec /index.htm. Questions can be sent to the email address realestate@dobi.state.nj.us.

REAL ESTATE COMMISSION

The New Jersey Real Estate Commission, a division of the Department of Banking and Insurance, is composed of eight members appointed by the governor. Five are real estate brokers who have been licensed as such for at least 10 years; two are chosen from the general public; and one represents a department of the state government. All members serve three-year terms, except the governmental member, who serves at the pleasure of the governor. The governor has the right to remove any member for cause.

REAL ESTATE LICENSES

Classes of Licenses

Under the Real Estate License Act, there are four types of licensees:

1. A **broker** is authorized to operate a real estate business, to hire salespersons, and to charge the public for services. Every real estate company must have one person who is the authorized broker for the entire company; this person is often referred to as the *broker of record*.

2. A **salesperson** works under a sponsoring licensed broker, doing business in the name of the broker and receiving compensation only from that broker. The supervising broker is required to furnish "guidance and direction" and is personally responsible for the real estate acts of salespersons under his or her supervision.

3. A **broker-salesperson** has fulfilled all of the requirements of a broker yet chooses to work in a sales capacity for and in the name of another broker.

4. A **salesperson licensed with a real estate referral company (SLWRERC)** is a licensee whose activities are restricted to only making referrals and not any other real estate activity. An SLWRERC must be licensed with a **real estate referral company**, not a real estate firm.

All initial, renewed, and reinstated licenses are issued on a biennial term that expires on June 30 of odd-numbered years. (The trademarked terms **REALTOR**® and **REALTOR-ASSOCIATE**® are used by members of the National Association of REALTORS®, a private trade association, and have no connection with state licensing.)

Activities Covered

When the work is being performed for another person and in anticipation of a fee or commission, a broker's license is required to

- list real estate for sale;

- sell, exchange, buy, auction, or rent real estate;

- collect rent;

- solicit prospective purchasers or sellers;
- negotiate a real estate loan;
- sell lots or other parcels for a developer;
- sell business opportunities that involve real estate; or
- attempt to do any of the previous activities.

A salesperson's license allows the holder to operate under the supervision of a licensed broker to assist in

- negotiating the purchase, sale, or exchange of real estate;
- negotiating real estate loans;
- leasing, renting, and collecting rent; and
- selling lots or other parcels for a developer.

Licensees are also permitted to handle the resale of mobile homes, but they must follow Motor Vehicle Commission regulations as well as ones set forth by the Real Estate Commission.

Exemptions

A real estate license is not required for

- owners handling their own property as unrepresented sellers (referred to as for sale by owner or FSBO);
- attorneys, executors, trustees, receivers, administrators, legal guardians, and others handling real estate under the order of a court;
- banks and trust companies; and
- insurance companies.

Attorneys are exempt while handling real estate in their normal practice of law, but an attorney who intends to engage in general real estate brokerage must obtain a real estate license.

Payment for Services

To collect a commission, one must be licensed at the time the service is performed. It is illegal for anyone to share in any portion of a commission without a real estate license. A broker may share commissions only with his or her associated salespersons and SLWRERCs or with another broker (in the event of a cooperative listing or a **referral**, including a broker who is licensed in another state). One exception, after a new law went into effect in early 2010, allows a selling broker to rebate part of the commission to the buyer in the form of either a credit or a check.

Finder's fees—money or gifts to unlicensed persons who refer buyers or sellers—are also forbidden. A broker is, however, allowed to pay other brokers.

Unlicensed Assistants

Salespersons and brokers often use assistants, secretaries, and similar support staff who are not allowed to perform activities that require a license. The Real Estate Commission has issued guidelines on what unlicensed assistants may and may not do. The lists paint a fairly complete picture of most tasks involved in real estate brokerage. In general, prohibited activities are those involving contact with clients or customers.

An unlicensed assistant or secretary may not

- show property;
- answer any questions about listed property;
- make "cold calls," by phone or in person, seeking business from potential listers, purchasers, tenants, or landlords;
- discuss or explain a contract or any other real estate document with anyone outside the brokerage firm;
- make telephone calls for rent collection; or
- except when accompanying a licensee, host open houses or promotional booths, distribute promotional material, or attend a home inspection.

An unlicensed assistant or secretary may

- answer phones and forward calls;
- process and submit listings and changes to the multiple listing system;
- place signs on properties, pick up keys, and deliver documents;
- schedule appointments for showing listed properties;
- set up files and track and secure documents;
- (only under the direction of a licensee) have keys made for company listings, write and place ads, type contract forms, order items or inspections, and prepare flyers and promotional materials;
- keep records of and deposit earnest money, security deposits, and rent;
- follow up on loan applications; or
- compute commission checks.

License Qualifications

To obtain a salesperson's license or an SLWRERC's license, the candidate must

- be 18 years of age or older;
- prove a high school education or its equivalent;
- furnish evidence of good moral character;
- successfully complete a 75-hour prelicensing course;
- disclose his or her Social Security number for child support enforcement purposes;
- pass a state examination; and
- be sponsored by a licensed real estate broker (to activate the license).

According to S2455, undocumented immigrants are eligible for professional licenses, provided that they meet all other requirements for licensure.

The applicant for a broker's license must

- be 18 years of age or older;
- prove the equivalent of a high school education;
- furnish evidence of good moral character;

■ have served three years full-time as a licensed salesperson;

■ successfully complete 150 hours of study, consisting of a 90-hour general broker prelicensing course, a 30-hour prelicensing course on brokers' ethics and agency law and relationships, and a 30-hour prelicensing course on office management and related topics;

■ disclose his or her Social Security number for child support enforcement purposes; and

■ pass a state examination.

Exceptions

The experience requirement for a broker's or broker-salesperson's license can be waived for an honorably discharged war veteran with a service-connected wound or disability. License and renewal fees also are waived.

The commission may agree to waive the education requirement for

■ a licensed broker from another state;

■ someone previously licensed as a New Jersey broker within the past five years;

■ someone who has taken equivalent real estate courses in college;

■ New Jersey attorneys; and

■ in some cases, certain applicants who took an equivalent prelicensing course in another state.

No license will be issued to anyone convicted within the preceding five years of forgery, burglary, robbery, any theft other than shoplifting, criminal conspiracy to defraud, "or any like offense."

New Jersey does not recognize licenses issued in any other state (no reciprocity).

Required Experience

A candidate for a broker's license must have been continuously employed on a full-time basis as a real estate salesperson during the three years immediately preceding the application. (*Full-time* means the applicant worked at least 40 hours per week, between the hours of approximately 10 am and 8 pm, and during that time was not employed elsewhere except on a part-time basis for no more than 25 hours a week.) The licensee must be able to show evidence that he or she had experience in listing, selling, and leasing property during the three-year period.

Time Limit on Application

Applications for a real estate license must be submitted to the commission within one year of the date when the candidate successfully completed the prelicense course. Otherwise, the course must be taken again.

Nonresidents

Someone who does not live in the state may obtain a New Jersey real estate license after qualifying in the usual way and also filing irrevocable consent to service of process (i.e., consent to be sued in this state).

Corporations

A corporation can be granted a real estate license only if one of its officers holds a broker's license. That person then becomes the broker of record for the corporation and is personally responsible for all transactions for which a real estate license is required.

Examination

Fees for the license examination are paid directly to the independent testing service that runs the examination. Special arrangements can be made for people who are blind, disabled, or have extreme language difficulty.

Temporary License

If a broker dies or becomes mentally or physically incapacitated and the office has no other broker to carry on transactions already in progress, a temporary broker's license may be issued to a salesperson with at least three years' experience immediately preceding the date of application.

The salesperson is expected to complete qualifications for a broker's license within one year; no extension of time is allowed. The application requesting the temporary license must be made within 30 days of the date of the broker's death and is effective for one year from the date of issuance.

Continuing Education Requirements for License Renewal

License renewal is on July 1 in odd-numbered years. All broker, broker-salesperson, and salesperson licensees must complete 12 hours of approved **continuing education** courses before each two-year license renewal. There is no exception for brokers who have been licensed for a long time. Completion between May 1 and June 30 of the renewal year may subject the licensee to a processing fee of $200.

The required courses should be completed on or before April 30 of the renewal year. The 12 hours must contain at least 6 hours of core topics, including 2 hours on ethics, 1 hour on fair housing and discrimination, and 3 hours of other core topics totaling 6 hours within the core topics. Credit may also be claimed for certain courses taken in other states upon the New Jersey Real Estate Commission's approval. Credit may also be claimed for courses approved as prelicense or continuing education in appraisal and banking professions related to real estate brokerage.

An SLWRERC is not required to complete any continuing education unless and until the SLWRERC wishes to convert to actively listing and selling real estate. The required number of continuing education hours is determined by how long the licensee has been an SLWRERC. (See https://www.state.nj.us/dobi/division_rec/licensing/splwrerc.pdf.) When upgrading to a salesperson, broker-salesperson, or broker license, the required continuing education courses will consist entirely of core courses.

Failure to Renew

If a broker's or salesperson's license is not renewed for two consecutive years or more after the expiration of the last license, it becomes void. At that point the salesperson must once more meet all original license qualifications. In some cases, a broker need not retake the courses.

License Fees

Costs for an initial license including application and Real Estate Guaranty Fund fees, where applicable, are as follows:

1. Salesperson $160
2. SLWRERC   160
3. Broker   270
4. Broker-salesperson   270
5. Branch office   150
6. Corporations, etc.   270

Renewal fees are $100 for a salesperson's or SLWRERC's license and $200 for a broker's.

License Transfer and Termination

Managing brokers can register for online reporting ("entitlement") at www.state.nj.us/dobi /onlineservices/DOBIOnlineServices.htm (click "Register for Real Estate Broker Online Services" under the **Real Estate Brokers** section). Once registered, the managing broker may print out licenses and report transfers or terminations at https://portal01.state.nj.us.

A broker who goes out of business must close out the escrow account, remove signs, notify clients, and provide the commission with a name and address where past records will be available for *six* years.

LICENSING PROCEDURE

To obtain a salesperson's or SLWRERC's license in New Jersey, the candidate follows three steps:

1. Successfully complete the required 75-hour pre-license course and the state license examination, and receive a Score Report. The school will notify the testing provider that the applicant has completed the course successfully.

2. Submit the Score Report (signed by the sponsoring broker) to the Real Estate Commission. At the same time a completed form is submitted allowing the commission to request a criminal-history check, as well as a certified check, cashier's check, or money order for $160, payable to the State Treasurer of New Jersey.

3. Complete a fingerprinting process and consent to a criminal history record check. The Department strongly suggests completing the fingerprinting process as soon as possible after passing the state examination.

The procedure is handled by Idemia, using the NJ Universal Fingerprint form. Appointments may be scheduled on the internet at www.bioapplicant.com/nj or by telephone at 877-503-5981. The website lists the different fingerprinting sites in the state. The fee for the criminal check and fingerprinting is $66.05, payable by money order, bank check, or credit card. Personal checks are not accepted. For the most recent information, consult the PSI candidate exam booklet for New Jersey.

Each applicant must bring to the fingerprinting site a completed Universal Form as well as a government-issued ID. Instructions for the fingerprinting procedure may be found at the website www.state.nj.us/dobi/division_rec/licensing/fingerprint.html.

SALESPERSON'S OR SLWRERC'S LICENSE EXAMINATION

Information

New Jersey's license examinations are administered by the testing service PSI Services, LLC. A candidate bulletin with information about New Jersey examination requirements and procedures is available online at www.psiexams.com. (Click on "Government/State Licensing Agencies," select "New Jersey" from the **Select Jurisdiction** drop-down menu, choose "NJ Real Estate" from the **Select Account** drop-down menu, and then click your classification type. Click to download the Candidate Information Bulletin.) An online practice exam is also offered.

Appointment

The salesperson's examination is administered at various locations throughout the state (see Figure 1.1). The administrator of the state test allows four hours to complete the exam. Reservations for the exam must be made at least four days in advance through www.psiexams .com or at least one day in advance by phone at 800-733-9267. Registration may be made by fax to 702-932-2666. A completed form may be faxed at any hour, including a Visa or MasterCard number and expiration date. The exam fee is $45 and is due at the time of reservation, payable by credit card, debit card, or electronic check. The candidate will receive a confirmation number to be used at the exam. The fee for the PSI examination is $50.

PSI and the New Jersey Real Estate Commission now offer the opportunity of taking a "remotely proctored online exam from a computer at a remote location." For the most current guidelines, consult the PSI NJ Exam booklet: https://home.psiexams.com/#/home

Figure 1.1: Examination Centers

Brick	**North Brunswick**
260 Chambersbridge Rd, Unit #1A Brick, NJ 08723	The Shoppes at North Brunswick 980 Shoppes BLVD, 2nd Floor North Brunswick, NJ 08902
Cherry Hill	**Northfield Area (Linwood)**
950 N. Kings Highway, Suite 301 Cherry Hill, NJ 08034	Central Park East 222 New Road, Suite 301 Linwood, NJ 08221
Hamilton Square Area	**Parsippany**
IBIS Plaza South 3525 Quakerbridge Rd, Suite 1000 Hamilton Township, NJ 08619	239 New Road, Suite A-203 Parsippany, NJ 07054
New Brunswick—Georges Road	**Rochelle Park**
825 Georges Road, Suite 2A New Brunswick, NJ 08902	365 W. Passaic St, Ste 180 Rochelle Park, NJ 07662
New Providence	**Secaucus**
Murray Hill Office Center 571 Central Avenue, Suite 117 New Providence, NJ 09074	110-B Meadowlands Parkway, Suite 204 Secaucus, NJ 07094

What to Bring

Candidates should bring to the exam two forms of identification (at least one with a government-issued photo ID).

The primary identification, with photo, may be one of the following: state-issued drivers license, state-issued identification card, U.S. government–issued passport, U.S. government–issued military identification card, U.S. government–issued alien registration card, or Canadian government-issued ID. The ID must contain the candidate's photo, and be valid and unexpired.

The secondary identification may be one of the following: a signed credit card, social security card, or United States–issued birth certificate with raised seal. Student IDs and employment IDs are not acceptable forms of identification.

The Examination

Candidates are asked to arrive at least 30 minutes before their scheduled appointment and are allowed up to four hours to complete the examination. The examination includes 80 general real estate questions (approximately 10% of them are math questions) and 30 questions specifically on New Jersey real estate. A passing grade is 70% and the examinations are scored immediately. In case of failure, re-takes are permitted after 24 hours. After successful completion of the state examination, the sponsoring broker will notify the state of the new salesperson's association. The new salesperson may begin working as soon as his or her name appears on the state's Licensee Name Search. The list is updated every 24 hours.

Through http://reconline.nj.gov, either the supervising broker or the new licensee may print out the license as a hard copy or download it to a cell phone as a photo.

GUARANTY FUND

The **Guaranty Fund** was established to reimburse members of the public who suffer a monetary loss due to wrongdoing in a real estate transaction by a licensed broker or salesperson or an unlicensed employee of a broker. The party must first obtain a court judgment, naming the Real Estate Commission as a party to the suit. If the party suffering the loss is unable to collect that judgment, he or she may apply within six years to the Real Estate Guaranty Fund for payment. A criminal claim must also be filed against the offending party. No spouse of a licensee may bring action against the licensee under the Guaranty Fund.

At time of initial issuance of license, each salesperson contributes $10 and each broker or broker-salesperson contributes $20 to the Guaranty Fund, which is maintained by the state treasurer and administered by the commission. Maximum payment for a single claim is $20,000 per offense. If there is not enough in the fund to pay all the claims against it, the commission may assess licensees an additional amount at the time of license renewal.

Once the fund pays a claim against a broker or salesperson, that person's license is revoked until the fund is reimbursed, with interest.

RENTAL REFERRAL COMPANIES

Every person working in rental referral companies who for a fee refers prospective tenants to rental units is required to have a real estate license and to enter into a written contract with each prospective tenant. This contract must specify such things as services to be performed, fees charged, date and term of contract, and refund policy.

No rental property may be offered without the landlord's consent; oral consent must be confirmed in writing within 24 hours.

Units that are advertised must be checked every day to see if they are still available; units that are simply listed must be checked every three days.

If prospective tenants are charged an advance fee of more than $25, regulations require deposit of the funds in an escrow account.

SUMMARY

Anyone assisting in a real estate transaction for another and for compensation must be licensed by the state of New Jersey. Licenses are administered by the New Jersey Real Estate Commission, whose eight members are appointed by the governor. Five are real estate brokers and two are members of the general public, all of whom serve three-year terms; a government representative serves at the governor's pleasure.

A *broker* may operate a real estate business and charge the public for services. A *salesperson* is licensed to assist one specific broker. A *broker-salesperson* is a fully qualified broker who chooses to maintain the position of a salesperson with some other broker. A *salesperson licensed with a real estate referral company (SLWRERC)* is licensed only to refer prospective buyers and sellers to the referral company.

The license law does not apply to owners handling their own property, attorneys in their normal course of business, those under court order (executors, trustees, legal guardians, and so on), banks, and insurance companies.

Any sharing of commissions with unlicensed persons is forbidden, with the exception of a possible rebate of part of the commission to a buyer. A salesperson may receive compensation only from his or her own supervising broker; brokers may share commissions only with their own salespersons and other licensed brokers.

An unlicensed assistant or secretary may perform support services for salespersons and brokers but is not allowed to show property or give information about it, explain documents, or host open houses.

Licensees must be 18 years of age or older, have the equivalent of a high school education, and be of good moral character. Salesperson applicants must successfully complete a 75-hour prelicensing course within one year before applying, must pass a state examination, and must be sponsored by a licensed broker. Licensure as a broker requires completion of 150 hours in prelicensing courses and three years' full-time employment as a salesperson immediately prior to licensure. Some exceptions are made for those licensed in other states, for certain disabled veterans, for attorneys, and for others.

License renewal, on July 1 of every odd-numbered year, requires completion of at least 12 hours of continuing education, with two hours or more on ethics. The courses should be taken prior to May 1, or the licensee could incur the possibility of an additional processing fee up to $200. The only exceptions are made for SLWRERCs, salespersons first licensed within the past year, and any licensee who completed a broker's prelicense course within the preceding two years.

Licensees contribute to a Guaranty Fund, which reimburses members of the public who have been defrauded or badly served by real estate licensees and who can collect damages in no other way.

Special regulations apply to rental referral companies and to the sale of out-of-state developments, major in-state subdivisions, and property involving common ownership.

USEFUL WEBSITES

New Jersey State Government: www.state.nj.us

New Jersey Real Estate Commission: www.state.nj.us/dobi/division_rec/index.htm

New Jersey State Legislature: www.njleg.state.nj.us

Online Licenses: http://reconline.nj.gov

Testing Service: www.psiexams.com

Fingerprinting: www.bioapplicant.com/nj

KEY TERMS REVIEW

Match the number of each key term with the corresponding letter.

_____ 1. Broker

_____ 2. Broker-salesperson

_____ 3. Continuing education

_____ 4. Guaranty Fund

_____ 5. New Jersey Real Estate Commission

_____ 6. Real Estate License Act

_____ 7. REALTOR®

_____ 8. REALTOR-ASSOCIATE®

_____ 9. Referral fee

_____ 10. Salesperson

_____ 11. Salesperson licensed with a real estate referral company (SLWRERC)

_____ 12. Title 11, Chapter 5

A. administrator of real estate licenses

B. state rules and regulations for real estate licensees

C. fully qualified broker who remains under another broker's supervision

D. individual licensed to charge the public for real estate services

E. law governing the practice of real estate in New Jersey

F. member of a private real estate trade organization

G. money paid another broker for sending a client or customer

H. one licensed to assist a broker in real estate transactions

I. reimburses people defrauded or badly served by licensees in real estate transactions

J. salesperson who joins a particular real estate trade group

K. licensee limited to presenting prospective clients and customers to the broker

L. classes required for license renewal

UNIT 1 REVIEW QUESTIONS

1. New Jersey's real estate license law is known as
   A. the Statute of Frauds.
   B. Title VII.
   C. Title 45.
   D. the Law of Agency.

2. An unlicensed New Jersey resident may
   A. help a neighbor sell his or her house in return for a used car.
   B. negotiate the purchase of vacant land on behalf of a developer in return for one lot.
   C. draw up a binding lease for a new tenant in a property the resident owns.
   D. charge a fee for selling someone else's pizza business, including name, ovens, truck, and small building.

3. A real estate license is valid for
   A. six months.
   B. one year.
   C. two years.
   D. life.

4. According to the law, to obtain a salesperson's license one must reach the age of
   A. 18.
   B. 19.
   C. 20.
   D. 21.

5. A broker must have completed how many hours of study in addition to the original salesperson's course?
   A. 30
   B. 75
   C. 150
   D. 165

6. The prelicense course must be taken over if the student does not apply for a license within
   A. six months.
   B. one year.
   C. two years.
   D. an unlimited amount of time.

7. A nonresident broker requesting a New Jersey license must
   A. post a bond.
   B. agree to be sued in New Jersey.
   C. open an office in the state.
   D. have a licensed New Jersey broker as a sponsor.

8. An honorably discharged war veteran with a service-connected wound or disability may
   A. sell real estate and charge commissions without holding a real estate license.
   B. be exempt from payment of license fees.
   C. obtain a license even if younger than 18.
   D. be excused from taking the state licensing examination.

9. If a principal broker dies, associated salespersons should promptly
   A. change their affiliation to another firm.
   B. have one of their members apply for a temporary broker's license.
   C. obtain broker's licenses.
   D. move the office to another location.

10. The Real Estate Commission has how many members?
    A. Three
    B. Five
    C. Eight
    D. Ten

11. Continuing education courses must be taken
    A. by all licensees.
    B. in every two-year period.
    C. for an initial broker's license.
    D. within a year after license renewal.

12. Which of the following are never allowed to sell real estate without a license?
    A. Banks
    B. Insurance brokers
    C. Attorneys
    D. Owners

13. The Guaranty Fund is funded by
    A. fines paid by brokers who violate license law.
    B. a 1% tax on real estate sales over $500,000.
    C. fees paid at first-license application.
    D. real property taxes.

14. Real estate brokers may need special registration when selling some
    A. out-of-state properties.
    B. previously owned condominiums.
    C. business opportunities.
    D. real estate at an auction.

15. Rental referral companies must
    A. charge prospective tenants no more than $25.
    B. check once a week to see if apartments are still available.
    C. obtain a special rental license.
    D. furnish prospective tenants with a written contract.

16. An unlicensed assistant is asked over the telephone, "How many bedrooms are there in that house at 78 Oak Street?" The assistant is allowed to
    A. read from the description in the written listing contract.
    B. repeat only what her broker has told her about the property.
    C. say that yesterday's classified ad (which she wrote) mentions four bedrooms.
    D. decline to answer questions about the property.

17. An apartment is listed with a rental referral company, but it is not actively advertised to the public. How frequently must the company check the apartment's availability?
    A. Every day
    B. Every other day
    C. Every three days
    D. Weekly

18. Certification that legal restrictions have been reviewed with the certifying broker is required for which license?
    A. Salesperson
    B. Salesperson-broker
    C. Broker
    D. SLWRERC

19. Continuing education requirements mandate at least two hours' instruction in
    A. ethics.
    B. law of agency.
    C. current financing options.
    D. local issues.

20. In order to avoid an additional processing fee, licensees should complete their required continuing education courses during the renewal year on or before
    A. April 30 of the renewal year.
    B. May 1 of the renewal year.
    C. June 1 of the renewal year.
    D. June 30 of the renewal year.

21. A broker who goes out of business must provide a name and address where past records will be available for
    A. six months.
    B. one year.
    C. three years.
    D. six years.

UNIT
2

Commission Rules and Regulations

LEARNING OBJECTIVES

When you have completed this unit, you will be able to accomplish the following.

> Identify the standards set by license law and commission rules regarding the brokerage business.
> Explain commission regulations for broker business relationships and advertising.
> Describe violations and penalties of the license law.

KEY TERMS

branch office	guilty knowledge	suspension
commingling	letter of intent	trust account
duplicate original	probation	Waiver of Broker
escrow account	revocation	Cooperation

LICENSE LAW AND RULES

Both the license law and the commission's rules set standards for licensees. Most of the obligations fall on the broker, with the understanding that a broker is responsible for associated salespersons' observance of the rules. A salesperson may not

■ accept any form of compensation except from his or her supervising broker;

■ maintain an escrow account or hold funds belonging to others; or

■ work for more than one New Jersey broker at a time.

PLACE OF BUSINESS

Main Office

Every broker who is a resident of New Jersey must maintain a place of business in the state. If the office is in the broker's own home it must have a separate area with its own entrance visible from the street. The office can never be in the home of a broker's associate. This avoids the practice known as *license lending*, in which a broker permits his or her license to be used by another person or business entity without actually supervising the business. A broker may not allow someone else to use the firm name.

The broker's name and the words "Licensed Real Estate Broker" must be conspicuously displayed on the exterior. The license of the broker and those of any associates should be prominently displayed in the main office.

The main office and the persons working in it must be under the full-time direct supervision of either the broker or a qualified broker-salesperson. *Full-time* means the supervising licensee is physically present at the office during usual business hours five days a week and is not otherwise employed.

Branch Office

Each **branch office** must be under the direct supervision of a broker or broker-salesperson and must have a duplicate license. Additionally, the names of all licensees and the branch office supervisor must be recorded with the commission and prominently displayed in the branch office, along with the office license. No branch office can be in the home of a salesperson or broker-salesperson.

TRUST ACCOUNT (ESCROW ACCOUNT)

A broker must establish a separate, special **trust account**, also known as an **escrow account**, in an authorized financial institution in New Jersey, to be used for the deposit of all money belonging to other persons (earnest money deposits, rent collections, and the like). The name of the financial institution and the account number must be reported to the commission both at license application and at the time of renewal.

There is no need for a separate account for each transaction, but careful books must be kept so it is always clear how much money belongs to each client or customer. The account must be clearly labeled so that it cannot be claimed by creditors in the event of a bankruptcy or by heirs at the broker's death.

Brokers are required to deposit funds coming into their keeping "promptly," which the commission defines as within five business days of acceptance. Salespersons should immediately give any escrow monies they receive to their broker.

Brokers are specifically prohibited from **commingling** (mixing) their own funds with money in the trust account. In some circumstances, the broker may be authorized to collect a commission directly from money held in the escrow account. In that case, the business ledger should document the source of the authorization and the amount and source of the commission, and the money should be taken out promptly after authorization. Leaving such money in the account for more than five business days might result in commingling. The broker is, however, allowed to leave a nominal amount of his or her own money in the account to cover service charges and keep the account open.

Advance Fees

When a client places advance fees of more than $25 with a broker—to assist with advertising costs, for example—the broker must give the client an account of how the money is being spent within 90 days.

Cash Deposits or Withdrawals

The customer or client who makes a cash deposit must be given a written receipt; the broker keeps a copy of the receipt. In accordance with federal law, any cash deposit of $10,000 or more must be reported to the Internal Revenue Service. Withdrawals from the trust account must be made payable to a specific person, never to "cash."

Permanent Records

Every broker must keep records of trust account activity for at least six years.

REGULATION OF DOCUMENTS

Sales Contracts

Every person who signs a listing contract, sales contract, or lease should immediately receive a **duplicate original** of the document; that is, licensees must provide multiple original copies for the parties signatures. Any additions or changes to a document after the original signing should be initialed by all parties and a copy given to each party.

Commissions are negotiable between client and broker. No contract can contain anything indicating a prescribed fee schedule. The commission requires the following statement be included in all listing contracts (or sales contracts if there is no listing contract on the property) for one- to four-family residences:

> As seller you have the right to individually reach an agreement on any fee, commission, or other valuable consideration with any broker. No fee, commission, or other consideration has been fixed by any governmental authority or by any trade association or multiple listing service.

Licensees can prepare sales contracts only for one- to four-family homes and single building lots. The sale or rental of commercial or industrial properties or businesses is accomplished on a **letter of intent**. A letter of intent is generally a nonbinding document that references what the parties plan to do; note that some provisions could be binding.

The commission requires that all sales contracts prepared by licensees contain an *Attorney Review Clause*, giving buyer and seller the right to consult an attorney, who may disapprove a contract within three business days after delivery of signed contracts to both parties. The specific language required is detailed in Unit 11. A similar clause is required in residential leases, as covered in Unit 12.

All written offers must be forwarded to sellers within 24 hours, and at the time of listing, owners of property must be furnished with a copy of the *Attorney General's memorandum* regarding the New Jersey Law Against Discrimination, as shown in Unit 10.

The New Jersey Supreme Court has ruled that buyers and sellers of residential real estate may choose whether or not to incur the cost of hiring a lawyer. If they choose not to hire a lawyer, real estate brokers and title agents may provide certain assistance in the title closing process provided the broker gave a mandatory notice to the buyer and seller advising them of their right to hire a lawyer. This notice must be attached as a cover page to any contract of sale prepared by licensees. (See Figure 11.1.)

If a real estate broker is also a licensed insurance broker, mention of the buyer's purchase of insurance from that broker, if included in a sales contract, must be confirmed separately in writing not less than five days before the actual closing of title.

Other Documents

The broker must keep copies of all unaccepted offers to purchase for *six months* from the date of the initial offer. All copies of contracts of sale and listing agreements must be kept for *six years*. Also, bills for brokerage services, records showing payment to salespersons and cooperating brokers, bank statements, canceled checks, and deposit slips from the broker's business account must be kept for six years.

All records and files must be available for inspection at any time by the commission, and they always remain the property of the broker. Salespersons may not remove anything from the broker's files if they leave that broker.

BROKER BUSINESS RELATIONSHIPS

Any licensee involved in the sale of residential real estate containing one- to four-dwelling units, or the sale of vacant one-family lots or residential lease transactions for more than 125 days, is required to supply information on business relationships to buyers and sellers (or landlords and tenants) in accordance with 11:5-6.9 of the New Jersey Administrative Code (in Appendix A). In addition to disclosing the nature of the licensee's relationship to all parties involved in any transaction (both verbally and in brokerage agreements, offers, contracts, or leases), the licensee must provide a copy of the Consumer Information Statement on New Jersey Real Estate Relationships, which is shown in Unit 3.

Listing Broker and Seller/Principal

Brokers are bound to specific duties to their principal. Their obligation to put the principal's interest first, however, still requires fair and honest dealing with other parties. Brokers—and all licensees, for that matter—are required to make reasonable efforts to ascertain all material information concerning the physical condition of every property for which they accept an agency or are retained to market as a transaction broker. They must also determine the financial qualifications of every person for whom they submit an offer to their client or principal. Reasonable effort includes inquiries to the seller (or the seller's agent) about any physical condition that may affect the property. The property should also be visually inspected.

To give sellers the best service possible, the commission expects brokers to cooperate with other firms that may want to show listed property. Any time a seller directs a broker not to cooperate, the licensee must have the seller sign a **Waiver of Broker Cooperation** form, which states:

WAIVER OF BROKER COOPERATION

I UNDERSTAND THAT COOPERATION AMONGST BROKERS PRODUCES WIDER EXPOSURE OF MY PROPERTY AND MAY RESULT IN IT BEING SOLD OR LEASED SOONER AND AT A HIGHER PRICE THAN WOULD

BE THE CASE WERE MY BROKER NOT TO COOPERATE WITH OTHER BROKERS. I FURTHER UNDERSTAND THAT WHEN MY BROKER COOPERATES WITH OTHER BROKERS, I CAN STILL HAVE THE ARRANGEMENTS FOR THE SHOWING OF THE PROPERTY AND ALL NEGOTIATIONS WITH ME OR MY ATTORNEY MADE ONLY THROUGH MY LISTING BROKER'S OFFICE, SHOULD I SO DESIRE.

However, despite my awareness of these factors, I direct that this property is to be marketed only through the efforts of the listing broker. This listing is not to be published in any multiple listing service. I will only consider offers on this property which are obtained by the listing broker, and I will only allow showings of this property to be conducted by the listing broker or his or her duly authorized representatives. THE LISTING BROKER IS HEREBY DIRECTED NOT TO COOPERATE WITH ANY OTHER BROKER.

By signing below, the parties hereto confirm that no pressure or undue influence has been exerted upon the owners as to how this property is to be marketed by the listing broker.

The owner(s) further confirm receipt of a fully executed copy of the listing agreement on this property, and of this waiver of broker cooperation form.

Dated: _____ Owner: _____

Owner: _____

Listing Broker: _____

By: Authorized Licensee or Broker: _____

Broker and Buyer/Principal

More and more licensees in New Jersey are functioning as *buyers' brokers*; in other words, they are being retained by buyers to help them find suitable properties. Again, these brokers and their associated salespersons are bound to specific duties to their principal. Their obligation to put the principals' interest first, however, still requires fair and honest dealing with other parties.

Broker as Disclosed Dual Agent

Although an agent cannot give first loyalty to two or more principals in the same transaction, the New Jersey Real Estate Commission allows a broker to represent both parties in a transaction, provided that the broker obtains the parties' *written, informed consent* to the dual agency.

Broker as Transaction Broker

The state has recognized that nowhere in the licensing laws is it mandated that licensees must act as agents when rendering real estate services. Licensees in New Jersey have the option of functioning as *transaction brokers*, without creating an agency relationship with any of the parties to a transaction (see Unit 3 or Appendix A, 11:5-6.9, for the commission's definition and discussion of this term).

BROKER AND SALESPERSON

Before a salesperson can begin working for a sponsoring broker, a written Broker-Salesperson Independent Contractor Agreement must be drawn up that includes

- the compensation rate paid the salesperson (straight salary and/or commission split, for example);

- a broker promise to turn over monies due the salesperson within ten days after a commission is received or as soon thereafter as the check has cleared;

- the rate of compensation to be paid the salesperson for transactions that close after the salesperson leaves that broker's firm; and

- a provision that any future changes to the contract will be binding only if in writing and signed by both parties.

A sample agreement is shown in Unit 3.

Any commission due on a transaction is paid to the broker and disbursed in accordance with the agreement the salesperson and broker entered into at the time the salesperson joined the company. If a salesperson leaves a company, the broker must make a complete written account of all monies due the salesperson within 30 days of termination.

ADVERTISING

The New Jersey Real Estate Commission has regulations regarding any advertisement offering to sell, buy, exchange, or rent real property. They are intended to let the public know exactly with whom they are dealing. The regulations cover all media, including publications, broadcasts, stationery, business cards, email, and web pages.

Real estate listings today are reproduced on websites by local newspapers classified ad departments, individual salespersons and brokers, local and regional MLS sites, and on national sites like www.realtor.com.

All ads must indicate the name of the brokerage company followed by a term such as REALTOR®, Realtist, real estate broker, or real estate agency. The licensee's name must appear exactly as it is on the license with the exception of any middle name or initial, which need not be used. A nickname may be added.

An ad that includes a salesperson's name must also include the name of the real estate company in larger type or more prominently. The salesperson's full first and last names must be used. A nickname may also be included. An individual salesperson's web page must display the phone number of the brokerage office or clearly indicate a link to the brokerage's web page. If an advertisement includes a licensee's home phone, it must be identified as such ("res." or "home") and the office phone number must be included and identified as such.

All ads must specify the property's *municipal location*, specifically named in the ad or at the head of the column in which the ad appears. Such phrases as "in the vicinity of" are prohibited, unless the body of the ad also contains the exact municipal location.

If, in an ad, the broker refers to membership in a multiple listing service (MLS), the full name of that service must be spelled out. Exceptions include spot ads (20 lines or fewer, no wider than one column), For Sale signs, and business cards.

Any advertisement that refers to a home warranty must state whether inspection is required, if the warranty is mandatory, and whether the purchaser is responsible for the payment of fees in connection with the warranty. Any ad offering a rebate to the purchaser of residential property must disclose the buyer's obligation to pay any applicable taxes and advise the purchaser to consult a tax professional.

An ad may not indiscriminately promise financing. All loan terms must contain the words "to a qualified buyer." Any sums mentioned in terms of payments or financing must be qualified by the word "approximate" or "estimated." If such a statement is not so qualified, the broker must have written proof of its validity and maintain this record for 12 months.

No advertising or sign may indicate that a property is "sold" until the sale has closed and title (ownership) has been transferred.

Any offer of a free item or service must be genuinely free and cannot be contingent upon any purchase or listing of property. A free offer cannot be linked to a lottery, contest, game, or drawing.

Advertising that offers free appraisals is also prohibited, although offering a comparative market analysis (CMA) is permissible (see Unit 10).

The commission regulations supplement the New Jersey Law Against Discrimination by specifying that no licensee may advertise or in any way express a discriminatory limitation (see Unit 4).

Any advertisement that mentions a specific commission rate or amount must also state that "In New Jersey, commissions are negotiable."

COMMISSION REBATES

To prevent fraud, license law has traditionally forbidden any sharing of commissions with unlicensed persons. In 2009, however, the Legislature passed an act allowing real estate brokers to provide a purchaser of real estate with a portion of the broker's commission in the form of a rebate. It can be in the form of a credit or a check.

Restrictions and limitations apply to the rebate. It cannot be dependent on any lottery, contest, or game.

Only a broker may pay the rebate, and it can be paid only to the purchaser. The arrangement must be agreed upon at the start of the relationship and included, for example, in the original buyer-agency agreement. The purchaser must be advised to contact a tax professional about the income tax consequences of a rebate, and all parties to the transaction, including any mortgage lender, must be made aware of it.

PRICE-FIXING

Any agreement between competing offices to establish standard commission rates is forbidden not only by the federal government (see Unit 3) but also by the Real Estate Commission. Any offer to share commissions with other firms must be made on the same terms to all who cooperate.

PROBATION, SUSPENSION, AND REVOCATION

The commission may investigate complaints against the action of licensees or investigate on its own. It may

■ place a licensee on **probation**;

■ suspend a license (**suspension**); or

■ revoke the license completely (**revocation**).

In addition, fines range from $5,000 for the first offense and $10,000 for subsequent offenses. The most a licensee may be fined is $25,000 total. Three violations and a license is revoked.

Note that the person filing charges in known as the *complainant*, while the person being investigated is known as the *respondent*.

Procedure

Before suspending or revoking a license, the commission must provide the licensee at least 10 days' advance notice of a hearing. The commission's ruling after a hearing can be appealed to the New Jersey Superior Court.

The commission may order that money be paid to someone who has been wronged before a license is reinstated. It can also require a licensee to pass another written examination in cases where merited.

When a salesperson is disciplined, the broker's license may or may not be affected, depending on whether the broker had **guilty knowledge**—in other words, knew what was going on and did not attempt to stop it. When brokers' licenses are suspended or revoked, their salespersons' licenses are suspended until the end of the current license period. During that time, salespersons are free to affiliate with another broker and can obtain a reissued license at no charge.

The commission can promptly revoke the license of anyone convicted of certain crimes, among them forgery, burglary, robbery, and theft, and for an indefinite period of time. The commission can also suspend a license for anyone awaiting trial for a number of serious crimes, including murder, kidnapping, robbery, criminal conspiracy, and so on.

Violations

The License Act specifically mentions the following offenses that are subject to disciplinary action:

■ Making false promises or substantial misrepresentation

■ Acting for more than one party in a transaction without the knowledge of all parties thereof

■ Pursuing a flagrant and continued course of misrepresentations or making of false promises

■ Failure to account for or pay over money belonging to others

■ Conduct demonstrating unworthiness, incompetence, dishonesty, or bad faith

■ Failing to provide a client with a copy of a contract at the time of signing, or failing to specify an expiration date in a listing

■ Using a lottery, contest, game, prize, or drawing to promote the sale of real estate

■ Being convicted of a crime of which the commission does not have knowledge

■ Collecting a commission as a broker in a transaction while simultaneously representing either party in a different capacity for a consideration (for instance, acting as attorney and broker)

- Using any trade name or insignia of a real estate organization while not being a member
- Paying any compensation or commission to an unlicensed person except in some circumstances to a buyer
- Any other conduct constituting fraud or dishonest dealing
- As a salesperson or broker-salesperson, accepting any commission or valuable consideration from anyone except the employing broker
- Procuring a real estate license through fraud or deceit
- Commingling the licensee's own money with that of clients and customers or failing to maintain and promptly deposit others' money in a special trust account
- Selling property in which the licensee has an interest without disclosing in the contract of sale that interest and the fact that the seller is a licensed real estate salesperson or broker
- Buying property without disclosing in the contract of sale that the buyer is a licensed real estate salesperson or broker
- Violating any of the rules regulating rental practices
- Failing to notify the commission within 30 days of conviction, indictment, or being charged with a crime, or of the suspension or revocation of any real estate license issued by another state, or of initiation of disciplinary proceedings
- Violating any of the previous items or the administrative rules adopted by the commission

If a licensee is guilty of a third violation of any of the listed articles, the person may be considered a *repeat offender* and denied ever again holding a real estate license.

SUMMARY

Licensees are governed by the *Real Estate License Act* and also the rules of the Real Estate Commission.

Salespersons may not accept compensation from anyone but their supervising broker. They may not hold deposits or maintain trust accounts. A salesperson may work for only one New Jersey broker at a time.

Every resident broker must have a place of business in the state. A branch office requires a duplicate license and a broker-salesperson as supervisor. No office may be located in the home of a salesperson who is in the broker's employ, thus avoiding the practice of *license lending*.

Each broker maintains a special *trust account*, also known as an *escrow account*, for funds belonging to other persons. Brokers must deposit such funds within *five business days* of receipt. Mixing escrow funds with the broker's own money is called *commingling* and is forbidden.

The broker must keep, for at least *six years*, copies of all financial records, listings, and contracts, as well as numerous other documents; unaccepted offers must be kept for *six months*. Every person signing a real estate document must immediately receive a *duplicate original*.

The broker must pay salespersons any commissions due within ten days after the broker receives the fees. When a salesperson leaves, commissions are paid in accordance with the agreement signed by the salesperson and the broker, and the broker must make an account in writing within 30 days of termination of any funds still due the salesperson.

Listing fees are negotiable between clients and brokers, and no contract can indicate that there is any set fee schedule. Every seller who lists real estate must receive a copy of the Attorney General's memorandum of the Law Against Discrimination.

Licensees can prepare sales contracts only on one- to four-family dwellings and one-family lots, and every contract or lease prepared by a licensee must carry specific language notifying the tenants or buyers and sellers that they have *three business days* in which to seek *attorney's review* of the contract. As a result of a New Jersey Supreme Court ruling in March 1995, all contracts prepared by licensees must have attached as the cover sheet the notice advising buyers and sellers of their right to hire an attorney.

Although brokers owe special duties to their principals if they are functioning as agents, they must deal fairly with all parties to any transaction.

Unless otherwise instructed by the client, brokers must *cooperate* with other firms to find buyers for a specific property. All *written* offers must be promptly transmitted to the seller.

All advertising by brokers must clearly state that it is being placed by a real estate company. All ads for property must name the municipality in which the property is located. No ads can refer to financing without including the words "to a qualified buyer." Rebate of part of the commission may be paid by a broker to a buyer, in the form of a credit or a check. The arrangement must be established at the start of the relationship, all parties, including mortgage lenders, must be aware of it, and the purchaser must be alerted to possible tax consequences.

The Real Estate Commission must give 10 days' notice of a hearing if a violation is suspected. It can put licensees on *probation*, or subject their licenses to *suspension* or *revocation*. Fines of $250–$50,000 are also possible.

USEFUL WEBSITES

New Jersey State Government: www.state.nj.us

New Jersey Real Estate Commission: www.state.nj.us/dobi/remnu.shtml

New Jersey State Legislature: www.njleg.state.nj.us

National Association of Exclusive Buyer Agents: www.naeba.org

Real Estate Buyer's Agent Council: www.rebac.net

KEY TERMS REVIEW

Match the number of each key term with the corresponding letter.

_____ 1. Branch office	A.	broker's additional place of business
_____ 2. Commingling	B.	copy of a real estate contract with original signatures
_____ 3. Duplicate original	C.	least severe discipline by the Real Estate Commission
_____ 4. Escrow account	D.	mixing broker's money with that of others
_____ 5. Guilty knowledge	E.	cancellation of a real estate license
_____ 6. Probation	F.	place for money belonging to clients and customers
_____ 7. Revocation	G.	awareness of wrongdoing with no attempt to stop it
_____ 8. Suspension	H.	temporary lifting of a real estate license
_____ 9. Trust account	I.	another name for escrow account
_____ 10. Waiver of Broker Cooperation	J.	form sellers must sign for an office-exclusive listing

UNIT 2 REVIEW QUESTIONS

1. A licensed salesperson is allowed to
   A. keep earnest money deposits in a special escrow account.
   B. leave one broker and affiliate with another.
   C. keep a license without a sponsoring broker.
   D. work for two brokers if each is informed and consents.

2. Under some circumstances, a real estate office may be in the home of
   A. a broker.
   B. a salesperson.
   C. a broker-salesperson.
   D. no one.

3. A broker wants to open a branch office in a new shopping mall in the next town. The office can be supervised by
   A. a salesperson with at least two years' experience.
   B. the broker by phone each day.
   C. a friendly broker in the next town.
   D. a broker-salesperson.

4. A salesperson accepts an earnest money deposit and turns it over to his broker. The broker must
   A. open a separate bank account for the deposit.
   B. keep it in the account used for the salesperson's transactions.
   C. promptly deposit it in the office's business account and keep a careful record so that it won't get confused with the broker's funds.
   D. deposit it within five days in a trust account.

5. An escrow account may be opened in
   A. any authorized New Jersey financial institution.
   B. a New Jersey stockbroker's office.
   C. a Texas bank that offers high interest.
   D. any of these.

6. A broker must keep copies of
   A. contracts for six years.
   B. documents for seven years.
   C. financial transactions only.
   D. leases for at least one year after they expire.

7. Every person who signs a contract is entitled to receive a duplicate original. When are they entitled to receive it?
   A. Immediately
   B. Within three days
   C. Within a week
   D. Within 10 days

8. Every sales contract prepared by a broker must contain a notice that
   A. the broker's commission rates do not exceed community standards.
   B. the buyer may not purchase insurance from the same company that sold the property.
   C. earnest money will be deposited in a trust account.
   D. the buyer and seller may seek attorney review within three business days.

9. Even when the broker is the seller's agent, buyers are entitled to
   A. preferential treatment.
   B. first loyalty.
   C. fair dealing.
   D. negotiated fees.

10. For a license law violation, the Real Estate Commission could fine a licensee as much as
    A. $10,000.
    B. $20,000.
    C. $35,000.
    D. $25,000.

11. The commission will rule that someone could never again get a license after how many violations?
    A. One
    B. Two
    C. Three
    D. Four

12. Rebate of part of a commission may be paid to a
    A. seller only.
    B. buyer only.
    C. home inspector.
    D. seller or buyer.

13. The Real Estate Commission must give a licensee how much notice before a hearing is held on a possible violation?
    A. No notice
    B. One week
    C. 10 days
    D. 30 days

14. A real estate firm holds a door-prize drawing at a weekend open house it runs. This practice
    A. violates the commission's rules.
    B. is acceptable because it is in the seller's best interest.
    C. is acceptable only if it is offered at every listed house.
    D. can offer only prizes worth less than $25.

15. A broker is offering her mother's house for sale and will charge no commission. Should she reveal that she is a licensed agent?
    A. No, because she is acting in a private capacity.
    B. Yes, but not until after the purchaser signs an offer.
    C. No, because no fee will be paid.
    D. Yes, as soon as she meets a prospective buyer.

16. A broker-run advertisement in a local newspaper
    A. must specify the complete address of the property.
    B. must be retained for six months if a qualifying word or words for attainable financing was used.
    C. must spell out the full name of the MLS with no exceptions.
    D. may not advertise a free appraisal, although a free CMA is permitted.

17. What is a *reasonable effort* for a seller's agent to determine material information about a property's physical condition?
    A. Ask questions while walking the property with the seller.
    B. Hire a home inspector prior to taking the listing.
    C. Suggest that the seller to sell "as is" to avoid making disclosures.
    D. Encourage the seller to complete a property disclosure statement.

18. A New Jersey licensee is permitted to represent both parties to a transaction if he or she obtains the
    A. written consent of the seller and at least the informed, oral consent of the buyer.
    B. informed, written consent of the seller, buyer, and any other agent involved.
    C. consent, whether written or oral, of either party to the transaction.
    D. permission of the New Jersey Real Estate Commission in accordance with the license law.

19. Any agreement between competing offices to establish standard commission rates is referred to as
    A. the preliminary marketing contract.
    B. price gouging.
    C. illegal price-fixing.
    D. legal industry practice under New Jersey law.

20. A salesperson working for a broker was disciplined for pursuing a flagrant and continued course of misrepresentations, making false promises, and failing to pay over money belonging to others. In this case, the broker's license
    A. will automatically be suspended, because the broker is responsible for the acts of all salespersons in her office.
    B. will not be suspended, because only the salesperson was disciplined for wrongdoing.
    C. will be suspended or revoked only if the broker knew about the salesperson's activities and did nothing about it.
    D. will be suspended, but the licenses of any other salespersons in her brokerage will not be affected.

UNIT 3

Agency, Brokerage, and Ethical Considerations

LEARNING OBJECTIVES

When you have completed this unit, you will be able to accomplish the following.

> Identify types of agency and fiduciary responsibilities.
> Describe the broker-salesperson relationships and compensation issues.
> Discuss the disclosures to sellers and buyers related to creating agency and providing material information.
> Describe misrepresentation, Consumer Fraud Act, antitrust laws, ethical considerations, and disciplinable offenses as forms of consumer protections.

KEY TERMS

agent
antitrust laws
attorney in fact
broker
buyer's agent
buyer's broker
client
Code of Ethics
commission
conflict of interest
Consumer Information
  Statement (CIS)
customer
disclosed dual agent
disclosure
dual agency
employee
errors and omissions
  (E&O) insurance

fiduciary
fiduciary relationship
fraud
fraudulent
  misrepresentation
general agent
Graduate REALTOR®
  Institute (GRI)
independent contractor
innocent
  misrepresentation
kickback
latent defect
law of agency
meeting of the minds
Megan's Law
National Association of
  REALTORS® (NAR)

negligent
  misrepresentation
New Jersey REALTORS®
  (NJR)
off-site conditions
power of attorney
principal
procuring cause
puffing
ready, willing, and able
  buyer
REALTOR®
salesperson
special agent
standard of card
subagent
transaction broker
universal agent

BROKERAGE DEFINED

The business of bringing buyers and sellers together in the marketplace is called *brokerage*. In the real estate business a **broker** is defined as a person who is licensed to assist others in real estate transactions and to receive compensation for those services. A real estate **salesperson** works on behalf of and is licensed to work under the supervision of a broker.

Years ago in New Jersey and elsewhere, the **principal** (known as the client) who employed the broker was almost always an owner who wished to sell a property. The real estate broker acted as the seller's **agent**, and was usually compensated with a **commission** if a ready, willing, and able purchaser was procured. In this traditional real estate transaction the seller was the **client**, to whom specific duties were owed; the buyer was the agent's **customer**, whom the agent must only treat fairly and honestly.

Today, however, agency relationships have become more complex than under the old seller-based model. A prospective buyer or a person seeking property to rent can also be a principal and hire a broker to act as a **buyer's broker** or **buyer's agent**. In this type of relationship, the buyer is the client (the person to whom specific duties are owed) and the seller is the agent's customer (whom the agent must simply treat honestly and fairly).

It is also possible for a licensee to function as a transaction broker, working with buyer, seller, or both, without representing either one but functioning as the manager of the transaction. In this case, *no agency relationship is created*. The creation of agency is determined not by who pays the commission but in most cases by a contractual agreement between the broker and the buyer or seller.

AGENCY

The role of a broker as the agent of his or her principal is a *fiduciary relationship* that falls within the requirements of the **law of agency**. A **fiduciary relationship** is one of *trust* and *confidence* in which an agent is responsible for the money and/or property of others. It requires putting the principal's interest above all others, including the broker's own interest. The agent is also known as a **fiduciary**.

Types of Agency

A **universal agent** has authority to represent the principal in all matters that can be delegated. He or she can enter into any contract on behalf of the principal without prior permission. Other agents may be classified as general agents or special agents, based on the scope of their authority.

A **general agent** is empowered to represent the principal in a *broad range* of matters. The general agent may bind the principal to any contracts within the scope of his or her authority. An example of a general agent would be a property manager responsible for running a large building: procuring tenants, collecting rents, and hiring and supervising maintenance personnel, among other duties.

A **special agent** is authorized to represent the principal in one *specific* capacity only. A real estate broker is traditionally a special agent hired by a buyer or seller to locate a willing seller of a suitable property or a willing buyer. As a special agent, the broker is not authorized to buy or sell the property or to bind the principal to any contract.

Often one person is authorized to act for someone else in a legally binding capacity. This type of agency is created by a **power of attorney**, a legal *written authorization* that stipulates the specific areas of authority in which the agent may act. The agent acting in such a capacity is known as an **attorney-in-fact**.

FIDUCIARY RESPONSIBILITIES

An agent has a fiduciary relationship with his or her principal; that is, a special relationship of trust and confidence. This confidential relationship carries with it certain duties that the agent must perform:

- Care
- Obedience
- Accounting
- Loyalty (confidentiality)
- Disclosure

These duties are easily remembered by the acronym COALD.

Care

The agent must exercise a reasonable degree of care and diligence while transacting business on behalf of the principal. Brokers and agents are expected, by virtue of their licenses, to have expertise in real estate matters greater than that possessed by the average person. As a result, they may be liable to the principal for any loss resulting from negligence or carelessness.

Breach of Duty of Care

The duty of care requires the seller's agent to, among other things, be knowledgeable about all aspects of the property to arrive at a reasonable listing price, to discover and investigate material facts, assist the owner with negotiating an offer that meets the seller's needs, and advise the seller on ways to effect the sale. Examples of a breach of the duty of care could include failure to inform the seller of how the property condition affects value, or failure to effectively navigate the transaction through to closing.

A buyer's agent is expected to inform the client of whatever problems can be discovered in the property, advise on probable market value, advise on financing options, help negotiate the lowest possible purchase price, and monitor the progress of the purchase until transfer of title.

The agent is expected to deliver the quality of service that a normal person would expect of a reasonably prudent agent. Actions breaching this obligation might be failing to present a written offer before it expires, neglecting to mention in the purchase contract any fixtures or personal property desired by one of the parties, neglecting property being managed for another, improperly handling escrow deposits, or failing to obtain all necessary signatures on a contract.

The courts set differing **standards of care** for brokers and for salespersons. Brokers are held to higher expectations than salespersons. Special training, designations, education, and experience may all increase the standard required of an agent. Brokers are unwise to represent themselves as, for example, experienced syndicators if they are unable to deliver service of acceptable quality. The rookie residential agent confronted with an opportunity to list a shopping plaza should probably approach an experienced commercial broker with a request that they work together to list and sell the property. Otherwise, the duty of observing an appropriate standard of care may be breached by the inexperienced agent.

Unit 3

Obedience

The agent is obligated to obey the principal's lawful instructions. The agent is not, however, required to obey unlawful or unethical instructions—for example, violating fair housing laws or misrepresenting a property's condition or a buyer's finances.

Breach of Duty of Obedience

The agent must obey all the client's lawful instructions, such as "24-hour notice for showing," or "all offers through listing broker," or "all contracts must be accompanied by a preapproved mortgage letter." Failing to do so constitutes a breach of the duty of obedience. However, some instructions must be disobeyed, such as any order to conceal a hidden defect or to practice discrimination in the sale or rental of a property. An agent may not advertise a property below the price stipulated by the seller; thus, "Try around ninety thousand" or "Make an offer" may be in violation of the duty of obedience. It is also a violation for a seller's agent to suggest that the buyer offer anything below the asking price unless the seller has authorized the broker to do whatever negotiating is necessary to effect a sale.

Accounting

The agent is obligated to safeguard and account for all money or property entrusted to his or her professional care. Real estate license laws require brokers to give duplicate originals of all documents to all parties affected by them and to keep copies of such documents on file for six years. In addition, the license laws require the broker to deposit all funds entrusted to him or her immediately into a special trust account. It is illegal for an agent to commingle (mix) such monies with personal funds or to retain any interest they earn. An agent may not make any *secret profit*.

Breach of Duty of Accounting

All monies received from a client or that is being held in trust for a client must be scrupulously accounted for. New Jersey's license law, rules, and regulations detail how to account for the money. A common source of trouble occurs when a prospective buyer who does not keep large sums in a checking account gives an agent a check to be held for a few days. Troubles may occur if the seller accepts the purchase offer based on the representation that the earnest money is in the broker's possession. Everyone is protected if the licensee informs the seller of the exact form and status of the deposit and has the seller initial an acknowledgment. The broker clearly owes the seller an accounting of the exact status of the deposit, and *disclosure* is again the key element.

Loyalty (Includes Confidentiality)

An agent must always place a principal's interests above those of other persons, including the agent's own interests. For instance, an agent cannot disclose such information as the principal's financial condition or disclose any confidential facts that might harm the principal's bargaining position. For example, disclosing that the seller will accept a price lower than the listing price might harm the principal. A buyer's broker, on the other hand, cannot reveal the buyer's readiness to pay more if necessary.

Brokers or salespersons must not buy property listed with them for themselves or for accounts in which they have a personal interest without first notifying the principal of such interest.

Neither brokers nor salespersons may sell property in which they have a personal interest without informing the purchaser of that interest. Such a disclosure must be made in writing as part of the purchase contract.

Breach of Duty of Loyalty

Because the agent may not advance his or her interest at the expense of the principals, any attempt to profit from a transaction except through the agreed-on commission signals a situation in which loyalty might be breached. Profiting from a client's misfortune is forbidden. The agent who subtly discourages efforts by co-brokers in a multiple listing system in hopes of securing a sale within the listing office is not acting in the client's best interest.

Disclosure (Notice)

It is the agent's duty to pass on to the principal all facts or information he or she obtains that could affect the principal's business or decisions. The agent must volunteer pertinent information whether or not the client asks. This includes any information that might affect the object of the agency, the true value of the property and/or possible legal consequences of contract provisions.

In certain instances the broker may be held liable for damages for failing to disclose such information. The fiduciary duty owed by a buyer's agent to the buyer/principal includes conveying to the buyer any information about the seller's willingness to accept a lower price, about other offers, or about the value of the property. No confidentiality would apply to the seller's disclosures if made to a buyer's broker.

Breach of Duty of Disclosure or Notice

The law considers that any notice given the agent has been given to the principal. The agent therefore has a duty to pass on any material information; all written offers must be presented immediately.

The broker who is a seller's agent must volunteer any facts that might be of value to the seller. Details of the buyer's financial condition should be disclosed, as well as any information that the buyer has indicated he or she might pay a higher price. The duty of notice also places on the broker an obligation to explain to the seller matters that might otherwise escape notice or be misunderstood, such as details of proposed financing or drawbacks in a purchase offer.

In similar fashion, the buyer's broker is obligated to pass on to the buyer any information that might help the buyer's negotiating position. If the sellers have indicated that they might take less for the house, or that they are facing foreclosure if they don't get a prompt offer, a buyer's broker need not keep the fact confidential. On the contrary, the buyer's broker must relay the information to his or her client.

General Duty of Fair Dealing

Although an agency relationship binds the agent to the principal with certain specific duties, remember that real estate licensees are required to deal fairly and honestly with all parties.

BROKER-SALESPERSON RELATIONSHIP

A person licensed to perform any real estate activities on behalf of a licensed real estate broker is known as a real estate salesperson. The *salesperson is responsible to the broker under whom he or she is licensed*. A salesperson can carry out only those responsibilities assigned by that broker.

Salesperson and Broker

A broker's license entitles the broker to enter into contractual agreements and collect commissions for performing his or her assigned duties either as an agent or as a transaction broker. A salesperson, on the other hand, has no authority to make contracts with or receive compensation directly from anyone other than his or her supervising broker. The broker is fully responsible for the actions of all salespeople licensed under him or her. All of a salesperson's activities must be performed in the name of the supervising broker.

The salesperson functions as an agent of the broker and as a **subagent** of a principal. In most cases today, sellers and their brokers do not offer subagency to other brokers who may produce a buyer (see Unit 10). Each agent usually owes fiduciary duties to the party by whom he or she is retained. Unless the buyer has specifically retained his or her agent, it is inaccurate to refer to the buyer as one's client.

Independent Contractor vs. Employee

Salespersons are engaged by brokers as either employees or independent contractors. The New Jersey Real Estate Commission requires the agreement between broker and salesperson to be in writing and to include a termination agreement.

The employer-employee relationship allows a broker to exercise certain controls over salespeople who are employees. The broker can require an **employee** to adhere to regulations such as working hours, office routine, and dress standards. As an employer, a broker is required by the federal government to withhold Social Security tax and income tax from wages paid to employees. The employee is also required to pay unemployment or workers' compensation tax on wages as defined by state and federal laws. A broker may provide employees with benefits such as health insurance.

Most real estate salespersons, however, act as **independent contractors**. Independent contractors assume responsibility for paying their own income and Social Security taxes and must provide their own health insurance if such coverage is desired (see Unit 2). Independent contractors receive nothing from their brokers that could be considered an employee benefit (see Figure 3.1). Brokers cannot require independent contractors to work certain hours or attend office meetings, nor can they pay them any salary. The greater the number of broker-imposed controls over an independent contractor's work, the greater the risk that the relationship will be construed as employer-employee with significant tax and regulatory consequences.

The Internal Revenue Service has provided safe *harbor* guidelines under which independent contractor status will not be challenged when the associate is licensed, has fluctuating income based on commissions, and works under a written contract *specifying independent contractor status*. A suggested independent contractor agreement is shown in Figure 3.2.

BROKER'S COMPENSATION

The broker's compensation is specified in the listing agreement, buyer-broker agreement, management agreement, or other contract with the principal and is subject to negotiation between the parties. Compensation is often computed as a *percentage* of the total amount of money involved, but it can be a *flat fee* or *hourly rate*. The commission or fee is usually considered to be earned when the broker has accomplished the work for which he or she was hired. Unless there is an agreement to the contrary, after a listing broker procures a **ready, willing, and able buyer**, the seller technically is liable for the broker's commission. A ready, willing, and able buyer is one who is prepared to buy on the seller's terms, is financially capable, and is ready to take positive steps toward consummation of the transaction.

Even though the fee is actually earned earlier, most contracts provide that the fee not be paid until the actual sale (transfer of title).

In some cases, even after the listing broker (or a cooperating broker) has produced a buyer who is ready, willing, and able to meet the listing terms, the deal falls through. If such occurs for any of the following reasons, the broker may still be entitled to a commission:

- The owner changes his or her mind and refuses to sell
- There are defects in the owner's title that are not corrected
- The owner commits fraud with respect to the transaction
- The owner is unable to deliver possession within a reasonable time
- The owner insists on terms not in the listing (for example, the right to restrict the use of the property)
- The owner and the buyer enter into a contract but later agree to cancel the transaction

In other words, a broker generally is due a commission if a sale is not finalized *because of the principal's default.*

Figure 3.1: Employee vs. Independent Contractor

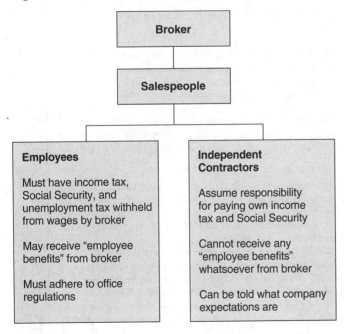

Figure 3.2: Sample of Independent Contractor Agreement

**NEW JERSEY REALTORS® STANDARD FORM OF
BROKER-SALESPERSON
INDEPENDENT CONTRACTOR AGREEMENT**

©2001, New Jersey Realtors®, Inc.

1   THIS AGREEMENT, is made and entered into this _____ day of _____, 20_____, by and between
2   _____ (hereinafter referred to as the "Broker"),
3   having its principal office at _____,
4   _____, and _____,
5   (hereinafter referred to as the "Salesperson"), residing at _____
6   _____
7
8
9   **WITNESSETH:**
10   WHEREAS, Broker is engaged in business as a real estate broker trading as _____
11   _____, with its principal office at _____
12   _____, and as such is duly licensed to engage in activities including, but
13   not limited to, selling, offering for sale, buying, offering to buy, listing and soliciting prospective purchasers, and negotiating loans on real
14   estate, leasing or offering to lease, and negotiating the sale, purchase or exchange of leases, renting or placing for rent, or managing real
15   estate or improvements thereon for another or others; and
16   WHEREAS, Broker has and does enjoy the goodwill of the public, and has a reputation for fair and honorable dealing with the public;
17   and
18   WHEREAS, Broker maintains an office in the State of New Jersey equipped with furnishings, listings, prospect lists and other equipment
19   necessary, helpful, and incidental to serving the public as a real estate broker; and
20   WHEREAS, Salesperson is duly licensed by the State of New Jersey as a real estate salesperson; and
21   WHEREAS, it is deemed to be to the mutual advantage of Broker and Salesperson to enter into this Agreement; and
22   WHEREAS, Salesperson acknowledges that he has not performed any acts on behalf of Broker nor has he been authorized to act on
23   behalf of Broker; and
24   WHEREAS, the parties acknowledge that they deem it desirable to enter into an agreement in compliance with the provisions of
25   N.J.A.C. 11:5-4.1;
26   NOW, THEREFORE, in consideration of the foregoing premises and the mutual covenants herein contained, it is mutually covenanted
27   and agreed by and between the parties hereto as follows:
28
29   1. **SERVICES.** Salesperson agrees to proceed diligently, faithfully, legally, and with his best efforts to sell, lease, or rent any and all real
30   estate listed with Broker, except for any listings which are placed by Broker exclusively with another salesperson(s), and to solicit additional
31   listings and customers for Broker, and otherwise to promote the business of serving the public in real estate transactions, and for the
32   mutual benefit of the parties hereto.
33
34   2. **OFFICE SPACE.** Broker agrees to provide Salesperson with work space and other facilities at its office presently maintained at __
35   _____, or at such other location
36   as determined by Broker at which Broker may maintain an office. The items furnished pursuant to this Paragraph 2 shall be for the
37   convenience of the Salesperson.
38
39   3. **RULES AND REGULATIONS.** Salesperson and Broker agree to conduct business and regulate habits and working hours in a
40   manner which will maintain and increase the goodwill, business, profits, and reputation of Broker and Salesperson, and the parties agree
41   to conform to and abide by all laws, rules and regulations, and codes of ethics that are binding on, or applicable to, real estate broker
42   and real estate salespeople. Salesperson and Broker shall be governed by the Code of Ethics of the NATIONAL ASSOCIATION OF
43   REALTORS®, the real estate laws of the State of New Jersey, the Constitution and By-Laws of the _____
44   _____ Board/Association of Realtors®, the rules and regulations of any Multiple Listing
45   Service with which Broker now or in the future may be affiliated with, and any further modifications or additions to any of the foregoing.
46   Salesperson acknowledges that it is his responsibility to familiarize himself with all current Code of Ethics, the Local Board/Association
47   By-Laws, the rules and regulations of any Multiple Listing Service with which Broker is now affiliated, the Rules and Regulations of the
48   Real Estate Commission and the License Law of the State of New Jersey. Broker agrees to maintain copies of all the foregoing and to
49   make the same available to Salesperson. Salesperson agrees also to abide by the rules, regulations, policies and standards promulgated by
50   Broker.
51   NJ REALTORS® Form-134-8/15   Page 1 of 5

Figure 3.2: Sample of Independent Contractor Agreement (continued)

51 52 53 54 55 56 57 58 59   **4. LICENSING AND ASSOCIATION MEMBERSHIP.** Salesperson represents that he is duly licensed by the State of New Jersey as a real estate salesperson. Salesperson acknowledges that Broker is a member of the _____ _____ Board/Association of Realtors®, the New Jersey Association of REALTORS® and the NATIONAL ASSOCIATION OF REALTORS®, and as a result thereof, Broker is subject to the rules and regulations of those organizations. Salesperson agrees to be subject to and act in accordance with said rules and regulations. If Broker requires Salesperson to become a member of any real estate organization, then Salesperson agrees that he shall become a member thereof and shall pay all applicable fees and dues required to maintain said membership. As a result of Broker being a member of the aforesaid groups, Broker and Salesperson agree to abide by all applicable rules, regulations and standards of such organizations, including, but without limitation, those pertaining to ethics, conduct and procedure.

61 62 63 64 65   **5. COMPENSATION.** Salesperson's sole compensation from Broker shall be in the form of commissions. The commissions for services rendered in the sale, rental, or leasing of any real estate and the method of payment, shall be determined exclusively by Broker. Commissions, when earned and collected by Broker, shall be divided between Broker and Salesperson after deduction of all expenses and co-brokerage commissions in accord with the Salesperson's Commission Schedule attached to this Agreement as Schedule A which is an outline of compensation to be paid by Broker to Salesperson during the Salesperson's affiliation with Broker.

67 68 69 70   **6. MULTIPLE SALESPEOPLE.** In the event that two (2) or more salespeople under contract with Broker participate in a sale and claim a commission thereon, then and in that event the amount of commissions allocable to each salesperson shall be divided in accordance with a written agreement among said salespeople. In the event that the salespeople shall be unable to agree, the dispute shall be submitted to and be determined by Broker, in his sole discretion.

72 73 74   **7. RESPONSIBILITY OF BROKER FOR COMMISSIONS.** In no event shall Broker be liable to Salesperson for any commissions not collected, nor shall Salesperson be personally liable for any commissions not collected. It is agreed that commissions collected shall be deposited with the Broker and subsequently divided and distributed in accordance with the terms of this Agreement.

76 77 78 79   **8. DIVISION AND DISTRIBUTION OF COMMISSIONS.** The division and distribution of the earned commissions as provided for in this Agreement which may be paid to or collected by the Broker, but from which Salesperson is due certain commissions, shall take place as soon as practicable after collection and receipt of such commissions, but in no event more than ten (10) business days after receipt by the Broker, or as soon thereafter as such funds have cleared the Broker's bank.

81 82 83   **9. RESPONSIBILITY FOR EXPENSES.** Unless otherwise agreed in writing, Broker shall not be liable to Salesperson for any expenses incurred by Salesperson or for any of his acts, nor shall Salesperson be liable to Broker for Broker's office help or expenses, or for any of Broker's acts other than as specifically provided for herein.

85 86 87 88 89 90 91 92 93 94 95   **10. ADVANCES.** Broker may from time to time and in his sole discretion make advances to Salesperson on account of future commissions; it being expressly agreed, however, that such advances are temporary loans by Broker for the accommodation of Salesperson which are due and payable on demand or as otherwise agreed to by the Broker, and are not compensation. Upon notice to Salesperson, Broker shall have the right to charge interest on any and all advances made to Salesperson, either at the time of making the advance or thereafter, at a rate chosen by Broker in his sole discretion, but not in excess of the maximum rate permitted by law. Upon receipt of payment of commissions, Broker shall credit the account of Salesperson (first toward interest, if any, and then toward principal) with the portion of such commissions due Salesperson. If at any time, the advances made to Salesperson together with interest thereon, if any, exceed the credits to his account for his share of commissions collected, then such excess shall be owing by Salesperson to Broker and shall be due and payable upon demand. After such demand, interest at the maximum rate permitted by law shall accrue upon the amount due Broker, notwithstanding the fact that any or all of the advances made to Salesperson have initially been interest free or at a reduced rate of interest.

97 98 99 100   **11. REAL ESTATE LICENSES, BONDS, DUES AND FEES.** Salesperson agrees to pay the cost of maintaining his real estate license, dues for membership in the NATIONAL ASSOCIATION OF REALTORS®, the New Jersey Association of REALTORS®, the local Board/Association of REALTORS® and other dues and fees related to the rendering of services by Salesperson as a real estate salesperson.

102 103 104 105   **12. AUTHORITY TO CONTRACT.** Salesperson shall have no authority to bind, obligate, or commit Broker by any promise or representation, either verbally or in writing, unless specifically authorized in writing by Broker in a particular transaction. However, Salesperson shall be and is hereby authorized to execute listing agreements for and on behalf of Broker as his agent subject to Broker's office policy.

107 108 109 110   **13. CONTROVERSIES WITH OTHERS.** In the event any transaction in which Salesperson is involved results in a dispute, litigation or legal expense, Salesperson shall cooperate fully with Broker. Broker and Salesperson shall share the payment of all judgments, awards, settlement and other expenses connected therewith, in the same proportion as they normally would share the commission resulting from such transaction if there were no dispute or litigation. It is the policy to avoid litigation wherever possible, and Broker, within his

Unit 3

Figure 3.2: Sample of Independent Contractor Agreement (continued)

111 sole discretion may determine whether or not any litigation or dispute shall be prosecuted, defended, compromised or settled, and the
112 terms and conditions of any compromise or settlement, or whether or not legal expense shall be incurred. Salesperson shall not have the
113 right to directly or indirectly compel Broker to institute or prosecute litigation against any third party for collection of commissions, nor
114 shall Salesperson have any cause of action against Broker for its failure to do so. In the event a commission is paid to Broker in which
115 Salesperson is entitled to share, but another real estate broker disputes or may dispute the right of Broker to receive all or any portion of
116 such commission, Salesperson agrees that Broker may hold said commission in trust until such dispute is resolved or sufficient time has
117 passed to indicate to Broker in his sole and absolute judgment that no action or proceeding will be commenced by such other real estate
118 broker regarding the subject commission. In the event Broker shall pay any commission to Salesperson and thereafter, either during or
119 subsequent to termination of this Agreement, Broker shall become obligated, either by way of final judicial determination, arbitration
120 award or good faith negotiation, to repay all or any part of such commission to others, Salesperson agrees to reimburse Broker his pro
121 rata share thereof. In any such instance, Broker agrees to keep Salesperson reasonably informed of any proceeding.
122
123 14. **OWNERSHIP OF LISTINGS.** Salesperson agrees that any and all listings of property, and all actions taken in connection with
124 the real estate business and in accordance with the terms of this Agreement shall be taken by Salesperson in the name of Broker. In the
125 event Salesperson receives a listing, it shall be filed with Broker no later than twenty four (24) hours after receipt of same by Salesperson.
126 Broker agrees, but is not obligated, to generally make available to Salesperson all current listings maintained by its office. However, all
127 listings shall be and remain the separate and exclusive property of Broker unless otherwise agreed to in writing by the parties hereto.
128
129 15. **DOCUMENTS.** Broker and Salesperson agree that all documents generated by and relating to services performed by either of
130 them in accordance with this Agreement, including, but without limitation, all correspondence received, copies of all correspondence
131 written, plats, listing information, memoranda, files, photographs, reports, legal opinions, accounting information, any and all other
132 instruments, documents or information of any nature whatsoever concerning transactions handled by Broker or by Salesperson or jointly
133 are and shall remain the exclusive property of the Broker.
134
135 16. **COMMUNICATIONS.** Broker shall determine and approve all correspondence from the Broker's office pertaining to transactions
136 being handled, in whole or in part, by the Salesperson.
137
138 17. **FORMS AND CONTRACTS.** Broker shall determine and approve the forms to be used and the contents of all completed
139 contracts and other completed forms before they are presented to third parties for signature.
140
141 18. **INDEPENDENT CONTRACTOR.** This Agreement does not constitute employment of Salesperson by Broker and Broker and
142 Salesperson acknowledge that Salesperson's duties under this Agreement shall be performed by him in his capacity as an independent
143 contractor. Nothing contained in this Agreement shall constitute Broker and Salesperson as joint ventures or partners and neither shall
144 be liable for any obligation incurred by the other party to this Agreement, except as provided herein. The Salesperson shall not be
145 treated as an employee for Federal, State or local tax purposes with respect to services performed in accordance with the terms of this
146 Agreement. Effective as of the date of this Agreement, Broker will not (i) withhold any Federal, State, or local income or FICA taxes
147 from Salesperson's commissions; (ii) pay any FICA or Federal and State unemployment insurance on Salesperson's behalf; or (iii) include
148 Salesperson in any of its retirement, pension, or profit sharing plans. Salesperson shall be required to pay all Federal, State, and local
149 income and self-employment taxes on his income, as required by law, and to file all applicable estimated and final returns and forms in
150 connection therewith.
151
152 19. **NOTICE OF TERMINATION.** This Agreement, and the relationship created hereby may be terminated by either party
153 hereto with or without cause, at anytime upon three (3) days written notice. However, this Agreement shall immediately terminate upon
154 Salesperson's death. Except as otherwise provided for herein, the rights of the parties hereto to any commissions which were accrued and
155 earned prior to the termination of this Agreement shall not be divested by the termination of this Agreement.
156
157 20. **SERVICES TO BE PERFORMED SUBSEQUENT TO TERMINATION.** Upon termination of this Agreement, all
158 negotiations commenced by Salesperson during the term of this Agreement shall continue to be handled through Broker and with such
159 assistance by Salesperson as is determined by Broker. The Salesperson agrees to be compensated for such services in accordance with
160 Schedule B attached hereto.
161
162 21. **LIST OF PROSPECTS.** Upon termination of this Agreement. Salesperson shall furnish Broker with a complete list of all
163 prospects, leads and foreseeable transactions developed by Salesperson, or upon which Salesperson shall have been engaged with respect to
164 any transaction completed subsequent to termination of this Agreement in which Salesperson has rendered assistance in accordance with
165 the terms of this Agreement. Except as expressly provided for in Paragraph 20 of this Agreement, Salesperson shall not be compensated
166 in respect of any transaction completed subsequent to termination of this agreement unless agreed to in writing by the Broker.
167
168 22. **DUTY OF NON-DISCLOSURE.** Salesperson agrees that upon termination of this Agreement, he will not furnish to any person,
169 firm, company, corporation, partnership, joint venture, or any other entity engaged in the real estate business, any information as to
170 Broker or its business, including, but not limited to, Broker's clients, customers, properties, prices,

Figure 3.2: Sample of Independent Contractor Agreement (continued)

171 terms of negotiations, nor policies or relationships with prospects, clients and customers. Salesperson, shall not, after termination of
172 this Agreement, remove from the files or from the office of the Broker, any information pertaining to the Broker's business, including, but
173 not limited to, any maps, books, publications, card records, investor or prospect lists, or any other material, files or data, and it is expressly
174 agreed that the aforementioned records and information are the property of Broker.

175
176 23. **COMPENSATION SUBSEQUENT TO TERMINATION.** Upon termination of this Agreement, Salesperson shall be
177 compensated only in accordance with the appended Schedule B.

178
179 24. **ESCROW DEPOSIT.** All contracts of sale shall be accompanied by an escrow deposit in an amount as determined by Broker.
180 Salesperson will, at all times, require purchaser or prospective purchasers, to put up such escrow deposit unless a higher or lower sum shall
181 be mutually agreed to by Broker and Salesperson. Salesperson is expressly prohibited from accepting a smaller escrow deposit, a post-
182 dated check, or agreeing not to deposit an escrow check, unless such action has been expressly authorized by Broker.

183
184 25. **AUTOMOBILE.** Salesperson agrees to furnish his own automobile, pay all expenses in connection with the operation
185 and maintenance of said automobile, and that Broker shall have no responsibility therefore. Salesperson agrees to carry
186 throughout the terms of this Agreement public liability insurance upon his automobile with minimum limits not less than
187 _____ ($ _____) for each person and
188 _____ ($ _____) for each accident,
189 and property damage insurance with a minimum limit of not less than _____
190 $ _____). Upon request, Salesperson agrees to furnish to Broker certificates certifying as to
191 such insurance prepared by the insurance company.

192
193 26. **ASSIGNABILITY AND BINDING EFFECT.** This Agreement is personal to the parties hereto and may not be assigned, sold or
194 otherwise conveyed by either of them.

195
196 27. **NOTICE.** Any and all notices, or any other communication provided for herein shall be in writing and shall be personally delivered
197 or mailed by registered or certified mail, return receipt requested prepaid postage, which shall be addressed to the parties at the addresses
198 indicated herein, or to such different address as such party may have fixed. Any such notice shall be effective upon receipt, if personally
199 delivered, or three (3) business days after mailing.

200
201 28. **GOVERNING LAW.** This Agreement shall be subject to and governed by the laws of the State of New Jersey, including the
202 conflicts of laws, irrespective of the fact that Salesperson may be or become a resident of a different state.

203
204 29. **WAIVER OF BREACH.** The waiver by the Broker of a breach of any provision of this Agreement by the Salesperson shall not
205 operate or be construed as a waiver of any subsequent breach by the Salesperson.

206
207 30. **ENTIRE AGREEMENT.** This Agreement constitutes the entire agreement between the parties and contains all of the agreement
208 between the parties with respect to the subject matter hereof; this Agreement supersedes any and all other agreements, either oral or in
209 writing between the parties hereto with respect to the subject matter hereof.

210
211 31. **GENDER.** When used in this Agreement, the masculine shall be deemed to include the feminine.

212
213 32. **SEPARABILITY.** If any provision of this Agreement is invalid or unenforceable in any jurisdiction, the other provisions herein
214 shall remain in full force and effect such jurisdiction and shall be liberally construed in order to effectuate the purpose and intent of this
215 Agreement, and the invalidity or unenforceability of any provision of this Agreement in any jurisdiction shall not affect the durability or
216 enforceability of any such provision in any other jurisdiction.

217
218 33. **MODIFICATION.** This Agreement may not be modified or amended except by an instrument in writing signed by the parties
219 hereto. Any modification to this Agreement between the parties after the date of the Agreement shall be of no effect unless such
220 modification is in writing and is signed by both Broker and Salesperson.

221
222 34. **PARAGRAPH HEADINGS.** The paragraph headings contained in this Agreement are for reference purposes only and shall not
223 affect in any way the meaning or interpretation of this Agreement.

224
225 35. **SURVIVAL OF PROVISIONS.** The provisions of this Agreement shall survive the termination of the Salesperson's services
226 under this Agreement.

227
228 36. **COPY RECEIVED.** Salesperson acknowledges receipt of a fully executed copy of this Agreement, duly signed by Broker and
229 Salesperson.

230

Figure 3.2: Sample of Independent Contractor Agreement (continued)

231	IN WITNESS WHEREOF, the undersigned have set their hands and seals, or if a corporation, has caused this Agreement to be signed
232	and sealed by its duly authorized corporate officer, the day and year first above written.
233	
234	WITNESS:
235	
236	
237	_____ _____
238	(Broker)
239	WITNESS:
240	
241	_____ _____
242	(Salesperson)

The broker is usually entitled to a fee if he or she is the **procuring cause** of sale, that is, produces a ready, willing, and able buyer; or brings about a meeting of the minds. Where several brokers disagree as to which one brought about a sale, the one with the best claim to be the procuring cause is often difficult to determine. In some cases it could be the one who first introduced the buyer to the property; in others, it would be the one who brought the parties into agreement, as evidenced by the sales contract. A **meeting of the minds** is said to have taken place when the parties are in agreement on price, down payment, and financing method. Compensation of the buyer's broker is discussed later in this unit.

The rate of a broker's commission is negotiable in every case, although a particular firm may have its own independent policy of rates or fees. Any attempt, no matter how subtle, to impose uniform commission rates among competing firms would be a clear violation of state and federal antitrust laws.

New Jersey's license laws make it illegal for a broker to share a commission with anyone who is not licensed as a salesperson or a broker except in some circumstances to a buyer. This has been construed to include any form of gift or compensation—for instance, giving a television to a friend for providing a valuable lead or paying finder's fees and portions of the commission. **Kickbacks**, the return of part of the commission as gifts or money to sellers, are also prohibited.

SALESPERSON'S COMPENSATION

The compensation of a salesperson is set by a mutual agreement between the broker and salesperson. A broker may agree to pay a salary or, more commonly, a share of the commissions (the "split") from transactions originated by a salesperson. The salesperson may never accept compensation from any buyer, seller, or broker except the one broker with whom he or she is associated.

The Real Estate Commission requires that a salesperson's share of commission be paid by the broker within ten days of receipt by the broker, the only exception being a case in which the commission check has not cleared.

AGENCY AND THE CONSUMER

Creation of Agency With Sellers and Buyers

In New Jersey real estate practice, the *special agency* relationship between a broker and a seller or a broker and a buyer is generally created by a written employment contract. With sellers this is commonly called an Exclusive Listing Agreement (see Unit 10). With buyers this is called an Exclusive Buyer Agency Agreement, one sample of which is shown in Figure 3.3. Neither agreement is required to be in writing by New Jersey regulation although it is prudent to have such agreements in writing.

A broker has the right to reject agency contracts that, in his or her judgment, violate the ethics or high standards of the office and, in fact, must reject contracts that would cause the broker to violate the law. However, after a brokerage relationship has been established, the broker owes the principal the duty to exercise care, skill, and integrity in carrying out instructions.

Figure 3.3: Exclusive Buyer Agency Agreement

NEW JERSEY REALTORS® STANDARD FORM OF
EXCLUSIVE BUYER AGENCY AGREEMENT

© 2001 New Jersey REALTORS®

1   **1. AGENCY:** _____ and _____ referred to in
2   (Buyer)   (Buyer)
3   this Agreement as "Buyer" hereby designate _____
4   (Brokerage Firm)
5   as Buyer's exclusive agent, referred to in this Agreement as "Buyer's Agent", for the purpose of searching for, locating, and purchasing
6   real estate by Buyer in the following, _____ (municipality(ies)), pursuant to all of the
7   terms and conditions set forth below.
8
9   **2. DOES BUYER HAVE A BUSINESS RELATIONSHIP WITH ANOTHER BROKER?** ❏ YES ❏ NO
10   Buyer represents to Buyer's Agent that no other buyer's agency agreement is presently in effect. Buyer agrees not to enter into any such
11   agreement during the term of this Agreement.
12
13   **3. DECLARATION OF BUSINESS RELATIONSHIP:** The real estate license law of the State of New Jersey requires every real
14   estate licensee to declare the basis of the business relationship being established between such licensee and Buyer. Accordingly,
15   I, _____ **AS AN AUTHORIZED REPRESENTATIVE OF**
16   (Name of Licensee)
17   _____ **INTEND, AS OF THIS TIME, TO WORK WITH YOU** (buyer)
18   (Name of Firm)
19   **AS A:** (choose one)
20   ❏ **BUYER'S AGENT ONLY** ❏ **BUYER'S AGENT AND DISCLOSED DUAL AGENT IF THE OPPORTUNITY ARISES.**
21
22   **4. TERM:** This Agency Agreement shall commence on _____ and shall expire at midnight on the _____ day
23   of _____ or three (3) days after receipt by Buyer's Agent of a written termination notice from Buyer, whichever
24   shall first occur.
25
26   **5. BROKERAGE FEE:** In consideration of the services rendered by Buyer's Agent on behalf of Buyer, Buyer agrees to pay to Buyer's
27   Agent a brokerage fee of _____. The brokerage fee shall be earned, due and payable by Buyer to Buyer's
28   Agent if any property introduced by Buyer's Agent to Buyer during the term of this Agreement is purchased by Buyer prior to the expira-
29   tion of this Agreement, or within _____ days after the termination of this Agreement. However, except where Buyer's Agent
30   is a disclosed dual agent in which case the entire brokerage fee must be paid by either Buyer or seller, if the seller of such property autho-
31   rizes the listing broker to pay a portion of the listing broker's brokerage fee to Buyer's Agent, that portion of such brokerage fee shall be
32   credited against Buyer's obligation to Buyer's Agent as set forth above. In such event, Buyer agrees to pay to Buyer's Agent, at closing, the
33   difference between the amount so received from the listing broker and the total brokerage fee due to Buyer's Agent as referred to in this
34   paragraph, unless, as a term or condition of the contract of sale, the seller has agreed to pay such difference to Buyer's Agent at closing.
35
36   **6. BUYER'S AGENT'S DUTY:** Buyer's Agent shall:
37   (a) Use diligence in its search to locate a property which is acceptable to Buyer.
38   (b) Use professional knowledge and skills to assist Buyer to negotiate for the purchase of such property.
39   (c) Assist the Buyer throughout the transaction and to represent Buyer's best interests.
40
41   **7. BUYER'S DUTY:** Buyer shall:
42   (a) Provide accurate and relevant personal information to Buyer's Agent regarding Buyer's financial ability to purchase real estate.
43   (b) Advise Buyer's Agent of any home offered for sale to Buyer where Buyer may have an interest in purchasing such property.
44   (c) Submit through Buyer's Agent, any offer to purchase or contract on a property which was shown to Buyer by Buyer's Agent.
45
46   **8. OTHER BUYERS:** Other potential buyers may be interested in the same properties as Buyer. It is agreed that Buyer's Agent may
47   represent such other potential buyers whether such representation arises prior to, during, or after the termination of this Agreement. In
48   any such situation, Buyer agrees that Buyer's Agent will not disclose to any other potential buyer the terms of the Buyer's offer or any other
49   confidential information concerning the Buyer and also will not disclose to Buyer the terms of any other buyer's offer or any confidential
50   information concerning the other buyer(s).

NJ REALTORS® | Form 121 | 08/19 Page 1 of 2

Figure 3.3: Exclusive Buyer Agency Agreement (continued)

51
52 **9. DUAL AGENCY:** Buyer understands that Buyer's Agent may elect to represent a seller as well as Buyer in the sale and purchase of
53 such seller's property. In such event, Buyer acknowledges that Buyer's Agent will be a dual agent, and pursuant to law, will have to obtain
54 the written informed consent of both the seller and Buyer for the Buyer's Agent to be a Disclosed Dual Agent. Buyer understands that by
55 consenting to the Buyer's Agent to be a Disclosed Dual Agent, there will be a limitation on the Buyer's Agent's ability to represent either
56 the Buyer or seller fully and exclusively. Buyer's Agent, when acting as a Disclosed Dual Agent, will not be able to put either the seller's
57 interests ahead of the Buyer's nor the Buyer's interests ahead of the seller's. **Buyer's consent to Buyer's Agent being a Disclosed**
58 **Dual Agent shall be deemed to have been given only when the "Informed Consent to Dual Agency" is signed by the**
59 **Buyer.**
60
61 10. Buyer acknowledges receipt of the Consumer Information Statement on New Jersey Real Estate Relationships.
62
63 **11.** Buyer hereby acknowledges receipt of a signed copy of this legally binding Agreement and agrees to be bound by and comply with
64 its terms and conditions.
65
66 IF BUYER DOES NOT UNDERSTAND ALL OF THE TERMS OF THIS AGREEMENT, LEGAL ADVICE SHOULD BE
67 SOUGHT BEFORE SIGNING.
68
69 By: _____   _____   _____
70   Buyer's Agent   BUYER   Date
71
72   _____   _____
73   BUYER   Date

Disclosure of Agency

New Jersey regulations require licensees to present a **Consumer Information Statement (CIS)**, a form of disclosure (reprinted in Figure 3.4), to all sellers, buyers, landlords, and tenants on the sale or rental of all one- to four-family residential properties or vacant one-family lots. (Short-term rentals—those held for not more than 125 consecutive days—are excluded from the formal written disclosure requirement, although licensees still must disclose their business relationship in the transaction.) Although a Consumer Information Statement (CIS) is not required for other transactions (commercial buildings or multi-unit apartments, for example), written disclosure of agency can be a prudent precaution for the broker in all situations.

The Consumer Information Statement describes the types of business relationships a real estate agent can enter into with a customer or client and the duties associated with each relationship. A real estate agent can function as (1) a seller's agent, (2) a buyer's agent, (3) a **disclosed dual agent**, (4) a **transaction broker**, or (5) a seller's agent on properties on which the firm is acting as a seller's agent and transaction broker on other properties.

The client or customer should understand in advance, before discussing matters that might injure a negotiating position, whether the licensee is legally obligated to keep financial information confidential or legally obligated to pass the information on to another party. Is the licensee able to divulge how much the seller would really take for the property or how much the buyer would really pay if necessary? These are prime examples of what should or should not be discussed with the licensee, depending on the type of business relationship the client or customer has entered into. In short, the public has a right to know whose agent they are dealing with. Requirements for dealing with sellers and buyers apply also to landlords and tenants.

Furnishing the Consumer Information Statement (CIS)

Real estate agents are required to furnish a CIS before any discussion of a seller's/landlord's or buyer's/tenant's motivation or financial situation is initiated. If the first discussion takes place by telephone or in a social setting, the seller or buyer must still be verbally informed about the possible agency relationships and alerted to their implications. The statement should then be furnished at the next meeting, or included with the first email, fax, mail, or delivered material. If no discussion of motivation or financial situation has taken place, the agent must furnish a CIS before any property (listed or unlisted) is shown.

The regulations do not require that the CIS be signed by the parties as to their acknowledgment of receipt of the CIS or by the licensee as to the declaration of business relationship. However, in the event that a broker's office policy requires that a CIS be signed, the regulations do provide language that a licensee may use as an option for obtaining the required signatures. If the CIS is signed, a copy of the signed CIS is to be retained by the broker when a sale or rental is consummated for six years. Sellers and buyers must acknowledge receipt of the CIS on all offers, contracts, and leases.

Further Written Disclosures of Agency

Every listing, offer, contract, and lease prepared by a licensee (except on real estate properties exempted from the disclosure requirements) must set forth the broker's relationship with the parties involved. If a signed CIS is not attached, offers, contracts, or leases (except short-term rentals) must also contain the client or customer's acknowledgment that the CIS was received prior to the first showing of the property. In addition, when more than one firm is involved, the licensee preparing the document must include a statement indicating how the other firm has described its agency status in that transaction.

Figure 3.4: Consumer Information Statement (CIS)

CONSUMER INFORMATION STATEMENT ON NEW JERSEY REAL ESTATE RELATIONSHIPS

In New Jersey, real estate licensees are required to disclose how they intend to work with buyers and sellers in a real estate transaction. (In rental transactions, the terms "buyers" and "sellers" should be read as "tenants" and "landlords", respectively.)

1. AS A SELLER'S AGENT OR SUBAGENT, I, AS A LICENSEE, REPRESENT THE SELLER AND ALL MATERIAL INFORMATION SUPPLIED TO ME BY THE BUYER WILL BE TOLD TO THE SELLER.

2. AS A BUYER'S AGENT, I, AS LICENSEE, REPRESENT THE BUYER AND ALL MATERIAL INFORMATION SUPPLIED TO ME BY THE SELLER WILL BE TOLD TO THE BUYER.

3. AS A DISCLOSED DUAL AGENT, I, AS A LICENSEE, REPRESENT BOTH PARTIES, HOWEVER, I MAY NOT, WITHOUT EXPRESS PERMISSION, DISCLOSE THAT THE SELLER WILL ACCEPT A PRICE LESS THAN THE LISTING PRICE OR THAT THE BUYER WILL PAY A PRICE GREATER THAN THE OFFERED PRICE.

4. AS A TRANSACTION BROKER, I, AS A LICENSEE, DO NOT REPRESENT EITHER THE BUYER OR THE SELLER. ALL INFORMATION I ACQUIRE FROM ONE PARTY MAY BE TOLD TO THE OTHER PARTY.

Before you disclose confidential information to a real estate licensee regarding a real estate transaction, you should understand what type of business relationship you have with that licensee. There are four business relationships: (1) seller's agent; (2) buyer's agent; (3) disclosed dual agent; and (4) transaction broker. Each of these relationships imposes certain legal duties and responsibilities on the licensee as well as on the seller or buyer represented. These four relationships are defined in greater detail below. Please read carefully before making your choice.

SELLERS' AGENT
A seller's agent WORKS ONLY FOR THE SELLER and has legal obligations, called fiduciary duties, to the seller. These include reasonable care, undivided loyalty, confidentiality and full disclosure. Seller's agents often work with buyers, but do not represent the buyers. However, in working with buyers a seller's agent must act honestly. In dealing with both parties, a seller's agent may not make any misrepresentations to either party on matters material to the transaction, such as the buyer's financial ability to pay, and must disclose defects of a material nature affecting the physical condition of the property, which a reasonable inspection by the licensee would disclose.

Seller's agents include all persons licensed with the brokerage firm, which has been authorized through a listing agreement to work as the seller's agent. In addition, other brokerage firms may accept an offer to work with the listing broker's firm as the seller's agents. In such cases, those firms and all persons licensed with such firms are called "sub-agents." Sellers who do not desire to have their property marketed through sub-agents should so inform the seller's agent.

BUYER'S AGENT
A buyer's agent WORKS ONLY FOR THE BUYER. A buyer's agent has fiduciary duties to the buyer, which include reasonable care, undivided loyalty, confidentiality and full disclosure. However, in dealing with sellers, a buyer's agent must act honestly. In dealing with both parties, a buyer's agent may not make any misrepresentations on matters material to the transaction, such as the buyer's financial ability to pay, and must disclose defects of a material nature affecting the physical condition of the property which a reasonable inspection by the licensee would disclose.

A buyer wishing to be represented by a buyer's agent is advised to enter into a separate written buyer agency contract with the brokerage firm, which is to work as their agent.

DISCLOSED DUAL AGENT
A disclosed dual agent WORKS FOR BOTH THE BUYER AND SELLER. To work as a dual agent, a firm must first obtain the informed written consent of the buyer and the seller. Therefore, before acting as a disclosed dual agent, brokerage firms must make written disclosure to both parties. Disclosed dual agency is most likely to occur when a licensee with a real estate firm working as a buyer's agent shows the buyer properties owned by sellers for whom that firm is also working as a seller's agent or sub-agent.

A real estate licensee working as a disclosed dual agent must carefully explain to each party, that, in addition to working as their agent, their firm will also work as the agent for the other party. They must also explain what effect their working as a disclosed dual agent will have on the fiduciary duties their firm owes to the buyer and to the seller. When working as a disclosed dual agent, a brokerage firm must have the express permission of a party prior to disclosing confidential information to the other party. Such information includes the highest price a buyer can afford to pay and the lowest price a seller will accept and the parties' motivation to buy or sell.

Figure 3.4: Consumer Information Statement (CIS) (continued)

Remember, a brokerage firm acting as a disclosed dual agent will not be able to put one party's interests ahead of those of the other party and cannot advise or counsel either party on how to gain an advantage at the expense of the other party on the basis of confidential information obtained from or about the other party.

If you decide to enter into an agency relationship with a firm, which is to work as a disclosed dual agent, you are advised to sign a written agreement with that firm.

TRANSACTION BROKER
The New Jersey Real Estate Licensing Law does not require licensees to work in the capacity of an "agent" when providing brokerage services. A transaction broker works with a buyer or a seller or both in the sales transaction without representing anyone. A TRANSACTION BROKER DOES NOT PROMOTE THE INTERESTS OF ONE PARTY OVER THOSE OF THE OTHER PARTY TO THE TRANSACTION. Licensees with such a firm would be required to treat all parties honestly and to act in a competent manner, but they would not be required to keep confidential any information. A transaction broker can locate qualified buyers for a seller or suitable properties for a buyer. They can then work with both parties in an effort to arrive at an agreement on the sale or rental of real estate and perform tasks to facilitate the closing of a transaction.

A transaction broker primarily serves as a manager of the transaction, communicating information between the parties to assist them in arriving at a mutually acceptable agreement and in closing the transaction, but cannot advise or counsel either party on how to gain an advantage at the expense of the other party. Owners considering working with transaction brokers are advised to sign a written agreement with that firm which clearly states what services that firm will perform and how it will be paid. In addition, any transaction brokerage agreement with a seller or landlord should specifically state whether a notice on the property to be rented or sold will or will not be circulated in any or all Multiple Listing System(s) of which that firm is a member.

YOU MAY OBTAIN LEGAL ADVICE ABOUT THESE BUSINESS RELATIONSHIPS FROM YOUR OWN LAWYER.
THIS STATEMENT IS NOT A CONTRACT AND IS PROVIDED FOR INFORMATIONAL PURPOSES ONLY.

ACKNOWLEDGEMENT OF RECEIPT OF CONSUMER INFORMATION STATEMENT (CIS)

FOR SELLERS AND LANDLORDS
"By signing this Consumer Information Statement, I acknowledge that I received this Statement from_____(name of brokerage Firm) prior to discussing my motivation to sell or lease or my desired selling or leasing price with one of its representatives."

Signed:_____

FOR BUYERS AND TENANTS
"By signing this Consumer Information Statement, I acknowledge that I received this Statement from _____(name of brokerage firm) prior to discussing my motivation or financial ability to buy or lease with one of its representatives."

Signed:_____
# # # #

DECLARATION OF BUSINESS RELATIONSHIP

I,_____, (name of licensee) as an authorized representative of _____, (name of brokerage firm) intend, as of this time, to work with you as a (indicate one of the following):

____ Seller's Agent Only

__ Buyer's Agent Only

__ Seller's Agent and Disclosed Dual Agent if the opportunity arises

____Buyer's Agent and Disclosed Dual Agent if the opportunity arises

____Transaction Broker Only

____Seller's Agent on properties on which this firm is acting as the seller's agent and transaction broker on other properties

DATE:_____

2012 CIS (A)

Listing agreements prepared by a seller's agent must state whether subagency is being offered to cooperating firms and whether the seller has authorized sharing the commission with subagents, buyer's brokers, or transaction brokers. If so, the agreement must state the amount of the share. An "Addendum to Real Estate Listing/Commission Agreement" must be included with every listing contract (see Figure 10.1). When other licensees inquire about a listing, it is the responsibility of the agent who listed the property to determine first whether the licensee is functioning as a buyer's broker, a subagent of the seller, a transaction broker, or a disclosed dual agent, in order to judge what confidential information may be shared.

Termination of Agency

The agency relationship may be terminated by any of the following:

- Death or incompetency of either party
- Destruction or condemnation of the property
- Expiration of the term of the agency
- Mutual agreement to terminate the agency
- Renunciation by the agent
- Revocation by the principal
- Bankruptcy of either party
- Completion or fulfillment of the purpose for which the agency was created

Generally, a seller or buyer, acting in good faith, has a right to fire a broker (for cause) or to rescind the brokerage agreement at any time if he decides not to sell. When a broker is discharged prior to the agreed upon date, the broker may be entitled to reimbursement for out-of-pocket expenses, such as advertising and multiple listing service fees.

Buyer as Principal

A buyer's broker should have a written employment contract and may be paid with a retainer, a flat fee, an hourly fee, or even out of the proceeds of the sale. The creation of agency is *not* determined by who pays the commission. Licensees are prohibited from receiving compensation from both parties under certain circumstances. If a broker represents *one* party to a transaction, whether a sale or lease, the broker can collect a fee from *both* parties, provided that the broker gives full written disclosure to and gets consent from both parties. But if a broker represents *both* parties in the same real estate transaction, the broker can collect from *only one* of them.

DUAL AGENCY

Dual agency occurs when the broker represents both parties in the same transaction. While dual agency in itself is not illegal, *undisclosed dual agency* is. Whenever possible, the broker should avoid any situation that might result in or be considered undisclosed dual agency, that is, representing both parties in a transaction at the same time without the prior knowledge and written consent of all parties. An agent cannot give the highest level of loyalty to two or more principals in the same transaction.

When working with a buyer as a seller's agent, a licensee must be careful not to give the buyer the impression that he or she is the agent's client. Simply giving a buyer the mandated Consumer Information Statement is not enough. Salespeople working with customers should be careful at all times not to use such terms as "my buyer," which could actually be construed as creating an *inadvertent dual agency* relationship.

Disclosed dual agency is legal in New Jersey if the broker

- explains fully the legal duties that will and will not be available from him or her;

- discloses any other business relationships that might affect the proposed transaction;

- obtains the buyer's and seller's written informed consent to the brokers acting as a dual agent (in addition to the CIS); and

- advises that each party may want to consult a lawyer.

A Consent to Dual Agency Agreement is shown as Figure 3.5.

Brokers representing sellers and multiple buyers are advised to consult with counsel on how their brokerage agreements and informed consent forms should be revised to cover the simultaneous representation of buyers, and if disclosure must be made to competing buyer clients.

Even when acting with written consent to dual agency, the broker is not allowed to accept compensation from both the buyer and the seller in the same transaction. The dual agent may be paid by either the buyer or the seller, but never by both.

Dual Agency and Conflict of Interest

In recent years surveys have disclosed that a large majority of the buying public thinks they are being represented by a selling broker. Even worse, some brokers have the same impression. Long discussions have been taking place on the question of dual agency, sometimes designated as the *subagency* question, because of the position of a cooperating broker in a multiple listing system.

In one state after another, legislatures have been wrestling with the problem of informing the public and controlling the agent's fiduciary position.

New Jersey's license law forbids an agent to represent both parties except with the informed *written* consent of both parties (*disclosed dual agency*; see Appendix A [11:5-6.9(a)4] for the requirements of how such disclosure must be made). A common situation is one in which the seller's agent comes to identify with the buyer and furnishes encouragement, advice, and assistance to the buyer.

Advising the buyer on how to negotiate with the seller may even put the listing agent in the position of serving two masters. Without some such advice, of course, most transactions would not take place at all. The seller's broker has been retained to produce a ready, willing, and able buyer; to accomplish this, negotiation and compromise are usually necessary. Nevertheless, an unintended result, commonly known as *dual agency*, may follow, with the agent now representing both parties. If the transaction falls through, either buyer or seller might claim damages, based on the broker's conflict of interest.

That the actions are performed with good intentions does not change the situation. The problem is a difficult one, faced daily by licensees, with no simple solution. One remedy might be to obtain the seller's authorization to divulge normally privileged information, such as the seller's motivation or lowest acceptable price, in order to secure an offer.

Figure 3.5: Dual Agency Agreement

**NEW JERSEY REALTORS® STANDARD FORM OF
INFORMED CONSENT TO DUAL AGENCY
(SELLER)**

©2001, NEW JERSEY REALTORS®, INC.

PROPERTY ADDRESS: _____

1 This Agreement evidences Seller's consent that the Brokerage Firm, as Seller's Agent, may act as a Disclosed Dual Agent in order to
2 represent both Seller and Buyer in the same real estate transaction, and seeks Seller's consent to allow Seller's Agent to act as a Disclosed
3 Dual Agent when the opportunity arises. Seller should be aware that a real estate licensee may legally act as a Disclosed Dual Agent only
4 with Seller's and Buyer's informed written consent.
5
6 Seller understands that Disclosed Dual Agency (representing more than one party to a transaction) has the potential of creating a conflict
7 of interest in that both Seller and Buyer may intend to rely on the Seller's Agent's advice, and their respective interests may be adverse to
8 each other. Therefore, when acting as a Disclosed Dual Agent, Seller's Agent will not represent the interests of Buyer to the exclusion or
9 detriment of the interests of a Seller; nor will Seller's Agent represent the interests of Seller to the exclusion and detriment of the interests
10 of Buyer.
11
12 As a Disclosed Dual Agent of both the Seller and the Buyer, Seller's Agent will be working equally for both parties to the real estate
13 transaction and will provide services to complete the transaction **without** the full range of fiduciary duties ordinarily owed by an agent
14 who represents Seller alone, or the Buyer alone. In the preparation of offers and counteroffers between Seller and Buyer, Seller's Agent
15 will act only as an intermediary to facilitate the transaction rather than as an active negotiator representing either the Seller or Buyer in a
16 fiduciary capacity. By consenting to this dual agency, Seller is giving up the right to undivided loyalty and will be owed only limited duties
17 of disclosure by the Seller's Agent.
18
19 For example, Seller acknowledges that Seller's Agent, as a Disclosed Dual Agent, is not permitted, under law, to disclose to either Seller or
20 Buyer any confidential information which has been, or will be communicated to Seller's Agent by either of the parties to the transaction.
21 Moreover, Seller's Agent is not permitted to disclose (without the express written permission of the Seller) to the Buyer that such Seller
22 will accept a price less than the full listing price. Nor will Seller's Agent disclose (without the express written permission of the Buyer) to
23 the Seller that Buyer will pay a sum greater than the price offered by Buyer. It is also impermissible for Seller's Agent to advise or counsel
24 either the Seller or Buyer on how to gain an advantage at the expense of the other party on the basis of confidential information obtained
25 from or about the other party.
26
27 Seller acknowledges receipt of the Consumer Information Statement on New Jersey Real Estate Relationships.
28
29 I, _____ AS AN AUTHORIZED REPRESENTATIVE OF
30   (Name of Licensee)
31 _____ INTEND, AS OF THIS TIME, TO WORK WITH
32   (Name of Firm)
33 YOU (SELLER) AS A SELLER'S AGENT AND DISCLOSED DUAL AGENT IF THE OPPORTUNITY ARISES.
34
35 **If Seller does not understand all of the provisions of this Informed Consent to Dual Agency, legal advice should be sought**
36 **before signing.**
37
38 By signing below, Seller acknowledges that Seller has read and understood this Informed Consent to Dual Agency and gives consent to
39 Seller's Agent to act as a Disclosed Dual Agent.
40
41
42 SELLER'S SIGNATURE   BROKERAGE FIRM
43
44
45 SELLER'S SIGNATURE   ADDRESS
46
47
48   CITY, STATE, ZIP CODE
49
50
51 DATE   SALESPERSON'S SIGNATURE

NJ REALTORS® Form-122B-8/15

Unit 3

Conflict of interest may occur when the agent is called to a listing interview and finds a seller ready to let the property go at a ridiculously low price. The courts have held that even though the property is not yet listed, the seller is relying on the broker's expertise and may become a principal. The licensee who decides to buy the property immediately without notifying the seller of its true value is operating under a conflict between his or her own interest and that of the seller.

A more subtle situation occurs when no financial advantage accrues to the agent, but the agent has an indirect interest in the transaction. The agent should disclose, for example, if he is a member of the Boy Scout committee looking for a campsite or if he is trying to locate a home for his mother to purchase.

DISCLOSURE ISSUES

Material Information

In New Jersey, real estate brokers and salespeople are responsible for disclosing to a buyer any defects of a material nature that affect the physical condition of the property. Material information is defined as a physical condition that a reasonable person attaches importance to, or information that the agent knows or suspects a buyer would want to know and would consider important before proceeding. It doesn't matter whether the agent or any hypothetical "reasonable person" would share that interest or agree that the information is important.

Licensees must disclose defects that would be discovered by a reasonable inspection. These defects would include such things as water seepage, unused oil tanks in the basement, and sloping floors. Sellers should be aware, however, that courts have ruled that they are responsible for revealing any hidden or **latent defects** to their real estate agents. A latent defect is one that is not discoverable by ordinary inspection. An example might be EIFS (exterior insulation finish systems), a specific form of stucco that has been linked, in recent years, to water leakage, rotted sheathing, and the growth of mold. The seller of a stucco home should be questioned about whether the finish is EIFS and buyers should be alerted to investigate. Because in such instances buyers have been able to either rescind the sales contract or receive damages, real estate agents should urge their sellers to disclose to them and to buyers any problems not evident but that might affect the buyer's desire to purchase or the price the buyer would be willing to pay. This information should be included in the Seller's Property Condition Disclosure Statement (see Figure 10.2).

Sellers can be encouraged to obtain and share their Comprehensive Loss Underwriting Exchange (CLUE) report from LexisNexis, the company that assembles the data from participating insurance companies. The CLUE lists insurance claims filed by the current owner for the past seven years. Not every insurance company participates and only the current property owner can access the report. There is no cost to the owner for an annual report. The report can be obtained at https://personalreports.lexisnexis.com/index.jsp.

Buyers can provide the report to their home inspector. If the damage was not properly corrected, on rare occasions, CLUE records have made it difficult for buyers to find the homeowner's insurance required by their mortgage lenders.

In the same fashion, a buyer's broker is required to disclose any material defect that would affect the buyer's ability to complete the transaction. This means that despite the fiduciary duty of confidentiality, a buyer's broker must immediately disclose any financial problem (an earnest money check that bounces, for example) to the seller.

The New Jersey Administrative Code says that social conditions and psychological impairments are not considered physical conditions. For instance, noisy dogs or unpleasant neighbors do not affect the property's physical condition. Suicide or other unpleasant events associated with a property are also nonphysical conditions. If asked, agents must pass along any information they possess but they are not required to investigate social or psychological conditions. Before the agent decides to pass along any of this kind of information, however, he or she should carefully consider how the communication might impact his or her fiduciary duties.

Off-Site Conditions

In 1995, several families sued a developer and broker, alleging that both had known that the development was located a half-mile from a hazardous waste dumping site and had failed to disclose this fact. The trial court ruled in favor of the developer and broker, stating that there is no duty to disclose to a potential purchaser the conditions of someone else's property. On appeal, however, the decision was reversed. The New Jersey Supreme Court ultimately held that conditions beyond the limits of a specific property may be considered material facts that must be disclosed to prospective purchasers.

As a result of this decision, two disclosures for **off-site conditions** are now included in all contracts. One refers to new construction; the other, to resales of existing properties. The new construction notice includes a five-day period in which the purchaser may cancel the contract; the resale notice does not include a similar right of rescission (see Figure 11.1).

Megan's Law

Megan's Law requires that a community be alerted to the presence of convicted sex offenders. Megan's Law was enacted in New Jersey in 1995, and similar laws have been adopted in most other states since then.

In New Jersey, all contracts and leases on residential real estate that are prepared by a licensee must include a Megan's Law Statement. This statement advises purchasers and lessees that the county prosecutor has a list of all known sex offenders who live in the area. Buyers and lessees can obtain this information from the county prosecutor after the sale or lease of the property has closed (again, see Figure 11.1). Licensees are not permitted to inquire about or give any information regarding the presence of convicted sex offenders in the neighborhood.

A buyer's broker can suggest that a concerned client check New Jersey State Police website www.njsp.org for a registry of sex offenders.

MISREPRESENTATION

Licensees must be careful about the statements they or their staff members make about a parcel of real estate. Extravagant statements of *opinion* ("This house has the most gorgeous view in the world!") are permissible, as long as they are offered as opinions and without any intention to deceive. Making such statements when selling real estate is called **puffing**.

Statements of *fact*, however, must be accurate, and questions must be answered honestly. The broker must be alert to ensure that none of his or her statements can in any way be interpreted as involving **fraud**, which encompasses all deceitful or dishonest practices intended to harm or take advantage of another person. If a contract to purchase real estate is obtained as a result of misstatements made by a broker or his or her salespersons, the contract may be disaffirmed or renounced by the purchaser. In such a case the broker would lose the commission. If either party suffers loss because of a broker's misrepresentations, the broker can be held liable for damages.

Misrepresentation covers more than a deliberate lie intended to mislead someone, which is called **fraudulent** (intentional) **misrepresentation**. There are two other classifications: **negligent** (unintentional) **misrepresentation** covers false statements made by someone who should have known better. **Innocent** (honest) **misrepresentation** is a false statement by someone who believes the information to be true but is not expected to have expertise in the subject.

Liability Criteria

For the agent to be liable for misrepresentation there must be

■ a false or misleading statement (or concealment of a material fact) by

■ a person who knows (or should have known) that the information is false, with

■ intent to deceive or defraud (or if, where there is no such intent, the effect is still to deceive or defraud) and

■ damages suffered by the party who relied on the information.

It is relatively easy for an agent to avoid intentional misrepresentation simply by sticking to the truth. But omissions and half-truths may misrepresent as readily as actual misstatements, and the offense may be committed inadvertently. The buyer looking at rural property may be told "The septic system works well," when, in fact, it does not. If the agent knows the true state of affairs, *intentional* misrepresentation has occurred. If the agent does not know the condition of the system, the potential buyer is still being misled by *negligent* misrepresentation. The half-truth that might mislead is a statement like "Septic systems are normal in this area, and there's probably nothing to worry about." True in itself, this skirts the issue in a manner that may be misleading to an ignorant buyer. No mention at all of the septic system may also be misleading, particularly to an urban buyer who may assume sewers are available everywhere.

That the broker knew nothing of the condition of that system will be little defense if brokers in that community *should* know about such matters. Even if the intention is not to defraud, the buyer who purchases the property and discovers the septic system to be faulty has suffered damages and may seek to recover them from the broker.

In recent years, buyers and sellers have become increasingly aware of the possible danger posed by radon, lead paint, asbestos building materials, toxic pollutants, urea-formaldehyde foam insulation (UFFI), and other environmental hazards.

Among areas where problems frequently arise are statements about the value of property ("Sure to go up 10% a year in this area"), title ("The judgments have all been cleared up"), utilities ("No problem hooking in to the sewers"), boundaries, zoning, and size. In a recent case in another state, the buyer of a house that contained 100 square feet fewer than stated in the listing data was awarded the current construction cost of 100 square feet in that area. The buyer may prefer to sue the broker, who still has an office in town and a vulnerable reputation, rather than the seller, who may have already moved out of town.

To Avoid Misrepresentation

Never present opinions as facts. Not "We can certainly get you $300,000 for this house," but "I don't see why we might not . . ." or "It should probably bring as much as these recent sales did." Absolute statements should be avoided. Not "All copper plumbing," but "It looks from here as if . . ." The phrases "I believe" or "I was told by the seller" are more accurate than "The roof is five years old," where the agent has no direct knowledge of its age.

Many requests for information should be met by referring the questioner directly to an expert source: city zoning bureau, mortgage counselor, building inspection engineer, or lawyer. The agent thus shifts responsibility and cuts down the chances of giving faulty information in specialized areas.

CONSUMER FRAUD ACT

New Jersey's Consumer Fraud Act lists in detail all sorts of misleading, fraudulent, and scam practices, and sets penalties that include fines up to three times the damages. Concealing or omitting material facts about real estate is considered an unlawful practice.

The act, however, offers an exemption from liability for a real estate licensee who can prove that

- the licensee had no actual knowledge that information provided was false or deceptive;

- a diligent effort was made to learn the truth, including the licensee's visual inspection of the property; and

- the broker or salesperson was relying on information provided by a home inspector or similar specialist, a government employee, or the seller's property condition disclosure statement.

ANTITRUST LAWS

The real estate industry is subject to federal and state **antitrust laws**. The most common antitrust violations that can occur in the real estate business are price-fixing and allocation of customers or markets.

Illegal *price-fixing* occurs when brokers conspire to set prices for the services they perform (sales commissions, management rates), rather than letting those prices be established through competition in the open market.

Real estate licensees must disassociate themselves immediately from the slightest discussion of commission rates with any member of a competing firm. In the past a number of brokers and real estate boards have suffered from charges under antitrust laws.

Allocation of customers or markets would involve an agreement between brokers to divide their markets and refrain from competing with each other's business. For example, allocations could take place on a geographic basis with brokers agreeing to specific territories within which they operate exclusively. Or the division could take place along other lines: for example, two brokers may agree that one handles only residential properties less than $250,000 in value and the other handles only residential properties greater than $250,000 in value. Any such arrangement is illegal.

Individual firms may, however, establish their own fee schedules and allocate sales territories between salespersons. Violations occur only when competing firms agree to act together in these matters.

The penalties for such acts are severe. Under the *Sherman Antitrust Act*, people who fix prices or allocate markets may be found guilty of a misdemeanor punishable by a maximum $1 million and up to 10 years in prison. In a civil suit a person who has suffered a loss because of such activities may recover triple the value of the actual damages plus attorney's fees and costs.

ETHICS, LIABILITY, AND DISCIPLINABLE OFFENSES

It is possible for a broker to incur liability even though acting in all honesty and with good will. Situations that may lead to professional liability fall under four main headings:

1. Breach of fiduciary duties

2. Failure to observe standard of care

3. Conflict of interest

4. Misrepresentation

Any of these can be a potentially serious infraction. Possible results include

- loss of client and listing;
- loss of customer and sale;
- loss of commission;
- civil lawsuit for damages;
- criminal prosecution; and
- suspension or loss of license.

In many of the following situations *full disclosure* in advance prevents liability. If, on the other hand, the problem is not immediately obvious, disclosure as soon as it is discovered may limit liability.

Disciplinable Offenses

An analysis of offenses for which licensees are usually disciplined includes the broker's failure to supervise a salesperson, a salesperson acting as a broker, misuse of escrow funds, and the broker using the services of an unlicensed person.

Other offenses that recently brought fines or suspension or revocation of license include

- racial steering,
- discrimination,
- violation of nonsolicitation orders,
- failure to disclose licensee's interest in a transaction,
- failure to disclose dual compensation,
- unauthorized practice of law,
- failure to deliver copies of documents,
- net listing,
- inducing breach of another's contract,
- material misstatement on a license application,
- deceptive and improper advertising,
- improper information on stationery and business cards, and
- personal offenses not necessarily related to real estate (fraud, failure to pay a judgment, conviction of a felony).

Brokers and salespersons were cited for breach of fiduciary duties (failure to explain the nature of exclusive-right-to-sell listing, failure to follow principal's directions).

DEFENSE AGAINST CLAIMS OF LIABILITY

Staying alert to situations that might pose problems is a first defense. Disclaimers that "the information furnished is believed correct but not warranted" are of little value. They cannot cover spoken repetition of the material and they cannot acquit the broker of liability. The fact that the misleading material may have been furnished by the seller is also of little value as a defense.

The broker's potential liability for undisclosed defects is somewhat lessened if the seller furnishes a written disclosure of property condition to the buyer (see Unit 10) and if the buyer retains the service of a home inspector before the contract becomes binding.

Errors and omissions (E&O) insurance is the real estate industry's equivalent of medical malpractice insurance. Subject to the limitations of a particular policy, it defends against many circumstances but does not cover fraud. It is carried by many brokers and some individual salespersons.

Dual Contracts

New Jersey specifically outlaws the use of *dual contracts* in a real estate sales transaction. Dual contracts, either oral or written, are two separate contracts concerning the same parcel of real estate, one stating the *true purchase price* and the other stating *a larger amount* as the purchase price. Such contracts are used to induce a lender to make a mortgage loan commitment for a larger amount based on the false, inflated purchase price quoted on the second contract.

The writing of such dual contracts is obviously a fraudulent act, and the license of a person found guilty of being a party to dual contracts could be suspended or revoked. Such action becomes a misdemeanor, punishable by fine and/or imprisonment of up to three years.

Ethics

Professional conduct involves much more than just complying with the law. In real estate, the state's licensing laws (and federal laws as well) establish those activities that are illegal and therefore prohibited. However, merely complying with the letter of the law may not be enough; licensees may perform legally yet not ethically. *Ethics* refers to a system of moral principles, rules, and standards of conduct. The ethical system of a profession establishes conduct that goes beyond merely complying with the law.

These moral principles address two sides of a profession:

1. They establish standards for integrity and competence in dealing with consumers of an industry's services.

2. They define a code of conduct for relations within the industry, among its professionals.

Most professions have codes of ethics for their members: the physician's Hippocratic Oath, for instance, or the attorney's Code of Professional Responsibility. A code of ethics is a written system of standards for ethical conduct. The code contains statements designed to advise, guide, and regulate job behavior. To be effective, a code of ethics must be specific by dictating rules that either prohibit or demand certain desirable behavior. Lofty statements of positive goals are not especially helpful. By including sanctions for violators, a code of ethics becomes more effective.

The National Association of REALTORS® (discussed later) adopted its Code of Ethics and Standards of Practice in 1913. All members of NAR are expected to subscribe to this code of conduct. The code has proved helpful, because it contains practical applications of business ethics. Other professional organizations in the real estate industry have codes of ethics as well, and many state commissions are required by law to establish codes or canons of ethical behavior for their states licensees.

PROFESSIONAL ORGANIZATIONS

Years ago real estate brokers realized the need for an organization to assist them in improving their business abilities and to educate the public to the value of qualified real estate brokers. The **National Association of REALTORS® (NAR)** was founded in 1908 to meet this need. This organization is made up of brokers and salespeople who are members of local boards/associations and state associations of REALTORS® that operate throughout the United States, and the professional activities of all REALTORS® active members of local boards that are affiliated with the national association are governed by the association's **Code of Ethics**, which NAR adopted in 1913 and updates as needed. The term **REALTORS®** is a registered trademark.

For more about NAR, visit their website at www.realtor.com. It has had a major impact on and has often served as a model for the licensing laws of many states, including New Jersey.

The National Association of Real Estate Brokers (NAREB), whose members are called Realtists, was founded in 1947 and is particularly active in the South. Its membership, generally composed of African-Americans, includes individual members as well as brokers who belong to state and local real estate boards affiliated with the organization. Members subscribe to a code of ethics that sets professional standards for all Realtists. The NAREB website is www.nareb.com.

New Jersey REALTORS®

The **New Jersey REALTORS® (NJR)**, formerly the **New Jersey Association of REALTORS® (NJAR)**, at www.njr.com, is the state branch of the NAR. Among other services, the NJR offers a variety of educational courses and programs to approximately 46,000 members. It also maintains many committees including a legislative study-action committee to advance the public's social, economic, and vocational interest in real estate through legislative efforts. The state association provides a standard sales contract form that may be adapted to the needs of any member's office, and agency and property-disclosure forms. These are private trade associations. Licensed brokers and salespersons are not required by law to join.

Designations

As a mark of expertise in various fields, professional organizations award designations after required experience, study, and examinations. The National Association of REALTORS®, together with its institutes, societies, and councils, offers many designations. Among the better-known designations are

- ABR (Accredited Buyers Representative), awarded through the NARs Real Estate Buyers Agent Council (REBAC);
- CCIM (Certified Commercial Investment Member), awarded by the REALTORS® National Marketing Institute;

- CRB (Certified Real Estate Broker), awarded by the REALTORS® National Marketing Institute;

- CRS (Certified Residential Specialist), awarded by the REALTORS® National Marketing Institute;

- Certified Property Manager (CPM), awarded by the Institute of Real Estate Management;

- GRI® (Graduate, REALTOR® Institute);

- SIOR (Society of Industrial and Office REALTOR®);

- CRE (Counselor of Real Estate);

- MRP (Military Relocation Professional);

- CIPS (Certified International Property Specialist);

- LTG (Leadership Training Graduate), awarded by the Women's Council of REALTORS®;

- DREI (Distinguished Real Estate Instructor), Real Estate Educators Association;

- SREA (Senior Real Estate Analyst), Appraisal Institute; and

- SRES (Seniors Real Estate Specialist), awarded by the NAR's Seniors Advantage Real Estate Council.

SUMMARY

Real estate brokerage is the bringing together, for a fee or commission, of people who wish to buy, sell, exchange, or lease real estate. In New Jersey a real estate agent can act as a (1) seller's agent, (2) buyer's agent, (3) disclosed dual agent, (4) transaction broker, or (5) seller's agent on properties on which the firm is acting as the seller's agent and transaction broker on other properties. A *transaction broker* works with buyer, seller, or both without representing either one in an agency relationship.

Real estate brokerage is commonly governed by the *law of agency*. The real estate broker is the agent, hired by either a buyer or a seller of real estate to find or sell a particular parcel of real estate. The person who hires the broker is the principal or client. The principal and the agent have a *fiduciary relationship* under which the agent owes the principal the duties of care, obedience, accounting, loyalty, and disclosure.

Agents are required to disclose material information about a property, as well as other disclosures required by Megan's Law and standard off-site condition notices.

Misrepresentation need not be intentional; unintentional or *negligent misrepresentation* is also possible. Ways to avoid misrepresentation include not stating opinions as facts and referring the questioner directly to expert sources. The best defense against claims arising from such situations is disclosure, either before the client has acted or as soon as the problem is discovered. Licensees may function as *dual agents*, but only after following strict rules governing disclosure of their role. Undisclosed dual agency is illegal.

New Jersey's Consumer Fraud Act sets strict penalties for anyone giving false or misleading information about real estate, but sets some exemptions for licensees who can prove they were not aware of the deception, had tried diligently to ascertain the true picture, and were relying on information supplied by professionals, government employees, or sellers.

The broker's compensation in a real estate sale generally takes the form of a *commission*, which is often (though not necessarily) a percentage of the real estate's selling price. The broker is considered to have earned a commission when he or she procures a *ready, willing, and able buyer* for a seller or brings about a *meeting of the minds*. Most contracts of sale, however, provide that the commission only be paid at the closing of title.

Salespeople may assist brokers as either *employees* or *independent contractors*. The salesperson is the broker's agent and usually the seller's subagent (or, if specifically retained as such, the buyer's subagent).

Many of the general operations of a real estate brokerage are regulated by the real estate license laws. In addition, state and federal *antitrust laws* prohibit brokers from conspiring to fix prices or allocate customers or markets.

Liability claims against brokers for damages caused to buyers or sellers may arise from breach of fiduciary duty, failure to observe standard of care, conflict of interest, or misrepresentation.

Professional organizations providing a code of ethics for their members include the National Association of REALTORS® (NAR), the National Association of Real Estate Brokers (Realtists), and state REALTOR® Associations. The New Jersey REALTORS® (NJR) offers a variety of educational courses, including a specific course leading to the designation of Graduate, REALTOR® Institute (GRI). Numerous other designations are available to REALTOR® members.

USEFUL WEBSITES

U.S. Department of Justice, Antitrust Division: www.usdoj.gov/atr

National Association of REALTORS®: www.nar.realtor

New Jersey REALTORS®: www.njrealtor.com

National Association of Real Estate Brokers: www.nareb.com

National Association of Exclusive Buyer Agents: www.naeba.org

Real Estate Buyer's Agent Council: www.rebac.net

KEY TERMS REVIEW 1

Match the number of each key term with the corresponding letter.

_____ 1. Agent G

_____ 2. Antitrust laws A

_____ 3. Attorney-in-fact H

_____ 4. Broker O

_____ 5. Buyer's broker B

_____ 6. Client K

_____ 7. Commission C

_____ 8. Consumer Information Statement P

_____ 9. Customer D

_____ 10. Disclosed dual agent Q

_____ 11. Disclosure E

_____ 12. Dual agency F

_____ 13. Employee I

_____ 14. Fiduciary M

_____ 15. Fiduciary relationship J

_____ 16. Fraud N

_____ 17. General agent L

A. regulations prohibiting price-fixing 2

B. agent who takes a buyer as the principal

C. broker's usual compensation

D. third party in a transaction, not the principal

E. revealing to another any pertinent information

F. brokers taking both parties as principals

G. one authorized to act for another 1

H. person authorized to act under a power of attorney 3

I. salesperson whose broker pays Social Security, regulates hours, etc.

J. trust and confidence between parties

K. principal who engages an agent

L. one empowered for a wide range of actions

M. a special relationship of trust and confidence between a principal and an agent

N. intentional misleading of another, who is harmed thereby

O. one authorized to act for another in real estate transactions 4

P. written explanation of a business relationship

Q. one who works for both the seller and the buyer 10

KEY TERMS REVIEW 2

Match the number of each key term with the corresponding letter.

_____ 1. Independent contractor

_____ 2. Kickback

_____ 3. Latent defect

_____ 4. Law of agency

_____ 5. Listing agreement

_____ 6. Meeting of the minds

_____ 7. Megan's Law

_____ 8. Power of attorney

_____ 9. Principal

_____ 10. Procuring cause

_____ 11. Puffing

_____ 12. Ready, willing, and able buyer

_____ 13. Salesperson

_____ 14. Special agent

_____ 15. Subagent

_____ 16. Transaction broker

A. agent of an agent

B. agreement between a buyer and seller on major points

C. contract by which the owner retains a broker to find a buyer

D. harmless exaggeration as salesmanship

E. illegal sharing of a commission with seller

F. one authorized to act for another in a specific transaction

G. one qualified and prepared to purchase

H. person licensed to assist a real estate broker

I. salesperson who sets own hours, pays own estimated income taxes, etc.

J. problem not discoverable by normal prudent inspection

K. rules governing conduct of agents

L. the one employing an agent; the client

M. the one who brings about a sale

N. written authorization allowing one person to act on behalf of another

O. one who facilitates a transaction without functioning as an agent

P. legislation requiring that communities be alerted to the presence of sex offenders

KEY TERMS REVIEW 3

Match the number of each key term with the corresponding letter.

_____ 1. Code of Ethics

_____ 2. Conflict of interest

_____ 3. Errors and omissions insurance

_____ 4. Fraudulent misrepresentation

_____ 5. Graduate, REALTOR® Institute

_____ 6. Innocent misrepresentation

_____ 7. National Association of REALTORS®

_____ 8. Negligent misrepresentation

_____ 9. New Jersey REALTORS®

_____ 10. REALTOR®

_____ 11. Standard of care

A. competence normally expected

B. fraud committed by someone who should have known better

C. intentional fraud

D. member of a private national organization

E. designation awarded for advanced study

F. private nationwide organization of brokers and salespersons

G. problem when serving best interests of both the client and oneself

H. real estate equivalent of malpractice coverage

I. standards of conduct adopted by REALTORS®

J. statewide group of real estate licensees who choose to join

K. unintentional deception committed in ignorance

UNIT 3 REVIEW QUESTIONS

1. The legal relationship between a broker and seller is generally a(n)
   A. special agency. ✓
   B. general agency.
   C. ostensible agency.
   D. universal agency.

2. A seller cannot be present for the closing. Instead, her parent will sign for her having been given
   A. a power of attorney. ✓
   B. assistance of general counsel.
   C. general counsel authority.
   D. universal authority.

3. The statement "a broker must be employed to recover a commission for his or her services" means
   A. the broker must work in a real estate office.
   B. someone must have agreed to pay a commission to the broker for selling the property. ✓
   C. the broker must have asked the seller the price of the property and then found a ready, willing, and able buyer.
   D. the broker must have a salesperson employed in the office.

4. The procuring cause of a sale is
   A. always the person who first shows the property.
   B. always the licensee who draws up the contract. ✓
   C. sometimes hard to determine.
   D. whomever the buyer wants to receive the commission.

5. A listing may be terminated when either broker or principal
   A. gets married.
   B. goes bankrupt. ✓
   C. overfinances other property.
   D. becomes 21 years of age.

6. When retained by the seller, the broker owes a prospective buyer
   A. obedience to lawful instructions.
   B. confidentiality about the buyer's financial situation.
   C. honest treatment. ✓
   D. first loyalty.

7. The salesperson who sincerely tries to represent both buyer and seller is practicing
   A. fraud.
   B. puffing.
   C. dual agency. ✓
   D. general agency.

8. A seller who wishes to cancel a listing agreement in New Jersey
   A. must cite a legally acceptable reason.
   B. may not cancel without the agent's consent.
   C. may be held liable for money and time expended by the broker. ✓
   D. may not sell the property for six months after.

9. In New Jersey, the buyer of residential property is entitled to find out about the presence of a convicted sex offender in the neighborhood
   A. in the listing information for the property.
   B. at the time the contract is signed. ✓
   C. after the sale of the property has closed.
   D. only if he or she can demonstrate a material need to know.

10. What are buyers who ask to see the owner's Comprehensive Loss Underwriting Exchange looking for?
    A. Nearby hazardous waste dumping sites
    B. Presence of a convicted sex offender
    C. Possible suicide in the home
    D. Insurance claims for the past five years ✓

11. An example of a latent defect is a
    A. large crack in the dining room ceiling.
    B. roof with warped shingles. ✓
    C. used-car lot next door.
    D. malfunctioning septic system.

12. An independent contractor may be paid
    A. a regular draw against earnings.
    B. reimbursed car expenses.
    C. commissions on sales.
    D. two-week vacations each year.

13. Commissions usually are earned when
    A. the buyer makes a purchase offer.
    B. the seller accepts the buyer's offer without conditions.
    C. a new mortgage has been promised by the lender.
    D. title to the property transfers.

14. Even if a proposed transaction does not go through, the broker sometimes may collect a commission where the
    A. buyer turned out to be financially unable.
    B. seller refused to do repairs required by the lender.
    C. seller simply backed out.
    D. lender did not appraise the house for the sales price.

15. A salesperson's commission on a real estate transaction is
    A. paid within ten days after the broker is paid for the transaction.
    B. paid at the rate set by the New Jersey Real Estate Commission.
    C. always paid in cash.
    D. generally determined, by custom, by the broker with no input from the salesperson.

16. To be entitled to collect a commission on a real estate transaction, an agent must
    A. be the procuring cause of the transaction.
    B. charge no more than the local "going rate" of commission.
    C. work a minimum number of hours.
    D. sign the sales contract as a witness.

17. The seller lists his house with a broker offering a bonus commission of $500 to the agent who brings a good buyer before Thanksgiving. An agent with a cooperating firm effects the sale on November 1. The buyer agent may collect that bonus from
    A. the seller.
    B. the listing broker.
    C. the selling broker.
    D. no one.

18. Commission rates are set by
    A. state law.
    B. local custom.
    C. the broker.
    D. agreement between seller and broker.

19. At a booth in the neighborhood coffee shop, a broker is seated with her friendly rival. Her rival says, "Did you hear about that firm that's charging a flat fee for selling property? Do you think they'll make it?" The broker's proper response is to
    A. explain to her rival that flat fees are allowed by law, just as commissions are.
    B. assure her rival that she will not be changing her commission rates.
    C. caution the rival about the dangers of discussing competing firms.
    D. point out to the rival that it is a violation of federal antitrust law for competing brokers to discuss any aspect of commission rates.

20. The transaction broker represents
    A. the seller.
    B. the buyer.
    C. the lending institution.
    D. no one.

21. A Consumer Information Statement (CIS) is required for transactions involving
    A. commercial property and vacant land.
    B. one- to four-family dwellings.
    C. farms and subdivisions.
    D. all real estate.

22. A dual agent cannot provide advice on
    A. available financing.
    B. the right price to accept.
    C. utility costs.
    D. hidden defects.

23. The seller may remain quiet about
    A. sagging floor joists.
    B. seasonal flooding.
    C. the previous owner's suicide.
    D. inadequate septic tank.

24. The duty of loyalty forbids the seller's broker to
    A. mention the condition of the house in ads.
    B. place a sign on the property.
    C. suggest an offer under the listed price.
    D. give information over the telephone.

25. When the buyer gives a seller's broker information about possible financial problems in completing the purchase, the broker should
    A. respect the confidence and let it go no further.
    B. inform the seller immediately.
    C. offer to lend the buyer extra funds needed.
    D. ask for a written confirmation of the situation.

26. If the agent in the previous question is acting as a buyer's broker, the most correct response for the broker is to
    A. say nothing to the seller because of the duty of confidentiality to the principal.
    B. explain to the buyer that not revealing the problem to the seller may constitute concealment of a material defect.
    C. tell the seller, at the same time asking the seller not to reveal to the buyer that confidentiality was breached.
    D. try to find another buyer for the property.

27. Negligent misrepresentation occurs when
    A. the speaker knows the statement is false.
    B. the speaker should know the statement is false.
    C. the speaker is not expected to have knowledge in the matter under discussion.
    D. no harm is done by the falsehood.

28. The term REALTOR® applies only to
    A. any licensed broker.
    B. any broker or salesperson.
    C. members of a private organization.
    D. graduates of the REALTOR® Institute.

29. New Jersey's Consumer Fraud Act
    A. does not apply to real estate.
    B. holds licensees liable for any misrepresentation.
    C. allows exemption from liability in some circumstances.
    D. doesn't cover omission of material facts.

UNIT
4

Fair Housing

LEARNING OBJECTIVES

When you have completed this unit, you will be able to accomplish the following.

> Identify protections of the federal fair housing laws, including enforcement.
> Describe the protections of the New Jersey Law Against Discrimination, including state regulations on rentals.
> Discuss the implications of the fair housing laws for brokers and salespeople.

KEY TERMS

Attorney General's
  memorandum
blockbusting
Civil Rights Act of 1866
Department of
  Housing and Urban
  Development (HUD)

Federal Fair Housing Act
  of 1968
Law Against
  Discrimination
Mount Laurel I and II
protected class
redlining

reverse discrimination
steering
tester
Title VIII

EQUAL OPPORTUNITY IN HOUSING

Brokers and salespeople who offer housing or land for sale or rent must be aware of the federal, state, and local laws pertaining to civil rights and nondiscrimination. These laws, under such titles as *open housing*, *fair housing*, or *equal opportunity housing*, prohibit undesirable and discriminatory activities. Their provisions affect every phase of the real estate sales process from listing to closing, and all brokers and salespersons must comply with them.

The goal of legislators who have enacted fair housing laws and regulations is to create a single, unbiased housing market—one in which every financially qualified homeseeker has the opportunity to buy any home in the area he or she chooses. As a potential licensee, the student of real estate must be aware of illegal and discriminating housing practices in order to avoid them. Failure to comply with fair housing practices is not only grounds for license revocation but also a criminal act.

FEDERAL FAIR HOUSING LAWS

Civil Rights Act of 1866

The efforts of the federal government to guarantee equal housing opportunities to all U.S. citizens began with the passage of the **Civil Rights Act of 1866**. This law, an outgrowth of the 14th Amendment, prohibits any type of discrimination based on race and color. "All citizens of the United States shall have the same right in every state and territory as is enjoyed by white citizens thereof to inherit, purchase, lease, sell, hold, and convey real and personal property." Because of the reference to "white citizens," this law has been widely interpreted to prohibit discrimination based on race and/or color.

In 1987, in a court case involving that old Civil Rights Act, the Supreme Court broadened the definition of race, implying that it may also apply to ethnic or even, in some cases, religious groups.

No exceptions are allowed to this federal law.

Federal Fair Housing Act of 1968

In 1968 two major events greatly advanced the progress of fair housing. The first was the passage of the **Federal Fair Housing Act of 1968**, which is contained in **Title VIII** of the Civil Rights Act of 1968. This law provides that it is unlawful to discriminate on the basis of *race, color, religion,* or *national origin* (including the origin of his or her ancestors) when selling or leasing *residential* property.

The Federal Fair Housing Act covers dwellings and apartments, as well as vacant land acquired for the construction of residential buildings, and prohibits the following discriminatory acts:

- Refusing to sell, rent, or negotiate with any person, or otherwise making a dwelling unavailable to any person

- Changing terms, conditions, or services for different individuals as a means of discrimination

- Practicing discrimination through any statement or advertisement that restricts the sale or rental of residential property

- Representing to any person, as a means of discrimination, that a dwelling is not available for sale or rental when in fact it is

- Making a profit by inducing owners of housing to sell or rent because of the prospective entry into the neighborhood of persons of a particular race, color, religion, national origin, disability, or familial status

- Altering the terms or conditions for a home loan to any person who wishes to purchase or repair a dwelling, or otherwise denying such a loan as a means of discrimination

- Denying people membership or limiting their participation in any multiple listing service, real estate broker's organization, or other facility related to the sale or rental of dwellings, as a means of discrimination

Exemptions to the Federal Fair Housing Act include the following:

- The sale or rental of a single-family home is exempted when the home is owned by an individual who does not own more than three such homes at one time and when (a) *a broker, salesperson, or agent is not used* and (b) discriminatory advertising is not used. If the owner is not living in the dwelling at the time of the transaction or was not the most recent occupant, only one such sale by an individual is exempt from the law within any 24-month period.

- The rental of rooms or units is exempted in an owner-occupied one- to four-family dwelling.

- Dwelling units owned by religious organizations may be restricted to people of the same religion if membership in the organization is not restricted on the basis of race, color, national origin, disability, or familial status.

- A private club that is not open to the public may restrict the rental or occupancy of lodgings that it owns to its members, as long as the lodgings are not operated commercially.

In 1974, an amendment added *sex* as a protected class (particularly in cases of sexual harassment in housing). In 1988, two new classes were added: those with *mental or physical disabilities* (including AIDS) and *familial status* (family members under 18 years of age). Although alcoholics and persons in treatment are considered a protected class, drug abusers are not, nor are those who pose a threat to the health or safety of others. Housing intended for older persons is exempt from the familial status requirements if it is solely occupied by persons 62 and older, or if 80% of its units are occupied by at least one person 55 or older and the housing facility or community publishes and adheres to policies and procedures that demonstrate this intent to be housing for older persons and also complies with occupancy rules issued by the Secretary of the U.S. Department of Housing and Urban Development. A licensee marketing such housing for older persons should make sure the facility states in writing that it complies with the requirements for the exemption

Jones v. Mayer

The second significant fair housing development of 1968 was the Supreme Court decision in the case of *Jones v. Alfred H. Mayer Company*, 392 U.S. 409 (1968). Jones, an African-American, sued Mayer, alleging that Mayer had refused to sell him a home in St. Louis County, Missouri, solely on the basis of race. In its ruling the court upheld the Civil Rights Act of 1866, which "prohibits all racial discrimination, private or public, in the sale and rental of property."

The importance of this decision rests in the fact that while the 1968 federal law exempts *individual* homeowners and certain groups, the 1866 law prohibits *all racial discrimination without exception*. So despite any exemptions in the 1968 law, an aggrieved person may seek a remedy for racial discrimination under the 1866 law against any homeowner, regardless of whether the owner employed a real estate broker and/or advertised the property. Where *race* is involved, *no exceptions apply*.

Equal Housing Opportunity Poster

An amendment to the Federal Fair Housing Act of 1968 instituted the use of an equal housing opportunity poster. This poster (illustrated in Figure 4.1), which can be obtained from the Department of Housing and Urban Development (HUD), features the equal housing opportunity slogan, an equal housing statement pledging adherence to the Fair Housing Act and support of affirmative marketing and advertising programs, and the equal housing opportunity logo.

When HUD investigates a broker for discriminatory practices, it considers failure to display the poster evidence of discrimination.

Unit 4

Figure 4.1: Equal Housing Opportunity Poster

U. S. Department of Housing and Urban Development

EQUAL HOUSING OPPORTUNITY

We Do Business in Accordance With the Federal Fair Housing Law

(The Fair Housing Amendments Act of 1988)

It is Illegal to Discriminate Against Any Person Because of Race, Color, Religion, Sex, Handicap, Familial Status, or National Origin

---

In the sale or rental of housing or residential lots

In the provision of real estate brokerage services

In advertising the sale or rental of housing

In the appraisal of housing

In the financing of housing

Blockbusting is also illegal

Anyone who feels he or she has been discriminated against may file a complaint of housing discrimination:
  1-800-669-9777 (Toll Free)
  1-800-927-9275 (TTY)
  www.hud.gov/fairhousing

U.S. Department of Housing and Urban Development
Assistant Secretary for Fair Housing and Equal Opportunity
Washington, D.C. 20410

Previous editions are obsolete

form HUD-928.1 (8/2011)

Blockbusting and Steering

Blockbusting and steering are illegal housing practices frequently discussed in connection with fair housing. While they are not mentioned by name in the Federal Fair Housing Act of 1968, both are prohibited by that law and by state law.

Blockbusting, also known as *panic peddling*, means inducing homeowners to sell by making representations regarding the entry or prospective entry of minority persons into the neighborhood. The blockbuster frightens homeowners into selling and makes a profit by listing the homes or buying them cheaply and selling them at considerably higher prices to persons of another race. The Federal Fair Housing Act prohibits this practice.

Steering is the channeling of homeseekers either to or away from particular areas on the basis of race, religion, country of origin, or other protected class. On these grounds, it is prohibited by the provisions of the Federal Fair Housing Act. Steering is often difficult to detect, because the steering tactics can be so subtle that the homeseeker is unaware that his or her choices have been limited. Steering may be done unintentionally by agents who are not aware of their own subconscious assumptions.

Redlining

Refusing to make mortgage loans or issue insurance policies in specific geographic areas without regard to the economic qualifications of the applicant is known as **redlining**. This practice, which often contributes to the deterioration of older, transitional neighborhoods, is frequently based on racial grounds, rather than on any individual financial objections to the applicant.

Disparate Impact; Disparate Treatment

Disparate impact, sometimes referenced as disparate treatment or adverse impact, is a policy or practice that seems to be neutral but, in fact, may disproportionately impact a certain group of people. This results in discriminatory practices, resulting in unequal treatment and hindering equal access. For example, a lender or property management company may require full-time employment. On the surface, this requirement seems fair enough; however, it discriminates against someone receiving public assistance, disability payments, etc.

The Department of Housing and Urban Development (HUD), which enforces the Fair Housing Act of 1968, has published guidance explaining that use of criminal history to exclude people from housing may violate the prohibitions in certain circumstances. Housing providers may not use criminal history as a pretext for intentionally discriminating based on race or national origin (e.g., applying criminal record–based restrictions against protected classes differently than they apply them to non-protected-housing applicants).

For example, a management company, with the intent of keeping all tenants safe, might reject an application based on [unspecified] criminal history. This ignores groups who are incarcerated at higher rates than the general population and may not result in a safer environment. Yet another example is zero tolerance of violence, without recognizing that perhaps up to 25% of women have experienced domestic assault, so this policy could negatively impact them.

Enforcement

A person who believes illegal discrimination has occurred has up to one year after the alleged act to file a charge with the **Department of Housing and Urban Development (HUD)** or two years to bring a federal suit. HUD will investigate, and if the department believes a discriminatory act has occurred or is about to occur, it may issue a charge. Any party involved (or HUD) may choose to have the charge heard in a federal district court. If no one requests the court procedure, the charge will be heard by an *administrative law judge* within HUD itself.

The administrative judge has the authority to issue an *injunction*. This would order the offender to take action—rent to the complaining party, for example—or to refrain from taking action. The Federal Civil Penalties Inflation Adjustment Act Improvements Act of 2015, as amended, requires federal agencies to make annual adjustments to civil monetary penalty (CMP) for inflation. The adjustment is updated annually. For example, penalties imposed for violations occurring after April 6, 2020, range from $21,410 for a first violation to $53,524 for a second violation within five years, and $107,050 for further violations within seven years. If the case is heard in federal court, an injunction and actual and punitive damages are possible, with no dollar limit. In addition to offended parties, the Department of Justice may itself sue anyone who seems to show a pattern of illegal discrimination.

In all such cases mentioned, the guilty party may be required to pay the other side's legal fees and court costs, which can add up to substantial amounts.

Complaints brought under the Civil Rights Act of 1866 must be taken directly to a federal court. The only time limit for action would be the state's statute of limitation for *torts*, injuries done by one individual to another. There would be no dollar limit on damages.

Threats or Acts of Violence

The Federal Fair Housing Act of 1968 contains criminal provisions that protect the rights of those who seek the benefits of the open housing law as well as owners, brokers, or salespeople who aid or encourage the enjoyment of open housing rights. Unlawful actions involving threats, coercion, and intimidation are punishable by appropriate civil action. In such cases the victim should report the incident immediately to the local police and to the nearest office of the Federal Bureau of Investigation.

NEW JERSEY LAW AGAINST DISCRIMINATION

New Jersey's **Law Against Discrimination**, originally passed by the state legislature in 1945 and broadened over the years, is one of the strongest laws of its kind. By 1966 it covered housing and public accommodation, as well as the original field—employment.

It's important to note that, while federal laws apply to residential housing, New Jersey's law applies to all real property.

Protected classes for housing under New Jersey law now include

- race, color;
- national origin, ancestry, nationality;
- creed (religion);
- sex, gender identity or expression, affectional or sexual orientation;
- marital status, civil union status, domestic partner status;
- familial status, pregnancy or breastfeeding;
- actual or perceived physical or mental disability;
- source of lawful income used for mortgage or rental payments; and
- liability for service in the Armed Forces of the United States.

Figure 4.2 summarizes protected classes under various laws.

Prohibited Activities

The Law Against Discrimination forbids

- refusing to sell, rent, lease, assign, or sublease as a means of discrimination;

- for licensees, refusing to offer property or to negotiate transactions as a means of discrimination, or lying about the availability of property;

- changing the terms of a real estate transaction or offering special facilities or services to any person or group as a means of discrimination; and

- being involved with any expression, direct or indirect, of any limitation based on discrimination. This includes statements, advertisements, publications, signs, rent applications, purchase offers, and records of inquiries.

Exceptions

The only exception to New Jersey's law applies to rentals: It allows rooms, apartments, or flats in certain types of housing to be restricted to members of one sex; religious-based organizations to discriminate on the basis of religion; and an owner-occupant to discriminate except for race in the rental of a duplex or an up/down two-family dwelling. Note that these exemptions are similar to those available under federal law. New Jersey's law does not contain the federal exceptions for homeowners selling their own homes and no exceptions apply when a broker is involved. There is never an exception for race, whether or not a broker is involved.

Figure 4.2: Fair Housing Protected Classes

Legislation	Race	Color	Religion	National Origin	Sex	Age	Marital Status	Disability	Familial Status	Lawful Source of Income	Ancestry	Affectional or Sexual Orientation	Nationality	Gender Identity or Expression	Pregnancy or Breastfeeding	Liability for Service in the U.S. Armed Forces
Civil Rights Act of 1866	•	•														
Fair Housing Act of 1968 (Title VIII)	•	•	•	•												
Housing and Community Development Act of 1974					•											
Fair Housing Amendments Act of 1988								•	•							
Equal Credit Opportunity Act of 1974 (lending)	•	•	•	•	•	•	•			•						
New Jersey Law Against Discrimination	•	•	• (creed)	•	•		• (marital or domestic partnership of civil union status)	•	•	• (source of lawful income or rent payment)	•	•	•	•	•	•

Financing

The Law Against Discrimination applies also to loans for real estate transactions, whether by institutions or private individuals, for financing construction or for repairs and maintenance.

Blockbusting and Record Keeping

The practice of blockbusting is forbidden by federal law and it is also specifically prohibited by the Law Against Discrimination and by the New Jersey Real Estate Commission. The commission requires any brokerage soliciting listings from more than three homeowners in a block during a single month whether by mail, telephone, or door-to-door canvassing—to keep permanent records of the activity for at least a year. The records must include names and addresses of those solicited, name of the licensee involved, and date of the activity, and they are to be available to the commission.

Poster

All real estate offices and rental offices in large apartment complexes in New Jersey must conspicuously display an antidiscrimination poster (Figure 4.3). Failure to display the poster is punishable by a fine of $100 or more.

Enforcement

Complaints brought under the New Jersey Law Against Discrimination must be filed with the state's attorney general within 180 days after the alleged offense. The attorney general's office investigates promptly and has 45 days to attempt conciliation. After that time, the Director of the Division of Civil Rights holds a hearing. The accused, if found guilty, will be ordered to comply with the law, to make restitution to those who were discriminated against, and to take any other action ordered by the director. The orders can be enforced by the New Jersey superior court, or they may be appealed to that court. The director may award reimbursement for medical expenses; awards for pain, suffering, and humiliation; and fines of up to $10,000 for a first offense, $25,000 for a second offense, and up to $50,000 for subsequent offenses.

Any person who willfully interferes with the activities or who violates an order of the attorney general or the Division on Civil Rights is guilty of a misdemeanor and is subject to a fine of up to $500 and/or imprisonment for up to one year.

Complaints brought under the New Jersey Law Against Discrimination may be filed at any of the offices of the attorney general.

Notice at Listing

A copy of the **Attorney General's memorandum** on discrimination must be given to the homeowner at the time the property is listed. It is good practice for the licensee to have the owners read the memorandum and then initial all copies to acknowledge their acceptance of it. A copy of the memorandum is shown in Figure 4.4. (The form is also available in Spanish at https://www.nj .gov/oag/dcr/downloads/fair-housing-dcr-letters-spa.pdf.) The memorandum must be printed in at least 12-point type, larger than reproduced here. Salespersons and brokers must refuse listings from owners who indicate that they intend to violate the Law Against Discrimination. In October, 2020, the New Jersey Attorney General released an updated letter, available at http://www.nj.gov/ oag/newsreleases20/2020-AG-Fair-Housing-Letter-Updates.pdf.

STATE REGULATIONS ON RENTALS

Source of Income, Children in Family

State statutes prohibit refusing to rent because of the would-be tenant's lawful source of income. This provision, covered only by state and not by federal law, forbids discrimination based on income derived from welfare or other subsidy, such as Section 8 housing funds. State statute also prohibits refusal to rent to families with children under 18 years old. This is covered again under federal law.

Figure 4.3:   New Jersey Antidiscrimination Poster

5 Things You Should Know About
The New Jersey Law Against Discrimination

1   The New Jersey Law Against Discrimination (LAD) prohibits discrimination and harassment based on actual or perceived race, religion, national origin, gender, sexual orientation, gender identity or expression, disability, and other protected characteristics. The law applies in employment, housing, and places of public accommodation (generally, places open to the public, including businesses, restaurants, schools, summer camps, medical providers, etc.).

2   The anti-discrimination provisions mean that an employer cannot fire someone, pay someone less money, or refuse to hire or promote someone because of their race. Similarly, a housing provider cannot refuse to rent an apartment to a couple because of their sexual orientation. And a place of public accommodation cannot refuse service to someone because of their religion.

3   The LAD also prohibits bias-based harassment. That means if someone is being subjected to bias-based harassment that creates a hostile environment, an employer, housing provider, or place of public accommodation must take reasonable steps to stop the harassment if they knew or should have known about it. That includes harassment between coworkers, tenants, or patrons, not just harassment by a landlord or by a supervisor at work. The LAD also prohibits "quid pro quo" sexual harassment—where a person in a position of power demands sex or sexual favors in exchange for favorable treatment, such as continued employment or a promotion.

4   The LAD prohibits retaliation against a person for complaining about discrimination or bias-based harassment, or otherwise exercising or attempting to exercise their rights under the law. For example, an employer cannot fire someone for reporting sexual harassment to human resources. And a housing provider cannot evict someone for reporting housing discrimination to DCR.

5   The New Jersey Division on Civil Rights (DCR) enforces the LAD and is tasked with preventing and eliminating discrimination and bias-based harassment in New Jersey. Anyone who believes their rights under the LAD have been violated may file a complaint with DCR within 180 days of the incident.

To find out more or to file a complaint, go to NJCivilRights.gov or call 973-648-2700

NJ Office of the Attorney General **DIVISION ON**
NJCivilRights.gov   **CIVIL RIGHTS**

02/04/20

Unit 4

Figure 4.4: **Attorney General's Memorandum on Law Against Discrimination and Federal Fair Housing Laws**

State of New Jersey
OFFICE OF THE ATTORNEY GENERAL
DEPARTMENT OF LAW AND PUBLIC SAFETY
DIVISION ON CIVIL RIGHTS
31 CLINTON STREET, 3RD FLOOR
NEWARK, NJ 07102

PHILIP D. MURPHY
Governor

SHEILA Y. OLIVER
Lt. Governor

GURBIR S. GREWAL
Attorney General

RACHEL WAINER APTER
Director

TO: Property Owners

FROM: Gurbir S. Grewal, Attorney General, State of New Jersey
             Rachel Wainer Apter, Director, NJ Division on Civil Rights

DATE: October 7, 2020

SUBJECT: Housing Discrimination Laws

The New Jersey Real Estate Commission (REC) requires every licensed broker or salesperson with whom you list your property to give you a copy of this notice. The purpose is to help you comply with the New Jersey Law Against Discrimination (LAD).

Under the LAD, it is illegal to discriminate against a prospective or current buyer or tenant because of actual or perceived race, national origin, religion, gender, gender identity or expression, marital status, civil union status, domestic partner status, affectional or sexual orientation, familial status, pregnancy or breastfeeding, physical or mental disability, or liability for service in the Armed Forces of the United States. It is also illegal to discriminate against a prospective or current buyer or tenant because of any source of lawful income to be used for rental or mortgage payments. Source of lawful income includes Section 8 housing choice vouchers, SRAP (State Rental Assistance Programs), and TRA (temporary rental assistance). It is also illegal to make, print, or publish any statement, including print advertisements and online postings, expressing any preference, limitation, or discrimination based on any of those protected characteristics.

The LAD applies to a wide range of activities, such as advertising, selling, renting, leasing, subleasing, assigning, and showing property (including open land). Here are some issues that come up frequently in enforcing the LAD:

• The prohibition on discrimination based on source of lawful income means, for example, that a landlord cannot reject a prospective tenant because they intend to pay with a Section 8 housing choice voucher, State Rental Assistance Program (SRAP), temporary rental assistance (TRA), or any other subsidy or voucher provided by federal, state, or local rental-assistance programs. A housing provider cannot advertise a property in any way that discriminates based on source of lawful income, including by posting advertisements that state, directly or indirectly, a refusal to accept, or express any limitation on, vouchers or subsidies. For example, advertisements that state "No Section 8," "TRA not accepted," or "This property not approved for Section 8" violate the LAD. In addition, housing providers must calculate any minimum income requirement, financial standard, or income standard based only on the portion of the rent to be paid by the tenant, rather than the entire rental amount.

www.njcivilrights.gov
New Jersey is an Equal Opportunity Employer · Printed on Recycled Paper and Recyclable

CIVIL RIGHTS

Figure 4.4: Attorney General's Memorandum on Law Against Discrimination and Federal Fair Housing Laws (continued)

- The LAD prohibits bias-based harassment in housing, including sexual harassment. If a tenant is being subjected to bias-based harassment that creates a hostile environment, and if the housing provider knew or should have known about it, the housing provider must take reasonable steps to stop it. That includes harassment by other tenants and by a housing provider's agents or employees. "Quid pro quo" sexual harassment—for example, where a building superintendent demands sex or sexual favors as a condition of making necessary repairs—is also prohibited.

- Housing providers must reasonably accommodate tenants with disabilities unless doing so would be an undue burden on their operations. For example, if a tenant shows they have a disability and that keeping an emotional support animal is necessary to afford them an equal opportunity to use and enjoy the dwelling, the housing provider must permit the emotional support animal, even despite a "no pets" policy, unless they can show that doing so would be an undue burden.

- A "no pets" rule cannot be enforced against a person with a disability who has a service or guide animal. A landlord may also not charge a tenant with a disability an extra fee for keeping a service or guide animal.

- Landlords must permit a tenant with a disability—at that tenant's own expense—to make reasonable modifications to the premises if such modifications are needed to give the tenant an equal opportunity to use or enjoy the dwelling.

- The LAD prohibits discrimination based on "familial status"—for example, discrimination against families with children under the age of 18 and pregnant women. Landlords similarly cannot use unreasonable occupancy restrictions to prevent families with children from moving in.

- Selectively inquiring about, or requesting information about and/or documentation of, a prospective tenant's or buyer's immigration or citizenship status because of the person's actual or perceived national origin, race, or ethnicity, or otherwise discriminating on such a basis, is a violation of the LAD.

- As explained in the U.S. Department of Housing and Urban Development's April 2016 Guidance document, because of widespread racial and ethnic disparities in the criminal justice system, blanket policies that make all individuals with any prior arrest or criminal conviction ineligible to rent violate fair housing laws because they have a disproportionate impact based on race or national origin and are not supported by a legitimate business necessity. And housing providers may not use criminal history as a pretext for intentionally discriminating based on race or national origin (for example, by applying criminal-record based restrictions against Black housing applicants but not white housing applicants).

Penalties. If you commit a discriminatory housing practice that violates the LAD, you may be subject to penalties not exceeding $10,000 for a first violation, not exceeding $25,000 for a second violation within five years of the first offense, and not exceeding $50,000 for two or more violations within seven years.

Other remedies. Victims of discrimination may recover economic damages related to the discrimination (such as having to pay higher rent for another unit), as well as damages for emotional distress, pain, and humiliation. In more egregious cases, a victim may also recover punitive damages.

Brokers. The broker or salesperson with whom you list your property must transmit to you every written offer they receive on your property. Brokers and salespersons are licensed by the New Jersey Real Estate Commission and their activities are subject to the LAD as well as general real estate laws of the State and the Commission's own rules and regulations. The broker or salesperson must refuse your listing if you indicate an intent to

Figure 4.4:   Attorney General's Memorandum on Law Against Discrimination and Federal Fair Housing Laws (continued)

discriminate on any basis prohibited by the LAD.

Exemptions. The sale or rental of property (including open land), whether for business or residential purposes, is covered by the LAD, subject to the following exemptions. Note that when an LAD exemption applies, other civil rights laws may nonetheless prohibit discrimination.

- The LAD does not apply to the rental of one unit in a two-family dwelling if the owner occupies the other unit, or to the rental of a room or rooms in a one-family owner-occupied dwelling.

- A religious organization can give preference to persons of the same religion when selling or renting real property.

- In certain types of housing designated for older persons, it is not unlawful to discriminate based on familial status.

For more information about the LAD, or if you have other questions about discrimination in the sale or rental of real property, including how to report a complaint, please visit **www.NJCivilRights.gov** or call our Housing Hotline at **(866) 405-3050**. DCR has a number of fair housing fact sheets that are available at https://www.nj.gov/oag/dcr/housing.html. Thank you.

Gurbir S. Grewal
Attorney General

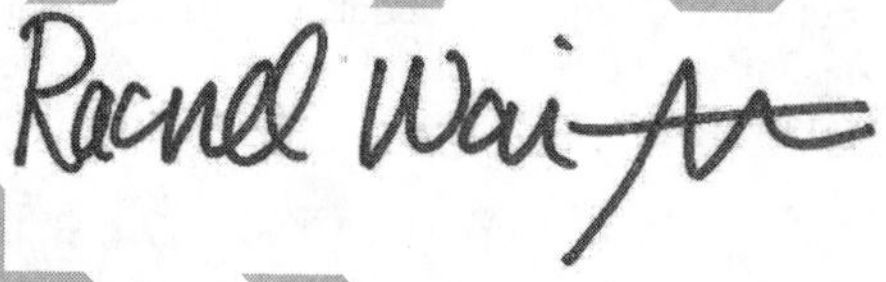

Rachel Wainer Apter
Director, Division on Civil Rights

Other Provisions

The following miscellaneous provisions govern rentals in New Jersey:

- A landlord cannot refuse to rent a one-bedroom apartment to two members of the same sex if the same apartment would be available to members of the opposite sex who were equally qualified.

  It is illegal to subject a tenant to sexual harassment.

- A lease may not provide that it will become null and void on the birth of a child.

- A facility that does not admit pets must permit a guide or service animal.

- A person with AIDS is considered a person with a disability under New Jersey laws and is entitled to protection against discrimination in housing. The LAD's protections continue to apply even if the conduct at issue is related to COVID-19. For example, a landlord cannot seek to evict because the tenant has or the landlord believes the tenant to have COVID-19. Likewise, a landlord cannot refuse to rent to someone who is Asian because they believe Asian people are responsible for spreading COVID-19.

Landlords are allowed to enforce health regulations limiting the number of persons allowed for the size of any given apartment. And it is, of course, always proper to accept or reject prospective tenants on the basis of their ability to pay the rent (income) and their likelihood of doing so (credit rating).

Multiple Dwelling Reporting

Owners of developments containing 25 or more apartments must file an annual report with the state Division of Civil Rights. The report covers racial composition of the tenants and methods of advertising and handling inquiries.

ZONING DISCRIMINATION: MOUNT LAUREL I AND II

In 1971, a lawsuit that came to be known as **Mount Laurel I** was filed by the NAACP against the town of Mount Laurel, New Jersey, for illegal discrimination against low-income and moderate-income persons through the use of exclusionary zoning. The court stated that all developing communities had to zone for their fair share of the regional needs for low-income and moderate-income families. In 1975, the court ruled that the poor may not be excluded from residential areas.

In 1983, **Mount Laurel II**, a second suit filed by the NAACP against Mount Laurel, resulted in the courts providing specific guidelines for all developing communities, and said that all municipalities have an obligation to provide a range of housing. This was accomplished by allowing for higher-density developments, a 20% set-aside, zoning for mobile homes, and a requirement that communities must cooperate with efforts to obtain subsidies. A panel of three judges, appointed by the chief justice, was set up to handle similar cases.

CODE FOR EQUAL OPPORTUNITY

The National Association of REALTORS® has adopted a *Code for Equal Opportunity*. The code sets forth suggested standards of conduct for REALTORS®, so that they may affirmatively pledge to offer equal service to all persons.

Unit 4

HUD/NAR Fair Housing Partnership

The *HUD/NAR Fair Housing Partnership* was founded on the principle of focusing attention on achieving fair housing through local community initiatives. The NAR, local REALTOR® Associations, and HUD field offices work together to develop fair housing partnerships based on the existing needs of their communities. REALTORS® are not required, under the partnership, to sign any declaration of adherence to fair housing principles, nor are individual REALTORS® or local boards monitored for performance. Rather, the NAR and HUD have developed a *Declaration of Fair Housing Principles* for REALTORS® to use to promote fair housing to the public and within the firm. Firms cannot simply point to their having signed the *Voluntary Affirmative Marketing Agreement* (VAMA), the partnership's predecessor program. Instead, firms must develop their own individual *Affirmative Fair Housing Marketing Plans* to obtain FHA financing, or adopt a model plan approved by HUD and NAR. Despite the loose structure of the partnership, penalties for violating fair housing laws are severe, and include the loss of a real estate license.

IMPLICATIONS FOR BROKERS AND SALESPERSONS

To a great extent the laws place the burden of responsibility for effecting and maintaining fair housing on real estate licensees—brokers and salespeople. The laws are clear and widely known. The complainant does not have to prove *guilty knowledge* or *specific intent*—only the fact that *discrimination occurred.*

How does a broker go about complying with the laws and making that policy known? HUD regulations suggest that a public statement in the form of an approved fair housing poster be displayed by a broker in any place of business where housing is offered for sale or rent (including model homes). HUD also offers guidelines for nondiscriminatory language and illustrations for use in real estate advertising.

In addition, the NAR suggests that a broker's position can be emphasized and problems can be avoided by the prominent display of a sign stating that it is against company policy as well as state and federal laws to offer any information on the racial, ethnic, or religious composition of a neighborhood or to place restrictions on listing, showing, or providing information on the availability of homes for any of these reasons.

If a prospect expresses a locational preference for housing based on race, the association's guidelines suggest the following response: "I cannot give you that kind of advice. I will show you several homes that meet your specifications. You will have to decide which one you want."

Discrimination involves a sensitive area, human emotions—specifically fear and self-preservation based on considerable prejudice and misconception. The broker or salesperson who keeps his or her own actions in check by complying with the law still has to deal in many cases with a general public whose attitudes cannot be altered by legislation alone. Therefore, a licensee who wishes to comply with the fair housing laws and also succeed in the real estate business must work to educate the public.

In recent years, brokers sometimes have been caught in the middle when local governments enacted well-meaning quotas that give rise to **reverse discrimination** regulations. Intended to preserve racial balance in given areas, local laws sometimes run counter to federal and state rules, posing a real problem for the conscientious licensee.

Advertising

There has been much confusion in the past about what types of property descriptions are and are not appropriate or legal to use in an advertisement. In an effort to clarify federal regulations regarding real estate advertising, HUD has issued detailed policy guidelines (see Figure 4.5).

- Race, color, national origin—Real estate advertisements should state no discriminatory preference or limitation on account of race, color, religion, or national origin. Use of words describing the housing, the current or potential residents, or the neighbors or neighborhood in racial or ethnic terms (for example, "white family home" or "no Irish") create liability. However, advertisements that are neutral ("master bedroom," or "good neighborhood") do not create liability.

- Religion—Advertisements should not contain anything explicitly preferencing, limiting, or discriminating on account of religion (for instance, "no Jews" or "good Christian home"). Advertisements that use the legal name of an entity that contains a religious reference (such as Roselawn Catholic Home) or that contain a religious symbol (i.e., a cross or menorah) standing alone, may indicate a religious preference. However, if such an ad includes a disclaimer (such as "This home does not discriminate on the basis of race, color, religion, national origin, sex, disability, or familial status"), it does not violate the act. Advertisements containing descriptions of properties ("apartment complex with chapel") or services ("kosher meals available") do not on their face state a preference for persons likely to make use of those facilities, and so do not violate the act.

- The use of secularized terms or symbols relating to holidays, such as Santa Claus, the Easter Bunny, or St. Valentine's Day images, or phrases such as "Merry Christmas" or "Happy Hanukkah" do not constitute violations of the act.

- Sex—Advertisements for single-family dwellings or separate units in a multifamily dwelling should contain no explicit preference, limitation, or discrimination based on sex. Use of the term "master bedroom" does not constitute a violation of either the sex discrimination or the race discrimination provisions. Terms such as "mother-in-law suite" and "bachelor apartment" are commonly used as physical descriptions of housing units and do not violate the act.

- Disability—Real estate advertisements should not contain specific exclusions, limitations, or other indications of discrimination based on disability (i.e., "no wheelchairs"). Advertisements containing descriptions of properties ("great view," "fourth-floor walk-up," or "walk-in closet"), services or facilities ("jogging trails") or neighborhood amenities ("walk to bus") do not violate the act. Advertisements describing conduct required of residents ("nonsmoking," "quiet") do not violate the act. Advertisements containing descriptions of accessibility features ("wheelchair ramp") are lawful.

- Familial status—Advertisements may not state an explicit preference, limitation, or discrimination based on familial status. Advertisements may not contain limitations on the number or ages of children or state a preference for adults, couples, or singles. Advertisements describing properties ("two-bedroom," "cozy," or "family room"), services and facilities ("no bicycles allowed"), or neighborhoods ("quiet streets") are not racially discriminatory and do not violate the act.

Testing

From time to time real estate offices may be visited by **testers**, or checkers, undercover volunteers who want to see whether all customers and clients are being treated with the same cordiality and are being offered the same free choice of housing within a given price range. The courts have held that such practice is permissible as the only way to test compliance with the fair housing laws that are of such importance to U.S. society.

When a real estate broker is charged with discrimination, it is no defense that the offense was unintentional. Citing past service to members of the same minority group is of little value as a defense.

Every broker should have a written policy on fair housing that all agents should be familiar with and follow. It is essential that all licensees develop sensitivity on the subject and follow routine practices designed to reduce the danger of unintentionally hurting any member of the public. These practices include careful record keeping for each customer, including financial analysis, properties suggested, houses shown, and check-back phone calls. Using a standard form for all qualifying interviews is recommended. Special care should be taken to be on time for appointments and to follow through on returning all phone calls. Besides helping to avoid civil rights violations, these practices are simply good business and should result in increased sales.

Figure 4.5: HUD's Advertising Guidelines

Category	Rule	Permitted	Not Permitted
Race Color National Origin	No discriminatory limitation/preference may be expressed	"master bedroom" "good neighborhood"	"white neighborhood" "no French"
Religion	No Religious discrimination religious preference/limitation	"chapel on premises" "kosher meals available" "Merry Christmas"	"no Muslims" "nice Christian family" "near great Catholic school"
Sex	No explicit preference based on sex	"mother-in-law suite" "master bedroom" "female roommate sought"	"great house for a man" "wife's dream kitchen"
Disability	No exclusions or limitations based on disability	"wheelchair ramp" "walk to shopping"	"no wheelchairs" "able-bodied tenants only"
Familial Status	No preference or limitation based on family size or nature	"two-bedroom" "family room" "quiet neighborhood"	"married couple only" "no more than two children" "retiree's dream house"
Photographs or Illustrations of People	People should be clearly representative and nonexclusive	Illustrations showing ethnic races, family groups, singles, etc.	Illustrations showing only singles, African American families, elderly white adults, etc.

SUMMARY

Federal regulations regarding equal opportunity in housing are principally contained in two laws. The *Civil Rights Act of 1866* prohibits all racial or color discrimination and the *Federal Fair Housing Act (Title VIII of the Civil Rights Act of 1968)* prohibits discrimination on the basis of race, color, religion, sex, national origin, disability, or familial status in the sale or rental of residential property. Discriminatory actions include refusing to deal with an individual or a specific group, changing any terms of a real estate or loan transaction, changing the services offered for any individual or group, making statements or advertisements that indicate discriminatory restrictions, or otherwise attempting to make a dwelling unavailable to any person or group because of membership in a protected class. Some exceptions apply to owners but *none apply to brokers*, and *none when the discriminatory act is based on race.*

Complaints under the Federal Fair Housing Act may be reported to and investigated by the *Department of Housing and Urban Development* and may be taken to a U.S. District Court. Complaints under the Civil Rights Act of 1866 must be taken to a federal court.

Protected classes under New Jersey's Law Against Discrimination include race, creed (religion), color, national origin, ancestry, nationality, marital or domestic partnership or civil union status, sex, gender identity or expression, disability, affectional or sexual orientation, family status, and source of lawful income or rent payment. A housing poster must be displayed in real estate and rental offices; records must be kept of solicitation that might be construed as *blockbusting*; each listing property owner must be given a summary of the Law

Against Discrimination; owners of multiple dwellings with 25 or more units must make annual reports on racial status of their tenants. Landlords may not refuse prospective tenants solely on the basis of *lawful source of income*.

The court cases known as *Mount Laurel I* and *II* mandate availability of low-income and middle-income housing in housing developments.

Licensees must take special care that their ads include no language that could be considered discriminatory.

The HUD/NAR Fair Housing Partnership Guide (replacing the Voluntary Affirmative Marketing Agreement) offers alternative suggestions for developing and implementing fair housing partnerships in the community. The Fair Housing Declaration developed by the NAR and HUD contains principles for REALTORS® to use to promote fair housing to the public and within the firm.

USEFUL WEBSITES

New Jersey Division of Civil Rights: www.nj.gov/oag/dcr/index/html

U.S. HUD: Fair Housing: http://portal.hud.gov/hudportal/HUD?src=/program_offices/fair_housing_equal_opp

U.S. HUD: Housing Discrimination Complaints: www.hud.gov/complaints/housediscrim.cfm

KEY TERMS REVIEW

Match the number of each key term with the corresponding letter.

_____ 1. Attorney General's memorandum

_____ 2. Blockbusting

_____ 3. Civil Rights Act of 1866

_____ 4. Department of Housing and Urban Development

_____ 5. Federal Fair Housing Act of 1968

_____ 6. Law Against Discrimination

_____ 7. Mount Laurel I and II

_____ 8. Protected class

_____ 9. Redlining

_____ 10. Reverse discrimination

_____ 11. Steering

_____ 12. Tester

_____ 13. Title VIII

A.   federal law setting many protected classes; some exceptions

B.   federal law; protected classes are race and color; no exceptions

C.   inducing panic selling based on prejudice

D.   New Jersey's law governing discrimination in real estate transactions

E.   refusal to lend in certain areas, usually inner-city

F.   section of federal Civil Rights Act that covers housing

G.   specific group that may not be discriminated against

H.   court cases covering moderate-income housing

I.   channeling homeseekers to or away from certain areas

J.   undercover checker who monitors fair housing compliance

K.   "benign" discrimination intended to correct past wrongs

L.   federal agency enforcing civil rights compliance

M.   statement about discrimination everyone listing property must receive

UNIT 4 REVIEW QUESTIONS

1. At the time the owner listed his home with a salesperson, he informs her of his general dislike of members of a particular ethnic group. The salesperson later shows the home to two prospective buyers, one of whom is a member of this group, and both make an offer. When the owner contacts the agent again, she does not present him with the lower offer, which was made by the member of the minority group. The salesperson has violated
   A. the Civil Rights Act of 1866.
   B. only the New Jersey real estate license law.
   C. the New Jersey Law Against Discrimination, federal fair housing laws, and New Jersey Real Estate License Law.
   D. only federal fair housing laws.

2. Which of the following acts is permitted under the Federal Fair Housing Act?
   A. Advertising property for sale only to a special group
   B. Altering the terms of a loan for a member of a minority group
   C. Refusing to sell a home to an individual because he or she has a poor credit history
   D. Telling a protected individual that an apartment has been rented when in fact it has not

3. The Civil Rights Act of 1866 is unique because the act
   A. protects all persons, male or female, based only on color.
   B. provides exceptions based on income.
   C. requires the complainant to file suit in a state court.
   D. covers only the areas of race and color.

4. "I hear they're moving in; there goes the neighborhood. Better list with me today!" is an example of
   A. steering.
   B. blockbusting.
   C. redlining.
   D. testing.

5. The act of channeling homeseekers to a particular area, either to maintain or to change the character of a neighborhood, is
   A. blockbusting.
   B. redlining.
   C. steering.
   D. permitted under the Fair Housing Act of 1968.

6. Which would NOT be permitted under the Federal Fair Housing Act?
   A. The Harvard Club in New York rents rooms only to graduates of Harvard who belong to the club.
   B. The owner of a 20-unit apartment building rents to women only.
   C. A convent refuses to furnish housing for a Jewish man.
   D. All of these.

7. Under federal law, families with children may be refused rental or purchase in buildings where occupancy is reserved exclusively for those aged at least
   A. 57.
   B. 60.
   C. 62.
   D. 65.

8. Guiding prospective buyers to a particular area because the agent feels they belong there may lead to
   A. blockbusting.
   B. redlining.
   C. steering.
   D. bird-dogging.

9. Refusal to rent to someone because they receive public assistance violates
   A. the New Jersey Law Against Discrimination.
   B. Executive Order 11063.
   C. the Fair Housing Act of 1968.
   D. the Civil Rights Act of 1866.

10. A policy of never renting to people whose income is derived from public assistance violates
    A. no law.
    B. the most recent presidential executive letter.
    C. the New Jersey Law Against Discrimination.
    D. the Civil Rights Act of 1866.

11. Refusing an apartment to a couple because they are unmarried violates
    A. no law.
    B. the New Jersey Executive Law.
    C. the Law Against Discrimination.
    D. the Civil Rights Act of 1866.

12. A mortgage company makes it a practice not to lend money to potential homeowners attempting to purchase property located in predominantly black neighborhoods. This practice is known as
    A. redlining.
    B. blockbusting.
    C. steering.
    D. qualifying.

13. A court found a landlord guilty of illegal discrimination and ordered him to rent his next available apartment to the person who was unfairly hurt. The court order is an example of
    A. punitive damages.
    B. actual damages.
    C. an injunction.
    D. a monetary penalty.

14. The seller who requests prohibited discrimination in the showing of a home should be told
    A. "As your agent I have a duty to warn you that such discrimination could land you in real trouble."
    B. "I am not allowed to obey such instructions."
    C. "If you persist, I'll have to refuse to list your property."
    D. "I cannot list your property."

15. A good precaution against even unintentional discrimination is
    A. detailed record keeping on each customer.
    B. use of a standard financial interview form.
    C. routine follow-up phone calls.
    D. all of these.

16. The Federal Fair Housing Amendments of 1988 added which of the following as new protected classes?
    A. Occupation and source of income
    B. Disability and familial status
    C. Political affiliation and country of origin
    D. Prison record and marital status

17. As of 2020, the fine for a first violation of the Federal Fair Housing Act could be as much as
    A. $12,300.
    B. $15,435.
    C. $19,787.
    D. $21,410.

18. The only defense against an accusation of illegal discrimination is proof that it
    A. was unintentional.
    B. didn't cause financial loss to anyone.
    C. arose because the agent was ignorant of the law.
    D. didn't occur.

19. Undercover investigation to see whether fair housing practices are being followed is sometimes made by
    A. testers.
    B. evaluators.
    C. operatives.
    D. conciliators.

20. Participation in the HUD/NAR Fair Housing Partnership is
    A. required by law.
    B. automatic when regular dues are paid.
    C. voluntary.
    D. open to brokers only.

21. Complaints brought under the New Jersey Law Against Discrimination
    A. must be filed with the New Jersey superior court.
    B. must be filed within 180 days after the alleged discriminatory action occurs.
    C. must be filed with the federal court.
    D. are also filed in the local court.

22. The New Jersey Law Against Discrimination
     A. requires the owner of a multiple dwelling of 35 units or less to file an annual report regarding the racial composition of the residents of the property.
     B. disregards discriminatory lending practices on the part of savings and loan associations and other institutions that make mortgage loans.
     C. permits an owner-occupant of a one- or two-family residence to deny housing to a tenant based on the applicant's age.
     D. is rarely enforced or observed.

23. The Mount Laurel court decisions attempt to correct housing discrimination based on
     A. race.
     B. income.
     C. religion.
     D. political affiliation.

24. At the time a property is listed, the homeowner must be given a copy of the
     A. HUD Fair Housing Poster.
     B. New Jersey Law Against Discrimination.
     C. Attorney General's memorandum on discrimination.
     D. Division of Civil Rights homeseller's information pamphlet.

25. If a New Jersey salesperson sent bright yellow postcards to all the homeowners in a neighborhood warning them that several immigrant families were planning to move into the neighborhood, and suggesting that property values were about to fall, the salesperson would be guilty of which of the following?
     A. Redlining
     B. Screening
     C. Testing
     D. Blockbusting

UNIT
5

What Is Real Estate?

LEARNING OBJECTIVES

When you have completed this unit, you will be able to accomplish the following.

› Identify the characteristics of real estate.
› Distinguish between the characteristics of personal property and fixtures.

KEY TERMS

accretion
air rights
alluvion
avulsion
bill of sale
bundle of rights
chattels
corporeal
devise
emblements

erosion
fixture
front foot
hereditament
improvement
incorporeal
land
littoral rights
mineral rights
parcel

personal property,
  personalty
real estate
real property, realty
reliction
riparian rights
subsurface rights
trade fixture

REAL ESTATE

Tens of thousands of men and women in New Jersey work in some aspect of the real estate industry as brokers, salespersons, appraisers, builders, developers, lawyers, or property managers. They aid buyers, sellers, and investors in completing transactions that involve billions of dollars in property each year. But what exactly is real estate? This unit discusses the nature of land, real estate, and real and personal property.

Real property ownership is often described as a **bundle of rights**. When a person purchases a parcel of real estate, he or she is actually buying the rights previously held by the seller. These rights (see Figure 5.1) include

■ the right of *possession*,

- the right to *use* the property in any legal manner,
- the right of *enjoyment*,
- the right of *exclusion* (to keep others from entering or occupying the property), and
- the right of *disposition* or *alienation* (to be able to sell or give away the property).

Figure 5.1: The Bundle of Legal Rights

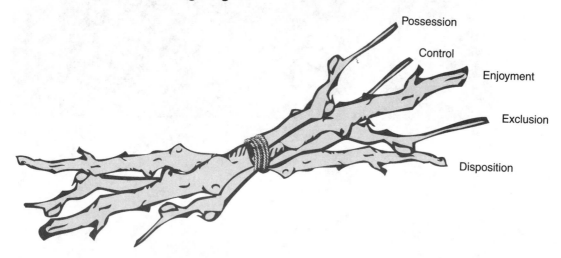

Within these ownership rights are included further rights to improve, **devise** (leave by will), mortgage, encumber, cultivate, explore, mine, build, lease, license, dedicate, give away, abandon, share, trade, or exchange the property.

LAND VS. REAL ESTATE

The terms *land* and *real estate*, though sometimes used to describe the same thing, have important differences in meaning.

Land

The term *land* refers to the surface of the earth, including water, and anything attached to it by nature, such as trees and bushes. It also includes the minerals and substances below the earth's surface, together with the airspace above the earth's surface, up to infinity.

Thus, **land** may be defined as the earth, extending downward from the surface to the center of the earth, and upward to infinity, including all things permanently attached by nature.

A specific tract of land is commonly referred to as a **parcel**, which can be of any size but has legally defined boundaries.

Real Estate

The term *real estate* includes land as defined previously and also all man-made improvements. The word **improvement** includes both buildings erected on the land and streets, utilities, sewers, and other manufactured additions to the property. The concept of real estate can also include all the legal rights that go with property ownership.

Real estate, then, is defined as the earth's surface extending downward to the center of the earth and upward into space, including all things permanently attached to it by nature or by people, and all rights, benefits, and interests in it. The terms **real estate**, **real property**, and **realty** are usually used interchangeably and include both **corporeal** (tangible) assets like buildings and trees and **incorporeal** (intangible) assets like views or rights.

Subsurface Rights

The rights to the natural resources lying below the earth's surface, called **subsurface** or **mineral rights**, may be owned separately (see Figure 5.2).

Figure 5.2: Surface and Subsurface Rights

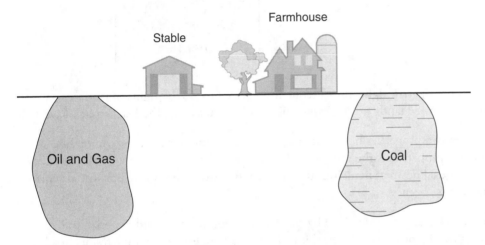

A landowner, for example, may sell his or her rights to any oil and gas found in the land to an oil company. The landowner could then sell the land to a purchaser and in the sale reserve the rights to all coal that may be found in the land. After these sales, three parties have ownership interests in this real estate:

1. The oil company owns all oil and gas.
2. The seller owns all coal.
3. The new landowner owns the rights to all the rest of the real estate.

Air Rights

The rights to use the air above the land may be sold or leased independently of the land itself. Such **air rights** are an increasingly important part of real estate, particularly in large cities, where air rights over railroads have been used to construct huge office buildings, such as New York City's Met-Life Building (the former Pan American Building) next to Grand Central Station. For the construction of such a building, the developer must obtain not only the air rights above the land but also numerous small portions of the actual land on which to construct the building's foundation supports. The Federal Aviation Agency has exclusive primary jurisdiction of airspace over 500 feet of the highest point of a property owned.

Water Rights

Land bordering on oceans, seas, or large lakes affected by tide currents is known as *littoral*. Land bordered or traversed by a stream or waterway is known as *riparian*. (An easy way to remember this distinction is that **littoral rights** refer to lakes and other large bodies of water; **riparian rights** refer to rivers, streams, and waterways.) If a stream is identified as not navigable on a federal survey map, its bed is owned by the owner or owners of the adjoining land, who have certain riparian rights that allow them to use the water (see Figure 5.3).

Figure 5.3: Riparian Rights

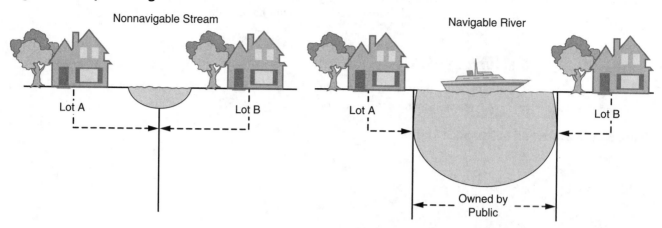

In New Jersey, the riparian rights most frequently referred to are the rights of landowners abutting on tide-flowed lands (for example, the meadowlands along the Hackensack River).

Normally, when two properties have a stream as their common border, the dividing line between the two properties is the middle of the stream. If the stream were suddenly to change its course, a process known as **avulsion**, the property line would not move but would remain where it had always been.

Accretion is an increase of land caused by the gradual depositing of solid material, called **alluvion**, by a contiguous body of water; it is the opposite of **erosion**, which results in a loss of property. **Reliction** is the creation of dry land by the gradual withdrawal of water from the land by the lowering of its surface level.

New Jersey contains approximately 124 miles of coastline. Approximately half is owned by municipalities, and one quarter is under private ownership. The state and federal governments each own about 14 miles (see Figure 5.4). Property that borders on water (river, lake, or ocean) is often priced by **front foot** (i.e., the width of the land on the water). Each front foot extends the depth of the lot.

Figure 5.4: Littoral Rights

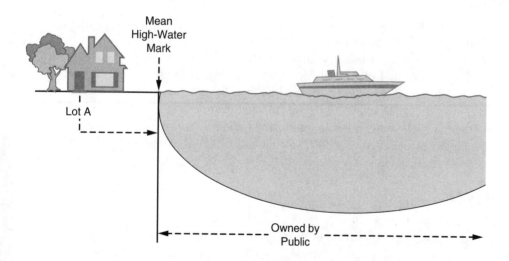

REAL PROPERTY VS. PERSONAL PROPERTY

Everything that can be owned may be classified as either real or personal property. And anything that can be inherited is a **hereditament**. Real estate, or real property, has already been defined as the earth's surface including the permanent additions or growing things attached to it, the airspace above it and the minerals below it.

Personal property, also called **personalty**, is all property that does not fit the definition of real property. While real estate is fixed and immovable, personal property is movable. *Tangible personal property* is also referred to as **chattels** and includes such items as furniture, clothing, refrigerators, and bonds (see Figure 5.5).

Figure 5.5: Real vs. Personal Property

Real Estate

Land and anything permanently attached to it

Personal Property

Movable items not attached to real estate; items severed from real estate

Fixture

Item of personal property converted to real estate by attaching it to the real estate with the intention that it become permanently a part thereof

Trade Fixture

Item of personal property attached to real estate that is owned by a tenant and is used in a business; legally removable by tenant

The distinction between personal and real property is of great importance to the real estate practitioner. Buyers and sellers must be guided to clear written agreements about what "goes with" property being sold, and methods of transfer of ownership differ for the two: real property ownership is transferred by **deed**, while personal property is transferred by **bill of sale**.

It is possible to change the status of an item of real estate to personal property. A tree is real estate, but if the owner cuts down the tree, severing it from the earth, the tree becomes personal property, a transformation process known as *severance*.

The reverse situation is also possible. Personal property can be changed to real property. If an owner buys cement, stones, and sand and constructs a concrete walk, then materials that were originally personal property are converted into real estate because they have become a permanent improvement to the land.

Vegetation falls into two classes: trees, perennial bushes, and grasses that do not require cultivation are considered real estate; annual crops such as wheat, corn, and garden vegetables are known as **emblements** and are considered personal property. One would expect a tenant farmer to return to harvest crops even after the farm had been sold.

A mobile home, unless it has been removed from its axle and permanently attached to the land by a foundation, is considered personal property. However, real estate brokers who are not licensed as motor vehicle dealers may legally broker the resale of mobile and manufactured homes that are titled as motor vehicles. The broker must strictly adhere to Division of Motor Vehicles requirements regarding the transfer.

Fixtures

An article that was once personal property but has been so attached to land or to a building that it is now considered to be part of the real estate is a **fixture**. Examples of fixtures are heating systems, elevator equipment, kitchen cabinets, built-in dishwashers, and light and plumbing fixtures. Almost any item that has been added as a permanent part of a building is considered a fixture.

Tenant and Trade Fixtures

An article owned by a tenant and attached to a rented space for use in conducting a business is a **trade fixture**. Examples of trade fixtures are barber chairs and sinks, store shelves, and restaurant and bar equipment. Agricultural fixtures such as chicken coops and tool sheds also fall into this category (see Figure 5.5). Tenants must remove their trade fixtures before the termination of their lease; any fixtures that are not removed after the lease expires become the real property of the landlord.

Trade fixtures differ from other fixtures in the following ways:

- Fixtures belong to the owner of the real estate, but trade fixtures are usually owned and installed by a tenant for his or her business use.
- Fixtures are considered a permanent part of a building, but trade fixtures are removable. (The tenant must, however, restore the property to its original condition before the end of the lease.)
- Fixtures are legally considered real estate, but trade fixtures are legally considered to be personal property.

Tenant fixtures can also be fixtures installed by a tenant in a residential rental property, including such items as bookcases, chandeliers, or even stoves. Without prior written agreement of the landlord, they become part of the real estate and belong to the landlord.

If tenants are allowed to remove the fixtures, they are expected to restore the property to its original condition before they vacate the premises.

Legal Tests of a Fixture

Courts apply four basic tests to determine whether a disputed article is a fixture (a part of the real estate) or removable personal property. These tests are based on

1. the intention of the party annexing the item,
2. the method of annexation of the item,
3. the adaptation of the article to the real estate, and
4. the relationship of the parties.

Although these tests seem simple, there is no uniformity in court decisions regarding what constitutes a fixture. Articles that appear to be permanently affixed sometimes have been held by the courts to be personal property, and items that do not appear to be permanently attached have been held to be fixtures. For example, the installation of wall-to-wall carpeting can be interpreted as an installation of an area rug; a seller could remove it even if that was not specifically stated in the listing agreement or contract. Items like the front door key, although not attached, are clearly fixtures that belong with a house. Licensees should be sure to ask sellers which items are and are not included in a real estate transaction.

SUMMARY

Even the simplest real estate transactions involve a complex body of laws. When a person purchases real estate, the person is purchasing not only the land itself but also a *bundle of legal rights* to use the land in certain ways that formerly were held by the seller.

Although most people think of land as the surface of the earth, the definition of this word really applies not only to the earth's surface but also to the mineral deposits under the earth and the air above it. The term *real estate* expands this definition to include all man-made *improvements* attached to the land and the rights that go with it.

The same parcel of real estate may be owned and controlled by different parties, one owning the *surface rights*, one owning the *air rights*, and another owning the *subsurface rights*.

All property that does not fit the definition of real estate is classified as *personal property*. When articles of personal property are permanently affixed to land, they may become *fixtures* and as such are considered a part of the real estate. However, personal property attached to real estate by a tenant for a business purpose is classified as a *trade fixture* and remains personal property.

USEFUL WEBSITE

Legal information: www.law.cornell.edu

Unit 5

KEY TERMS REVIEW 1

Match the number of each key term with the corresponding letter.

_____ 1. Accretion

_____ 2. Air rights

_____ 3. Littoral rights

_____ 4. Avulsion

_____ 5. Bundle of rights

_____ 6. Chattels

_____ 7. Corporeal

_____ 8. Devise

_____ 9. Emblements

_____ 10. Riparian rights

_____ 11. Fixture

_____ 12. Hereditament

_____ 13. Improvement

A. belong to owner of land below

B. the wearing away of land usually due to the action of wind or water

C. leave real estate to someone by will

D. tangible

E. annual crops

F. tangible personal property

G. rights of landowners to use waters adjoining streams or waterways not affected by tidal currents

H. once personal property, now real estate

I. sudden change of the course of a stream

J. anything that can be inherited

K. an increase of land caused by the gradual depositing of solid material by the action of water

L. rights of landowners to use bodies of water affected by tidal currents

M. solid material deposited by a body of water

KEY TERMS REVIEW 2

Match the number of each key term with the corresponding letter.

_____ 1. Incorporeal

_____ 2. Land

_____ 3. Littoral rights

_____ 4. Mineral rights

_____ 5. Parcel

_____ 6. Personal property, personalty

_____ 7. Real estate

_____ 8. Real property, realty

_____ 9. Reliction

_____ 10. Riparian rights

_____ 11. Subsurface rights

_____ 12. Trade fixture

A. creation of dry land by the gradual withdrawal of water

B. everything that is not real property

C. specific tract of land

D. subsurface rights

E. removable by tenants

F. land, improvements, and bundle of rights

G. use of water by adjoining landowners

H. intangible

I. the earth, including air above

J. synonyms for real estate

K. ownership of minerals, oil, and so on

L. land bordering bodies of water affected by tides

UNIT 5 REVIEW QUESTIONS

1. Which of the following is included in the traditional bundle of rights?
   A. Payment of rent
   B. Use of the property for any legal purpose
   C. Prohibit a person from another country from ownership
   D. Condemnation rights

2. Which of the following is NOT included in the definition of real estate?
   A. Chattels
   B. Fixtures
   C. Trees
   D. Minerals in the earth

3. A specific tract of land is known as a
   A. bundle.
   B. parcel.
   C. chattel.
   D. riparian.

4. The owner of a large farm may lease to a gas-drilling company his
   A. riparian rights.
   B. subsurface rights.
   C. air rights.
   D. littoral rights.

5. Manufactured, permanent additions to land are called
   A. chattels.
   B. parcels.
   C. improvements.
   D. trade fixtures.

6. One would have to look at a federal map to identify
   A. riverfronts.
   B. major lakes.
   C. navigable waterways.
   D. uplands.

7. A person owns land along the Passaic River. As a result, this person may possess certain
   A. riparian rights.
   B. subsurface rights.
   C. air rights.
   D. solar rights.

8. Which of the following items would be considered personal property?
   A. Fences
   B. Permanent buildings
   C. Farm equipment
   D. Growing trees

9. A tenant in a small house is under a one-year lease. Without consulting his landlord, the tenant installs awnings over the building's front windows to keep the sun away from some delicate hanging plants. Which of the following is TRUE?
   A. By law, the tenant's landlord must pay for the awnings before the rental period is over.
   B. Because of their permanent nature, the awnings are considered to be personal property.
   C. The awnings have become part of the real estate and cannot be removed.
   D. The awnings are removable trade fixtures.

10. When furnishing a beauty salon, the hairdresser installed three shampoo basins, four large plate-glass mirrors, and custom workstation counters. Just before the expiration of the lease, the hairdresser has the right to remove
    A. everything but the shampoo basins, because they are attached to the plumbing.
    B. only the mirrors, and then only if holes in the walls are repaired.
    C. everything.
    D. nothing, because all the items became fixtures when they were attached.

11. The owners are building a new enclosed front porch on their home. The lumber dealer with whom they are contracting has just unloaded a truckload of lumber to be used to build the porch in front of their house. At this point, the lumber is considered
    A. a chattel.
    B. real estate.
    C. a fixture.
    D. a trade fixture.

12. When the new front porch is completed, the lumber that the dealer originally delivered will be considered
    A. a chattel.
    B. real estate. ✓
    C. personalty.
    D. a trade fixture.

13. Personal property differs from real property in its
    A. variety.
    B. mobility. ✓
    C. adaptation.
    D. improvements.

14. A functioning furnace in the basement of a home would be considered a
    A. trade fixture.
    B. fixture. ✓
    C. chattel.
    D. severance.

15. Courts apply four basic tests to determine whether an item is a fixture or personal property. These include all of the following EXCEPT
    A. the way in which the item is attached to the real estate.
    B. the intention of the person who attached the item.
    C. the way in which the item has been adapted to the real estate.
    D. the opinion of the person purchasing the real estate to which the item is attached. ✓

16. After a railroad sells air rights for construction of a building over its tracks, trains usually can
    A. operate normally. ✓
    B. no longer run under the building.
    C. operate only with permission of the building owners.
    D. operate unless they create a noise hazard.

17. A rancher owns land on which oil is discovered by a drilling company. Based on these facts alone, which of the following statements is TRUE?
    A. If the owner has not previously conveyed the mineral rights, he owns the oil. ✓
    B. The drilling company owns the oil by finder's right.
    C. Both the property owner and the oil company own rights to the oil jointly.
    D. The underground oil is a littoral asset and may be subject to government ownership.

18. A mobile home can be sold as real estate if it is
    A. appraised at $50,000 or more.
    B. located in rented space for more than two years.
    C. permanently attached to the land by a foundation. ✓
    D. more than 15 feet long.

19. The rights of the owner of property along the ocean are known as
    A. emblements.
    B. avulsions.
    C. littoral rights. ✓
    D. chattel rights.

20. Ownership rights to real estate do NOT include
    A. buildings located on the property.
    B. air space above the property.
    C. minerals found under the property.
    D. navigable rivers running through the property. ✓

UNIT 6

Estates and Interests

LEARNING OBJECTIVES

When you have completed this unit, you will be able to accomplish the following.

› Identify the characteristics of estates in land.
› Describe the characteristics of encumbrances, such as liens, easements, and encroachments.

KEY TERMS

construction lien	encumbrance	lis pendens
convey	estate in land	mortgage lien
curtesy	fee determinable	party wall
dominant estate	fee simple	priority
dower	freehold estate	remainderman
easement	general lien	reversionary interest
easement appurtenant	involuntary lien	servient estate
easement by necessity	leasehold estate	specific lien
easement by prescription	license	tacking
easement in gross	lien	voluntary lien
encroachment	life estate	

ESTATES IN LAND

Not all forms of ownership of real estate are equal. An owner may or may not be able to pass property on to heirs. Sometimes ownership may exist only as long as property is used for one specific purpose. In addition, other persons may possess certain *interests* (legal claims or rights) in one's real estate.

The amount and kind of ownership interest that a person has in real property is an **estate in land**. Estates in land are divided into two major classifications:

1. Freehold estates

2. Less-than-freehold, or leasehold, estates

Freehold estates are estates of indeterminable length: a person may own that estate for a lifetime or forever. Three freehold estates are recognized in New Jersey. They are

1. fee simple,

2. fee determinable, and

3. life estates.

The first two of these estates continue for an indefinite period and are inheritable by the heirs of the owner. The third estate ends on the death of the person on whose life it is based.

Leasehold estates involve tenants and are estates for a period of time. Leaseholds are considered to be personal property, not real property, and are discussed in greater detail in Unit 12.

Fee Simple Estate

An estate in **fee simple** is the highest type of interest in real estate recognized by law. A fee simple estate is one in which the holder is entitled to all rights in the property. There is no time limit on a fee simple estate: it is said to run forever. On the owner's death, the estate passes to his or her heirs. The terms *fee*, *fee simple*, and *fee simple absolute* are used interchangeably.

Fee Determinable

In New Jersey, a **fee determinable** (also known as a *conditional fee* or *defeasible fee*) is an estate in land that can terminate on the occurrence or nonoccurrence of a specified event. For example, Owner A **conveys** (transfers title to) 1,000 acres to the Open Space Foundation "so long as it is maintained as a wildlife preserve." Five years later the Foundation decides to build its corporate headquarters on this land. Title (ownership) to the land reverts to Owner A or Owner A's heirs. This future interest is called a *possibility of reverter*. If the original owner's conveyance stated that the land would go to Owner B or his heirs if the Jones Foundation violated the terms, then Owner B would become the **remainderman**, a third party named in the instrument.

Life Estate

A **life estate** is *limited to the life of a specific person*. The owner of a normal life estate does not have the right to pass ownership to heirs, because the life estate ends with the death of the owner. For example, Person A gives a life estate to Person B for as long as Person B lives. Upon Person B's death, the disposition of the property is governed by Person A's original conveyance. If Person A maintained a **reversionary interest**, the property will revert to Person A or his heirs (see Figure 6.1). If Person A specified that Person C would receive the property on Person B's death, then Person C would be the remainderman (see Figure 6.2).

Figure 6.1: Reversionary Interest

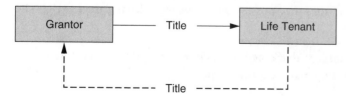

Figure 6.2: Remainder Interest

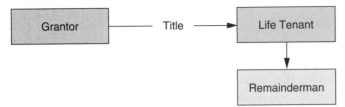

Life estates can also be tied to the life of a third party. Person A could have given the property to Person B's son for as long as his mother was alive. Then Person B's son would have a life estate *pur autre vie* (for another's life). When Person B dies, Person B's son's interest in the property ends.

The holder of a life estate has true ownership of real property. The life tenant cannot, however, *waste* the property; that is, the tenant cannot perform any acts that would permanently harm the land or property or destroy its value. A life tenant is entitled to all income and profits arising from the property and is responsible for paying taxes on it. A life interest may be sold, leased, mortgaged, or given away, but it always ends on the death of the person against whose life the estate is measured.

Dower and Curtesy

Dower is an ancient right under which a wife has certain interests upon her husband's death in any real estate he owned during their marriage. **Curtesy** is a similar right that a husband retains in his wife's estate. As of May 28, 1980, New Jersey abolished the creation of any new dower or curtesy rights and, instead, now gives both husband and wife the right of joint possession of the property that is their main marital residence. The real estate broker must learn which rules apply in any specific case in order to judge whether both spouses need to sign documents when only one owns the real estate. Where both the husband and the wife are listed as owners, both must, of course, sign any relevant documents. In many cases, a nonowning spouse must agree to release claims of dower, curtesy, or possession by signing a listing contract, sales contract, or deed:

■ For real estate owned during their marriage by one spouse *before* May 28, 1980, a surviving spouse has rights of dower or curtesy. Any document relating to the property should be signed *by both spouses*, no matter which one is the owner.

■ If the family home is being sold, *all documents must be signed by both spouses*, even if only one is listed as owner.

All real estate acquired after May 28, 1980, that is *not* the family home may be sold by the owner only, without the signature of a spouse. The seller should, however, consult an attorney before signing any documents without the spouse.

ENCUMBRANCES

An **encumbrance** is a claim, lien, charge, or liability attached to and binding on real property; it affects or limits its use, value, or title. Encumbrances may be divided into two general classifications:

1. *Liens*, which are financial claims against the property

2. *Physical* or *usage encumbrances*, which include restrictions, easements, licenses, and encroachments

All liens are encumbrances, but not all encumbrances are liens; there are several other types of encumbrances.

Liens

A **lien** is a financial claim against property that provides security for a debt or obligation of the property owner. If the obligation is not repaid, the lienholder, or creditor, has the right to have it paid out of the property, usually from the proceeds of a court sale. Real estate taxes have first claim against the proceeds of such a sale. Liens are classified as either *voluntary* or *involuntary*, and as *general* or *specific*.

A **voluntary lien** is created by the property owner, who, for example, gives a bank a claim against the real estate in return for a mortgage loan. An **involuntary lien** is a financial claim against the property that is imposed without the owner's consent. Property taxes, for example, are involuntary liens.

A **general lien** affects *all* the property someone owns; a **specific lien** is placed against one parcel of real estate only. If someone receives a court judgment for a large unpaid bill or unpaid child support, for example, this judgment can be placed as a lien against all the real estate owned by the debtor. A judgment lien, then, is general. A mortgage, on the other hand, is a claim only on the property pledged for the loan. A mortgage is a specific lien.

Property taxes are specific liens against individual parcels of real estate. Specific liens are illustrated in Figure 6.3.

Figure 6.3: Specific Liens

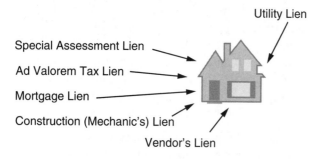

General liens include money judgments, federal estate and state inheritance taxes, debts of a person who has died, and Internal Revenue Service taxes. These can be placed against all the debtor's real and personal property, as illustrated in Figure 6.4.

Effects of Liens on Title

The owner is still free to sell to someone who is willing to take the encumbrances along with the property. Encumbrances (liens and other kinds) *run with the land* (go with the real estate) and are still binding after a sale, but liens (except property taxes and special assessments) do not survive foreclosure.

Liens attach to the property, not the property owner. Although in most cases the next owner is not personally responsible for the debt secured by a lien, he or she could lose the property if a creditor took court action to enforce payment of the financial claim.

Figure 6.4: General Liens

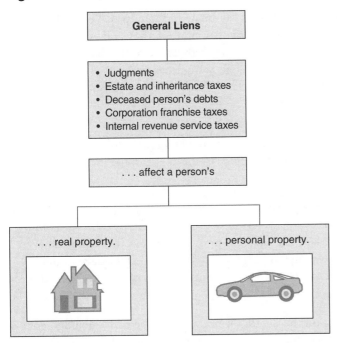

Priority of Liens

The **priority** of a lien determines the order in which debts will be paid off in case of a foreclosure. Real estate taxes and special assessments for improvements that enhance the value of the property generally take priority over all other liens. Other outstanding liens are paid in the order of their priority, which is normally determined by the date of recording in the public records of the county where the property is located (see Figure 6.5).

Figure 6.5: Priority of Liens

First Priority   Real Estate Taxes/Special Assessments

Next Priority
According to
Order of Filing
in Public Record

Property   1024 First St.
                  Anytown USA

10-14-93 First Mortgage lien...
USA---Federal Savings & Loan
2-17-94--Mechanic's lien filed
J.W. Adams Construction
3-1-95--Second Mortgage lien--
American Finance Co.

Mortgage Liens

A **mortgage lien** is a voluntary lien on real estate given to a lender by a borrower as security for a mortgage loan. It becomes a lien on real property when the mortgage funds are disbursed and the lender files or records the mortgage with the clerk or registrar of the county where the property is located. Mortgage lenders generally require a preferred lien, referred to as a first mortgage lien; this means that (aside from taxes) no other major liens against the property take priority over the mortgage lien. This requirement does not apply to second mortgages or home equity loans.

Construction Liens

Also known as mechanics' liens, **construction liens** can be placed against real estate by workers who have contributed labor or material to that specific property and who have not been paid. Construction liens are unique, in that they are retroactive to the date when the work in question originally began or when the materials were delivered.

Judgments

A judgment is a *decree issued by a court*. When the decree provides for the awarding of money and sets forth the amount of money owed by the debtor to the creditor, the judgment is referred to as a *money judgment*.

A judgment becomes a *general, involuntary lien on real property* owned by the debtor when it is docketed (filed) with the county clerk. A lien covers only property located within the county in which the judgment is issued. Transcripts of the lien must be filed in other counties when a creditor wishes to extend the lien coverage. A judgment differs from a mortgage in that a specific parcel of real estate was not given as security at the time that the debtor-creditor relationship was created.

A judgment takes its priority as a lien on the debtor's property from the date the judgment was docketed in the county clerk's office. Judgments are enforced through the sale of the debtor's real or personal property by the sheriff. When the property is sold and the sale yields enough to satisfy the debt, the debtor may demand a legal document known as a *satisfaction of judgment*, or *satisfaction piece*, which should be filed with the clerk of the court and the county clerk where the judgment was docketed so that the record will be cleared of the judgment.

A judgment can be enforced by issuance of a writ of execution and sale of the real estate by the sheriff in order to pay the judgment amount and related costs.

Other Liens

Federal *estate taxes* and state *inheritance taxes* (as well as the debts of deceased persons) are general, involuntary liens that encumber a deceased person's real and personal property.

An *Internal Revenue Service (IRS) tax lien* results from a person's failure to pay any portion of his or her federal IRS taxes, such as income and withholding taxes. A federal tax lien is a general, involuntary lien on all real and personal property held by the delinquent taxpayer.

Lis Pendens

A judgment or other decree affecting real estate is rendered at the conclusion of a lawsuit. Generally, considerable time elapses between the filing of a lawsuit and the rendering of a judgment. When any suit is filed that potentially affects title to a specified parcel of real estate (such as a foreclosure suit), a notice known as a **lis pendens** is recorded. A lis pendens is not a lien but rather a notice of possible future legal action against the property. Recording of the lis pendens gives notice to all interested parties, such as prospective purchasers and lenders, and establishes a priority for the later lien, which is dated back to the date the lis pendens was filed for record. The lis pendens creates a cloud on the title until the lawsuit is settled.

Unit 6

Easements

A right acquired by one party to use the land of another party for a particular purpose is an **easement**. A party may also have an easement right in the air above a parcel of real estate or land. The holder of an easement has only a right, not an estate or ownership interest, in the land over which the easement exists. An easement may be either *appurtenant* or *in gross*.

Easement Appurtenant

An easement that grants rights to the owner of an adjacent parcel of land is an **easement appurtenant**. For example, if A and B own adjacent properties in a resort community and only A's property borders the lake, A may grant B a right-of-way across A's property to the beach and B may grant A a right-of-way from the paved road to A's property (see Figure 6.6).

Figure 6.6: Easements

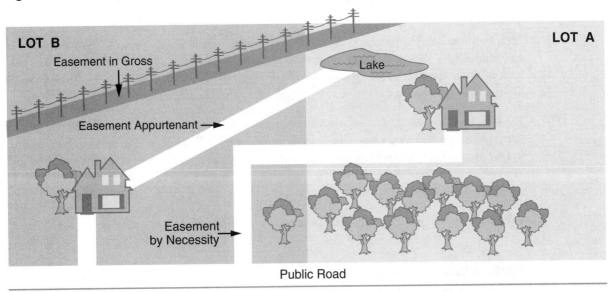

The owner of Lot B has an *easement appurtenant* across Lot A to gain access to the lake. Lot B is dominant and Lot A is servient. The utility company has an *easement in gross* across both parcels of land for its power lines.

For an easement appurtenant to exist, there must be two adjacent tracts of land owned by different parties. The tract over which the easement runs is known as the **servient estate**; the tract that is to benefit from the easement is known as the **dominant estate**.

Because an easement is said to run with the land, if A sells his or her lakefront property, the new owner acquires the same right to use B's land for access. If B sells, the new owner of the roadside parcel must honor the easement belonging to property A. In the same way, the easement from B's property to the lake belongs permanently to lot B, no matter who owns the two parcels. However, if one person acquired title to both parcels of land, the resulting *merger* would abolish the easements because there would no longer be a need for them.

Easement in Gross

A simple right to use the land of another is an **easement in gross**. In Figure 6.6, the power company owns an easement in gross on the boundary line of both lots. No adjoining lands are involved. If the need for the easement were to cease, the easement would cease to exist.

Easement by Necessity

In certain cases, if the only access to a parcel is through another's property, the owner may acquire an **easement by necessity** to reach his or her land. An easement by necessity can sometimes be acquired to gain access to real estate that would otherwise be landlocked. In Figure 6.6, A owns an easement by necessity, for the purpose of *ingress* and *egress* (entrance and exit).

Easement by Prescription

When someone has used another person's land for a certain period of time as defined by state law, an **easement by prescription** may be claimed. The claimant's use must have been continuous, hostile, adverse to owner's title, exclusive, and without the owner's approval. Additionally, the use must be visible, open, and notorious. New Jersey law is silent as to the required number of years, although court cases appear to support a minimum of 30 years of adverse use.

An owner can halt the process by specifically granting permission for use or by cutting off continuous use. That is, a homeowner might give a neighbor written permission to garden the back of the homeowner's lot. The owner of a shopping mall or plaza often closes the area one night a year, to avoid any claim that the public has gained an easement.

Through **tacking**, successive periods of continuous, uninterrupted occupation by different parties may be combined to reach the prescriptive period. To tack on one person's possession to that of another, the parties must have been *successors in interest,* such as an ancestor and his or her heir, a landlord and a tenant, or a seller and a buyer. Regardless, legal action must be taken to perfect the easement.

The user may also sue for actual title (ownership) as discussed in Unit 20.

Party Walls

A **party wall** is a wall of a building that straddles the boundary lines between two owners' lots. Each lot owner owns half of the wall (on his or her own side), and each has an easement right in the other half of the wall for support of the building. A written party wall agreement should be used to create these easement rights. Each owner must pay half of the expenses to maintain the wall.

Creating an Easement

Easements are commonly created by written agreement between the parties establishing the easement right. They also may be created

- by *express grant* from the owner of the property over which the easement will run;
- by the grantor in a *deed of conveyance,* either reserving an easement over the sold land or granting the new owner an easement over the grantor's remaining land;
- by *longtime usage,* as in an easement by prescription;
- by *necessity*; or
- by *implication,* that is, the situation of the parties' actions may imply that they intend to create an easement. Court action is necessary to perfect the easement created by implication.

Terminating an Easement

Easements may be terminated

■   when the purpose for which the easement was created no longer exists;

■   when the owner of either the dominant or the servient tenement becomes the owner of the other, provided there is an expressed intention of the parties to extinguish the easement (this is called a merger);

■   by release of the right of easement to the owner of the servient tenement; and

■   by abandonment of the easement (again, the intention of the parties is the determining factor).

Licenses

A permission to enter the land of another for a specific purpose is a **license**. It is not a permanent right and may be withdrawn. Examples of license include permission to park in a neighbor's driveway and permission to erect a billboard. Licenses may be written or oral.

Encroachments

When all or part of a building, fence, driveway, or any other installation illegally extends beyond the land of its owner and covers some land of an adjoining owner or a street or alley, an **encroachment** arises. Encroachments usually are disclosed by either a physical inspection of the property or a survey. A survey shows the location of all improvements on a property and whether any improvements extend over the lot lines. If a building encroaches on neighboring land, the neighbor may be able to recover damages or secure removal of the portion of the building that encroaches. Encroachments of long standing (for a 20-year period) may give rise to easements by prescription.

Deed Restrictions

Deed restrictions (discussed in Unit 9) are restrictive clauses added to a deed when property is conveyed that are established by the seller to restrict future owners' use of the property.

SUMMARY

An estate is the amount and kind of interest a person holds in land. *Freehold estates* are estates of indeterminate length. Less-than-freehold estates are those for which the length can be accurately determined. These are called *leasehold estates*, and they concern landlords and tenants.

Freehold estates are further divided into fee estates and life estates. Estates of inheritance include *fee simple* and *fee determinable estates*. Life estates can be granted for the life of the new owner or for the life of some third party (*pur autre vie*). At the end of the life estate, ownership can go back to the original owner (*reverter*) or pass to a designated third party (*remainder*).

The rights of *dower* and *curtesy* ceased to be created in New Jersey as of 1980. Currently, the only individually owned real estate that does not require a spouse's signature to release remaining rights is property acquired after May 28, 1980, that is not a family's main residence.

Encumbrances against real estate may be in the form of liens, deed restrictions, easements, licenses, and encroachments.

Liens are financial claims against a parcel of real property. They are either *general*, covering all real and personal property of a debtor-owner, or *specific*, covering only the specific parcel of real estate described in the mortgage, tax bill, building or repair contract, or other document.

With the exception of real estate tax liens and construction liens, the priority of liens is generally determined by the order in which they are placed in the public record of the county in which the debtors property is located.

Mortgage liens are voluntary, specific liens given to lenders to secure payment for mortgage loans. *Construction liens* protect general contractors, subcontractors, and materials suppliers whose work enhances the value of real estate.

A judgment is a court decree obtained by a creditor, usually for a monetary award from a debtor. *Lis pendens*, or notice of pendency, is a recorded notice that a lawsuit is awaiting trial in court and may result in a judgment that will affect title to a parcel of real estate.

Federal estate taxes and state inheritance taxes are general liens against a deceased owner's property.

Liens for water charges or other municipal utilities and surety bail bond liens are specific liens, and corporation franchise tax liens are general liens against a corporation's assets.

IRS tax liens are general liens against all property of a person who is delinquent in payment of income tax.

An *easement* is the permanent right acquired by one person to use another's real estate.

Easements appurtenant involve two separately owned tracts. An *easement in gross* is a right such as that granted to utility companies to maintain poles, wires, and pipelines. Easements run with the land and are binding on future owners of the property. An *easement by necessity* can sometimes be acquired to gain access to real estate that would otherwise be landlocked. An *easement by prescription*, a permanent right to use the land, is sometimes granted by the courts when land has been used by a nonowner for 20 years and certain other requirements have been met.

Easements may be created by agreement, express grant, grant, or reservation in a deed, implication, necessity, prescription, or party wall agreement. They can be terminated when the purpose of the easement no longer exists, by merger of both interests with an express intention to extinguish the easement, by release, or by an intention to abandon the easement.

A *license* is permission to enter another's property for a specific purpose. A license usually is created orally, is of a temporary nature, and can be revoked.

An *encroachment* is physical intrusion of some improvement upon another's land.

USEFUL WEBSITE

Real estate law: http://realestate.findlaw.com/

KEY TERMS REVIEW 1

Match the number of each key term with the corresponding letter.

_____ 1. Construction lien

_____ 2. Convey

_____ 3. Curtesy

_____ 4. Dominant estate

_____ 5. Dower

_____ 6. Easement

_____ 7. Easement appurtenant

_____ 8. Easement by necessity

_____ 9. Easement by prescription

_____ 10. Easement in gross

_____ 11. Encroachment

_____ 12. Encumbrance

_____ 13. Estate in land

_____ 14. Fee determinable

_____ 15. Fee simple

_____ 16. Freehold estate

A. right sometimes acquired through usage

B. any easement, encroachment, etc.

C. right of access to a landlocked parcel

D. amount of ownership

E. building intruding on another's land

F. property that benefits from an easement

G. most complete ownership of land possible

H. husband's rights in wife's property

I. ownership lasting indefinitely

J. placed against real estate by a worker who has not been paid

K. ownership "as long as"

L. permanent right to use another's land

M. right that runs with the land

N. transfer by sale or gift

O. right used for utility lines on another's land

P. wife's rights in husband's property

KEY TERMS REVIEW 2

Match the number of each key term with the corresponding letter.

_____ 1. General lien

_____ 2. Involuntary lien

_____ 3. Leasehold estate

_____ 4. License

_____ 5. Lien

_____ 6. Life estate

_____ 7. Lis pendens

_____ 8. Mortgage lien

_____ 9. Party wall

_____ 10. Priority

_____ 11. Remainderman

_____ 12. Reversionary interest

_____ 13. Servient estate

_____ 14. Specific lien

_____ 15. Tacking

_____ 16. Voluntary lien

A. adding successive periods of usage

B. the tract over which an easement runs

C. temporary permission

D. claim against one parcel of real estate

E. the order in which liens are paid

F. right to use and possess for limited time

G. complete ownership until someone's death

H. third party who will gain eventual ownership

I. financial claim against real estate

J. lender's claim against real estate

K. property taxes are one

L. mortgage or equity loan, for example

M. claim against all property someone owns

N. notice that a lien may be filed

O. structure owned by two adjoining landowners

P. future interest of an owner

UNIT 6 REVIEW QUESTIONS

1. The most complete ownership recognized by law is a(n)
   A. life estate.
   B. fee simple estate.
   C. leasehold estate.
   D. estate at will.

2. A man devises a parcel of land to the local university "so long as it is used for an experimental farm." Two years after the man's death, the university begins to build a cafeteria on the land. In this case, the man's heirs
   A. automatically become owners.
   B. are joint tenants with the university.
   C. own the land but the university owns the cafeteria.
   D. have no claim on the land.

3. Which one of the following BEST describes a life estate?
   A. An estate conveyed to A for the life of Z, and on Z's death to B
   B. An estate held by A and B in joint tenancy with right of survivorship
   C. An estate on condition
   D. An estate given by law to a husband

4. A woman inherited her cousin's house, but it is hers only as long as the dog is alive, well, and living in the house. When the dog dies, the house goes to her cousin's grandson. The cousin's grandson is a
   A. beneficiary.
   B. remainderman.
   C. life tenant.
   D. limited partner.

5. A woman owns a house and wants to sell it. Her husband must also sign the sales contract if
   A. he furnished any of the money when she bought it.
   B. he cosigned the mortgage.
   C. she bought the property after May 28, 1980.
   D. it is their family home.

6. Encumbrances include all of the following EXCEPT
   A. encroachments.
   B. liens.
   C. easements.
   D. estates.

7. Deed restrictions are created by a
   A. seller.
   B. buyer.
   C. neighborhood association.
   D. governmental agency.

8. In certain circumstances, the owner of landlocked property can go to court and request a permanent right to go over a neighbors land for access in the form of an
   A. easement in gross.
   B. estate for life.
   C. encroachment.
   D. easement by necessity.

9. The buyer of a house automatically receives the same right the seller had to use a party wall. The buyer owns an
   A. encumbrance.
   B. emblement.
   C. encroachment.
   D. easement.

10. The right to run a power line across the back of someone's property is an example of an easement
    A. in gross.
    B. by prescription.
    C. by necessity.
    D. in common.

11. The owner of a small country house gives a neighboring farmer permission to plant crops on the two acres around his house. The owner changes his mind and decides to put in a lawn. He may withdraw the permission because the farmer had only a(n)
    A. encroachment.
    B. easement by necessity.
    C. license.
    D. life estate.

12. A license is an example of a(n)
    A. easement.
    B. encroachment.
    C. encumbrance.
    D. restriction.

13. Two adjacent buildings share a central wall. This wall is known as a(n)
    A. encroachment.
    B. necessity wall.
    C. party wall.
    D. easement right.

14. Which of the following is considered a lien on real estate?
    A. An easement running with the land
    B. An unpaid mortgage loan
    C. A public footpath
    D. A license to erect a billboard

15. A lis pendens is
    A. a voluntary lien on real estate, given as security in an ongoing legal action.
    B. a decree issued by a court that becomes a lien against real property when docketed with the county clerk.
    C. a type of federal tax lien.
    D. a recorded notice of possible future legal action against a property.

16. Which of the following liens usually would be given highest priority?
    A. A mortgage dated last year
    B. The current real estate tax
    C. A construction lien for work started before the mortgage was made
    D. A judgment rendered yesterday

17. To acquire an easement by prescription in New Jersey, a person must use the land owned by another person
    A. openly and without the owner's permission.
    B. for a period of at least 15 years.
    C. by permission of a lease.
    D. for a right-of-way.

18. The neighbor mistakenly built a new garage two feet onto the neighboring lot. This mistake results in an
    A. implied deed of partial conveyance.
    B. incorporeal right.
    C. easement.
    D. encroachment.

19. A license differs from an easement in that it
    A. runs with the land.
    B. requires a court order.
    C. may be withdrawn.
    D. allows use of someone else's land.

20. After a buyer had purchased his house and moved in, he discovered that his neighbor regularly used the owner's driveway to reach a garage located on the neighbor's property. The owner's attorney explained that ownership of the neighbor's real estate includes an easement over the driveway and this property is called
    A. the dominant tenement.
    B. a tenement.
    C. a leasehold.
    D. the servient tenement.

UNIT
7

Ownership of Real Estate

LEARNING OBJECTIVES

When you have completed this unit, you will be able to accomplish the following.

> Describe different forms of ownership.
> Explain the differences between condominiums, cooperatives, and time-sharing.

KEY TERMS

board of directors
common elements
condominium
conversion
cooperative
corporation
devisee
general partnership
homeowners' association

Horizontal Properties Act
joint tenancy
limited liability company
  (LLC)
limited partnership
partition
partnership
proprietary lease
reserves

right of survivorship
sole proprietorship
tenancy by the entirety
tenancy in common
tenancy in severalty
time-sharing
title
town house

FORMS OF OWNERSHIP

Title to a parcel of real estate may be held by one person or there may be two or more *co-owners* of the property.

Tenancy in Severalty

If title is held by one person (or entity), that person is said to possess *sole ownership* or **tenancy in severalty**. (The term *severalty* means all interest is *severed* from others.) When that person dies, title to the property will pass to his or her heirs or **devisees** (persons named in a will).

Figure 7.1: Remembering Legal Terminology: "OR" vs. "EE"

Throughout this unit and the rest of the book, we will be referring to people as grantor and grantee, trustor and trustee, mortgagor and mortgagee, and so on. Because the terminology can be confusing, we've included this figure to help you remember who's who in a transaction. Refer back to this figure when the terms come up in other units, too.

Product	Person Giving the Product	Person Receiving the Product
Devise	Devisor	Devisee
Grant	Grantor	Grantee
Legacy	Legator	Legatee
Lease	Lessor	Lessee
Mortgage*	Mortgagor	Mortgagee
Offer	Offeror	Offeree
Option	Optionor	Optionee
Sublease	Sublessor	Sublessee
Trust	Trustor	Trustee

*Note that a mortgage is a written agreement that pledges real estate as security for the payment of a debt. The mortgagor is the borrower. This person (the mortgagor) gives the mortgagee (the lender) a mortgage or deed of trust (property interest) on the property used to secure the loan.

Tenancy in Common

When two or more people own property, they do so as tenants in common. In a **tenancy in common**, each owner has an undivided interest in the whole property. Although a tenant in common may hold, say, a one-half or one-third interest in a property, it is impossible to distinguish physically which specific half or third of the property is owned. Tenants in common do not necessarily have equal shares. For example, one could have a one-third interest and the other, a two-thirds interest.

In a tenancy in common, each owner can sell, convey, mortgage, or transfer that interest *without the consent* of the other co-owners. Upon the death of a tenant in common, that interest passes to his or her heirs or devisees (see Figure 7.2).

Figure 7.2: Tenancy in Common

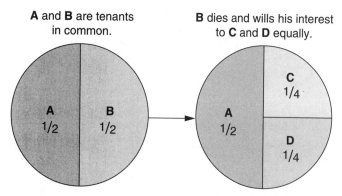

A and **B** are tenants in common.

B dies and wills his interest to **C** and **D** equally.

If a tenant in common wants to dissolve a co-ownership but the other parties do not voluntarily agree to its termination, he or she may file a suit in court to **partition** the property. If possible, the land itself may be divided into separate parcels (physical partition). If the court determines that the land cannot actually be divided into parts, it orders the real estate sold and the proceeds divided among the co-owners, according to their fractional interests (judicial partition).

In New Jersey a conveyance to two or more persons not married to each other creates a tenancy in common, unless otherwise stated in the deed. The tenants' shares would be equal unless otherwise described.

Joint Tenancy

Two or more people can also choose to own property as *joint tenants*. The main feature of **joint tenancy** is that it carries with it a **right of survivorship**. The death of one joint tenant of a property simply means there is one less person in the group; the remaining joint tenants receive the share owned by the deceased tenant (see Figure 7.3). This transfer occurs automatically.

Figure 7.3: Joint Tenancy With Right of Survivorship

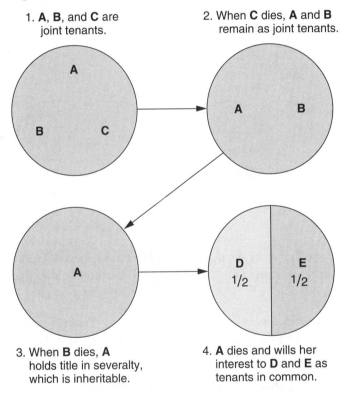

1. **A**, **B**, and **C** are joint tenants.

2. When **C** dies, **A** and **B** remain as joint tenants.

3. When **B** dies, **A** holds title in severalty, which is inheritable.

4. **A** dies and wills her interest to **D** and **E** as tenants in common.

In contrast to tenants in common, joint tenants cannot devise their interest in a property. As each successive joint tenant dies, the surviving joint tenants acquire the interest of the deceased joint tenant. Only the last survivor may dispose of the property by will, because that person now has an estate in severalty.

Creating Joint Tenancies

To create a joint tenancy in New Jersey, language in the deed must expressly state that title is to be taken in that form of ownership.

Four unities are required to create a joint tenancy:

1. Unity of *time*: all joint tenants must acquire their interests at the same time.

2. Unity of *title*: all joint tenants must acquire their interests by the same deed.

3. Unity of *interest*: all joint tenants hold equal ownership interests.

4. Unity of *possession*: all joint tenants hold undivided possession of the property.

These four unities are present when title is acquired by *one deed, signed and delivered at one time,* and conveying *equal interests* to all the owners who hold *undivided possession of the property as joint tenants.*

Terminating Joint Tenancies

A joint tenancy is destroyed when any one of the essential unities of joint tenancy is broken. Thus, while a joint tenant is free to convey his or her interest in the jointly held property, doing so will destroy the unity of interest and, in turn, the joint tenancy. For example, if Person A, Person B, and Person C hold title as joint tenants and Person A sells her interest to Person D, then Person D owns a one-third interest as a tenant in common with Person B and Person C, who continue to hold their one-third interests as joint tenants (see Figure 7.4).

Figure 7.4: Combination of Tenancies

A, B, and C are joint tenants.   A sells her interest to D.

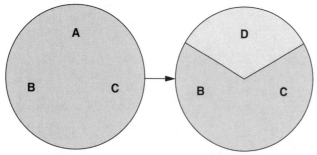

D becomes a tenant in common with **B** and **C** as joint tenants.

Because Person D is a tenant in common, her share would go to her heirs if she dies. Because Person B and Person C remain as joint tenants, should either die, the other would acquire that person's share.

If Person B dies, Person C would own two-thirds, as a tenant in common with Person D. He would no longer have a joint tenant as co-owner. Then, if Person C dies, his share would go to his heirs.

Joint tenancies also may be terminated by operation of law, as in bankruptcy or foreclosure-sale proceedings.

Like tenants in common, joint tenants may sue for partition if the other parties do not voluntarily agree to terminate the tenancy.

Tenancy by the Entirety

A **tenancy by the entirety** is a special tenancy between husband and wife. The distinguishing characteristics of this tenancy are

- the owners must be husband and wife when they receive the property;
- the owners have rights of survivorship; and
- there is no right to partition.

In New Jersey, a conveyance to a couple who are legally married to each other creates a tenancy by the entirety unless the deed expressly states otherwise. When a couple gets divorced, the tenancy by the entirety is broken and they become tenants in common. (New Jersey does not recognize common-law marriages.)

BUSINESS OWNERSHIP OF REAL ESTATE

Ownership of real estate by an organization is treated differently from ownership by people. Some such forms of ownership provide for the real estate to be owned by the entity itself; others provide for direct ownership of the real estate by its members. Business organizations may be categorized as

- partnerships, or
- corporations.

The purchase or sale of real estate by any business organization involves complex legal questions, and legal counsel usually is required.

All of the following types of business organizations are contrasted with **sole proprietorship**, a business owned by one individual.

Partnerships

An association of two or more people to carry on a business as co-owners and share in the business profits and losses is a **partnership**. Partnerships are classified as *general* and *limited*.

In a **general partnership** all partners participate to some extent in the operation and management of the business and may be held *personally* liable for business's losses and obligations, even *beyond the amount of their initial investment*.

A **limited partnership** includes a general partner as well as limited partners. The business is run by the general partner or partners. The limited partners do not participate in the operation of the business, and each can be held liable for the business's losses *only to the extent of his or her investment*. The limited partnership is a popular method of organizing investors in a real estate project.

Corporations

A **corporation** is an artificial person or legal entity created under the laws of the state from which it receives its charter. Because the corporation is a legal entity, real estate ownership by a corporation is in *severalty*, or as a *tenant in common* if it is partial ownership. Because of its possible perpetual existence, a corporation cannot hold real estate as a joint tenant.

As a legal entity, a corporation exists until it is formally dissolved. The death of one of the officers or directors does not affect title to property that is owned by the corporation.

A corporation is managed and operated by its **board of directors**. Individuals participate, or invest, in a corporation by purchasing stock. Because stock is personal property, shareholders do not have a direct ownership interest in real estate. Each shareholder's liability for the corporation's losses usually is limited to the amount of his or her investment.

Investors may opt for an alternative corporate ownership form called an *S corporation*. Like a corporation, this form is a legal entity, but its investors avoid double taxation. Only the shares of the profits passed to the shareholders are taxed, while the profits of the S corporation are not. However, S corporations are subject to strict requirements regulating their structure, membership, and operation.

Limited Liability Companies

A **limited liability company (LLC)** is a form of business organization in which LLC members have the tax advantages offered by partnerships, and at the same time the limited liability offered by the corporate form of ownership. The LLC also offers its members flexible management structure without the complicated restrictions common to S corporations and limited partnerships.

Other Forms of Ownership

A *syndicate* is a joining together of two or more people to carry out a particular business project. Syndicates are not legal entities. A *joint venture* is an organization of people or firms designed to carry out a single project. Joint ventures last for a limited period of time and do not establish a continuing relationship. A *real estate investment trust (REIT)* is a form of organization that is useful for taking advantage of certain tax benefits. REITs, syndicates, and joint ventures are discussed in detail later, in Unit 17, "Investment and Business Brokerage."

GROWTH OF CONDOMINIUMS AND COOPERATIVES

Condominium and **cooperative** ownership of housing has risen in the second half of the 20th century. Together with town houses and planned unit developments (PUDs), condos and co-ops offer the emotional, financial, and tax advantages of home ownership combined with various advantages of apartment living.

As opposed to traditional single-family homes, condos and co-ops offer more efficient use of ever-scarcer building land, lower costs for lot development, less outlay for construction per living unit, and some savings in maintenance and heating bills.

Contributing to the growth of condos and co-ops are changes in population patterns, with increasing numbers of single homeowners, one-parent families, and senior citizens. To such groups, community living offers security and sociability, ease of maintenance, and sometimes the opportunity for sharing expensive recreational facilities like swimming pools and exercise rooms.

The terms *condominium* and *cooperative* refer to forms of ownership; looking at a shared-housing complex gives no clue as to whether it is a condo, a co-op, or (in some cases) a PUD. The buildings themselves may be high-rises, town houses, patio homes, garden apartments, or even single detached houses. The differences arise from the legal forms of ownership.

Condominium ownership is not limited to residential dwellings. There has been a rise in recent years in commercial and office condominiums.

CONDOMINIUM OWNERSHIP

Buyers of a condominium receive a deed conveying fee simple ownership of two things: their living unit (from the paint on the interior walls inward) and a proportionate undivided interest in the common elements. Chief among the common elements are the land and the exteriors of the buildings. Common property can also include hallways, basements, elevators, stairwells, driveways, private roads, sidewalks, lawns, landscaping, and recreational facilities (see Figure 7.5).

Figure 7.5: **Condominium Ownership**

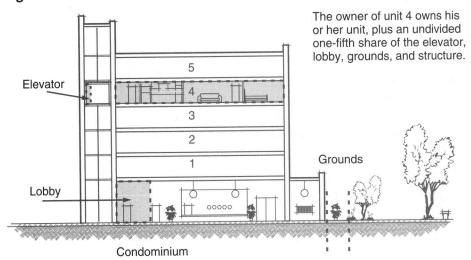

The owner of unit 4 owns his or her unit, plus an undivided one-fifth share of the elevator, lobby, grounds, and structure.

Elevator

Lobby

Grounds

Condominium

In many respects a condominium owner may be regarded in the same light as the owner of a single detached house. Title may be held in severalty, by the entirety, as joint tenants, or as tenants in common. The unit receives an individual tax bill and may be mortgaged as a house would be. The owners place a separate insurance policy on their living space. Income tax advantages are identical to those for single-family homes. The owners are free to sell the property, lease it, give it away, or leave it to heirs. Each unit is a financial entity, and if an adjoining unit is foreclosed, no obligation is incurred by the other owners.

Owners are, however, bound by the bylaws of a **homeowners' association**, to which all belong. As long as the rules are not unreasonable, New Jersey law permits associations to enforce their rules by fining residents who fail to comply. Monthly fees are levied for the maintenance, insurance, and management of **common elements**. If unpaid, these common charges become a lien against the individual unit and may even be enforced by foreclosure. The bylaws also set up covenants, conditions, and restrictions (CC&Rs), which, for example, may prohibit the display of For Sale signs or painting a front door bright red.

A condominium is usually managed by an elected board of managers. A board with more than 25 units often hires professional management.

Establishing a Condominium

In New Jersey, the creation of condominiums is regulated by the state's **Horizontal Properties Act** and the Condominium Act.

First, the owners of the property execute and record a master deed and file it in the public record of the county in which the property is located. Many items must be contained in or attached to the master deed, including a legal description of the land; a graphic description of the buildings and the other improvements, which identifies the individual units by letter, name, or number and specifies the percentage of the common elements (if any) included in the ownership of each unit; a description of the common elements; provision for an association of unit owners; and a list of the bylaws.

Condominium Conversion

The landlord who desires to convert a rental apartment building into a condominium must obtain approval of the planned conversion by the state of New Jersey at least three years and two months before **conversion** may start.

Certain tenants with disabilities and those aged 62 years or older may not be evicted during a condominium conversion. The tenants so protected must have occupied the premises for at least two years before the conversion and have incomes no higher than three times their county's per capita income (or, in any case, no higher than $50,000). If they meet the qualifications, they are allowed to continue as tenants for up to 40 years.

COOPERATIVE OWNERSHIP

Cooperative ownership, common in New York City, is also found in certain areas of New Jersey. Under the usual cooperative arrangement, title to the land and building is held by a corporation. Each purchaser of an apartment in the building receives stock in the corporation and a **proprietary lease**, which gives the purchaser the right to occupy his or her apartment.

The cooperative building's real estate taxes are assessed against the corporation as owner. There is usually one underlying mortgage on the entire parcel of real estate. Taxes, mortgage principal and interest, and operating and maintenance expenses of the property are shared by the tenant-shareholders in the form of monthly maintenance charges.

Thus, even though co-op owners do not actually own real estate (they own stock, which is personal property), for all practical purposes they control the property through their stock ownership and their voice in the management of the corporation. Co-op bylaws generally provide that each prospective owner must be approved by the board of directors.

One disadvantage of cooperative ownership is the possibility that if enough owner-occupants become financially unable to make prompt payment of their monthly assessments, the corporation might be forced to allow mortgage and tax payments to go unpaid. Through such defaults the entire property could be ordered sold by court order in a foreclosure suit. Such a sale might destroy the interests of all owners, even those who paid their assessments. Accumulation of a substantial fund of **reserves** for future repairs and emergency payments offers some protection to the cooperative as a whole.

As with a condominium, the owner of a cooperative has all the income tax advantages of the owner of a single-family home. That portion of maintenance charges attributable to property taxes and mortgage interest may be taken as income tax deductions. Interest paid to finance the stock purchase is also deductible.

Many co-ops do not permit rentals, because if the ratio of rentals is too high, a prospective buyer might have difficulty obtaining adequate financing. However, a New Jersey law provides that owners of co-ops in buildings with ten or more units may rent their units if they have been trying to sell for four or more months at a price no greater than their investment. That is, under certain circumstances a co-op unit owner may rent his or her unit if unable to sell it.

Cooperative living tends to develop somewhat differently from condominium occupancy. Long-term stability of tenants is common. The corporation's right to accept or reject any new owner is aimed at safeguarding present owners, who would share financial responsibility for a defaulting neighbor, but it is often used to maintain a particular level of occupancy.

TOWN HOUSES

The term **town house** is used to describe an architectural style in which buildings share a party wall. Town house developments can be condominiums, or all elements can be owned in fee simple, including the land beneath the building. In some cases, the town house owner owns a share in common elements.

TIME-SHARING

The buyer of a time-share receives a fraction of a year's ownership or use of a property, which might be a hotel, town house, single-family detached home, campground, or even a motel. In some cases only right-to-use is purchased; in others the owner has a true fee simple interest in the real estate.

Although the concept is most popular in resort areas such as the Caribbean, Colorado, Vermont, and Florida, it has been used in Long Island, the Poconos, and other nearby resort areas. An owner can exchange, sell, or rent the time slot, subject only to any restrictions in the prospectus of the organization administering the property. It is not unusual for an interval to be for a specified week of each year.

The New Jersey Timeshare laws apply to all timeshares sold in New Jersey, as well as those located outside New Jersey but sold in the state. The act requires that certain disclosures be made when certain types of out-of-state properties, such as subdivided land sales, condominiums, and common interest ownership properties, are offered in New Jersey. A timeshare buyer has the right to cancel a timeshare contract up to seven days after signing the contract or after receiving the receipt of the public offering statement, whichever is later. The buyer may cancel by certified mail, or in person, whereupon the seller must refund all payments within 30 days.

The developer or timeshare salesperson is required to provide honest, not false, information; to not make any predictions of increases in value; or misrepresent how the buyer may use or exchange the times share. The New Jersey Real Estate Timeshare Act does not apply to ten or fewer timeshare interests, investments of less than $3,000, to resales. The Bureau of Subdivided Land Sales Control (BSLSC) is a part of the New Jersey Real Estate Commission that enforces the registration and anti fraud provisions of the New Jersey Real Estate Sales Full Disclosure Act.

SUMMARY

Sole ownership or ownership in *severalty* indicates that *title* is held by one person or entity.

There are three ways in which *title* to real estate can be held at the same time by more than one person, with each having an undivided interest. Under *tenancy in common*, an individual owner may sell his or her interest and has the right to leave the share to any designated heirs. When two or more persons not married to each other hold title to real estate, they own it as tenants in common, unless their deed specifically states some other intention. *Joint tenancy* involves two or more owners with the *right of survivorship*. Upon the death of one owner, that person's share passes to the remaining co-owner or co-owners. The intention of the parties to establish joint tenancy with right of survivorship must be clearly stated in their deed, and four unities must exist. Both tenants in common and joint tenants have the right to force a sale by *partition*.

Tenancy by the entirety is a special joint tenancy for property acquired jointly by husband and wife. Unless their deed specifically states that they wish to own the property as tenants in common, they will own it by the entirety. Both must sign a deed for complete title to pass to a purchaser, and neither can force a sale by partition. Divorce changes their ownership to tenancy in common.

Various types of business organizations may own real estate. A *corporation* is a legal entity and holds title to real estate in severalty. A *partnership* may own real estate in its own name.

Condominium and *cooperative* arrangements for home owning are becoming more frequent because of scarcity of land, the need for economical construction and operation, and changing lifestyles.

Both terms refer to forms of ownership and not to the type of buildings involved.

Condominiums provide fee simple ownership of the living unit and an undivided interest in *common elements*. The owner may mortgage the unit, receives individual tax bills, and arranges homeowner's insurance. Owners bear no direct financial liability for adjoining units.

Management of common elements is administered by a *homeowners' association*, which levies monthly fees. Bylaws provide reasonable regulations binding on all owners in the form of covenants, conditions, and restrictions.

The owner of a cooperative apartment receives shares in a corporation that owns the entire building and a *proprietary lease* to his or her apartment. Each owner shares responsibility for the debts of the corporation. The *board of directors* has the right to reject prospective buyers for financial and other reasons that are not discriminatory, and to prohibit rentals except under certain circumstances.

The term *town house* refers to an architectural style. There are some town house developments with fee simple ownership of the living unit and the land beneath it but with common elements that are owned by a homeowners' association in which owners are members.

Time-sharing involves the purchase of a resort or vacation property for a portion of the year.

USEFUL WEBSITES

New Jersey Condominium Act: www.lawrev.state.nj.us/ucioa/dtrpt4a.pdf

Community Associations Institute: www.caionline.org

KEY TERMS REVIEW 1

Match the number of each key term with the corresponding letter.

_____ 1. Corporation

_____ 2. Devisee

_____ 3. General partnership

_____ 4. Joint tenancy

_____ 5. Limited partnership

_____ 6. Partition

_____ 7. Partnership

_____ 8. Right of survivorship

_____ 9. Sole proprietorship

_____ 10. Tenancy by the entirety

_____ 11. Tenancy in common

_____ 12. Tenancy in severalty

_____ 13. Title

A. default form of ownership for those who are unmarried and not in a civil union

B. legal entity considered to be an artificial person

C. business owned by one person or entity

D. court-ordered sale and division

E. process by which co-owner automatically receives share of co-owner who dies

F. group with each partner completely liable

G. co-owners joined together to carry on a business

H. nonmarried persons with right of survivorship

I. person named in a will to inherit real estate

J. group with only general partner fully liable

K. ownership

L. real estate ownership by only one

M. special ownership by married couple

KEY TERMS REVIEW 2

Match the number of each key term with the corresponding letter.

_____ 1. Board of directors

_____ 2. Common elements

_____ 3. Condominium

_____ 4. Conversion

_____ 5. Cooperative

_____ 6. Homeowners' association

_____ 7. Horizontal Properties Act

_____ 8. Proprietary lease

_____ 9. Reserves

_____ 10. Time-sharing

_____ 11. Town house

A. all owners in one condominium complex

B. regulates the creation of condominiums

C. apartment house changed to condos

D. architectural term

E. apartment whose buyer receives a proprietary lease/stock in corporation

F. co-op owner's right to apartment

G. group elected to manage a cooperative

H. fee simple ownership of living unit

I. money set aside for future repairs

J. ownership for part of a year

K. stairwells, roofs, etc., owned by all

UNIT 7 REVIEW QUESTIONS

1. When buying a property, one party paid one-third of the cost and the other paid the balance. The seller's deed received at the closing conveyed the property to the two parties without further explanation. As a result, the two owners are
   A. joint tenants.
   B. tenants in common, each owning a one-half undivided interest.
   C. tenants in common, with each owning an undivided one-third interest.
   D. general partners in a joint venture.

2. If property is held by two or more owners as tenants in common, upon the death of one owner the ownership of his or her share passes to the
   A. remaining owner or owners.
   B. heirs or whoever is designated under the deceased owner's will.
   C. surviving owner and/or his or her heirs.
   D. deceased owner's surviving spouse.

3. In New Jersey, a deed conveying property to a married couple creates a
   A. joint tenancy.
   B. tenancy by the entirety.
   C. tenancy in common.
   D. periodic tenancy.

4. Which of the following statements applies equally to joint tenants and tenants by the entirety?
   A. There is no right to file a partition suit.
   B. The survivor becomes complete owner.
   C. Sale of one share creates a tenancy in common.
   D. A deed must state the type of tenancy desired.

5. Two cousins inherited their grandfather's farm. The cousin who lives on the farm does not pay rent and refuses to pay the taxes. The nonoccupant cousin can
   A. establish a joint tenancy.
   B. sue for partition.
   C. inherit automatically when one cousin dies.
   D. exercise her right of reverter.

6. Owners A and B own an apartment building as joint tenants. If Owner A sells his interest to Person C,
   A. Person C becomes a joint tenant with Owner B.
   B. Person C becomes a joint tenant with Owner A.
   C. Person C and Owner B become tenants in common.
   D. the sale is invalid, and Owner B becomes sole owner.

7. Shortly after their marriage, a couple buys a home together. If the deed states nothing to the contrary, they are
   A. tenants by the entirety.
   B. joint tenants.
   C. tenants in common.
   D. tenants in severalty.

8. Two people buy a small shopping plaza together. If the deed states nothing to the contrary, they are
   A. tenants by the entirety.
   B. joint tenants.
   C. tenants in common.
   D. cooperative owners.

9. X, Y, and Z are joint-tenant owners of a hunting lodge. Z dies, leaving everything to his wife. Which statement is TRUE?
   A. X and Y are now joint tenants with Mrs. Z.
   B. X and Y are joint tenants, with Mrs. Z as tenant in common.
   C. X and Y are now the only owners of the property.
   D. X, Y, and Mrs. Z are now tenants in common.

10. Two friends want to buy a house together and ensure that if one dies the other inherits automatically. They should take title as
    A. tenants by the entirety.
    B. joint tenants.
    C. tenants in common.
    D. life tenants.

11. Two friends buy a store together as joint tenants. One party dies, leaving everything she owns to her daughter. The original owner now owns the store
    A. jointly with her friend's daughter.
    B. as a tenant in common.
    C. as a life tenant.
    D. in severalty.

12. An artificial person created by legal means is known as a
    A. trust.
    B. corporation.
    C. limited partnership.
    D. joint tenancy.

13. The four unities required to create a joint tenancy in New Jersey include all of the following EXCEPT
    A. time.
    B. title.
    C. partnership.
    D. interest.

14. X, Y, and Z each invest $1,000 in a new business. X and Y do not participate in the operation of the new venture, but agree to let Z make all the decisions regarding its day-to-day management. If the business experiences a $6,000 loss, how is liability shared under these facts?
    A. As partners, X, Y, and Z are equally liable for the loss: $2,000 each.
    B. This is a limited partnership, in which the partners cannot be held liable for more than the $3,000 original total investment.
    C. As general partner, Z is liable for any loss; X and Y have no liability.
    D. As limited partners, X and Y are liable only to the extent of their investment.

15. Common elements include
    A. stairwells.
    B. the swimming pool.
    C. foyers.
    D. all of these.

16. The term *CC&R* refers to
    A. clubhouse, courts, and recreation.
    B. covenants, conditions, and restrictions.
    C. condominiums, cooperatives, and resort time-shares.
    D. contracts, citations, and releases.

17. The owner of a cooperative apartment receives
    A. a deed.
    B. a property tax bill.
    C. a life estate.
    D. shares in a corporation.

18. The right to reject prospective new owners is held by the board of directors of a
    A. town house.
    B. time-share.
    C. cooperative.
    D. condominium.

19. A man owns a fee simple interest in his apartment, together with a specified undivided percentage of common elements. The man's building is organized as a
    A. condominium.
    B. real estate investment trust.
    C. cooperative.
    D. syndicated venture.

20. The buyer of an apartment received shares in a corporation and a proprietary lease to her apartment. Her building is organized as a
    A. cooperative.
    B. condominium.
    C. joint venture.
    D. syndicate.

21. A board of directors commonly reserves the right to approve or disapprove of potential buyers in which form of joint ownership?
    A. Cooperative
    B. Condominium
    C. Joint venture
    D. Tenancy in common

22. Stock in a cooperative apartment is usually considered
    A. real property.
    B. personal property.
    C. proprietary property.
    D. a common element.

23. The term reserves refers to
    A. tenants willing to invest in a conversion.
    B. weeks of the year owned by a time-share purchaser.
    C. percentage of ownership for each condominium deed.
    D. funds set aside for major repairs in the future.

24. Long-term stability of residence is most characteristic of
    A. a cooperative.
    B. time-sharing.
    C. a condominium.
    D. an apartment.

25. A couple has the right to live in unit 6B only between March 3 and March 15 of every year. For the rest of the year, others have the exclusive right to live in the unit. The type of ownership arrangement described by these facts is most likely
    A. a cooperative apartment building.
    B. a time-share.
    C. illegal under New Jersey law.
    D. a rental apartment.

UNIT
8

Real Estate Taxes

LEARNING OBJECTIVES

When you have completed this unit, you will be able to accomplish the following.

> Describe the differences between a general real estate tax and special assessment taxes.
> Explain the taxation process.

KEY TERMS

ad valorem tax	mill	tax foreclosure
assessed value	ratable	tax lien
assessment roll	redemption period	tax sale
equalization factor	revaluation	
full-value assessment	special assessment	

TAX LIENS

The ownership of real estate is subject to certain government powers. One of these powers is the right of state and local governments to impose (levy) **tax liens** to pay for governmental functions. Because the location of real estate is permanently fixed, the government can levy taxes with a rather high degree of certainty that the taxes will be collected. Because the annual taxes levied on real estate usually have priority over other previously recorded liens, they may be enforced by the court-ordered sale of the real estate.

Real estate taxes can be divided into two types:

1. General real estate tax or ad valorem tax

2. Special assessment or improvement tax

Both taxes are levied against specific parcels of property and automatically become liens on those properties.

Ad Valorem Tax (General Tax)

The general real estate tax is made up of the taxes levied on real estate by various governmental agencies and municipalities. These taxing bodies include

- states;

- counties;

- cities, towns, townships, boroughs, and villages;

- school districts (local public elementary and high schools, publicly funded junior colleges, and community colleges);

- park districts, forest preserves, and recreation districts; and

- water, sanitary, and drainage districts.

Ad valorem is Latin for "according to value." **Ad valorem taxes** are based on the value of the property being taxed. General real estate taxes are levied to fund the operation of the governmental agencies that impose the taxes.

Exemptions from General Taxes

In New Jersey, homeowners aged at least 65 or disabled (who meet certain income and residency requirements) may take annual deductions of up to $250 from property taxes. An annual deduction of up to $250 from taxes due on real or personal property is available to qualified war veterans and their unmarried surviving spouses. Totally disabled war veterans or unmarried surviving spouses of such veterans may be granted a full property tax exemption on their dwelling house and the lot on which it is situated. A "Senior Freeze" program allows homeowners aged 65 or older who meet rather generous income limits to apply for reimbursement of any increase in property taxes.

Residents who own and pay property taxes on a principal residence in New Jersey may qualify for rebates. A rebate is also available to homeowners and tenants who pay property taxes (for tenants, 18% of rent) and whose gross income does not exceed a certain amount. Some property tax reimbursement is also available for owners of mobile homes located in mobile home parks.

Details on these programs, and information on how to apply, are available at https://www .state.nj.us/treasury/taxation/pdf/lpt/ptbenefitsbrochure.pdf.

Farmland Reassessment Act

To encourage the preservation of open spaces, the state allows a different assessment rate for farmlands. The preferential treatment is available only for genuine agricultural property, which must meet the following requirements:

- It must be at least five acres in size, exclusive of homesite.

- It must earn at least $500 per year in gross sales for the first five acres. In addition, gross sales must average $5 per acre on qualified agricultural land and $500 per acre on woodland and wetland for the first five acres.

- It must have been actively used as farmland for two years immediately prior to the year for which preferential tax treatment is requested.

Most properties used for religious, charitable, and other not-for-profit purposes are totally *exempt* from property taxes. To qualify for exemption, the homeowner must file an application with the local tax assessor by December 1 each year, stating that the property was a principal residence as of the previous October 1.

The real estate broker must be alert for the possibility of such exemptions, so that when property is offered to the public, potential buyers will know the *true tax* figure, the amount a new owner will have to pay, rather than the sometimes reduced amount paid by the present owner.

Special Assessments (Improvement Taxes)

Special assessments are special taxes that require property owners to pay for improvements that benefit the real estate they own. These taxes are often levied to pay for streets, alleys, street lighting, curbs, and similar items and are enforced in the same manner as general real estate taxes. The proper authority spreads the assessment over the various parcels of real estate that will benefit. The assessment usually varies from parcel to parcel, as all will not benefit equally from the improvement.

In practice, licensees should be very careful when selling property that includes a special assessment. Many times, the improvement has been financed over a number of years, and the new property owner may incur financial liability for continuing the payments.

THE TAXATION PROCESS

In each community a certified tax assessor lists the values of all property as of October 1 for the tax year that begins the next January 1. This **assessed value** is what the year's taxes are based on. New Jersey has set a goal of **full-value assessment** (almost impossible to attain), that is, of assessing real estate at 100% of true market value. Periodically municipalities must have a **revaluation**: An outside appraisal firm is hired to assess every **ratable** (taxable property) in the municipality, to bring everyone's assessment up to current market value. The New Jersey Division of Taxation Property Administration has published an excellent brochure "How Property is Valued for Property Tax Purposes." (Revised on 4/2016.) Another outstanding brochure is "Understanding Revaluations" available at https://www.state.nj.us /treasury/taxation/pdf/lpt/revaluationbrochure.pdf.

Appealing the Assessed Value

Taxpayers who believe an assessment is unfair start with an informal appeal to the tax assessor. The time frame for an appeal varies by county. The Division of Taxation Property Administration has produced an excellent brochure that answers many questions about assessments, revaluation and compliance plans, added and omitted assessments, and the appeal process. The brochure is available at https://www.state.nj.us/treasury/taxation/pdf/lpt /ptassessment.pdf.

To be successful, an appeal should be based on solid data. If it can be shown that several similar neighboring properties have recently sold for less than the assessment of the parcel in question, the appeal is most likely to result in an adjustment. The assessed value that results from this process remains in effect for three years. Further appeals can, however, be made all the way to the New Jersey Supreme Court.

Equalization

Because not every district assesses exactly at market value, the State Division of Taxation publishes tables of Equalization Rates to achieve uniformity among tax districts. An equalization factor may be used to raise or lower assessments in a particular district or county.

The equalization issue is important to local governments, because state funding of programs (such as aid to education) is based on the assessed value of local real estate. The assessed value of each property in the area is multiplied by the **equalization factor**, and the tax rate is then applied to the equalized assessment.

These rates allow adjustments to distribute property tax revenue equitably among individual school districts. For example, the assessments in one county are 20% lower than average assessments throughout the rest of the state. This under-assessment can be corrected by applying an equalization factor of 125% to each assessment in that county. A parcel of land assessed for tax purposes at $98,000 has an equalized value of $122,500 ($98,000 × 1.25 = $122,500). $122,500 is 20% greater than $98,000 ($122,500 × 20% = $24,500; $98,000 + $24,500 = $122,500).

Tax Rates

The process of arriving at a real estate tax rate begins with the adoption of a budget by each county, city, school board, or other taxing district. Each budget covers the financial requirements of the taxing body for the coming fiscal year, which may be the January-to-December calendar year or some other 12-month period. The budget must include an estimate of all expenditures for the year and indicate the amount of income expected from all fees, revenue-sharing, and other sources. The net amount remaining to be raised from real estate taxes is then determined from these figures.

The next step is *appropriation*, the action taken by each taxing body that authorizes the expenditure of funds and provides for the sources of such monies. Appropriation involves the adoption of an ordinance or the passage of a law setting forth the specifics of the proposed taxation.

The amount to be raised from the general real estate tax is then imposed on property owners through a *tax levy*, the formal action taken to impose the tax, by a vote of the taxing districts governing body.

The *tax rate* for each individual taxing body is computed separately. To arrive at a tax rate, the total monies needed for the coming fiscal year are divided by the total assessments of all real estate located within the jurisdiction of the taxing body (called the **assessment roll**, also known as ratables). For example, a taxing district's budget indicates that $300,000 must be raised from real estate tax revenues, and the assessment roll of all taxable real estate within this district equals $10 million. The tax rate is computed thus:

$300,000 ÷ $10,000,000 = 0.03, or 3%

The tax rate may be stated in a number of different ways. In many areas it is expressed in mills.

A **mill** is one one-thousandth of a dollar, or $0.001. The tax rate may be expressed as a mill ratio, in dollars per hundred or dollars per thousand. The tax rate computed in the foregoing example could be expressed as:

30 mills (per $1 of assessed value)

or

$3 per $100 of assessed value

or

$30 per $1,000 of assessed value

In New Jersey, however, the tax rate can only be expressed as dollars per hundred of assessed value.

Tax Bills

A property owner's tax bill is computed by applying the tax rate to the assessed valuation of the property. For example, on property assessed for tax purposes at $90,000, at a tax rate of 3%, or 30 mills, the tax will be $2,700 ($90,000 × 0.030 = $2,700). If an equalization factor is used, the computation on a property with an assessed value of $120,000 and a tax rate of 4% with an equalization factor of 120% would be as follows:

$120,000 × 1.20 = $144,000

$144,000 × 0.040 = $5,760 tax

Tax Liens

Taxes on real property become a lien on January 1. Taxes are due starting on February 1, and additional payments may be made quarterly on the first of May, August, and November.

Tax Sale

When taxes are unpaid six months after the end of the tax year, the taxing body can resort to **tax foreclosure**. The local tax collector is required to hold a **tax sale** of the property. Advance notices of the sale must be posted in five places in the municipality and advertised in a local newspaper for four weeks. Owners of the property should receive notice of the forthcoming sale by mail; if they do not, the sale is still valid.

Right of Redemption

The purchaser at a tax sale receives a *tax sale certificate*, but is not entitled to occupy or use the property and does not receive title. If a municipality purchases the certificate, the delinquent homeowner has six months in which to pay the money due and redeem the property. If the certificate is bought by a private party, the **redemption period** is two years. The homeowner trying to regain the property must pay reasonable legal costs and interest on the overdue taxes. After the redemption period has passed without the owners redeeming the property, the holder of the certificate may obtain clear title by the legal process of foreclosure any time within 20 years.

If the municipality forecloses on a tax sale certificate, it is through judicial foreclosure, before a court. The action is called *in rem* proceedings (against the property), and this type of proceeding is available only to municipalities; it does not affect the tax debtor's credit rating.

INCOME TAX ISSUES FOR HOMESELLERS

Although sellers should be referred to their accountants or attorneys for specific information, many ask the real estate broker about the regulations on profit from the sale of real estate. Both the federal government and New Jersey provide an exclusion from capital gains tax of up to $500,000 profit on the sale of a principal residence by married taxpayers who file jointly. Single filers are entitled to a $250,000 exclusion.

This exclusion may be reused as often as every two years if the homesellers have owned and occupied the property as a principal residence for at least two of the five years before the sale. In the case of the couple, only one need to have owned the residence, but both must have occupied it for at least two years. When the home is sold after less than the required two years, a portion of the exclusion may be used if the sale is mandated by an unexpected event. In that category the IRS includes a job transfer, health reasons, death, divorce, or multiple births.

First-time homebuyers may make penalty-free withdrawals from their individual retirement fund (IRA). The limit on such withdrawals for a first time down payment is $10,000.

SUMMARY

Real estate taxes are levied by local authorities. *Tax liens* are generally given priority over other liens. Payments are required before stated dates, after which penalties accrue. An owner may lose title to his or her property for nonpayment of taxes because such tax-delinquent property can be sold at a *tax sale*. New Jersey allows a time period during which a defaulted owner can redeem his or her real estate from a tax sale.

Special assessments are levied to spread the cost of improvements such as new sidewalks, curbs, or paving to the real estate that benefits from them.

The valuation process begins with assessment of the taxable value of each parcel. New Jersey mandates *full-value assessment* with variations from one jurisdiction to another adjusted through the use of equalization rates. The money budgeted to be raised through taxation is then divided by the total *assessment roll* to arrive at the tax rate. The tax bill for each parcel is determined by multiplying the tax rate by assessed valuation. Periodically municipalities must have a *revaluation* to bring every *ratable* up to current market value.

Unpaid taxes become a lien against property, usually taking precedence over other liens, and may be enforced through *tax foreclosure* or sale.

Married homesellers may take up to $500,000 capital gain ($250,000 for single sellers) on the sale of a principal residence free of any federal tax. The home must have been owned and occupied as a main residence for at least two of the five years before the sale. The exclusion may be used as often as every two years.

USEFUL WEBSITES

U.S. Internal Revenue Service: www.irs.gov

New Jersey Property Tax Programs: https://www.state.nj.us/treasury/taxation/lpt/lpt-appeal.shtml

KEY TERMS REVIEW

Match the number of each key term with the corresponding letter.

_____ 1. Ad valorem tax

_____ 2. Assessed value

_____ 3. Assessment roll

_____ 4. Equalization factor

_____ 5. Full-value assessment

_____ 6. Mill

_____ 7. Ratable

_____ 8. Redemption period

_____ 9. Revaluation

_____ 10. Special assessment

_____ 11. Tax foreclosure

_____ 12. Tax lien

_____ 13. Tax sale

A. adjusts for assessment variations

B. list of all taxable property

C. estimate based on probable sales price

D. tax set according to value

E. value used for tax purposes

F. collection of overdue taxes through public auction of property

G. one-thousandth of a dollar

H. seizing of property for unpaid taxes

I. reassessment of all a municipality's ratables

J. municipality's financial claim against real property

K. a taxable property

L. tax only on property directly benefiting from an improvement

M. time in which a foreclosed owner can regain property

UNIT 8 REVIEW QUESTIONS

1. New Jersey offers partial property tax exemptions to
   A. churches.
   B. homeowners 65 and older.
   C. licensed physicians.
   D. owners of unused farmland.

2. In New Jersey, the tax rate is expressed as
   A. millage.
   B. dollars per hundred of assessed value.
   C. dollars per thousand of assessed value.
   D. tax levies.

3. Property taxes become a lien on the land
   A. as soon as the assessment roll is confirmed.
   B. at change of title.
   C. only if payment is more than 30 days late.
   D. every January 1.

4. Real estate is evaluated for property tax purposes by a(n)
   A. appraiser.
   B. building inspector.
   C. assessor.
   D. zoning board.

5. A house valued at $120,000 is assessed for 80% of its value. The tax rate is $26.34 per $1,000. How much is the property tax bill?
   A. $252.86
   B. $2,528.64
   C. $316.08
   D. $3,160.80

6. A tax on the houses in one small neighborhood, to pay for new street lamps in that area, would take the form of
   A. an ad valorem tax.
   B. eminent domain.
   C. a special assessment.
   D. a conditional-use tax.

7. Some exemptions from real estate taxes may be granted to certain
   A. veterans.
   B. senior citizens.
   C. religious organizations.
   D. Any of these.

8. Which of these types of property is eligible for a different assessment rate?
   A. Park districts
   B. Forest preserves
   C. Certain agricultural properties
   D. Churches

9. An example of a special assessment is a tax to
   A. build a bypass around the city.
   B. pay for street lighting.
   C. construct a new school.
   D. expand a community college.

10. During the statutory period of redemption, New Jersey property sold for delinquent taxes may
    A. be redeemed by payment of back taxes, penalties, and interest.
    B. be redeemed by payment of four times the delinquent taxes.
    C. be redeemed only through a court proceeding.
    D. not be redeemed.

11. The chance to take at least $250,000 profit free of federal tax on the sale of one's home is available to any seller who
    A. is over the age of 55 on the date of the sale.
    B. buys a replacement home of equal or greater value within two years of the sale.
    C. owned and occupied the home for two of the five years prior to the sale.
    D. is married on the date of the sale.

12. A single person who bought her home 18 months ago is moving to take a new job in another city. A married couple who file jointly have owned their nine-bedroom home for only three years, and now they want to move to a small condominium unit. Another single person owned his home for 17 years wants to use the proceeds from his sale to purchase a larger house. Which of these people is entitled to the $250,000 exclusion from the federal capital gains tax?
    A. The single person who bought her home 18 months ago
    B. The single person who owned his home for 17 years
    C. The married couple who have owned their home for three years
    D. Both of the single persons

13. For purposes of determining capital gains tax liability, all of the following factors are relevant considerations EXCEPT
    A. the marital or filing status of the taxpayer.
    B. the profit realized on the sale of the home.
    C. how long the taxpayer has lived in the home.
    D. whether or not the taxpayer is over 55 years old.

14. What is the federal capital gains tax exclusion available to home sellers who file their income taxes singly?
    A. $125,000
    B. $225,000
    C. $250,000
    D. $500,000

15. Which of the following taxpayers is permitted to make a penalty-free withdrawal from their IRA to assist with their purchase?
    A. A married couple selling their large home to buy a small condominium
    B. A single person buying her first home
    C. A single person selling a small condominium to buy a larger home
    D. Any single person

UNIT 9

Land-Use Regulations and Environmental Issues

LEARNING OBJECTIVES

When you have completed this unit, you will be able to accomplish the following.

> Distinguish between private land-use controls and government powers relating to public land-use controls.
> Describe environmental issues and hazardous substances, especially those subject to federal legislation and landmark preservation.

KEY TERMS

asbestos
building codes
building permit
carbon monoxide
CERCLA
certificate of compliance
certificate of occupancy
  (CO)
condemnation

deed restriction
Department of
  Environmental
  Protection (DEP)
eminent domain
escheat
exclusionary zoning
inverse condemnation
lead-based paint

master plan
nonconforming use
police power
radon
urea-formaldehyde
variance
zoning ordinances

LAND-USE CONTROLS

The ownership rights a person possesses in a parcel of real estate are subject to public and private land-use controls such as zoning ordinances, building codes, and deed restrictions. This unit discusses private land-use controls, government powers, and environmental issues.

PRIVATE LAND-USE CONTROLS

Deed Restrictions

It is important to note that **deed restrictions** are placed on property by *private parties*, not by governments. An owner might stipulate that only one house may be built on the large next-door lot she is selling. A grandfather could give a house to a grandson with the provision that no intoxicating liquors ever be used on the property. The restriction is set up in the deed that transfers the property by use of a statement known as a *restrictive covenant*. Unless otherwise stated, it is binding on all future owners.

More commonly, deed restrictions are placed on an entire subdivision by the original developer to protect certain features that add value to the subdivision, like size of lots, exterior design, or minimum square footage of houses. The developer's restrictions may be recorded once with the original map of the subdivision and simply referred to, without being restated, in the individual deeds when each lot is sold.

In the past, deed restrictions might have forbidden any future sale of the property to a member of a particular religious or ethnic group. Such restrictions are now in violation of laws and are not enforceable. Restrictions that prohibit the next owners from selling the property are also not enforceable.

Some restrictions have a time limitation—for example, "effective for a period of 25 years from this date." Frequently, the effective term of the restrictions may be extended with the consent of a majority (or sometimes two-thirds) of the owners in a subdivision.

When a deed restriction and a zoning provision cover the same subject, the more *limiting* restriction will prevail. If deed restrictions say lots in a subdivision must measure at least two acres but the town allows half-acre lots, the two-acre restriction is enforceable.

Enforcement

Neighbors or the original subdivider may enforce deed restrictions through court action.

GOVERNMENT POWERS

Although an individual in the United States has maximum rights in the land he or she owns, these ownership rights are subject to certain powers, or rights, held by federal, state, and local governments. Because they are for the general welfare of the community, these limitations on the ownership of real estate supersede the rights of the individual. Government rights include the following:

■ **Police power** is the power vested in a state to establish legislation to preserve order, protect the public health and safety, and promote the general welfare. A state's police power is passed on to municipalities and counties. The use and enjoyment of property is subject to restrictions, including environmental protection laws and zoning and building ordinances regulating the use, occupancy, size, location, construction, and rental of real estate.

■ **Eminent domain** enables a government to exercise its right to acquire privately owned real estate for public use through the process of **condemnation**. The taking must be *for the public good*, and the owner must receive *just compensation*. If, after negotiation, the owner does not agree to the taking, or a fair price cannot be agreed upon, then a *condemnation suit* can be instituted. If, after a condemnation hearing, agreement is still not reached, the case can go to Superior Court, for trial either by a jury or before a judge in open court.

The right of eminent domain is granted by state laws not only to public agencies and governmental bodies but also to railroads, public utility companies, and quasi-public bodies such as land-clearance commissions and public housing or redevelopment authorities.

Another type of *taking* occurs when the government changes the rules that severely limits how the property may be used. The property owner may bring an *inverse condemnation* suit when governmental action takes away all or substantially all reasonable uses of the property and it appears that the government does not intend to bring eminent domain proceedings or offer compensation.

■ Taxation is a charge to raise funds to meet the public needs of a government.

■ State laws provide for ownership of real estate to **escheat** (revert) to the state when an owner dies leaving no will disposing of his or her estate and no heirs can be located.

The four government powers are easy to remember using the acronym PETE (**P**olice powers, **E**minent domain, **T**axation, **E**scheat).

PUBLIC LAND-USE CONTROLS

Our large urban population and the increasing demands placed on our limited natural resources have made it necessary for municipalities to increase their limitations on the private use of real estate. We now have controls over noise, air, and water pollution, and population density. Regulations on privately owned real estate include

■ planning;

■ zoning;

■ subdivision regulations;

■ codes that regulate building construction, safety, and public health; and

■ environmental protection legislation.

Planning

The primary method by which local governments recognize development goals is through the formulation of a comprehensive **master plan**, also sometimes referred to as a *general plan*. Municipalities and counties develop master plans to ensure that social and economic needs are balanced against environmental and aesthetic concerns.

Both economic and physical surveys are essential in preparing a master plan. Countywide plans must also include the coordination of numerous civic plans and developments to ensure orderly city growth with stabilized property values. City plans are put into effect by enactment and enforcement of zoning ordinances.

Zoning

Zoning ordinances are laws of local government authorities (such as municipalities and counties) that regulate and control the use of land and structures within designated districts (zones). Zoning regulates and affects such things as use of the land, lot sizes, types of structures permitted, building heights, setbacks (the minimum distance away from streets or sidewalks that structures may be built), and density (the ratio of land area to structure area or population).

Often the purpose of zoning is to implement a local master plan. New Jersey has given zoning powers to municipal governments.

Zoning ordinances generally divide land use into five classifications:

1. Residential
2. Commercial
3. Industrial
4. Institutional
5. Recreational

Many communities now include *cluster zoning* and *multiple-use zoning*, which permit planned unit developments. A *buffer zone* is sometimes established to serve as a separation between two different areas. An expanse of *greenbelt*, for example, might be left wild to serve as a boundary between a residential development and an industrial area.

To ensure adequate control, land-use areas are further divided into subclasses. For example, residential areas may be subdivided to provide for detached single-family dwellings, semi-detached structures containing not more than four dwelling units, walk-up apartments, highrise apartments, and so forth. Variations exist between municipalities, and some may have as many as 15 classifications.

Zoning laws are enforced through local requirements that building permits be obtained before property owners build on their land. A permit is not issued unless a proposed structure conforms to the permitted zoning, among other requirements.

Exclusionary zoning, sometimes used in the past to keep low-income and moderate-income families out of suburban communities, has been outlawed by the New Jersey Supreme Court. The Mt. Laurel decisions, discussed in Unit 4, mandate master plans and zoning that provide for a mix of housing types within the community.

Nonconforming Use

A frequent occurrence is a building that does not conform to the zoning use because it was erected before the enactment of the zoning law. Such a **nonconforming use** is allowed to continue (grandfathered). If the use is abandoned or the building is destroyed or torn down, any new structure must comply with the current zoning ordinance. Local laws may say that the right to a nonconforming use is lost if such use is discontinued for a certain period, usually one year. In general, though, courts have held that simple nonuse does not constitute abandonment.

Zoning Boards

A zoning appeals board has been established in most communities to hear complaints about the effects of zoning ordinances on specific parcels of property. Petitions may be presented to the board of adjustment for exceptions to the zoning law. Determinations can be challenged in state courts.

Zoning Variations

Each time a plan is created or a zoning ordinance enacted, some owners are inconvenienced and want to change the use of a property. Generally, such owners may appeal for a **variance** from existing regulations to allow a use that does not meet zoning requirements. A variance may be sought by a property owner who has suffered *hardship* as a result of a zoning ordinance. For example, if an owner's lot is level next to a road but slopes steeply 30 feet back from the road, the zoning board may be willing to allow a variance so the owner can build closer to the road than normally would be allowed.

Subdivision Regulations

Most communities have adopted *subdivision regulations*, often as a part of a master plan. Subdivision regulations usually provide for the following:

- Location, grading, alignment, surfacing, and widths of streets, highways, and other rights-of-way
- Installation of sewers and water mains
- Minimum dimensions of lots
- Building and setback lines
- Areas to be reserved or dedicated for public use, such as parks or schools
- Easements for public utilities

Subdivision regulations, like all other forms of zoning or building regulations, must be flexible to meet the ever-changing needs of society.

Building Codes

Municipalities have enacted ordinances to specify construction standards that must be met when repairing or erecting buildings. These are called **building codes** and they set the requirements for kinds of materials, sanitary equipment, electrical wiring, fire prevention standards, and the like.

Most communities require the issuance of a **building permit** by the building department or other authority before a person can build a structure or alter or repair an existing building on property within the municipality. Through the permit requirement, officials can verify compliance with building codes and zoning ordinances by examining the plans and inspecting the work. After the new structure has been inspected and found satisfactory, the inspector issues a **certificate of occupancy** (CO or C of O) or, for an altered building, a **certificate of compliance**. In some municipalities, a certificate of continuing occupancy may also be required for transfers of existing buildings.

ENVIRONMENTAL ISSUES

Most states, like New Jersey, have recognized the need to balance the legitimate commercial use of land with the need to preserve vital resources and protect the quality of the state's air, water, and soil. Many homebuyers base their decisions in part on the desire for fresh air, clean water, and outdoor recreational opportunities. Preservation of a state's environment both enhances the quality of life and helps strengthen property values. The prevention and cleanup of pollutants and toxic wastes not only revitalizes the land, but creates greater opportunities for responsible development.

Environmental issues have become an important factor in the practice of real estate. Consumers are becoming more health conscious and safety concerned and are enforcing their rights to make informed decisions. Scientists are learning more about our environment, and consumers are reacting by demanding that their surroundings be free of chemical hazards.

These developments affect not only sales transactions, but also appraisers, developers, lending institutions, and property managers.

The Environmental Protection Agency publishes a brochure called "Healthy Home Action." In plain language, the brochure covers mold, radon, carbon monoxide, allergies, second-hand smoke, and volatile organic compounds (VOCs). The brochure can be accessed at https://www.epa.gov/sites/production/files/2014-05/documents/healthy_homes_brochure _english.pdf; and accessed in Spanish at https://19january2017snapshot.epa.gov/sites /production/files/2014-05/documents/healthy_homes_brochure_spanish.pdf.

HAZARDOUS SUBSTANCES

Pollution and hazardous substances in the environment are of interest to real estate licensees because they affect the attractiveness, desirability, and market value of cities, neighborhoods, and backyards. A toxic environment is not a place where anyone would want to live (see Figure 9.1).

Figure 9.1: Environmental Hazards

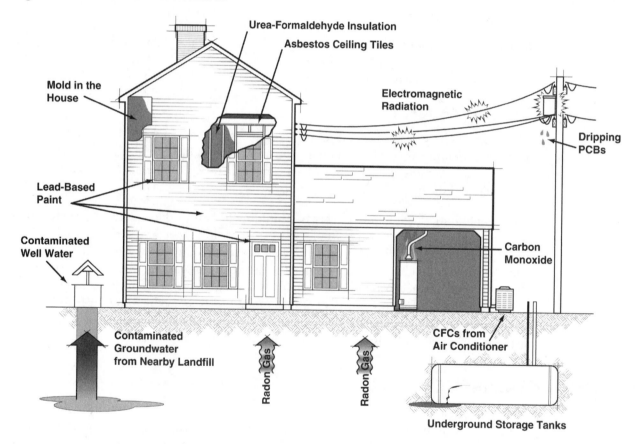

Asbestos

Asbestos is a mineral once used as insulation because it was resistant to fire and contained heat effectively. Before 1978 (the year when the use of asbestos insulation was banned), asbestos was found in most residential construction. It was a component of more than 3,000 types of building materials.

The Environmental Protection Agency (EPA) estimates that about 20% of the nation's commercial and public buildings contain asbestos. So long as the asbestos is contained, it poses little risk. However, when disturbed, as often occurs during renovation or remodeling, older asbestos fibers break down into tiny filaments and particles, a condition known as friable. When these particles become airborne, they pose a risk to humans. If the asbestos fibers in the indoor air of a building reach a dangerous level, the building becomes difficult to lease, finance, or insure.

The fire-resistant properties of asbestos made it a popular material for use in floor tile, exterior siding, and roofing products. It was used as insulation to cover pipes, ducts, and heating and hot water units in residential and commercial properties. Though it may be easy to identify asbestos when it is visible (for instance, when it is wrapped around heating and water pipes), identification may be more difficult when it is behind walls or under floors.

No safe level of asbestos exposure has been determined. Asbestos is costly to remove because the process requires state-licensed technicians and specially sealed environments. In addition, removal itself may be dangerous: improper removal procedures may further contaminate the air within the structure. The waste generated should be disposed of at a licensed facility, which further adds to the cost of removal. *Encapsulation*, or the sealing off of disintegrating asbestos, is an alternate method of asbestos control that may be preferable to removal in certain circumstances.

Tests can be conducted to determine the level of airborne asbestos to provide an accurate disclosure in a sales transaction. A more thorough analysis of a building can be performed by an engineer skilled in identifying the presence of materials that contain asbestos. Either of these approaches can satisfy the concerns of a consumer. Appraisers also should be aware of the possible presence of asbestos.

Lead-Based Paint and Other Lead Hazards

An elevated level of lead in the body can cause serious damage to the brain, kidneys, nervous system, and red blood cells on anyone, but it is especially in children under the age of six, who are still developing. The degree of harm is related to the amount of exposure and the age at which a person is exposed.

Lead was used as a pigment and drying agent in alkyd oil-based paint. Lead-based paint may be on any interior or exterior surface, but it is particularly common on doors, windows, and other woodwork in much of the housing constructed before 1978. Lead-based paint is not a problem so long as it is not disturbed.

When disturbed, such as during renovation, lead dust can become airborne but it quickly settles. It may be ingested from the hands by a crawling infant, inhaled by any occupant of a structure, or ingested from the water supply because of lead pipes or lead solder. Soil and groundwater may be contaminated by everything from lead plumbing in leaking landfills to discarded skeet and bullets from an old shooting range. High levels of lead have been found in the soil near waste-to-energy incinerators. The air may be contaminated by leaded gasoline fumes from gas stations or automobile exhausts.

The use of lead-based paint was banned in 1978. No federal law requires that homeowners test for the presence of lead-based paint. However, under the Lead-Based Paint Hazard Reduction Act, persons selling or leasing residential housing constructed before 1978 must disclose the presence of known lead-based paint and provide purchasers or lessees with any relevant records or reports. A lead hazard pamphlet (Figure 9.2) must be distributed to all buyers and tenants, and a lead-based paint disclosure statement (see Figure 9.3) must be attached to all sales contracts and leases regarding residential properties built before 1978. Note that the New

Jersey Seller's Property Condition Disclosure Statement in Figure 10.2 does not include the federally mandated Lead-Based Paint Disclosure.

Purchasers must be given 10 days in which to conduct risk assessments or inspections for lead-based paint or lead-based paint hazards. Purchasers are not bound by any real estate contract until the 10 days have expired. However, buyers can shorten the period or even give up their lead-inspection rights entirely. The regulations specifically require real estate agents to ensure that all parties comply with the law.

Figure 9.2: Lead Hazard Pamphlet

Radon

Radon is a radioactive gas produced by the natural decay of other radioactive substances. Although radon can occur anywhere, some areas are known to have abnormally high amounts. The state of New Jersey has mapped areas of high and low probabilities (see Figure 9.4). If radon dissipates into the atmosphere, it is not likely to cause harm. However, when radon enters buildings and is trapped in high concentrations (usually in basements with inadequate ventilation), it can cause health problems.

Remediation is indicated if radon levels measure 4 picocuries (pci) or more. Recent evidence suggests that radon may be the most underestimated cause of lung cancer, particularly for children, individuals who smoke, and those who spend considerable time indoors.

Because radon is odorless, colorless, and tasteless, it is impossible to detect without testing. Care should be exercised in the manner in which tests are conducted to ensure that the results are accurate.

Radon levels vary, depending on the amount of fresh air that circulates through a house, the weather conditions, and the time of year. It is relatively easy to reduce levels of radon by installing ventilation systems or exhaust fans.

According to New Jersey State law, a seller must reveal to a prospective buyer the results of all radon testing and any mitigation work when the contract of sale is entered into. The New Jersey Real Estate Commission advises seller's agents that they have a duty to keep confidential any information about radon test results or mitigation work until the contract of sale is entered into, unless the seller has authorized the agent in writing to discuss the matter with buyers.

Urea-Formaldehyde

Urea-formaldehyde was first used in building materials, particularly insulation, in the 1970s. Gases may leak out of the urea-formaldehyde foam insulation (UFFI) as it hardens and become trapped in the interior of a building. In 1982, the Consumer Product Safety Commission banned the use of UFFI. The ban was reduced to a warning after courts determined that there was insufficient evidence to support a ban. Urea-formaldehyde is known to cause cancer in animals, though the evidence of its effect on humans is inconclusive.

Mold

Concern has been growing about the presence of mold in buildings. Some types of mold are considered toxic; many are not.

Mold requires three elements in order to begin growing and multiply: (1) a food source of organic matter commonly used in building materials such as wood, wallpaper, or cloth; (2) moderate temperature conditions; and (3) most important, a source of moisture. Any intrusions of water in a house should be promptly addressed so that mold spores do not take hold.

NJAR's Sellers Property Condition Disclosure Statement has been amended to include under Environmental Issues a question regarding mold and its remediation. The EPA's Brief Guide to Mold, Moisture and Your Home" is available through https://www.epa.gov/. When listing a house, licensees should note signs of moisture or standing water and ask homeowners if they know of any mold in the home. If water conditions are present, buyers should be advised to have an inspection to determine if mold exists.

Carbon Monoxide

Carbon monoxide (CO) is a colorless, odorless gas that occurs as a by-product of burning such fuels as wood, oil, and natural gas due to incomplete combustion. Furnaces, water heaters, space heaters, fireplaces, and wood stoves all produce CO as a natural result of their combustion of fuel. However, when these appliances function properly and are property ventilated, their CO emissions are not a problem. Also, annual maintenance of heating systems helps avoid CO exposure. When improper ventilation or equipment malfunctions permit large quantities of CO to be released into a residence or commercial structure, it poses a significant health hazard. Its effects are compounded by the fact that CO is so difficult to detect. CO is quickly absorbed by the body. It inhibits the blood's ability to transport oxygen and results in dizziness and nausea. As the concentrations of CO increase, the symptoms become more severe. More than 200 deaths from carbon monoxide poisoning occur each year.

New Jersey requires carbon monoxide detectors in every dwelling unit, where the building contains three or more units.

Unit 9

Figure 9.3: Lead Disclosure

Disclosure of Information on Lead-Based Paint and/or Lead-Based Paint Hazards

Lead Warning Statement

Every purchaser of any interest in residential real property on which a residential dwelling was built prior to 1978 is notified that such property may present exposure to lead from lead-based paint that may place young children at risk of developing lead poisoning. Lead poisoning in young children may produce permanent neurological damage, including learning disabilities, reduced intelligence quotient, behavioral problems, and impaired memory. Lead poisoning also poses a particular risk to pregnant women. The seller of any interest in residential real property is required to provide the buyer with any information on lead-based paint hazards from risk assessments or inspections in the seller's possession and notify the buyer of any known lead-based paint hazards. A risk assessment or inspection for possible lead-based paint hazards is recommended prior to purchase.

Seller's Disclosure

(a) Presence of lead-based paint and/or lead-based paint hazards (check (i) or (ii) below):

   (i) _____ Known lead-based paint and/or lead-based paint hazards are present in the housing (explain).

   _____

   (ii) _____ Seller has no knowledge of lead-based paint and/or lead-based paint hazards in the housing.

(b) Records and reports available to the seller (check (i) or (ii) below):

   (i) _____ Seller has provided the purchaser with all available records and reports pertaining to lead-based paint and/or lead-based paint hazards in the housing (list documents below).

   _____

   (ii) _____ Seller has no reports or records pertaining to lead-based paint and/or lead-based paint hazards in the housing.

Purchaser's Acknowledgment (initial)

(c) _____ Purchaser has received copies of all information listed above.

(d) _____ Purchaser has received the pamphlet *Protect Your Family from Lead in Your Home.*

(e) Purchaser has (check (i) or (ii) below):

   (i) _____ received a 10-day opportunity (or mutually agreed upon period) to conduct a risk assessment or inspection for the presence of lead-based paint and/or lead-based paint hazards; or

   (ii) _____ waived the opportunity to conduct a risk assessment or inspection for the presence of lead-based paint and/or lead-based paint hazards.

Agent's Acknowledgment (initial)

(f) _____ Agent has informed the seller of the seller's obligations under 42 U.S.C. 4852d and is aware of his/her responsibility to ensure compliance.

Certification of Accuracy

The following parties have reviewed the information above and certify, to the best of their knowledge, that the information they have provided is true and accurate.

Seller	Date	Seller	Date
Purchaser	Date	Purchaser	Date
Agent	Date	Agent	Date

Figure 9.4: New Jersey Radon Map

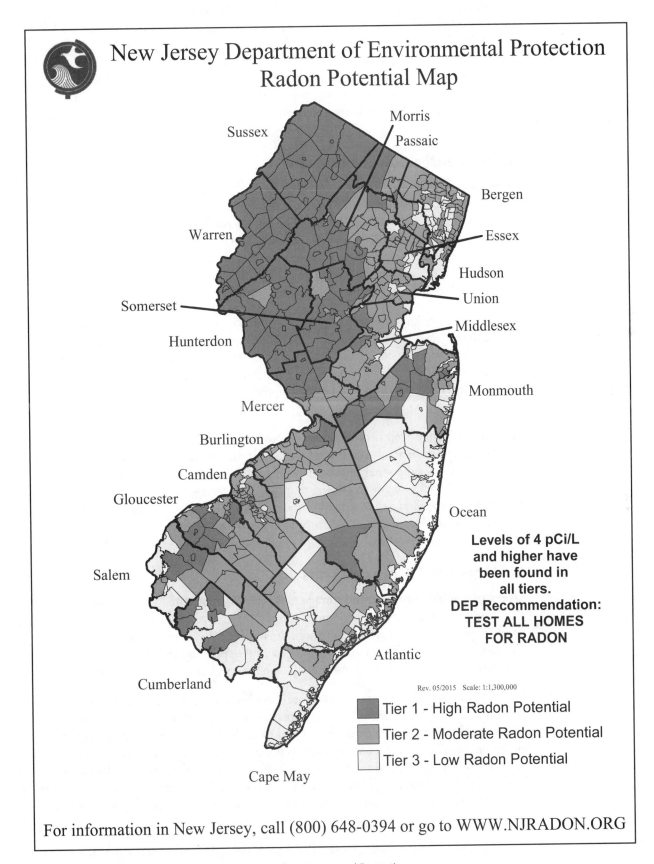

New Jersey Department of Environmental Protection
Radon Potential Map

Sussex

Morris

Passaic

Bergen

Warren

Essex

Hudson

Union

Somerset

Middlesex

Hunterdon

Monmouth

Mercer

Burlington

Camden

Gloucester

Ocean

**Levels of 4 pCi/L
and higher have
been found in
all tiers.
DEP Recommendation:
TEST ALL HOMES
FOR RADON**

Salem

Atlantic

Cumberland

Rev. 05/2015   Scale: 1:1,300,000

Tier 1 - High Radon Potential

Tier 2 - Moderate Radon Potential

Tier 3 - Low Radon Potential

Cape May

For information in New Jersey, call (800) 648-0394 or go to WWW.NJRADON.ORG

Reprinted with permission from New Jersey Department of Environmental Protection.

Unit 9

Electromagnetic Fields

Electromagnetic fields (EMFs) are generated by the movement of electrical currents. The use of any electrical appliance creates a small field of electromagnetic radiation: clock radios, blow-dryers, televisions, and computers all produce EMFs. The major concern regarding electromagnetic fields involves high-tension power lines. There is considerable controversy about whether EMFs actually pose a health hazard. Buyers may be worried about purchasing property near power lines or transformers. As research into EMFs continues, real estate licensees should stay informed about current findings.

Groundwater Contamination

Groundwater is the water that exists under the earth's surface within the tiny spaces or crevices in geological formations. Groundwater forms the water table, the natural level at which the ground is saturated. This may be near the surface (in areas where the water table is very high) or several hundred feet underground. Surface water can also be absorbed into the groundwater. Any contamination of the underground water can threaten the supply of pure, clean water for private wells or public water systems. Numerous state and federal laws have been enacted to preserve and protect the water supply.

Water can be contaminated from a number of sources. Run-off from waste disposal sites, leaking underground storage tanks, and pesticides and herbicides are some of the main culprits. Because water flows from one place to another, contamination can spread far from its source. Once contamination has been identified, its source can be eliminated. The water may eventually become clean. However, the process can be time-consuming and extremely expensive.

New Jersey's Private Well Testing Act applies to every contract of sale where the source of potable water is from an on-site private well, or under certain conditions, an off-site well. It mandates testing of the water in accordance with the Act. Closing may not take place unless both buyer and seller certify in writing that they have received and reviewed a copy of the test results. The law applies also to rented properties. For more information review the following resource at https://www.state.nj.us/dep/watersupply/pw_pwta.html.

Underground Storage Tanks

Over half a million underground storage tanks (USTs) exist in the United States. Underground storage tanks are commonly found on sites where petroleum products are used or where gas stations and auto repair shops are located. They also may be found in other commercial and industrial establishments—including printing and chemical plants, wood treatment plants, paper mills, paint manufacturers, dry cleaners, and food processing plants.

Military bases and airports are also common sites for underground tanks. In residential areas, they are used to store heating oil. Some tanks are currently in use, but many are long forgotten. Over time, however, neglected tanks may leak hazardous substances into the environment. This permits contaminants to pollute not only the soil around the tank, but also adjacent parcels and groundwater. Licensees should be particularly alert to the presence of fill pipes, vent lines, stained soil, and fumes or odors, any of which may indicate the presence of a UST. Detection, removal, and cleanup of surrounding contaminated soil can be an expensive operation.

Recent state and federal laws impose strict requirements on landowners where underground storage tanks are located, to detect and correct leaks in an effort to protect the groundwater.

The federal UST program is regulated by the EPA. The regulations apply to tanks that contain hazardous substances or liquid petroleum products and that store at least 10% of their volume underground. UST owners are required to register their tanks and adhere to strict technical and administrative requirements that govern

- installation,
- maintenance,
- corrosion prevention,
- overspill prevention,
- monitoring, and
- recordkeeping.

Owners are also required to demonstrate that they have sufficient financial resources to cover any damage that might result from leaks.

COMPREHENSIVE ENVIRONMENTAL RESPONSE, COMPENSATION, AND LIABILITY ACT (CERCLA)

Although the EPA was created at the federal level to oversee environmental problems, several other federal agencies areas of concern generally overlap. The federal laws were created to encourage state and local governments to enact their own legislation. The Comprehensive Environmental Response, Compensation, and Liability Act (**CERCLA**) established a fund of $9 billion, called the Superfund, to clean up uncontrolled hazardous waste sites and to respond to spills. It created a process for identifying potential responsible parties (PRPs) and ordering them to take responsibility for the cleanup action. CERCLA is administered and enforced by the EPA.

Liability

A landowner is liable under CERCLA when a release or a threat of release of a hazardous substance has occurred on his or her property. Regardless of whether the contamination is the result of the landowner's actions or those of others, the owner can be held responsible for the cleanup. This liability includes the cleanup not only of the landowner's property, but also of any neighboring property that has been contaminated. A landowner who is not responsible for the contamination can seek recovery reimbursement for the cleanup cost from previous landowners, any other responsible party, or the Superfund. However, if other parties are not available, even a landowner who did not cause the problem could be solely responsible for the costs.

Once the EPA determines that hazardous material has been released into the environment, it is authorized to begin remedial action. First, it attempts to identify the PRPs. If the PRPs agree to cooperate in the cleanup, they must agree about how to divide the cost. If the PRPs do not voluntarily undertake the cleanup, the EPA may hire its own contractors to do the necessary work.

The EPA then bills the PRPs for the cost. If the PRPs refuse to pay, the EPA can seek damages in court for up to three times the actual cost of the cleanup.

Liability under the Superfund is considered to be strict, joint and several, and retroactive. *Strict liability* means that the owner is responsible to the injured party without excuse. *Joint and several liability* means that each of the individual owners is personally responsible for the total damages. If only one of the owners is financially able to handle the total damages, that owner must pay the total and collect the proportionate shares from the other owners whenever possible. *Retroactive liability* means that the liability is not limited to the current owner, but includes people who have owned the site in the past.

Superfund Amendments and Reauthorization Act

In 1986, the U.S. Congress reauthorized the Superfund. The amended statute contains stronger cleanup standards for contaminated sites and five times the funding of the original Superfund.

The amended act also sought to clarify the obligations of lenders. As mentioned, liability under the Superfund extends to both the present and all previous owners of the contaminated site. Real estate lenders found themselves either as present owners or somewhere in the chain of ownership through foreclosure proceedings.

The amendments created a concept called innocent landowner immunity. It was recognized that in certain cases, a landowner in the chain of ownership was completely innocent of all wrongdoing and therefore should not be held liable. The innocent landowner immunity clause established the criteria by which to judge whether a person or business could be exempted from liability. The criteria included the following:

- The pollution was caused by a third party.
- The property was acquired after the fact.
- The landowner had no actual or constructive knowledge of the damage.
- Due care was exercised when the property was purchased (the landowner made a reasonable search, called an environmental site assessment) to determine that no damage to the property existed.
- Reasonable precautions were taken in the exercise of ownership rights.

Industrial Site Recovery Act (ISRA) and Wetlands Protection

The New Jersey Industrial Site Recovery Act (ISRA) provides for mandatory cleanup of industrial and some commercial sites when they are closed, sold, or otherwise change ownership. Recognizing the necessity of preserving the ecological balance of the area between the sea and the land, "one of the most vital and productive areas of our natural world," the New Jersey Legislature enacted the Wetlands Act of 1970. Under this act the **Department of Environmental Protection (DEP)** regulates certain activities in designated wetlands areas. Riparian owners who wish to conduct any of the regulated activities must apply to the commissioner of environmental protection for a permit. Regulated activities include, but are not limited to, draining, dredging, excavating, or removing soil, mud, or sand; dumping or depositing any rubbish or similar material; discharging any liquid wastes; and erecting structures, driving pilings (for piers), or placing obstructions, whether or not they change the tidal ebb and flow.

Additional legislation has been enacted that requires persons to apply to the commissioner for a permit to erect manufacturing, processing, or housing facilities in the coastal area that might tend to pollute the marine environment. Permits are granted on the basis of the applicant's preparation for meeting established environmental standards and preserving the natural ecological balance of the area as much as possible.

Regulation of nonmarine waters is administered by DEP's separate Division of Water Resources.

Public Access to Beach Areas

The state supreme court has ruled that municipal beaches, whether dry or wet, should be open to the general public on an equal basis.

LANDMARK PRESERVATION

Local governments may enact regulations intended to preserve individual buildings and areas of historical or architectural significance. Regulations setting up local historic areas or landmark preservation districts may restrict an owner's right to alter certain old buildings on the exterior. Interior remodeling is typically free from regulation. Individual buildings located outside a historic area also may be designated as landmarks.

DIRECT PUBLIC OWNERSHIP

Over the years the government's general policy has been to encourage private ownership of land. A certain amount of land is owned by the government for use as municipal buildings, state legislature houses, schools, and military stations. Direct public ownership is a means of land control.

Publicly owned streets and highways serve a necessary function for the entire population. In addition, public land is often used for such recreational purposes as parks and wildlife preserves.

SUMMARY

The control of land use is exercised through public controls, through private (or nongovernment) controls, and through public ownership.

Private controls are exercised by owners, generally subdividers, who control use of subdivision lots by *deed restrictions* that are made to apply to all lot owners. The usual recorded restrictions may be enforced by adjoining lot owners obtaining a court injunction to stop a violator.

Government powers, held by federal, state, and local governments, are for the purpose of protecting the general welfare. Government powers limiting private rights in land include *eminent domain*, *police power*, *taxation*, and *escheat*.

Public controls are ordinances based on the state's police power to protect the public health, safety, and welfare. Through power conferred by the state, cities, and municipalities enact master plans and zoning ordinances.

Zoning ordinances segregate residential areas from business and industrial zones and control not only land use, but height and bulk of buildings and density of population. Zoning enforcement problems involve zoning boards of appeal, *variances*, and *nonconforming uses*. *Subdivision regulations* maintain control of the development of expanding community areas so that growth is harmonious with community standards.

Building codes control construction of buildings by specifying standards for construction, plumbing, sewers, electrical wiring, and equipment. A building inspector issues a *certificate of occupancy* when a completed building meets standards, and, where required by a municipality, a certificate of continuing occupancy on every transfer of title on existing buildings.

In recent years, testing has become common for environmental concerns, such as *radon*, *asbestos*, and *underground oil tanks*. A seller or lessor lead-based paint disclosure is required

Unit 9

before a buyer or lessee may sign a contract or lease on any residential dwelling built prior to 1978.

State and federal governments occasionally have intervened to preserve natural resources through environmental legislation. In particular, the federal government requires disclosure of the presence of lead-based paint.

USEFUL WEBSITES

U.S. Environmental Protection Agency: www.epa.gov

CERCLA: www.epa.gov/superfund/policy/index.htm

A Citizen's Guide to Radon, 2nd ed.: www.epa.gov/radon

New Jersey Department of Environmental Protection: www.njradon.org/radonin.htm

KEY TERMS REVIEW

Match the number of each key term with the corresponding letter.

_____ 1. Asbestos

_____ 2. Building codes

_____ 3. Building permit

_____ 4. CERCLA

_____ 5. Certificate of occupancy

_____ 6. Condemnation

_____ 7. Deed restriction

_____ 8. Department of Environmental Protection

_____ 9. Eminent domain

_____ 10. Escheat

_____ 11. Exclusionary zoning

_____ 12. Lead-based paint

_____ 13. Master plan

_____ 14. Nonconforming use

_____ 15. Police power

_____ 16. Radon

_____ 17. Variance

_____ 18. Zoning ordinance

A. court action by which government takes property

B. discriminatory local regulations

C. Comprehensive Environmental Response, Compensation, and Liability Act of 1980

D. government's power to take property for public use

E. inspector's approval for human habitation

F. limit on use of property set by seller

G. a use that does not meet zoning requirements

H. New Jersey agency overseeing natural resources

I. permission for construction

J. reversion of property to the state when intestate owner dies without heirs

K. standards for construction

L. now-banned hazardous mineral once used for insulation

M. government's right to regulate for health and safety

N. existing use that doesn't meet current zoning standards

O. municipal restriction on uses of real estate in various areas

P. a naturally occurring radioactive gas

Q. primary method by which local governments recognize development goals

R. once widely used wall covering containing a now-banned metal

UNIT 9 REVIEW QUESTIONS

1. Every parcel in the subdivision has a deed restriction forbidding basketball backboards on front-facing garages. A homeowner puts one up anyhow. The neighbors may force him to remove it by
   A. calling the police.
   B. notifying the original developer of the subdivision.
   C. sending a petition to the town or city hall.
   D. going to court.

2. The grantor of real estate may place effective deed restrictions forbidding
   A. any future sale of the property.
   B. rental of the property to a member of a particular ethnic group.
   C. division of the parcel into small building lots.
   D. any of these.

3. The developer of an exclusive subdivision placed a restriction in the deeds requiring 250 feet of road frontage for each building lot. The town building code requires only 100 feet. One property owner obtains permits to construct two houses on his 250-foot lot. His neighbors can
   A. ask the court to order one house torn down.
   B. act only before he has obtained certificates of occupancy.
   C. do nothing because he complied with all town regulations.
   D. enforce their rights by calling the police.

4. The government's police power allows it to regulate
   A. law enforcement.
   B. fire codes.
   C. zoning.
   D. all of these.

5. The state needs to run a new expressway through a farm. The farmer does not agree to sell the necessary land. The state then may try to exert its right of eminent domain through a court proceeding known as
   A. escheat.
   B. variance.
   C. condemnation.
   D. downzoning.

6. The right of escheat allows New Jersey to acquire land
   A. through an act of condemnation.
   B. when someone dies without leaving a will or heirs.
   C. through a gift from a donor.
   D. when property taxes are not paid as due.

7. A real estate salesman shows a pre-World War I house to a prospective buyer who has two toddlers and is worried about potential health hazards. In this situation
   A. there is a risk that urea-formaldehyde foam insulation was used in the original construction.
   B. the licensed real estate salesman can offer to inspect for lead and remove any lead risks.
   C. because the house was built before 1978, there is a good likelihood of the presence of lead-based paint, and federal disclosure laws must be complied with.
   D. there is a possibility of lead poisoning only if there are paint chips to chew and swallow.

8. A nonconforming use is allowed
   A. only after a condemnation suit.
   B. if it is for a public purpose.
   C. with the approval of two-thirds of the neighbors.
   D. if it existed before the area was zoned.

9. A physician goes before his local zoning board asking for permission to open an office in his residential neighborhood because the area has no medical facilities. He is asking for a
   A. variance.
   B. nonconforming use.
   C. special-use permit.
   D. restriction.

10. A homeowner asks the zoning board to allow him to build a fence to keep his children out of traffic on a busy corner. Since the owner does not have room for the required ten-foot setback, he is asking for a
    A. variance.
    B. nonconforming use.
    C. special-use permit.
    D. restriction.

11. An example of a private land-use control is
    A. subdivision regulations.
    B. deed restrictions.
    C. environmental protection laws.
    D. master plan specifications.

12. The building inspector who has determined that construction is satisfactory may issue a
    A. certificate of occupancy.
    B. subdivision regulation.
    C. restrictive covenant.
    D. conditional-use permit.

13. The purpose of a building permit is to
    A. override a deed restriction.
    B. maintain municipal control over the volume of building.
    C. provide evidence of compliance with municipal regulations.
    D. regulate area and bulk of buildings.

14. A Greek Revival home is located in a historic preservation district. The owner probably may NOT change
    A. the number of living units in the building.
    B. the exterior of the building.
    C. the interior of the building.
    D. either the exterior or interior.

15. Liability under the Superfund is
    A. limited to the owner of record.
    B. joint and several and retroactive, but not strict.
    C. voluntary.
    D. strict, joint and several, and retroactive.

16. The Lead-Based Paint Hazard Reduction Act
    A. is a federal law that requires homeowners to conduct certain tests for the presence of lead-based paint hazards prior to selling residential properties.
    B. requires that known lead-based paint hazards be disclosed to potential purchasers and renters.
    C. requires purchasers of residential properties to conduct risk assessments or inspections for lead-based paint hazards.
    D. permits purchasers of residential properties to void any sale if lead-based paint hazards are discovered within ten days after closing.

17. Which of the following materials is considered an environmental hazard due to its friable nature?
    A. Asbestos
    B. Lead
    C. Radon
    D. Urea-formaldehyde

18. Which of these is suspected but NOT proven to be hazardous to human health?
    A. Asbestos
    B. Lead-based paint
    C. Electromagnetic fields
    D. Carbon monoxide

19. The most common source of lead contamination in residential property is
    A. water in the basement.
    B. chipping paint.
    C. insulation.
    D. groundwater gas.

20. Buyers and sellers should be alerted to the possibility of mold when a house has
    A. insulation-wrapped heating ducts.
    B. groundwater contamination.
    C. an underground storage tank.
    D. signs of moisture.

UNIT
10

Listing Agreements

LEARNING OBJECTIVES

When you have completed this unit, you will be able to accomplish the following.

> Describe different types of listing agreements.
> Identify the information necessary for disclosure and properly pricing the property.

KEY TERMS

comparative market
    analysis (CMA)
exclusive agency listing

exclusive right-to-sell
    listing
multiple listing service
    (MLS)

net listing
open listing

LISTING PROPERTY

To acquire their inventories, brokers and salespeople must obtain *listings*, which are the properties they are authorized to offer for sale. Only a *broker* can act as an agent to list, sell, or rent another person's real estate. These acts must be done in the name and under the supervision of the broker, never in the name of the salesperson. *Listing agreements* generally are written contracts of employment.

The New Jersey statute of frauds stipulates that to be entitled to a commission on a real estate transaction, a listing broker must have a *written authorization* to act as the client's broker. The agreement must state the rate or exact amount of commission to be earned by the broker and must specify a *definite termination date* for the agreement.

If the agreement is entered into orally, the broker must deliver a written memorandum of the agreement to the client within five days of the agreement. With an oral agreement the broker cannot earn a commission if he or she effects a sale before the memorandum is delivered to the client or if the client revokes or terminates the oral agreement before the memorandum is delivered.

Listing Agreements

The different kinds of listings that are used in New Jersey are

- open listing,
- exclusive-**Subagency** agency listing, and
- exclusive-right-to-sell listing.

Open Listing

In an **open listing** a seller agrees to pay a broker a commission only if the broker procures a buyer for the property. A seller can enter into open listings with any number of brokers, all acting as agents.

The seller is obligated to pay a commission only to that broker who successfully produces a ready, willing, and able buyer. If the seller personally sells the property *without the aid of any of the brokers*, he or she is not obligated to pay any of them a commission. Because an open listing does not restrict the seller, it does not have to include a termination date. A subsequent exclusive listing with another broker would automatically terminate an open listing.

Exclusive-Agency Listing

In an **exclusive-agency listing** only one broker is specifically authorized to act as the exclusive agent of the principal. If any other broker brings a buyer, the listing agent is still due a commission, which he or she then splits with the selling broker. However, under this form of agreement if the seller finds a buyer with no help from any broker, the seller retains the right to sell the property himself or herself *without obligation to the broker*.

Exclusive-Right-to-Sell Listing

In an **exclusive-right-to-sell listing**, one broker is appointed as sole agent of the seller and is given the exclusive authorization to represent the property in question. The seller must pay the broker a commission *regardless of who sells the property* if it is sold while the listing is in effect. If the seller gives a broker an exclusive-right-to-sell listing but finds a buyer without the broker's assistance, the seller must still pay the broker a commission.

Net Listing (Illegal in New Jersey)

A **net listing** is based on the amount of money the seller will receive if the property is sold. The broker is free to offer the property for sale at any price. If the property is sold, the broker pays the seller only the net amount previously agreed on and keeps the rest. *This type of listing is illegal in New Jersey*. It lends itself to fraud and is not in the seller's best interest.

Multiple Listing Service

A **multiple listing service (MLS)** is usually organized within a geographic area by a group of brokers or board of REALTORS' for the purpose of sharing listings. Online multiple listing services make listings available on the internet to enormous numbers of consumers and brokers.

The multiple-listing agreement is in effect an exclusive-right-to-sell or exclusive-agency agreement with an additional authority to distribute the listing to other brokers *who belong to the MLS*. The contractual obligations among the member brokers of an MLS vary widely.

The listing broker states how the listing is offered (that is, to subagents, buyer brokers, or transaction brokers) as well as what compensation is offered to the selling broker.

An MLS offers advantages to broker, buyer, and seller. Brokers develop a sizable inventory of properties to be sold and are assured of a portion of the commission if they list the property or participate in its sale. Seller's gain because all members of the MLS work to sell their property. Buyers have efficient access to a large selection of listings.

Subagency

When a broker accepts a listing from a seller, the agency relationship is clear: the broker becomes the seller's agent. By extension, any salespersons who work for the broker become subagents of the seller, because they are agents of the broker. The situation is less clear, however, in the case of another broker who procures a buyer for the property. Is the other broker acting as a subagent of the seller, an agent of the buyer, or an agent of the listing broker?

If a seller does not wish to offer subagency to MLS members but still wants to gain exposure through an MLS, he or she can direct that the listing agent may split the commission with another broker who produces the buyer, without the other broker acting as the seller's subagent. The seller agrees to pay the selling broker part of the commission but does not risk being held liable for any statements or actions on the part of the selling broker. Since the creation of buyer agency, subagency has become antiquated and is rarely practiced in New Jersey.

Termination of Listings

As discussed in Unit 3, a listing agreement, which creates an agency relationship, may be terminated for any of the following reasons:

- Performance by the broker
- Expiration of the time period stated in the agreement
- Abandonment by the broker if he or she spends no time on the listing
- Revocation by the owner (although the owner may be liable for the broker's expenses)
- Cancellation by the broker
- Cancellation by mutual consent
- Bankruptcy, death, or insanity of either party
- Destruction of the property
- A change in property use by outside forces (such as a change in zoning)

Obtaining Listings

All legal owners of the listing property, their spouses (if required; see Unit 6), or their authorized agents, as well as the listing salesperson and/or broker, should sign the listing agreement. The listing salesperson can sign the contract in the broker's name if authorized by the broker.

All listing agreements must include a statement acknowledging receipt by the seller of the Consumer Information Statement and a declaration of business relationship.

The seller must be given a copy of the Attorney General's memorandum on the New Jersey Law Against Discrimination (see Figure 4.4).

A typical listing agreement is shown in Figure 10.1.

Figure 10.1: Sample Listing Agreement

Residential   MLS # _____

County: _____   Town: _____   Block: _____   Suffix: _____   Lot: _____   Suffix: _____

Street #: _____ N,S,E,W: _____   Name: _____   Mode: _____   Price: _____   Zip: _____

Directions: _____   Listing Date: _____   Expiration Date: _____

Owner (Last, First Name): _____   Exceptions: _____

Owner Address (if different): _____   Owner Phone #: _____

Listing Broker ID #: _____   Listing Salesperson ID #: _____   Co-Listing Salesperson ID #: _____

Agency Disclosure   Seller's Agent: _____   Transaction Broker: _____

Comp. BA (Buyer's Agent): _____   Comp. TA (Transaction Agent): _____   Comp. Sub (Subagent): _____

Dual Commission Arrangement: _____   Exclusive Agency: _____

Rooms: _____   Bedrooms: _____   Full Baths: _____   Half Baths: _____   Solar Yes/No: _____   Solar Leased/Owned: _____

Style: _____   Substyle: _____   Taxes: _____   Approx. Lot Dimensions: _____

Approx. Lot Sq. Ft.: _____   Approx. Lot Frontage: _____   Sewer : _____   Water Source: _____

Ground Floor: _____   **Schools**

1st Floor: _____   EL: _____

2nd Floor: _____   JH: _____

3rd Floor: _____   SH: _____

Basement: _____

Items Included: _____   Easements: _____

Items Not Included: _____   Municipal Assessments: _____

Possession: _____   For Lease: _____

Showing Instructions/Agent Remarks: (Will not appear on Customer Report)

Customer Remarks

Sample

Exclusive Listing Agreement between Broker and Seller from: Listing Date: _____   **Expiration Date:** _____

In consideration of listing and endeavoring to procure a purchaser for the property described above at the listed price of _____ with a possession date of _____, Seller (the word "Seller" includes all owners whose signatures appear on the bottom of this Listing Agreement) hereby grant to the Broker the Sole and Exclusive Right to Sell the above described property based on the terms and conditions contained in this Agreement.

Seller further agrees to pay the Broker a compensation of _____ . If the compensation is a percentage, it shall be a percentage of the offering price or of any sales price accepted by the Seller. This compensation shall be earned by the Broker and payable to the Broker if the property is sold by the Seller, the Broker, or through any other source, during the term of this Exclusive Right to Sell Listing Agreement.

<u>Seller represents that this property is not and will not be Exclusively Listed with any other Broker during the term of this Listing Agreement. Seller further represents that the property is not and will not be listed for Rent during the term of this Listing Agreement unless mutually agreed upon terms and conditions are negotiated with the Broker.</u>

"As a Seller you have the right to individually reach an agreement on any fee, compensation, or other valuable consideration with any Broker. No fee, compensation, or other consideration has been fixed by any governmental authority or by any trade association or multiple listing service." Nothing in this Agreement is intended to prohibit an individual Broker from independently establishing a policy regarding the amount of fee, compensation, or other valuable consideration to be charged in transactions by the Broker.

I, _____ (name of licensee), as an authorized representative of _____ (name of firm), intend, as of this time, to work with you as a:

_____ **Seller's Agent Only**, _____ **Transaction Broker**, _____ **Seller's Agent and Disclosed Dual Agent if the opportunity arises.****

**Separate informed consent form must be executed by Broker/Seller/Buyer

In the event that the property, or any part of it, described in this Agreement becomes subject to a written or other agreement by the Buyer and Seller or their designees, or is sold, conveyed, leased or in any way transferred within _____ days after the expiration of this Agreement to anyone to whom the Seller, Broker or the Broker's salesperson, sub-agent (participating Broker/cooperating Broker) or a Buyers' Broker/Buyers' Agent or a Transaction Broker/Transaction Agent had introduced the property during the term of this Exclusive Right to Sell Listing, the compensation as indicated above shall be earned by the Broker and payable to the Broker by the Seller, unless the Seller executes a new Exclusive Right to Sell Listing Agreement during the protection period.

Seller represents that Seller is the Owner of the above described property and Seller has the full authority to enter into this Agreement. If this Agreement is executed by anyone other than the Owner of the property, Owner represents that the individual or individuals is/are acting on behalf of the Owner and that the individual or individuals has/have furnished the Broker with a copy of that written authorization. Seller and Broker further represent that no other terms or conditions exist other than those that are contained in this Agreement.

Seller acknowledges that he/she has read this Agreement, the New Jersey Attorney General's Memorandum, the Key Box Agreement printed on the reverse side, and has received the Consumer Information Statement and a fully executed copy of this Agreement which contains accurate information.

Authorization is hereby granted by Seller to submit this listing to the New Jersey Multiple Listing Service for distribution to all Broker members.

☐ Unless this box is checked, Seller authorizes listing to appear on all real estate web sites authorized by the Board of Directors.

☐ Unless this box is checked, the property address <u>will</u> appear on all web sites.

Sales Associate Signature _____   Owner Signature _____

Broker/Manager Signature _____   Owner Signature _____

Print Owner Name _____   Owner Phone # _____   Realtor Phone # _____

Print Owner Name _____   Date _____

Information herein deemed reliable but not guaranteed.   Revised 04/2018   **New Jersey Multiple Listing Service, Inc.**
160 Terrace St., PO Box U, Haworth, NJ 07641

Figure 10.1: Sample Listing Agreement (continued)

PHILIP D. MURPHY *Governor* SHEILA Y. OLIVER *Lt. Governor*	*State of New Jersey* OFFICE OF THE ATTORNEY GENERAL DEPARTMENT OF LAW AND PUBLIC SAFETY DIVISION ON CIVIL RIGHTS 31 CLINTON STREET, 3RD FLOOR NEWARK, NJ 07102	GURBIR S. GREWAL *Attorney General* RACHEL WAINER APTER *Director*

TO: Property Owners
FROM: Gurbir S. Grewal, Attorney General, State of New Jersey
             Rachel Wainer Apter, Director, NJ Division on Civil Rights
DATE: October 7, 2020
SUBJECT: Housing Discrimination Laws

The New Jersey Real Estate Commission (REC) requires every licensed broker or salesperson with whom you list your property to give you a copy of this notice. The purpose is to help you comply with the New Jersey Law Against Discrimination (LAD).

Under the LAD, it is illegal to discriminate against a prospective or current buyer or tenant because of actual or perceived race, national origin, religion, gender, gender identity or expression, marital status, civil union status, domestic partner status, affectional or sexual orientation, familial status, pregnancy or breastfeeding, physical or mental disability, or liability for service in the Armed Forces of the United States. It is also illegal to discriminate against a prospective or current buyer or tenant because of any source of lawful income to be used for rental or mortgage payments. Source of lawful income includes Section 8 housing choice vouchers, SRAP (State Rental Assistance Programs), and TRA (temporary rental assistance). It is also illegal to make, print, or publish any statement, including print advertisements and online postings, expressing any preference, limitation, or discrimination based on any of those protected characteristics.

The LAD applies to a wide range of activities, such as advertising, selling, renting, leasing, subleasing, assigning, and showing property (including open land). Here are some issues that come up frequently in enforcing the LAD:

- The prohibition on discrimination based on source of lawful income means, for example, that a landlord cannot reject a prospective tenant because they intend to pay with a Section 8 housing choice voucher, State Rental Assistance Program (SRAP), temporary rental assistance (TRA), or any other subsidy or voucher provided by federal, state, or local rental-assistance programs. A housing provider cannot advertise a property in any way that discriminates based on source of lawful income, including by posting advertisements that state, directly or indirectly, a refusal to accept, or express any limitation on, vouchers or subsidies. For example, advertisements that state "No Section 8," "TRA not accepted," or "This property not approved for Section 8" violate the LAD. In addition, housing providers must calculate any minimum income requirement, financial standard, or income standard based only on the portion of the rent to be paid by the tenant, rather than the entire rental amount.

- The LAD prohibits bias-based harassment in housing, including sexual harassment. If a tenant is being subjected to bias-based harassment that creates a hostile environment, and if the housing provider knew or should have known about it, the housing provider must take reasonable steps to stop it. That includes harassment by other tenants and by a housing provider's agents or employees. "Quid pro quo" sexual harassment—for example, where a building superintendent demands sex or sexual favors as a condition of making necessary repairs—is also prohibited.

- Housing providers must reasonably accommodate tenants with disabilities unless doing so would be an undue burden on their operations. For example, if a tenant shows they have a disability and that keeping an emotional support animal is necessary to afford them an equal opportunity to use and enjoy the dwelling, the housing provider must permit the emotional support animal, even despite a "no pets" policy, unless they can show that doing so would be an undue burden.

- A "no pets" rule cannot be enforced against a person with a disability who has a service or guide animal. A landlord may also not charge a tenant with a disability an extra fee for keeping a service or guide animal.

- Landlords must permit a tenant with a disability—at that tenant's own expense—to make reasonable modifications to the premises if such modifications are needed to give the tenant an equal opportunity to use or enjoy the dwelling.

- The LAD prohibits discrimination based on "familial status"—for example, discrimination against families with children under the age of 18 and pregnant women. Landlords similarly cannot use unreasonable occupancy restrictions to prevent families with children from moving in.

- Selectively inquiring about, or requesting information about and/or documentation of, a prospective tenant's or buyer's immigration or citizenship status because of the person's actual or perceived national origin, race, or ethnicity, or otherwise discriminating on such a basis, is a violation of the LAD.

- As explained in the U.S. Department of Housing and Urban Development's April 2016 Guidance document, because of widespread racial and ethnic disparities in the criminal justice system, blanket policies that make all individuals with any prior arrest or criminal conviction ineligible to rent violate fair housing laws because they have a disproportionate impact based on race or national origin and are not supported by a legitimate business necessity. And housing providers may not use criminal history as a pretext for intentionally discriminating based on race or national origin (for example, by applying criminal-record based restrictions against Black housing applicants but not white housing applicants).

Penalties. If you commit a discriminatory housing practice that violates the LAD, you may be subject to penalties not exceeding $10,000 for a first violation, not exceeding $25,000 for a second violation within five years of the first offense, and not exceeding $50,000 for two or more violations within seven years.

Other remedies. Victims of discrimination may recover economic damages related to the discrimination (such as having to pay higher rent for another unit), as well as damages for emotional distress, pain, and humiliation. In more egregious cases, a victim may also recover punitive damages.

Brokers. The broker or salesperson with whom you list your property must transmit to you every written offer they receive on your property. Brokers and salespersons are licensed by the New Jersey Real Estate Commission and their activities are subject to the LAD as well as general real estate laws of the State and the Commission's own rules and regulations. The broker or salesperson must refuse your listing if you indicate an intent to discriminate on any basis prohibited by the LAD.

Exemptions. The sale or rental of property (including open land), whether for business or residential purposes, is covered by the LAD, subject to the following exemptions. Note that when an LAD exemption applies, other civil rights laws may nonetheless prohibit discrimination.

- The LAD does not apply to the rental of one unit in a two-family dwelling if the owner occupies the other unit, or to the rental of a room or rooms in a one-family owner-occupied dwelling.

- A religious organization can give preference to persons of the same religion when selling or renting real property.

- In certain types of housing designated for older persons, it is not unlawful to discriminate based on familial status.

For more information about the LAD, or if you have other questions about discrimination in the sale or rental of real property, including how to report a complaint, please visit **www.NJCivilRights.gov** or call our Housing Hotline at **(866)-405-3050**. DCR has a number of fair housing fact sheets that are available at www.nj.gov/oag/dcr/housing.html. Thank you.

Gurbir S. Grewal
Attorney General

Rachel Wainer Apter
Director, Division on Civil Rights

www.njcivilrights.gov
New Jersey is an Equal Opportunity Employer · Printed on Recycled Paper and Recyclable

CIVIL⚖️RIGHTS

NJMLS's Keybox Information Disclosure
A key box is a small safe, which is secured to the outside of the house. Within the box is placed a key to the house, which will permit access to the premises. The key box itself is locked and can only be opened with non-duplicative entry cards. These entry cards are distributed to each Broker's office, which is a participant in the New Jersey Multiple Listing Service, Inc. The major advantage of a key box system, to the homeowner, is that it permits Brokers to show the house to prospective purchasers even when the owner is not at home. Since a home may be visited by a Broker and prospective customers when the owner is not present, the owner is encouraged not to leave articles such as money, small jewelry items, etc., in the open. From time to time the MLS has been advised that items have been found to be missing during the term of a listing. The homeowner is urged to take precautions as he or she deems appropriate. Although most of the homes that are listed through the New Jersey Multiple Listing Service, Inc. employ the key box operation because of its great advantage to the homeowner, there is no obligation on any individual owner to do so.

Figure 10.1: Sample Listing Agreement (continued)

NJ REAL ESTATE COMMISSION
ADDENDUM TO LISTING AGREEMENT

MLS Number: _____

Property Address: _____

Town: _____

LISTING BROKERS USUALLY COOPERATE WITH OTHER BROKERAGE FIRMS BY SHARING INFORMATION ABOUT THEIR LISTINGS AND OFFERING TO PAY PART OF THEIR COMMISSION TO THE FIRM THAT PRODUCES A BUYER. THIS IS GENERALLY REFFERED TO AS THE "COMMISSION SPLIT."

SOME LISTING BROKERS OFFER TO PAY COMMSSION SPLITS OF A PORTION OF THE GROSS COMMISSION, USUALLY EXPRESSED AS A PERCENTAGE OF THE SELLING PRICE, LESS A SIGNIFICANT DOLLAR AMOUNT. OTHER LISTING BROKERS OFFER A PORTION OF THE GROSS COMMISSION LESS ONLY A MINIMAL LISTING FEE OR LESS ZERO.

THE AMOUNT OF COMMISSION SPLIT YOUR BROKER OFFERS CAN AFFECT THE EXTENT TO WHICH YOUR PROPERTY IS EXPOSED TO PROSPECTIVE BUYERS WORKING WITH LICENSEES FROM OTHER BROKERAGE FIRMS.

ON THIS LISTING, THE BROKER IS OFFERING A COMMISSION SPLIT OF _____
TO POTENTIAL COOPERATING BROKERS.

IF YOU FEEL THAT THIS MAY RESULT IN YOUR PROPERTY RECEIVING LESS THAN MAXIMUM EXPOSURE TO BUYERS, YOU SHOULD DISCUSS THOSE CONCERNS WITH THE LISTING SALESPERSON OR HIS/HER SUPERVISING BROKER.

BY SIGNING THIS LISTING AGREEMENT, THE OWNER(S) ACKNOWLEDGE HAVING READ THIS STATEMENT ON COMMISSION SPLITS.

Sample

Sales Associate Signature _____   Owner Signature _____

Broker/Manager Signature _____   Owner Signature _____

Print Owner Name _____   Owner Phone _____   Realtor Phone _____

Print Owner Name _____   Date _____

Information herein deemed reliable but not guaranteed.   New Jersey Multiple Listing Service, Inc.
                                                                          160 Terrace St., PO Box U, Haworth, NJ 07641

Revised 01/2020_A

Property Information for Listings

When taking a listing it is important to obtain as much information as possible concerning a parcel of real estate. This ensures that all possible contingencies can be anticipated, particularly when the listing is shared with other brokers and salespeople in a multiple-listing arrangement. The following list includes some of the information a licensee might obtain; some of the items are essential, while others are not appropriate in every case.

- Names and addresses of owners
- Adequate description of the property
- A survey or dimensions of the lot (frontage and depth)
- Number, size, and layout of rooms
- Square footage
- Construction and age of the building
- Information relative to the neighborhood (schools, houses of worship, transportation)
- Current taxes
- Special assessments
- Dues (if a condominium or in a private community)
- Amount of existing financing (including interest, payments, and other costs)
- Utilities and average payments
- Septic and/or well information, if applicable
- Appliances to be included in the transaction
- Date of occupancy or possession
- Possibility of seller financing
- Zoning classification (especially important for vacant land)
- Flood zone information
- A detailed list of exactly what is and is not included in the sales price
- Seller's Property Condition Disclosure Statement
- EPA's Lead Hazard Pamphlet, if applicable

The licensee might also want to obtain a copy of the sellers' deed and their title policy.

Responsibility for Disclosure

A real estate broker, as an agent of the seller, is responsible for the disclosure of any material information regarding the property. Getting as much initial information from the seller as possible—even if asking penetrating and possibly embarrassing questions—pays off in the long run by saving both principal and agent from potential legal difficulties. The agent also should assume the responsibility of searching the public records for such pertinent information as zoning, lot size, and yearly taxes.

The *true tax* figure should be used, disregarding any present veterans, aged, or religious exemptions, or any addition for unpaid water bills. In the sale of multiple dwellings the seller should be ready to present a statement of rents and expenses, preferably prepared by an accountant. Prospective buyers want statements on leases and security deposits. The listing agent should verify zoning and the legality of existing use.

The seller should be informed of any necessity for a certificate of occupancy at transfer. Arranging with tenants to show the property at reasonable times is also of vital importance.

Sellers of properties located in flood-prone areas should be prepared to provide an elevation map since flood insurance will most likely be a requirement for any federally-related mortgage loan. For more information, consult Unit 21.

Some municipalities may have restrictive ordinances such as aquifer protection zones, wetlands protection, or steep slope ordinances. Listing agents should keep current with all potential restrictions on use of land.

Many brokers now require every seller to fill out a disclosure form at the time the listing agreement is signed. This form should eventually be signed by the buyer and attached to the sales contract so both attorneys are aware of its contents. A sample disclosure form is provided in Figure 10.2.

Responsibility for Investigation

The more information an agent has concerning a piece of property, the easier it is to negotiate with prospective purchasers and the smaller the chance that the sale is hindered by unexpected problems. The New Jersey Real Estate Commission rules and regulations clearly require the licensee to ascertain all pertinent information on a property that has been accepted for listing. The results of the licensee's investigation must be made known to all prospective purchasers.

Failure to disclose any known defects or any defect that would have been apparent if a reasonable investigation had been made may make the licensee liable for any claims levied by the purchaser of the property. The rules also require the licensee to investigate the financial qualifications of every person for whom he or she submits an offer to a client (principal).

The New Jersey Real Estate License Act further requires that

- a fully executed (signed) copy of any sole or exclusive sale or rental listing be provided to the owner at the time of execution; and
- the listing contain a definite date of termination.

Cooperation With Other Licensees

Every licensee must fully cooperate with all other New Jersey licensees in the sale of listed property, unless specifically ordered not to do so by the seller (see the *Waiver of Broker Cooperation* in Unit 2). Any MLS must receive a listing within 48 hours of signing. Any written offer must be transmitted to the seller within 24 hours.

Each listing contract must contain an explanation of the fee arrangements under which the real estate firm cooperates on the sale of listings. The amount of commission offered to a cooperating office that provides the buyer ("the split") must be specified in the listing contract. The required wording can be found as part of the contract in Figure 10.1.

Negotiability of Commission

Commission rates are negotiated between client and broker. No listing contract may prescribe or predetermine a fee or percentage. All listing agreements for the sale of one- to four-family dwelling units must contain in print larger than the predominant type size the language *"As seller you have the right to individually reach an agreement on any fee, commission, or other valuable consideration with any broker. No fee, commission, or other consideration has been fixed by any governmental authority or by any trade association or multiple listing service."*

Figure 10.2: Seller's Property Condition Disclosure Statement

SELLER'S PROPERTY CONDITION DISCLOSURE STATEMENT

© 2018, New Jersey REALTORS®

NEW JERSEY REALTORS®

1   **Property Address:** _____

2

3   _____

4

5   **Seller:** _____

6

7   _____

8

9   The purpose of this Disclosure Statement is to disclose, to the best of Seller's knowledge, the condition of the Property, as of the date set

10 forth below. The Seller is aware that he or she is under an obligation to disclose any known material defects in the Property even if not

11 addressed in this printed form. Seller alone is the source of all information contained in this form. All prospective buyers of the Property

12 are cautioned to carefully inspect the Property and to carefully inspect the surrounding area for any off-site conditions that may adversely

13 affect the Property. Moreover, this Disclosure Statement is not intended to be a substitute for prospective buyer's hiring of qualified experts

14 to inspect the Property.

15

16 If your property consists of multiple units, systems and/or features, please provide complete answers on all such units, systems and/or

17 features even if the question is phrased in the singular, such as if a duplex has multiple furnaces, water heaters and fireplaces.

18

19

20 **OCCUPANCY**

21   Yes No Unknown

22   [ ] 1. Age of House, if known _____

23   [ ] [ ]   2. Does the Seller currently occupy this property?

24   If not, how long has it been since Seller occupied the property? _____

25   3. What year did the seller buy the property? _____

26   [ ] [ ]   3a. Do you have in your possession the original or a copy of the deed evidencing your ownership of the

27   property? If "yes," please attach a copy of it to this form.

28

29 **ROOF**

30   Yes No Unknown

31   [ ] 4. Age of roof _____

32   [ ] [ ]   5. Has roof been replaced or repaired since seller bought the property?

33   [ ] [ ]   6. Are you aware of any roof leaks?

34   7. Explain any "yes" answers that you give in this section: _____

35

36

37 **ATTIC, BASEMENTS AND CRAWL SPACES** (Complete only if applicable)

38   Yes No Unknown

39   [ ] [ ]   8. Does the property have one or more sump pumps?

40   [ ] [ ]   8a. Are there any problems with the operation of any sump pump?

41   [ ] [ ]   9. Are you aware of any water leakage, accumulation or dampness within the basement or crawl spaces

42   or any other areas within any of the structures on the property?

43   [ ] [ ]   9a. Are you aware of the presence of any mold or similar natural substance within the basement or crawl

44   spaces or any other areas within any of the structures on the property?

45   [ ] [ ]   10. Are you aware of any repairs or other attempts to control any water or dampness problem in the

46   basement or crawl space? If "yes," describe the location, nature and date of the repairs:

47   _____

48

49   [ ] [ ]   11. Are you aware of any cracks or bulges in the basement floor or foundation walls? If "yes," specify

50   location. _____

NJ REALTORS® | Form 140 | 10/2019   Page 1 of 9

Unit 10

Figure 10.2: Seller's Property Condition Disclosure Statement (continued)

51	[] []	12. Are you aware of any restrictions on how the attic may be used as a result of the manner in which
52		the attic or roof was constructed?
53	[] []	13. Is the attic or house ventilated by: ❑ a whole house fan? ❑ an attic fan?
54	[] []	13a. Are you aware of any problems with the operation of such a fan?
55		14. In what manner is access to the attic space provided?
56		❑ staircase ❑ pull down stairs ❑ crawl space with aid of ladder or other device
57		❑ other _____
58		15. Explain any "yes" answers that you give in this section:
59		_____
60		_____
61		

TERMITES/WOOD DESTROYING INSECTS, DRY ROT, PESTS

	Yes	No	Unknown	
63				
64	[]	[]		16. Are you aware of any termites/wood destroying insects, dry rot, or pests affecting the property?
65	[]	[]		17. Are you aware of any damage to the property caused by termites/wood destroying insects, dry rot,
66				or pests?
67	[]	[]		18. If "yes," has work been performed to repair the damage?
68	[]	[]		19. Is your property under contract by a licensed pest control company? If "yes," state the name and
69				address of the licensed pest control company: _____
70				
71	[]	[]		20. Are you aware of any termite/pest control inspections or treatments performed on the property in
72				the past?
73				21. Explain any "yes" answers that you give in this section:
74				_____
75				_____
76				

STRUCTURAL ITEMS

	Yes	No	Unknown	
78				
79	[]	[]		22. Are you aware of any movement, shifting, or other problems with walls, floors, or foundations,
80				including any restrictions on how any space, other than the attic or roof, may be used as a result of
81				the manner in which it was constructed?
82	[]	[]		23. Are you aware if the property or any of the structures on it have ever been damaged by fire, smoke,
83				wind or flood?
84	[]	[]		24. Are you aware of any fire retardant plywood used in the construction?
85	[]	[]		25. Are you aware of any current or past problems with driveways, walkways, patios, sinkholes, or
86				retaining walls on the property?
87	[]	[]		26. Are you aware of any present or past efforts made to repair any problems with the items in this
88				section?
89				27. Explain any "yes" answers that you give in this section. Please describe the location and nature of the
90				problem.
91				_____
92				_____
93				

ADDITIONS/REMODELS

	Yes	No	Unknown	
95				
96	[]	[]		28. Are you aware of any additions, structural changes or other alterations to the structures on the
97				property made by any present or past owners?
98	[]	[]	[]	29. Were the proper building permits and approvals obtained? Explain any "yes" answers you give in this
99				section:
100				_____
101				_____
102				

PLUMBING, WATER AND SEWAGE

	Yes	No	Unknown	
104				
105				30. What is the source of your drinking water?
106				❑ Public ❑ Community System ❑ Well on Property ❑ Other (explain)_____
107	[]	[]		31. If your drinking water source is not public, have you performed any tests on the water?
108				If so, when?_____
109				Attach a copy of or describe the results.
110				

Figure 10.2:   Seller's Property Condition Disclosure Statement (continued)

111	[]	[]	[]	32. Does the wastewater from any clothes washer, dishwasher, or other appliance discharge to any location other than the sewer, septic, or other system that services the rest of the property?

113   [] — 33. When was well installed? _____

114   [] — Location of well? _____

115   [] [] — 34. Do you have a softener, filter, or other water purification system? ❑ Leased ❑ Owned

116   35. What is the type of sewage system?

117   ❑ Public Sewer ❑ Private Sewer ❑ Septic System ❑ Cesspool ❑ Other (explain): _____

118   [] [] — 36. If you answered "septic system," have you ever had the system inspected to confirm that it is a true septic system and not a cesspool?

120   [] — 37. If Septic System, when was it installed? _____

121   Location? _____

122   [] — 38. When was the Septic System or Cesspool last cleaned and/or serviced? _____

123   [] [] [] — 39. Are you aware of any abandoned Septic Systems or Cesspools on your property?

124   [] [] [] — 39a. If "yes," is the closure in accordance with the municipality's ordinance? (explain): _____

126   [] [] — 40. Are you aware of any leaks, backups, or other problems relating to any of the plumbing systems and fixtures (including pipes, sinks, tubs and showers), or of any other water or sewage related problems? If "yes," explain: _____

130   [] [] — 41. Are you aware of any shut off, disconnected, or abandoned wells, underground water or sewage tanks, or dry wells on the property?

132   [] [] [] — 42. Is either the private water or sewage system shared? If "yes," explain: _____

134   43. Water Heater: ❑ Electric ❑ Fuel Oil ❑ Gas

135   [] — Age of Water Heater _____

136   [] [] — 43a. Are you aware of any problems with the water heater?

137   44. Explain any "yes" answers that you give in this section: _____

HEATING AND AIR CONDITIONING

Yes   No   Unknown

143   45. Type of Air Conditioning:

144   ❑ Central one zone ❑ Central multiple zone ❑ Wall/Window Unit ❑ None

145   46. List any areas of the house that are not air conditioned: _____

147   [] — 47. What is the age of Air Conditioning System? _____

148   48. Type of heat: ❑ Electric ❑ Fuel Oil ❑ Natural Gas ❑ Propane ❑ Unheated ❑ Other

149   49. What is the type of heating system? (for example, forced air, hot water or base board, radiator, steam heat) _____

151   50. If it is a centralized heating system, is it one zone or multiple zones? _____

153   [] — 51. Age of furnace _____ Date of last service: _____

154   52. List any areas of the house that are not heated: _____

156   [] [] [] — 53. Are you aware of any tanks on the property, either above or underground, used to store fuel or other substances?

158   [] [] — 54. If tank is not in use, do you have a closure certificate?

159   [] [] — 55. Are you aware of any problems with any items in this section? If "yes," explain: _____

WOODBURNING STOVE OR FIREPLACE

Yes   No   Unknown

164   [] [] — 56. Do you have ❑ wood burning stove? ❑ fireplace? ❑ insert? ❑ other

165   [] [] — 56a. Is it presently usable?

166   [] [] [] — 57. If you have a fireplace, when was the flue last cleaned? _____

167   [] [] [] — 57a. Was the flue cleaned by a professional or non-professional? _____

168   [] [] [] — 58. Have you obtained any required permits for any such item?

169   [] [] — 59. Are you aware of any problems with any of these items? If "yes," please explain: _____

Unit 10

Figure 10.2: Seller's Property Condition Disclosure Statement (continued)

ELECTRICAL SYSTEM

Yes	No	Unknown	
			60. What type of wiring is in this structure? ❑ Copper ❑ Aluminum ❑ Other ❑ Unknown
			61. What amp service does the property have? ❑ 60 ❑ 100 ❑ 150 ❑ 200 ❑ Other ❑ Unknown
[]	[]	[]	62. Does it have 240 volt service? Which are present ❑ Circuit Breakers, ❑ Fuses or ❑ Both?
[]	[]		63. Are you aware of any additions to the original service?
			If "yes," were the additions done by a licensed electrician? Name and address:
			_____
			_____
[]	[]	[]	64. If "yes," were proper building permits and approvals obtained?
[]	[]		65. Are you aware of any wall switches, light fixtures or electrical outlets in need of repair?
			66. Explain any "yes" answers you give in this section:
			_____
			_____
			_____

LAND (SOILS, DRAINAGE AND BOUNDARIES)

Yes	No	Unknown	
[]	[]		67. Are you aware of any fill or expansive soil on the property?
[]	[]		68. Are you aware of any past or present mining operations in the area in which the property is located?
[]	[]		69. Is the property located in a flood hazard zone?
[]	[]		70. Are you aware of any drainage or flood problems affecting the property?
[]	[]	[]	71. Are there any areas on the property which are designated as protected wetlands?
[]	[]		72. Are you aware of any encroachments, utility easements, boundary line disputes, or drainage or other easements affecting the property?
[]	[]		73. Are there any water retention basins on the property or the adjacent properties?
[]	[]		74. Are you aware if any part of the property is being claimed by the State of New Jersey as land presently or formerly covered by tidal water (Riparian claim or lease grant)? Explain:
			_____
[]	[]		75. Are you aware of any shared or common areas (for example, driveways, bridges, docks, walls, bulkheads, etc.) or maintenance agreements regarding the property?
			76. Explain any "yes" answers to the preceding questions in this section:
			_____
			_____
[]	[]		77. Do you have a survey of the property?

ENVIRONMENTAL HAZARDS

Yes	No	Unknown	
[]	[]		78. Have you received any written notification from any public agency or private concern informing you that the property is adversely affected, or may be adversely affected, by a condition that exists on a property in the vicinity of this property? If "yes," attach a copy of any such notice currently in your possession.
[]	[]		78a. Are you aware of any condition that exists on any property in the vicinity which adversely affects, or has been identified as possibly adversely affecting, the quality or safety of the air, soil, water, and/ or physical structures present on this property? If "yes," explain:
			_____
			_____
[]	[]		79. Are you aware of any underground storage tanks (UST) or toxic substances now or previously present on this property or adjacent property (structure or soil), such as polychlorinated biphenyl (PCB), solvents, hydraulic fluid, petro-chemicals, hazardous wastes, pesticides, chromium, thorium, lead or other hazardous substances in the soil? If "yes," explain:
			_____
[]	[]		80. Are you aware if any underground storage tank has been tested? (Attach a copy of each test report or closure certificate if available).
[]	[]	[]	81. Are you aware if the property has been tested for the presence of any other toxic substances, such as lead-based paint, urea-formaldehyde foam insulation, asbestos-containing materials, or others? (Attach copy of each test report if available).
			82. If "yes" to any of the above, explain:
			_____
			_____

Figure 10.2: Seller's Property Condition Disclosure Statement (continued)

231	[]	[]	82a. If "yes" to any of the above, were any actions taken to correct the problem? Explain:
232			_____
233			_____
234	[]	[]	[]	83. Is the property in a designated Airport Safety Zone?

DEED RESTRICTIONS, SPECIAL DESIGNATIONS, HOMEOWNERS ASSOCIATION/CONDOMINIUMS AND CO-OPS

Line	Yes	No	Unknown	
238	Yes	No	Unknown	
239	[]	[]		84. Are you aware if the property is subject to any deed restrictions or other limitations on how it may be used due to its being situated within a designated historic district, or a protected area like the New Jersey Pinelands, or its being subject to similar legal authorities other than typical local zoning ordinances?
243	[]	[]		85. Is the property part of a condominium or other common interest ownership plan?
244	[]	[]		85a. If so, is the property subject to any covenants, conditions, or restrictions as a result of its being part of a condominium or other form of common interest ownership?
246	[]	[]		86. As the owner of the property, are you required to belong to a condominium association or homeowners association, or other similar organization or property owners?
248	[]	[]		86a. If so, what is the Association's name and telephone number?
250	[]	[]	[]	86b. If so, are there any dues or assessments involved? If "yes," how much? _____
252	[]	[]		87. Are you aware of any defect, damage, or problem with any common elements or common areas that materially affects the property?
254	[]	[]		88. Are you aware of any condition or claim which may result in an increase in assessments or fees?
255	[]	[]	[]	89. Since you purchased the property, have there been any changes to the rules or by-laws of the Association that impact the property?
256				90. Explain any "yes" answers you give in this section:

_____

_____

MISCELLANEOUS

Line	Yes	No	Unknown	
262	Yes	No	Unknown	
263	[]	[]		91. Are you aware of any existing or threatened legal action affecting the property or any condominium or homeowners association to which you, as an owner, belong?
265	[]	[]		92. Are you aware of any violations of Federal, State or local laws or regulations relating to this property?
266	[]	[]		93. Are you aware of any zoning violations, encroachments on adjacent properties, non-conforming uses, or set-back violations relating to this property? If so, please state whether the condition is pre-existing non-conformance to present day zoning or a violation to zoning and/or land use laws.
271	[]	[]		94. Are you aware of any public improvement, condominium or homeowner association assessments against the property that remain unpaid? Are you aware of any violations of zoning, housing, building, safety or fire ordinances that remain uncorrected?
274	[]	[]	[]	95. Are there mortgages, encumbrances or liens on this property?
275	[]	[]		95a. Are you aware of any reason, including a defect in title, that would prevent you from conveying clear title?
277	[]	[]		96. Are you aware of any material defects to the property, dwelling, or fixtures which are not disclosed elsewhere on this form? (A defect is "material," if a reasonable person would attach importance to its existence or non-existence in deciding whether or how to proceed in the transaction.) If "yes," explain: _____
282	[]	[]		97. Other than water and sewer charges, utility and cable tv fees, your local property taxes, any special assessments and any association dues or membership fees, are there any other fees that you pay on an ongoing basis with respect to this property, such as garbage collection fees?
285				98. Explain any other "yes" answers you give in this section:

_____

_____

Figure 10.2: Seller's Property Condition Disclosure Statement (continued)

291 **RADON GAS** Instructions to Owners
292 By law (N.J.S.A. 26:2D-73), a property owner who has had his or her property tested or treated for radon gas may require that information
293 about such testing and treatment be kept confidential until the time that the owner and a buyer enter into a contract of sale, at which time
294 a copy of the test results and evidence of any subsequent mitigation or treatment shall be provided to the buyer. The law also provides that
295 owners may waive, in writing, this right of confidentiality. As the owner(s) of this property, do you wish to waive this right?

296 Yes No
297 [] [] _____   _____
298   (Initials)   (Initials)
299
300 If you responded "yes," answer the following questions. If you responded "no," proceed to the next section.
301
302 Yes No Unknown
303 [] []   99. Are you aware if the property has been tested for radon gas? (Attach a copy of each test report if
304   available.)
305 [] []   100. Are you aware if the property has been treated in an effort to mitigate the presence of radon gas?
306   (If "yes," attach a copy of any evidence of such mitigation or treatment.)
307 [] []   101. Is radon remediation equipment now present in the property?
308 [] []   101a. If "yes," is such equipment in good working order?
309
310
311 **MAJOR APPLIANCES AND OTHER ITEMS**
312 The terms of any final contract executed by the seller shall be controlling as to what appliances or other items, if any, shall be included
313 in the sale of the property. Which of the following items are present in the property? (For items that are not present, indicate "not
314 applicable.")
315
316 Yes No Unknown N/A
317 [] []   [] 102. Electric Garage Door Opener
318 [] []   [] 102a. If "yes," are they reversible? Number of Transmitters _____
319 [] [] [] [] 103. Smoke Detectors
320   ❏ Battery ❏ Electric ❏ Both How many _____
321   ❏ Carbon Monoxide Detectors How many _____
322   Location _____
323 [] []   [] 104. With regard to the above items, are you aware that any item is not in working order?
324   104a. If "yes," identify each item that is not in working order or defective and explain the nature
325   of the problem: _____
326   _____
327
328 [] []   [] 105. ❏ In-ground pool ❏ Above-ground pool ❏ Pool Heater ❏ Spa/Hot Tub
329 [] [] [] [] 105a. Were proper permits and approvals obtained?
330 [] []   [] 105b. Are you aware of any leaks or other defects with the filter or the walls or other structural or
331   mechanical components of the pool or spa/hot tub?
332 [] []   [] 105c. If an in-ground pool, are you aware of any water seeping behind the walls of the pool?
333   106. Indicate which of the following may be included in the sale? (Indicate Y for yes N for no.)
334   [ ] Refrigerator
335   [ ] Range
336   [ ] Microwave Oven
337   [ ] Dishwasher
338   [ ] Trash Compactor
339   [ ] Garbage Disposal
340   [ ] In-Ground Sprinkler System
341   [ ] Central Vacuum System
342   [ ] Security System
343   [ ] Washer
344   [ ] Dryer
345   [ ] Intercom
346   [ ] Other
347 [] [] [] 107. Of those that may be included, is each in working order?
348   If "no," identify each item not in working order, explain the nature of the problem:
349   _____
350

Figure 10.2: Seller's Property Condition Disclosure Statement (continued)

351 **SOLAR PANEL SYSTEMS**
352 By completing this section, Seller is acknowledging that the Property is serviced by a Solar Panel System, which means a system of solar
353 panels designed to absorb the sunlight as a source of energy for generating electricity or heating, any and all inverters, net meter, wiring,
354 roof supports and any other equipment pertaining to the Solar Panels (collectively, the "Solar Panel System"). This information may be
355 used, among other purposes, to prepare a Solar Panel Addendum to be affixed to and made a part of a contract of sale for the Property.
356

357 **Yes   No   Unknown**
358   []   108. When was the Solar Panel System Installed? _____
359 []   []   []   109. Are SRECs available from the Solar Panel System?
360   []   109a. If SRECs are available, when will the SRECs expire? _____
361 []   []   []   110. Is there any storage capacity on your Property for the Solar Panel System?
362 []   []   111. Are you aware of any defects in or damage to any component of the Solar Panel System? If yes,
363   explain: _____
364
365   **112. Choose one of the following three options:**
366 []   112a. The Solar Panel System is financed under a power purchase agreement or other type of financing
367   arrangement which requires me/us to make periodic payments to a Solar Panel System provider
368   in order to acquire ownership of the Solar Panel System ("PPA")? If yes, proceed to **Section A**
369   below.
370 []   112b. The Solar Panel System is the subject of a lease agreement. If yes, proceed to **Section B** below.
371 []   112c. I/we own the Solar Panel System outright. If yes, you do not have to answer any further questions.
372
373   **SECTION A - THE SOLAR PANEL SYSTEM IS SUBJECT TO A PPA**
374   []   113. What is the current periodic payment amount? $ _____
375   []   114. What is the frequency of the periodic payments (check one)?   ❏ Monthly ❏ Quarterly
376   []   115. What is the expiration date of the PPA, which is when you will become the owner of the Solar Panel
377   System? _____ ("PPA Expiration Date")
378 []   []   116. Is there a balloon payment that will become due on or before the PPA Expiration Date?
379   []   117. If there is a balloon payment, what is the amount? $ _____
380
381   **118. Choose one of the following three options:**
382 []   118a. Buyer will assume my/our obligations under the PPA at Closing.
383 []   118b. I/we will pay off or otherwise obtain cancellation of the PPA as of the Closing so that the Solar
384   Panel System can be included in the sale free and clear.
385 []   118c. I/we will remove the Solar Panel System from the Property and pay off or otherwise obtain
386   cancellation of the PPA as of the Closing.
387
388   **SECTION B - THE SOLAR PANEL SYSTEM IS SUBJECT TO A LEASE**
389   []   119.   What is the current periodic lease payment amount? $ _____
390   []   120.   What is the frequency of the periodic lease payments (check one)?   ❏ Monthly ❏ Quarterly
391   []   121.   What is the expiration date of the lease? _____
392
393   **122. Choose one of the following two options:**
394 []   122a. Buyer will assume our obligations under the lease at Closing.
395 []   122b. I/we will obtain an early termination of the lease and will remove the Solar Panel System prior to
396   Closing.
397
398 **ACKNOWLEDGMENT OF SELLER**
399 The undersigned Seller affirms that the information set forth in this Disclosure Statement is accurate and complete to the best of Seller's
400 knowledge, but is not a warranty as to the condition of the Property. Seller hereby authorizes the real estate brokerage firm representing
401 or assisting the seller to provide this Disclosure Statement to all prospective buyers of the Property, and to other real estate agents. Seller
402 alone is the source of all information contained in this statement. If the Seller relied upon any credible representations of another, the
403 Seller should state the name(s) of the person(s) who made the representation(s) and describe the information that was relied upon.
404 _____
405 _____
406 _____
407
408
409
410

Figure 10.2: Seller's Property Condition Disclosure Statement (continued)

411
412
413
414 SELLER _____ DATE _____
415
416
417
418 SELLER _____ DATE _____
419
420
421
422 SELLER _____ DATE _____
423
424
425
426 SELLER _____ DATE _____
427
428 **EXECUTOR, ADMINISTRATOR, TRUSTEE**
429 (If applicable) The undersigned has never occupied the property and lacks the personal knowledge necessary to complete this Disclosure
430 Statement.
431
432
433
434 _____ DATE _____
435
436
437
438 _____ DATE _____
439
440
441 **RECEIPT AND ACKNOWLEDGMENT BY PROSPECTIVE BUYER**
442 The undersigned Prospective Buyer acknowledges receipt of this Disclosure Statement prior to signing a Contract of Sale pertaining to
443 this Property. Prospective Buyer acknowledges that this Disclosure Statement is not a warranty by Seller and that it is Prospective Buyer's
444 responsibility to satisfy himself or herself as to the condition of the Property. Prospective Buyer acknowledges that the Property may be
445 inspected by qualified professionals, at Prospective Buyer's expense, to determine the actual condition of the Property. Prospective Buyer
446 further acknowledges that this form is intended to provide information relating to the condition of the land, structures, major systems and
447 amenities, if any, included in the sale. This form does not address local conditions which may affect a purchaser's use and enjoyment of
448 the property such as noise, odors, traffic volume, etc. Prospective Buyer acknowledges that they may independently investigate such local
449 conditions before entering into a binding contract to purchase the property. Prospective Buyer acknowledges that he or she understands
450 that the visual inspection performed by the Seller's real estate broker/broker-salesperson/salesperson does not constitute a professional
451 home inspection as performed by a licensed home inspector.
452
453
454
455 PROSPECTIVE BUYER _____ DATE _____
456
457
458
459 PROSPECTIVE BUYER _____ DATE _____
460
461
462
463 PROSPECTIVE BUYER _____ DATE _____
464
465
466
467 PROSPECTIVE BUYER _____ DATE _____
468
469
470

Figure 10.2: Seller's Property Condition Disclosure Statement (continued)

471 **ACKNOWLEDGMENT OF REAL ESTATE BROKER/BROKER-SALESPERSON/SALESPERSON**
472 The undersigned Seller's real estate broker/broker-salesperson/salesperson acknowledges receipt of the Property Disclosure Statement
473 form and that the information contained in the form was provided by the Seller.
474 The Seller's real estate broker/broker-salesperson/salesperson also confirms that he or she visually inspected the property with reasonable
475 diligence to ascertain the accuracy of the information disclosed by the seller, prior to providing a copy of the property disclosure statement
476 to the buyer.
477 The Prospective Buyer's real estate broker/broker-salesperson/salesperson also acknowledges receipt of the Property Disclosure Statement
478 form for the purpose of providing it to the Prospective Buyer.
479
480 _____   _____
481 SELLER'S REAL ESTATE BROKER/   DATE
482 BROKER-SALESPERSON/SALESPERSON:
483
484
485 _____   _____
486 PROSPECTIVE BUYER'S REAL ESTATE BROKER/   DATE
487 BROKER-SALESPERSON/SALESPERSON:

Unit 10

Attorney General's Memorandum

The attorney general of New Jersey has published a one-page official summary of the New Jersey Law Against Discrimination. The New Jersey Real Estate Commission requires brokers and salespeople to furnish *each listing owner* with a copy of this memorandum. In addition, *a licensee must refuse to take a listing from any owner who indicates an intention to violate the Law Against Discrimination*. A discussion of this law and a copy of the Attorney General's memorandum are included in Unit 4.

Expiration of Listing Period

All exclusive listings must specify a definite period of time during which the broker is to be employed, with an exact termination date.

PRICING THE PROPERTY

The pricing of the real estate is of primary importance. Even though it is the responsibility of the broker or salesperson to advise, counsel, and assist, it is ultimately the seller who must determine a listing price for his or her property. However, because the average seller usually does not have the background to make an informed decision about a fair market price, the real estate agent must be prepared to offer knowledge, information, and expertise in this area.

A broker or salesperson can help the seller determine a listing price for the property through a **comparative market analysis (CMA)**. This is a comparison of the prices of recently sold homes that are similar in location, style, and amenities to the property of the listing seller.

Although it has some resemblance to an appraisal, a CMA differs in several important ways. It is usually offered as a complimentary service by a salesperson or broker, in contrast to the paid appraisal rendered by an appraiser. Both studies analyze recent sales of similar properties, but the CMA does so in a more superficial manner. The CMA includes material not usually considered in regular appraisals: information on nearby properties that *failed* to sell, for example, and a list of competing properties currently on the market. It also includes significant *DOM* (days on market) information.

License laws dictate that a CMA must never be called a free appraisal. It should contain a statement that it "should not be considered the equivalent of any appraisal prepared by a New Jersey licensed or certified real estate appraiser." The statement must be in print with type as large as the predominant size type in the CMA. A partial comparative market analysis form is illustrated in Figure 10.3.

The broker should convey to the seller the fact that the eventual selling price is set by the buying public through the operation of supply and demand in the open market. Among factors that should not determine listing price are the original cost, assessed value, replacement cost, and the amount the seller needs to realize from the property.

Figure 10.3: Comparative Market Analysis Form

ADDRESS	STYLE	CONST.	AGE	#RMS	#BRMS	#BATHS	GAR	FPLC	POOL	C/A	SIZE PROPERTY	AREA	TAXES	COMMENTS & EXTRAS			SUGGESTED LIST PRICE
																	FAIR MARKET VALUE

1. Similar homes recently sold: These tell us what people are willing to pay . . . for this kind of home . . . in this area . . . at this time.

														CLOSED PRICE	DATE		ADJUSTED PRICE

2. Similar homes for sale now: These tell us what we are competing against. Buyers will compare your home against these homes.

														ASKING PRICE			DAYS ON MARKET

3. Expired listings — Similar homes unsold for 90 days or more: These illustrate the problems of overpricing.

														ASKING PRICE			DAYS ON MARKET

Problems of Overpricing: A. HARD to get sales people excited.
                            B. HARD to get people to make an offer.
                            C. HARD to get good buyers to look.
                            D. HARD to get financing.

Prepared by:

_____

Date _____

SUMMARY

Listing agreements are agreements by which a seller authorizes a broker to offer property for sale and agrees to pay a commission. If the listing is not written, the broker must deliver a memorandum of the agreement to the seller within five days. All listings must be taken in the name of the broker.

New Jersey recognizes three types of listings. An *open listing* may be given to any number of agents, with the commission going to the one who effects the sale. The owners may sell on their own without owing any commission.

An *exclusive-agency listing* authorizes one broker to handle the property with the owner reserving the right to sell on his or her own without paying commission.

An *exclusive-right-to-sell listing* authorizes one broker to handle the property and to receive commission if the property is sold by anyone during the listing period.

A *net listing*, illegal in New Jersey, allows the broker to keep anything received above a certain sales price set by the owner.

A *multiple listing service* is organized by a group of brokers who cooperate in the sale of each other's listings. Sellers may choose not to allow their property into multiple listing, if they wish.

Every listing must contain a definite expiration date and must be signed by all owners. A signed copy must be given to the owner immediately, along with the Attorney General's memorandum on the New Jersey Law Against Discrimination.

A broker should furnish the seller with a *comparative market analysis* to aid in establishing the listing price.

KEY TERMS REVIEW

Match the number of each key term with the corresponding letter.

_____ 1. Comparative market analysis

_____ 2. Exclusive-agency listing

_____ 3. Exclusive-right-to-sell listing

_____ 4. Multiple listing service

_____ 5. Net listing

_____ 6. Open listing

A. illegal listing; broker keeps everything above a certain figure

B. listing given to any number of brokers; only selling broker is paid

C. listing that promises broker will be paid unless owners sell on their own

D. listing that states broker will be paid no matter who sells

E. organization of brokers who work to sell each other's listings

F. price comparison for seller's use when listing

UNIT 10 REVIEW QUESTIONS

1. A seller promised a commission to Broker A if she sold the property, then turned around and made the same arrangement with Broker B. The seller must be entering into a(n)
   A. open listing.
   B. exclusive-agency listing.
   C. exclusive-right-to-sell listing.
   D. multiple listing.

2. A seller arranged to let a broker be his only broker, but when the seller sold the property himself, he owed the broker nothing. Their agreement must have been a(n)
   A. multiple listing.
   B. exclusive-agency listing.
   C. exclusive-right-to-sell listing.
   D. net listing.

3. In the preceding question, the broker could have claimed a commission if their agreement had been a(n)
   A. open listing.
   B. exclusive-agency listing.
   C. exclusive-right-to-sell listing.
   D. net listing.

4. In New Jersey, an exclusive-listing agreement must include a(n)
   A. provision that states the price the owner wishes to receive for the sale and stipulates that the brokers commission will be any amount above that price for which the property can be sold.
   B. definite termination date.
   C. lease option.
   D. option for renewal.

5. A broker entered into an oral agreement to act as broker for the sellers. To collect a commission for finding a buyer for the house, the broker must
   A. deliver a written memorandum of the agreement to the sellers, complete with all details, within five days.
   B. notify the sellers' attorney of the agreement within five days.
   C. file with the courts for payment.
   D. obtain agreement from the buyers.

6. A salesperson is taking a listing for a home owned by a married couple. The salesperson should
   A. include the reason for selling on the listing.
   B. request a bill of sale for personal items included in the sale.
   C. start the title search.
   D. obtain the signatures of both husband and wife.

7. Under a multiple-listing system, if Broker A lists the property and Broker B with another firm sells it,
   A. no commission is paid.
   B. Broker A is entitled to the full commission.
   C. Broker B receives the full commission.
   D. the commission is shared between the two offices.

8. A house was purchased in 1940 for $4,500. The elderly owner's daughter asks a broker to list it, instructing him to see if he can get as much as $85,000 "because she's heard houses have gone up in value." The broker knows the property might bring $250,000. The broker should
   A. take the listing as instructed, knowing he can produce a prompt, trouble-free sale for the daughter.
   B. buy the house himself for the full $85,000, making sure his purchase contract reveals that he is a licensed broker.
   C. buy the house only through his cousin, who has a different last name, to avoid a breach of fiduciary duty.
   D. tell the daughter that he believes the house is worth much more.

9. In the final analysis, selling price for real estate is determined by
   A. the seller.
   B. the broker.
   C. the buying public.
   D. comparative market analysis.

10. For which of the following reasons does the Attorney General require that the licensee must refuse to take a listing?
    A. Seller is overpricing the listing
    B. Seller prohibits showing the home to immigrants
    C. Seller requires 36 hour notice to show
    D. Property needs to be cleaned up

UNIT
11

Real Estate Contracts

LEARNING OBJECTIVES

When you have completed this unit, you will be able to accomplish the following.

> Describe the essential elements of a valid contract including the effect of the statute of frauds.
> Identify different types of contracts and issues that affect the validity of the contract.
> Distinguish among various contracts used in the real estate business.

KEY TERMS

addendum	equitable title	parol evidence rule
ammendment	escape clause	rescission
assignment	executed contract	specific performance
bilateral contract	executory contract	statute of frauds
breach of contract	express contract	statute of limitations
competent parties	implied contract	time is of the essence
consideration	land contract	unenforceable contract
contingency	liquidated damages	unilateral contract
contract	novation	valid contract
counteroffer	offer and acceptance	voidable contract
earnest money	option	void contract

CONTRACT LAW

Brokers and salespeople use many types of contracts and agreements in the course of their business to carry out their responsibilities to sellers, buyers, and the general public. Among these are listing agreements, sales contracts, option agreements, and leases.

The general body of law that governs the operations of such agreements is known as *contract law*. A **contract** may be defined as a voluntary agreement between legally competent parties to perform or refrain from performing some legal act, supported by legal consideration.

ESSENTIAL ELEMENTS OF A VALID CONTRACT

The essentials of a valid contract vary somewhat from state to state. Certain elements are uniformly required, however:

1. **Competent parties**—To enter into a binding contract in New Jersey, a person must be at least 18 years old and of sound mind. A married person under 18 is considered an adult. Persons under 18 may enter into a valid contract, but the contract is voidable by the minor until a reasonable time after he or she reaches the age of 18.

2. Offer and acceptance—This requirement, also called mutual assent, means that there must be a meeting of the minds on each term of the contract. The wording of the contract must express all the agreed-on terms and must be clearly understood by the parties.

3. Consideration—The agreement must be based on good or valuable **consideration**. Consideration is what the parties promise in the agreement to give to or receive from each other. Consideration may consist of legal tender, exchange of value, or love and affection. The price or amount must be definitely stated and payable in exchange for the deed or right received. In a sales contract, the consideration is the entire purchase price.

4. Legality of object—To be valid and enforceable, a contract must not involve a purpose that is illegal or against public policy.

A valid contract may be oral or written. The **parol evidence rule**, however, states that the written contract takes precedence over oral agreements or promises.

Amendments and Addenda

Either party may propose changes to the already agreed upon contract, but to be effective (binding), both parties must agree, in writing, to any change. An **amendment** is a change used by the signing parties to correct or clarify something in the original contract, such as extending the term of the agreement, changing the closing date, or even changing the sales price. An amendment does not invalidate the entire contract. The change may be made in the contract itself, often with different ink, but it can be a separate document added at the end of the contract. The change(s) must be dated and signed by all parties.

An **addendum** is a separate document that alters the terms of the original contract. Either party can originate an addendum, but it must be signed by all parties to be legally binding. Examples include inspections; HOA documents; disclosures; updates to the terms; and modifications, clarifications, or nullifications of a portion of the original agreement.

STATUTE OF FRAUDS

New Jersey's **Statute of Frauds** states that a contract for the sale of real estate (and any lease for more than three years) must be in writing and signed in order to be enforceable. In most other states, the statute requires the same thing.

Exception

In 1996, the New Jersey Statute of Frauds was changed so that it also allowed oral contracts to be enforced where there was "clear and convincing evidence" that buyer and seller had agreed orally on the exact real estate to be transferred, the "nature of the interest to be transferred, the existence of the agreement, and the identity of the transferee."

While licensees should be aware of this situation, it would be extremely risky to rely on the validity of oral contracts for the sale (or long-term lease) of real estate. To do so would be inviting litigation.

A real estate broker's authorization must be *in writing and signed* for either a sale or lease transaction, whether the broker is acting on behalf of the seller, the buyer, the landlord, or the tenant.

TYPES OF CONTRACTS

Depending on the situation and the nature or language of the agreement, a contract may be

- express or implied;
- unilateral or bilateral;
- executory or executed; and
- valid, unenforceable, voidable, or void.

Express and Implied Contracts

Depending on how a contract is created, it may be express or implied. In an **express contract**, the parties state the terms and show their intentions in words. An express contract may be either oral or written. In an **implied contract**, the agreement of the parties is demonstrated by their acts and conduct. The patron who orders a meal in a restaurant has implied a promise to pay for the food. In an agency relationship, a listing agreement is an *express* contract between the principal (buyer or seller) and the broker that names the broker as the principal's fiduciary representative.

Bilateral and Unilateral Contracts

According to the nature of the agreement made, contracts also may be classified as either bilateral or unilateral. In a **bilateral contract**, both parties promise to do something; one promise is given in exchange for another. A real estate sales contract is a bilateral contract because the seller promises to sell a parcel of real estate and deliver title to the property to the buyer, who promises to pay a certain sum of money for the property. "I will do this *and* you will do that." "Okay."

A **unilateral contract**, on the other hand, is a one-sided agreement whereby one party makes a promise to induce a second party to do something. The second party is not legally obligated to act; however, if the second party does comply, the first party is obligated to keep the promise. An option is generally considered a unilateral contract. The buyer (optionee) pays a certain fee to the seller (optionor) for the promise to convey title within a certain time frame, provided that the buyer wants to proceed. The buyer is not under obligation to buy, but the seller must sell if the buyer wishes to proceed.

Executed and Executory Contracts

A contract may be classified as either executed or executory, depending on whether the agreement is completely performed. A fully **executed contract** is one in which both parties have fulfilled their promises and thus performed the contract. An **executory contract** exists when something remains to be done by one or both parties. A real estate sales contract is executory before final settlement; after the closing, it is an executed contract.

There is also a second meaning of the term *executed* as it applies to contracts: an *executed* contract can be a signed contract; a fully executed contract would be one that has been *signed* by all parties.

Validity of Contracts

A contract can be described as *valid, void, voidable,* or *unenforceable,* depending on the circumstances. A **valid contract** contains all essential elements (discussed later in this unit) and is binding on and enforceable by both parties.

A **void contract** is one that has no legal force or effect because it does not meet the essential elements of a contract. One of the essential conditions for a contract to be valid is that it be for a legal purpose; thus, a contract to commit a crime would be void. The term is, in essence, self-contradictory; in the eyes of the law, a void contract is not a contract at all.

A **voidable contract** is one that seems on the surface to be valid but may be rescinded, or disaffirmed, by one of the parties. For example, a contract entered into with a minor usually is voidable; a minor generally is permitted to disaffirm a real estate contract within a reasonable time after reaching legal age. A voidable contract is considered by the courts to be a valid contract if the party who has the option to disaffirm the agreement does not do so within a prescribed period of time.

An **unenforceable contract** also seems on the surface to be valid; however, neither party can successfully sue the other to force performance. An unenforceable contract is said to be "valid as between the parties," because if both desire to go through with it, they can do so. For example, a man may have been drunk when he agreed to buy his friend's property. Because the man was not a competent party when he signed, the contract is not enforceable. But there is nothing to stop them from complying with its terms, if when he sobers up he still wants to go through with the purchase and the owner still wants to sell. The contract is "valid between the parties."

Undue Influence and Duress

Contracts signed by a person under duress (force) or undue influence (being taken advantage of) are voidable (may be canceled) by such person or by a court. Extreme care should be taken when one or more of the parties to a contract is elderly, sick, in great distress, or under the influence of drugs or alcohol. To be valid, every contract must be signed as the free and voluntary act of each party.

Performance of Contract

Occasionally a contract may call for a specific time at or by which the agreed-on acts must be completely performed. In addition, many contracts provide that **time is of the essence**. This means that the contract must be performed within the time limit specified, and any party who has not performed on time is guilty of a breach of contract. This powerful phrase is a two-edged sword, and licensees should leave its use to attorneys.

When a contract does not specify a date for performance, the acts it requires should be performed within a reasonable time. In the most common situation, a real estate sales contract stipulates a target date and place for closing. If that date comes and goes without settlement, the contract is still valid. Either party may later make time of the essence; again, that action should be taken only with a lawyer's advice.

Assignment and Novation

Often, after a contract has been signed, one party may want to withdraw without actually terminating the agreement. This may be accomplished through either assignment or novation.

Assignment refers to a transfer of rights and/or duties under a contract. Unless a contract specifically forbids it, rights may be assigned to a third party. Most contracts include a clause that either permits or forbids assignment.

In the case of assignment, *the assignor maintains secondary liability* if the assignee breaches the contract. A contract also may be modified by **novation**, or the substitution of a new contract for an existing agreement. The new agreement may be between the same parties or a new party may be substituted for either (this is *novation of the parties*).

In the case of novation, the old contract no longer has any force.

Discharge of Contract

A contract may be completely performed, with all terms carried out, or it may be breached (broken) if one of the parties defaults. In addition, there are various other methods by which a contract may be discharged. These include

- *partial performance* of the terms along with a written acceptance by the person for whom acts have not been done or to whom money has not been paid;

- *substantial performance*, in which one party has substantially performed the contract but does not complete all the details exactly as the contract requires (such performance may be sufficient to force payment with certain adjustments for any damages suffered by the other party);

- *impossibility of performance*, in which an act required by the contract cannot be legally accomplished;

- *mutual agreement* of the parties to cancel; and

- *operation of law*, as in the voiding of a contract by a minor, as a result of fraud, by expiration of the statute of limitations, or as a result of a contracts being altered without the written consent of all parties involved.

Default—Breach of Contract

A **breach of contract** is a violation of any of the terms or conditions of a contract without legal excuse; for example, a seller breaches a sales contract by not delivering title to the buyer under the conditions stated in the agreement.

If the seller defaults, the buyer has three alternatives:

1. The buyer may *rescind*, or *cancel*, the contract and recover the earnest money deposit.

2. The buyer may file a court suit known as an action for **specific performance**. Specific performance is a legal remedy seeking to force the other party to perform the actions they specifically promised to do in the contract. A buyer filing an action for specific performance would therefore be seeking to force the seller to sell the property as specifically promised in the contract.

3. The buyer may sue the seller for *compensatory damages*.

If the buyer defaults, the seller may pursue one of four courses:

1. The seller may *declare the contract forfeited.* The right to forfeit may be provided for in the contract, and according to the terms of the contract, the seller may be entitled to retain the earnest money and all payments received from the buyer as *liquidated damages*.

2. The seller may *rescind* the contract; that is, he or she may cancel, or terminate, the contract as if it had never been made. This requires the seller to return all payments the buyer has made.

3. The seller may sue for *specific performance*. This may require the seller to offer, or tender, a valid deed to the buyer to show the seller's compliance with the contract terms.

4. The seller may sue for *compensatory damages*.

Statute of Limitations

New Jersey allows a specific time limit of *six years* during which parties to a contract may bring legal suit to enforce their rights. Any party who does not take steps to enforce his or her rights within this **statute of limitations** may lose those rights. The *six-year* period applies to *contracts*, *foreclosures*, *mortgages*, and *cases of fraud*. *Lawsuits to recover real property* have a *ten-year* statute of limitations in New Jersey.

CONTRACTS USED IN THE REAL ESTATE BUSINESS

The written agreements most commonly encountered by brokers and salespersons are listing agreements, real estate sales contracts, and leases.

Preparation of Documents

New Jersey allows brokers (or their agents) to complete residential leases and standard approved sales contracts for one- to four-family residences and vacant single lots. To avoid the unauthorized practice of law, brokers (and their salespersons) *may not* draft commercial leases, option agreements, or sales contracts on tracts of vacant land, commercial property, or industrial property.

New Jersey Requirements

All offers, contracts, or leases prepared by licensees must indicate the business relationship the firm has with respect to parties named in the document (see 11:5-6.9 of the New Jersey Administrative Code in Appendix A).

Attached to a proposed contract of sale as a cover page must be the notice that is included as the first page of Figure 11.1, appropriately revised if the broker represents the buyer or is functioning as a dual agent or as a transaction broker. Because the broker/agent has a monetary interest in the transaction, the buyer could void the contract if this fact is not disclosed.

New Jersey also requires that the following language appear in exactly this form at the top of the first page of a sales contract:

THIS IS A LEGALLY BINDING CONTRACT THAT WILL BECOME FINAL WITHIN THREE BUSINESS DAYS. DURING THIS PERIOD YOU MAY CHOOSE TO CONSULT AN ATTORNEY WHO CAN REVIEW AND CANCEL THE CONTRACT. SEE SECTION ON ATTORNEY REVIEW FOR DETAILS.

The following section must appear within the contract:

ATTORNEY REVIEW:

1. *Study by Attorney*. *The Buyer or the Seller may choose to have an attorney study this contract. If an attorney is consulted, the attorney must complete his or her review of the contract within a three-day period. This contract will be legally binding at the end of this three-day period unless an attorney for the Buyer or the Seller reviews and disapproves of the contract.*

2. *Counting the Time*. *You count the three days from the date of delivery of the signed contract to the Buyer and the Seller. You do not count Saturdays, Sundays, or legal holidays. The Buyer and the Seller may agree in writing to extend the three-day period for attorney review.*

3. *Notice of Disapproval*. *If an attorney for the Buyer or the Seller reviews and disapproves of this contract, the attorney must notify the broker(s) and the*

other party named in this contract within the three-day period. Otherwise this contract will be legally binding as written. The attorney must send the notice of disapproval to the broker(s) by certified mail, by telegram, or by delivering it personally. The telegram or certified letter will be effective upon sending. The personal delivery will be effective upon delivery to the broker's office. The attorney may also, but need not, inform the broker(s) of any suggested revision(s) in the contract that would make it satisfactory.

The state also requires an equivalent notice on leases. Other required disclosures, such as the off-site conditions, lead-based paint, and Megan's Law disclosures, are considered part of the contract.

Federal Requirement

The buyer of residential property constructed before 1978 must be offered, in the sales contract, a 10-day opportunity to conduct a lead-based paint survey of the property, with the right to void the contract if hazardous paint is found. Buyers may choose to shorten the 10-day period or waive the right altogether.

Contract Forms

Printed forms are used for all kinds of contracts because most transactions basically are similar in nature. The use of printed forms raises three problems:

1. What to *write in the blanks*
2. What printed matter is not applicable to a particular sale and can be *ruled out* by drawing lines through the unwanted words
3. What additional clauses or agreements (called *riders*) are to be *added*

All changes and additions usually are initialed by both parties. If changes are made, the rule is that *typing* takes precedence over the *printed* form, and *handwriting* takes precedence over *typed* changes.

Listing Agreements

Listing agreements are contracts that establish the rights of the broker as agent and of the seller as principal. Explanations of the types of listing agreements were covered in Unit 10. They must indicate the business relationship the firm intends to have with the other party to the agreement.

Buyer Brokerage Agreements

Buyer brokerage agreements are contracts that establish the rights of the broker as agent and of the buyer as principal. They should clearly set forth when, in what manner, and by whom the agent is to be compensated. They must also indicate the business relationship the firm intends to have with the other party to the agreement. On the reverse side of the standard exclusive buyer agency agreement developed by the New Jersey Association of REALTORS®, there is an Informed Consent to Dual Agency agreement that must be signed by the buyer in the event a dual agency arises.

Transaction Broker and Dual Agency Agreements

N.J.A.C. 11:5-6.9 (in Appendix A) specifically regulates contracts that constitute any written agreement between a brokerage firm and a party describing the terms under which that firm is performing brokerage services as specified in the licensing laws.

Figure 11.1: Sample Sales Contract

NOTICE
TO BUYER AND SELLER
READ THIS NOTICE BEFORE SIGNING THE CONTRACT

The Law requires real estate brokers to give you the following information before you sign this contract. It requires us to tell you that you must read all of it before you sign. The purpose is to help you in this purchase or sale.

1) As a real estate broker, I represent: ☐ the seller, not the buyer;   ☐ the buyer, not the seller; ☐ both the seller and the buyer; ☐ neither the seller nor the buyer. The title company does not represent either the seller or the buyer.

2) You will not get any legal advice unless you have your own lawyer. Neither I nor anyone from the title company can give legal advice to either the buyer or the seller. If you do not hire a lawyer, no one will represent you in legal matters now or at the closing. Neither I nor the title company will represent you in those matters.

3) The contract is the most important part of the transaction. It determines your rights, risks, and obligations. Signing the contract is a big step. A lawyer would review the contract, help you to understand it, and to negotiate its terms.

4) The contract becomes final and binding unless your lawyer cancels it within the following three business days. If you do not have a lawyer, you cannot change or cancel the contract unless the other party agrees. Neither can the real estate broker nor the title insurance company change the contract.

5) Another important service of a lawyer is to order a survey, title report, or other important reports. The lawyer will review them and help to resolve any questions that may arise about the ownership and condition of the property. These reports and survey can cost you a lot of money. A lawyer will also prepare the documents needed to close title and represent you at the closing.

6) A buyer without a lawyer runs special risks. Only a lawyer can advise a buyer about what to do if problems arise concerning the purchase of this property. The problems may be about the seller's title, the size and shape of the property, or other matters that may affect the value of the property. If either the broker or the title company knows about the problems, they should tell you. But they may not recognize the problem, see it from your point of view, or know what to do. Ordinarily, the broker and the title company have an interest in seeing that the sale is completed, because only then do they usually receive their commissions. So, their interests may differ from yours.

7) Whether you retain a lawyer is up to you. It is your decision. The purpose of this notice is to make sure that you have the information needed to make your decision.

SELLER	DATE	BUYER	DATE
SELLER	DATE	BUYER	DATE
SELLER	DATE	BUYER	DATE
SELLER	DATE	BUYER	DATE

Listing Broker   Selling Broker

Prepared by: _____
                        Name of Real Estate Licensee

New Jersey REALTORS® Form 118-Statewide | 10/2020 Page 1 of 13

Figure 11.1: Sample Sales Contract (continued)

STATEWIDE NEW JERSEY REALTORS® STANDARD FORM
OF REAL ESTATE SALES CONTRACT

©2018 New Jersey REALTORS®, Inc.

THIS FORM MAY BE USED ONLY IN THE SALE OF A ONE TO FOUR-FAMILY RESIDENTIAL PROPERTY
OR VACANT ONE-FAMILY LOTS. THIS FORM IS SUITABLE FOR USE ONLY WHERE THE SELLER HAS
PREVIOUSLY EXECUTED A WRITTEN LISTING AGREEMENT.

**THIS IS A LEGALLY BINDING CONTRACT THAT WILL BECOME FINAL WITHIN THREE BUSINESS DAYS.
DURING THIS PERIOD YOU MAY CHOOSE TO CONSULT AN ATTORNEY WHO CAN REVIEW AND CANCEL THE
CONTRACT. SEE SECTION ON ATTORNEY REVIEW FOR DETAILS.**

TABLE OF CONTENTS

1. PARTIES AND PROPERTY DESCRIPTION:

_____ ("**Buyer**"), _____, ("**Buyer**"),

_____ ("**Buyer**"), _____, ("**Buyer**"),

whose address is/are _____

AGREES TO PURCHASE FROM

_____ ("**Seller**"), _____, ("**Seller**"),

_____ ("**Seller**"), _____, ("**Seller**"),

whose address is/are _____

**THROUGH THE BROKER(S) NAMED IN THIS CONTRACT AT THE PRICE AND TERMS STATED BELOW, THE
FOLLOWING PROPERTY**:

Property Address: _____

shown on the municipal tax map of _____ County_____

as Block _____ Lot _____ (**the "Property"**) Qualifier _____ (if the Property is a condominium).

THE WORDS "BUYER" AND "SELLER" INCLUDE ALL BUYERS AND SELLERS LISTED ABOVE.

2. PURCHASE PRICE:

TOTAL PURCHASE PRICE . . . . $ _____

   INITIAL DEPOSIT . . . . $_____

   ADDITIONAL DEPOSIT . . . . $ _____

   MORTGAGE . . . . $ _____

   BALANCE OF PURCHASE PRICE . . . . $ _____

Buyer's Initials: _____   Seller's Initials: _____

Figure 11.1: Sample Sales Contract (continued)

51 **3. MANNER OF PAYMENT:**
52 (A) **INITIAL DEPOSIT** to be paid by Buyer to ☐ Listing Broker ☐ Participating Broker ☐ Buyer's Attorney ☐ Title Company
53 ☐ Other _____, on or before _____ (date) (if left blank, then within five (5)
54 business days after the fully signed Contract has been delivered to both the Buyer and the Seller).
55
56 (B) **ADDITIONAL DEPOSIT** to be paid by Buyer to the party who will be responsible for holding the escrow who is identified below
57 on or before _____ (date) (if left blank, then within ten (10) calendar days after the fully signed Contract has been
58 delivered to both the Buyer and the Seller).
59
60 (C) **ESCROW:** All initial and additional deposit monies paid by Buyer shall be held in escrow in the NON-INTEREST
61 BEARING TRUST ACCOUNT of _____, ("Escrowee"), until the Closing, at which time all
62 **monies shall be paid over to Seller.** The deposit monies shall not be paid over to Seller prior to the Closing, unless otherwise agreed
63 in writing by both Buyer and Seller. If Buyer and Seller cannot agree on the disbursement of these escrow monies, the Escrowee may
64 place the deposit monies in Court requesting the Court to resolve the dispute.
65
66 (D) **IF PERFORMANCE BY BUYER IS CONTINGENT UPON OBTAINING A MORTGAGE:**
67 If payment of the purchase price requires a mortgage loan other than by Seller or other than assumption of Seller's mortgage,
68 Buyer shall apply for the loan through any lending institution of Buyer's choice in writing on lender's standard form within ten (10)
69 calendar days after the attorney-review period is completed or, if this Contract is timely disapproved by an attorney as provided in the
70 Attorney-Review Clause Section of this Contract, then within ten (10) calendar days after the parties agree to the terms of this Contract,
71 and use best efforts to obtain it. Buyer shall supply all necessary information and fees required by the proposed lender and shall authorize
72 the lender to communicate with the real estate brokers(s) and involved attorney(s). Buyer shall obtain a written commitment from the
73 lending institution to make a loan on the property under the following terms:
74
75 Principal Amount $_____ Type of Mortgage: ☐VA ☐FHA ☐Conventional ☐Section 203(k) ☐Other _____
76 Term of Mortgage: _____ years, with monthly payments based on a _____ year payment schedule.
77
78 The written mortgage commitment must be delivered to Seller's agent, who is the Listing Broker identified in Section 30, and Seller's
79 attorney, if applicable, no later than _____ (date) (if left blank, then within thirty (30) calendar days after
80 the attorney-review period is completed or, if this Contract is timely disapproved by an attorney as provided in the Attorney-Review
81 Clause Section of this Contract, then within thirty (30) calendar days after the parties agree to the terms of this Contract). Thereafter,
82 if Buyer has not obtained the commitment, then either Buyer or Seller may void this Contract by written notice to the other party and
83 Broker(s) within ten (10) calendar days of the commitment date or any extension of the commitment date, whichever is later. If this
84 Contract is voided, the deposit monies paid by Buyer shall be returned to Buyer notwithstanding any other provision in this Contract,
85 provided, however, if Seller alleges in writing to Escrowee within said ten (10) calendar days of the commitment date or any extension of
86 the commitment date, whichever is later, that the failure to obtain the mortgage commitment is the result of Buyer's bad faith, negligence,
87 intentional conduct or failure to diligently pursue the mortgage application, then Escrowee shall not return the deposit monies to Buyer
88 without the written authorization of Seller. If Buyer has applied for Section 203(k) financing this Contract is contingent upon mortgage
89 approval and the Buyer's acceptance of additional required repairs as determined by the lender.
90
91 (E) **BALANCE OF PURCHASE PRICE:** The balance of the purchase price shall be paid by Buyer in cash, or by certified, cashier's
92 or trust account check.
93
94 Payment of the balance of the purchase price by Buyer shall be made at the closing, which will take place on _____
95 _____(date) at the office of Buyer's closing agent or such other place as Seller
96 and Buyer may agree ("the Closing").
97
98 **4. SUFFICIENT ASSETS:**
99 Buyer represents that Buyer has or will have as of the Closing, all necessary cash assets, together with the mortgage loan proceeds, to
100 complete the Closing. Should Buyer not have sufficient cash assets at the Closing, Buyer will be in breach of this Contract and Seller shall
101 be entitled to any remedies as provided by law.
102
103 **5. ACCURATE DISCLOSURE OF SELLING PRICE:**
104 Buyer and Seller certify that this Contract accurately reflects the gross sale price as indicated in Section 2 of this Contract. Buyer and
105 Seller understand and agree that this information shall be disclosed to the Internal Revenue Service and other government agencies as
106 required by law.
107
108 **6. ITEMS INCLUDED IN SALE:**
109 The Property includes all fixtures permanently attached to the building(s), and all shrubbery, plantings and fencing, gas and electric
110 fixtures, cooking ranges and ovens, hot water heaters, flooring, screens, storm sashes, shades, blinds, awnings, radiator covers, heating

Buyer's
Initials: _____   Seller's
Initials: _____

Figure 11.1: Sample Sales Contract (continued)

111 apparatus and sump pumps, if any, except where owned by tenants, are included in this sale. All of the appliances shall be in working
112 order as of the Closing. Seller does not guarantee the condition of the appliances after the Deed and affidavit of title have been delivered
113 to Buyer at the Closing. The following items are also specifically included (If reference is made to the MLS Sheet and/or any other
114 document, then the document(s) referenced should be attached.):
115
116
117
118
119 **7. ITEMS EXCLUDED FROM SALE:** (If reference is made to the MLS Sheet and/or any other document, then the document(s)
120 referenced should be attached.):
121
122
123
124
125 **8. DATES AND TIMES FOR PERFORMANCE:**
126 Seller and Buyer agree that all dates and times included in this Contract are of the essence. This means that Seller and Buyer must satisfy
127 the terms of this Contract within the time limits that are set in this Contract or will be in default, except as otherwise provided in this
128 Contract or required by applicable law, including but not limited to if the Closing has to be delayed either because a lender does not timely
129 provide documents through no fault of Buyer or Seller or for three (3) business days because of the change of terms as required by the
130 Consumer Financial Protection Bureau.
131
132 If Seller requests that any addendum or other document be signed for a property it owns in connection with this Contract, "final execu-
133 tion date," "acknowledgement date," or similar language contained in such document that sets the time period for the completion of any
134 conditions or contingencies, including but not limited to inspections and financing, shall mean that the time will begin to run after the
135 attorney-review period is completed or, if this Contract is timely disapproved by an attorney as provided in the Attorney-Review Clause
136 Section of this Contract, then from the date the parties agree to the terms of this Contract.
137
138 **9. CERTIFICATE OF OCCUPANCY AND ZONING COMPLIANCE:**
139 Seller makes no representations concerning existing zoning ordinances, except that Seller's use of the Property is not presently in violation
140 of any zoning ordinances.
141
142 Some municipalities may require a Certificate of Occupancy or Housing Code Letter to be issued. If any is required for this Property,
143 Seller shall obtain it at Seller's expense and provide to Buyer prior to Closing and shall be responsible to make and pay for any repairs
144 required in order to obtain the Certificate or Letter. However, if this expense exceeds $_____ (if left blank, then 1.5% of the
145 purchase price) to Seller, then Seller may terminate this Contract and refund to Buyer all deposit monies plus Buyer's reasonable expenses,
146 if any, in connection with this transaction unless Buyer elects to make repairs in excess of said amount at Buyer's expense, in which event
147 Seller shall not have the right to terminate this Contract. In addition, Seller shall comply with all New Jersey laws, and local ordinances,
148 including but not limited to smoke detectors, carbon monoxide detectors, fire extinguishers and indoor sprinklers, the cost of which shall
149 be paid by Seller and not be considered as a repair cost.
150
151 **10. MUNICIPAL ASSESSMENTS:** (Seller represents that Seller ☐ has ☐ has not been notified of any such municipal assessments as
152 explained in this Section.)
153
154 Title shall be free and clear of all assessments for municipal improvements, including but not limited to municipal liens, as well as
155 assessments and liabilities for future assessments for improvements constructed and completed. All confirmed assessments and all
156 unconfirmed assessments that have been or may be imposed by the municipality for improvements that have been completed as of the
157 Closing are to be paid in full by Seller or credited to Buyer at the Closing. A confirmed assessment is a lien against the Property. An
158 unconfirmed assessment is a potential lien that, when approved by the appropriate governmental entity, will become a legal claim against
159 the Property.
160
161 **11. QUALITY AND INSURABILITY OF TITLE:**
162 At the Closing, Seller shall deliver a duly executed Bargain and Sale Deed with Covenant as to Grantor's Acts or other Deed satisfactory
163 to Buyer. Title to the Property will be free from all claims or rights of others, except as described in this Section and Section 12 of this
164 Contract. The Deed shall contain the full legal description of the Property.
165
166 This sale will be subject to utility and other easements and restrictions of record, if any, and such state of facts as an accurate survey
167 might disclose, provided such easement or restriction does not unreasonably limit the use of the Property. Generally, an easement is a
168 right of a person other than the owner of property to use a portion of the property for a special purpose. A restriction is a recorded
169 limitation on the manner in which a property owner may use the property. Buyer does not have to complete the purchase, however,
170 if any easement, restriction or facts disclosed by an accurate survey would substantially interfere with the use of the Property for

Buyer's
Initials: _____

Seller's
Initials: _____

Figure 11.1: Sample Sales Contract (continued)

171 residential purposes. A violation of any restriction shall not be a reason for Buyer refusing to complete the Closing as long as the title
172 company insures Buyer against loss at regular rates. The sale also will be made subject to applicable zoning ordinances, provided that
173 the ordinances do not render title unmarketable.
174
175 Title to the Property shall be good, marketable and insurable, at regular rates, by any title insurance company licensed to do business
176 in New Jersey, subject only to the claims and rights described in this Section and Section 12. Buyer agrees to order a title insurance
177 commitment (title search) and survey, if required by Buyer's lender, title company or the municipality where the Property is located,
178 and to furnish copies to Seller. If Seller's title contains any exceptions other than as set forth in this Section, Buyer shall notify Seller
179 and Seller shall have thirty (30) calendar days within which to eliminate those exceptions. Seller represents, to the best of Seller's
180 knowledge, that there are no restrictions in any conveyance or plans of record that will prohibit use and/or occupancy of the Property
181 as a _____ family residential dwelling. Seller represents that all buildings and other improvements on the Property are
182 within its boundary lines and that no improvements on adjoining properties extend across boundary lines of the Property.
183
184 If Seller is unable to transfer the quality of title required and Buyer and Seller are unable to agree upon a reduction of the purchase
185 price, Buyer shall have the option to either void this Contract, in which case the monies paid by Buyer toward the purchase price shall
186 be returned to Buyer, together with the actual costs of the title search and the survey and the mortgage application fees in preparing for
187 the Closing without further liability to Seller, or to proceed with the Closing without any reduction of the purchase price.
188
189 **12. POSSESSION, OCCUPANCY AND TENANCIES:**
190 **(A) Possession and Occupancy.**
191 Possession and occupancy will be given to Buyer at the Closing. Buyer shall be entitled to possession of the Property, and any rents or
192 profits from the Property, immediately upon the delivery of the Deed and the Closing. Seller shall pay off any person with a claim or right
193 affecting the Property from the proceeds of this sale at or before the Closing.
194
195 **(B) Tenancies.** ☐ Applicable   ☐ Not Applicable
196 Occupancy will be subject to the tenancies listed below as of the Closing. Seller represents that the tenancies are not in violation of any
197 existing Municipal, County, State or Federal rules, regulations or laws. Seller agrees to transfer all security deposits to Buyer at the Closing
198 and to provide to Brokers and Buyer a copy of all leases concerning the tenancies, if any, along with this Contract when it is signed by
199 Seller. Seller represents that such leases can be assigned and that Seller will assign said leases, and Buyer agrees to accept title subject to
200 these leases.
201
202 **TENANT'S NAME   LOCATION   RENT   SECURITY DEPOSIT   TERM**
203
204 _____
205 _____
206 _____
207
208 **13. LEAD-BASED PAINT AND/OR LEAD-BASED PAINT HAZARD: (This section is applicable only to all dwellings**
209 **built prior to 1978.)**   ☐ Applicable ☐ Not Applicable
210 **(A) Document Acknowledgement.**
211 Buyer acknowledges receipt of the EPA pamphlet entitled "Protect Your Family From Lead In Your Home." Moreover, a copy of a
212 document entitled "Disclosure of Information and Acknowledgement Lead-Based Paint and Lead-Based Paint Hazards" has been fully
213 completed and signed by Buyer, Seller and Broker(s) and is appended to and made a part of this Contract.
214
215 **(B) Lead Warning Statement.**
216 Every purchaser of any interest in residential real property on which a residential dwelling was built prior to 1978 is notified that such
217 property may present exposure to lead from lead-based paint that may place young children at risk of developing lead poisoning. Lead
218 poisoning in young children may produce permanent neurological damage, including learning disabilities, reduced intelligence quotient,
219 behavioral problems, and impaired memory. Lead poisoning also poses a particular risk to pregnant women. The seller of any interest
220 in residential real property is required to provide the buyer with any information on lead-based paint hazards from risk assessments or
221 inspections in the seller's possession and notify the buyer of any known lead-based paint hazards. A risk assessment or inspection for
222 possible lead-based paint hazards is recommended prior to purchase.
223
224 **(C) Inspection.**
225 The law requires that, unless Buyer and Seller agree to a longer or shorter period, Seller must allow Buyer a ten (10) calendar day period
226 within which to complete an inspection and/or risk assessment of the Property as set forth in the next paragraph. Buyer, however, has the
227 right to waive this requirement in its entirety.
228
229 This Contract is contingent upon an inspection and/or risk assessment (the "Inspection") of the Property by a certified inspector/risk
230 assessor for the presence of lead-based paint and/or lead-based paint hazards. The Inspection shall be ordered and obtained by Buyer at

Figure 11.1: Sample Sales Contract (continued)

231 Buyer's expense within ten (10) calendar days after the attorney-review period is completed or, if this Contract is timely disapproved by an
232 attorney as provided in the Attorney-Review Clause Section of this Contract, then within ten (10) calendar days after the parties agree to
233 the terms in this Contract ("Completion Date"). If the Inspection indicates that no lead-based paint or lead-based paint hazard is present
234 at the Property, this contingency clause shall be deemed null and void. If the Inspection indicates that lead-based paint or lead-based paint
235 hazard is present at the Property, this contingency clause will terminate at the time set forth above unless, within five (5) business days from
236 the Completion Date, Buyer delivers a copy of the inspection and/or risk assessment report to Seller and Brokers and (1) advises Seller
237 and Brokers, in writing that Buyer is voiding this Contract; or (2) delivers to Seller and Brokers a written amendment (the "Amendment")
238 to this Contract listing the specific existing deficiencies and corrections required by Buyer. The Amendment shall provide that Seller
239 agrees to (a) correct the deficiencies; and (b) furnish Buyer with a certification from a certified inspector/risk assessor that the deficiencies
240 have been corrected, before the Closing. Seller shall have _____ (if left blank, then 3) business days after receipt of the Amendment
241 to sign and return it to Buyer or send a written counter-proposal to Buyer. If Seller does not sign and return the Amendment or fails to
242 offer a counter-proposal, this Contract shall be null and void. If Seller offers a counter-proposal, Buyer shall have _____ (if left
243 blank, then 3) business days after receipt of the counter-proposal to accept it. If Buyer fails to accept the counter-proposal within the time
244 limit provided, this Contract shall be null and void.

245
246 **14. POINT-OF-ENTRY TREATMENT ("POET") SYSTEMS:** ☐ Applicable   ☐ Not Applicable
247 A point-of-entry treatment ("POET") system is a type of water treatment system used to remove contaminants from the water entering a
248 structure from a potable well, usually through a filtration process. Seller represents that a POET system has been installed to an existing
249 well on the Property and the POET system was installed and/or maintained using funds received from the New Jersey Spill Compensation
250 Fund Claims Program, N.J.S.A. 58:10-23.11, et seq. The Buyer understands that Buyer will not be eligible to receive any such funds for the
251 continued maintenance of the POET system. Pursuant to N.J.A.C. 7:1J-2.5(c), Seller agrees to notify the Department of Environmental
252 Protection within thirty (30) calendar days of executing this Contract that the Property is to be sold.

253
254 **15. CESSPOOL REQUIREMENTS:** ☐ Applicable   ☐ Not Applicable
255 **(This section is applicable if the Property has a cesspool, except in certain limited circumstances set forth in N.J.A.C.**
256 **7:9A-3.16.)** Pursuant to New Jersey's Standards for Individual Subsurface Sewage Disposal Systems, N.J.A.C. 7:9A (the "Standards"), if
257 this Contract is for the sale of real property at which any cesspool, privy, outhouse, latrine or pit toilet (collectively "Cesspool") is located,
258 the Cesspool must be abandoned and replaced with an individual subsurface sewage disposal system at or before the time of the real
259 property transfer, except in limited circumstances.

260
261 **(A)** Seller represents to Buyer that ☐ no Cesspool is located at or on the Property, or ☐ one or more Cesspools are located at or on the
262 Property. **[If there are one or more Cesspools, then also check EITHER Box 1 or 2 below.]**

263
264 1. ☐ Seller agrees that, prior to the Closing and at its sole cost and expense, Seller shall abandon and replace any and all Cesspools
265 located at or on the Property and replace such Cesspools with an individual subsurface sewage disposal system ("System") meeting all
266 the requirements of the Standards. At or prior to the Closing, Seller shall deliver to Buyer a certificate of compliance ("Certificate of
267 Compliance") issued by the administrative authority ("Administrative Authority") (as those terms are defined in N.J.A.C. 7:9A-2.1) with
268 respect to the System. Notwithstanding the foregoing, if the Administrative Authority determines that a fully compliant system cannot
269 be installed at the Property, then Seller shall notify Buyer in writing within three (3) business days of its receipt of the Administrative
270 Authority's determination of its intent to install either a nonconforming System or a permanent holding tank, as determined by the
271 Administrative Authority ("Alternate System"), and Buyer shall then have the right to void this Contract by notifying Seller in writing
272 within seven (7) business days of receipt of the notice from Seller. If Buyer fails to timely void this Contract, Buyer shall have waived its
273 right to cancel this Contract under this paragraph, and Seller shall install the Alternate System and, at or prior to the Closing, deliver
274 to Buyer such Certificate of Compliance or other evidence of approval of the Alternate System as may be issued by the Administrative
275 Authority. The delivery of said Certificate of Compliance or other evidence of approval shall be a condition precedent to the Closing; or

276
277 2. ☐ Buyer agrees that, at its sole cost and expense, Buyer shall take all actions necessary to abandon and replace any and all Cesspools
278 located at or on the Property and replace such Cesspools with a System meeting all the requirements of the Standards or an Alternate
279 System. Buyer shall indemnify and hold Seller harmless for any and all costs, damages, claims, fines, penalties and assessments (including
280 but not limited to reasonable attorneys' and experts' fees) arising from Buyer's violation of this paragraph. This paragraph shall survive
281 the Closing.

282
283 **(B)** If prior to the Closing, either Buyer or Seller becomes aware of any Cesspool at or on the Property that was not disclosed by Seller
284 at or prior to execution of this Contract, the party with knowledge of the newly identified Cesspool shall promptly, but in no event later
285 than three (3) business days after receipt of such knowledge, advise the other party of the newly identified Cesspool in writing. In such
286 event, the parties in good faith shall agree, no later than seven (7) business days after sending or receiving the written notice of the newly
287 identified Cesspool, or the day preceding the scheduled Closing, whichever is sooner, to proceed pursuant to subsection (A) 1 or 2 above
288 or such other agreement as satisfies the Standards, or either party may terminate this Contract.

289
290

Buyer's
Initials: _____   Seller's
Initials: _____

Figure 11.1: Sample Sales Contract (continued)

16. INSPECTION CONTINGENCY CLAUSE:

(A) Responsibilities of Home Ownership.

Buyer and Seller acknowledge and agree that, because the purchase of a home is one of the most significant investments a person can make in a lifetime, all aspects of this transaction require considerable analysis and investigation by Buyer before closing title to the Property. While Brokers and salespersons who are involved in this transaction are trained as licensees under the New Jersey Licensing Act they readily acknowledge that they have had no special training or experience with respect to the complexities pertaining to the multitude of structural, topographical and environmental components of this Property. For example, and not by way of limitation, Brokers and salespersons have no special training, knowledge or experience with regard to discovering and/or evaluating physical defects, including structural defects, roof, basement, mechanical equipment, such as heating, air conditioning, and electrical systems, sewage, plumbing, exterior drainage, termite, and other types of insect infestation or damage caused by such infestation. Moreover, Brokers and salespersons similarly have no special training, knowledge or experience with regard to evaluation of possible environmental conditions which might affect the Property pertaining to the dwelling, such as the existence of radon gas, formaldehyde gas, airborne asbestos fibers, toxic chemicals, underground storage tanks, lead, mold or other pollutants in the soil, air or water.

(B) Radon Testing, Reports and Mitigation.

(Radon is a radioactive gas which results from the natural breakdown of uranium in soil, rock and water. It has been found in homes all over the United States and is a carcinogen. For more information on radon, go to www.epa.gov/radon/pubs/citguide.html and www.nj.gov/dep/rpp/radon or call the NJ Radon Hot Line at 800-648-0394 or 609-984-5425.)

If the Property has been tested for radon prior to the date of this Contract, Seller agrees to provide to Buyer, at the time of the execution of this Contract, a copy of the result of the radon test(s) and evidence of any subsequent radon mitigation or treatment of the Property. In any event, Buyer shall have the right to conduct a radon inspection/test as provided and subject to the conditions set forth in paragraph (D) below. If any test results furnished or obtained by Buyer indicate a concentration level of 4 picocuries per liter (4.0 pCi/L) or more in the subject dwelling, Buyer shall then have the right to void this Contract by notifying Seller in writing within seven (7) business days of the receipt of any such report. For the purposes of this Section 16, Seller and Buyer agree that, in the event a radon gas concentration level in the subject dwelling is determined to be less than 4 picocuries per liter (4.0 pCi/L) without any remediation, such level of radon gas concentration shall be deemed to be an acceptable level ("Acceptable Level") for the purposes of this Contract. Under those circumstances, Seller shall be under no obligation to remediate, and this contingency clause as it relates to radon shall be deemed fully satisfied.

If Buyer's qualified inspector reports that the radon gas concentration level in the subject dwelling is four picocuries per liter (4.0 pCi/L) or more, Seller shall have a seven (7) business day period after receipt of such report to notify Buyer in writing that Seller agrees to remediate the gas concentration to an Acceptable Level (unless Buyer has voided this Contract as provided in the preceding paragraph). Upon such remediation, the contingency in this Contract which relates to radon shall be deemed fully satisfied. If Seller fails to notify Buyer of Seller's agreement to so remediate, such failure to so notify shall be deemed to be a refusal by Seller to remediate the radon level to an Acceptable Level, and Buyer shall then have the right to void this Contract by notifying Seller in writing within seven (7) calendar days thereafter. If Buyer fails to void this Contract within the seven (7) business day period, Buyer shall have waived Buyer's right to cancel this Contract and this Contract shall remain in full force and effect, and Seller shall be under no obligation to remediate the radon gas concentration. If Seller agrees to remediate the radon to an Acceptable Level, such remediation and associated testing shall be completed by Seller prior to the Closing.

(C) Infestation and/or Damage By Wood Boring Insects.

Buyer shall have the right to have the Property inspected by a licensed exterminating company of Buyer's choice, for the purpose of determining if the Property is free from infestation and damage from termites or other wood destroying insects. If Buyer chooses to make this inspection, Buyer shall pay for the inspection unless Buyer's lender prohibits Buyer from paying, in which case Seller shall pay. The inspection must be completed and written reports must be furnished to Seller and Broker(s) within ____ (if left blank, then 14) calendar days after the attorney-review period is completed or, if this Contract is timely disapproved by an attorney as provided in the Attorney-Review Clause Section of this Contract, then within ____ (if left blank, then 14) calendar days after the parties agree to the terms of this Contract. This report shall state the nature and extent of any infestation and/or damage and the full cost of treatment for any infestation. Seller agrees to treat any infestation and cure any damage at Seller's expense prior to Closing, provided, however, if the cost to cure exceeds 1% of the purchase price of the Property, then either party may void this Contract provided they do so within ____ (if left blank, then 7) business days after the report has been delivered to Seller and Brokers. If Buyer and Seller are unable to agree upon who will pay for the cost to cure and neither party timely voids this Contract, then Buyer will be deemed to have waived its right to terminate this Contract and will bear the cost to cure that is over 1% of the purchase price, with Seller bearing the cost that is under 1% of the purchase price.

(D) Buyer's Right to Inspections.

Buyer acknowledges that the Property is being sold in an "as is" condition and that this Contract is entered into based upon the knowledge of Buyer as to the value of the land and whatever buildings are upon the Property, and not on any representation made by Seller, Brokers or their agents as to character or quality of the Property. Therefore, Buyer, at Buyer's sole cost and expense, is granted the right to have the dwelling and all other aspects of the Property, inspected and evaluated by "qualified inspectors" (as the term is defined in subsection G below) for the purpose of determining the existence of any physical defects or environmental conditions such as outlined above. If Buyer

Buyer's Initials: _____ Seller's Initials: _____

Figure 11.1: Sample Sales Contract (continued)

351 chooses to make inspections referred to in this paragraph, such inspections must be completed, and written reports including a list of
352 repairs Buyer is requesting must be furnished to Seller and Brokers within _____ (if left blank, then 14) calendar days after the attorney-
353 review period is completed or, if this Contract is timely disapproved by an attorney as provided in the Attorney-Review Clause Section
354 of this Contract, then within _____ (if left blank, then 14) calendar days after the parties agree to the terms of this Contract. If Buyer fails
355 to furnish such written reports to Seller and Brokers within the _____ (if left blank, then 14) calendar days specified in this paragraph,
356 this contingency clause shall be deemed waived by Buyer, and the Property shall be deemed acceptable by Buyer. The time period for
357 furnishing the inspection reports is referred to as the "Inspection Time Period." Seller shall have all utilities in service for inspections.
358
359 **(E) Responsibility to Cure.**
360 If any physical defects or environmental conditions (other than radon or woodboring insects) are reported by the qualified inspectors to
361 Seller within the Inspection Time Period, Seller shall then have seven (7) business days after the receipt of such reports to notify Buyer
362 in writing that Seller shall correct or cure any of the defects set forth in such reports. If Seller fails to notify Buyer of Seller's agreement
363 to so cure and correct, such failure to so notify shall be deemed to be a refusal by Seller to cure or correct such defects. If Seller fails to
364 agree to cure or correct such defects within the seven (7) business day period, or if the environmental condition at the Property (other
365 than radon) is incurable and is of such significance as to unreasonably endanger the health of Buyer, Buyer shall then have the right to
366 void this Contract by notifying Seller in writing within seven (7) business days thereafter. If Buyer fails to void this Contract within the
367 seven (7) business day period, Buyer shall have waived Buyer's right to cancel this Contract and this Contract shall remain in full force,
368 and Seller shall be under no obligation to correct or cure any of the defects set forth in the inspections. If Seller agrees to correct or cure
369 such defects, all such repair work shall be completed by Seller prior to the closing of title. Radon at the Property shall be governed by
370 the provisions of subsection (B), above.
371
372 **(F) Flood Hazard Area (if applicable).**
373 The federal and state governments have designated certain areas as flood areas. If the Property is located in a flood area, the use of the
374 Property may be limited. If Buyer's inquiry reveals that the Property is in a flood area, Buyer may cancel this Contract within ten (10)
375 calendar days after the attorney-review period is completed or, if this Contract is timely disapproved by an attorney as provided in the
376 Attorney-Review Clause Section of this Contract, then within ten (10) calendar days after the parties agree to the terms of this Contract.
377 If the mortgage lender requires flood insurance, then Buyer shall be responsible for obtaining such insurance on the Property. For a flood
378 policy to be in effect immediately, there must be a loan closing. There is a thirty (30) calendar day wait for flood policies to be in effect for
379 cash transactions. Therefore, cash buyers are advised to make application and make advance payment for a flood policy at least thirty
380 (30) calendar days in advance of closing if they want coverage to be in effect upon transfer of title.
381
382 Buyer's mortgage lender may require Buyer to purchase flood insurance in connection with Buyer's purchase of this Property. The
383 National Flood Insurance Program ("NFIP") provides for the availability of flood insurance but also establishes flood insurance policy
384 premiums based on the risk of flooding in the area where properties are located. Due to amendments to federal law governing the
385 NFIP, those premiums are increasing and, in some cases, will rise by a substantial amount over the premiums previously charged for
386 flood insurance for the Property. As a result, Buyer should not rely on the premiums paid for flood insurance on this Property previously
387 as an indication of the premiums that will apply after Buyer completes the purchase. In considering Buyer's purchase of this Property,
388 Buyer is therefore urged to consult with one or more carriers of flood insurance for a better understanding of flood insurance coverage,
389 the premiums that are likely to be required to purchase such insurance and any available information about how those premiums may
390 increase in the future.
391
392 **(G) Qualifications of Inspectors.**
393 Where the term "qualified inspectors" is used in this Contract, it is intended to refer to persons or businesses that are licensed or certified
394 by the State of New Jersey for such purpose.
395
396 **17. MEGAN'S LAW STATEMENT:**
397 Under New Jersey law, the county prosecutor determines whether and how to provide notice of the presence of convicted sex offenders
398 in an area. In their professional capacity, real estate licensees are not entitled to notification by the county prosecutor under Megan's Law
399 and are unable to obtain such information for you. Upon closing, the county prosecutor may be contacted for such further information
400 as may be disclosable to you.
401
402 **18. MEGAN'S LAW REGISTRY:**
403 Buyer is notified that New Jersey law establishes an Internet Registry of Sex Offenders that may be accessed at www.njsp.org. Neither
404 Seller nor any real estate broker nor salesperson make any representation as to the accuracy of the registry.
405
406 **19. NOTIFICATION REGARDING OFF-SITE CONDITIONS: (Applicable to all resale transactions.)**
407 Pursuant to the New Residential Construction Off-Site Conditions Disclosure Act, N.J.S.A. 46:3C-1, et. seq, the clerks of municipalities
408 in New Jersey maintain lists of off-site conditions which may affect the value of residential properties in the vicinity of the off-site
409 condition. Buyers may examine the lists and are encouraged to independently investigate the area surrounding this property in order
410

New Jersey REALTORS® Form 118-Statewide | 10/2020 Page 8 of 13

Buyer's
Initials: _____

Seller's
Initials: _____

Figure 11.1: Sample Sales Contract (continued)

411 to become familiar with any off-site conditions which may affect the value of the property. In cases where a property is located near the
412 border of a municipality, buyers may wish to also examine the list maintained by the neighboring municipality.
413
414 **20. AIR SAFETY AND ZONING NOTICE:**
415 Any person who sells or transfers a property that is in an airport safety zone as set forth in the New Jersey Air Safety and Zoning Act of
416 1983, N.J.S.A. 6:1-80, et seq., and appearing on a municipal map used for tax purposes, as well as Seller's agent, shall provide notice to
417 a prospective buyer that the property is located in an airport safety zone prior to the signing of the contract of sale. The Air Safety and
418 Zoning Act also requires that each municipality in an airport safety zone enact an ordinance or ordinances incorporating the standards
419 promulgated under the Act and providing for their enforcement within the delineated areas in the municipality. Buyer acknowledges
420 receipt of the following list of airports and the municipalities that may be affected by them and that Buyer has the responsibility to
421 contact the municipal clerk of any affected municipality concerning any ordinance that may affect the Property.
422

Municipality	Airport(s)	Municipality	Airport(s)
Alexandria Tp.	Alexandria & Sky Manor	Manalapan Tp. (Monmouth Cty.)	Old Bridge
Andover Tp.	Aeroflex-Andover & Newton	Mansfield Tp.	Hackettstown
Bedminster Tp.	Somerset	Manville Bor.	Central Jersey Regional
Berkeley Tp.	Ocean County	Medford Tp.	Flying W
Berlin Bor.	Camden County	Middle Tp.	Cape May County
Blairstown Tp.	Blairstown	Millville	Millville Municipal
Branchburg Tp.	Somerset	Monroe Tp. (Gloucester Cty.)	Cross Keys & Southern Cross
Buena Bor. (Atlantic Cty.)	Vineland-Downtown	Monroe Tp. (Middlesex Cty.)	Old Bridge
Dennis Tp.	Woodbine Municipal	Montgomery Tp.	Princeton
Eagleswood Tp.	Eagles Nest	Ocean City	Ocean City
Ewing Tp.	Trenton-Mercer County	Old Bridge Tp.	Old Bridge
E. Hanover Tp.	Morristown Municipal	Oldmans Tp.	Oldmans
Florham Park Bor.	Morristown Municipal	Pemberton Tp.	Pemberton
Franklin Tp. (Gloucester Cty.)	Southern Cross & Vineland Downtown	Pequannock Tp.	Lincoln Park
Franklin Tp. (Hunterdon Cty.)	Sky Manor	Readington Tp.	Solberg-Hunterdon
Franklin Tp. (Somerset Cty.)	Central Jersey Regional	Rocky Hill Boro.	Princeton
Hammonton Bor.	Hammonton Municipal	Southampton Tp.	Red Lion
Hanover Tp.	Morristown Municipal	Springfield Tp.	Red Wing
Hillsborough Tp.	Central Jersey Regional	Upper Deerfield Tp.	Bucks
Hopewell Tp. (Mercer Cty.)	Trenton-Mercer County	Vineland City	Kroelinger & Vineland Downtown
Howell Tp.	Monmouth Executive	Wall Tp.	Monmouth Executive
Lacey Tp.	Ocean County	Wantage Tp.	Sussex
Lakewood Tp.	Lakewood	Robbinsville	Trenton-Robbinsville
Lincoln Park Bor.	Lincoln Park	West Milford Tp.	Greenwood Lake
Lower Tp.	Cape May County	Winslow Tp.	Camden County
Lumberton Tp.	Flying W & South Jersey Regional	Woodbine Bor.	Woodbine Municipal

450 The following airports are not subject to the Airport Safety and Zoning Act because they are subject to federal regulation or within the
451 jurisdiction of the Port of Authority of New York and New Jersey and therefore are not regulated by New Jersey: Essex County Airport,
452 Linden Airport, Newark Liberty Airport, Teterboro Airport, Little Ferry Seaplane Base, Atlantic City International Airport, and
453 Maguire Airforce Base and NAEC Lakehurst.
454
455 **21. BULK SALES:**
456 The New Jersey Bulk Sales Law, N.J.S.A. 54:50-38, (the "Law") applies to the sale of certain residential property. Under the Law,
457 Buyer may be liable for taxes owed by Seller if the Law applies and Buyer does not deliver to the Director of the New Jersey Division
458 of Taxation (the "Division") a copy of this Contract and a notice on a form required by the Division (the "Tax Form") at least ten
459 (10) business days prior to the Closing. If Buyer decides to deliver the Tax Form to the Division, Seller shall cooperate with Buyer by
460 promptly providing Buyer with any information that Buyer needs to complete and deliver the Tax Form in a timely manner. Buyer
461 promptly shall deliver to Seller a copy of any notice that Buyer receives from the Division in response to the Tax Form.
462
463 The Law does not apply to the sale of a simple dwelling house, or the sale or lease of a seasonal rental property, if Seller is an
464 individual, estate or trust, or any combination thereof, owning the simple dwelling house or seasonal rental property as joint tenants,
465 tenants in common or tenancy by the entirety. A simple dwelling house is a one or two family residential building, or a cooperative or
466 condominium unit used as a residential dwelling, none of which has any commercial property. A seasonal rental property is a time
467 share, or a dwelling unit that is rented for residential purposes for a term of not more than 125 consecutive days, by an owner that has a
468 permanent residence elsewhere.
469
470 If, prior to the Closing, the Division notifies Buyer to withhold an amount (the "Tax Amount") from the purchase price proceeds for

Buyer's Initials: _____   Seller's Initials: _____

Figure 11.1: Sample Sales Contract (continued)

471   possible unpaid tax liabilities of Seller, Buyer's attorney or Buyer's title insurance company (the "Escrow Agent") shall withhold the Tax
472   Amount from the closing proceeds and place that amount in escrow (the "Tax Escrow"). If the Tax Amount exceeds the amount of
473   available closing proceeds, Seller shall bring the deficiency to the Closing and the deficiency shall be added to the Tax Escrow. If the
474   Division directs the Escrow Agent or Buyer to remit funds from the Tax Escrow to the Division or some other entity, the Escrow Agent
475   or Buyer shall do so. The Escrow Agent or Buyer shall only release the Tax Escrow, or the remaining balance thereof, to Seller (or as
476   otherwise directed by the Division) upon receipt of written notice from the Division that it can be released, and that no liability will be
477   asserted under the Law against Buyer.

478

479   **22. NOTICE TO BUYER CONCERNING INSURANCE:**
480   Buyer should obtain appropriate casualty and liability insurance for the Property. Buyer's mortgage lender will require that such insurance
481   be in place at Closing. Occasionally, there are issues and delays in obtaining insurance. Be advised that a "binder" is only a temporary
482   commitment to provide insurance coverage and is not an insurance policy. Buyer is therefore urged to contact a licensed insurance agent
483   or broker to assist Buyer in satisfying Buyer's insurance requirements.

484

485   **23. MAINTENANCE AND CONDITION OF PROPERTY:**
486   Seller agrees to maintain the grounds, buildings and improvements, in good condition, subject to ordinary wear and tear. The premises
487   shall be in "broom clean" condition and free of debris as of the Closing. Seller represents that all electrical, plumbing, heating and air
488   conditioning systems (if applicable), together with all fixtures included within the terms of the Contract now work and shall be in proper
489   working order at the Closing. Seller further states, that to the best of Seller's knowledge, there are currently no leaks or seepage in the
490   roof, walls or basement. Seller does not guarantee the continuing condition of the premises as set forth in this Section after the Closing.

491

492   **24. RISK OF LOSS:**
493   The risk of loss or damage to the Property by fire or otherwise, except ordinary wear and tear, is the responsibility of Seller until
494   the Closing.

495

496   **25. INITIAL AND FINAL WALK-THROUGHS:**
497   In addition to the inspections set forth elsewhere in this Contract, Seller agrees to permit Buyer or Buyer's duly authorized
498   representative to conduct an initial and a final walk-through inspection of the interior and exterior of the Property at any reasonable
499   time before the Closing. Seller shall have all utilities in service for the inspections.

500

501   **26. ADJUSTMENTS AT CLOSING:**
502   Seller shall pay for the preparation of the Deed, realty transfer fee, lien discharge fees, if any, and one-half of the title company charges
503   for disbursements and attendance allowed by the Commissioner of Insurance; but all searches, title insurance premium and other
504   conveyancing expenses are to be paid for by Buyer.

505

506   Seller and Buyer shall make prorated adjustments at Closing for items which have been paid by Seller or are due from Seller, such as real
507   estate taxes, water and sewer charges that could be claims against the Property, rental and security deposits, association and condominium
508   dues, and fuel in Seller's tank. Adjustments of fuel shall be based upon physical inventory and pricing by Seller's supplier. Such determi-
509   nation shall be conclusive.

510

511   If Buyer is assuming Seller's mortgage loan, Buyer shall credit Seller for all monies, such as real estate taxes and insurance premiums paid
512   in advance or on deposit with Seller's mortgage lender. Buyer shall receive a credit for monies, which Seller owes to Seller's Mortgage
513   lender, such as current interest or a deficit in the mortgage escrow account.

514

515   If the Property is used or enjoyed by not more than four families and the purchase price exceeds $1,000,000, then pursuant to N.J.S.A.
516   46:15-7.2, Buyer will be solely responsible for payment of the fee due for the transfer of the Property, which is the so-called "Mansion
517   Tax", in the amount of one (1%) percent of the purchase price.

518

519   Unless an exemption applies, non-resident individuals, estates, or trusts that sell or transfer real property in New Jersey are required to
520   make an estimated gross income tax payment to the State of New Jersey on the gain from a transfer/sale of real property (the so-called
521   "Exit Tax,") as a condition of the recording of the deed.

522

523   If Seller is a foreign person (an individual, corporation or entity that is a non-US resident) under the Foreign Investment in Real
524   Property Tax Act of 1980, as amended ("FIRPTA"), then with a few exceptions, a portion of the proceeds of sale may need to be
525   withheld from Seller and paid to the Internal Revenue Service as an advance payment against Seller's tax liability.

526

527   Seller agrees that, if applicable, Seller will (a) be solely responsible for payment of any state or federal income tax withholding amount(s)
528   required by law to be paid by Seller (which Buyer may deduct from the purchase price and pay at the Closing); and (b) execute
529   and deliver to Buyer at the Closing any and all forms, affidavits or certifications required under state and federal law to be filed in
530   connection with the amount(s) withheld.

Buyer's
Initials: _____

Seller's
Initials: _____

Figure 11.1: Sample Sales Contract (continued)

531 There shall be no adjustment on any Homestead Rebate due or to become due.
532

533 **27. FAILURE OF BUYER OR SELLER TO CLOSE:**
534 If Seller fails to close title to the Property in accordance with this Contract, Buyer then may commence any legal or equitable action
535 to which Buyer may be entitled. If Buyer fails to close title in accordance with this Contract, Seller then may commence an action
536 for damages it has suffered, and, in such case, the deposit monies paid on account of the purchase price shall be applied against such
537 damages. If Buyer or Seller breach this Contract, the breaching party will nevertheless be liable to Brokers for the commissions in the
538 amount set forth in this Contract, as well as reasonable attorneys' fees, costs and such other damages as are determined by the Court.
539

540 **28. CONSUMER INFORMATION STATEMENT ACKNOWLEDGMENT:**
541 By signing below, Seller and Buyer acknowledge they received the Consumer Information Statement on New Jersey Real Estate
542 Relationships from the Broker(s) prior to the first showing of the Property.
543

544 **29. DECLARATION OF BROKER(S)'S BUSINESS RELATIONSHIP(S):**
545 (A)_____, (name of firm) and its authorized
546 representative(s) _____
547 _____
548 (name(s) of licensee(s))
549

550 **ARE OPERATING IN THIS TRANSACTION AS A (indicate one of the following)**
551 ☐ **SELLER'S AGENT**   ☐ **BUYER'S AGENT**   ☐ **DISCLOSED DUAL AGENT**   ☐ **TRANSACTION BROKER.**
552

553 **(B) (If more than one firm is participating, provide the following.) INFORMATION SUPPLIED BY**_____
554 _____ (name of other firm.) **HAS INDICATED THAT IT IS**
555 **OPERATING IN THIS TRANSACTION AS A (indicate one of the following)**
556 ☐ **SELLER'S AGENT**   ☐ **BUYER'S AGENT**   ☐ **TRANSACTION BROKER.**
557

558 **30. BROKERS' INFORMATION AND COMMISSION:**
559 The commission, in accord with the previously executed listing agreement, shall be due and payable at the Closing and payment by Buyer
560 of the purchase consideration for the Property. Seller hereby authorizes and instructs whomever is the disbursing agent to pay the full
561 commission as set forth below to the below-mentioned Brokerage Firm(s) out of the proceeds of sale prior to the payment of any such
562 funds to Seller. Buyer consents to the disbursing agent making said disbursements. The commission shall be paid upon the purchase price
563 set forth in Section 2 and shall include any amounts allocated to, among other things, furniture and fixtures.
564

565

566 **Listing Firm**_____   REC License ID_____
567

568

569 **Listing Agent**_____   REC License ID_____
570

571 Address_____
572

573

574 Office Telephone_____   Fax_____   Agent Cell Phone_____
575   (Per Listing Agreement)
576 E-mail_____   **Commission due Listing Firm**_____
577

578

579 **Participating Firm**_____   REC License ID_____
580

581 **Participating Agent**_____   REC License ID_____
582

583

584 Address_____
585

586 Office Telephone_____   Fax_____   Agent Cell Phone_____
587

588

589 E-mail_____   **Commission due Participating Firm**_____
590

Buyer's
Initials: _____

Seller's
Initials: _____

Figure 11.1: Sample Sales Contract (continued)

591
592
593
594
595
596
597
598
599
600
601
602
603
604
605
606
607
608
609
610
611
612
613
614
615
616
617
618
619
620
621
622
623
624
625
626
627
628
629
630
631
632
633
634
635
636
637
638
639
640
641
642
643
644
645
646
647
648
649
650

31. EQUITABLE LIEN:

Under New Jersey law, brokers who bring the parties together in a real estate transaction are entitled to an equitable lien in the amount of their commission. This lien attaches to the property being sold from when the contract of sale is signed until the closing and then to the funds due to seller at closing, and is not contingent upon the notice provided in this Section. As a result of this lien, the party who disburses the funds at the Closing in this transaction should not release any portion of the commission to any party other than Broker(s) and, if there is a dispute with regard to the commission to be paid, should hold the disputed amount in escrow until the dispute with Broker(s) is resolved and written authorization to release the funds is provided by Broker(s).

32. DISCLOSURE THAT BUYER OR SELLER IS A REAL ESTATE LICENSEE: ☐ Applicable ☐ Not Applicable

A real estate licensee in New Jersey who has an interest as a buyer or seller of real property is required to disclose in the sales contract that the person is a licensee. _____ therefore discloses that he/she is licensed in New Jersey as a real estate ☐ broker ☐ broker-salesperson ☐ salesperson ☐ referral agent.

33. BROKERS TO RECEIVE CLOSING DISCLOSURE AND OTHER DOCUMENTS:

Buyer and Seller agree that Broker(s) involved in this transaction will be provided with the Closing Disclosure documents and any amendments to those documents in the same time and manner as the Consumer Financial Protection Bureau requires that those documents be provided to Buyer and Seller. In addition, Buyer and Seller agree that, if one or both of them hire an attorney who disapproves this Contract as provided in the Attorney-Review Clause Section, then the attorney(s) will notify the Broker(s) in writing when either this Contract is finalized or the parties decide not to proceed with the transaction.

34. PROFESSIONAL REFERRALS:

Seller and Buyer may request the names of attorneys, inspectors, engineers, tradespeople or other professionals from their Brokers involved in the transaction. Any names provided by Broker(s) shall not be deemed to be a recommendation or testimony of competency of the person or persons referred. Seller and Buyer shall assume full responsibility for their selection(s) and hold Brokers and/or salespersons harmless for any claim or actions resulting from the work or duties performed by these professionals.

35. ATTORNEY-REVIEW CLAUSE:

(1) Study by Attorney.

Buyer or Seller may choose to have an attorney study this Contract. If an attorney is consulted, the attorney must complete his or her review of the Contract within a three-day period. This Contract will be legally binding at the end of this three-day period unless an attorney for Buyer or Seller reviews and disapproves of the Contract.

(2) Counting the Time.

You count the three days from the date of delivery of the signed Contract to Buyer and Seller. You do not count Saturdays, Sundays or legal holidays. Buyer and Seller may agree in writing to extend the three-day period for attorney review.

(3) Notice of Disapproval.

If an attorney for the Buyer or Seller reviews and disapproves of this Contract, the attorney must notify the Broker(s) and the other party named in this Contract within the three-day period. Otherwise this Contract will be legally binding as written. The attorney must send the notice of disapproval to the Broker(s) by fax, email, personal delivery, or overnight mail with proof of delivery. Notice by overnight mail will be effective upon mailing. The personal delivery will be effective upon delivery to the Broker's office. The attorney may also, but need not, inform the Broker(s) of any suggested revision(s) in the Contract that would make it satisfactory.

36. NOTICES:

All notices shall be by certified mail, fax, email, recognized overnight courier or electronic document (except for notices under the Attorney-Review Clause Section) or by delivering it personally. The certified letter, email, reputable overnight carrier, fax or electronic document will be effective upon sending. Notices to Seller and Buyer shall be addressed to the addresses in Section 1, unless otherwise specified in writing by the respective party.

37. NO ASSIGNMENT:

This Contract shall not be assigned without the written consent of Seller. This means that Buyer may not transfer to anyone else Buyer's rights under this Contract to purchase the Property.

38. ELECTRONIC SIGNATURES AND DOCUMENTS:

Buyer and Seller agree that the New Jersey Uniform Electronic Transaction Act, N.J.S.A. 12A:12-1 to 26, applies to this transaction, including but not limited to the parties and their representatives having the right to use electronic signatures and electronic documents that are created, generated, sent, communicated, received or stored in connection with this transaction. Since Section 11 of the Act provides that acknowledging an electronic signature is not necessary for the signature of such a person where all other information required to be included is attached to or logically associated with the signature or record, such electronic signatures, including but not limited to an electronic signature of one of the parties to this Contract, do not have to be witnessed.

Buyer's Initials: _____   Seller's Initials: _____

Figure 11.1: Sample Sales Contract (continued)

39. CORPORATE RESOLUTIONS:

If Buyer or Seller is a corporate or other entity, the person signing below on behalf of the entity represents that all required corporate resolutions have been duly approved and the person has the authority to sign on behalf of the entity.

40. ENTIRE AGREEMENT; PARTIES LIABLE:

This Contract contains the entire agreement of the parties. No representations have been made by any of the parties, the Broker(s) or its salespersons, except as set forth in this Contract. This Contract is binding upon all parties who sign it and all who succeed to their rights and responsibilities and only may be amended by an agreement in writing signed by Buyer and Seller.

41. APPLICABLE LAWS:

This Contract shall be governed by and construed in accordance with the laws of the State of New Jersey and any lawsuit relating to this Contract or the underlying transaction shall be venued in the State of New Jersey.

42. ADDENDA:

The following additional terms are included in the attached addenda or riders and incorporated into this Contract (check if applicable):

☐ Buyer's Property Sale Contingency ☐ Private Well Testing
☐ Condominium/Homeowner's Associations ☐ Properties With Three (3) or More Units
☐ Coronavirus ☐ Seller Concession
☐ FHA/VA Loans ☐ Short Sale
☐ Lead Based Paint Disclosure (Pre-1978) ☐ Solar Panel
☐ New Construction ☐ Swimming Pools
☐ Private Sewage Disposal (Other than Cesspool) ☐ Underground Fuel Tank(s)

43. ADDITIONAL CONTRACTUAL PROVISIONS:

WITNESS:

_____   _____   _____
                                BUYER   Date

_____   _____   _____
                                BUYER   Date

_____   _____   _____
                                BUYER   Date

_____   _____   _____
                                BUYER   Date

_____   _____   _____
                                SELLER   Date

_____   _____   _____
                                SELLER   Date

_____   _____   _____
                                SELLER   Date

                                _____   _____
                                SELLER   Date

Sales Contracts

A real estate sales contract sets forth all details of the agreement between a buyer and a seller for the purchase and sale of a parcel of real estate. Depending on the locality, this agreement may take one of a number of forms and be known as an *offer to purchase, contract of purchase and sale, earnest money agreement, binder and deposit receipt*, or other variations of these titles. Figure 11.1 illustrates a form of contract often used in New Jersey.

The contract of sale is the most important document in the sale of real estate because it sets out in detail the agreement between the buyer and the seller and establishes their legal rights and obligations.

The contract, in effect, *dictates the contents of the deed.*

Offer and Acceptance

One of the essential elements of a valid contract of sale is a *meeting of the minds* whereby the buyer and seller agree on the terms of the sale. This usually is accomplished through the process of **offer and acceptance**.

A broker lists an owner's real estate for sale at the price and conditions set by the owner. A prospective buyer is found who wants to purchase the property at those terms or some other terms.

An offer to purchase is drawn up, signed by the prospective buyer, and presented by the broker to the seller. This is an *offer*. If the seller agrees to the offer *exactly* as it was made and signs the contract, the offer has been *accepted* and the contract is *valid*, pending attorney review. The broker then must advise the buyer of the seller's acceptance, obtain attorney's review if the parties wish, and deliver a duplicate original of the contract to each party.

Any attempt by the seller to change the terms proposed by the buyer creates a **counteroffer**. The buyer is relieved of his or her original offer because the seller has, in effect, rejected it. The buyer can accept the seller's counteroffer or can reject it and, if he or she wishes, make another counteroffer. Any change in the last offer made results in a counteroffer, until one party finally agrees to the other party's last offer and both parties sign the final contract (see Figure 11.2).

Figure 11.2: The Negotiation Process: Offer, Counteroffer, and Acceptance

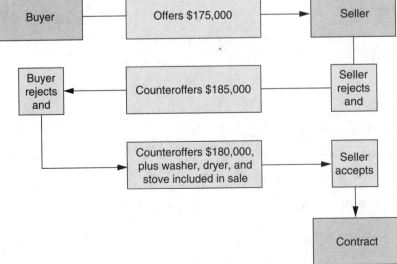

An offer is not considered accepted until the person making the offer has been *notified of the other party's acceptance*. When the parties are communicating through an agent or at a distance, questions may arise regarding whether an acceptance, rejection, or counteroffer has effectively taken place. The real estate broker or salesperson must transmit all written offers, acceptances, or other responses as soon as possible to avoid such problems. Legally binding signatures may be obtained via fax machines, but they should be followed up with original signatures as soon as possible.

Earnest Money Deposits

It is customary, but not essential, for a purchaser to provide a cash deposit (a check) when making an offer to purchase real estate. This cash deposit, commonly referred to as **earnest money** or a *good faith deposit*, gives evidence of the buyer's intention to carry out the terms of the contract. This deposit is given to the broker, and the sales contract typically provides that the broker or seller's attorney holds the deposit until closing. If the offer is not accepted, the earnest money deposit is returned to the would-be buyer immediately.

The amount of the deposit is a matter to be agreed on by the parties. Generally, the deposit should be sufficient to discourage the buyer from defaulting and to compensate the seller for taking the property off the market and cover any expenses the seller might incur if the buyer defaults. A purchase offer with no earnest money, however, is valid. Most contracts provide that the deposit becomes the seller's property if the buyer defaults (as *liquidated damages*). In certain cases the seller might claim damages in excess of the earnest money.

Earnest money must be deposited by a broker within five days in a special *trust*, or *escrow, bank account*. This money cannot be *commingled*, or mixed, with a broker's personal funds. A broker may not use such funds for personal use; this illegal act is known as *conversion*. A broker need not open a special escrow account for each earnest money deposit received. One account into which all such funds are deposited is sufficient. A broker should maintain full, complete, and accurate records of all earnest money deposits. Under no circumstances does the money belong to the broker, who must maintain it in his or her trust account. The uncertain nature of earnest money deposits makes it absolutely necessary that such funds be properly protected pending a final decision on their disbursement.

Any cash deposit of $10,000 or more must be reported to the Internal Revenue Service.

Parts of a Sales Contract

The essentials of a valid contract for the sale of real property are

- contract in writing,
- competent parties,
- agreement to buy and sell,
- adequate description of the property,
- consideration (price and terms of payment),
- grantor's agreement to convey (type of deed specified),
- place and time of closing, and
- signatures of the parties.

Usually included, but not essential for a valid contract, are provisions covering

- encumbrances to which the deed is made subject;
- earnest money deposit;
- mortgage financing the buyer plans to obtain and other contingencies;
- possession by the buyer;
- title evidence;
- prorations and adjustments;
- destruction of the premises before closing;
- default by either party; and
- contingencies.

The signature of a witness is *not* essential for a valid contract.

Before signing any purchase contract, the buyer of a house built before 1978 must have received and acknowledged a copy of the EPA booklet on lead paint dangers. If the property is to be financed by an FHA mortgage, the buyer must receive and acknowledge, before signing, a notice that the FHA recommends the use of a home inspector, and that its appraisal is concerned with overall value, not details of condition of the property, as well as a notice about potential mold and radon problems.

Home inspectors must now be licensed by the state. When suggesting the names of home inspectors, an agent should check to make sure they are properly licensed.

Contingencies

When the purchaser intends to secure an FHA or VA loan, special clauses must be included in the sales contract that provide that the contract may be voided if the property appraises below the sales price. Provisions may be added stipulating that the seller furnish satisfactory reports on such matters as termite or insect infestation, quality of a private water supply, or condition of plumbing or heating equipment. In some transfers a certificate of occupancy must be obtained from a municipality; the contract should make it clear whose responsibility this is. The purchaser may add a stipulation that allows a walk-through inspection of the property shortly before settlement.

Among common provisions in the "subject to" section of the contract are the purchasers need to secure a specific loan; the purchaser's right to a satisfactory report on the property by a licensed home inspector within a specified few days; approval of the contract by a family member, again within a short period of time; or the purchaser's need to sell a present home before buying the next residence. The buyer cannot be required to complete the purchase if any such **contingency** is not satisfied. Where the purchaser has another home that must be sold first, the seller may insist on an **escape clause** (also called a *kickout* or *knockout clause*). Such a provision allows the seller to look for a more favorable offer, with the original purchaser retaining the right, if challenged, either to firm up the first sales contract (waiving the contingency) or to void the contract.

Liquidated damages are an amount of money, agreed to in advance by buyer and seller, that serves as compensation if one party does not live up to the contract. If a sales contract specifies that the earnest money deposit serves as liquidated damages in case of default by the buyer, the seller is entitled to keep the deposit if the buyer refuses to perform for no good reason.

The seller who does choose to keep the deposit as liquidated damages may not sue for any further damages.

Plain-Language Requirement

New Jersey law requires that certain written agreements for the sale or lease of residential property be written in a clear and coherent manner with words that are common in everyday usage.

Rescission of Contract

Sales contracts for the purchase of planned unit developments and other developments that are promoted with comprehensive advertising or incentive programs may be rescinded by the purchaser for any reason within seven calendar days of signing. This **rescission** period applies *only* to real estate covered under the New Jersey Planned Real Estate Development Full Disclosure Act and not to all real estate transactions. In the usual one- to four-family dwelling or condominium transaction, the buyer and seller have three days in which to seek attorney review of a contract. An attorney need give no reason for disapproving (and thereby voiding) a contract.

Borrowers who change their minds about a mortgage loan have three days in which to cancel the transaction if the mortgage was for *refinancing* of presently owned property. No right of rescission, however, applies to mortgage loans used for the purchase of real estate.

Option Agreements

An **option** is a contract by which an *optionor* (generally an owner) gives an *optionee* (a prospective purchaser or lessee) the right to buy or lease the owner's property at a fixed price within a stated period of time. The optionee pays an agreed-on consideration for this option right and assumes no other obligation until deciding, within the specified time, either to (1) exercise his or her option right (to buy or lease the property) or (2) allow the option right to expire. The owner may be bound to sell; the optionee is not bound to buy. A common application of an option is a lease that includes an option for the tenant to purchase the property. Such options must contain all the terms and provisions required for a valid contract of sale, and in New Jersey they should be prepared by attorneys.

Land Contracts

A real estate sale can be made under a **land contract**, sometimes called a *contract for deed* or an *installment sales contract*. Land contracts are typically used as a means of seller financing. Under a typical land contract, the seller, also known as the *vendor*, retains fee ownership; and the buyer, known as the *vendee*, secures possession and an *equitable interest* in the property. The buyer agrees to give the seller a down payment and pay regular monthly installments of principal and interest over a number of years. The buyer also agrees to pay real estate taxes, insurance premiums, repairs, and upkeep on the property. Although the buyer obtains possession when the contract is signed by both parties and the buyer has **equitable title**, the seller does not execute and deliver a deed to the buyer until the terms of the contract have been satisfied. This frequently occurs when the buyer has made a sufficient number of payments to obtain a mortgage loan and pay off the balance due on the contract.

Real estate is occasionally sold with the new buyer assuming an existing land contract from the original buyer/vendee. Generally, the seller/vendor must approve the new purchaser.

Unit 11

Land contracts require extensive legal input from experienced real estate lawyers. The broker who negotiates a land contract should consult attorneys for both parties at every step of the way and refrain from specifying any detailed terms in the agreement.

SUMMARY

A *contract* is defined as an agreement made by *competent parties*, with adequate *consideration*, to *take* or to *refrain* from some *action*.

Contracts may be classified according to whether the parties' intentions are *expressed* or are *implied* by their actions. They also may be classified as *bilateral*, when both parties have obligated themselves to act, or *unilateral*, when one party is obligated to perform only if the other party acts. In addition, contracts may be classified according to their legal enforceability as *valid, void, voidable,* or *unenforceable.*

Many contracts specify a time for performance. In any case all contracts must be performed within a reasonable time. An *executed* contract is one that has been fully performed. An *executory* contract is one in which some act remains to be performed.

The *essentials of a valid contract* are (1) *competent parties*, (2) *offer and acceptance*, (3) *consideration*, and (4) *legality of object*. The New Jersey statute of frauds traditionally requires that contracts for the sale of real estate must be *in writing and signed* to be enforceable in court.

A valid real estate contract also must include a description of the property.

In many types of contracts, either party may transfer his or her rights and obligations under the agreement by *assignment* of the contract or *novation* (substitution of a new contract).

Contracts usually provide that the seller has the right to declare a sale canceled if the buyer defaults. If either party has suffered a loss because of the other's default, he or she may sue for damages to cover the loss. If one party insists on completing the transaction, he or she may sue the defaulter for specific performance of the terms of the contract; a court can order the other party to comply with the agreement.

Contracts frequently used in the real estate business include listing agreements, sales contracts, options, land contracts (installment contracts), and leases.

A real estate sales contract binds a buyer and a seller to a definite transaction as described in detail in the contract. The buyer is bound to purchase the property for the amount stated in the agreement.

The seller is bound to deliver title, free from liens and encumbrances (except those allowed by the "subject to" clause of the contract). Additionally, if the contract has been prepared by a real estate licensee, the buyer and seller have three days in which to seek *attorney's review* of a contract.

Under an *option* agreement, the optionee purchases from the optionor, for a limited time period, the exclusive right to purchase or lease the optionor's property. For a potential purchaser or lessee, an option is a means of buying time to consider or complete arrangements for a transaction. A *land contract*, or *installment contract*, is a sales/financing agreement under which a buyer purchases a seller's real estate on time. The buyer takes possession of and responsibility for the property but does not receive the deed immediately.

USEFUL WEBSITES

List of Licensed Home Inspectors and Licensed Associates: https://www.njconsumeraffairs.gov/hom/Pages/default.aspx

American Society of Home Inspectors: www.homeinspector.org

KEY TERMS REVIEW 1

Match the number of each key term with the corresponding letter.

_____ 1. Assignment

_____ 2. Bilateral contract

_____ 3. Breach of contract

_____ 4. Competent parties

_____ 5. Consideration

_____ 6. Contingency

_____ 7. Contract

_____ 8. Counteroffer

_____ 9. Earnest money

_____ 10. Equitable title

_____ 11. Escape clause

_____ 12. Executed contract

_____ 13. Executory contract

_____ 14. Express contract

_____ 15. Implied contract

_____ 16. Land contract

A. agreement between two parties to perform some legal act(s)

B. violation of a contract

C. buyer's deposit with purchase contract

D. certain happening on which a contract depends

E. contract not put into words but shown by actions

F. contract set down in so many words

G. contract that has been fulfilled or one that has been signed, depending on the contract

H. contract that has not yet been performed

I. contract with a promise by each party

J. interest acquired by buyer with land contract

K. offer returned to offeror with changes by offeree

L. protection for seller when buyer has another house to sell

M. something of value given in exchange

N. those legally qualified to enter into contracts

O. transfer of interest in a contract to a third party

P. agreement under which buyer pays in installments and waits for deed

KEY TERMS REVIEW 2

Match the number of each key term with the corresponding letter.

_____ 1. Liquidated damages

_____ 2. Novation

_____ 3. Offer and acceptance

_____ 4. Option

_____ 5. Parol evidence rule

_____ 6. Rescission

_____ 7. Specific performance

_____ 8. Statute of frauds

_____ 9. Statute of limitations

_____ 10. Time is of the essence

_____ 11. Unenforceable contract

_____ 12. Unilateral contract

_____ 13. Valid contract

_____ 14. Void contract

_____ 15. Voidable contract

A. contract binding one party; other party free to act or not

B. seemingly valid contract but neither party can sue to force performance

C. contract clause requiring punctual performance

D. return to the status quo

E. contract that does not meet all legal requirements

F. contract that is binding, but one party may disaffirm it

G. contract that meets all legal requirements

H. court action usually asking that the seller be forced to sell as agreed

I. time within which one is allowed to assert a legal right

J. law requiring certain contracts to be in writing

K. another name for an option contract

L. convention that a written contract overrides spoken promises

M. substitution of a new contract for an existing one

N. sum agreed on to serve as damages in case of future default

O. the process of reaching a meeting of the minds

UNIT 11 REVIEW QUESTIONS

1. A legally enforceable agreement under which two parties agree to do something for each other is known as a(n)
   A. escrow agreement.
   B. legal promise.
   C. valid contract.
   D. option agreement.

2. A person drives into a filling station and tops off her gas tank. She is obligated to pay for the fuel through what kind of contract?
   A. Express
   B. Implied
   C. Oral
   D. Voidable

3. A contract is said to be bilateral if
   A. one of the parties is a minor.
   B. the contract has yet to be fully performed.
   C. only one party to the agreement is bound to act.
   D. all parties to the contract are bound to act.

4. A seller gave an open listing to several brokers, specifically promising that if one of the brokers found a buyer for the seller's real estate, the seller then would be obligated to pay a commission to that broker. This offer by the seller is a(n)
   A. executed agreement.
   B. discharged agreement.
   C. implied agreement.
   D. unilateral agreement.

5. During the period of time after a real estate sales contract is signed but before title actually passes, the status of the contract is
   A. voidable.
   B. executory.
   C. exculpatory.
   D. implied.

6. A 17-year-old New Jersey resident signs a contract to buy a home for himself and his wife. The contract is
   A. voidable.
   B. valid.
   C. fulfilled.
   D. unilateral.

7. A broker has found a buyer for a man's home. The buyer has indicated in writing his willingness to buy the property for $1,000 less than the asking price and has deposited $5,000 earnest money with the broker. The buyer is out of town for the weekend and the broker has been unable to inform him of the signed document. At this point the document is a(n)
   A. voidable contract.
   B. offer.
   C. executory agreement.
   D. implied contract.

8. Consideration given in exchange for a sales contract might take the form of
   A. a down payment and note.
   B. a purchase-money mortgage.
   C. cash.
   D. any of the above.

9. A buyer makes a written offer to buy an apartment building for $900,000, with the closing to be on December 30. The seller, who has income tax concerns, signs his consent to sell for that amount, agreeing to all her terms except that "the sale shall not be closed until January." At this point, who is free to walk away and forget the whole thing?
   A. Either seller or buyer
   B. Neither seller nor buyer
   C. The seller
   D. The buyer

10. The seller told the buyer she'd leave the washing machine but instead took it with her. The written contract made no mention of the washing machine. The buyer has no right to complain because of the rule of
    A. partial performance.
    B. novation.
    C. undue influence.
    D. parol evidence.

11. New Jersey real estate brokers and their salespersons may fill in sales contract forms for
    A. one- to four-family properties.
    B. any residential properties.
    C. residential properties and vacant land.
    D. residential and industrial property only.

12. A broker must deposit funds received as earnest money deposits in a special separate bank account within
    A. 3 days.
    B. 5 business days.
    C. 7 days.
    D. 30 days.

13. Buyers have a seven-day period in which they may cancel sales contracts on
    A. certain condominiums.
    B. all one- to four-family dwellings.
    C. any commercial properties.
    D. leased property.

14. If a real estate sales contract does not state that time is of the essence and the stipulated date of transfer comes and goes without a closing, the contract is then
    A. binding for only 30 more days.
    B. novated.
    C. still valid.
    D. automatically void.

15. A buyer has a contract to buy a commercial building but would rather let his friend buy it instead. If the contract allows, the friend can take over the buyer's obligation by the process known as
    A. assignment.
    B. substantial performance.
    C. subordination.
    D. mutual consent.

16. A suit for specific performance of a real estate contract asks for
    A. money damages.
    B. a new contract.
    C. a deficiency judgment.
    D. a forced sale or purchase.

17. In filling out a sales contract, someone crossed out several words and inserted others. To eliminate future controversy as to whether the changes were made before or after the contract was signed, the usual procedure is to
    A. write a letter to each party listing the changes.
    B. have each party write a letter to the other approving the changes.
    C. redraw the entire contract.
    D. have both parties initial or sign in the margin near each change.

18. The buyer's offer in writing to purchase a house for $120,000, drapes included, with the offer to expire Saturday at noon. The sellers reply in writing on Thursday, accepting $120,000 but excluding the drapes. On Friday, while the buyers are considering this counteroffer, the sellers decide to accept the original offer, drapes included, and state that in writing. At this point, the buyers
    A. must buy and have a right to insist on the drapes.
    B. are not bound to buy and can forget the whole thing.
    C. must buy but are not entitled to the drapes.
    D. must buy and can deduct the value of the drapes from the $120,000.

19. In New Jersey a valid contract for the sale of real estate must include
    A. an earnest money deposit.
    B. an adequate description of the property.
    C. the signatures of witnesses.
    D. all of the above.

20. The sales contract says the buyer will purchase only if his wife flies up and approves the sale by the following Saturday. The approval by the buyer's wife is a
    A. contingency.
    B. reservation.
    C. warranty.
    D. consideration.

UNIT 12

Leases: Landlord and Tenant

LEARNING OBJECTIVES

When you have completed this unit, you will be able to accomplish the following.

> Explain characteristics of four leasehold estates.
> Describe standard lease provisions, including various forms of eviction and the effect of Truth-in-Renting and the Americans with Disabilities Act.
> Discuss differences between various types of leases.
> Identify functions of the property manager.

KEY TERMS

actual eviction	ground lease	periodic estate
Americans with Disabilities Act (ADA)	holdover tenancy	property manager
assignment	implied warranty of habitability	sublease
Certified Property Manager (CPM)	lease	suit for possession
constructive eviction	lessee	summary proceeding
demise	lessor	tenancy at sufferance
estate for years	management agreement	tenancy at will
gross lease	net lease	Truth-in-Renting
	percentage lease	

LEASING REAL ESTATE

A **lease** from an owner of real estate (known as the **lessor**) to a tenant (the **lessee**) transfers the right to possession and use of the owner's property to the tenant for a specified period of time. This agreement sets forth the length of time the contract is to run, the amount to be paid by the lessee for the right to use the property, and other rights and obligations of the parties. A transfer of property by lease is known as a **demise**.

The landlord grants the tenant the right to occupy the premises and use them for purposes stated in the lease. In return the landlord retains the right to receive payment for the use of

199

the premises as well as the right to retake possession after the lease term has expired. A lease is both a *contract* (in that it sets forth conditions for both parties to follow) and a *conveyance* (in that it grants a leasehold estate).

The New Jersey Statute of Frauds requires that leases for a period of *more than three years be in writing*. A lease may be *recorded* if it is for *two years or more*. Also, a recent amendment to the statute provides that, in order for a broker to successfully sue for a commission on a lease transaction, the authorization must be in writing and signed by the principal. The requirement applies regardless of the length of time of the leasehold interest being transferred.

LEASEHOLD ESTATES

A tenant's right to occupy land is called a *leasehold estate*. Just as there are several types of freehold (ownership) estates, there are various leasehold estates. The four most important are

1. estate for years;

2. periodic estate, or estate from period to period;

3. tenancy at will; and

4. tenancy at sufferance (see Figure 12.1).

Figure 12.1: Leasehold Estates

Type of Estate	Distinguishing Characteristics
Estate for years	For a definite period of time
Estate from period to period	Automatically renews
Estate at will	For an indefinite period of time
Estate at sufferance	Without landlord's consent

Estate for Years

A leasehold estate that continues for a *definite period of time* with a *specific termination date* is an **estate for years**. When a definite term is specified in a written or oral lease and that period of time has expired, the tenant is required to vacate the premises. No notice is required to terminate such a lease at the end of the term. A lease for years may be terminated prior to the expiration date by the mutual consent of both parties, but otherwise, neither party may terminate without showing that the lease agreement has been breached.

An estate for years need not necessarily last for years or even for one year. For example, it could be for six weeks or for ten months. Its distinguishing characteristic is that it begins and ends at a specific time.

Periodic Estate

Periodic estates, sometimes called *estates from period to period*, are created when the landlord and tenant enter into an agreement that continues for an indefinite length of time without a specific expiration date; rent, however, is payable at definite intervals. These tenancies generally run for a certain amount of time; for instance, month to month or year to year. The agreement is automatically renewed for similar succeeding periods until one of the parties gives notice to terminate.

A *month-to-month tenancy* is created when a tenant takes possession with no definite termination date and pays rent on a monthly basis. A tenancy from year to year is created when a tenant for a term of years remains in possession, or holds over, after the expiration of the lease term. When no new lease agreement has been made, the landlord may either evict the tenant or accept the **holdover tenancy**.

A New Jersey tenant who remains in possession of leased premises after giving notice of intention to quit the premises may be held liable for double rent. When the lease term is longer than one month, the landlord may commence proceedings to remove a tenant who has held over. The subsequent acceptance of rent by the landlord creates a tenancy from month to month.

To terminate a periodic estate, either the landlord or the tenant must give proper notice. To end a month-to-month tenancy, New Jersey requires one month's written notice before the date the rent is due. Local rent control regulations may set different requirements.

Tenancy at Will

An estate that gives the tenant the right to possess with the consent of the landlord for an indefinite period is a **tenancy at will**. It may be created by express agreement or by operation of law, and during its existence the tenant has all the rights and obligations of a lessor/lessee relationship, including the payment of rent at regular intervals.

For example, at the end of a lease period a landlord informs a tenant that in a few months the city is going to demolish the apartment building to make way for an expressway. The landlord gives the tenant the option of occupying the premises until demolition begins. If the tenant agrees to stay, a tenancy at will is created. The term of an estate at will is indefinite, but the estate may be terminated by giving three months' notice. An estate at will is automatically terminated by the death of either the landlord or the tenant.

Tenancy at Sufferance

A **tenancy at sufferance** arises when a tenant who lawfully came into possession of real property continues, after his or her rights have expired, to hold possession of the premises *without the consent of the landlord*. A tenant at sufferance can be evicted at any time. Just as fee simple absolute is the highest estate in land, tenancy at sufferance is the lowest estate in land.

STANDARD LEASE PROVISIONS

A lease may be written, oral, or implied, depending on the circumstances. A standard form of residential lease is now available in New Jersey (see Figure 12.2). The requirements for a valid lease are essentially the same as those for any other real estate contract. The essentials of a valid lease include the following:

- Capacity to contract—the parties must be sane adults.
- A demising clause—the lessor to let and the lessee to take the premises.
- Description of the premises—a description of the leased premises should be clearly stated; If the lease covers land, the legal description of the real estate should be used; If, on the other hand, the lease is for a part of the building, such as office space or an apartment, the space itself should be clearly and carefully described; If supplemental space is to be included, the lease should clearly identify it.
- A clear statement of the term (duration) of the lease must be provided.
- The rent and how it is to be paid must be specified.
- The lease must be in writing if for a term of more than three years.
- Signatures: a lease should be signed by all parties.

Figure 12.2: Residential Lease

NEW JERSEY REALTORS® STANDARD FORM OF
RESIDENTIAL LEASE

©2001 NEW JERSEY REALTORS®, INC.

THIS IS A LEGALLY BINDING LEASE THAT WILL BECOME FINAL WITHIN THREE BUSINESS DAYS. DURING THIS PERIOD YOU MAY CHOOSE TO CONSULT AN ATTORNEY WHO CAN REVIEW AND CANCEL THE LEASE. SEE SECTION ON ATTORNEY REVIEW FOR DETAILS.

TABLE OF CONTENTS

RESIDENTIAL LEASE AGREEMENT

1
2
3 BETWEEN LANDLORD(S): _____
4
5 _____
6
7 whose address is/are _____
8
9 _____
10
11 AND TENANT(S): _____
12
13 _____
14
15 whose address is/are _____
16
17 _____
18
19 The word "Landlord" as used in this Lease means all of the landlords above listed. In all instances in which the
20 Landlord may exercise rights or perform obligations under this Lease, it may do so through its authorized agents or
21 representatives.
22
23 The word "Tenant" as used in this Lease means all of the tenants above listed.
24
25 **1. CONDOMINIUM/CO-OPERATIVE RIGHT OF TERMINATION:** (The following statement generally, as required
26 by law, must be included in a lease for a condominium or cooperative unit.) THIS BUILDING IS BEING CONVERTED
27 TO OR IS A CONDOMINIUM OR COOPERATIVE. YOUR TENANCY CAN BE TERMINATED UPON 60 DAYS NOTICE
28 IF YOUR APARTMENT IS SOLD TO A BUYER WHO SEEKS TO PERSONALLY OCCUPY IT. IF YOU MOVE OUT AS A
29 RESULT OF RECEIVING SUCH A NOTICE, AND THE LANDLORD ARBITRARILY FAILS TO COMPLETE THE SALE,
30 THE LANDLORD SHALL BE LIABLE FOR TREBLE DAMAGES AND COURT COSTS.
31
32 **2. PROPERTY:** The Tenant agrees to lease from the Landlord and the Landlord agrees to lease to the Tenant (the single family home)
33 (apartment # _____) (condominium unit #_____) (townhouse unit #_____) having a street address of _____
34 _____ located in _____
35 _____, New Jersey (referred to as the "Property").
36
37
38
39 NJ REALTORS® Form 125 | 09/2020   Page 1 of 8   Tenant's Initials: _____   Landlord's Initials: _____

Figure 12.2: Residential Lease (continued)

40 **3. TERM:** The Term of this Lease is for _____ (months) (years) starting on _____
41 _____ and ending on _____. This is referred to as
42 the "Term". If the Landlord is unable to give possession of the Property to the Tenant on the first day of the Term, the Landlord shall
43 not have any liability to the Tenant. However, the Tenant shall not be liable for the payment of rent until the Landlord gives possession of
44 the Property to the Tenant. If the Landlord fails to give possession of the Property within 30 days of the start date set forth above, then
45 the Tenant may terminate this Lease by giving notice to Landlord. If the first day of the Term is delayed, then the last day of the Term
46 shall be adjusted accordingly, so that the Term remains for the number of months or years above stated.

48 **4. RENT:** The rent for the Term of this Lease is $ _____, to be paid as follows: $_____ per month, which is
49 due on the _____ day of each month. Rent shall be payable to: _____
50 _____.
51 <center>(NAME AND ADDRESS)</center>

52 **5. INITIAL DEPOSIT:** Tenant has paid an initial deposit of $ _____ received on _____ that will be
53 credited towards _____ the first month's rent or _____ the Security Deposit. The balance shall be paid as follows: First
54 month's rent $_____ Due on _____, Security Deposit $_____ Due
55 on _____.

57 **6. SECURITY DEPOSIT:** The Tenant shall pay to the Landlord the sum of $_____ (the "Security Deposit," which cannot
58 exceed one and one-half months rent) to assure that the Tenant performs all of the Tenant's obligations under this Lease. If the Landlord
59 collects any additional Security Deposit, the additional security collected annually shall not be greater than 10 percent of the current
60 Security Deposit. Landlord shall comply with the Rent Security Deposit Act, N.J.S.A. 46:8-19 et seq. (the "Act"), unless this Lease is
61 for owner occupied Property with not more than two rental units or is a seasonal tenancy of not more than 125 consecutive days. Any
62 attempt to waive the requirements of the Act is prohibited and void as a matter of law.

64 The Act requires depositing the Security Deposit into a banking institution or investment company in New Jersey and notifying the Tenant in
65 writing of the name and address of the banking institution or investment company, the type of account in which the Security Deposit is deposited
66 or invested (for example, interest bearing or money market), the amount of the Security Deposit, and the current rate of interest for the account
67 within 30 days of each of the following: (a) the Landlord's receipt of the Security Deposit from the Tenant; (b) the Landlord moving the deposit
68 from one institution or fund to another (unless the move is due to a merger, in which case a notice to the Tenant must be within 30 days of receipt of
69 notice by the Landlord of the merger if the merger occurs more than 60 days prior to the annual interest payment); or (c) the transfer or conveyance
70 of ownership or control of the Property. Such notice also must be provided at the time of each annual interest payment. All interest earned on
71 the Security Deposit shall be paid to the Tenant in cash or be credited toward the payment of rent due under this Lease upon the anniversary date
72 of this Lease, the renewal of the Term or on January 31, if the Landlord gives the Tenant written notice that interest will be paid on January 31.

74 The Act also provides that, if the Landlord sells or conveys the Property during the Term of this Lease, the Landlord will transfer the
75 Security Deposit plus the undistributed interest to the new owner. The Landlord shall notify the Tenant of the sale or conveyance, as
76 well as the name and address of the new owner. The notice shall be given by registered or certified mail within five days after conveyance
77 of title. After acquisition of the Property, the new owner shall be liable for investing the Security Deposit, making all interest payments,
78 giving all notices and returning the Security Deposit as required under the Act, even if the Landlord fails to transfer the Security Deposit.

79 The Landlord shall inspect the Property after the Tenant vacates at the end of the Term. Within 30 days of the termination of this Lease,
80 the Landlord shall return the Security Deposit plus the undistributed interest to the Tenant, less any charges expended by the Landlord
81 for damages to the Property resulting from the Tenant's occupancy. The interest and deductions shall be itemized in a statement by the
82 Landlord, and shall be forwarded to the Tenant with the balance of the Security Deposit by personal delivery, or registered or certified
83 mail. The Security Deposit may not be used by the Tenant for the payment of rent without the written consent of the Landlord.

85 **7. LATE PAYMENT PENALTY:** If the Tenant does not pay the rent by the _____ day of the month, the Tenant shall pay a
86 late charge of _____ until the rent is received by Landlord. The late charge shall be added to the rent, and shall be considered
87 as additional rent, which is defined in Section 8. In the event any rent check is returned unpaid due to insufficient funds, the Tenant agrees
88 to pay the Landlord a $_____ processing charge. In such event, the Landlord reserves the right to demand that future rent
89 payments be made in cash, bank or certified check.

91 **8. ADDITIONAL RENT:** Landlord may perform any obligations under this Lease which are Tenant's responsibility and which Tenant
92 fails to perform. The cost to Landlord for such performance may be charged to tenant as "additional rent" which shall be due and payable
93 with the next installment of monthly rent. Landlord has the same rights against Tenant for failure to pay additional rent as Landlord has
94 for Tenant's failure to pay monthly rent. This means that the Landlord may evict Tenant for failure to pay additional rent.

96 **9. POSSESSION AND USE:** The Landlord shall give possession of the Property to the Tenant for the Term of this Lease except as
97 otherwise provided in this Lease. The Tenant shall occupy the Property only as a private residence, and will not use the Property for any
98 business, trade or profession. The Tenant shall not store any flammable, dangerous or hazardous materials at the Property, other than
99 ordinary household cleaning materials. The Property shall not be allowed to be vacant for any extended period of time.

NJ REALTORS® Form 125 | 09/2020   Page 2 of 8   Tenant's Initials: _____   Landlord's Initials: _____

Figure 12.2: Residential Lease (continued)

100 **10. UTILITIES:** The Tenant shall arrange to have the utilities transferred into Tenant's name prior to occupancy, and shall be responsible
101 for paying the following utility services: ☐ Gas ☐ Electric ☐ Water ☐ Heat ☐ Sewer ☐ General Trash Disposal
102 ☐ (Other) _____.
103 The Landlord shall provide and pay for the following utility services: ☐ Gas ☐ Electric ☐ Water ☐ Heat ☐ Sewer
104 ☐ General Trash Disposal ☐ (Other) _____. The Tenant agrees
105 not to waste or unreasonably use any utility or appliance that is provided by the Landlord. Landlord shall not be responsible for any
106 damage or loss caused to Tenant or Tenant's property because of an interruption in utility services over which Landlord has no reasonable
107 means of control. Any such interruption shall not be grounds for Tenant to reduce or stop paying rent.
108

109 **11. NO ASSIGNMENT OR SUBLETTING:** The Tenant may not assign this Lease, sublet all or any part of the Property, or permit
110 any other person to use the Property without the prior written permission of the Landlord. The Landlord may withhold such permission
111 in Landlord's sole and absolute discretion.
112

113 **12. VIOLATION, EVICTION AND RE-ENTRY:** The Landlord reserves the right of re-entry. This means that if the Tenant violates
114 the terms of this Lease, the Landlord may terminate this Lease and regain possession of the Property. This is done by a court proceeding
115 known as an eviction. A complaint is served upon the Tenant and the Tenant must appear in court. The Landlord may also evict the
116 Tenant for any other cause which is permitted by applicable law. When the eviction proceeding is concluded, the Landlord may regain
117 possession of the Property.
118

119 **13. DAMAGES:** The Tenant is liable for all the Landlord's damages caused by the Tenant's breach of this Lease. Such damages may
120 include loss of rent, the cost of preparing the Property for re-renting and a brokerage commission incurred finding a new tenant as a result
121 of the Tenant's eviction or if the Tenant moves out prior to the end of the Term.
122

123 **14. QUIET ENJOYMENT:** The Tenant may occupy the Property without interference, subject to Tenant's compliance with the Terms
124 of this Lease.
125

126 **15. TENANT'S REPAIRS AND MAINTENANCE:** The Tenant shall:
127 (a) Pay for all repairs, replacements and damages caused by the act or neglect of the Tenant, the Tenant's family, domestic employees,
128   guests or visitors, which includes but is not limited to sewer and plumbing drainage problems caused by the Tenant.
129 (b) Keep and maintain the Property in a neat, clean, safe and sanitary condition.
130 (c) Cut the grass and maintain the shrubbery.
131 (d) Drive and park vehicles only in designated areas, if any.
132 (e) Take good care of the Property and all equipment, fixtures, carpeting and appliances located in it.
133 (f) Keep the furnace clean, and regularly change the furnace filters, if applicable.
134 (g) Keep nothing in the Property which is flammable, dangerous or which might increase the danger of fire or other casualty.
135 (h) Promptly notify the Landlord of any condition which requires repairs to be done.
136 (i) Use the electric, plumbing and other systems and facilities in a safe manner.
137 (j) Promptly remove all garbage and recyclables from the Property and place it at the curb (or other designated area) in the proper
138   containers in accordance with the prescribed pick-up schedule.
139 (k) Not engage in any activity which may cause a cancellation or an increase in the cost of the Landlord's insurance coverages.
140 (l) Use no more electricity than the receptacles, wiring or feeders to the Property can safely carry.
141 (m) Obey all instructions, written or otherwise, of the Landlord for the care and use of appliances, equipment and other personal
142   property.
143 (n) Do nothing to destroy, deface or damage any part of the Property.
144 (o) Promptly comply with all orders and rules of the Board of Health or any other governmental authority which are directed to the
145   Tenant.
146 (p) Do nothing which interferes with the use and enjoyment of neighboring properties.
147 (q) Do nothing to cause any damage to any trees or landscaping on the Property.
148 (r) Keep the walks and driveway free from dirt, debris, snow, ice and any hazardous objects.
149 (s) Comply with such rules and regulations that may be published from time to time by the Landlord.
150

151 **16. LANDLORD REPAIRS:** The Landlord shall make any necessary repairs and replacements to the vital facilities serving the
152 Property, such as the heating, plumbing and electrical systems, within a reasonable time after notice by the Tenant. The Tenant may be
153 liable for the cost of such repairs and replacements pursuant to Section 15. The Landlord shall not be liable for interruption of services
154 or inconvenience resulting from delays in making repairs or replacements if due to circumstances beyond Landlord's reasonable control.
155

156 **17. ACCESS TO THE PROPERTY:** The Landlord shall have access to the Property on reasonable notice to the Tenant in order to
157 (a) inspect the interior and exterior of the Property, (b) make necessary repairs, alterations, or improvements, (c) supply services, and (d)
158 show it to prospective buyers, appraisers, contractors or insurers. The Landlord may enter the Property without prior notice in the event
159 of an emergency or if the Tenant is not home for more than seven consecutive days. If this Lease is not renewed as per Section 27 of this

Figure 12.2: Residential Lease (continued)

160 Lease Agreement, Landlord shall then be allowed access to the Property at any time prior to the end of the Term for showing of Property
161 to prospective tenants.
162
163 **18. NO ALTERATIONS OR INSTALLATION OF EQUIPMENT:** The Tenant may not alter or change the Property without first
164 obtaining Landlord's written consent. By way of example, the Tenant may not:
165   (a) Install any improvement such as carpeting, paneling, floor tiles, or any other improvement which is nailed or tacked down, cemented
166   or glued in;
167   (b) Install any locks or chain guards;
168   (c) Wallpaper, affix wall coverings or other permanent type decorations;
169   (d) Install or change the electrical, plumbing, heating or air cooling system.
170
171 When painting (whether interior or exterior), the Tenant must have the Landlord's permission regarding paint colors. All painting must
172 be done in a professional and workmanlike manner. The Tenant shall repair all walls and ceilings which had pictures or fixtures attached,
173 prior to vacating. Any and all changes, additions or improvements made without the Landlord's written consent shall be removed by the
174 Tenant on demand by the Landlord. The Property shall be in substantially the same condition at the end of the Term as it was at the
175 beginning of the Term, reasonable wear and tear excepted.
176
177 All permitted changes, additions and improvements shall become the property of the Landlord when completed, shall be fully paid for by
178 the Tenant, and shall remain as part of the Property at the end of the Term of this Lease, unless the Landlord demands that the Tenant
179 remove them. The Tenant shall not allow any construction lien or other claim to be filed against the Property. If any such lien or claim is
180 filed against the Property, the Tenant shall have it promptly removed.
181
182 **19. INSPECTION:** If the municipality requires a continued use inspection or certificate of occupancy prior to occupancy, the Landlord
183 shall be responsible for obtaining such inspections and certificates as well as making the necessary repairs.
184
185 **20. INSURANCE:** The Tenant shall be responsible for obtaining, at Tenant's own cost and expense, a tenant's insurance policy for the
186 Tenant's furniture, furnishings, clothing and other personal property. The Tenant's personal property shall not be the responsibility of the
187 Landlord, and will not be insured by the Landlord. The Tenant's insurance policy must also include liability coverage. Upon request, the
188 Tenant shall periodically furnish Landlord with evidence of Tenant's insurance policy.
189
190 **21. FIRE AND OTHER CASUALTY:** Immediate notice shall be given by the Tenant to Landlord of any fire or other casualty which
191 occurs at the Property. If the Property is uninhabitable, Tenant's obligation to pay rent shall cease until the time that the Property is
192 restored by the Landlord. If only a part of the Property is uninhabitable, then the rent shall be adjusted proportionately.
193
194 If only part of the Property is damaged, the Landlord shall repair the Property within a reasonable period of time. Landlord shall not be
195 obligated to repair or restore any improvements that Tenant has made to the Property.
196
197 Either party may cancel this Lease if the Property is so damaged by fire or other casualty that the property cannot be repaired within 90
198 days. The Landlord's determination in such regard shall be final, conclusive and binding on both parties.
199
200 The Lease shall end if the Property is totally destroyed. The Tenant shall pay rent to the date of destruction.
201
202 If the fire or other casualty is caused by the act or neglect of the Tenant, the Tenant's family, domestic employees, guests or visitors, the
203 Tenant shall pay for all repairs and other damages.
204
205 **22. LIABILITY OF LANDLORD AND TENANT:** The Landlord is not legally responsible for any loss, injury or damage to any
206 person or property unless such loss, injury or damage is directly caused by the Landlord's negligence. The Tenant is legally responsible
207 for loss, injury or damage to any person or property caused by the negligence of the Tenant, the Tenant's family members, domestic
208 employees, guests or visitors.
209
210 **23. PETS:** No dogs, cats or other pets shall be permitted on the Property without the prior written consent of the Landlord, which the
211 Landlord may withhold in the Landlord's sole and absolute discretion. Failure to obtain written permission from landlord to have, keep,
212 or allow others to bring any type of pet upon the Property will result in a fine of $25 per day that the pet is present without prior written
213 permission and may result in termination of the Lease for breach of the Lease at Landord's sole discretion.
214
215 **24. NOTICES:** All notices given under this Lease must be in writing in order to be effective. Delivery of notices may not be refused. If
216 any notice is refused, it shall be considered to have been effectively given. Notices shall be given by (a) personal delivery, or (b) certified
217 mail, return receipt requested, unless applicable law requires a different means of notice. Notices to the Landlord shall be at the address
218 on the first page of this Lease, and to the Tenant at the Property.
219

Figure 12.2: Residential Lease (continued)

25. NO WAIVER: The Landlord's failure to enforce any obligation of the Tenant contained in this Lease in any one instance shall not prevent the Landlord from enforcing the obligation at a later time.

26. SEVERABILITY: If any term or condition of this Lease is contrary to law, the remainder of the Lease shall be unaffected and shall continue to be binding upon the parties.

27. RENEWAL OF LEASE: The Tenant must be offered a renewal of this Lease by the Landlord, unless the Landlord has good cause not to do so under applicable law. Reasonable changes may be included in the renewal Lease. Not less than _____ days before the expiration of the Term of this Lease, the Landlord shall notify the Tenant of the proposed terms for the renewal Lease. Within _____ days after the Tenant receives the Landlord's renewal notice, Tenant shall notify Landlord whether Tenant accepts or rejects the proposed renewal Lease. If the Tenant does not notify the Landlord of Tenant's acceptance, then the Landlord's proposal shall be considered to have been rejected. If the Tenant does not accept the renewal Lease, the Tenant must vacate the Property at the end of the Term.

28. FURNITURE: If the Property is leased in furnished condition, or if the Landlord leaves personal property to be used by the Tenant, the Tenant shall maintain the furniture and furnishings in good condition and repair. A list of such items shall be attached to this Lease and signed by the Landlord and the Tenant.

29. END OF TERM: At the end of the Term, the Tenant shall (a) leave the Property clean, (b) remove all of the Tenant's property, (c) repair any damage including that caused by moving, (d) make arrangements for final utility readings and pay all final utility bills and (e) vacate the Property and return it with all keys to the Landlord in the same condition as it was at the beginning of the Term, except for normal wear and tear.

30. ASSOCIATION BYLAWS, RULES AND REGULATIONS: If Property is subject to any Association Bylaws and Rules and Regulations, Tenant agrees to comply with such Association Bylaws and Rules and Regulations including any amendments.

31. BINDING: This Lease is binding on the Landlord and the Tenant and all parties who lawfully succeed to their rights and responsibilities.

32. ENTIRE AGREEMENT: This Lease contains the entire agreement of the Landlord and Tenant. No representations have been made by the Landlord or its real estate broker or agents except as set forth in this Lease. This Lease can only be changed in writing by an agreement signed by both the Landlord and the Tenant.

33. ATTORNEY REVIEW CLAUSE:

(1) Study by Attorney.
The Tenant or the Landlord may choose to have an attorney study this Lease. If an attorney is consulted, the attorney must complete his or her review of the Lease within a three-day period. This Lease will be legally binding at the end of this three-day period unless an attorney for the Tenant or the Landlord reviews or disapproves of the Lease.

(2) Counting the Time.
You count the three days from the date of delivery of the signed Lease to the Tenant and the Landlord. You do not count Saturdays, Sundays or legal holidays. The Tenant and the Landlord may agree in writing to extend the three-day period for attorney review.

(3) Notice of Disapproval.
If an attorney for the Tenant or Landlord reviews and disapproves of this Lease, the attorney must notify the Broker(s) and the other party named in this Lease within the three-day period. Otherwise this Lease will be legally binding as written. The attorney must send the notice of disapproval to the Broker(s) by fax, email, personal delivery, or overnight mail with proof of delivery. Notice by overnight mail will be effective upon mailing. The personal delivery will be effective upon delivery to the Broker's office. The attorney may also, but need not, inform the Broker(s) of any suggested revision(s) in the Lease that would make it satisfactory.

34. BROKER'S COMMISSION: The Broker's Commission is earned, due and payable upon signing of a fully executed Lease Agreement and satisfaction of the Attorney Review Period set forth in Section 33 of this Lease. The Commission shall be paid by the

❏ Landlord in accord with previously executed Listing Agreement.

❏ Tenant and shall be payable as follows: _____

_____

_____

Listing Broker

Figure 12.2: Residential Lease (continued)

280	
281	
282	Address	Telephone#
283	
284	
285	
286	Email Address	Cell Phone#	Fax#
287	
288	
289	Participating Broker	Commission
290	
291	
292	Address	Telephone #
293	
294	
295	Email Address	Cell Phone#	Fax#

296

297 **35. LEAD-BASED PAINT DOCUMENT ACKNOWLEDGMENT: (Applies to dwellings built before 1978)**
298 The Tenant acknowledges receipt of the EPA pamphlet, "Protect Your Family From Lead In Your Home". Moreover, a copy of the
299 document entitled, "Disclosure of Information on Lead-Based Paint and Lead-Based Paint Hazards" has been fully completed, signed by
300 Tenant, Landlord and Broker(s) and is appended to and made a part of this Agreement.
301

302 **36. WINDOW GUARD NOTIFICATION:**
303 THE OWNER (LANDLORD) IS REQUIRED BY LAW TO PROVIDE, INSTALL AND MAINTAIN WINDOW GUARDS
304 IN THE APARTMENT IF A CHILD OR CHILDREN 10 YEARS OF AGE OR YOUNGER IS, OR WILL BE, LIVING IN
305 THE APARTMENT OR IS, OR WILL BE, REGULARLY PRESENT THERE FOR A SUBSTANTIAL PERIOD OF TIME
306 IF THE TENANT GIVES THE OWNER (LANDLORD) A WRITTEN REQUEST THAT THE WINDOW GUARDS BE
307 INSTALLED. THE OWNER (LANDLORD) IS ALSO REQUIRED, UPON THE WRITTEN REQUEST OF THE TENANT,
308 TO PROVIDE, INSTALL AND MAINTAIN WINDOW GUARDS IN THE HALLWAYS TO WHICH PERSONS IN
309 THE TENANT'S UNIT HAVE ACCESS WITHOUT HAVING TO GO OUT OF THE BUILDING. IF THE BUILDING
310 IS A CONDOMINIUM, COOPERATIVE OR MUTUAL HOUSING BUILDING, THE OWNER (LANDLORD) OF THE
311 APARTMENT IS RESPONSIBLE FOR INSTALLING AND MAINTAINING WINDOW GUARDS IN THE APARTMENT
312 AND THE ASSOCIATION IS RESPONSIBLE FOR INSTALLING AND MAINTAINING WINDOW GUARDS IN
313 HALLWAY WINDOWS. WINDOW GUARDS ARE ONLY REQUIRED TO BE PROVIDED IN FIRST FLOOR WINDOWS
314 WHERE THE WINDOW SILL IS MORE THAN SIX FEET ABOVE GRADE OR THERE ARE OTHER HAZARDOUS
315 CONDITIONS THAT MAKE INSTALLATION OF WINDOW GUARDS NECESSARY TO PROTECT THE SAFETY OF
316 CHILDREN.
317

318 **37. MEGAN'S LAW STATEMENT:**
319 UNDER NEW JERSEY LAW, THE COUNTY PROSECUTOR DETERMINES WHETHER AND HOW TO PROVIDE
320 NOTICE OF THE PRESENCE OF CONVICTED SEX OFFENDERS IN AN AREA. IN THEIR PROFESSIONAL CAPACITY,
321 REAL ESTATE LICENSEES ARE NOT ENTITLED TO NOTIFICATION BY THE COUNTY PROSECUTOR UNDER
322 MEGAN'S LAW AND ARE UNABLE TO OBTAIN SUCH INFORMATION FOR YOU. UPON CLOSING, THE COUNTY
323 PROSECUTOR MAY BE CONTACTED FOR SUCH FURTHER INFORMATION AS MAY BE DISCLOSABLE TO YOU.
324

325 **38. CONSUMER INFORMATION STATEMENT ACKNOWLEDGMENT:** By signing below, the Landlord and Tenant
326 acknowledge they received the Consumer Information Statement on New Jersey Real Estate Relationships from the brokerage firms
327 involved in this transaction prior to the first showing of the Property.
328

329 **39. DECLARATION OF LICENSEE BUSINESS RELATIONSHIP(S):**
330 A. _____, (name of firm)
331 AND _____ (name(s) of licensee(s))
332 AS ITS AUTHORIZED REPRESENTATIVE(S) ARE WORKING IN THIS TRANSACTION AS (choose one)
333 ❏ LANDLORD'S AGENTS ❏ TENANT'S AGENTS ❏ DISCLOSED DUAL AGENTS ❏ TRANSACTION BROKERS.
334
335 B. INFORMATION SUPPLIED BY _____(name of other firm)
336 HAS INDICATED THAT IT IS OPERATING IN THIS TRANSACTION AS A (choose one)
337 ❏ LANDLORD'S AGENT ONLY ❏ TENANT'S AGENT ONLY ❏ DISCLOSED DUAL AGENT ❏ TRANSACTION BROKER.
338
339

Tenant's
Initials: _____

Landlord's
Initials: _____

Figure 12.2: Residential Lease (continued)

340
341
342
343
344
40. ACKNOWLEDGMENT OF TRUTH IN RENTING STATEMENT: (**Applies to all Tenants with a rental term of at least one month living in residences with more than two dwelling units or more than three if the Landlord occupies one.**) By signing below, Tenant acknowledges receipt of the booklet, "Truth In Renting - A guide to the rights and responsibilities of residential tenants and landlords in New Jersey".

345
346
347
348
41. SMOKE DETECTORS, CARBON MONOXIDE ALARM AND PORTABLE FIRE EXTINGUISHER COMPLIANCE: The Certificate of smoke detectors, carbon monoxide alarm and portable fire extinguisher compliance (CSDCMAPFEC), as required by law, shall be the responsibility of the Landlord. If such alarms are battery operated, the Tenant shall be responsible for their maintenance.

349
350
351
352
353
354
355
356
357
358
359
42. PRIVATE WELL TESTING: (**This section is applicable if the Property's potable water supply is provided by a private well for which testing of the water is not required by any State law other than the Private Well Testing Act (the "Act" - N.J.S.A. 58:12A-26 to 37).**) By March 14, 2004, and at least once every five years thereafter, the Landlord is required to test the potable water supply for the Property in accordance with the Act. Within thirty (30) days after receiving the test results, the Landlord shall provide a written copy thereof to the Tenant. Also, the Landlord is required to provide a written copy of the most recent test results to any new tenant at the Property. If the Property is for "seasonal use or rental," the Landlord shall either post the tests results in a readily visible location inside of the Property or provide a written copy thereof to the tenant. A "seasonal use or rental" means use or rental for a term of not more than 125 consecutive days for residential purposes by a person having a permanent place of residence elsewhere. By signing below, Tenant acknowledges receipt of a written copy of the test results, or in the case of a seasonal rental, if it has not received the test results, acknowledges the posting thereof inside of the Property in accordance with the Act.

360
361
362
363
364
365
366
367
368
43. SECURITY CAMERAS:
If there are any security cameras on the Property, including but not limited to what often are called "nanny cams" or other video or audio taping equipment, the Landlord represents that the security cameras will be disabled and not functioning during the Term of this Lease unless only the Tenant has the use of the security cameras and neither the Landlord nor any other party has access to or the use of it. The Landlord acknowledges that any use or access to the security system by the Landlord or any other party during the tenancy may constitute an invasion of privacy of the Tenant and subject the Landlord to civil damages and criminal charges. Specifically excluded from this Section are such security cameras in multi-family housing that are in common areas, such as common hallways, the exterior of the building(s), entrance ways to the building(s), common laundry rooms, or common parking lots or garages.

369
370
371
44. MEGAN'S LAW REGISTRY: Tenant is notified that New Jersey law establishes an Internet Registry of Sex Offenders that may be accessed at www.njsp.org.

372
373
374
375
376
377
378
45. NEW MULTIPLE DWELLING RENT CONTROL / LEVELING EXEMPTION: If this box ❏ is checked, then the Property is exempt from rent control or rent leveling for such time as remains in the exemption period as provided in N.J.S.A. 2A:42-84.1, et seq., and Tenant acknowledges that Landlord has provided Tenant with a separate written notice about this exemption before Tenant signed this Lease. The period for this exemption shall not exceed the period of amortization of any initial mortgage loan obtained for the multiple dwelling or for thirty (30) years from the completion of construction, whichever is less. If the box in this section is not checked, then Tenant may contact the municipal clerk to determine if there is any rent control or rent leveling that applies to the Property.

379
380
381
382
46. ADDENDA:
The following additional terms are included in the attached addenda or riders and incorporated into this Lease (check if applicable):
❏ Addendum Permitting Pets

383
384
385
386
387
388
389
390
391
392
393
394
395
396
397
398
399
47. OTHER LEASE PROVISIONS, IF ANY:

Figure 12.2: Residential Lease (continued)

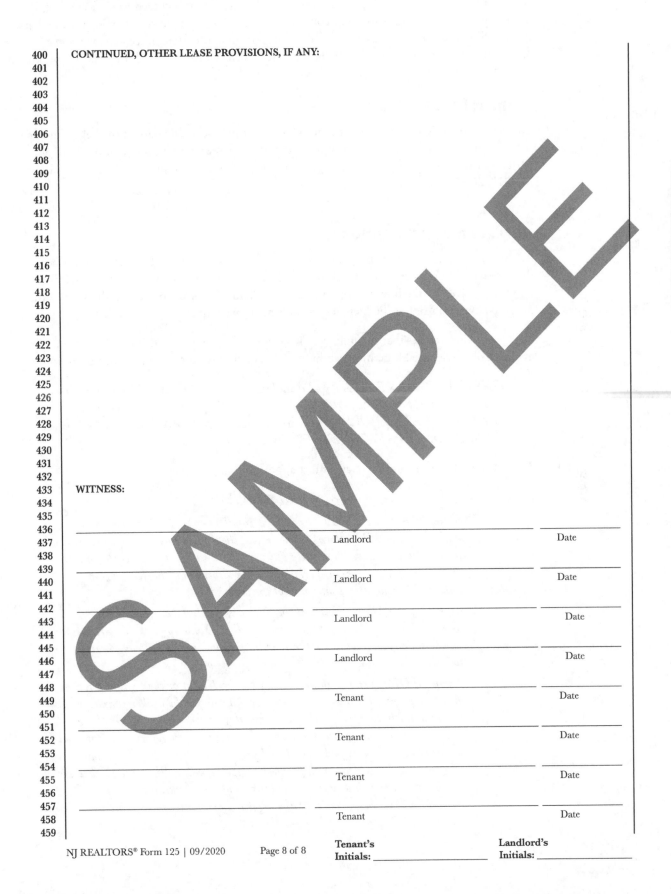

400	CONTINUED, OTHER LEASE PROVISIONS, IF ANY:
401	
402	
403	
404	
405	
406	
407	
408	
409	
410	
411	
412	
413	
414	
415	
416	
417	
418	
419	
420	
421	
422	
423	
424	
425	
426	
427	
428	
429	
430	
431	
432	
433	WITNESS:
434	
435	
436	_____ Landlord Date
437	
438	
439	_____ Landlord Date
440	
441	
442	_____ Landlord Date
443	
444	
445	_____ Landlord Date
446	
447	
448	_____ Tenant Date
449	
450	
451	_____ Tenant Date
452	
453	
454	_____ Tenant Date
455	
456	
457	_____ Tenant Date
458	
459	

NJ REALTORS® Form 125 | 09/2020   Page 8 of 8   Tenant's Initials: _____   Landlord's Initials: _____

Unit 12

Use of Premises

A lessor may restrict a lessee's use of premises through provisions included in the lease. This is most important in leases for stores or commercial space. For example, a lease may provide that the leased premises are to be used *only* for the purpose of a real estate office *and for no other purpose*. In the absence of such limitations, a lessee may use the premises for any lawful purpose.

Term of Lease

The period for which the lease runs should be set out precisely. The date of the beginning of the term and the date of its ending should be stated together with a statement of the total period of the lease: for example, "for a term of one year beginning June 1, 2021, and ending May 31, 2022."

New Jersey Requirements

All offers, contracts, or leases prepared by licensees must indicate the business relationship the firm has with respect to parties named in the document and acknowledgment that the CIS was received by the buyers/tenants and sellers/landlords prior to the first showing of the property. (See 11:5-6.9 of the New Jersey Administrative Code in Appendix A.)

New Jersey also requires that the following language appear in exactly this form at the top of the first page of a residential lease prepared by a real estate licensee for a term of one year or more:

THIS IS A LEGALLY BINDING LEASE THAT WILL BECOME FINAL WITHIN THREE BUSINESS DAYS. DURING THIS PERIOD YOU MAY CHOOSE TO CONSULT AN ATTORNEY WHO CAN REVIEW AND CANCEL THE LEASE. SEE SECTION ON ATTORNEY REVIEW FOR DETAILS.

The following language and form also must appear *within* the text:

ATTORNEY REVIEW:

1. *Study by Attorney. The Tenant or the Landlord may choose to have an attorney study this lease. If an attorney is consulted, the attorney must complete his or her review of the lease within a three-day period. This lease will be legally binding at the end of this three-day period unless an attorney for the Tenant or the Landlord reviews and disapproves of the lease.*

2. *Counting the Time. You count the three days from the date of delivery of the signed lease to the Tenant and the Landlord. You do not count Saturdays, Sundays, and legal holidays. The Tenant and the Landlord may agree in writing to extend the three-day period for attorney review.*

3. *Notice of Disapproval. If an attorney for the Tenant or the Landlord reviews and disapproves of this lease, the attorney must notify the broker(s) and the other party named in this lease within the three-day period. Otherwise this lease will be legally binding as written. The attorney must send the notice of disapproval to the broker(s) by certified mail, by telegram, or by delivering it personally. The telegram or certified letter will be effective upon sending. The personal delivery will be effective upon delivery to the broker's office. The attorney may, but need not also, inform the broker(s) of any suggested revision(s) in the lease that would make it satisfactory.*

Federal Lead-Based Paint Disclosure

Under the Lead-Based Paint Hazard Reduction Act (discussed in detail in Unit 9), persons leasing residential housing constructed before 1978 must disclose the presence of known lead-based paint and provide lessees with any relevant records or reports. A lead-based paint disclosure statement must be attached to all leases regarding residential properties built before 1978, and a lead hazard pamphlet must be distributed to all tenants before a lease is signed (refer to Figure 9.2).

The Environmental Protection Agency (EPA) conducts unannounced inspections of transaction files and leases in brokers' offices and it has levied substantial fines when there was no proof of the required disclosures having been made.

Security Deposits

Many leases require the tenant to provide some form of security. This security guarantees payment of rent and safeguards against a tenant's destruction of the premises. Residential landlords may charge no more than *one-and-a-half month's rental figure* as a security deposit; for commercial leases there is no maximum amount of security fixed by law. The tenant is to be notified where the money has been placed in a special interest-bearing account used only for security deposits. The tenant is entitled to all of the interest as a credit toward rent on the anniversary of the lease.

If the property is sold, the landlord turns over security deposits to the new owner and notifies the tenant. The landlord must return the security deposit, minus itemized deductions for damages done by the tenant, within 30 days after the end of the lease. The penalty for violation of this requirement is double the security. The tenant is not entitled to apply the deposit to the last month's rent, nor can the landlord keep the deposit if the only damage to the apartment can be construed as normal wear and tear.

Late Payments

Unless otherwise stated in the lease, rent is due at the end of each month ("in arrears," the opposite of "in advance"). For this reason, most leases clearly state that rent is due and payable at the beginning of the month. Landlords may charge a penalty for late payment of rent, except that senior citizens receiving Social Security, old-age railroad retirement pensions, or any other government pensions must be given a five-day grace period free of late charges.

LEGAL PRINCIPLES OF LEASES

When legal documents are involved, it may help to distinguish between the words *lessor* and *lessee* to recall this classic real estate story: The landlord of a two-family house with a gambling den on one side and a house of ill repute on the other is called the "'lessor' of two evils." New Jersey provides that leases can be recorded in the county in which the property is located when a lease runs for a period of *two years* or longer. The recording of a long-term lease places the world on notice of the long-term rights of the tenant. The recordation of such a lease is usually required if the tenant intends to mortgage his or her leasehold interest.

Possession of Leased Premises

Leases carry the implied covenant that the landlord gives the tenant possession of the premises. Thus, if the premises are occupied by a holdover tenant at the beginning of a new tenant's lease period, it is the landlord's duty to bring whatever action is necessary to recover possession and to bear the expense of this action.

Improvements

The tenant may make improvements with the landlord's permission, but any such alterations generally become the property of the landlord; that is, they become fixtures. However, a tenant may be given the right to install trade or chattel fixtures by the terms of the lease. It is customary to provide that such trade fixtures may be removed by the tenant before the lease expires, provided the tenant restores the premises to the same condition as when he or she took possession.

Maintenance of Premises

Every residential lease, oral or written, is considered to contain an **implied warranty of habitability**. The landlord guarantees that the leased property is fit for human habitation and that the tenant is not subjected to any conditions that could endanger life, health, or safety. The landlord is required to maintain dwelling units in a habitable condition and to make any necessary repairs to common elements such as hallways, stairs, or elevators. The tenant does not have to make any repairs (unless otherwise provided in the lease) but must return the premises in the same condition they were received, with allowances for wear and tear occasioned by ordinary use.

A landlord must make necessary repairs within a reasonable time after notification. The *Department of Community Affairs* inspects buildings with three or more apartments at least every five years for compliance with building and construction standards.

If a landlord fails to make repairs, New Jersey does recognize the tenant's right to *repair and deduct*—the tenant may withhold rent until the repairs have been made or, if repairs are vital and the landlord does not make them within a reasonable amount of time, have the repairs done and deduct their cost from the rent. If rent is withheld, it should be put in an escrow account. Such measures should not be undertaken without consulting an attorney first.

Where the landlord furnishes heat, between October 1 and May 1, all rooms must be heated to at least 68 degrees from 6 am to 11 pm, and to at least 65 degrees at night.

Assignment and Subleasing

The tenant may assign the lease or may sublease if the lease terms do not prohibit it. A tenant who transfers the entire lease *assigns* the lease. One who transfers most of the term but retains a small part of it, or transfers only a portion to the premises, *sublets*. The sublessor then has a *sandwich lease* and is in a middle position without occupying the property. In most cases the **sublease** or assignment of a lease does not relieve the original tenant of the obligation to make rental payments, unless the landlord agrees to waive such liability. If nothing states otherwise in the lease, the tenant has the right to assign it or sublet. Most leases prohibit the tenant from assigning or subletting without the landlord's consent; this allows the landlord to retain control over the occupancy of the leased premises.

When there is an **assignment** of a lease, the new tenant has primary responsibility for paying rent, though the original tenant maintains secondary liability in case of default. When the property is subleased, the original tenant is still responsible for seeing that rent is paid.

Destruction of Premises

Liability of either party in the event of destruction of leased premises is controlled largely by the terms of the lease. Carefully prepared leases generally include a provision covering the subject.

Termination of Lease

A written lease for a definite period of time expires at the end of that time period; no separate notice is required to terminate the lease when it expires. Oral and written leases that do not specify a definite expiration date (such as month-to-month or year-to-year tenancy or a tenancy at will) may be terminated by giving proper written notice.

When the conditions of a lease are breached, or broken, a landlord may terminate the lease and evict the tenant. This action must be handled through a court proceeding according to state law. The landlord who wishes to be rid of a tenant is not allowed to use threats of violence, change locks, discontinue essential services like water or heat, or seize the tenant's possessions.

It is possible for the parties to a lease to agree to cancel the lease. The tenant may offer to surrender the lease, and acceptance by the landlord results in termination. A tenant who abandons leased property remains liable for the terms of the lease—including the rent. The landlord is required, however, to try to mitigate damages by renting the property as soon as possible to another tenant. But if a tenant can only be found who will pay a lower rent, the original tenant is liable for the difference in rents.

The advance notice to be given by either landlord or tenant who wants to end the relationship varies according to the type of leasehold:

- An *estate for years* requires *no advance notice of termination* by either landlord or tenant; it ends automatically at the end of the stated term.
- A *tenancy at will* in New Jersey may be terminated by giving *three months' notice*.

Periodic estates have varying requirements:

- an estate from year to year requires three months' notice;
- a month-to-month tenancy requires one month's notice; and
- a week-to-week tenancy requires one week's notice.

If no intention to end the tenancy is expressed, periodic tenancies are automatically renewed for the same term—week, month, or year.

Death terminates a lease if a survivor notifies the lessor within 90 days of the death.

Unless a lease states otherwise, it *survives a sale*. That is, it is binding on the purchaser of the property, who takes title *subject* to present leases. Tenants have the same legal relationship with the new owner that they had with the old one.

TRUTH-IN-RENTING

The New Jersey Department of Community Affairs publishes an annual updated statement on the rights and duties of residential landlords and tenants. Included is information on eviction procedures, building maintenance requirements, and rent and lease provisions. Landlords must give a copy to every tenant and post a copy on the property.

The booklet, Truth in Renting, is no longer available for sale through the Department of Community Affairs. The booklet is available free at https://www.nj.gov/dca/divisions/codes /publications/pdf_lti/t_i_r.pdf in English and at https://www.nj.gov/dca/divisions/codes /publications/pdf_lti/spanish_tir.pdf in Spanish. Hard copies may be printed directly from the website.

The **Truth-in-Renting** requirement applies to residential property, including mobile homes, but not to commercial real estate. The booklet explains the rights and responsibilities of tenants and landlords and provides information about leases, security deposits, discrimination, safety, health and up-do-date information on New Jersey rental laws and regulations. Exceptions, under which the landlord is not required to distribute the statement, are for transient tenants with terms of less than one month and those in single-family or two-family houses (three-family if the landlord lives in one).

Disclosure of Owners and Managers

Landlords are required to inform tenants of the names and addresses of owners of the property, officers of a corporation that may own the building, resident managers, managing agents, superintendents, and mortgage holders. The disclosure also must be filed with local government and state agencies.

Federal Crime Insurance

Owners of all dwellings with ten or more units must provide tenants with information, obtainable from the federal Department of Housing and Urban Development, about special crime insurance available in high-risk areas that might not qualify for other insurance coverage.

THE AMERICANS WITH DISABILITIES ACT

The **Americans with Disabilities Act (ADA)** has had a significant impact on the responsibilities of the property manager, both in building amenities and in employment issues. The ADA was passed in 1990 and went into effect in 1992.

Title I of the ADA provides for the employment of qualified job applicants regardless of their disability. Any employer with 15 or more employees must adopt nondiscriminatory employment procedures. In addition, employers must make reasonable accommodations to enable individuals with disabilities to perform essential job functions.

Property managers must also be familiar with Title III of the ADA, which prohibits discrimination in commercial properties. The ADA requires that managers ensure that people with disabilities have full and equal access to facilities and services. The property manager typically is responsible for determining whether a building meets the ADA's accessibility requirements. The property manager must also prepare and execute a plan for restructuring or retrofitting a building that is not in compliance. ADA experts and architectural designers may need to be consulted.

To protect owners of existing structures from the massive expense of extensive remodeling, the ADA recommends *reasonably achievable accommodations* to provide access to the facilities and services. New construction and remodeling, however, must meet higher standards because new design costs less than retrofitting. An unexpected benefit to new owners is that many of the accessible design features and accommodations benefit everyone.

Existing barriers must be removed when this can be accomplished in a readily achievable manner—that is, with little difficulty and at low cost. (See Figure 12.3) The following are typical examples of readily achievable modifications:

■ Ramping or removing an obstacle from an otherwise accessible entrance

■ Lowering wall-mounted public telephones

■ Adding raised letters and braille markings on elevator buttons

■ Installing auditory signals in elevators

■ Reversing the direction in which doors open

Handicap parking spaces for people with disabilities can be set aside where appropriate.

Alternative methods can be used to provide reasonable accommodations if extensive restructuring is impractical or if retrofitting is unduly expensive. For instance, installing a cup dispenser at a water fountain that is too high for an individual in a wheelchair may be more practical than installing a lower unit.

Figure 12.3: Reasonable Modifications to Public Facilities or Services

Provide doors with automatic opening mechanisms

Provide menus (and real estate listings) in a large-print or braille format

Install an intercom so customers can contact a second-floor business in a building without an elevator

Lower public telephones

Add grab bars to public restroom stalls

Permit guide dogs to accompany customers

Provide a shopper's assistant to help disabled customers

Provide ramps in addition to entry stairs

RENTAL REFERRAL SERVICES

As discussed in Unit 1, those involved with rental referrals must be licensed. Every person working in rental referral agencies who for a fee refers prospective tenants to rental units is required to have a written contract with every prospective tenant. This contract must specify such things as services to be performed, fees charged, date and term of contract, and refund policy. The service should charge no more than $25 until the tenant actually secures an apartment listed with the broker. If prospective tenants are charged an advance fee of more than $25, regulations require deposit of the funds in an escrow account. No rental property may be offered without the landlord's consent; oral consent must be confirmed in writing within 24 hours.

Units that are advertised must be checked every day to see if they are still available; units that are simply listed in the MLS must be checked every three days. If prospective tenants are charged an advance fee of more than $25, regulations require deposit of the funds in an escrow account.

RENT CONTROL

Individual communities set their own rent control regulations, and some form of rent control is in effect in almost one-quarter of the state's municipalities. Most limit allowable yearly rent increases. To encourage construction of more housing units, new construction is exempt from rent control while an initial mortgage is in effect.

Although rent control clearly benefits tenants, many argue that in the long run it can hurt them because it can discourage investors from putting up rental housing and can cause hardship to landlords who cannot bring rents up to fair market value, encouraging them to let buildings deteriorate and eventually be abandoned.

EVICTION

A landlord may not evict a tenant without a court ruling. In cases of hardship, the court may allow a tenant as long as six months to find other accommodations. The law lists specific causes for eviction, with failure to pay rent and damage to property among the most common.

Landlords may not evict a tenant because the tenant made a complaint to a government agency. When property is being converted to a condominium or cooperative, certain tenants with disabilities and those aged 62 years or older may not be evicted. The tenants so protected must have occupied the premises for at least two years before the conversion and have income no higher than three times their county's per capita income (or, in any case, no higher than $50,000). If they meet the qualifications, they are allowed to continue as tenants for up to 40 years.

Constructive Eviction

Contrasted with the more familiar process of actual eviction is *constructive eviction*. If a landlord fails to provide such basic services necessary for human habitation as heat, electricity, or water, and the premises become uninhabitable, a tenant may claim **constructive eviction**, *move out*, and cease paying rent. The tenant must vacate the property before claiming constructive eviction. If asked for advice in such a case, a licensee should always recommend that the tenant consult an attorney first.

Suit for Possession—Actual Eviction

When a tenant breaches a lease or improperly retains possession of leased premises, the landlord may regain possession through a **suit for possession** or **summary proceeding** to recover possession of real estate. This process is known as **actual eviction**. Law requires the landlord to serve notice on the tenant before commencing the suit, except in a suit based on nonpayment of rent. The summary proceeding is often called a *dispossess proceeding*.

Causes for Eviction

In New Jersey, the landlord may sue for eviction on the following grounds:

- Nonpayment of rent—notice to quit need not be given before the suit is filed

- Tenant's disorderly conduct—three days' notice must be given before suit may be filed

- Destruction or damage to premises due to tenant's gross negligence—three days' notice is required

- Tenant's continued violation of landlord's regulations, provided they were included in the lease or in some other document that the tenant accepted and signed—one month's notice is required after a second written notice to cease

- Tenant's substantial violation or breach of any reasonable covenant of the lease agreement—one month's notice is required

- Tenant's failure to pay rent and/or an increase in rent after notice to quit and/or notice of increase is given, provided that the increase complies with all laws governing rent increases—no notice is required

- A landlord or owner cited for violations of local or state housing codes wants to permanently board up or demolish the property if the violations cannot be corrected without tenant removal—three months' notice is required

- Landlord's removing property from the rental market—six months' notice is required, unless the tenant has a lease for one year or more

- Tenant's failure to comply with new lease terms after written notice of such terms is given, provided such terms are reasonable—one month's notice is required, after a second notice to accept the changes

- Tenant's habitual failure to pay rent promptly after receiving written notice to cease—one month's notice is required

- Conversion of a building or mobile home park to a condominium, cooperative, or more dwelling units—three years and two months' notice is required

- An owner of three or fewer condominiums or cooperatives or a building of three or fewer residential units wants to personally occupy it—two months' notice is required

- Landlord's termination of a tenant's employment when this employment is the basis for the tenancy—three days' notice is required; Note: the employee must be discharged first for the notice to be effective in court

- Certain cases of conviction for a drug-related offense

New Jersey's Anti-Eviction Act provides, with only a few exceptions, that tenants who are current with their rent payments may not be evicted solely on the grounds of foreclosure. That is true whether or not a tenant has a written lease.

TYPES OF LEASES

Three primary types of leases are outlined in Figure 12.4.

Figure 12.4: Types of Leases

Type of Lease	Lessee	Lessor
Gross lease (residential)	Pays basic rent	Pays property charges (taxes, repairs, insurance, etc.)
Net lease (commercial/industrial)	Pays basic rent plus all or most property charges	May pay some property charges
Percentage lease (retail)	Pays basic rent plus percent of gross sales (may pay property costs)	May pay some or all property charges

Gross Lease

In a **gross lease** the tenant's obligation is to pay a *fixed rent*, and the landlord pays all taxes, insurance, mortgage payments, repairs, and the like connected with the property (usually called *property charges*). This type of lease most often is used for residential rentals.

Net Lease

The **net lease** provides that in addition to the rent, the tenant pays *some or all of the property charges*. The monthly rental paid to the landlord is in addition to these charges and so is net income for the landlord. Leases for entire commercial or industrial buildings and the land on which they are located, ground leases, and long-term leases are usually net leases. With a *triple-net lease*, the tenant pays taxes, insurance, and all other expenses except debt services.

Percentage Lease

A **percentage lease** provides that the rental be based on a *percentage of the gross income* received by the tenant doing business on the leased property. This type of lease is most commonly found in shopping malls.

The percentage lease usually provides for a minimum fixed rental fee plus a percentage of that portion of the tenant's business income that exceeds a stated minimum. For example, a lease might provide for a minimum monthly rental of $1,200 with the further agreement that the tenant pay an additional amount each month equivalent to 5% of all gross sales in excess of $30,000. The percentage charged in such leases varies widely with the nature of the business and is negotiable between landlord and tenant. A tenant's bargaining power is determined by the volume of business.

Other Lease Types

Variable Leases

Several types of leases allow for increases in the fixed rental charge during the lease period. Two of the more common ones are the *graduated lease*, which provides for increases in rent at set future dates, and the *index lease*, which allows rent to be increased or decreased periodically, based on changes in the government cost-of-living index.

Ground Leases

When a landowner leases his or her land to a tenant who agrees to erect a building on it, the lease is referred to as a **ground lease**. Such a lease must be for a long enough term to make the transaction desirable to the tenant making the investment in the building. These leases are generally *net leases* that require the lessee to pay rent as well as real estate taxes, insurance, upkeep, and repairs. Net ground leases often run for terms of 50 years or longer, and a lease for 999 years is not impossible. Although leases are considered to be personal property, the law may give these leaseholders some of the rights and obligations of real property owners. The lease may state what happens to the building at the end of the lease term, whether it reverts to the property owner or the tenant is responsible for demolishing it.

Oil and Gas Leases

When oil companies lease land to explore for oil and gas, a special lease agreement must be negotiated. Usually the landowner receives a cash payment for executing the lease. If no well is drilled within the period stated in the lease, the lease expires; however, most oil and gas leases provide that the oil company may continue its rights by paying another flat rental fee. Such rentals may be paid annually until a well is produced. If oil and/or gas is found, the landowner usually receives a fraction of its value as a royalty. In this case the lease continues for as long as oil or gas is obtained in significant quantities.

PROPERTY MANAGEMENT

In recent years the increased size of buildings; the technical complexities of construction, maintenance, and repair; and the trend toward absentee ownership by individual investors and investment groups have led to the expanded use of professional property managers for both residential and commercial properties.

Property management has become so important that many brokerage firms maintain separate management departments staffed by carefully selected, well-trained people. Many corporate and institutional owners of real estate have also established property management departments. Many real estate investors still manage their own property, however, and thus must acquire the knowledge and skills of a property manager. In some instances, property managers must be licensed real estate brokers.

FUNCTIONS OF THE PROPERTY MANAGER

In the simplest terms, a **property manager** is someone who *preserves the value* of an investment property *while generating income* as an agent for the owners. A property manager is expected to merchandise the property and control operating expenses so as to maximize income. A property manager chooses the best possible means to carry out an agents responsibilities and has more authority and discretion than an employee. A manager should maintain and modernize the property to preserve and enhance the owner's capital investment. The manager carries out these objectives by

- securing suitable tenants,
- collecting the rents,
- caring for the premises,
- budgeting and controlling expenses,
- hiring and supervising employees, and
- keeping proper accounts and making periodic reports to the owner.

The Management Agreement

The first step in assuming the management of any property is to enter into a **management agreement** with the owner. This agreement creates an agency relationship between the owner and the property manager. A property manager is usually considered a *general agent,* whereas most real estate brokers function as *special agents* because the property manager may be given authority to make decisions about the property and its expenses. Of course, the property manager is charged with the same fundamental responsibilities of agency—*Care, Obedience, Accounting, Loyalty,* and *Disclosure* (agency responsibilities are discussed at length in Unit 3).

The management agreement should be in writing and should cover the following points:

- Description of the property

- Time period the agreement will be in force

- Definition of management's responsibilities; all of the manager's duties should be stated in the contract, with exceptions noted

- Extent of manager's authority as an agent—This provision should state what authority the manager is to have in such matters as hiring, firing, and supervising employees; fixing rental rates for space; and making expenditures and authorizing repairs within the limits established previously with the owner (repairs that exceed a certain expense limit may require the owner's written approval)

- Reporting—Agreement should be reached on the frequency and detail of the manager's periodic reports on operations and financial position; these reports serve as a means for the owner to monitor the manager's work and as a basis for both the owner and the manager to assess trends that can be used in shaping future management policy

- Management fee—The fee can be based on a percentage of gross or net income, a commission on new rentals, a fixed fee, or any combination of these

- Allocation of costs—The agreement should state which of the property management expenses, such as custodial and other help, advertising, supplies, and repairs, are to be charged to the property's expenses and paid by the owner

Budgeting Expenses

Operating Expenses

Before attempting to rent any property, a property manager should develop an operating budget based on anticipated revenues and expenses and reflecting the long-term goals of the owner. In preparing a budget, a manager should begin by allocating money for such continuous *fixed expenses* as employees' salaries, management fees, property taxes, and insurance premiums.

Next, the manager should establish a *cash reserve fund* for such *variable expenses* as repairs, decorating, and supplies. The amount allocated for the reserve fund can be computed from the previous yearly costs of variable expenses.

Capital Expenditures

If an owner and a property manager decide that modernization or renovation of the property enhances its value, the manager should budget money to cover the costs of remodeling. In the case of large-scale construction, the expenses charged against the property's income should be spread over several years.

Renting the Property

The role of the manager in managing a property should not be confused with that of the broker, who acts as a leasing agent and is solely concerned with renting space. The property manager may use the services of a leasing agent, but that agent does not undertake the full responsibility of maintenance and management of the property.

Setting Rental Rates

In establishing rental rates for a property, a basic concern must be that in the long term, the income from the rentable space covers the fixed charges and operating expenses and also provides a fair return on the investment. Consideration also must be given to the prevailing rates in comparable buildings and the current level of vacancy in the property to be rented—supply and demand. Following a detailed survey of the competitive space available in the neighborhood, prices should be noted and adjusted for differences between neighboring properties and the property being managed. Annual rent adjustments are usually warranted. Apartment rental rates are stated in monthly amounts, but office and commercial space rentals are usually stated as either an annual or a monthly rate per square foot of space.

If a high level of vacancy exists, an immediate effort should be made to determine why. A high level of vacancy does not necessarily indicate that rents are too high. The trouble may be inept management or defects in the property. The manager should attempt to identify and correct the problems first, rather than immediately lowering rents. Conversely, a high percentage of occupancy may appear to indicate an effective rental program, but it could also mean that rental rates are too low. With an apartment house or office building, any time the occupancy level exceeds 95%, serious consideration should be given to raising the rents.

Tenant Selection

Generally, the highest rents can be secured from satisfied tenants. A broker may sell a property and then have no further dealings with the purchaser, whereas a building manager's success depends on retaining sound, long-term relationships. In selecting prospective commercial or industrial tenants, a manager should be sure that each tenant "fits the space." In selecting tenants, the property manager must comply with all federal and local antidiscrimination and fair housing laws.

Collecting Rents

The best way to minimize problems with rent collection is to make a careful selection of tenants in the first place. A property manager should investigate financial references given by the prospect, local credit bureaus, and, when possible, the prospective tenant's former landlord.

The terms of rental payment should be spelled out in detail in the lease agreement. A *firm* and *consistent* collection plan with a sufficient system of notices and records should be established. In cases of delinquency, every attempt must be made to collect without resorting to legal action. For those cases in which it is required, a property manager must be prepared to initiate and follow through with legal counsel.

Maintaining the Property

One of the most important functions of a property manager is supervision of property maintenance. A manager must learn to balance the provided services with the costs they entail so as to satisfy the tenants needs while minimizing operating expenses.

Hiring Employees vs. Contracting for Services

One of the major decisions a property manager faces is whether to contract for maintenance services from an outside firm or hire on-site employees to perform such tasks. This decision should be based on a number of factors, including size of the building, complexity of tenant's requirements, and availability of suitable labor.

Insurance

One of the most important responsibilities of a property manager is to protect the property owner against all major insurable risks. In some cases a property manager or a member of the management firm may be a licensed insurance broker. In any case a competent, reliable insurance agent who is well versed in all areas of insurance pertaining to property should be selected to survey the property and make recommendations. If the manager is not completely satisfied with these recommendations, additional insurance surveys should be obtained. Final decisions, however, must be made by the property owner. An insurance broker *must pass a state examination* to secure a special license to sell insurance.

THE MANAGEMENT FIELD

For those interested in pursuing a career in property management, most large cities have local associations of building and property owners and managers that are affiliates of regional and national associations. The Institute of Real Estate Management (IREM) was founded in 1933 and is part of the National Association of REALTORS®. Members may earn the designation **Certified Property Manager (CPM)**. The Building Owners and Managers Association International (BOMA International) is a federation of local associations of owners and managers, primarily of office buildings. Participation in groups like these allows property managers to gain valuable professional knowledge and to discuss their problems with other managers facing similar issues.

A growing field is the management of cooperatives and condominiums. The manager hired by a homeowners' organization must develop different techniques because owners and tenants are one and the same. The Community Associations Institute (CAI) is a nonprofit organization founded in 1974 to research and distribute information on association living and offers training and designation for specialized management.

SUMMARY

A *lease* grants one person the right to use the property of another for a certain period in return for consideration.

A leasehold estate that runs for a specific length of time creates an *estate for years*, whereas one that runs for an indefinite period creates a *periodic estate* (year to year, month to month) or a *tenancy at will*. A leasehold estate is generally classified as personal property.

The requirements of a valid lease include the capacity to contract, a demising clause, description of premises, statement of terms, rent, and signatures. The state statute of frauds requires that any lease for more than three years be in writing. Most leases also include clauses relating to rights and obligations of the landlord and tenant, such as the use of the premises, subletting, judgments, maintenance of the premises, and termination of the lease period. Under the Lead-Based Paint Hazard Reduction Act, persons leasing residential housing constructed before 1978 must disclose the presence of known lead-based paint and provide lessees with any relevant records or reports along with a special information pamphlet.

New Jersey residential landlords are allowed to charge up to one-and-one-half months' rent as a security deposit and must return any deposit due within 30 days after the end of the lease. Tenants are entitled to all of the interest earned on security deposits.

The state's *Truth-in-Renting* law requires landlords to furnish most residential tenants with a yearly statement of rights and duties of landlords and tenants, as issued by the *Department of Community Affairs*. Landlords must also inform tenants of the names and addresses of owners and managers of the property.

Upon a tenant's breach of any of the lease provisions, a landlord may sue for a money judgment or for *actual eviction* where a tenant has improperly retained possession of the premises. If the premises have become uninhabitable due to the landlord's negligence, the tenant may exercise *constructive eviction*, the right to abandon the premises and refuse to pay rent until the premises are repaired.

Basic types of leases include *net leases*, *gross leases*, and *percentage leases*, classified according to the method used in determining the rental rate of the property.

Property management is a specialized service to owners of income-producing properties, in which the managerial function may be delegated to an individual or a firm with particular expertise in the field. The *property manager*, as agent of the owner, becomes the administrator of the property.

A *management agreement* must be carefully prepared to define and authorize the manager's duties and responsibilities. The first step a property manager should take when managing a building is to draw up a budget of estimated variable and fixed expenses. The budget should allow for any proposed expenditures for major renovations or modernizations. These projected expenses, combined with the manager's analysis of the condition of the building and the rent patterns in the neighborhood, will form the basis on which rental rates for property are determined.

After a rent schedule is established, the property manager is responsible for soliciting tenants whose needs are suited to the available space and who are financially capable of meeting the proposed rents. The manager usually is obligated to collect rents, maintain the building, hire necessary employees, pay taxes for the building, and deal with tenant problems.

One of the manager's primary responsibilities is supervising maintenance. Maintenance includes safeguarding the physical integrity of the property and performing routine cleaning and repairs, as well as adapting the interior space and overall design of the property to suit the tenants' needs and meet the demands of the market.

In addition, the manager is expected to secure adequate insurance coverage for the premises.

USEFUL WEBSITES

Building Owners and Managers Association: www.boma.org

N.J. DCA Landlord/Tenant Lawsuits: www.judiciary.state.nj.us/civil/civ-04.htm

Institute of Real Estate Management: www.irem.org

Americans with Disabilities Act Information: www.usdoj.gov/crt/ada

KEY TERMS REVIEW 1

Match the number of each key term with the corresponding letter.

_____ 1. Actual eviction

_____ 2. Assignment

_____ 3. Certified Property Manager

_____ 4. Constructive eviction

_____ 5. Demise

_____ 6. Estate for years

_____ 7. Gross lease

_____ 8. Ground lease

_____ 9. Holdover tenancy

_____ 10. Implied warranty of habitability

_____ 11. Lease

_____ 12. Lessee

A.   a transfer of only a portion of the lease

B.   designation by the Institute of Real Estate Management

C.   landlord's responsibility for decent conditions

D.   lease for a definite period of time

E.   lease under which landlord pays taxes, insurance, and other expenses

F.   a transfer of property by lease

G.   tenant is forced to move because apartment becomes uninhabitable

H.   rental of land on which tenants erect their own buildings

I.   situation when tenant remains after lease period has expired

J.   suit for possession; legal removal of a tenant

K.   tenant

L.   transfer of primary responsibility for a lease to another party

KEY TERMS REVIEW 2

Match the number of each key term with the corresponding letter.

_____ 1. Lessor

_____ 2. Management agreement

_____ 3. Net lease

_____ 4. Percentage lease

_____ 5. Periodic estate

_____ 6. Property manager

_____ 7. Sublease

_____ 8. Suit for possession

_____ 9. Summary proceeding

_____ 10. Tenancy at sufferance

_____ 11. Tenancy at will

_____ 12. Truth-in-Renting

A.   a transfer of only a portion of the lease

B.   another term for dispossess proceeding

C.   landlord's court action to evict tenant

D.   lease in which landlord shares in gross receipts of tenant's business

E.   lease in which tenant pays expenses like property taxes, insurance, and so forth

F.   lease with regular rent payments and no stated ending date

G.   landlord

H.   person who looks after another's rental real estate

I.   property manager's employment agreement

J.   state requirements that tenants be notified of their rights

K.   tenancy that may be terminated when landlord or tenant wishes

L.   tenants remaining after lease term without landlord's consent

UNIT 12 REVIEW QUESTIONS

1. A licensee-written lease must contain notice of the right to attorney review if it
   A. requires a security deposit.
   B. contains an automatic renewal clause.
   C. provides for holdover tenancy.
   D. is for a period of one year or more.

2. A lead-based paint disclosure statement must be included in the lease for any
   A. residential property.
   B. living unit to be occupied by a child under the age of ten.
   C. residential building constructed before 1978.
   D. residential or commercial property.

3. A lease is considered to be
   A. a freehold estate.
   B. personal property.
   C. a reversionary interest.
   D. real property.

4. A woman agrees to rent her upstairs apartment to a friend for only the next six months. The friend has a(n)
   A. estate for years.
   B. periodic estate.
   C. tenancy at will.
   D. tenancy at sufferance.

5. The owner agrees to rent his upstairs apartment, which is not subject to rent control, to a friend from month to month. To end the arrangement, the owner must
   A. file a court suit to recover possession.
   B. give at least 60 days' notice from the day the rent is due.
   C. give at least one month's notice before the day the rent is due.
   D. simply refuse to accept the next month's rent on the day it is due.

6. A tenant's lease has expired, the tenant has neither vacated nor negotiated a renewal lease, and the landlord has declared that she does not want the tenant to remain in the building. The tenancy is called
   A. estate for years.
   B. periodic estate.
   C. tenancy at will.
   D. tenancy at sufferance.

7. The owner sells her six-unit apartment building in Trenton to a buyer. All tenants have leases and have paid security deposits. Now
   A. the buyer may give all the tenants 30 days' notice.
   B. tenants should collect their security deposits from the previous owner.
   C. the new owner must renegotiate all leases with the tenants.
   D. the original owner must turn over security deposits to the new owner.

8. A lease, properly acknowledged, may be recorded if it is for a period of more than
   A. one year.
   B. two years.
   C. three years.
   D. four years.

9. The prospective tenant is entitled to an attorney's review of a licensee-written residential lease that runs for as short a term as
   A. three years.
   B. two years.
   C. one year.
   D. six months.

10. A tenant who transfers the entire remaining term of his or her lease to a third party is
    A. a sublessor.
    B. assigning the lease.
    C. automatically relieved of any further obligation under it.
    D. giving the third party a sandwich lease.

11. An apartment lease agreement states that it expires on April 30, 2022. When must the landlord give notice that the tenancy is to end?
    A. January 31, 2022
    B. March 31, 2022
    C. April 1, 2022
    D. No notice is required.

12. If a tenant falls three months behind in rent payments, a landlord may
    A. turn down the heat.
    B. move out the tenant's possessions, storing them carefully.
    C. start a court suit for possession.
    D. do all of the above.

13. Even when there is a lease, if a landlord turns the heat down to 55 degrees, the tenant may move out and stop paying rent because of
    A. the demising clause.
    B. constructive eviction.
    C. a summary proceeding.
    D. secondary liability.

14. A property manager may be reimbursed with
    A. a percentage of rentals.
    B. rebates from suppliers.
    C. key money.
    D. any of the above.

15. In New Jersey, rent security deposits
    A. must be placed in an interest-bearing account.
    B. belong to the landlord while in his or her possession and may be kept in the landlord's personal savings account.
    C. may be double the rent.
    D. must be placed in the bank within 15 days of acceptance.

16. After a landlord has properly placed a tenant's security deposit in a bank account,
    A. annual interest earned must be credited to the tenant.
    B. the landlord may keep, for expenses, 2% of the annual interest earned on the deposit.
    C. the tenant can demand its return at any time.
    D. no other tenant's security deposit can be added to that account.

17. An owner wants to sell a rental residential property that is currently under lease for another 16 months. Regarding the security deposit made by the current tenants, the seller
    A. may keep it, as the new owner can collect a new security deposit from the tenants.
    B. must return the deposit and interest earned to the tenants.
    C. must deliver the deposit to the purchaser and notify the tenants.
    D. must immediately terminate the current lease.

18. A tenant signed an apartment lease calling for $1,000 rent per month. According to New Jersey law, the landlord may also require a maximum security deposit of
    A. $500.
    B. $1,000.
    C. $1,250.
    D. $1,500.

19. A woman owns a 24-unit apartment building. The building is managed by a professional management company, and a superintendent lives on the premises. As the landlord, the woman is responsible for furnishing certain information to each of her tenants. Which of the following is NOT her responsibility to provide?
    A. Her name and address, as well as those of the managing agent and the superintendent
    B. Information regarding the Federal Crime Insurance Program, including how the tenant may obtain coverage
    C. A copy of the Truth-in-Renting Statement
    D. The name of the local housing inspector and health officer

20. A gross lease is most likely to be used for rental of
    A. an apartment.
    B. a factory building.
    C. land under a post office.
    D. a farm.

21. With a triple-net lease, the tenant pays
    A. rent only.
    B. rent plus a share of business profits.
    C. rent plus any increase in property taxes.
    D. everything but the mortgage.

22. A percentage lease provides for a
    A. rental of a percentage of the value of a building.
    B. definite periodic rent not exceeding a stated percentage.
    C. definite monthly rent plus a percentage of the tenant's gross receipts in excess of a certain amount.
    D. graduated amount due monthly and not exceeding a stated percentage.

23. A ground lease is usually
    A. terminable with 30 days' notice.
    B. based on percentages.
    C. long term.
    D. a gross lease.

24. In the absence of rent regulations, the amount of rent charged is determined by the
    A. management agreement.
    B. principle of supply and demand.
    C. operating budget.
    D. toss of a coin.

25. The initials CPM stand for
    A. chargeback percentage mortgage.
    B. contract priority maintenance.
    C. Certified Property Manager.
    D. cardiopulmonary manipulation.

UNIT
13

LEARNING OBJECTIVES

When you have completed this unit, you will be able to accomplish the following.

› Describe the provisions of a note, a mortgage, and a trust deed.
› Explain various methods of satisfying or transferring a mortgage, including the process of foreclosure.

KEY TERMS

acceleration clause	hypothecation	satisfaction of mortgage
alienation clause	mortgage	sheriff's deed
bond	mortgagee	sheriff's sale
default	mortgagor	short sale
defeasance clause	note	subordination agreement
deficiency judgment	prepayment	usury
estoppel certificate	real estate owned (REO)	
foreclosure	reduction certificate	

NOTE AND MORTGAGE

A **mortgage** is a pledge of real property that serves as security or collateral for a loan. Two documents are involved:

1. A **note** (or, in some areas, a similar document known as a **bond**) is the financing instrument signed by the borrower, who states, "I promise to repay the money you have just lent me, at the following rate and terms . . ." It is the note that makes the borrower *personally liable* for the *entire amount* borrowed, even if the property goes down in value. While the mortgage creates a *lien*, the note creates a personal obligation and the mortgage creates a lien.

2. The *mortgage* itself is a security instrument signed by the borrower, which states, "If I don't keep my promise to repay you as agreed, you may foreclose" (have the property sold at public auction and use the proceeds to pay the debt).

It is the borrower who signs the mortgage, who does the mortgaging. It is incorrect to say to a buyer, "We will find a bank to give you a mortgage." What the bank gives is a *loan*, money; in return it takes a mortgage, *holds* a mortgage.

The **mortgagor** is the owner of the property. In other words, the mortgagor is the borrower, who can pledge the property as security to the lender, who is the **mortgagee**. Remember that when you see the "-or," it refers to the owner of the property.

Hypothecation is the term used to describe the pledging of property as security for payment of a loan without surrendering possession of the property.

TRUST DEEDS

In some areas of the country and in certain situations, lenders prefer to use a three-party instrument known as a *trust deed* or *deed of trust*, rather than a mortgage document. A trust deed conveys the real estate as security for the loan to a third party, called the *trustee*. In case of default, the lender with a trust deed can gain possession of the property more promptly and more simply than a lender who forecloses on a mortgage. In most aspects, a trust deed operates like a mortgage. When the borrower has made the last payment, title is returned by way of a deed of reconveyance or release deed.

PROVISIONS OF THE NOTE OR BOND

The promissory note (or bond) executed by a borrower (known as the *maker* or *payor*) states the amount of the debt, the time and method of payment, and the rate of interest, if any. The bond, like the mortgage, should be signed by all parties who have an interest in the property.

PROVISIONS OF THE MORTGAGE DOCUMENT

The mortgage document refers to the terms of the note and clearly establishes that the land is security for the debt. It identifies the lender as well as the borrower, and it includes an accurate legal description of the property. It should be signed by all parties who have an interest in the real estate. It also sets forth the obligations of the borrower and the rights of the lender.

Duties of the Mortgagor

The borrower's obligations usually include the following:

- Paying the debt in accordance with the terms of the note
- Paying all real estate taxes on the property given as security
- Maintaining adequate insurance to protect the lender if the property is destroyed or damaged by fire, windstorm, or other hazard
- Obtaining lender's authorization before making any major alterations on the property
- Maintaining the property in good repair at all times
- Until the mortgage has been in place for 30 days, obtaining lender's authorization before placing a second mortgage (junior lien) against the property

Failure to meet any of these obligations can result in a borrower's **default** on the note. When this happens, the mortgage usually provides for a grace period (30 days, for example) during which the borrower can meet the obligation and cure the default. If he or she does not do so, the lender has the right to foreclose the mortgage and collect on the note. The most frequent cause of default is the borrower's failure to pay monthly installments.

Provisions for Default

A mortgage may include an **acceleration clause** to assist the lender in a foreclosure. If a borrower defaults, the lender has the right to accelerate the maturity of the debt—to declare the *entire* debt due and owing *immediately*. The acceleration clause is the first step used in foreclosure.

Other Clauses

Other clauses in a mortgage enable the lender to take care of the property in the event of the borrower's negligence or default. If the borrower does not pay taxes or insurance premiums or make necessary repairs on the property, the lender may step in and do so to protect his or her security (the real estate). Any money advanced by the lender to cure such defaults is either added to the unpaid debt or declared immediately due and owing from the borrower.

In New Jersey mortgages, a **defeasance clause** ensures that when the debt is repaid, the mortgagee has no further claim on the property.

Assignment of the Mortgage

A note or bond is usually a *negotiable instrument*; as such it may be sold by the lender to a third party, or *assignee*. An **estoppel certificate** executed by the borrower verifies the amount that remains to be repaid and the interest rate. On payment in full, or satisfaction of the debt, the assignee is required to execute the satisfaction, or release, of the mortgage. In the event of a foreclosure, the assignee (not the original mortgagee) files the suit.

Recording Mortgages

The mortgage document should be recorded in the proper office of the county in which the real estate is located. This establishes the lien's priority over future mortgages or other liens. To be recorded, the signature on the document must be acknowledged before a notary public.

INTEREST RATES

Usury

The charging of an unreasonably high rate of interest is known as **usury**. Various state laws protect borrowers. The federal government, in an effort to make mortgage money freely available, has exempted most regular lending institutions from mortgage limits. Two private sources for mortgage money, however, are bound by state usury laws:

1. The seller who "takes back financing" or holds the mortgage
2. Third parties (real estate broker, grandfather, investor), who may lend the buyer money to purchase someone else's property

In New Jersey, *sellers* may charge no more than 16% on a first mortgage; however, they may charge as much as 30% when they are selling their own primary residences. If the seller is taking back a second mortgage, the limits are 16% on the first $50,000 lent and up to 30% beyond that amount.

When a private *third party*, someone not the seller and not an institutional lender, makes a mortgage loan, it is *essential* to find out ahead of time *what usury limits apply*. A mortgage that charges an illegal rate of interest is not legally enforceable; the borrower might have a good case for not repaying the debt at all. Maximum rates are set by the New Jersey commissioner of banking and are changed as the money market changes.

Imputed Interest

The Internal Revenue Service (IRS), on the other hand, is concerned about artificially low interest rates, sometimes used as a trade-off by a seller who prefers a higher sales price, with favorable capital gains treatment.

If seller financing is at an artificially low interest rate, the IRS "imputes" a higher rate and taxes the recipient accordingly. If the amount of seller financing in a transaction is $2.8 million or less, the seller must charge no less than 9% interest or a rate equal to the applicable federal rate (AFR), whichever is lower. The AFR is set monthly by the federal government and reflects current rates around the country. If the seller charges a rate lower than required, he or she is taxed as if income had been received at the required rate. An exception is made for certain transfers of vacant land within a family.

Prepayment

A prepayment is any amount paid before it is due. The most common example is the seller paying the remainder of the mortgage loan so the seller can convey the property to the new buyer. Under New Jersey law an institutional lender may not impose a prepayment fee or penalty if a mortgage is fully paid off earlier than was originally planned.

FIRST AND SECOND MORTGAGES

Mortgages and other liens normally have priority in the order in which they have been recorded. A mortgage on land that has no prior mortgage lien on it is a *first mortgage*. When the owner of this land later executes another mortgage for additional funds, the new mortgage becomes a *second mortgage*, or *junior lien*, when recorded. The first mortgage has prior claim to the value of the land pledged as security. A home equity loan is usually a second mortgage.

The priority of mortgage liens may be changed by the execution of a **subordination agreement** in which the first lender subordinates his or her lien.

The holder of the first mortgage would then drop back in priority, allowing a later mortgage to move up. This is sometimes done to allow further financing when the first lender feels the additional loan would benefit all concerned.

SATISFACTION OF THE MORTGAGE LIEN

When all mortgage loan payments have been made and the note paid in full, the mortgagee (lender) is usually required to execute a *release of mortgage*, or **satisfaction of mortgage**.

By having this release entered in the public record, the owner shows that the mortgage lien has been removed from his or her property. Neglecting to do so can lead to irritating legal problems in later years.

New Jersey law requires the mortgagee to record the satisfaction or discharge of mortgage document. The borrower (mortgagor) may be charged for the recording fee (see Figure 13.1).

Figure 13.1: Mortgages

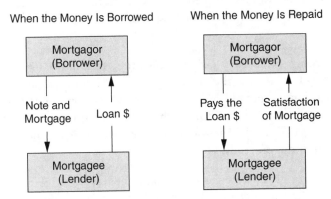

ASSUMING A SELLER'S MORTGAGE

Anyone who purchases real estate that has an assumable mortgage on it may be able to *assume* it and *agree to pay the debt*. The new owner then becomes personally obligated for payment of the debt. If the mortgage is foreclosed in such a case and the court sale does not bring enough money to pay the debt in full, a deficiency judgment against *both* the assumer and the original borrower can be obtained for the unpaid balance. While the assignee has become responsible for the debt, the assignor *retains secondary liability* if the lender cannot collect the full amount owed from the assignee.

When a mortgage is being assumed or paid off, the borrower requires a statement from the mortgagee detailing the amount currently due. This **reduction certificate** is often—and wrongly—referred to as an estoppel certificate.

BUYING SUBJECT TO A SELLER'S MORTGAGE

Anyone who purchases real estate *subject to* a mortgage is not assuming a note or bond and is not *personally obligated* to pay the debt. The new owner has bought the real estate knowing that he or she must make the loan payments and that on default the lender forecloses and the property is sold by court order to pay the debt. If the sale does not pay off the entire debt, the new owner is *not liable* for the difference.

Alienation Clause

Frequently, when a real estate loan is made, the lender wishes to prevent some future purchaser of the property from being able to assume that loan, particularly at its old rate of interest. For this reason some lenders include an **alienation clause** (also known as a *resale clause* or *due-on-sale clause*) in the note. An alienation clause provides that on the sale of the property, the lender has the choice of either declaring the entire debt to be immediately due and owing or permitting the buyer to assume the loan.

FORECLOSURE

When a borrower defaults in making payments or fulfilling any of the obligations set forth in the mortgage, the lender can ask the court to order a **foreclosure** sale. The mortgagee must search the public records to find other parties who have claims against the property and to find out whether tenants are involved. All must be notified that the suit is in progress, a *lis pendens* is placed in the public records, and a public auction, a **sheriff's sale**, is advertised in local newspapers.

Back property taxes and special assessments have first claim on the property, and whoever buys the real estate has to pay them. *Junior liens* to the one being foreclosed, however, are *wiped out by the sale*. For this reason, junior lienholders (usually those with second mortgages, construction liens, and the like) attend the auction to protect their interests. If necessary, they may bid the price up high enough to pay their claims as well. If someone else bids higher, they can expect their debts to be paid out of the proceeds.

The successful bidder must pay cash, at least 20% at the auction and the rest within ten days. Until a **sheriff's deed** is delivered to the buyer at the end of the ten days, the defaulting borrower can redeem the property by paying the full amount due, including back taxes and legal costs. After that time, no further right of redemption exists in New Jersey.

In some other states the former owner has a *statutory right of redemption* for up to one year after the foreclosure sale.

Deed in Lieu of Foreclosure

An alternative to foreclosure is for the lender to accept a *deed in lieu of foreclosure* from the borrower. This is sometimes known as a *friendly foreclosure* because it is by agreement rather than by civil action. The major disadvantage to the lender is that it takes the real estate subject to all junior liens, while foreclosure eliminates all such liens. However, because foreclosure is a time-consuming and expensive procedure, lenders will sometimes agree to accept a "deed in lieu."

Short Sale

During the recent recession, rising unemployment and falling prices left some homeowners unable to make their mortgage payments and unable to sell for enough to pay off the whole debt. In that situation, lenders sometimes agreed to a short sale rather than foreclosing on the loan. The lender would agree to accept whatever the house brought on the open market and remove the mortgage lien so that title could be transferred.

Rarely, the lender might then seek a deficiency judgment for the shortfall. Often, though, the debt was simply listed as satisfied. The lender reserved the right to approve or disapprove of the sale contract, and the process was often lengthy and complicated. But, for a homeowner facing foreclosure, a short sale did somewhat less damage to a credit record.

Deficiency Judgment

If the foreclosure sale does not produce sufficient cash to pay the loan balance in full after deducting expenses and accrued unpaid interest, the mortgagee may be entitled to seek a *personal judgment* against the signer of the note for the unpaid balance. Such a judgment is called a **deficiency judgment**. It may be obtained against any endorsers or guarantors of the note and any owners of the mortgaged property who may have assumed the debt by written agreement. If, on the other hand, there are any surplus proceeds from the foreclosure sale after the debt is paid off and expenses are deducted, they are paid to the borrower.

Real Estate Owned

In recent years, many homeowners owe more than their houses can be sold for, a situation often referred to as being "underwater" with an "upside-down" mortgage. When the mortgage is foreclosed, no outsider will bid enough to take the property, and it defaults to the lender.

Real estate owned (REO) is used to describe such properties acquired by lenders through foreclosure. Some real estate brokers specialize in handling REO properties for lending institutions.

SUMMARY

The borrower who pledges real estate is known as a *mortgagor*; the lender is a **mortgagee**. The borrower signs a personal promise to repay as a *note* or *bond*, and also pledges the property in a *mortgage*.

The borrower who fails to live up to the provisions of the mortgage is said to be in *default*. An *acceleration clause* allows the mortgagee to declare the whole debt due and payable in case of default. A *defeasance clause*, on the other hand, provides that when the debt has been paid, the mortgagee has no further claim on the property.

An *estoppel certificate* is the borrower's statement of the remaining debt and interest rate. A *reduction certificate* is the lender's acknowledgment that the debt has been paid down to a certain amount.

The charging of a higher rate of interest than is legally allowed is known as *usury*. Lending institutions are free of usury limits. New Jersey sets high limits for sellers taking back financing on their own property and market-rate limits for third parties who make mortgage loans. The IRS imputes interest income to sellers who set artificially low interest rates on mortgages they hold.

A *first mortgage* is the first one placed against the property in the public records. A further mortgage loan would become a second or *junior lien*. Priority is set by the date of recording, unless one lender agrees to subordinate a loan to another. Full payment of the loan is acknowledged by the lender's signing of a *satisfaction of mortgage* certificate, which should be entered in the public records.

One who takes over property *subject* to an existing loan is not personally responsible in case of default. The buyer who assumes an existing loan makes a personal promise to repay. An *alienation clause* provides that a mortgage cannot be assumed by anyone else but must be paid off if the property is sold.

When a borrower is in default, the mortgagee may ask the court to order a *foreclosure*, with a *public auction* of the property, known as a *sheriff's sale*. The successful bidder receives a *sheriff's deed* after ten days. Until the deed is delivered, the original owner can redeem the property by coming forward with all the money due.

If the sale yields more than enough to pay the debts, the original owner receives any money that is left. If the sale does not yield enough, the mortgagee may seek a *deficiency judgment* against the borrower.

Unit 13

KEY TERMS REVIEW

Match the number of each key term with the corresponding letter.

_____ 1. Acceleration clause

_____ 2. Alienation clause

_____ 3. Bond

_____ 4. Default

_____ 5. Defeasance clause

_____ 6. Deficiency judgment

_____ 7. Estoppel certificate

_____ 8. Foreclosure

_____ 9. Hypothecation

_____ 10. Mortgage

_____ 11. Mortgagee

_____ 12. Mortgagor

_____ 13. Note

_____ 14. Reduction certificate

_____ 15. REO property

_____ 16. Satisfaction of mortgage

_____ 17. Sheriff's deed

_____ 18. Sheriff's sale

_____ 19. Short sale

_____ 20. Subordination agreement

_____ 21. Usury

A. borrower

B. borrower's statement of how much remains on mortgage debt

C. arrangement by which mortgage holder gives up priority

D. charging higher interest than is allowed by law

E. clause ensuring that after repayment, lender has no claim on property

F. clause stating that if property is sold, debt is immediately payable

G. pledging of property as security without surrendering possession

H. clause stating that in case of default, the whole debt is immediately payable

I. court order that borrower pay money lost by lender after foreclosure

J. document given to purchaser of foreclosed property

K. failure to live up to any part of a mortgage agreement

L. lender

M. lender's statement of how much remains on a debt

N. lender's statement that debt has been repaid in full

O. personal promise to repay a loan; similar to a bond

P. personal promise to repay money; similar to a note

Q. proceeding to auction foreclosed real estate

R. to seize and sell property pledged for a debt

S. written pledge of real estate as security for a loan

T. lender agrees to accept sale proceeds, even if less than the debt

U. property acquired by lenders

UNIT 13 REVIEW QUESTIONS

1. All on the same parcel: Person A gives Person B a mortgage in return for a loan of $100,000. Person B fails to record the mortgage. Person A then borrows an additional $40,000 from Person C, who records the mortgage. Person A then persuades Person D to lend him $150,000 and Person D records his mortgage. Which is now the first mortgage against the property?
   A. Person B's, because it was the loan first made
   B. Person C's, because it was the one first recorded
   C. Person D's, because it was for the largest amount
   D. Person B's and Person C's, sharing priority

2. An owner allows the buyer to take over the mortgage on her property when he buys the house. She receives the *MOST* protection if the buyer
   A. takes the property subject to the existing loan.
   B. assumes the existing loan.
   C. acknowledges the present loan.
   D. subordinates the loan.

3. A mortgage document requires the mortgagor to perform certain duties. Which of the following is NOT one of these?
   A. Maintain the property in good condition at all times
   B. Obtain the mortgagee's permission before renting a room to a boarder
   C. Maintain adequate insurance on the property
   D. Obtain the lender's permission before making major alterations to the property

4. A buyer borrows $120,000 to buy a house. The local factory closes down and real estate values fall. At a foreclosure auction the property sells for only $80,000. To make up its loss, the lender may seek a deficiency judgment against
   A. the original buyer.
   B. the new owner.
   C. the appraiser.
   D. no one.

5. In a friendly foreclosure, the lender agrees to
   A. forgive the loan.
   B. accept the deed in lieu of foreclosure.
   C. reduce the amount owed on the loan.
   D. a short sale.

6. The bond accompanying a mortgage is signed by the
   A. mortgagor.
   B. mortgagee.
   C. grantor.
   D. lessee.

7. The IRS taxes income not really received if a mortgage interest rate is
   A. above federal usury limits.
   B. charged by a seller.
   C. set by the state.
   D. below the applicable rate.

8. New Jersey's usury limits apply to interest on mortgage loans by
   A. state-chartered banks.
   B. sellers and third parties.
   C. regular lending institutions.
   D. the FHA.

9. The two instruments signed by someone who pledges real estate for a loan are known as the
   A. note and mortgage.
   B. abstract and conveyance.
   C. estoppel and note.
   D. note and bond.

10. A mortgagor is the one who
    A. pays transfer tax.
    B. lends the money.
    C. signs the note.
    D. holds the note.

11. A homeowner has just made the final payment on his mortgage loan. His lender must record a(n)
    A. satisfaction of the mortgage.
    B. reconveyance with a quit claim deed.
    C. alienation.
    D. reversion.

12. The clause that could require a mortgagor to pay the whole debt, interest, and charges immediately is called a(n)
    A. escalation clause.
    B. amendatory clause.
    C. acceleration clause.
    D. lock-in clause.

13. A homeowner defaulted on his mortgage, which had a remaining principal balance of $100,000. At the foreclosure sale, the house brought only $82,000. To recover the remaining $18,000, the lender may
    A. seek a deficiency judgment.
    B. sue for specific performance.
    C. sue for damages.
    D. get a default judgment.

14. A homeowner defaulted on his mortgage, which had a remaining balance of $165,000. At the foreclosure sale, the property brought $180,000. After the debt and the costs of foreclosure are met, who receives the remaining money?
    A. The sheriff's office
    B. The mortgagor
    C. The mortgagee
    D. The purchaser

15. An interest rate that exceeds the legal rate is called
    A. usury.
    B. deficiency.
    C. escheat.
    D. void.

16. A homeowner paid off the whole of her mortgage loan several years ahead of schedule. According to New Jersey law, her bank may impose a prepayment penalty of
    A. nothing.
    B. 1% of the remaining debt.
    C. paperwork fees only.
    D. a flat $1,000 charge.

17. A mortgage may be recorded
    A. to establish the priority of the lender's lien.
    B. even though the borrower has not received a copy of it.
    C. to bar a construction lien.
    D. to prevent a personal levy.

18. An existing mortgage loan may be changed to a junior lien by
    A. a subordination agreement.
    B. satisfaction of the loan.
    C. court order.
    D. acceleration.

19. To establish a mortgage lien's priority, the mortgage document should be
    A. witnessed.
    B. sealed.
    C. recorded.
    D. considered.

20. The successful bidder at a foreclosure auction must pay for the property with
    A. a credit card.
    B. hypothecation.
    C. a junior lien.
    D. cash.

21. A short sale is one in which the
    A. purchase contract is signed within the first week the property is on the market.
    B. owner agrees to sell at 10% or more off the listing price.
    C. seller and the agent negotiate a cut-rate commission.
    D. lender accepts whatever the property brings on the market.

22. Borrowers decided to accelerate their mortgage payments. This process is called
    A. leverage.
    B. prepayment.
    C. rate locking.
    D. hypothecation.

UNIT 14

Financing I: Conventional, FHA, and VA Loans

LEARNING OBJECTIVES

When you have completed this unit, you will be able to accomplish the following.

› Describe issues concerning mortgage financing, including various payment plans.
› Distinguish differences among conventional loans, insured loans, guaranteed loans, and New Jersey's homebuyers' programs.

KEY TERMS

adjustable-rate mortgage (ARM)
amendatory clause
amortization schedule
amortized loan
assumable
biweekly mortgage
broker's price opinion (BPO)
budget loan
buydown
cap
ceiling

Certificate of Reasonable Value (CRV)
equity
Federal Housing Administration (FHA)
FHA 203(b)
index
interest
loan-to-value (LTV) ratio
margin
negative amortization
New Jersey Housing and Mortgage Finance Agency (NJHMFA)

PITI
points
private mortgage insurance (PMI)
rate lock
straight (term) loan
target area
Your Home Loan Toolkit: A Step-by-Step Guide
VA (Veterans Affairs) mortgage

MORTGAGE FINANCING

Few buyers approach the real estate transaction with all the money they need to purchase the real estate, whether a home or an investment property. Most loans require a down payment. At the time of purchase, the buyers' **equity** is equal to the down payment. Their equity grows as the property increases in value and the mortgage payments reduce the loan amount. **Interest** is the "rent" the borrower pays the lender for the use of the lender's money.

The amount of a mortgage loan in relation to the value of a home, the **loan-to-value (LTV) ratio**, has increased from 40% in 1920 to as much as 95 or 100% today. Payment periods have also lengthened from five years in the 1920s to as much as 30 years or more today.

Interest rates charged by lending institutions on home mortgage loans vary as changes occur in the money market. As interest rates move up, an established fixed-rate mortgage with a low interest rate may be a plus in selling a home if the new owner is able to assume the existing mortgage. On the other hand, if mortgage interest rates fall, homeowners may seek to pay off their loan and refinance at a lower rate.

To buffer the effects of an unstable money market, lenders have been offering many alternative forms of mortgages in recent years, such as adjustable interest rate mortgages. Seller financing gains popularity in times of tight mortgage money.

For years, potential homeowners have been able to receive assistance in obtaining low down-payment mortgage loans through the government programs of the Federal Housing Administration (FHA) and the Department of Veterans Affairs (VA). In addition, private mortgage insurance companies offer programs that enable loan applicants to receive higher LTV ratios from private lenders than they could otherwise obtain.

PAYMENT PLANS

Most mortgage loans are **amortized loans**. The word *amortize* means "to kill off slowly over time." That's what an amortized loan does: it slowly "kills off" a debt over time through periodic payments to the lender. Regular payments are applied first to the interest owed, and the balance is applied to the principal amount over a term of perhaps 15 to 30 years. At the end of the term, the full amount of the principal has been paid off. Such loans are also called *self-liquidating loans*.

Most amortized mortgage loans are paid in monthly installments. These payments may be computed based on a number of payment plans, which tend to gain and lose favor as the cost and availability of mortgage money fluctuates.

Fixed-Rate Loans

■ A *fully amortized loan* is the most frequently used plan. It requires the mortgagor to pay a constant amount, usually each month. The mortgagee credits each payment first to the interest due and then applies the balance to reduce the principal of the loan. While each payment is the same, the portion applied toward repayment of the principal grows and that applied to the interest due declines as the unpaid balance of the loan is reduced. (See Figure 14.1.)

■ A *straight payment plan* calls for periodic payments of interest only, with the principal to be paid in full at the end of the loan term. This is known as a **straight (term) loan**. Such plans are generally used for home improvement loans and second mortgages rather than for residential first mortgage loans.

■ When a mortgage loan requires periodic payments that do not fully amortize the amount of the loan by the time the final payment is due, the final payment is a larger amount than the others. This is called a *balloon payment*, and this type of loan is called a *partially amortized loan*.

■ **Biweekly mortgages** involve half-payments every two weeks instead of monthly. Some borrowers misunderstand this as "twice a month" but it involves 26 half-payments, the equivalent of 13 monthly payments a year. The extra money, applied entirely to principal, can reduce time on a fixed-rate loan from 30 years to 22 or 23 years.

Figure 14.1: Level-Payment Amortized Plan

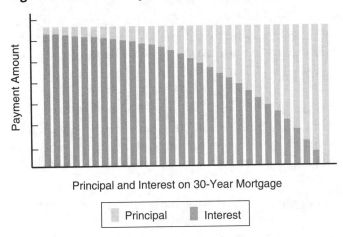

Principal and Interest on 30-Year Mortgage

Principal   Interest

Adjustable-Rate Mortgages

Adjustable-rate mortgages shift the risk—or reward—of changing interest rates from the lender to the borrower, with corresponding changes in the monthly payment.

The ARM shifts the risk of changing interest rates to the borrower, who also stands to benefit if rates drop during the period of the loan. (See Figure 14.2.)

Figure 14.2: Adjustable-Rate Mortgage

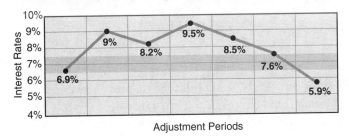

The vocabulary of ARMs includes the following terms.

Adjustment Period

This is the anniversary on which interest rate adjustments may be made. Most borrowers elect one-year adjustments, although they might be made more frequently or after three, five, or even ten years.

Index

The interest rate on the loan may go up or down, following the trend for interest rates across the country. The lender must key changes to some national indicator of current rates. The most commonly chosen **index** is the rate paid on one-year U.S. Treasury bills or London Interbank Offered Rates (LIBORs).

Unit

Margin

If treasury bills are the chosen index and they are selling at 2% interest at the time the loan is adjusted, the borrower pays a specific percentage above that index. That percentage is known as the **margin**. With a 2% margin over treasury bills, the borrower would be charged 4%.

Cap

The loan agreement may set a **cap** of, for example, 2% on any single adjustment. If interest rates (as reflected by the index) went up 3% by the time of adjustment, the interest rate could be raised only 2%. Depending on the particular mortgage, the extra 1% might be treated one of three ways:

1. It could be saved by the lender to be used at the next adjustment period, even though rates had fallen in the meantime.

2. It could be absorbed by the lender with no future consequences to the borrower.

3. The shortfall (the unpaid 1%) could be added to the amount borrowed so that the principal would increase instead of decreasing (negative amortization).

Ceiling

A **ceiling** (sometimes called a *lifetime cap*) is a maximum allowable interest rate. Typically, a mortgage may offer a five-point ceiling. If the interest rate started at 8%, it could never go beyond 13%, no matter what happened to national rates. A ceiling allows the borrower to calculate the *worst case*.

Worst Case

If a 30-year adjustable loan for $150,000 costs $1,100 a month for principal and interest at 8% and if the ceiling is 5%, the worst that could happen is that the rate would go to 13%. The borrower can calculate in advance what that would cost—$1,659 a month.

Negative Amortization

When the monthly payment isn't enough to cover the interest due, the shortfall is sometimes added to the principal amount. As a result, the debt increases (rather than taking its normal downward path). This process is known as negative amortization. Not all mortgage plans include the possibility of **negative amortization**. Sometimes the lender agrees to absorb any shortfalls. The possibility must always be explored, however, when an ARM is being evaluated.

Convertibility

This feature may offer the best of both worlds. The borrower may choose to change the mortgage to a fixed-rate mortgage at then-current interest levels. With some plans any favorable moment may be chosen. More commonly the option is available on the third, fourth, or fifth anniversary of the loan.

Cash outlay for the conversion is low, compared with the costs of placing a completely new mortgage: One point, or 1% of the loan, is typical. The borrower, however, may be charged a slightly higher interest rate all along for this privilege.

Initial Interest Rate

With many loan plans the rate during the first year, or the first adjustment period, is set artificially low ("teaser" rate) to induce the borrower to enter into the agreement. This enables some buyers, whose income might not otherwise qualify, to place new mortgage loans. Buyers who plan to be in a house for only a few years may be delighted with such arrangements, especially if no interest adjustment is planned for several years. Other borrowers, however, may end up with negative amortization and payment shock at the first adjustment.

Assumability

Some ARMs are **assumable** by the next owner of the property, usually with the lender's approval and the payment of one point or more in service fees.

To help consumers compare different ARMs, lenders must give anyone considering a specific adjustable-rate mortgage a uniform disclosure statement that lists and explains indexes, history of past interest rate changes, and other information. A method for calculating the worst case is included.

The disclosures must be furnished before the loan applicant has paid any nonrefundable application fee.

Hybrid Mortgage Loans

A combination of fixed-rate and adjustable-rate loans, hybrids offer an initial fixed interest rate, usually for three to seven years, followed by annual rate adjustments for the balance of the term.

Interest-Only Loans

When high interest rates or zooming property values make it impossible for many homebuyers to afford traditional mortgage loans, some lenders offer interest-only mortgages which have lower monthly payments because the debt is not being amortized. Many financial experts consider these risky because the homeowner is not reducing the debt. If prices stop rising or even fall, owners who had to sell might find themselves "underwater" or "upside down"—owing more than the house would bring in a sale. With some plans, the interest-only provision lasts for only a given number of years and a new amortization schedule at the end of that time requires much higher monthly payments.

Interest

A charge for the use of someone else's money is called **interest**. A lender charges a borrower a certain percentage of the principal as interest for each year the debt is outstanding. The amount of interest due on any one installment payment date is calculated by computing the total yearly interest, based on the unpaid balance, and dividing that figure by the number of payments made each year.

Unit

On an amortized loan of $100,000 for 30 years at an annual interest rate of 7% and monthly payments of $665.31, the amount due after the first month's payment has been made can be calculated in four steps, as follows:

1. $100,000 × 7% = $7,000 annual interest

2. $7,000 ÷ 12 = $583.33 first month's interest

   $665.31 monthly payment made

3. −583.33 interest due first month

   $81.97 available to pay down principal

   $100,000.00 debt at start of month

4. −81.97 principal repayment

   $99,918.03 remaining debt after first month

The following month, because less is now being borrowed, not quite so much interest is due, and the principal can be reduced by a slightly larger amount.

Figure 14.3 shows an **amortization schedule** for the first and last three months of this 360-payment loan. Interest is usually due at the *end* of each payment period (payment *in arrears*, as opposed to payment *in advance*). Figure 14.4 shows the amount of monthly payment needed to amortize a given loan. Many real estate salespersons and brokers carry special hand calculators with built-in amortization tables.

Figure 14.3: Amortization Table for the First and Last Few Months of a 30-Year Loan of $100,000 at 7% with Monthly Payment of $665.30

Month	Payment	Interest	Principal	Remaining Balance
1	$665.30	$583.33	81.97	$99,918.03
2	665.30	582.36	82.44	99,835.59
3	665.30	582.37	82.93	99,752.66
358	665.30	11.51	653.79	1,318.92
359	665.30	7.69	657.61	666.31
360	665.30	3.86	661.31	0.00

TAX-DEDUCTIBLE INTEREST PAYMENTS

The Tax Cuts and Jobs Act (TCJA), which is in effect from 2018 to 2025, allows homeowners to deduct interest on qualified home loans up to $750,000 (down from $1 million in 2017). For taxpayers who use married filing separate status, the home acquisition debt limit is $375,000. The new law ended the deduction for interest on home equity lines of credit until 2026, unless one condition is met—the HELOCs or home equity loans are used to pay for improvements to the home.

The upper limit to state and local taxes deduction (SALT) is now $10,000. This limit has been particularly hard on property owners in New Jersey, New York, and California because these states have high property taxes.

Different income tax regulations apply to mortgage loans on investment property. Licensees should always recommend that clients consult with a qualified tax person about current tax regulations.

Figure 14.4: Monthly Payment Needed to Amortize a Loan of $1,000

How to Use This Chart

To use this chart, start by finding the appropriate interest rate. Then follow that row over to the column for the appropriate loan term. This number is the payment required each month to amortize a loan. To calculate the principal and interest payment, multiply the payment by the number of 1,000s in the total loan.

For example, if the interest rate is 8% for a term of 30 years, the payment is 7.34. If the total loan is $100,000, the loan contains 100 1,000s. Therefore, 100 × 7.34 = $734 PI only.

Rate	Term 10 Years	Term 15 Years	Term 20 Years	Term 25 Years	Term 30 Years
3	9.65	6.90	5.54	4.74	4.21
3¼	9.77	7.02	5.67	4.87	4.35
3½	9.88	7.14	5.79	5.00	4.49
3¾	10.00	7.27	5.92	5.14	4.63
4	10.13	7.40	6.06	5.28	4.78
4¼	10.25	7.53	6.20	5.42	4.92
4½	10.37	7.65	6.33	5.56	5.07
4¾	10.49	7.78	6.47	5.71	5.22
5	10.61	7.91	6.60	5.85	5.37
5¼	10.73	8.04	6.74	6.00	5.53
5½	10.86	8.18	6.88	6.15	5.68
5¾	10.98	8.31	7.03	6.30	5.84
6	11.10	8.44	7.16	6.44	6.00
6¼	11.23	8.57	7.31	6.60	6.16
6½	11.35	8.71	7.46	6.75	6.32
6¾	11.48	8.85	7.60	6.91	6.49
7	11.61	8.98	7.75	7.06	6.65
7¼	11.74	9.12	7.90	7.22	6.82
7½	11.87	9.27	8.05	7.38	6.99
7¾	12.00	9.41	8.20	7.55	7.16
8	12.14	9.56	8.37	7.72	7.34
8¼	12.27	9.71	8.53	7.89	7.52
8½	12.40	9.85	8.68	8.06	7.69
8¾	12.54	10.00	8.84	8.23	7.87
9	12.67	10.15	9.00	8.40	8.05

POINTS

When a new mortgage is placed, the lending institution may compensate for an interest rate below the current true cost of money by asking for extra prepaid interest in the form of upfront **points** (also called *discount points*). Each point is 1% of the new loan. On an $80,000 loan each point would be $800; a charge of two points would total $1,600. Payment of points is a one-time affair, usually at the time of closing but occasionally at mortgage application or issuance of a mortgage commitment by the lender.

Points may be paid by either buyer or seller, depending on the terms of the sales contract. The buyer's points are interest payments, income-tax deductible in the year they are paid. When the seller pays points to help the buyer obtain financing, the IRS allows the buyer to deduct them. The seller may not, because they are not paid on the seller's own loan. Points paid by investors or by refinancing homeowners must be *capitalized* or *amortized* (deducted gradually over the period of the loan).

RATE LOCK

Because interest rates change constantly, lenders may offer the borrowers the opportunity to lock in at a quoted rate. In this situation, the lender agrees to hold the quoted rate for a certain period of time. If the interest goes up, the borrower is protected. Unfortunately, if the interest rate goes down, the borrower often cannot take advantage. Borrowers typically can lock the rate for 30, 45, 60 days and hope that they get to closing before the rate lock expires.

BUYDOWNS

With some mortgage plans, lending institutions are willing to lower the interest rate in return for extra payment of points. The arrangement is known as a **buydown**. Permanent buydowns keep the interest rate low for the entire life of the loan. Often sellers pay points for the buyer to lower the rate for a period of time, for example, by 3% the first year of the loan, 2% the second year, and 1% the third year (3-2-1 buydown). Because the buyer's qualification for the loan is calculated using the initial interest rate, such an action by the seller enables the buyer to pay a higher purchase price by qualifying for a larger mortgage.

TAX AND INSURANCE RESERVES

Most lenders require borrowers to provide a reserve, or escrow, fund to meet future real estate taxes and, in some cases, insurance premiums. When the mortgage loan is made, the borrower starts the reserve by depositing funds to cover partial payment of the following year's tax bill and property insurance premium. Thereafter the monthly loan payments required of the borrower include *principal, interest,* and *tax* and *insurance* reserves (**PITI**).

To be certain that these important bills are being met, the lender accumulates the borrower's money in the escrow account. Property tax bills and insurance premium bills are sent directly to the lending institution, which pays them and renders accounting to the borrower. In most cases, the borrower is entitled to 2% interest on the money thus held. When the mortgage loan is eventually paid off, any money remaining in the escrow account is returned to the borrower. A PITI loan is sometimes referred to as a **budget loan**. RESPA, the federal Real Estate Settlement and Procedures Act, limits the amount of tax and insurance reserves that a lender may require.

YOUR HOME LOAN TOOLKIT: A STEP-BY-STEP GUIDE

Real estate licensees can provide their buyers the *Your Home Loan Toolkit: A Step-by-Step Guide* created by the Consumer Financial Protection Bureau (CFPB). Although lenders are obligated to provide the booklet to borrowers within three business days of their completed loan application, no one is actually responsible for explaining the contents of the booklet. The CFPB suggests that real estate licensees provide and discuss the booklet with their buyers as soon as practical, even before the buyers consult a lender.

The Toolkit includes easy-to-understand information on a number of topics:

- How to determine affordability

- How credit scores affect the availability of mortgage money
- How to choose the right mortgage and down payment
- Understand the trade-off between points and interest rate
- Value of shopping several lenders
- How to avoid pitfalls and handle problems

The Toolkit is available for download in English at https://files.consumerfinance.gov/f/201503 _cfpb_your-home-loan-toolkit-web.pdf and in Spanish at https://files.consumerfinance.gov/f /documents/cfpb_your-home-loan-toolkit_es.pdf

The Toolkit can also be purchased in bulk from https://bookstore.gpo.gov/agency/224.

CONVENTIONAL, INSURED, AND GUARANTEED LOANS

Mortgage loans fall into several classifications:

- *Conventional loans* are those arranged entirely between borrower and lending institution.
- *Government-backed loans* include those *insured* by the Federal Housing Administration (FHA) or *guaranteed* by the Department of Veterans Affairs (VA). With both types *the actual loan comes from a local lending institution.*
- *Loans directly from the government* include New Jersey Housing and Mortgage Finance Agency mortgages and Rural Economic Community Development (RECD) (the former Farmer's Home Administration) loans. In addition, in certain rural areas of the country where there are no banks who place VA loans, the VA lends money directly to the veteran.

Conventional Loans

In making conventional loans, lending institutions set their own standards within the scope of banking regulations. As a result, a variety of mortgage plans are often offered and some flexibility is occasionally available. Conventional mortgages may be fixed rate, adjustable rate, or a combination. Most conventional mortgages are not assumable by a subsequent buyer of the property or are assumable only with the lender's approval.

Private Mortgage Insurance

In general, conventional loans call for higher down payments (lower LTV ratio) than do government-backed mortgages. Banking theory holds that it risks depositors' money to lend more than 80% of the value of real estate. With any down payment less than 20%, therefore, a conventional loan must be accompanied by **private mortgage insurance (PMI)**. The borrower pays a monthly premium for insurance that protects the *lender* in case of loss at a foreclosure. This is not life insurance.

For conventional loans placed after July 29, 1999, the federal government requires that lenders drop PMI coverage at the borrower's request when equity reaches 20%, and that coverage be dropped automatically when it reaches 22%. Equity is the difference between the market value of the property and the amount still owed on it. A new appraisal may be required. In some cases, the lender may accept instead a BPO (broker's price opinion). This written estimate of value resembles a CMA (comparative market analysis). Like a CMA, it should contain, in type at least as large as that used in the main body of the document, a statement that it "should not be considered the equivalent of an appraisal prepared by a New Jersey licensed or certified real estate appraiser." As with other commissions and fees, any payment the licensee receives for providing a BPO must be paid to the agent's supervising broker.

FHA-Insured Loans

The **Federal Housing Administration (FHA)** which operates under the Department of Housing and Urban Development (HUD), neither builds homes nor lends money itself. Rather, it insures loans on real property made by approved lending institutions. It does not insure the property, but it does insure the lender against loss. The common term FHA *loan*, then, refers to a loan that is *not made* by the agency, but is *insured* by it.

Most FHA loans are processed through direct endorsement, with lenders handling the paperwork within their own organizations. Borderline cases are forwarded to the FHA for final decision; this can add several weeks to the loan process. Borrowers are often attracted to FHA loans because they require a low down payment, and allow relatives or the seller to furnish some of the cash required at closing.

FHA 203(b)

The most widely used FHA mortgage is **FHA 203(b)**, which may be placed on one- to four-family residences. Certain requirements are set by the FHA before it will insure a loan.

An upfront single mortgage insurance premium (MIP) is charged at closing. It may be paid in cash or added to the loan. For 30-year mortgages, this lump-sum premium is 1.75% of the loan amount.

The FHA allows any or all of the down payment and closing costs to be a gift (not a loan) from the borrower's relatives. In addition, a willing seller may pay the points and furnish money to establish the escrow account for payment of future property taxes and insurance premiums. The seller's contribution ("seller concession") may not exceed 6% of the loan.

In addition to the lump-sum payment, FHA borrowers also pay as much as 1.55% a year as additional mortgage insurance premium in some cases, depending on the amount of down payment and term of the loan.

The FHA requires that most borrowers (those who make less than a 10% down payment) continue to pay annual premiums for the life of the loan, up to 30 years. The only way to cancel the annual MIP is to pay off the loan or refinance.

Estimate of Value

The real estate must be evaluated by an FHA-approved appraiser. The maximum loan is a percentage of the appraised value. If the purchase price is higher than the FHA appraisal, the buyer must pay the difference in a higher cash down payment or may decide not to purchase.

The FHA allows down payments as low as 3.5% and will consider applicants with credit scores as low as 580 in some circumstances.

FHA borrowers are allowed to finance a portion of their closing costs. The amount of the financed closing costs is added to the base loan amount. Therefore, the total amount borrowed, including the upfront mortgage insurance premium, may exceed the purchase price of the property in some cases. The FHA sets top limits on its loans, depending on price levels in different areas of the country.

Repair Requirements

The FHA may stipulate repairs to be completed before issuing mortgage insurance on a specific property. Before the purchase contract is signed, however, the FHA requires the buyer to be notified in writing that its appraisal is concerned mainly with the value of the property, and that the use of a home inspector is recommended.

Occupancy Requirement

With certain exceptions, the borrower must intend to occupy the property. Certain energy-saving improvements may be financed along with an FHA mortgage. No prepayment penalties are charged if an FHA loan is paid off before the end of the term.

Assumability

An older FHA loan, one made before December 15, 1989, may be *assumed* (taken over along with the house) by any next owner of the property, with no change in interest rate, no credit check on the buyer, and only a small charge for paperwork. The original borrower is never released from liability, however, unless the new borrower is willing to go through a *formal assumption*, which involves the lender's approval of credit and income.

FHA mortgages placed after December 15, 1989, are assumable if the new borrower, who must intend to occupy the house, qualifies by the lender's standards.

Other FHA Programs

Among other FHA programs, which may or may not be available at any given time, are adjustable-rate mortgages and special plans intended for veterans, teachers, and law enforcement officers, for rehabilitation of housing being purchased, and for no-down-payment purchase of modest homes.

Other FHA programs are sometimes available to finance mobile homes, manufactured housing, condominiums, and rehabilitation construction of housing.

FHA Section 203(k) mortgages allow one loan to cover both the purchase price and extensive rehabilitation work. Section 203(k) mortgages may also be used for refinancing to cover the existing loan plus remodeling jobs like a garage or addition to a house.

For either an FHA or VA mortgage loan, an extra **amendatory clause** must be included in the sale contract. It states that if the property appraises for less than the agreed upon sale price, the buyer is not obligated to complete the purchase.

VA-Guaranteed (GI) Loans

The Department of Veterans Affairs (VA) can guarantee lending institutions against loss on mortgage loans to eligible veterans. Because the VA guarantees the top 25% of the loan, *no down payment is required* (though individual lenders may sometimes ask for a small down payment). Although no top limit is set for the loan, the VA will guarantee a loan on a single-family house in New Jersey up to $510,000 in lower-cost counties and up to $765,608 in more-expensive counties.

VA mortgages, formerly known as GI mortgages, are intended only for *owner-occupied* property owned or co-owned by the veteran, and may be placed on one- to four-family residences. Although the guarantee comes from the federal government, the loan itself is made by a local lending institution.

As with FHA loans, the contract must contain a clause stating that if the appraisal comes in lower than the purchase price, the veteran can get out of the contract at no penalty—or, at the veteran's option, make up the difference in cash at closing. A VA appraisal is called a **Certificate of Reasonable Value (CRV)**. It is also possible for the veteran to get a no-points mortgage by paying a higher interest rate. Any discount points may be paid by the seller or the buyer alone, or shared between them.

The veteran pays a *funding fee* directly to the Department of Veterans Affairs, the amount varying depending on the size of the down payment.

Any veteran with a service-connected disability is exempt from funding fees, and National Guardsmen and Reservists pay higher funding fees.

The seller can pay the funding fee for the veteran, or the veteran can finance the fee by adding it to the mortgage amount.

Eligibility

The right to a VA guarantee does not expire. To qualify, a veteran must have a discharge that is "other than dishonorable" and the required length of service:

- 90 consecutive days of active service during wartime
- 181 days of active service during peacetime
- Six years in the Reserves or the National Guard

In-service VA loans are available to those still on active duty.

The veteran applying for a VA loan must furnish a *certificate of eligibility*.

Even though the veteran has used some or all of his or her eligibility to guarantee one loan, it is sometimes possible to place another VA mortgage. Entire or partial eligibility may still be available if

- the first loan has used up only part of the guarantee;
- the original VA loan has been paid off; or
- the original VA loan was formally assumed by another veteran.

Depending on the size of the down payment, reusers of VA eligibility may be charged a higher funding fee.

The widow or widower of a veteran who died of a service-connected disability and who has not remarried may use the veterans eligibility.

Information is available at http://www.benefits.va.gov/homeloans/.

Assumability

Any VA mortgage loan made before March 1, 1988, may be assumed by the next owner of the property, who need not be a veteran and need not prove qualification to the lender or the VA. For loans made after March 1, 1988, the assumer (who need not be a veteran) must prove creditworthiness, and a fee of up to 1% may be charged. For VA loans made after 1989, the veteran is free of liability after a good-faith assumption.

NEW JERSEY HOMEBUYERS' PROGRAM

The **New Jersey Housing and Mortgage Finance Agency (NJHMFA)** offers below-market-interest loans, with low or no down payment, to qualified buyers who purchase homes in urban **target areas**, located mainly in inner cities. Outside the target areas, these loans may be available to first-time homebuyers.

The loans are possible on one- to four-family dwellings and are not available to investors. Maximum allowable family income ranges apply depending on the size of the family and the county in which the property is located.

Application is made through various local lenders handling the program. An informative brochure can be ordered by calling 800-NJ-HOUSE. The website is www.state.nj.us/dca/hmfa; 800-564-6873.

FARMER'S HOME LOAN

For the purchase of inexpensive homes in rural areas and small towns, the former *Farmer's Home Administration (FmHA)*, now the *Rural Economic and Community Development (RECD)*, is an agency of the federal Department of Agriculture that makes direct loans to borrowers.

For low-income first-time homebuyers, mortgage interest may be subsidized as low as 1%. Only modest homes qualify. Sales are handled through local real estate brokers, but the loan comes directly from the Department of Agriculture. Information and the location of local offices is available at https://www.usda.gov/topics/rural/housing-assistance.

SUMMARY

The note for most common forms of mortgage loans provides for amortization, the gradual repayment of principal borrowed along with interest. The note also sets the rate of *interest* that the mortgagor must pay as a charge for borrowing the money.

In an *adjustable-rate mortgage*, the interest rate is changed each adjustment period to a stipulated *margin* above a national *index* of current mortgage rates. A *cap* may limit the size of possible adjustments, and a *ceiling* may limit the maximum adjustment over the life of the loan. In instances where monthly payments do not cover the interest due, negative amortization is possible, with the total debt increasing instead of decreasing as it does with normal amortization.

Mortgage loans include conventional loans, those insured by the FHA or an independent mortgage insurance company, and those guaranteed by the VA. FHA and VA loans must meet certain requirements for the borrower to obtain the benefits of the government backing that induces the lender to lend its funds. Lenders may charge discount *points*; each point is 1% of the new mortgage. FHA and VA mortgages are generally *assumable*, with some exceptions and regulations.

The *New Jersey Housing and Mortgage Finance Agency (NJHMFA)* offers favorable mortgage terms to those who buy homes in urban target areas and to first-time homebuyers. The Consumer Finance Protection Bureau (CFPB) created the *Your Home Loan Toolkit: A Step-by-Step Guide* to educate consumers about critical issues to consider when obtaining a home loan. Lenders are required to provide the Toolkit to prospective borrowers, but they are not required to discuss or explain it with their borrowers. The CFPB encourages real estate agents to provide the booklet and to assist their buyers understand how to obtain the best mortgage loan.

Unit

USEFUL WEBSITES

Your Home Loan Toolkit (English): http://files.consumerfinance.gov/f/201503_cfpb_your -home-loan-toolkit-web.pdf

Your Home Loan Toolkit (Spanish): http://files.consumerfinance.gov/f/201503_cfpb_your -home-loan-toolkit-web-spanish.pdf

VA Loan Eligibility: http://www.benefits.va.gov/homeloans/

New Jersey Homebuyers Program: www.state.nj.us/dca/hmfa

U.S. Department of Agriculture Rural Development: www.usda.gov/topics/rural/housing -assistance

U.S. FHA Mortgage Programs: www.hud.gov

FHA Mortgage Limits: https://entp.hud.gov/idapp/html/hicostlook.cfm

KEY TERMS REVIEW 1

Match the number of each key term with the corresponding letter.

_____ 1. Adjustable-rate mortgage

_____ 2. Amendatory clause

_____ 3. Amortization schedule

_____ 4. Amortized loan

_____ 5. Assumable

_____ 6. Biweekly mortgage

_____ 7. CMA

_____ 8. Budget loan

_____ 9. Buydown

_____ 10. Cap

_____ 11. Ceiling

_____ 12. Certificate of Reasonable Value

_____ 13. Federal Housing Administration

_____ 14. FHA 203(b)

A. low down-payment insured mortgage loan

B. insured loan with monthly payments including property taxes and insurance

C. mortgage can be taken over by next buyer

D. VA appraisal statement

E. highest interest rate ever allowed on a specific adjustable loan

F. listing of each payment: interest, principal paid, remaining debt

G. payment of extra points in return for lower interest rate

H. states that a buyer getting an FHA loan can rescind the contract if the appraisal is lower than the purchase price

I. percentage beyond which interest rate cannot be raised at adjustment

J. plan with interest rate changed either up or down periodically

K. repayment plan including principal payments; gradually reduces debt

L. repayment plan, the equivalent of 13 monthly payments per year

M. U.S. agency that insures mortgage to protect lending institutions

N. written estimate of value by a real estate licensee, not to be confused with an appraisal

KEY TERMS REVIEW 2

Match the number of each key term with the corresponding letter.

_____ 1. Index

_____ 2. Interest

_____ 3. Loan-to-value ratio

_____ 4. Margin

_____ 5. New Jersey Housing and Mortgage Finance Agency

_____ 6. PITI

_____ 7. Point

_____ 8. Private mortgage insurance

_____ 9. Straight loan

_____ 10. Target area

_____ 11. VA mortgage

_____ 12. Equity

_____ 13. *Your Home Loan Toolkit*

_____ 14. Rate lock

A. charge for the use of other people's money

B. guide to national mortgage trends, used for adjustable mortgage rates

C. lender of low-interest money in certain areas

D. mortgage payment, including interest, amortization, and certain expenses

E. mortgage with payments of interest only

F. loan guaranteed by federal government

G. neighborhoods in which the state wishes to strengthen housing stock

H. 1% of the loan amount, charged as extra up-front interest when loan is made

I. percentage charged by lender above index rate

J. percentage of a property's market value that may be borrowed

K. protection for the lender on a low-down-payment conventional mortgage loan

L. lender agrees to hold the interest rate for a certain period of time

M. difference between current value and money owed

N. explanation of financing terms

UNIT 14 REVIEW QUESTIONS

1. A savings and loan institution offers a mortgage plan with an 80% LTV ratio. On the purchase of a $240,000 property, how much down payment is required?
    A. $40,000
    B. $48,000
    C. $80,000
    D. $160,000

2. A borrower obtains a $150,000 mortgage loan at 5% interest. If the monthly payments of $805.15 are credited first on interest and then on principal, what is the balance of the principal after the borrower makes the first payment?
    A. $150,000
    B. $149,819
    C. $149,250
    D. $149,194

3. A seller took back a 30-year note and mortgage from the buyer. However, the seller wants the whole remaining debt paid off at the end of the fifth year. The buyer has a
    A. graduated payment.
    B. shared-equity payment.
    C. balloon payment.
    D. blanket payment.

4. With some exceptions, a homeowner may take as an income tax deduction
    A. the mortgage insurance premium.
    B. the mortgage interest paid.
    C. the property insurance premium.
    D. all of the above.

5. The terms index, margin, and cap are used in evaluating what type of mortgage?
    A. Package
    B. Blanket
    C. Conventional
    D. Adjustable rate

6. The seller sells his home for $300,000 and agrees to pay three points to his buyer's lending institution. The buyer is putting 20% down on the property. How much will the points cost the seller?
    A. $240
    B. $1,800
    C. $7,200
    D. $9,000

7. A lending institution may require the buyer to send in extra money to cover future bills for
    A. property taxes and insurance premiums.
    B. major repairs.
    C. possible default in monthly payments.
    D. all of the above.

8. Which of the following is an example of a conventional loan?
    A. A mortgage loan insured by the Federal Housing Administration
    B. A second loan for home improvements secured through a credit union
    C. A mortgage obtained through a private lender with a VA guarantee
    D. All of the above

9. Private mortgage insurance (PMI) is required whenever the
    A. loan is to be placed with the FHA.
    B. property covers more than 2.5 acres.
    C. loan exceeds $77,197.
    D. buyer is putting less than 20% down on a conventional loan.

10. The Department of Housing and Urban Development insures mortgage loans made through
    A. the FHA.
    B. the VA.
    C. Fannie Mae.
    D. Freddie Mac.

11. No down payment is required for loans made through
    A. the FHA.
    B. the VA.
    C. Fannie Mae.
    D. Freddie Mac.

12. Money for FHA and VA mortgages comes from
    A. different departments of the federal government.
    B. qualified local lending institutions.
    C. the Federal Reserve Bank.
    D. the secondary mortgage market.

13. The government normally lends money directly in which kind of loan?
    A. FHA
    B. VA
    C. RECD
    D. All of the above

14. The bank that makes a lower-rate loan in return for the payment of extra points is offering a
    A. reduced loan-to-value ratio.
    B. graduated payment loan.
    C. buydown.
    D. second mortgage.

15. Negative amortization refers to a situation in which the
    A. debt is gradually reduced through monthly payments.
    B. debt grows larger instead of smaller.
    C. regular adjustments reduce the interest rate.
    D. interest rate may rise or fall according to an index.

16. The borrower with a biweekly mortgage makes how many half-payments every year?
    A. 12
    B. 13
    C. 24
    D. 26

17. In an amortized loan, how are monthly payments applied?
    A. Principal and interest payments remain constant.
    B. Principal payment decreases as interest decreases.
    C. Principal increases as interest decreases.
    D. Total monthly payment decreases each year.

18. If the monthly interest at 5% is $1,250, what is the principal amount of the loan?
    A. $250,000
    B. $300,000
    C. $408,500
    D. $625,000

19. The amount of a loan expressed as a percentage of the value of the real estate used as security is known as the
    A. depreciation.
    B. loan-to-value ratio.
    C. amortization.
    D. principal balance.

20. Borrowers with a 30-year mortgage loan pay
    A. twice as much per month as for a 20-year loan.
    B. less per month than for a 20-year loan.
    C. one-third more than for a 20-year loan.
    D. the same per month as for a 20-year loan.

21. Who pays points?
    A. The lender
    B. Either the buyer or seller
    C. Only the seller
    D. Only the buyer

22. Who is responsible for explaining mortgage financial concepts to buyers who need a mortgage?
    A. Buyer's broker
    B. Closing officer
    C. Lender taking the mortgage application
    D. No one

23. The buyers purchased their first home for $250,000. Their down payment was $50,000 and they took a first mortgage for $200,000. At the time of purchase, their equity was
    A. $250,000
    B. $200,000
    C. $50,000
    D. Not enough information to determine equity

24. The homeowners purchased their home for $250,000, using a conventional loan of $200,000. They now want to refinance their home to take advantage of lower interest rates. The appraisal comes in at $275,000 but they still owe about $185,000 on their mortgage. How much equity, if any, have they built up?
    A. $90,000
    B. $50,000
    C. $185,000
    D. Not enough information to determine equity

UNIT 15

Financing II: Primary and Secondary Markets

LEARNING OBJECTIVES

When you have completed this unit, you will be able to accomplish the following.

› Describe various financing techniques.
› Identify the sources of real estate financing (i.e., the primary mortgage market).
› Explain government influences on mortgage lending.

KEY TERMS

ALIENS	jumbo loan	Regulation Z
blanket mortgage	Loan Estimate (LE)	reverse mortgage
construction loan	mortgage banker	sale-leaseback
credit history	mortgage broker	shared equity mortgage
credit union	open-end mortgage	TRID
Fannie Mae	package mortgage	triggering terms
Freddie Mac	portfolio loan	Truth in Lending Act
Ginnie Mae	primary mortgage market	underwriting
home equity loan	purchase-money	wraparound mortgage
intent to proceed	mortgage	
interim financing	qualifying ratio	

FINANCING TECHNIQUES

Strictly speaking, a **purchase-money mortgage** is any mortgage placed when property is bought. This is in contrast to *refinancing*, further borrowing after the realty is already owned. In many areas, however, the term *purchase-money mortgage* is used for a mortgage taken by the seller to enable the buyer to purchase ("seller take-back financing"). A purchase-money mortgage may be given to cover all or a portion of the purchase price and may be a first or second mortgage.

A **reverse mortgage** is one in which regular monthly payments are made *to* the borrower, based on the equity the homeowner has in the property given as security for the loan. A reverse mortgage allows senior citizens on fixed incomes to tap the equity buildup in their homes without having to sell. The loan accumulates interest and is eventually paid, usually from the sale of the property, when the owner moves out or dies. Information is available at www.reversemortgage.org.

Home equity loans, a form of second mortgage, have grown in popularity in recent years. Homeowners whose property has appreciated in value may borrow up to new loan-to-value ratios or, in one popular version, establish a line of credit, borrowing against it as they choose. Home equity loans usually carry adjustable interest rates.

The homeowner who is selling one residence and buying another may find it necessary to purchase the new home before the closing date on the present one. In that situation a temporary loan, variously called a *bridge loan, swing loan*, or **interim financing** may be arranged. Such loans usually provide for interest-only payments and are intended for no more than six months.

Under a **shared equity mortgage** the purchaser receives some financial help in the form of a contribution toward the down payment, a concessionary interest rate, or assistance with monthly payments. The "partner" may be a lending institution, the seller, the government, or a relative. Typically the partner receives a share of profit when the property is sold.

A **package mortgage** covers not only the real estate but also *all fixtures and appliances on the premises*. In recent years this kind of loan has been used extensively in financing furnished condominium units.

A **blanket mortgage** covers *more than one parcel or lot* and is used to finance subdivision developments. These mortgages often include a provision, known as a *partial release clause*, that the borrower may obtain the release of any one lot or parcel from the lien by repaying a definite amount of the loan.

A **wraparound mortgage** is frequently used as a method of refinancing real property or financing the purchase of real property when an existing mortgage is to be retained. The buyer gives a wraparound mortgage to the seller, who collects payments on the new loan, usually at a higher interest rate, and continues to make payments on the old loan. The buyer should require a protective clause in the document granting him or her the right to make payments directly to the original lender in the event of a default by the seller. Wraparound mortgages, like all unusual arrangements, require careful study by the buyer's and seller's attorneys. The broker who negotiates one should exercise special care not to give legal advice.

An **open-end mortgage** is frequently used by borrowers to obtain additional funds to improve their property. The borrower "opens" the mortgage to increase the debt after it has been reduced by payments over a period of time. The lender is not obligated to advance the additional funds.

A **construction loan**, or *building loan agreement*, is made to *finance the construction of improvements* on real estate (homes, apartments, office buildings, and so forth). Under a construction loan the lender disburses the loan proceeds while the building is being constructed. A building loan can be difficult to secure if an individual is not working through a recognized builder or contractor. Payments are made from time to time to the *general contractor* or owner for that part of the construction work that has been completed since the previous payment. Prior to each payment the lender usually inspects the work. This kind of mortgage loan generally bears a higher interest rate because of the risk assumed by the lender.

It is short-term. The borrower is expected to arrange for a permanent loan (called *take-out financing*) when the work is completed.

Sale-leaseback arrangements are sometimes used as a means of financing large commercial or industrial plants. The land and building used by the seller for business purposes are sold to an investor such as an insurance company. The real estate is then leased back by the buyer (the investor) to the seller, who continues to conduct business on the property as a tenant. The buyer becomes the lessor and the original owner becomes the lessee. This enables a business firm that has money invested in a plant to free that money for working capital. The buyer benefits from an assured long-term tenant.

Sale-leaseback arrangements are complex. They involve complicated legal procedures and their success is usually related to the effects the transaction has on the firm's income-tax liability. A real estate broker should consult with legal and tax experts when involved in this type of transaction.

As discussed in Unit 11, real estate can be purchased under a *land contract*, also known as a *contract for deed* or *installment contract*. Real estate is usually sold on contract in one of two situations:

1. when mortgage financing is not available or is too expensive, or

2. when the purchaser does not have a sufficient down payment to secure a mortgage loan.

SELLER-BUYER ARRANGEMENTS

Several different financing arrangements are possible between buyer and seller.

■ *Seller financing* and *land contracts*: The buyer makes agreed upon payments to the seller, not a lender, until the total sum has been paid at which time the seller issues a satisfaction of the mortgage lien.

■ *Lease-option*: The buyers are tenants who have a binding contract to buy the property if they choose to do so; in the meantime, the seller is the owner and their landlord.

■ *Sale-leaseback*: The buyer receives a deed and immediately becomes full owner. The former owner, meanwhile, continues to occupy the property as a tenant.

SOURCES OF REAL ESTATE FINANCING—THE PRIMARY MORTGAGE MARKET

The funds used to finance the purchase of real estate come from a variety of sources that make up the **primary mortgage market**—lenders who supply funds to borrowers as an investment. Lenders may originate loans for the purpose of selling them to other investors as part of what is termed the *secondary mortgage market*. The secondary mortgage market is discussed later in this unit.

Mortgage loans are generally made by *institutional lenders* such as *savings and loan associations, commercial banks, mutual savings banks, life insurance companies, mortgage banking companies, mortgage brokers, credit unions, pension and trust funds*, and *finance companies*. Individuals (sellers, investors, employers, brokers, and relatives) occasionally are sources for financing.

Insurance companies amass large sums of money from the premiums paid by their policyholders. A certain portion of this money is held in reserve to satisfy claims and cover operating expenses, but much of it is invested in profit-earning enterprises, such as long-term real estate loans.

Most insurance companies like to invest their money in large, long-term loans that finance commercial and industrial properties. They also invest in residential mortgage loans by purchasing large blocks of government-backed loans (FHA-insured and VA-guaranteed loans) from the Federal National Mortgage Association and other agencies that warehouse such loans for resale in the secondary mortgage market.

In addition, many life insurance companies seek to further ensure the safety of their investments by insisting on equity (part-ownership) positions in many projects they finance. This means that the company requires a partnership arrangement with, for example, a project developer or subdivider as a condition of making a loan. This is called *participation financing*.

Mortgage bankers use money borrowed from other institutions and funds of their own to make real estate loans that may later be sold to investors (with the mortgage company receiving a fee for servicing the loans). Mortgage bankers are involved in all types of real estate loan activities.

Mortgage banking companies are subject to considerably fewer lending restrictions than are commercial banks or savings and loans. Mortgage bankers originate about one-quarter of all home loans.

Mortgage brokers are individuals who are licensed to act as intermediaries in bringing borrowers and lenders together. Mortgage brokers charge a fee, often of the borrower, for their services.

Credit unions are cooperative organizations in which members place money in savings accounts, usually at higher interest rates than other savings institutions offer. In the past most credit unions made only short-term consumer and home-improvement loans, but in recent years they have been branching out into originating longer-term first and second mortgage loans.

APPLICATION FOR CREDIT

All mortgage lenders require prospective borrowers to file an application for credit that provides the lender with basic information needed to evaluate the proposed loan. The application includes information regarding the purpose of the loan, the amount, rate of interest, and the proposed terms of repayment.

A prospective borrower must submit personal information to the lender, including age, family status, employment, earnings, assets, and financial obligations. Details of the real estate that is the security for the loan must be provided, including legal description, improvements, title, survey, and taxes. For loans on income property or those made to corporations, additional information is required, such as financial and operating statements, schedules of leases and tenants, and balance sheets. Those self-employed are asked to show two years' income tax returns. Through the process known as **underwriting**, the lender carefully investigates the application information, studying **credit history** (how timely the applicant has repaid debts), credit reports and an appraisal of the property before deciding whether to grant the loan. The lender's acceptance of the application is written in the form of a *loan commitment*, which creates a contract to make a loan and sets forth the details.

Preapproved Loans

The buyer who wants to be in a strong negotiating position with sellers sometimes goes through the process of obtaining *preapproval* for a mortgage loan from a lending institution rather than merely a *prequalification*. Prequalification simply estimates the maximum amount the borrower is likely to qualify for.

Preapproval, on the other hand, is usually a solid written commitment from the lender to hold a mortgage up to a given amount. Unless the borrower's financial situation changes before closing, the loan is available as long as the property being sought appraises at the purchase price or higher.

In recent years, stricter regulations for mortgage lending have been implemented. Among other requirements, lenders must reverify credit and employment information at the last minute before closing, a requirement that often takes borrowers by surprise.

FICO Credit Scores

With the rise of underwriting decisions, or at least recommendations, made by computer programs, lenders have adopted a system of *credit scoring*. The most common index is called a FICO score, named for the company, Fair, Isaac and Co., that developed the statistical analysis.

The FHA will, in rare cases, accept a score as low as 620. Borrowers who score less than 600 are considered "subprime" risks.

Qualifying Ratios

With each mortgage plan offered, a lender specifies certain **qualifying ratios** to be applied to each borrower. A typical ratio might be 28/36—the borrower is allowed to spend up to 28% of gross monthly income for housing expense (PITI) or up to 36% of income including other payments on long-term debts. The lender calculates the maximum monthly payment each way and allows only the lower figure. With certain mortgage payments, a ratio of up to 43% is sometimes allowed.

GOVERNMENT INFLUENCE IN MORTGAGE LENDING

Aside from FHA-insured and VA-guaranteed loan programs, the federal government influences mortgage lending through the Federal Reserve System, as well as through various federal agencies, such as RECD (the former Farmer's Home Administration). It also deals in the secondary mortgage market through the Federal National Mortgage Association, the Government National Mortgage Association, and the Federal Home Loan Mortgage Corporation.

Federal Reserve System

The Federal Reserve System (the Fed) helps to maintain sound credit conditions, helps counteract inflationary and deflationary trends, and creates a favorable economic climate. The Fed regulates the flow of money and interest rates in the marketplace indirectly through its member banks by controlling their *reserve requirements and discount rates*.

Unit 15

Government Influence in the Secondary Market

Mortgage lending takes place in both the primary and secondary mortgage markets. The *primary market*, which this unit has dealt with thus far, includes

- lenders who supply funds to borrowers as an investment and keep the loans in their own portfolio; and

- lenders who originate loans for the purpose of selling them to investors.

Loans are bought and sold in the *secondary market* after they have been originated. A lender may wish to sell a number of loans to raise immediate funds when it needs more money to meet the mortgage demands in its area.

A major source of secondary mortgage market activity is *warehousing agencies*, which purchase large numbers of mortgage loans and assemble them into one or more packages of loans for resale to investors. The major warehousing agencies are Fannie Mae (formerly the Federal National Mortgage Association, or FNMA), the Government National Mortgage Association (GNMA), and the Federal Home Loan Mortgage Corporation (FHLMC).

Fannie Mae

Fannie Mae is a shareholder-owned company operating under a congressional charter. that provides a secondary market for mortgage loans. The corporation raises funds to purchase loans by selling government-guaranteed FNMA bonds at market interest rates. Mortgage bankers are actively involved with FNMA, originating loans and selling them to FNMA while retaining the servicing functions for which they are paid a fee by Fannie Mae. FNMA is the nation's largest purchaser of mortgages.

Because FNMA eventually purchases one mortgage out of every ten, it has great influence on lending policies. Loans that meet Fannie Mae's guidelines are called *conforming loans*. When Fannie Mae announces that it will buy a certain type of loan, local lending institutions often change their own regulations to meet the stated criteria. When lenders are experimenting with new types of loans, a Fannie Mae announcement can result in standardization of innovative mortgage plans.

Government National Mortgage Association

The Government National Mortgage Association, also known as **Ginnie Mae**, is a government corporation, was formed primarily to assist with low-income, moderate-income, and high-risk mortgages. Ginnie Mae does not issue, buy, or sell mortgage loans. The *Ginnie Mae pass-through certificate* lets small investors buy a share in a pool of mortgages that provides for a monthly "pass-through" of principal and interest payments directly to the certificate holder. The certificates are guaranteed by Ginnie Mae.

Federal Home Loan Mortgage Corporation

The Federal Home Loan Mortgage Corporation, or **Freddie Mac**, is a shareholder-owned company operating under a congressional charter. It provides a secondary market for member savings and loan associations mortgage loans, primarily conventional loans. Freddie Mac has the authority to purchase mortgages, pool them, and sell bonds in the open market with the mortgages as security.

Nonconforming Loans

Because each participant in the secondary market sets standards for the packages of mortgages it will buy, loans offered by local institutions tend toward uniformity. When Fannie Mae and Freddie Mac announce that they will buy loans up to a certain amount, many local lenders set that as their limit.

Loans higher than the secondary market's limit are known as **jumbo** (nonconforming) **loans**, and the borrower who wants to place one would search for a local lending institution that is making **portfolio loans**—lending its own money and taking mortgages it intends to hold into its own portfolio without selling them to secondary investors. Portfolio loans, known as *nonconforming mortgages* because they do not have to meet uniform underwriting standards, can be flexible in their guidelines. The borrower with an unusual credit situation or the unique house may need a portfolio loan. A lending institution may want such loans at one time but not at other times. Following the rapidly changing mortgage market is often a very large part of a real estate broker's work.

FINANCING LEGISLATION

The federal government regulates the lending practices of mortgage lenders through the *Truth in Lending Act*, *Equal Credit Opportunity Act*, the *Real Estate Settlement Procedures Act*, and the TILA-RESPA Integrated Disclosure (TRID).

Regulation Z

The **Truth in Lending Act**, which is implemented by **Regulation Z**, requires credit institutions to inform consumers of the true cost of obtaining credit so the consumer can compare the costs of various lenders and avoid the uninformed use of credit. All real estate transactions made for personal or agricultural loans that are financed are covered. The regulation does *not* apply to cash transactions or business or commercial loans.

Regulation Z requires that the borrower be fully informed of all finance charges, as well as the true annual interest rate, before a transaction is consummated. In the case of a mortgage loan made to finance the purchase of a dwelling, the lender must compute and disclose the annual percentage rate (APR). The rules do not apply to Home Equity Lines of Credit (HELOC), reverse mortgages, and land loans (mortgage secured by a dwelling not attached to the property).

TRID requires delivery or mailing of early disclosures about the proposed loan within three business days of completed mortgage application. Until disclosure has been made, the lender can not charge any fees except for a credit report. A loan application is considered complete when the prospective borrowers provide the Address of the property, Loan amount requested, Income, Estimated property value, Name of borrower(s), and their Social security numbers (ALIENS).

The consumer must be notified that he or she has the right to cancel the transaction even after loan application has been made and the disclosure received. This allows the consumer to compare various lenders' offerings, and the lender must allow at least seven business days after disclosure, before actually making the loan. (In an emergency like threatened foreclosure, the consumer may choose to take the loan earlier than that.) There must be at least seven business days between the delivery of the Loan Estimate and closing. For more detail, consult the TILA-RESPA Integrated Disclosure Guide at https://files.consumerfinance.gov/f/201404 _cfpb_tila-respa-integrated-disclosure-form.pdf.

Annual Percentage Rate (APR)

If a mortgage loan is made at 5% but also requires 3% in prepaid interest (points) and other fees, the loan really costs the borrower more than 5%. The true figure is nowhere near 8% (5 plus 3) because those points and fees are paid only once, at the start of the loan. The exact cost depends on complicated calculations, and the result, the annual percentage rate (APR) is a bit more than 5%.

Federal regulations require that the borrower be advised of the APR in advertisements and when the loan is placed. It is intended to help prospective borrowers compare the true cost of various types of loans, but is widely misunderstood and often ends up confusing borrowers. ("They told me I was getting a 5% mortgage and now they tell me it's 5.19%?")

Creditor

Regulation Z must be observed by any lender who is classified as a creditor. The regulation defines a creditor as one who extends consumer credit more than 25 times a year, or more than 5 times a year if the transaction involves a dwelling as security. The loan must be subject to a finance charge or payable in more than four installments by written agreement.

Three-Day Right of Rescission

In the case of most consumer credit transactions covered by Regulation Z, the borrower has three business days, including Saturday, in which to rescind (cancel) the transaction merely by notifying the lender. *This right of rescission does not apply to residential purchase-money first mortgage loans.*

Advertising

Regulation Z provides for the strict regulation of real estate advertisements that include mortgage financing terms. General phrases such as "liberal terms available" may be used, but if certain details are given they must comply with this act. The annual percentage rate (APR), which includes all charges rather than the interest rate alone, must be stated.

Regulation Z applies to all credit advertising. If any one of the following **triggering terms** is used, three further items of information also must be included. The triggering terms are

- amount or percentage of down payment (unless none is required);
- number of payments or period of repayment;
- amount of any payment; and
- amount of any finance charge.

If any of the items listed is mentioned, the advertisement also must include

- amount or percentage of down payment;
- number of payments or term of loan; and
- the words "annual percentage rate," so identified, and whether that rate is to be increased after consummation.

For example, full disclosure would be necessary if any of the following terms were used:

- 30-year loan available

- Payment $1,432 including principal and interest
- Only 5% down

These terms would *not* trigger the required disclosures:

- Financing available
- Terms negotiable
- Owner may finance
- Assume 5% annual percentage rate loan
- Attractive financing
- $400,000 mortgage available

Any offer of financing must include the words "to a qualified buyer."

Penalties

Regulation Z provides penalties for noncompliance. The penalty for violation of an administrative order enforcing Regulation Z is $10,000 for each day the violation continues. A fine of up to $10,000 may be imposed for engaging in an unfair or deceptive practice. In addition, a creditor may be liable to a consumer for twice the amount of the finance charge, for a minimum of $100 and a maximum of $1,000, plus court costs, attorney's fees, and any actual damages. Willful violation is a misdemeanor punishable by a fine of up to $5,000 or one year's imprisonment, or both.

Equal Credit Opportunity Act

The federal *Equal Credit Opportunity Act* (ECOA) prohibits lenders and others who grant or arrange credit to consumers from discriminating against credit applicants on the basis of race, color, religion, national origin, sex, marital status, age (provided the applicant is of legal age), or dependence on public assistance. Lenders must inform all rejected credit applicants in writing of the principal reasons why credit was denied or terminated.

Real Estate Settlement Procedures Act

The federal Real Estate Settlement Procedures Act (RESPA) was created to ensure that the buyer and seller in a residential real estate transaction involving a new first mortgage loan have knowledge of all settlement costs.

TILA-RESPA Integrated Disclosure (TRID)

The Consumer Financial Protection Bureau (CFPB) merged forms that were previously required by the Real Estate Settlement Procedures Act (RESPA) and the Truth in Lending Act (TILA) into the new TILA-RESPA Integrated Disclosure (TRID). TRID requirements became effective for most residential loans initiated after October 3, 2015.

Lenders are responsible for the delivery of documents to consumers within specific time frames. Lenders are liable if certain costs exceed the tolerance limitations imposed by TRID.

TRID rules do not apply to the following transactions:

- HELOCS (Home Equity Lines of Credit)

- Mortgage secured by mobile homes or other "movable" dwellings that are not permanently attached to real estate
- Reverse mortgages
- Cash transactions
- Loans for commercial purposes

The old forms—HUD-1, GFE, and TIL disclosures—are still used for most HELOCS and reverse mortgages. Lenders will determine the forms used in other lending transactions.

Intent to Proceed

Borrowers are encouraged to meet with several lenders to discuss different types of loans. At the initial meeting, lenders may require only a reasonable credit report fee. At this time, buyer/borrowers are neither approved nor denied. The lender may charge additional fees (such as an application fee and appraisal fees) only after the consumer indicates an **intent to proceed**. The borrower must acknowledge receipt of the LE. A loan application is considered complete when the borrower provides the lender with the following information. The acronym ALIENS helps to remember the required information:

- **A**ddress of the property
- **L**oan amount requested
- **I**ncome
- **E**stimated property value
- **N**ame
- **S**ocial Security number

Loan Estimate (LE)

Since October 2015, lenders are required to provide the buyer(s) with a Loan Estimate (LE) within three business days after completed loan application when making federally related first or second mortgage loans.

See Figure 15.1 for a sample Loan Estimate. It is filled out according to a sample transaction in *Your Home Loan Toolkit*: "This is a sample of a completed Loan Estimate for a fixed rate loan. This loan is for the purchase of property at a sale price of $180,000 and has a loan amount of $162,000, a 30-year loan term, a fixed interest rate of 3.875%, and a prepayment penalty equal to 2.00% of the outstanding principal balance of the loan for the first two years after consummation of the transaction. The consumer has elected to lock the interest rate. The creditor requires an escrow account and that the consumer pay for private mortgage insurance."

Under the TRID rule, lenders are held to a good faith standard in disclosing fees and changes to the LE. If the borrowers or the lender make certain changes, the lender must reissue the Loan Estimate, thus triggering a new-three day waiting period.

These are the changes that will trigger a new LE:

- Consumer requested a change (i.e., changing the loan program or the amount of their down payment)
- Appraisal came in higher or lower than expected
- Changed circumstances that affected the applicants' eligibility such as applicants took out a new loan or missed a payment that changed their credit score

- Lender could not document the applicant's overtime, bonus, or other income
- Costs changed for the services that the borrower cannot shop for
- Interest rate changed because the consumer did not opt for a rate lock or the rate lock expired
- Prepayment penalty was added
- Loan product was changed
- APR increased beyond the allowable limit, that is, more than ⅛% for fixed-rate loans or more than ¼% for adjustable-rate loans

Figure 15.1: Sample Loan Estimate

FEBRUARY 7, 2014

TILA RESPA Integrated Disclosure

H-24(B) Mortgage Loan Transaction Loan Estimate – Fixed Rate Loan Sample

This is a sample of a completed Loan Estimate for a fixed rate loan. This loan is for the purchase of property at a sale price of $180,000 and has a loan amount of $162,000, a 30-year loan term, a fixed interest rate of 3.875 percent, and a prepayment penalty equal to 2.00 percent of the outstanding principal balance of the loan for the first two years after consummation of the transaction. The consumer has elected to lock the interest rate. The creditor requires an escrow account and that the consumer pay for private mortgage insurance.

cfpb   Consumer Financial
Protection Bureau

Figure 15.1: Sample Loan Estimate (continued)

FICUS BANK

4321 Random Boulevard • Somecity, ST 12340

Save this Loan Estimate to compare with your Closing Disclosure.

Loan Estimate

DATE ISSUED	2/15/2013
APPLICANTS	Michael Jones and Mary Stone
	123 Anywhere Street
	Anytown, ST 12345
PROPERTY	456 Somewhere Avenue
	Anytown, ST 12345
SALE PRICE	$180,000

LOAN TERM	30 years
PURPOSE	Purchase
PRODUCT	Fixed Rate
LOAN TYPE	☒ Conventional ☐ FHA ☐ VA ☐ _____
LOAN ID #	123456789
RATE LOCK	☐ NO ☒ YES, until 4/16/2013 at 5:00 p.m. EDT

*Before closing, your interest rate, points, and lender credits can change unless you lock the interest rate. All other estimated closing costs expire on **3/4/2013** at 5:00 p.m. EDT*

Loan Terms

		Can this amount increase after closing?
Loan Amount	$162,000	NO
Interest Rate	3.875%	NO
Monthly Principal & Interest *See Projected Payments below for your Estimated Total Monthly Payment*	$761.78	NO

		Does the loan have these features?
Prepayment Penalty		YES • As high as $3,240 if you pay off the loan during the first 2 years
Balloon Payment		NO

Projected Payments

Payment Calculation	Years 1-7	Years 8-30
Principal & Interest	$761.78	$761.78
Mortgage Insurance	+ 82	+ —
Estimated Escrow *Amount can increase over time*	+ 206	+ 206
Estimated Total Monthly Payment	$1,050	$968

		This estimate includes	In escrow?
Estimated Taxes, Insurance & Assessments *Amount can increase over time*	$206 a month	☒ Property Taxes ☒ Homeowner's Insurance ☐ Other:	YES YES
		See Section G on page 2 for escrowed property costs. You must pay for other property costs separately.	

Costs at Closing

Estimated Closing Costs	$8,054	Includes $5,672 in Loan Costs + $2,382 in Other Costs – $0 in Lender Credits. *See page 2 for details.*
Estimated Cash to Close	$16,054	Includes Closing Costs. *See Calculating Cash to Close on page 2 for details.*

Visit **www.consumerfinance.gov/mortgage-estimate** for general information and tools.

Figure 15.1: Sample Loan Estimate (continued)

Closing Cost Details

Loan Costs

A. Origination Charges	$1,802
.25 % of Loan Amount (Points)	$405
Application Fee	$300
Underwriting Fee	$1,097

B. Services You Cannot Shop For	$672
Appraisal Fee	$405
Credit Report Fee	$30
Flood Determination Fee	$20
Flood Monitoring Fee	$32
Tax Monitoring Fee	$75
Tax Status Research Fee	$110

C. Services You Can Shop For	$3,198
Pest Inspection Fee	$135
Survey Fee	$65
Title – Insurance Binder	$700
Title – Lender's Title Policy	$535
Title – Settlement Agent Fee	$502
Title – Title Search	$1,261

D. TOTAL LOAN COSTS (A + B + C)	$5,672

Other Costs

E. Taxes and Other Government Fees	$85
Recording Fees and Other Taxes	$85
Transfer Taxes	

F. Prepaids	$867
Homeowner's Insurance Premium (6 months)	$605
Mortgage Insurance Premium (months)	
Prepaid Interest ($17.44 per day for 15 days @ 3.875%)	$262
Property Taxes (months)	

G. Initial Escrow Payment at Closing			$413
Homeowner's Insurance	$100.83 per month for 2 mo.	$202
Mortgage Insurance	per month for mo.	
Property Taxes	$105.30 per month for 2 mo.	$211

H. Other	$1,017
Title – Owner's Title Policy (optional)	$1,017

I. TOTAL OTHER COSTS (E + F + G + H)	$2,382

J. TOTAL CLOSING COSTS	$8,054
D + I	$8,054
Lender Credits	

Calculating Cash to Close

Total Closing Costs (J)	$8,054
Closing Costs Financed (Paid from your Loan Amount)	$0
Down Payment/Funds from Borrower	$18,000
Deposit	– $10,000
Funds for Borrower	$0
Seller Credits	$0
Adjustments and Other Credits	$0
Estimated Cash to Close	$16,054

Figure 15.1: Sample Loan Estimate (continued)

Additional Information About This Loan

LENDER	Ficus Bank	**MORTGAGE BROKER**	
NMLS/__ LICENSE ID		**NMLS/__ LICENSE ID**	
LOAN OFFICER	Joe Smith	**LOAN OFFICER**	
NMLS/__ LICENSE ID	12345	**NMLS/__ LICENSE ID**	
EMAIL	joesmith@ficusbank.com	**EMAIL**	
PHONE	123-456-7890	**PHONE**	

Comparisons		Use these measures to compare this loan with other loans.
In 5 Years	$56,582	Total you will have paid in principal, interest, mortgage insurance, and loan costs.
	$15,773	Principal you will have paid off.
Annual Percentage Rate (APR)	4.274%	Your costs over the loan term expressed as a rate. This is not your interest rate.
Total Interest Percentage (TIP)	69.45%	The total amount of interest that you will pay over the loan term as a percentage of your loan amount.

Other Considerations	
Appraisal	We may order an appraisal to determine the property's value and charge you for this appraisal. We will promptly give you a copy of any appraisal, even if your loan does not close. You can pay for an additional appraisal for your own use at your own cost.
Assumption	If you sell or transfer this property to another person, we ☐ will allow, under certain conditions, this person to assume this loan on the original terms. ☒ will not allow assumption of this loan on the original terms.
Homeowner's Insurance	This loan requires homeowner's insurance on the property, which you may obtain from a company of your choice that we find acceptable.
Late Payment	If your payment is more than *15* days late, we will charge a late fee of *5% of the monthly principal and interest payment.*
Refinance	Refinancing this loan will depend on your future financial situation, the property value, and market conditions. You may not be able to refinance this loan.
Servicing	We intend ☐ to service your loan. If so, you will make your payments to us. ☒ to transfer servicing of your loan.

Confirm Receipt	

By signing, you are only confirming that you have received this form. You do not have to accept this loan because you have signed or received this form.

_____   _____
Applicant Signature   Date   Co-Applicant Signature   Date

Changes that do NOT trigger delays include

- Unexpected discoveries discovered during the walkthrough
- Necessary changes at closing, such as the amount of the real estate commission, changes to tax and utility prorations, and the amount paid into escrow

Borrowers are expected to compare their LE to the Closing Disclosure (CD) that the lender will provide at least three business days before the closing. The CD is discussed in detail in Unit 21.

Business Days

Two definitions exist for "business day." One definition of a business day is any day that the lender is open for business and the other definition is any calendar day except Sunday and federal legal holidays. Thus, depending on the lender (creditor), Saturdays might or might not be considered.

Loan Estimate

To determine when the LE must be provided, the creditor may use the first definition (i.e., a business day is one when the creditor's office is open to the public). The LE must be delivered or placed in the mail no later than the third business day after the lender has received the completed application from the borrowers. There must be at least seven business days between the delivery of the Loan Estimate and closing.

Closing Disclosure

For other purposes, such as providing the CD, a business day is all calendar days except Sundays and legal holidays. The CD must be delivered to the consumer no later than three business days before the consumer signs the loan.

SUMMARY

Other types of real estate financing include shared equity loans, reverse mortgages, blanket mortgages, package mortgages, open-end mortgages, wraparound mortgages, construction loans, sale-leaseback agreements, land contracts, and investment group financing.

The federal government affects real estate financing money and interest rates through the Federal Reserve Board's discount rate and reserve requirements; it also participates in the secondary mortgage market. The secondary market is composed of investors who ultimately purchase and hold the loans as investments. These include insurance companies, investment funds, and pension plans. Fannie Mae (Federal National Mortgage Association), Ginnie Mae (Government National Mortgage Association), and Freddie Mac (Federal Home Loan Mortgage Corporation) take an active role in creating a secondary market by regularly purchasing mortgage loans from originators and retaining, or warehousing, them until investment purchasers are available.

Regulation Z, which implements the federal Truth in Lending Act, requires institutional lenders to inform prospective borrowers of all finance charges involved in the loan. Severe penalties are imposed for noncompliance. The federal Equal Credit Opportunity Act prohibits creditors from discriminating against credit applicants on the basis of race, color, religion, national origin, sex, marital status, age, or dependence on public assistance. The Real Estate Settlement Procedures Act requires lenders to inform both buyers and sellers in advance of all fees and charges for the settlement or closing of a residential real estate transaction. The Consumer Financial Protection Bureau (CFPB) merged forms that were previously required by RESPA and the Truth in Lending Act (TILA) into the new TILA-RESPA Integrated Disclosures (TRID). TRID rules apply to federally related first and second mortgage home loans. The old forms may be used for HELOCs, mortgages secured by a moveable dwelling, reverse mortgages, and cash sales. Under TRID, lenders may only charge a small amount for a credit report until the applicant has indicated an intent to proceed.

USEFUL WEBSITES

Fannie Mae: www.fanniemae.com

Freddie Mac: www.freddiemac.com

Ginnie Mae: www.ginnemae.gov

U.S. Federal Reserve: www.federalreserve.gov

KEY TERMS REVIEW 1

Match the number of each key term with the corresponding letter.

_____ 1. Blanket mortgage

_____ 2. Construction loan

_____ 3. Credit union

_____ 4. Fannie Mae

_____ 5. Freddie Mac

_____ 6. Ginnie Mae

_____ 7. Home equity loan

_____ 8. Interim financing

_____ 9. Jumbo loan

_____ 10. Mortgage banker

_____ 11. Mortgage broker

_____ 12. Open-end mortgage

_____ 13. Package mortgage

A. agent who brings together lender and borrower for a fee

B. bridge or swing loan for short-term financing before a sale

C. cooperative organization for members who save and borrow

D. Federal Home Loan Mortgage Corporation; warehouses packages of mortgages originated by member savings and loan associations

E. a privately owned corporation that sets standards and buys mortgages

F. Government National Mortgage Association; pools mortgages for investors

G. mortgage that provides possibility for further borrowing

H. mortgage covering both real and personal property

I. agent who makes real estate loans

J. loan higher than those usually bought by the secondary market

K. mortgage covering more than one parcel of real estate

L. additional financing for homeowner; usually a type of second mortgage

M. straight loan for short building period

KEY TERMS REVIEW 2

Match the number of each key term with the corresponding letter.

_____ 1. Portfolio loan

_____ 2. Primary mortgage market

_____ 3. Purchase-money mortgage

_____ 4. Qualifying ratio

__K__ 5. Regulation Z

_____ 6. Reverse mortgage

_____ 7. Sale-leaseback

_____ 8. Shared equity mortgage

_____ 9. Triggering term

_____ 10. Truth in Lending Act

_____ 11. Underwriting

_____ 12. Wraparound mortgage

_____ 13. ALIENS

_____ 14. TRID

_____ 15. Loan Estimate

A. percentage of income borrower may spend on housing expense

B. arrangement by which seller becomes tenant

C. larger loan that does not disturb underlying mortgage

D. lending institutions that make mortgage loans to the public

E. regulates consumer loans

F. loan in which investor shares payments and profits

G. loan not intended for resale on the secondary market

H. words in an ad that require full disclosure of financing conditions

I. mortgage in which lender sends regular checks, building up debt

J. process of deciding whether to make specific loans

K. implements the Truth in Lending Act

L. seller financing

M. detailed loan costs

N. required items before lender can proceed

O. merges TILA and RESPA disclosures

1. The term purchase-money mortgage applies
   A. to any mortgage used to finance the purchase of real estate.
   B. to any mortgage for which real estate is pledged as security other than for refinancing purposes
   C. only to a mortgage loan made by a regular lending institution.
   D. only to a mortgage loan "taken back" by the seller.

2. An elderly widow is on Social Security and a small fixed income. She wants to stay in her longtime home, which now has a market value of more than $200,000, but she cannot afford rising property taxes, and the house needs a new roof. This person is a perfect candidate for a(n)
   A. equity-sharing arrangement.
   B. reverse mortgage.
   C. home equity loan.
   D. interim finance loan.

3. Real estate brokers should be particularly careful to seek an attorney's assistance when a real estate transaction involves a
   A. home equity loan.
   B. construction loan.
   C. package mortgage.
   D. wraparound mortgage.

4. The buyer does NOT immediately receive a deed when purchasing with a
   A. sale-leaseback.
   B. seller-financed mortgage.
   C. balloon mortgage.
   D. land contract.

5. What is the function of mortgage brokers?
   A. Make mortgage loans.
   B. Bring borrowers and lenders together.
   C. Service mortgage loans.
   D. Sell packages of mortgages to investors.

6. When a bank allows a buyer to spend up to 28% of gross income on housing costs, it is applying a formula known as a
   A. loan-to-value ratio.
   B. qualifying ratio.
   C. PMI guarantee.
   D. low-income subsidy.

7. A couple purchased a residence for $375,000. They made a down payment of $45,000 and agreed to assume the seller's existing mortgage, which had a current balance of $123,000. The couple financed the remaining $207,000 of the purchase price by giving a mortgage and note to the seller. This type of loan, by which the seller becomes a mortgagee, is called a
   A. wraparound mortgage.
   B. package mortgage.
   C. balloon note.
   D. purchase-money mortgage.

8. A developer obtains one mortgage for a whole subdivision. As he sells each lot, he obtains a release of one parcel from the
   A. package mortgage.
   B. reverse mortgage.
   C. balloon mortgage.
   D. blanket mortgage.

9. An investor buys a local factory from a company that intends to remain and rent the building from him. The investor has put together a(n)
   A. equity-sharing transaction.
   B. sale-leaseback.
   C. secondary market.
   D. reserve for escrow.

10. Which of the following BEST defines the secondary market?
    A. Lenders who exclusively deal in second mortgages
    B. Lenders who buy and sell mortgages after they have been originated
    C. The major lender of residential mortgages
    D. The major lender of FHA and VA loans

11. What is Fannie Mae?
    A. The leading purchaser of mortgages on the secondary market
    B. A lender for homes in rural areas
    C. A government agency that regulates interest rates
    D. An old woman who lives in a cave

12. The public can invest in mortgage pools by buying certificates issued by the
    A. Federal Reserve Bank.
    B. Farmer's Home Administration.
    C. Government National Mortgage Association.
    D. Guaranteed Mortgage Fund.

13. Which of the following is NOT a participant in the nation's secondary mortgage market?
    A. FmHA
    B. Ginnie Mae
    C. Fannie Mae
    D. FHLMC

14. Which of the following represents the purpose of Freddie Mac?
    A. Guarantees mortgages by the full faith and credit of the federal government
    B. Buys and pools blocks of conventional mortgages, selling bonds with such mortgages as security
    C. Affects the mortgage market through adjustment of the discount rate
    D. Forbids the charging of more than one point to the buyer

15. Regulation Z protects the consumer from
    A. misleading advertising.
    B. fraudulent mortgage plans.
    C. discrimination in lending.
    D. substandard housing.

16. Regulation Z provides that
    A. buyers must be provided with information on heating costs.
    B. brokers must clear all ads with the Real Estate Commission.
    C. if certain financing terms are mentioned, others also must be included.
    D. vague, misleading geographic terms must not be used.

17. Which of the following is a triggering term that mandates inclusion of full details in an advertisement?
    A. Assume 4% FHA loan
    B. Less than 10% down
    C. Owner may finance
    D. Affordable terms

18. If a triggering term is included, an ad must go on to explain
    A. the amount or percentage of down payment.
    B. the number of payments.
    C. the annual percentage rate.
    D. all of the above.

19. Under Regulation Z, the borrower who places a mortgage
    A. has 3 days in which to cancel the loan.
    B. must be notified at least 12 days before closing of all costs.
    C. may not be discriminated against because of dependence on public assistance.
    D. must be quoted the APR as well as simple interest rate.

20. At what point is the lender required to provide a Loan Estimate to prospective borrowers?
    A. Immediately
    B. Upon payment of an application fee
    C. Within three business days of completed loan application
    D. Depends on the amount of the loan

21. A few changes were made to the original Loan Estimate. Which of the following is one that will trigger the need for a new Loan Estimate and a delay in closing?
    A. Walkthrough revealed a damage that the seller will repair
    B. Loan product was changed
    C. Increased taxes required a change to the escrow account
    D. Brokers had a dispute over the commission split

22. The borrowers want to talk with several lenders about various loan products before making a final decision. At this point, how much money may each lender require from the buyer borrowers?
    A. Nothing
    B. Up to $200 application fee
    C. Enough for a credit report
    D. There is no limit

UNIT 16

Appraisal

LEARNING OBJECTIVES

When you have completed this unit, you will be able to accomplish the following.

› Describe the differences among various types of value.
› Explain the three approaches to value.
› Discuss the profession of appraising in New Jersey.

KEY TERMS

amenity	gross income multiplier (GIM)	reconciliation
appraisal		replacement cost
appraiser	gross rent multiplier (GRM)	reproduction cost
capitalization rate		sales comparison approach
comparables	highest and best use	
cost approach	income approach	situs
depreciation	market price	subject property
external obsolescence	market value	substitution
functional obsolescence	physical deterioration	value

REAL ESTATE—THE BUSINESS OF VALUE

The real estate industry provides a setting in which supply and demand can establish price levels for real property. To understand that, it is helpful to take a look at the fundamentals of the real estate markets and real estate economic principles.

THE REAL ESTATE MARKET

A *market* is a place where goods can be bought and sold, where a price can be established, and where it becomes advantageous for buyers and sellers to trade. The market provides a setting in which supply and demand can establish price levels.

It is commonly agreed that land possesses these five attributes:

1. It is finite in its supply.
2. It is physically immobile.
3. It is durable.
4. Each parcel of land has its own unique location and characteristics.
5. It is useful to people.

Supply and Demand

The economic forces of supply and demand continually interact in any market to establish and maintain price levels. Essentially *when supply increases, prices drop; when demand increases, prices rise.*

Supply can be defined as *the amount of goods offered for sale within the market at a given price during a given time period.* Factors that tend to affect supply in the real estate market include labor supply, construction costs, and government controls and financial policies.

Demand can be defined as *the number of people willing and able to accept the available goods at any given price during a given time period.* Factors that tend to affect demand in the real estate market include population, employment and wage levels, and vacancy levels.

Because real estate is immobile and each parcel is unique, the real estate market is said to be an *inefficient market*; that is, it is relatively slow to adjust to changes in supply and demand. The product cannot be removed from the market or transferred to another market, so an oversupply usually results in a lowering of price levels. Because development and construction of real estate take a considerable period of time from conception to completion, however, increases in demand may not be met immediately. Building and housing construction may occur in uneven spurts of activity.

VALUE

Value can be defined as the monetary present worth of goods, products, or services in relationship to the perceived *worth of future benefits arising from the ownership of real property*. In real estate, value has different meanings, depending on context. It does not rise in exact proportion to either inflation or the cost of living. Value is not the same as *price*, nor is it the same as *cost*. In real estate, cost generally relates to the past, price to the present, and *value* to the future.

The value of real property *does not remain the same over time*. Changes in the cost of construction material can increase the objective value of property, and differing standards and needs can alter an estimate of value. A housing shortage may increase the market value even of older, less-desirable houses, whereas building a better road may cause the value of commercial property along an older road to decrease. Availability of financing also may affect the property's value.

The location of a particular property and people's preferences for particular locations (i.e., **situs**) is another critical factor that affects value. It's been said that the three most important factors in determining the value of real estate are *location, location, location*.

For a property to have value in the real estate market it must have four basic economic characteristics (DUST):

1. *Demand*: Being needed or desired by someone who can afford to buy it.
2. *Utility*: Capable of satisfying human needs and desires.
3. *Scarcity*: Being only available in a limited supply.
4. *Transferability*: Having ownership rights easily transferred from one person to another.

Market Value

While a given parcel of real estate may have many different kinds of value at the same time, often the goal of an appraisal is an estimate of **market value**. An **appraisal** is an estimate or opinion of value based on supportable evidence and approved methods. An **appraiser** is an independent person trained to provide an unbiased estimate of value. Appraising is a professional service performed for a fee. The practice of real estate appraisal is subject to licensing and professional regulation.

The market value of real estate has been defined as the *price* a ready, willing, and able *buyer* who is *not forced to buy* will pay a *seller* who is *not forced to sell* after the property has had a reasonable *exposure on the market*. Included in this definition are the following key points:

- Market value is the most probable price a property will bring.
- Payment must be made in cash or its equivalent.
- Both buyer and seller must act without undue pressure.
- A reasonable length of time must be allowed for the property to be exposed in the open market.
- Both buyer and seller must be well-informed of the property's assets, defects, and potential.

Market value assumes an *arm's-length transaction*, that is, one between relative strangers, each of whom is trying to do the best for himself or herself.

Value vs. Price

Market value is an estimate based on an analysis of comparable sales and other pertinent market data. **Market price**, on the other hand, is *what a property actually sells for*—its selling price. Theoretically, the ideal market price is the same as the market value. There are circumstances under which a property may be sold below market value, however, as when a seller is forced to sell quickly or when a sale is arranged between relatives. Thus, the market price can be taken as accurate evidence of current market value only after considering the circumstances and relationship of the buyer and the seller, the terms and conditions of the market, and the effect of the passage of time since the sale was made.

Market Value vs. Cost

It is important also to distinguish between *market value* and *cost*. Cost and market value may be equal, and often are, when the improvements on a property are new and represent the highest and best use of the land.

More often, cost does not equal market value. Two homes may be similar in every respect except that one is located on a street with heavy traffic and the other on a quiet, residential street. The value of the former may be less than that of the latter, although the cost to construct each was exactly the same, as would be the cost to rebuild them.

Basic Principles of Value

A number of economic principles affect the value of real estate. The most important of these principles are defined in the following paragraphs.

Highest and Best Use

The most profitable use to which the property can be adapted or the use that is most likely to be in demand in the reasonably near future is its **highest and best use**. For example, a highest-and-best-use study may show that a parking lot in a busy downtown area should, in fact, be replaced by an office building. To place a value on the property based on its present use would be wrong because a parking lot is not the highest and best use of the land. Any **amenity** (tangible or intangible benefit to the property) or contribution to owner satisfaction—an unusual view of the ocean, for instance—may be a key factor in determining highest and best use.

Substitution

The principle of **substitution** states that the maximum value of a property tends to be set by the cost of purchasing another, equally desirable property, assuming no undue cost because of delay. For example, if two similar houses are for sale in an area, generally, the less expensive one sells first.

Supply and Demand

This principle states that the value of a property increases if the supply of such property decreases and the demand for it either increases or remains constant—and vice versa. For example, the last lot sold in a desirable residential area would probably be worth more than the first lot sold in that area, because the person who wants to live in that development has no other choice.

Conformity

Maximum value is realized if there is a reasonable degree of conformity along social and economic lines. In residential areas of single-family houses, for example, buildings should be similar in design, construction, size, and age to other buildings in the neighborhood, and they usually house families of similar social and economic status. Subdivision restrictions rely on the principle of conformity to protect maximum future value.

Regression and Progression

Less expensive neighboring houses hold down the value of a better property. This appraisal principle is known as regression. It's the reason why homeowners aren't likely to get their investment back if they improve their home so that it costs much more than others on the same street. On the other hand, the principle of progression states that the worth of a lesser property is increased if its neighbors are more valuable. That is why the least expensive house in a neighborhood is traditionally considered a good investment.

Anticipation

This principle holds that the expectation of future benefits creates value. For example, multifamily income properties are bought by investors in anticipation of the rents to be collected every month; or the value of a house may be affected by rumors that an adjacent parcel may be converted to commercial use in the near future.

Increasing and Diminishing Returns

Improvements to land and structures eventually reach a point at which they no longer have an effect on property values. As long as money spent on improvements produces an increase in income or value, the *law of increasing returns* applies. But at the point where additional improvements do not produce a proportionate increase in income or value, the *law of diminishing returns* applies.

Adding another bathroom to a house that has only one usually increases its market value; adding a fourth bath to a house that already has three may not make any difference in eventual sale price.

Contribution

The value of any component of a property is not what it costs, but what its addition contributes to the value of the whole or what its absence detracts from that value. For example, the cost of installing an air-conditioning system and remodeling an older office building may be greater than the increase in market value (a function of expected rent increases) that would result from the improvement to the property; or an owner who spends $15,000 on an in-ground pool may not add anything to the resale value of the house.

Competition

This principle states that profits attract competition but excess profits tend to attract ruinous competition. For example, the success of a retail store may cause investors to open similar stores in the area, resulting in less profit for all stores concerned.

Change

No physical or economic condition remains constant. Real estate is subject to natural phenomena, such as tornadoes, fires, and routine wear and tear by the elements. The real estate business also is subject to changes in the demands of its market, just as any business is. It is an appraiser's job to be knowledgeable about the past and predictable effects of natural phenomena and the behavior of the marketplace.

THE THREE APPROACHES TO VALUE

To arrive at an accurate estimate of value, three basic approaches or techniques are traditionally used by appraisers: the *sales comparison approach*, the *cost approach*, and the *income approach*. Each method serves as a check against the others. Each method is generally considered most suitable for certain types of property.

The Sales Comparison Approach

The sales comparison approach is essential in almost every appraisal of real estate. It is considered the most reliable of the three approaches in appraising residential property, where the amenities are so difficult to measure.

In the **sales comparison approach**, also called the market data approach, an estimate of value is obtained by comparing the **subject property** (the property under appraisal) with recently sold similar properties (**comparables** or *comps*). This approach is most often used by brokers and salespeople when helping a seller set a price for residential real estate in an active market. Because no two parcels of real estate are exactly alike, each comparable property must be compared with the subject property and the sales price adjusted for any dissimilar features. The principal factors for which adjustments must be made fall into four basic categories:

1. **Date of sale**—An adjustment must be made if economic changes occur between the date of sale of the comparable property and the date of the appraisal.

2. **Location**—An adjustment may be necessary to compensate for locational differences. For example, similar properties might differ in price from neighborhood to neighborhood, or even within the same neighborhood, if certain locations are considered more or less desirable.

3. **Physical features**—Physical features that may require adjustments include age of building; size of lot; landscaping; construction; number of rooms; square feet of living space; interior and exterior condition; presence or absence of a garage, fireplace, or air-conditioning; and so forth.

4. **Terms and conditions of sale**—This consideration becomes important in the case of special financing arrangements.

After a careful analysis of the differences between comparable properties and the subject property, an appraiser assigns a dollar value to each of these differences. On the basis of their knowledge and experience, appraisers estimate dollar adjustments that reflect actual values assigned in the marketplace. The adjusted sales price represents the probable value range of the subject property.

From this range a single market value estimate can be calculated, using a weighted average to emphasize those properties most closely comparable.

An example is shown in Figure 16.1. In the figure, the first column describes the subject property, the one being appraised, for which no sale price is yet known. Sale prices of the nearby comparable sales are listed in the first line of the chart.

Those sale prices are adjusted to reach an estimate of the value of the subject property. Property C, for example, has a larger lot. The appraiser's local experience is that buyers might pay $5,000 more for the extra land. That amount is subtracted from the sale price of C, to estimate what the subject property might bring.

After all adjustments have been made (next to bottom line), each comparable sale has an adjusted sale price that can be used in appraising the subject property.

A useful reminder about adjustments is found in the acronyms CBS (Comparable Better, Subtract) and CPA (Comparable Poorer, Add).

Figure 16.1: Sales Comparison Approach to Value

| | Subject Property | Comparable Properties | | |
		A	B	C
Sales price		$262,000	$252,000	$265,000
Financing concessions		none	none	none
Date of sale	none	current	current	current
Location	good	same	poorer +4,500	same
Age	6 years	same	same	same
Size of lot	60' × 135'	same	same	larger –5,000
Landscaping	good	same	same	same
Construction	brick	same	same	same
Style	ranch	same	same	same
No. of rooms	8	same	same	same
No. of bedrooms	4	same	poorer +4,500	same
No. of baths	2½	same	same	better –500
Sq. ft. of living space	2,500	same	same	better –2,000
Other space (basement)	full basement	same	same	same
Condition—exterior	average	better –2,500	poorer +2,000	better –2,500
Condition—interior	good	same	same	better –1,000
Garage	3-car attached	same	same	same
Other improvements	none	none	none	none
Net adjustments		–2,500	+11,000	–11,000
Adjusted value		$259,500	$263,000	$254,000

Note: The value of a feature that is present in the subject but not in the comparable property is *added* to the sales price of the comparable. The value of a feature that is present in the comparable but not in the subject property is *subtracted from the sales price of the comparable*. A good way to remember this is as follows: CBS stands for "comp better, subtract"; and CPA stands for "comp poorer, add." The adjusted sales prices of the comparables represent the probable range of value of the subject property. From this range, a single market value estimate can be selected.

The Cost Approach

Uses of the Cost Approach

The **cost approach** is most helpful in the appraisal of special-purpose buildings such as schools, churches, and public buildings. Such properties are difficult to appraise using other methods because there are seldom many local sales to use as comparables, and the properties do not ordinarily generate income.

The cost approach to value is based on the principle of substitution, which states that the maximum value of a property tends to be set by the cost of acquiring an equally desirable and valuable substitute property. The cost approach is sometimes called *appraisal by summation*. The cost approach consists of five steps.

1. Estimate the value of the land as if it were vacant and available to be put to its highest and best use.

2. Estimate the current cost of constructing the building(s) and site improvements.

3. Estimate the amount of *accrued depreciation* resulting from physical deterioration, functional obsolescence and/or external (economic) obsolescence.

4. Deduct accrued depreciation from the estimated construction cost of new building(s) and site improvements.

5. Add the estimated land value to the depreciated cost of the building(s) and site improvements to arrive at the total property value.

Land value (step 1) is estimated by using the sales comparison approach; that is, the location and improvements of the subject site are compared to those of similar nearby sites that have sold recently, and adjustments are made for significant differences.

There are two ways to look at the construction cost of a building for appraisal purposes (step 2): reproduction cost and replacement cost. **Reproduction cost** is the dollar amount required to construct an *exact duplicate* of the subject building at current prices. **Replacement cost** of the subject property would be the construction cost at current prices of a building that is not necessarily an exact duplicate, but serves the same purpose or function as the original.

Replacement cost is more often used in appraising, because it eliminates obsolete features and takes advantage of current construction materials and techniques.

An example of the cost approach to value is shown in Figure 16.2.

Figure 16.2: Cost Approach to Value

Subject Property: 155 Potter Drive		
Land Valuation: Size 60' × 135' @ $450 per front foot	=	$27,000
Plus site improvements: driveway, walks, landscaping, etc.	=	8,000
Total		$35,000
Building Valuation: Replacement Cost		
1,500 sq. ft. @ $85 per sq. ft. =	$127,500	
Less Depreciation:		
Physical depreciation		
Curable		
(items of deferred maintenance)		
exterior painting	$4,000	
Incurable (structural deterioration)	9,750	
Functional obsolescence	2,000	
External depreciation	0	
Total Depreciation	$15,750	
Depreciated Value of Building		$111,750
Indicated Value by Cost Approach		$146,750

Determining Reproduction or Replacement Cost

An appraiser using the cost approach computes the reproduction or replacement cost of a building using one of the following methods:

■ *Square-foot method*: The cost per square foot of a recently built comparable structure is multiplied by the number of square feet in the subject building. This is the most common method of cost estimation. The example in Figure 16.2 uses the square-foot method. (For some property, the cost per cubic foot of a recently built comparable structure is multiplied by the number of cubic feet in the subject structure.)

■ *Unit-in-place method*: The replacement cost of a structure is estimated based on the construction cost per unit of measure of individual building components, including material, labor, overhead, and builder's profit. Most components are measured in square feet, although items like plumbing fixtures are estimated by unit cost.

■ *Quantity-survey method*: An estimate is made of the quantities of raw materials needed to replace the subject structure (lumber, plaster, brick, and so on), as well as of the current price of such materials and their installation costs. These factors are added to indirect costs (building permit, survey, payroll taxes, builder's profit) to arrive at the total replacement cost of the structure.

■ *Index method*: A factor representing the percentage increase to the present time of construction costs is applied to the original cost of the subject property.

Depreciation

In a cost-approach real estate appraisal, **depreciation** refers to a loss in value due to any cause or any condition that adversely affects the value of an improvement to real property. As a general rule, land does not depreciate (except in such rare cases as misused farmland, downzoned urban parcels, or improperly developed land). For *appraisal* purposes, as opposed to depreciation for *tax* purposes, depreciation is divided into three classes, according to its cause:

1. **Physical deterioration**: This represents normal wear and tear. It may be
   - *curable*: that is, repairs are economically feasible and would result in an increase in appraised value equal to or exceeding their cost. Routine maintenance, such as painting, falls in this category.
   - *incurable*: the overall value of the structure does not justify the repairs required.

2. **Functional obsolescence**: This refers to physical or design features that are no longer considered desirable by property buyers. It may be
   - *curable*: that is, outmoded fixtures, such as plumbing, are usually easily replaced; room function might be redefined at no cost if the basic room layout allows it. A bedroom adjacent to a kitchen, for instance, may be converted to a family room.
   - *incurable*: that is, currently undesirable physical or design features cannot be easily remedied. An office building that cannot be air-conditioned suffers from functional obsolescence.

3. **External obsolescence**: Also known as *economic* or *locational obsolescence*, this is caused by factors not on the subject property, so this type of obsolescence is almost always *incurable*. Proximity to a nuisance, such as a polluting factory, would be an unchangeable factor that could not be expected to be cured by the owner of the subject property.

The Income Approach

The **income approach**, or *income capitalization approach*, to value is based on the present worth of the future rights to income. It assumes that the income derived from a property controls the value of that property. The income capitalization approach is used for valuation of income-producing properties—apartment buildings, office buildings, shopping centers, and the like. In using the income capitalization approach to estimate value, an appraiser must go through the following steps:

- Estimate annual potential *gross rental income*.

- Add income from other sources, such as concessions and vending machines, then based on market experience, deduct an appropriate allowance for vacancy and rent collection losses to arrive at the *effective gross income*

- Based on appropriate operating standards, deduct the annual operating expenses of the real estate from the effective gross income to arrive at the *annual net operating income*. Management costs are always included as operating expenses, even if the current owner also manages the property. Mortgage payments (including principal and interest), however, are debt service and not considered operating expenses.

- Estimate the price a typical investor would pay for the income produced by this particular type and class of property. This is done by estimating the rate of return (or yield) that an investor demands for the investment of capital in this type of building. This rate of return is called the **capitalization** (or "cap") **rate** and is determined by comparing the relationship of net operating income to the sales price of similar properties that have sold in the current market. For example, a comparable property that is producing an annual net income of $15,000 is sold for $187,500. The capitalization rate is $15,000 divided by $187,500, or 8%. If other comparable properties have sold at prices that yield substantially the same rate, it may be assumed that 8% is the rate that the appraiser should apply to the subject property.

- Finally, the capitalization rate is applied to the property's annual net income, resulting in the appraiser's estimate of the property value.

With the appropriate capitalization rate and the projected annual operating net income, the appraiser can obtain an indication of value by the income capitalization approach in the following manner:

Net Operating Income ÷ Capitalization Rate = Value

EXAMPLE

$15,000 income ÷ 8% cap rate = $187,500 value

This formula and its variations are important in dealing with income property.

$$\frac{\text{Income}}{\text{Rate}} = \text{Value}$$

$$\frac{\text{Income}}{\text{Value}} = \text{Rate}$$

Value × Rate = Income

A simplified version of the computations used in applying the income capitalization approach is illustrated in Figure 16.3.

Figure 16.3: Income Capitalization Approach to Value

Potential Gross Annual Income	$60,000
Market rent (100% capacity)	
Income from other sources (vending machines and pay phones)	+600
	$60,600
Less vacancy and collection losses (estimated) @4%	–2,424
Effective Gross Income	$58,176

Expenses:

Real estate taxes	$9,000
Insurance	1,000
Heat	2,500
Maintenance	6,400
Utilities, electricity, water, gas	800
Repairs	1,200
Decorating	1,400
Replacement of equipment	800
Legal and accounting	600
Advertising	300
Management	3,000
Total	$27,000
Annual Net Operating Income	$31,176

Capitalization rate = 10% (overall rate)

Capitalization of annual net income: $31,176 ÷ 0.10 = $311,760

Indicated Value by Income Approach = $311,760

Gross Rent or Income Multipliers

When appraising an investment property that produces rent or income, the sales comparison approach can include comps based on the income of similar properties that sold recently. A **gross rent multiplier (GRM)** relates the sales price of a property to its rental income. (Gross *monthly* income is used for residential property; gross *annual* income is used for commercial and industrial property.) The formula is

$$\frac{\text{Sales Price}}{\text{Rental Income}} = \text{Gross Rent Multiplier}$$

For example, if a home recently sold for $200,000 and its monthly rental income was $1,400, the GRM for the property would be computed in the following way:

$$\frac{\$200,000}{\$1,400} = 142.86 \text{ GRM}$$

To establish an accurate GRM, an appraiser should have recent sales and rental data from at least four properties similar to the subject property. The most appropriate GRM can then be applied to the estimated fair market rental of the subject property to arrive at its market value. The formula would then be

Rental Income × GRM = Estimated Market Value

If a property's income also comes from nonrental sources (such as sales concessions), a **gross income multiplier (GIM)** is similarly used.

Much skill is required to use multipliers accurately, because there is no fixed multiplier for all areas or all types of properties. Therefore, many appraisers view the technique simply as a quick, informal way to arrive at an approximate property value. It does not take expenses into account.

The most difficult step in the income approach to value is determining the appropriate capitalization rate for the property. This rate must be selected to recapture the original investment over the building's economic life, give the owner an acceptable rate of return on investment, and provide for the repayment of borrowed capital. An income property that carries with it a great deal of risk as an investment generally requires a higher rate of return than would a property that is considered a safe investment.

Reconciliation

If more than one of the three approaches to value are applied to the same property, they normally produce as many separate indications of value. **Reconciliation** is the art of analyzing and effectively weighing the findings from the different approaches used, because certain approaches are more valid and reliable with some kinds of properties than with others.

For example, in appraising a home the income approach is rarely used and the cost approach is of limited value unless the home is relatively new; therefore, the sales comparison approach usually is given greatest weight in valuing single-family residences. In the appraisal of income or investment property, the income approach normally would be given the greatest weight. In the appraisal of churches, libraries, museums, schools, and other special-use properties where there is little or no income or sales revenue, and often no comparable sales data, the cost approach usually would be assigned a single estimate of market value is produced.

Before-and-After Method

If an appraisal is being made because of a *partial taking* (only part of a property is to be taken) by eminent domain (see Unit 9), the value of the property before the taking is determined, as is what it would be after the taking; the difference between the two is the just compensation the owner is entitled to.

APPRAISING

In the real estate business, the highest level of appraisal activity is conducted by professional real estate appraisers who are recognized for their knowledge, training, skill, and integrity in this field. Formal appraisal reports are relied on in important decisions made by mortgage lenders, investors, public utilities, government agencies, businesses, and individuals.

Not all estimates of real estate value are made by professional appraisers; the real estate licensee often must help a seller estimate a market value for his or her property without the aid of a formal appraisal report. It is necessary that everyone engaged in the real estate business—even those who are not experts in appraisal—possess at least a fundamental knowledge of real estate valuation. Formal or informal appraisals may be required in numerous situations, such as for

- *estate purposes*—to establish taxable value or facilitate fair division among heirs;
- *divorce proceedings*—where real estate forms part of property to be shared;
- *financing*—when the amount to be loaned depends on the value of the property;
- *taxation*—to furnish documentation for a taxpayer's protest of assessment figures;
- *relocation*—to establish the amount to be guaranteed to a transferred employee;
- *condemnation*—to arrive at fair compensation for property taken by government;
- *insurance*—to estimate possible replacement expense in cases of loss;
- *damage loss*—to support income tax deductions; and
- *feasibility*—to study possible consequences of a particular use for property.

A *fee appraiser* works as an independent contractor who offers services to a number of different clients. A *staff appraiser* is an in-house employee of organizations like the FHA, a lending institution, or a large corporation. New Jersey now requires that appraisers who work on federally related appraisals be either licensed or certified by the state.

THE APPRAISAL PROCESS

The key to an accurate appraisal lies in the methodical collection of data. The appraisal process is an orderly set of procedures used to collect and analyze data to arrive at an ultimate value conclusion. The data are divided into two basic classes:

1. General data—covering the nation, region, city, and neighborhood; of particular importance is the neighborhood, where an appraiser finds the physical, economic, social, and political influences that directly affect the value and potential of the subject property

2. Specific data—covering details of the subject property as well as comparative data relating to costs, sales, income, and expenses of properties similar to and competitive with the subject property

Figure 16.4 outlines the steps an appraiser takes in carrying out an appraisal assignment.

Once the approaches have been reconciled and an opinion of value has been reached, the appraiser prepares a report for the client. The report should

- identify the real estate and real property interest being appraised;
- state the purpose and intended use of the appraisal;
- define the value to be estimated;
- state the effective date of the value and the date of the report;
- state the extent of the process of collecting, confirming, and reporting the data;
- list all assumptions and limiting conditions that affect the analysis, opinion, and conclusions of value;
- describe the information considered, the appraisal procedures followed, and the reasoning that supports the report's conclusions (if an approach was excluded, the report should explain why);
- describe any additional information that may be appropriate to show compliance with the specific guidelines established in the *Uniform Standards of Professional Appraisal Practice (USPAP)* or to clearly identify and explain any departures from these guidelines; and
- include a signed certification, as required by the Uniform Standards.

Figure 16.4: The Appraisal Process

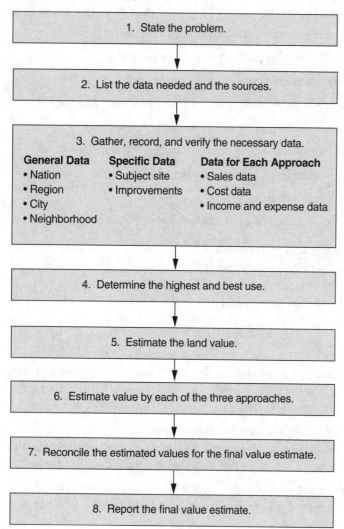

1. State the problem.

2. List the data needed and the sources.

3. Gather, record, and verify the necessary data.

General Data	**Specific Data**	**Data for Each Approach**
• Nation	• Subject site	• Sales data
• Region	• Improvements	• Cost data
• City		• Income and expense data
• Neighborhood		

4. Determine the highest and best use.

5. Estimate the land value.

6. Estimate value by each of the three approaches.

7. Reconcile the estimated values for the final value estimate.

8. Report the final value estimate.

Figure 16.5 shows part of the *Uniform Residential Appraisal Report,* the form required by many government agencies. It illustrates the types of detailed information required of an appraisal of residential property.

Figure 16.5: Uniform Residential Appraisal Report

Uniform Residential Appraisal Report

File #

| There are | comparable properties currently offered for sale in the subject neighborhood ranging in price from $ | to $ | . |

| There are | comparable sales in the subject neighborhood within the past twelve months ranging in sale price from $ | to $ | . |

FEATURE	SUBJECT	COMPARABLE SALE # 1		COMPARABLE SALE # 2		COMPARABLE SALE # 3	
Address							
Proximity to Subject							
Sale Price	$		$		$		$
Sale Price/Gross Liv. Area	$ sq. ft.	$ sq. ft.		$ sq. ft.		$ sq. ft.	
Data Source(s)							
Verification Source(s)							
VALUE ADJUSTMENTS	DESCRIPTION	DESCRIPTION	+(-) $ Adjustment	DESCRIPTION	+(-) $ Adjustment	DESCRIPTION	+(-) $ Adjustment
Sale or Financing Concessions							
Date of Sale/Time							
Location							
Leasehold/Fee Simple							
Site							
View							
Design (Style)							
Quality of Construction							
Actual Age							
Condition							
Above Grade Room Count	Total Bdrms. Baths	Total Bdrms. Baths		Total Bdrms. Baths		Total Bdrms. Baths	
Gross Living Area	sq. ft.	sq. ft.		sq. ft.		sq. ft.	
Basement & Finished Rooms Below Grade							
Functional Utility							
Heating/Cooling							
Energy Efficient Items							
Garage/Carport							
Porch/Patio/Deck							
Net Adjustment (Total)		☐ + ☐ - $		☐ + ☐ - $		☐ + ☐ - $	
Adjusted Sale Price of Comparables		Net Adj. % Gross Adj. % $		Net Adj. % Gross Adj. % $		Net Adj. % Gross Adj. % $	

I ☐ did ☐ did not research the sale or transfer history of the subject property and comparable sales. If not, explain

My research ☐ did ☐ did not reveal any prior sales or transfers of the subject property for the three years prior to the effective date of this appraisal.

Data source(s)

My research ☐ did ☐ did not reveal any prior sales or transfers of the comparable sales for the year prior to the date of sale of the comparable sale.

Data source(s)

Report the results of the research and analysis of the prior sale or transfer history of the subject property and comparable sales (report additional prior sales on page 3).

ITEM	SUBJECT	COMPARABLE SALE # 1	COMPARABLE SALE # 2	COMPARABLE SALE # 3
Date of Prior Sale/Transfer				
Price of Prior Sale/Transfer				
Data Source(s)				
Effective Date of Data Source(s)				

Analysis of prior sale or transfer history of the subject property and comparable sales

Summary of Sales Comparison Approach

Indicated Value by Sales Comparison Approach $

Indicated Value by: Sales Comparison Approach $ Cost Approach (if developed) $ Income Approach (if developed) $

This appraisal is made ☐ "as is", ☐ subject to completion per plans and specifications on the basis of a hypothetical condition that the improvements have been completed, ☐ subject to the following repairs or alterations on the basis of a hypothetical condition that the repairs or alterations have been completed, or ☐ subject to the following required inspection based on the extraordinary assumption that the condition or deficiency does not require alteration or repair:

Based on a complete visual inspection of the interior and exterior areas of the subject property, defined scope of work, statement of assumptions and limiting conditions, and appraiser's certification, my (our) opinion of the market value, as defined, of the real property that is the subject of this report is $, as of   , which is the date of inspection and the effective date of this appraisal.

(Vertical left margin labels: SALES COMPARISON APPROACH, RECONCILIATION)

THE PROFESSION OF APPRAISING

Although estimating the value (appraising) of property has existed since the concept of property ownership, appraising as an organized profession began as a result of the huge numbers of foreclosures during the Great Depression of the 1930s. Appraising has now become a highly specialized branch of real estate.

Professional designation of qualified appraisers is traditionally made through membership in appraisal societies. Different designations require varying levels of education, specific courses in appraisal, examinations, demonstration appraisals, experience, and continuing education.

The leading professional society is the Appraisal Institute, which awards the designations MAI (Member of the Appraisal Institute) and SRA (Senior Residential Appraiser) for general and residential appraisers, respectively. Specific credentials may be required when expert testimony is provided for court proceedings or before a public body such as a zoning board.

New Jersey requires that appraisals performed as part of a federally related transaction comply with state standards and be performed by a state-licensed or state-certified appraiser. An exception is allowed where a broker's price opinion (BPO) is acceptable to a lender. The BPO should include a statement indicating that the report "should not be considered the equivalent of an appraisal prepared by a New Jersey licensed or certified real estate appraiser." The statement should appear in a print size as large as the main text in the report. Any fees involved are payable to the agent's broker of record. All real estate appraisals for any purpose must be done by licensed or certified real estate appraisers. The only exceptions are for CMAs provided to sellers or buyers (see Unit 10) and BPOs ordered by lenders (see Unit 14).

Real estate salespersons and brokers may get partial experience credit toward appraisal licensing and certification in the performance of *Comparative Market Analyses (CMAs)*. Certification and licensing are handled by the Department of Law and Public Safety, Division of Consumer Affairs, State Board of Real Estate Appraisers, 124 Halsey Street, 6th Floor, Newark, NJ 07101, 973-504-6480. Detailed information is available at www.njconsumeraffairs.gov/rea.

To begin accumulating the required hours for licensure as an appraiser, a beginner may earn the status of *apprentice/trainee* after 90 hours of appraisal study and a successful examination.

To become *licensed as a residential appraiser*, New Jersey students must complete 150 classroom hours in approved courses and have 2,000 hours of experience in no fewer than 12 months.

The applicant for *certification as a residential appraiser* must have an associate degree or higher. (Applicants without a degree may substitute at least 21 semester credits in specific English, economics, mathematics, business, or law courses.) The student must also complete 200 hours in approved appraisal courses and have 2,500 hours of experience in a period of at least 24 months.

Both licensed and certified residential appraisers must pass examinations, and may conduct appraisals of no more than $1 million.

In order to become a *certified general appraiser*, the student must have a bachelor's degree or higher. (An applicant without a degree may substitute 30 semester credit hours in the courses mentioned previously, and two elective courses in accounting, geography, ag-economics, business management, or real estate.) In addition, 300 hours of approved appraisal courses are required, and an apprenticeship of 3,000 hours of experience over a period of 2½ years or more. At least 1,500 of those hours should be spent on non-residential properties. Unlike residential appraisers, certified general appraisers have no monetary caps on the properties they can appraise.

In every case, the required course of study must include a 15-hour national *USPAP* course (*Uniform Standards of Professional Appraisal Practice*).

The Real Estate Appraiser License Law requires that individuals who wish to be licensed or certified as appraisers must undergo a criminal background check.

SUMMARY

To appraise real estate is to estimate its value. Although there are many types of value, the most common objective of an *appraisal* is to estimate market value—the most probable sales price of a property.

While appraisals are concerned with values, prices and costs, it is vital to understand the distinctions among the terms. *Value* is concerned with the present worth of future benefits, *cost* represents a measure of past expenditures, and *price* reflects the actual amount of money paid for a property.

Basic to appraising are certain underlying economic principles such as *highest and best use*, *substitution*, *supply and demand*, *conformity*, *anticipation*, *increasing and diminishing returns*, *contribution*, *competition*, and *change*.

A professional appraiser analyzes a property through three approaches to value. In the *sales comparison approach*, the value of the subject property is compared with the values of others like it that have sold recently. Because no two properties are exactly alike, adjustments must be made to account for any differences. With the *cost approach*, an appraiser calculates the cost of building a similar structure on a similar site. Then the appraiser subtracts depreciation (loss in value), which reflects the differences between new properties of this type and the present condition of the subject property. The *income approach* is an analysis based on the relationship between the rate of return that an investor requires and the net income that a property produces.

The application of the three approaches normally results in three different estimates of value. In the process of *reconciliation*, the appraiser weighs the validity and reliability of each approach objectively to arrive at the best and most supportable conclusion of value.

USEFUL WEBSITES

New Jersey Board of Real Estate Appraisers: https://www.njconsumeraffairs.gov/rea

Appraisal Foundation: www.appraisalfoundation.org

Appraisal Institute: www.appraisalinstitute.org

KEY TERMS REVIEW 1

Match the number of each key term with the corresponding letter.

_____ 1. Amenity

_____ 2. Appraisal

_____ 3. Appraiser

_____ 4. Capitalization rate

_____ 5. Comparables

_____ 6. Cost approach

_____ 7. Depreciation

_____ 8. External obsolescence

_____ 9. Functional obsolescence

_____ 10. Gross income multiplier

_____ 11. Gross rent multiplier

_____ 12. Highest and best use

_____ 13. Income approach

A. analysis of income including rental and other factors

B. analysis of rental income, used roughly in sales comparison approach

C. use of land that yields the most money

D. appraisal technique that analyzes the cost to build

E. analysis of value of property using return on investment

F. extra that contributes to owner satisfaction: clean air, view, and so on

G. loss of value due to any cause

H. loss of value due to factors beyond the property boundaries

I. loss of value due to worn or outmoded features

J. process of estimating value

K. rate of return demanded by investors in a particular area

L. similar nearby property recently sold

M. an independent person trained to provide an unbiased estimate of value

KEY TERMS REVIEW 2

Match the number of each key term with the corresponding letter.

_____ 1. Market price

_____ 2. Market value

_____ 3. Physical deterioration

_____ 4. Reconciliation

_____ 5. Replacement cost

_____ 6. Reproduction cost

_____ 7. Sales comparison approach

_____ 8. Situs

_____ 9. Subject property

_____ 10. Substitution

_____ 11. Value

A. analysis of values received by different appraisal approaches

B. cost to rebuild exactly, using materials like the original

C. cost to rebuild using today's materials and techniques

D. what a property actually sells for

E. location; buyers' willingness to pay more for certain locations

F. loss of value due to wear and tear

G. parcel of real estate being appraised

H. present worth of future benefits

I. price that would be paid by an informed buyer

J. principle that no one pays more if the same can be had for less

K. appraisal technique that analyzes sale prices of comparable properties

UNIT 16 REVIEW QUESTIONS

1. What does an appraiser do?
   A. Discovers value
   B. Insures value
   C. Estimates value
   D. Sets value

2. No two parcels of land
   A. are worth exactly the same amount.
   B. can be combined.
   C. have the same highest and best use.
   D. are identical.

3. The appraiser who works for a number of different clients is known as a(n)
   A. fee appraiser.
   B. freelance appraiser.
   C. staff appraiser.
   D. in-house appraiser.

4. What is value?
   A. A relationship between desired object and the seller
   B. The future value of present benefits
   C. The amount a seller is willing to give up
   D. The power of an object to command other goods in exchange

5. A house should bring $400,000 but is sold for $350,000 by a hard-pressed seller in a hurry. It is then mortgaged for $300,000 and insured for $375,000. Its market value is
   A. $300,000.
   B. $350,000.
   C. $375,000.
   D. $400,000.

6. An example of an arm's-length transaction is one between
   A. father and daughter.
   B. employer and employee.
   C. broker and salesperson.
   D. two strangers.

7. An amenity that contributed to a property's value might be its
   A. updated plumbing.
   B. ocean frontage.
   C. sale price.
   D. replacement cost.

8. Market value and cost are often equal when property
   A. remains in the family a long time.
   B. was recently constructed.
   C. is sold in an arm's-length transaction.
   D. receives a weighted appraisal.

9. Highest and best use of real estate is defined as the use that produces the MOST
   A. benefit to the community.
   B. conformity.
   C. progression.
   D. money.

10. "Why should I pay more when I can buy almost the same house new for less?" is an example of the principle of
    A. substitution.
    B. conformity.
    C. anticipation.
    D. change.

11. Houses are likely to reach their maximum value when
    A. a wide range of price levels is represented.
    B. neighbors hold a mix of executive, blue-collar, and white-collar jobs.
    C. each house is unique.
    D. jobs, houses, and price levels are similar.

12. The cost approach is MOST useful for
    A. a library.
    B. insurance purposes.
    C. new construction.
    D. all of the above.

13. From the reproduction or replacement cost of the building an appraiser deducts depreciation, which represents
    A. the remaining useful economic life of the building.
    B. remodeling costs to increase rentals.
    C. loss of value due to any cause.
    D. costs to modernize the building.

14. The difference between reproduction cost and replacement cost involves
    A. functional obsolescence.
    B. estimated land value.
    C. modern versus obsolete methods and materials.
    D. effective gross income.

15. The appraised value of a residence with five bedrooms and one bathroom would probably be reduced because of
    A. locational obsolescence.
    B. functional obsolescence.
    C. curable physical deterioration.
    D. incurable physical deterioration.

16. The term economic obsolescence refers to
    A. poor landscaping.
    B. faulty floor plan.
    C. wear and tear.
    D. problems beyond the property line.

17. If a property's annual net income is $37,500 and it is valued at $300,000, what is its capitalization rate?
    A. 8%
    B. 12.5%
    C. 15%
    D. 18%

18. Expenses are subtracted from gross rental figures to arrive at
    A. debt service.
    B. cash flow.
    C. net operating income.
    D. depreciation.

19. Capitalization is the process by which the estimated future annual net income is used as the basis to
    A. determine cost.
    B. estimate value.
    C. establish depreciation.
    D. determine potential tax value.

20. Which of the following factors would NOT be important in comparing properties under the sales comparison approach to value?
    A. A difference in the dates of sale
    B. A difference in real estate taxes
    C. A difference in appearance and condition
    D. A difference in the original cost

21. Reconciliation refers to which of the following?
    A. Loss of value due to any cause
    B. Separating the value of the land from the total value of the property in order to compute depreciation
    C. Analyzing the results obtained by the three approaches to value to determine a final estimate of value
    D. The process by which an appraiser determines the highest and best use for a parcel of land

22. In order to become a certified general appraiser, one must have a
    A. fellowship.
    B. brokerage.
    C. bachelor's degree.
    D. designation.

23. Some of the country's foremost appraisers have earned the designation
    A. MAI.
    B. REA.
    C. SRE.
    D. ARE.

24. Real estate appraisals must be performed by a licensed or certified real estate appraiser
    A. regardless of the value of the property involved in the transaction.
    B. only if the value of the property involved in the transaction is greater than $150,000.
    C. only if the property's fair market value is less than $1 million
    D. whenever a CMA has not been previously prepared by a real estate broker or salesperson.

25. To be certified as a residential appraiser in New Jersey, an applicant must complete
    A. 2,000 hours of apprenticeship under a residential broker and undergo a physical examination.
    B. 165 hours of education in approved courses, and undergo a criminal background check.
    C. 1,500 hours of apprenticeship under a licensed or certified residential appraiser, and undergo a thorough psychological examination.
    D. 200 hours in approved real estate and appraisal courses, and have 2,500 hours of experience in no less than two years.

26. An apartment building has $65,000 in potential gross annual income. The vacancy rate is estimated at 5%. Total operating expenses are $29,000. The capitalization rate is 9%. What would be the value of the building using the income approach?
    A. $324,773
    B. $363,889
    C. $372,895
    D. $392,367

27. An appraiser has been asked to appraise a two-unit apartment building. In this neighborhood, the accepted gross rent multiplier is 144. The annual income on the building is $16,800 (both units rented). The monthly expenses are $300. What is the estimated market value if it is based on the sales comparison approach?
    A. $201,600
    B. $232,500
    C. $224,800
    D. $258,600

UNIT 17

Investment and Business Brokerage

LEARNING OBJECTIVES

When you have completed this unit, you will be able to accomplish the following.

> Explain the advantages and disadvantages of investing in real estate.
> Describe the tax benefits of real estate investments and the effect of the New Jersey Uniform Commercial Code.

KEY TERMS

adjusted basis
appreciation
basis
bill of sale
boot
Bulk Transfer Act
capital gain
cash flow
depreciation

exchange
income property
installment sale
leverage
marginal tax rate
pyramiding
real estate investment
  syndicate

real estate investment
  trust (REIT)
return
syndicate
tax-credit
uniform Commercial
  Code (UCC)

INVESTING IN REAL ESTATE

Often customers expect a real estate broker or salesperson to act as an investment counselor. The broker or salesperson should always refer a potential real estate investor to a competent tax accountant, attorney, or investment specialist who can give expert advice.

Advantages of Real Estate Investment

Traditionally, real estate investments have shown an overall rate of **return** generally higher than the prevailing interest rate charged by mortgage lenders. *Return* includes total income, both direct cash flow and indirect benefits such as depreciation and appreciation. Often, investors borrow money to finance a real estate purchase with the expectation that, if held long enough, the asset will yield a greater return than it costs to finance the purchase. Using borrowed money this way is called **leverage**.

Real estate markets vary widely, with real estate prices keeping pace with inflation in some areas, holding their own in other states, and dropping sharply elsewhere. Any real estate investor must take local conditions into account before making decisions.

Disadvantages of Real Estate Investment

Unlike stocks and bonds, real estate is *not highly liquid* over a short period of time. This means that an investor cannot usually sell real estate quickly without taking some sort of loss. Even though a real estate investor may be able to raise a limited amount of cash by refinancing the property, for a quick sale the investor may have to sell at a substantially lower price than full market value.

In addition, it is difficult to invest in real estate without some degree of expert advice. Investment decisions must be made based on a careful study of all the facts in a given situation, reinforced by a broad and thorough knowledge of real estate and the manner in which it affects and is affected by the marketplace—the human element. *All investors should seek legal and tax counsel before making any real estate investments.*

Rarely can a real estate investor sit idly by and watch his or her money grow. Management decisions must be made. For example, can the investor effectively manage the property personally, or would it be better to hire a professional property manager? How much rent should be charged? How should repairs and tenant grievances be handled? "Sweat equity" (physical improvements accomplished by the investor personally) may be required to make the asset profitable.

Finally, a high degree of risk is often involved in real estate investment. There is always the possibility that an investor's property will decrease in value during the period it is held or that it will not generate income sufficient to make it profitable.

THE INVESTMENT

Property held for **appreciation** is generally expected to increase in value and to show a profit when sold at some future date. **Income property** is just that—property held for producing income as well as for a profit on its sale.

Income

The wisest initial investment for a person who wishes to buy and personally manage real estate may be the purchase of rental income property.

Cash Flow

The object of owning income property is to generate spendable income, usually called **cash flow**. The cash flow is the total amount of money remaining after all expenditures have been paid, including taxes, operating costs, and mortgage payments. The cash flow produced by any given parcel of real estate is determined by at least three factors: amount of rent received, operating expenses, and method of debt repayment.

Generally, the amount of *rent* (income) that a property commands depends on a number of factors, including location, physical appearance, and amenities. If the cash flow from rents is not enough to cover all expenses, a *negative cash flow* results.

Pyramiding Through Refinancing

By holding and refinancing using equity and appreciation buildup, rather than selling or exchanging already-owned properties, an investor's holdings can be increased without investment of any additional capital. This practice is known as **pyramiding**. By reinvesting and doubling his or her holdings periodically, it is conceivable that an investor who started out with a small initial cash down payment could own (heavily mortgaged) properties worth hundreds of thousands or millions of dollars. With sufficient cash flow to cover all costs, *if market values hold steady or increase*, the income derived from such assets could pay off the various mortgage debts and show a handsome profit. In a steadily declining market, however, investors could find that properties are worth less than they paid for them and they have to dip into their cash reserves to make up for a negative cash flow.

TAX BENEFITS

One of the main reasons real estate investments were popular—and profitable—in the past was that federal law allowed investors to use losses generated by the investments to shelter income from other sources.

Internal Revenue Service regulations, however, are subject to frequent change. Too much tax shelter can backfire by making the investor subject to *tax alternative minimum tax*. Without additional training and possible licensure, real estate licensees should avoid making comments about tax benefits and refer any questions to qualified tax advisors.

Exchanges

Real estate investors can defer taxation of capital gains (profit on a sale) by a like-kind property **exchange**. Note that the tax is deferred, not eliminated. If the investor sells the property, the capital gain is taxed.

To qualify as a tax-deferred exchange, the properties involved must be of *like kind*—that is, income or investment property. For example, a landlord moving across the country wants to sell an apartment house and buy another that she can manage in the new location. If she has to pay capital gains tax on the sale of the present building, she won't have enough left to reinvest in a similar property.

By using a tax-deferred exchange, however, she can in effect "swap" the two properties with no immediate tax consequences. Gain on the first sale is not tax-exempt, but tax can be postponed indefinitely, then added to the gain on the second property when it is sold some time in the future.

It is not always necessary for the two sellers to make a direct exchange of properties. A Section 1031 exchange allows an investor to sell one investment and buy another outright, with no necessity to find an owner who wants to swap. Money involved is held by a third party until the two transactions are completed. The documentation is complicated. The investor must identify the intended purchase within 45 days of selling the first parcel and complete the purchase within 180 days. There are strict regulations about what is done with the money in the meantime. The transaction should not be undertaken without advance planning under the guidance of an accountant, broker, or lawyer who is familiar with the procedure.

When the property being bought, the replacement property, costs less than the one being sold, the difference in price is known as **boot**. That leftover cash may be immediately taxable, as part of the investor's capital gain on the first property. Tax on the rest of the gain, however, can be postponed by an adjustment to the cost basis of the new property.

Capital Gains

Capital gain is taxable profit on an investment; in real estate, it is the difference between the adjusted basis of property and its net selling price. At various times, tax law has excluded a portion of capital gains from income tax. In order to qualify for favorable long-term capital gains tax treatment, the asset must have been owned for a required length of time (referred to as the holding period). Capital gains tax rates fluctuate frequently. As of December 2020, the rates for 2021 could be 0%, 15%, or 20%, depending on income. Consult a tax accountant for authoritative and current information.

Basis

A property's cost basis determines the amount of gain to be taxed. The **basis** of property is the investor's initial cost for the real estate. The investor adds to the basis the cost of any capital (physical) *improvements* subsequently made to the property, and subtracts from the basis the amount of any depreciation claimed as a tax deduction (explained later) to derive the property's adjusted basis. When the property is sold by the investor, the amount by which the sales price exceeds the property's **adjusted basis** is the capital gain taxable as income.

For example, many years ago, an investor purchased a one-family dwelling for use as a rental property. The purchase price was $45,000. The investor is now selling the property for $100,000. Shortly before the sale date, the investor made $3,000 worth of capital improvements to the home. Depreciation of $10,000 on the property improvements has been taken during the term of the investor's ownership. The investor is paying a broker's commission of 7% of the sales price and closing costs of $600. The investor's capital gain is computed as follows:

Selling price:		$100,000
Less:		
7% commission	7,000	
closing costs	+ 600	
	7,600	− 7,600
Net sales price:		92,400
Basis:		
Original cost	45,000	
Improvements	+ 3,000	
	48,000	
Less:		
Depreciation	− 10,000	
Adjusted basis:	38,000	− 38,000
Total capital gain:		$54,400
(of which $44,400 is taxable at 15%, and $10,000 at 25%)		

Depreciation

Depreciation is an accounting concept that allows an investor to recover the cost of an income-producing asset by way of tax deductions over the period of the asset's useful life. Only costs of *improvements* to land may be recovered, *not* costs for the land itself. On residential property the cost of the building is divided by 27.5 years. The quotient is the amount chargeable each year for depreciation. (Commercial property is depreciated over 39 years.)

Deductions and Federal Tax Laws

Federal tax law limits the deductibility of losses from rental property, provided that the investor *actively participates* in the management and operation of the property and has taxable income that falls within certain guidelines. Tax laws on the deductibility of losses from rental property are complicated. In some cases, they are classified as passive losses, with limited value against other income. The investor's particular situation should be discussed with a Certified Public Accountant (CPA).

An investor may not use a loss from a passive activity (one in which the taxpayer is not an active participant) to shelter active income (such as wages) or portfolio income (such as stock dividends, bank interest, and capital gains). An example of a passive investor is a limited partner, someone who contributes investment monies but has no voice in the operation of the investment.

Tax Credits

A **tax credit** is a direct reduction in tax due, rather than a deduction from income before tax is computed. A tax credit is therefore of far greater value. Investors in older building renovations and low-income housing projects may use tax credits to offset tax on up to $25,000 of other income. Even passive investors can take advantage of the tax credits. The maximum income level at which the credits can be taken is also higher: Investors with adjusted gross incomes of up to $200,000 are entitled to the full $25,000 offset, which is reduced by $0.50 for every additional dollar of income and eliminated entirely for incomes above $250,000.

Tax credits have been provided for taxpayers who renovate historic property. (Historic property is so designated by the Department of the Interior and listed in the *National Register of Historic Landmarks*, or property of historic significance located in a state-certified historic district.) The allowable credit is 20% of the money spent on renovation.

The work must be accomplished in accordance with federal historic property guidelines and certified by the Department of the Interior. After renovation, the property must be used as a place of business or rented—it cannot be used as the personal residence of the person taking the tax credit.

There is a credit of 10% of rehabilitation costs for nonhistoric buildings placed in service before 1936. Nonhistoric buildings must be nonresidential property. The law also provides tax credits ranging from 4% to 9% each year over a ten-year period for expenditures on new construction or renovation of certain low-income housing.

Installment Sales

A taxpayer who sells real property and receives payment on an installment basis, in which the purchase price is paid over a period of years, may report any profit on the transaction year by year as it is collected. Complex tax rules apply to **installment sales**.

Income tax calculations are figured at the investor's **marginal tax rate**, the rate at which the top dollar is taxed.

REAL ESTATE INVESTMENT SYNDICATES

Generally, a **syndicate** is a joining together of two or more people or firms to carry out one or more business projects. A syndicate is not in itself a legal entity. It may be organized into a number of ownership forms, including partnership, trust, or corporation. A *joint venture* is an organization of two or more people or firms to carry out a single project. A joint venture lasts for a limited time and is not intended to establish a permanent relationship.

The real estate practitioner who organizes or promotes a real estate venture involving investors who expect to benefit without active participation should be alert for special registration or licensing required for syndication activity.

A **real estate investment syndicate** is a form of business venture in which a group of people pool their resources to own and/or develop a particular piece of property. In this manner, people with only modest capital can invest in large-scale, high-profit operations, such as highrise apartment buildings and shopping centers. A certain amount of profit is realized from rents collected on the investment, but the main return usually comes when the syndicate sells the property after sufficient appreciation.

Syndicate participation can take many different legal forms, from tenancy in common and joint tenancy to various kinds of partnerships, corporations, and trusts. *Private* syndication, which generally involves a small group of closely associated and/or widely experienced investors, is distinguished from *public* syndication, which generally involves a much larger group of investors who may or may not be knowledgeable about real estate as an investment. If one is considering raising money through the issuance of stock, there are many laws that must be complied with and professional advice should be sought.

Securities laws include provisions to control and regulate the offering and sale of securities. This is to protect members of the public who are not sophisticated investors but may be solicited to participate. Real estate securities must be registered with state officials and/or with the federal Securities and Exchange Commission (SEC) when they meet the defined conditions of a public offering. *Salespeople of such real estate securities may be required to obtain special licenses and registration.*

Forms of Syndicates

As discussed in Unit 7, a *general partnership* is organized so that *all members of the group share equally in the managerial decisions, profits, and losses involved with the investment.* A certain member (or members) of the syndicate is designated to act as trustee for the group and holds title to the property and maintains it in the syndicate's name.

Under a *limited partnership* agreement, *one party* (or parties), usually a property developer or real estate broker, *organizes, operates, and is responsible for the entire syndicate.* This person is called the general partner. The other members of the partnership are merely investors; they have no voice in the organization and direction of the operation. These passive investors are called *limited partners.*

The limited partners share in the profits and compensate the general partner out of such profits. The limited partners stand to lose only as much as they invest—nothing more. Any general partners are totally personally responsible for excess losses incurred by the investment.

The sale of a limited partnership interest involves the sale of an *investment security*, as defined by the SEC.

REAL ESTATE INVESTMENT TRUSTS

By directing their funds into **real estate investment trusts (REITs)**, real estate investors can take advantage of the same tax benefits as mutual fund investors. A REIT must have at least 100 investors and at least 75% of the trust's income must come from real estate.

BUSINESS OPPORTUNITY SALES

Every business, no matter how small, must have a place of operation. Whether it is a small, direct-mail sales enterprise operated from the owner's home or a large manufacturing concern with numerous factories and sales offices, the operation of a business involves the use of real estate. Consequently, when a business is sold, the title or lease to real estate used in the business is usually included in the sale. For this reason a person who sells or negotiates the sale of businesses for others for a fee *is required to be licensed as a real estate broker*. The exception is when a business is sold without any real estate interest in any form.

Besides title to real estate or a present lease, the business may also be selling

- fixtures and stock in inventory;
- the business name;
- customer lists;
- goodwill; and
- special rights such as copyrights, patents, franchises, and licenses. (A lottery license, with the right to operate a "Pick-It" machine, cannot be transferred.)

The items just listed are personal property. They can be included in a sales contract and may even be covered by a mortgage, but they are not included in the deed, which transfers ownership of real estate only.

The statute of frauds requires that all sales of personal property worth $500 or more be evidenced by a written contract. At the closing of a business sales transaction a separate **bill of sale** should be executed by the seller for all chattel, stock, materials, and other personal property that is included in the sale.

The broker should gather as complete information as possible about the business. Accountants' statements and past income tax returns are essential. In addition, the following questions should be asked—and answered:

- Are fixtures and equipment owned? What is their fair market value?
- Are fixtures and equipment leased? What are the terms of the lease and can it be assigned?
- Is the inventory as accurate as possible?
- What liabilities will be taken over by the buyer?
- How much will the accounts receivable (money owed to the business) be discounted for noncollectible debts?
- What is the depreciated value of used items and of any licenses or copyrights that have a limited life?
- Can the buyer take over unpaid bank notes, installment contracts, and chattel mortgages?

Because federal law can hold an innocent purchaser responsible for the cleanup of environmental hazards, the sale of any business that involves real estate should be made subject to a satisfactory environmental review before any agreement becomes firm. For unpaid bills owed to suppliers, the Uniform Commercial Code (UCC) sets specific regulations.

FINANCING

Business opportunities are usually sold with the buyer giving a substantial down payment and the seller providing a purchase-money mortgage for the balance of the selling price. To secure this loan the buyer pledges as collateral the business, personal property, and merchandise just purchased. If the buyer defaults on the loan, the seller is usually able to take back the business, personal property, and merchandise or stock.

UNIFORM COMMERCIAL CODE—BULK TRANSFERS

New Jersey has adopted the **Uniform Commercial Code (UCC)**, which regulates the transfer of personal property. The section of this code that is most applicable to the real estate business is Article 6, known as the **Bulk Transfer Act**.

In most businesses, supplies, goods, and services are constantly being purchased on credit and paid for as the suppliers submit their bills. The Bulk Transfer Act is designed to protect creditors from the fraud perpetrated by a business owner who sells the business, including equipment and stock, and then disappears, leaving creditors unpaid. In such a case the creditors cannot demand payment from the new owner unless it can be proved that the new owner had actual knowledge of the fraud. To prevent such a fraud, Article 6 requires that the following steps be taken when a business is sold:

- The purchaser should require the seller to prepare a list of existing creditors, including their names and business addresses and the amounts owed to each. This list should be signed and affirmed, or sworn to, by the seller, and it should include all persons who have possible claims against the business, whether or not the claims are valid.

- The parties to the transaction (purchaser and seller) should prepare a list of all real and personal property that is included in the sale.

- The purchaser should preserve the seller's list of creditors for at least six months after the date of sale and make the list available for inspection by any of the seller's creditors or record it in the public record of the county in which the business is located or in the office of the secretary of state of New Jersey.

The seller is obligated to prepare the list of creditors and is responsible for its completeness and truthfulness. It is against the law to make false statements on such a list.

After receiving this list, the purchaser is obligated to notify all listed creditors of the details of the pending sale and the details of how their debts will be paid, at least ten days before the sale takes place. The New Jersey statute of limitation on bulk transfers is six months; unless the transfer has been concealed, creditors have six months to file any claim on title to personal property after this notice to creditors has been sent. If the notice to creditors is not sent and the business is sold without first paying existing creditors, a creditor may enforce a lien on the goods and equipment of the business as if they still belonged to the original owner.

The requirements of the Bulk Transfer Act are designed to protect the interests of the buyer as well as those of the seller's creditors in the sale of a business. Noncompliance with this law is a *criminal offense* in New Jersey. Real estate is not covered under the Bulk Transfer Act, just business personal property.

Real estate brokers and salespersons are never allowed to draw up contracts for any commercial transactions. Licensees involved in a business or commercial sale should advise the parties to consult their tax experts and attorneys before committing themselves.

SUMMARY

Traditionally, real estate investment has offered a high rate of *return* while at the same time acting as an effective inflation hedge and allowing an investor to use other people's money to make investments through *leverage*. There may also be tax advantages to owning real estate. On the other hand, real estate is not a highly liquid investment and often carries with it a high degree of risk. Also, it is difficult to invest in real estate without expert advice, and a certain amount of involvement is usually required to establish and maintain the investment.

Investment property held for *appreciation* purposes is generally expected to increase in value to a point where its selling price is enough to cover holding costs and show a profit as well. The two main factors affecting appreciation are inflation and the property's present and future intrinsic value. *Income property*, real estate held for income purposes, is generally expected to generate a steady flow of income, called *cash flow*, and to show a profit upon its sale.

An investor hoping to use maximum leverage in financing an investment should make a small down payment, pay low interest rates, and spread mortgage payments over as long a period as possible. By holding and refinancing properties, known as *pyramiding*, an investor may substantially increase investment holdings without contributing additional capital.

By exchanging one property for another with an equal or greater selling value, an investor can defer paying tax on the gain realized until a sale is made. A total tax deferment is possible only if the investor receives no cash or other incentive to even out the exchange. If received, such cash or property is called *boot* and is taxed. Depreciation is a concept that allows an investor to recover in tax deductions the basis of an asset over the period of its useful life. Only costs of improvements to land may be recovered, not costs for the land itself.

An investor may defer federal income taxes on gain realized from the sale of an investment property through an *installment sale* of property.

Individuals may also invest in real estate through an investment syndicate; these generally include general and limited partnerships. Another form of real estate investment is the *real estate investment trust (REIT)*.

The real estate broker and salesperson should be familiar with the rudimentary tax implications of real property ownership, but should refer clients to competent tax advisers for answers to questions on specific matters.

A real estate license is required for the sale of any business that involves an interest in real estate (freehold or leasehold). Sales of personal property are handled by a *bill of sale*. Under the *Bulk Transfer Act of the Uniform Commercial Code*, the seller must notify the buyer about suppliers who have not been paid, and the purchaser notifies the creditors about the sale, at least ten days before the transfer of ownership. Creditors have up to six months to file claims on the chattels involved.

USEFUL WEBSITE

Commercial Investment Real Estate Institute: www.ccim.com

KEY TERMS REVIEW 1

Match the number of each key term with the corresponding letter.

A___ 1. Adjusted basis

D___ 2. Appreciation

E___ 3. Basis

B___ 4. Bill of sale

C___ 5. Boot

F___ 6. Bulk Transfer Act

H___ 7. Capital gain

G___ 8. Cash flow

K___ 9. Depreciation

J___ 10. Exchange

I___ 11. Income property

A. cost plus improvements, minus depreciation

B. document transferring ownership of personal property

C. extra money or property received by one party in an exchange

D. increase in value

E. initial cost of real estate

F. law regulating sale and financing of business personal property

G. money left from rental income after expenses are paid

H. taxable profit on the difference between the adjusted basis and net selling price of an asset

I. real estate held for rental income

J. tax-deferred mutual transfers of income property

K. yearly bookkeeping charge for part of initial cost

KEY TERMS REVIEW 2

Match the number of each key term with the corresponding letter.

J___ 1. Installment sale

C___ 2. Leverage

H___ 3. Marginal tax rate

I___ 4. Pyramiding

E___ 5. Real estate investment syndicate

D___ 6. Real estate investment trust

A___ 7. Return

F___ 8. Syndicate

B___ 9. Tax credit

G___ 10. Uniform Commercial Code

A. cash flow plus income tax saving plus appreciation

B. direct deduction from income tax due

C. extensive use of borrowed money for purchases

D. fund making real estate investments and selling shares

E. group pooling resources to buy real estate

F. a joining together of two or more people to carry out business projects

G. law regulating transfer of business personal property

H. rate at which investor's top dollar is taxed

I. refinancing property to buy more

J. sale in which seller receives purchase price over period of years

UNIT 17 REVIEW QUESTIONS

1. Among the advantages of real estate investment is
   A. illiquidity.
   B. need for expert advice.
   C. hedge against inflation.
   D. degree of risk.

2. Among the disadvantages of real estate investment is
   A. leverage.
   B. need for physical and mental effort.
   C. tax shelter.
   D. equity buildup.

3. The investor's initial cost for the real estate is called
   A. capital gains.
   B. basis.
   C. adjusted depreciation.
   D. boot.

4. Of these, the beginning investor would be wise to start with the purchase of
   A. vacant land.
   B. resort property.
   C. a shopping center.
   D. a nearby multiple dwelling.

5. A small multifamily property generates $50,000 in rental income with expenses of $45,000 annually, including $35,000 in debt service. The property appreciates about $25,000 a year. The owner realizes another $5,000 through income tax savings. On this property, the cash flow is
   A. $5,000.
   B. $15,000.
   C. $25,000.
   D. $35,000.

6. A small multifamily property generates $50,000 in rental income with expenses of $45,000 annually, including $35,000 in debt service. The property appreciates about $25,000 a year. The owner realizes another $5,000 through income tax savings. The owner's return is
   A. $5,000.
   B. $15,000.
   C. $25,000.
   D. $35,000.

7. Leverage involves the extensive use of
   A. cost recovery.
   B. borrowed money.
   C. government subsidies.
   D. alternative taxes.

8. A property's equity represents its current value less which of the following?
   A. Depreciation
   B. Mortgage indebtedness
   C. Physical improvements
   D. Selling costs and depreciation

9. An investor's marginal tax rate is the
   A. total tax bill divided by net taxable income.
   B. extra tax if he has too many tax shelters.
   C. top applicable income tax bracket.
   D. percentage taxable on an installment sale.

10. The primary source of tax shelter in real estate investments comes from the accounting concept known as
    A. recapture.
    B. boot.
    C. depreciation.
    D. net operating income.

11. For tax purposes the initial cost of an investment property plus the cost of any subsequent improvements to the property, less depreciation, represents the investment's
    A. adjusted basis.
    B. capital gains.
    C. basis.
    D. salvage value.

12. The money left in an investor's pocket after expenses, including debt service, have been paid is known as
    A. net operating income.
    B. gross income.
    C. cash flow.
    D. internal rate of return.

13. The investor who secures what the IRS regards as excessive tax shelter may be subject to
    A. recovery.
    B. recapture.
    C. alternative minimum tax.
    D. pyramiding.

14. A property owner is exchanging her apartment building for an apartment building of greater market value and must include a $10,000 boot to even out the exchange. Which of the following may she use as a boot?
    A. $10,000 cash
    B. Common stock with a current market value of $10,000
    C. A parcel of raw land with a current market value of $10,000
    D. Any of the above if acceptable to the exchangers

15. Two parties exchange properties that include a $10,000 boot payment. In this situation,
    A. the party who makes the boot payment may owe income tax on $10,000.
    B. each party to the exchange may owe tax on $10,000.
    C. the investor receiving the boot may owe tax on $10,000.
    D. no one owes any tax at this time.

16. An investment syndicate in which all members share equally in the managerial decisions, profits, and losses involved in the venture is an example of which of the following?
    A. Real estate investment trust
    B. Limited partnership
    C. Real estate mortgage trust
    D. General partnership

17. The buyer purchased a dilapidated 50-year-old row house that is 50 years old and has no particular historic value. Helen intends to renovate the row house and live in it. On her renovation expenditures, this buyer is entitled to tax credits of
    A. $25,000.
    B. $0.
    C. $12,500.
    D. 25%.

18. If the sale of a business involves any interest in real estate, handling the transaction requires a
    A. UCC filing.
    B. bulk transfer certificate.
    C. depreciation allowance.
    D. real estate license.

19. The Bulk Transfer Act requires that the purchaser of a business
    A. have a real estate license.
    B. notify creditors before the sale.
    C. conduct a careful inventory of goods.
    D. have an environmental review before closing.

20. After learning of the sale of a business, suppliers who have NOT been paid should take action within
    A. ten days.
    B. one month.
    C. six months.
    D. one year.

UNIT
18

LEARNING OBJECTIVES

When you have completed this unit, you will be able to accomplish the following.

> Describe various methods of developing and subdividing land.
> Identify the impact of environmental regulations and other laws on sales, health and safety building regulations.

KEY TERMS

assemblage
Bureau of Subdivided
    Land Sales Control
clustering
construction permit
dedication
density zoning
environmental impact
    statement (EIS)
Highlands Water
    Protection and
    Planning Act

impact fees
Interstate Land Sales Full
    Disclosure Act
moratorium
percolation test
Pinelands Protection Act
Planned Real Estate
    Development Act
planned unit
    development (PUD)
planning board
plat

plottage
Real Estate Sales Full
    Disclosure Act
subdivision
Uniform Construction
    Code
Warranty and Builders
    Registration Act
Wetlands Act

DEVELOPING AND SUBDIVIDING LAND

A developer may sometimes combine two or more lots into one larger parcel, a process known as **assemblage**. When the resulting large tract is worth more than the total of the individual lots had been, the increase is known as **plottage** value.

Land in large tracts must receive special attention before it can be converted into sites for homes, stores, or other uses. A *subdivider* buys undeveloped acreage and divides it into smaller lots for sale to individuals or developers or for the subdivider's own use. A *developer* (who may

311

also be a subdivider) builds homes or other buildings on the lots and sells them. A developer selling homes in a new subdivision may have a sales staff or use the services of local real estate brokerage firms.

Subdivisions

In New Jersey, as soon as a second lot is sold off a larger parcel, the development is classed as a **subdivision**. Subdivisions must meet certain standards set by the New Jersey Municipal Land Use Law. New Jersey gives authority to local planning boards for approving plans and issuing zoning permits. A minor subdivision consists of one or more lots that do not involve planned development, new streets or extension of any off-tract improvement. A major subdivision involves a planned development, new street(s), or extension of an off-tract improvement. The individual municipalities can decide what is a *minor subdivision*, which does not require a public hearing, and what constitutes a *major subdivision*.

LAND PLANNING

The recording of a plat of subdivision of land before public sale for residential or commercial use is usually required, but land planning precedes the actual subdividing process. The development plan must comply with any overall local *master land plan* adopted by a county, city, village, town, township, or borough. In doing so, the developer must consider zoning laws and land-use restrictions adopted for health and safety purposes. Basic municipal planning and zoning requirements are not inflexible, but long, expensive, frequently complicated hearings are usually required before alterations can be authorized.

Most villages, cities, and other areas that are incorporated under state laws have **planning boards** or *planning commissioners*. Communities establish strict criteria before approving new subdivisions. The following are frequently included:

- *Dedication* of land for streets, schools, parks
- Assurance by *bonding* that sewer and street costs will be paid
- *Compliance with zoning ordinances* governing use and lot size along with fire and safety ordinances

Local authorities usually require land planners to submit information on how they intend to satisfy sewage-disposal and water-supply requirements. Development and/or septic tank installation may first require a **percolation test** of the soil's absorption and drainage capacities. Frequently a planner also has to submit an *environmental impact report*.

Subdividing

During the initial planning stage the subdivider seeks out raw land in a suitable area that he or she can profitably subdivide. After the land is located the property is analyzed for its highest and best use, and preliminary subdivision plans are drawn up accordingly. As previously discussed, close contact is initiated between the subdivider and local planning and zoning officials: If the project requires zoning variances, negotiations begin along these lines. The subdivider also locates financial backers and initiates marketing strategies.

Next, plans are prepared, approval is sought from local officials, permanent financing is obtained, the land is purchased, final budgets are prepared, and marketing programs are designed.

The plans are then recorded with local officials, and streets, sewers, and utilities are installed. Buildings, open parks, and recreational areas may then be constructed and landscaped if they are part of the subdivision plan.

Title to the individual parcels of subdivided land is transferred as the lots are sold.

Subdivision Plans

In plotting out a subdivision according to local planning and zoning controls, a subdivider determines the size as well as the location of the individual lots. The size of the lots, front footage, depth, and square footage are generally regulated by local ordinances. Ordinances frequently regulate both the minimum and the maximum lot sizes.

The land itself must be studied, usually in cooperation with a surveyor, so that the subdivision can be laid out with consideration of natural drainage and land contours. A site planner and an engineer also are employed.

In laying out a subdivision a subdivider should provide for *utility easements* as well as easements for water and sewer mains. Water and sewer mains are usually laid in the street with connecting junction boxes available for each building site. When a city, town, or village installs the water and sewer mains that connect a new building with the junction box in the street, a tie-in or connection fee is frequently charged to help the authority defray the cost of such installation.

A large development may also be charged **impact fees**, intended to help a community cope with increased demand for schools and other services.

Most subdivisions are laid out by use of *lots and blocks*. An area of land is designated as a block, and the area making up this block is divided into lots. Both lots and blocks are numbered consecutively.

Street Patterns

By varying street patterns and clustering housing units, a subdivider can dramatically increase the amount of open or recreational space in a development. Two possible patterns are the *gridiron* and *curvilinear* patterns. (See Figure 18.1.) Curvilinear developments avoid the uniformity of the gridiron and are quieter and more secure. However, getting from place to place may be more challenging.

Figure 18.1: Street Patterns

Gridiron   Curvilinear

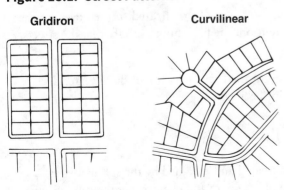

Clustering for Open Space

By slightly reducing lot sizes and **clustering** them around varying street patterns, a developer can house as many people in the same area as could be done using traditional subdividing plans but with substantially increased tracts of open space.

For example, compare the two subdivisions illustrated in Figure 18.2. Both subdivisions are equal in size and terrain. But when lots are reduced in size and clustered around limited-access cul-de-sacs, the number of housing units remains nearly the same (366), with less street area (17,700 linear feet) and dramatically increased open space (23.5 acres).

Figure 18.2: Subdivision Styles

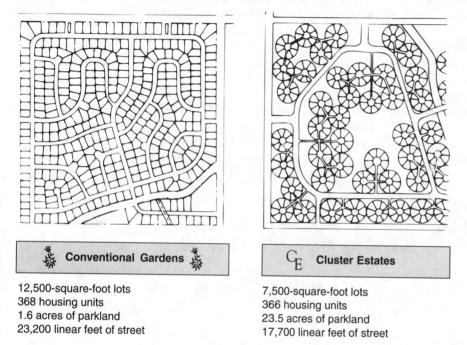

Conventional Gardens

12,500-square-foot lots
368 housing units
1.6 acres of parkland
23,200 linear feet of street

C_E Cluster Estates

7,500-square-foot lots
366 housing units
23.5 acres of parkland
17,700 linear feet of street

Plat of Subdivision

The subdivider's completed **plat** *of subdivision,* a map of the development indicating the location and boundaries of individual properties, must contain all necessary approvals of public officials and must be recorded in the county where the land is located. (See Figure 18.3.)

All areas that have been set aside for street purposes are to be **dedicated** (turned over) to the municipality. If this is not the subdivider's intention, the plat should specify that the streets are private.

Filing the map protects the developer in the event the local government should later declare a **moratorium**, a halt to further development in the area.

Covenants and Restrictions

Deed restrictions, discussed in Unit 9, are originated and recorded by the subdivider as a means of *controlling and maintaining* the desirable quality and character of the subdivision. These restrictions can be included in the subdivision plat or they may be set forth in a separate recorded instrument, commonly referred to as a *declaration of restrictions.*

Figure 18.3: Subdivision Plat Map

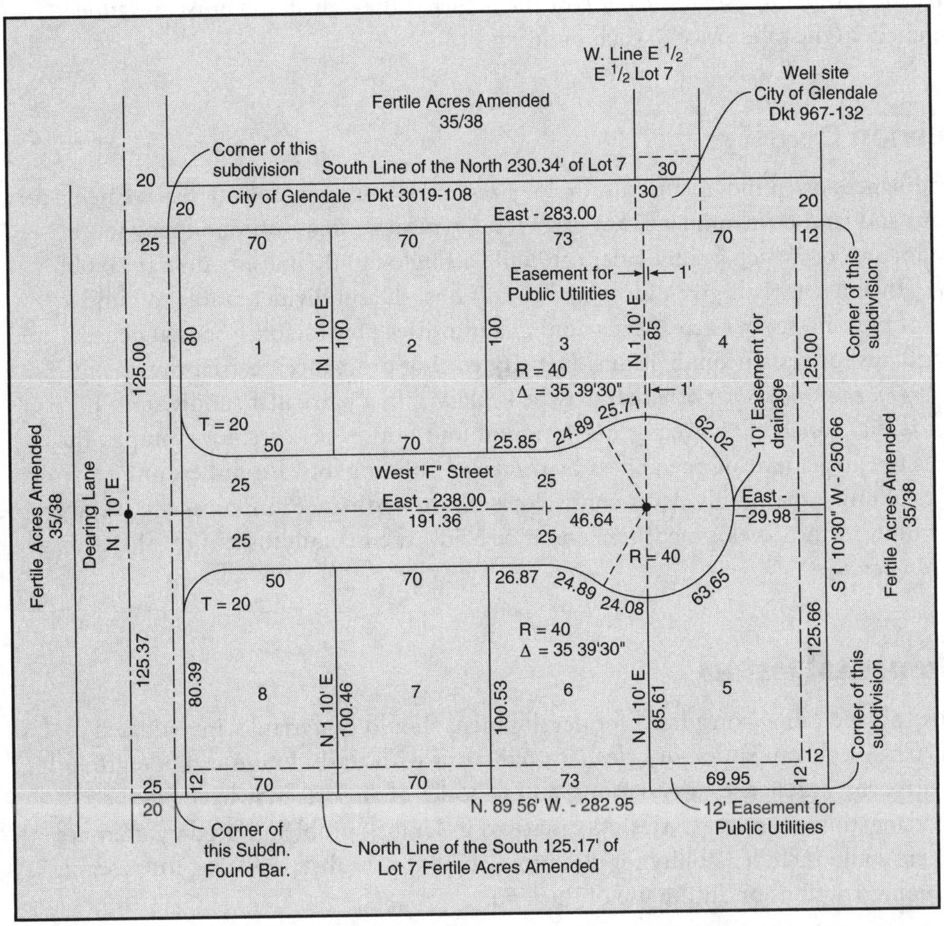

FHA Standards

FHA minimum standards have been established for residential area subdivisions that are to be submitted for approval for FHA loan insurance.

FHA standards also are applicable to building construction. FHA allows local building codes (where preapproved by HUD, the Department of Housing and Urban Development) to serve as standards. Exceptions generally include site conditions, thermal (insulation) standards, and certain other materials standards.

Development Costs

The subdivider, developer, and builder frequently invest many hundreds of thousands of dollars (and in larger developments, perhaps several million dollars) before the subdivision is even announced to the public. An analysis of these development costs substantiates the sales price for a typical building lot of four to six times the cost of the raw land.

In the subdivision of a typical parcel of raw land, a lot's sales price reflects such expenses as cost of land; installation of sewers or septic systems, water mains or wells, storm drains, landscaping, and streetlights; earthworks (mass dirt removal, site grading, and similar operations); paving; engineering and surveying fees; brokers' commissions; inspections; bonding costs; filing and legal fees; sale costs; and overhead. In certain areas a subdivider also may be required to give financial assistance to school districts, park districts, and the like, either in the form of donated school or park sites or in the form of a fixed subsidy per subdivision lot. Should such further costs be incurred they must, of course, be added proportionately to the sales price of each building site.

Subdivision Density

Zoning ordinances often include minimum lot sizes and population density requirements for subdivisions and land developments. For example, a typical zoning restriction may set the minimum lot area on which a subdivider can build a single-family housing unit at 10,000 square feet. This means that, given ideal land conditions, the subdivider is able to build a maximum of four houses per acre. Many zoning authorities now establish special density zoning standards for certain subdivisions. **Density zoning** ordinances restrict the *average maximum number of houses per acre* that may be built within a particular subdivision. If the area is density zoned at an average maximum of four houses per acre, for example, the developer is free to achieve an open effect by *clustering* building lots. Regardless of lot size or the number of units, the subdivider is consistent with the ordinance as long as the average number of units in the development remains at or below the maximum density. This average is called *gross density*.

Environmental Issues

Previous use of land being considered for development should be carefully investigated at the outset. Chemical companies, dry cleaners, old farms with trash dumps or underground gas tanks, airports, warehouses, gas stations, and factories of all sorts may have produced potentially dangerous chemical wastes. As discussed in Unit 9, problems faced by unaware future owners could include liability for cleanup, liability for health problems, unfavorable publicity, and restrictions on future use of the land.

Federal agencies are required to conduct studies called environmental impact statements (EIS) for any federal project that can affect the quality of life, especially projects located in floodplains, wetlands, steep slopes, or other environmentally fragile areas. The EIS requires information about the planned project as well as possible alternatives.

NEW JERSEY ENVIRONMENTAL REGULATIONS

Developers and builders should consult "Before You Buy, Before You Build" to determine if any part of the "site" being considered is regulated by the Division of Land Use Regulation (http://www.state.nj.us/dep/landuse/bybob.html). Licensees should avoid answering any questions about the viability of using any site for building a structure. Instead, they should encourage the questioner to consult the Division of Land Resource Licensees should avoid answering any questions about the viability using any site for building a structure. Instead, they should encourage the questioner to consult the Division of Land Resource Protection.

Licensees should avoid answering any questions about the viability using any site for building a structure. Instead, they should encourage the questioner to consult the Division of Land Resource Protection.

A proposed development site is ranked according to the New Jersey State Development and Redevelopment Plan in one of five categories, ranging from metropolitan (area 1) to environmentally sensitive (area 5). The amount of the area that can be developed as "impervious" ranges from 80% down to 3%, not counting any included dunes, wetlands, wetland buffers, coastal bluffs, and the like. The regulations also set out specific percentages for the preservation of existing forest vegetation or the planting of new trees.

The **Highlands Water Protection and Planning Act** protects New Jersey's drinking water. Developments involving one acre or more or the paving over or covering of a quarter-acre or more are regulated in the Highlands area by the Department of Environmental Protection (DEP). The supervision is intended to protect steep slopes, upland forests, and the areas around open waters.

The **NJ Pinelands Protection Act** regulates 22% of the state's land area. The Pineland National Reserve, also known as Pine Barrens, consists of oak-pine forests, extensive wetlands, and historic villages and berry farms. Human activities must respect the natural and cultural resources. See https://www.nj.gov/dep/landuse/lu_pl.html for more information about the act.

The New Jersey Department of Environmental Protection (DEP) regulates development in marshes and other wetlands under the Freshwater Wetlands Protection Act. Excavation, fill, or building on areas listed on DEP maps requires a permit. DEP maps cover both coastal areas and inland freshwater areas.

Stringent regulations for the development of coastal areas, which comprise about 20% of the state's land area are contained in the **Coastal Area Facilities Review Act (CAFRA)**. The CAFRA is authorized to regulate residential, commercial, public or industrial development within the CAFRA area. The width of the CAFRA area varies from a few thousand feet to 24 miles and is divided into zone with different regulatory thresholds for each zone.

Waterfront Development Law regulates areas outside the CAFRA area and requires that the DEP must approve plans for the development of any waterfront property on any navigable water or stream. This includes buildings, docks, wharfs, piers, and the like. After Superstorm Sandy, the Federal Emergency Management Agency (FEMA) redrew flood maps that affect where and how owners can build in a flood zone and/or meet new construction standards.

INTERSTATE LAND SALES FULL DISCLOSURE ACT

The **Interstate Land Sales Full Disclosure Act** requires those engaged in the *interstate* sale or leasing of 25 or more lots to file a *statement of record* and register the details of the land with the Consumer Financial Protection Bureau (CFPB). The rules are intended to protect the public from unscrupulous developers or marketers, or from undue sales pressure.

The New Jersey Real Estate Commission rules are complex requirements that must be met before any out-of-state land can be sold in New Jersey to New Jersey residents. The regulations, contained in the **Real Estate Land Sales Full Disclosure Act** requires prior approval and registration with the **Bureau of Subdivided Land Sales Control** for certain new out-of-state properties being offered to New Jersey residents. It includes substantially the same requirements as the Interstate Land Sales Full Disclosure Act, which regulates subdivided land on the federal level. Buyers have *up to seven calendar days* to cancel contracts for the purchase or lease of such lands.

Similar regulations apply to sales within the state of large subdivisions or when ownership of common areas is involved (in the case of condominiums and cooperatives, for instance). Real estate licensees should be alert to the possible need for special registration and fees before working on the original (that is, the first) sale of any out-of-state property. Before handling in-state developments, a broker should confirm that the project has been properly approved and registered.

Recent Real Estate Commission rules also address non-New Jersey properties that are advertised in New Jersey in languages other than English. Subsequent forms must be made available to prospective purchasers in the same language as was used in the original advertisement.

Unit 18

NEW JERSEY LAND SALES

For certain subdivisions within the state—primarily those that involve common elements (most condominiums, cooperatives, **planned unit developments (PUDs)**, and town house developments)—and for subdivisions with more than 100 lots or with a homeowners association, the **Planned Real Estate Development Act** sets requirements similar to those in the *Real Estate Sales Full Disclosure Act*. Disclosure statements must be approved and registered with the Bureau and a prospectus furnished to potential buyers. If a New Jersey subdivision falls within the requirements of the act, the buyer again has the right to cancel a contract *within seven calendar days*.

The registration and disclosure requirements apply to original offerings, not to single resales.

BUILDING REGULATIONS

Uniform Construction Code

New Jersey has adopted a statewide **Uniform Construction Code** that must be followed by local communities. The commissioner of the Department of Community Affairs regulates construction, alteration, renovation, occupancy, and use of all buildings.

Existing buildings do not have to conform unless they are found unsafe. When alterations or repairs cost more than half the value of an existing building, however, the *entire building* must be brought up to code. When alterations amount to between 25% and 50% of the buildings value, only the new construction must conform.

Warranty and Builders Registration

Under the New Home **Warranty and Builders Registration Act**, all builders of new homes must register a warranty against new home defects for varying periods up to 10 years with the Department of Community Affairs.

At closing or occupancy, whichever comes first, the builder must give the buyer a warranty insuring against various types of defects for periods of one, two, or ten years. The regulation applies to all owner-occupied one- or two-family buildings, cooperatives, condominiums, and modular or factory-built dwellings. It does not apply to resales, newly constructed rental units, remodeled houses, or mobile homes. The remaining years on the warranty can be transferred to the next owners if the building is sold.

Enforcement

Each county or municipality appoints its own construction agency to issue construction permits and enforce compliance with the regulations. If the local government does not appoint such an agency, the Department of Community Affairs assumes the task of administering and enforcing the code.

Construction Permits

The Uniform Construction Code requires a **construction permit** to be issued by each county or municipality before any construction, alteration, demolition, or change of use of a building can be undertaken. The application must contain such information as location of the property, construction plans, estimated cost of the work, and names and addresses of owners and designated contractors.

The local construction official then must inspect the application and the property to determine whether it conforms to the requirements of the code. Within 20 days the official either approves the plans and issues a permit or notifies the applicant in writing of the causes for rejection. If rejected, the applicant may revise the plans to meet the requirements or appeal his or her rejection to the Construction Board of Appeals.

Once issued, the construction permit may be revoked if the application is found to contain any false or misleading statements or omissions. In addition, the permit may be revoked if the proposed construction is not commenced within 12 months of the issue date or if work is suspended three months or longer after work has begun.

Certificate of Occupancy

No new or altered buildings in New Jersey can be used or occupied until a *certificate of occupancy* has been issued by the local construction official. A written application for a certificate must include the final cost of construction, any amendments to the plans registered at the time the construction permit was issued, and a statement of the proposed and/or current uses of the building. Before issuing a certificate, the local construction official must conduct an inspection to determine whether the structure complies with all local ordinances and the regulations of the Uniform Construction Code. Many municipalities now require a certificate of occupancy for transfer of title or change of tenants. All one-family and two-family homes must be inspected for the presence of smoke detectors prior to transfer of title or change in occupancy.

Existing Buildings

On the request of an owner a construction official may conduct an inspection of any existing building and issue a *certificate of continuing occupancy*. This certificate evidences that a general inspection of the visible structure has not revealed any apparent code violations. Existing buildings may continue to be put to any previously authorized use. However, if any change in use is initiated, the building must comply with the standards of the Uniform Construction Code.

Safety Requirements

In New Jersey, a change of occupancy for any one-family or two-family dwelling requires that the building have smoke detectors on each level of the dwelling and within ten feet of every sleeping quarter. Each municipality has the right to require more than this minimum; some require hardwired detectors with battery backups. The state also requires at least one properly installed carbon monoxide detector and an approved fire extinguisher.

HOTEL AND MOTEL MULTIPLE DWELLING HEALTH AND SAFETY LAW

This remedial legislation was enacted to assure the residents of New Jersey "decent, standard, and safe units of dwelling space." It is administered and enforced by the commissioner of community affairs, in consultation with the Hotel and Multiple Dwelling Health and Safety Board (in the Division of Urban Renewal of the Department of Community Affairs). The law applies to multiple dwellings with three or more units of dwelling space and hotels with 10 or more units of dwelling space or sleeping facilities for 25 or more persons.

The commissioner may issue rules and regulations regarding building and construction standards for multiple dwellings and hotels. Such properties may be entered and inspected without prior notice to see if they are in compliance with these standards. Multiple dwellings are inspected at least once every five years and hotels at least once every three years. In addition, the plans and specifications for all proposed new hotel and multiple-dwelling structures, alterations of existing structures, and conversions of buildings to use as hotels or multiple dwellings must be submitted to the commissioner and approved before the work is begun. The commissioner's jurisdiction in this area includes the power to enter complaints, hold hearings, issue fines to violators, and instigate court proceedings against continued violators.

SUMMARY

A subdivider buys undeveloped acreage, divides it into smaller parcels, and sells it. A land developer builds homes on the lots and sells them, either through an in-house sales organization or through local real estate brokerage firms. City planners and land developers, working together, plan whole communities that are later incorporated into cities, towns, or villages.

Land development must generally comply with master land plans adopted by counties or municipalities. This entails approval of land-use plans by local *planning boards*.

The process of *subdivision* includes dividing the tract of land into lots and blocks and providing for utility easements, as well as laying out street patterns and widths. A subdivider must generally record a completed *plat of subdivision* with all necessary approvals of public officials in the county where the land is located. Subdividers usually place restrictions on the use of all lots in a subdivision as a general plan for the benefit of all lot owners.

By varying street patterns and housing *density* and *clustering* housing units, a subdivider can dramatically increase the amount of open and recreational space within a development.

The state sets a *Uniform Construction Code* that must be followed by local communities. New home builders must give buyers of one- or two-family residences a warranty of from one to ten years on various parts of the construction.

New Jersey's *Real Estate Sales Full Disclosure Act* requires registration of out-of-state subdivided land offered to New Jersey residents. Buyers have up to seven calendar days to cancel contracts for purchase or lease of such lands. Brokers who handle out-of-state subdivisions must register and pay a fee.

No new or altered building may be occupied until a local construction official issues a *certificate of occupancy*.

All one- and two-family homes must be inspected for the presence of smoke detectors prior to transfer of title or change in occupancy.

In New Jersey, multiple dwellings of three or more units are inspected by the state every five years, and hotels every three years, for decent and safe conditions.

USEFUL WEBSITES

Pinelands Commission: www.state.nj.us/pinelands

Highlands Water Protection: www.highlands.state.nj.us

New Jersey Land Use Regulations: www.state.nj.us/dep/landuse

KEY TERMS REVIEW

Match the number of each key term with the corresponding letter.

_____ 1. Bureau of Subdivided Land Sales Control

_____ 2. Clustering

_____ 3. Construction permit

_____ 4. Dedication

_____ 5. Density zoning

_____ 6. Environmental impact statement (EIS)

_____ 7. Impact fees

_____ 8. Interstate Land Sales Full Disclosure Act

_____ 9. Moratorium

_____ 10. Percolation test

_____ 11. Planned Real Estate Development Act

_____ 12. Planned unit development

_____ 13. Planning board

_____ 14. Plat

_____ 15. Real Estate Sales Full Disclosure Act

_____ 16. Subdivision

_____ 17. Uniform Construction Code

_____ 18. Warranty and Builders Registration Act

A. putting living units close together to leave more open space

B. charges to developers for extra roads, schools, and so forth

C. community with dense zoning and developer's plan for entire land use

D. local municipality's authorization for building plans

E. engineering reports often required before building permits are issued

F. group setting standards for local subdivisions

G. test of soils absorption and drainage capacities

H. law requiring registration of certain developments within New Jersey

I. map of a town, section, or subdivision

J. New Jersey's standards for building

K. U.S. requirement for some developments to be registered with the CFPB

L. division of property into more than one building lot

M. a halt to development

N. state regulations for builders of new homes

O. turning over of private property (subdivision streets) to a municipality

P. zoning that allows more living units per acre than usual

Q. permits buyers up to seven calendar days to cancel contracts for lease or purchase of such lands

R. New Jersey state agency that approves and registers some out-of-state property

UNIT 18 REVIEW QUESTIONS

1. A person who buys farmland near the city and turns it into building lots is a
   A. site planner.
   B. developer.
   C. surveyor.
   D. subdivider.

2. Overall subdivision guidelines are set by
   A. the federal government.
   B. New Jersey Municipal Land Use Law.
   C. the Department of Health.
   D. the Department of Environmental Conservation.

3. Local governments often regulate subdivision through their
   A. planning boards.
   B. conservationists.
   C. site planners.
   D. building inspectors.

4. A particular subdivision plan may require the services of
   A. a surveyor.
   B. a site planner.
   C. an engineer.
   D. all of the above.

5. A map illustrating the sizes and locations of streets and lots in a subdivision is called a
   A. gridiron pattern.
   B. survey.
   C. plat of subdivision.
   D. property report.

6. Which of the following items are usually NOT designated on the plat for a new subdivision?
   A. Easements for sewer and water mains
   B. Land to be used for streets, schools, and civic facilities
   C. Numbered lots and blocks
   D. Prices of residential and commercial lots

7. A subdivider turns over streets to public ownership through
   A. development.
   B. eminent domain.
   C. dedication.
   D. condemnation.

8. Deed restrictions are usually placed on an entire subdivision by the
   A. building inspector.
   B. state government.
   C. planning board.
   D. subdivider.

9. Which of the following would NOT be a part of the development cost of land?
   A. Curbs and gutters
   B. Installation of telephone lines
   C. Raw land cost
   D. Developers overhead

10. Gross density refers to which of the following?
    A. The maximum number of residents that may, by law, occupy a subdivision
    B. The average maximum number of houses per acre that may, by law, be built in a subdivision
    C. The maximum size lot that may, by law, be built in a subdivision
    D. The minimum number of houses that may, by law, be built in a subdivision

11. The longest a new home builder must warranty some parts of the construction against defects is
    A. one year.
    B. two years.
    C. five years.
    D. ten years.

12. In New Jersey, subdivision regulations may apply as soon as anyone splits off the
    A. first lot.
    B. second lot.
    C. third lot.
    D. fourth lot.

13. A builder found a buyer for the new ranch home he has just finished, but the buyers need occupancy right away, before their mortgage loan comes through. Before letting the buyers move in, the builder must obtain
    A. subdivider's registration.
    B. a certificate of occupancy.
    C. a construction permit.
    D. a UCC filing.

14. Multiple dwellings are inspected by the state every five years if they have at LEAST
    A. two units.
    B. three units.
    C. four units.
    D. six units.

15. A subdivider can increase the amount of open and/or recreational space in a development by
    A. establishing outlots.
    B. meeting FHA standards.
    C. clustering housing units.
    D. dedicating roads.

16. In New Jersey, which projects are obligated to provide an environmental impact statement?
    A. Federal projects
    B. State projects
    C. Any developer of more than 10 acres
    D. Municipal projects

17. About 22% of New Jersey's land area, including historic villages and berry farms, is protected by the
    A. NJ Pinelands Protection Act.
    B. Environmental Protection Agency (EPA).
    C. Coastal Area Facilities Review Act (CAFRA).
    D. Federal Emergency Management Agency (FEMA).

18. The owner of a home built in 1925 suffered extensive damages during recent high winds and hail. The insurance adjuster estimated that more than half the building would need to be rebuilt. Under the Uniform Construction Code, what is the status of making repairs to existing buildings?
    A. Repairs do not have to meet code.
    B. Only the new construction must meet the code.
    C. Entire building must meet latest code standards.
    D. Building must be torn down and then rebuilt.

19. No new or altered buildings in New Jersey can be used or occupied until the local construction official issues a
    A. certificate of adequate completion.
    B. license to occupy.
    C. certificate of occupancy.
    D. permit to occupy.

20. All builders of new homes must provide a
    A. warranty against defects for varying periods up to 10 years.
    B. warranty of quiet enjoyment.
    C. certificate of reasonable value (CRV).
    D. certificate of reasonable occupancy.

21. In New Jersey, what is required by Uniform Construction Code before any construction, alteration, demolition, or change of use of the building can be undertaken?
    A. Certificate of occupancy
    B. Certificate of continuing occupancy
    C. Construction permit
    D. Authorization to build

22. New Jersey requires the broker who sells out-of-state subdivided lands to
    A. register with the state.
    B. obtain a securities license.
    C. consent to be sued in the state.
    D. file a certificate of occupancy.

23. In New Jersey, the buyer who purchases out-of-state subdivided land may cancel the contract for no reason within
    A. three days.
    B. seven calendar days.
    C. ten days.
    D. one month.

24. A developer advertises properties for sale in Vermont to New Jersey residents. The advertisements are all in French. Any additional forms, contracts or other materials that are made available to prospective purchasers must be in
    A. English.
    B. French.
    C. French and English.
    D. The developer has violated New Jersey law by offering out-of-state properties for sale in a language other than English or Spanish.

25. New Jersey real estate brokers may need special registration when selling some
    A. out-of-state properties.
    B. previously owned condominiums.
    C. business opportunities.
    D. real estate at auction.

UNIT
19

Legal Descriptions and Deeds

LEARNING OBJECTIVES

When you have completed this unit, you will be able to accomplish the following.

› Discuss three methods of describing real property.
› Identify the types of deeds used in New Jersey and the effect of various clauses.

KEY TERMS

acknowledgment
bargain and sale deed
bargain and sale deed
   with covenants
benchmark
covenant
datum
deed
delivery and acceptance

grantee
granting clause
grantor
habendum clause
legal description
metes and bounds
monuments
point of beginning (POB)
quitclaim deed

rectangular survey system
section
township
warranty deed (general
   warranty deed, full
   covenant and warranty
   deed)

LEGAL DESCRIPTIONS

A *deed* is the instrument that conveys title to real property, the document that transfers ownership. One of the essential elements of a valid deed is an adequate description of the *land* being conveyed (the deed usually does not describe improvements on the land). A **legal description** is an *exact way of describing real estate in a contract, deed, mortgage, or other document that is accepted by a court of law.*

Land can be described by three methods: by metes and bounds, by government survey, or by reference to a plat (map) filed in the county clerk's office in the county where the land is located. In New Jersey a legal description may combine different descriptive methods.

Legal descriptions should not be changed, altered, or combined without adequate information from a competent authority such as a surveyor or title attorney. Legal descriptions always should include the name of the county and state in which the land is located.

Street address and property tax account identification number, although helpful for quick reference to what is being described, are not usually acceptable as legal descriptions. They are often used in real estate contracts, and tax numbers, when available, are often added to legal descriptions used in deeds.

Metes and Bounds

A **metes-and-bounds** description makes use of the boundaries and measurements of the land in question. Such a description starts at a definitely designated point called the **point of beginning (POB)** and proceeds clockwise around the boundaries of the tract by reference to measurements and directions. A metes-and-bounds description always ends at the point where it began (the POB).

A tract of land located in the Township of Kingston, County of Burlington, State of New Jersey, may be described as follows: Beginning at the intersection of the east line of Jones Road and the south line of Skull Drive; thence east along the south line of Skull Drive 200 feet; thence south 15° east 216.5 feet, more or less, to the center thread of Red Skull Creek; thence northwesterly along the center line of said creek to its intersection with the east line of Jones Road; thence north 105 feet, more or less, along the east line of Jones Road to the place of beginning. This parcel is pictured in Figure 19.1.

Figure 19.1: Metes-and-Bounds Tract

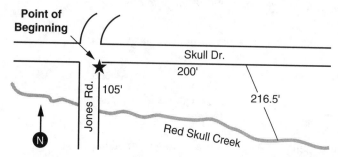

In a metes-and-bounds description, **monuments** are fixed objects used to establish real estate boundaries. In the past, natural objects such as stones, large trees, lakes, streams, and intersections of major streets or highways, as well as man-made markers placed by surveyors, were commonly used as monuments. Today, man-made markers—usually reinforcing bars, called *rebars*, bearing the surveyor's initials—are the more common monuments, because it is recognized that natural objects may change or be removed.

Rectangular Survey System

The **rectangular survey system**, sometimes called the *government survey method*, was established by Congress in 1785 as early pioneers moved westward. This method of describing real property is not used in New Jersey or in any other of the original 13 states. In New Jersey, the term township references towns and boroughs, each one of which is a totally separate entity and are unrelated to the other, complete with separate administrations, police departments, and the like.

The rectangular survey system is based on sets of two intersecting lines: *principal meridians* and *base lines*, located by reference to degrees of longitude and latitude.

Townships

Using these meridians and base lines, land is surveyed into six-mile-square **townships**, each with identifying reference numbers. Each township contains 36 square miles.

Sections

A township is further divided into 36 numbered **sections**. Sections are numbered 1 through 36, as shown in Figure 19.2. The township labeled 16 was always reserved for establishing a school.

Figure 19.2: Sections in a Township

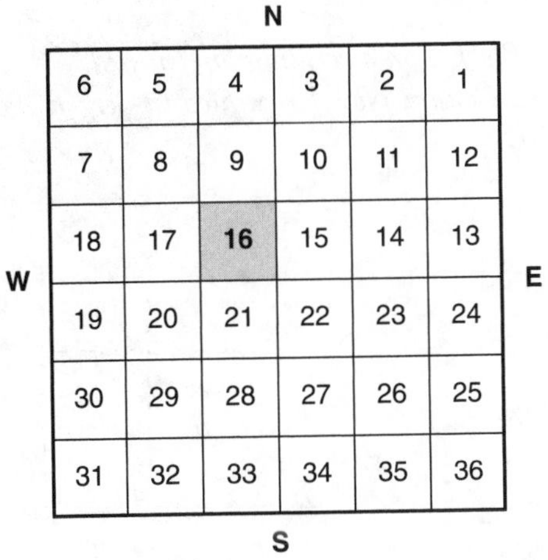

		N			
6	5	4	3	2	1
7	8	9	10	11	12
18	17	**16**	15	14	13
19	20	21	22	23	24
30	29	28	27	26	25
31	32	33	34	35	36

W (left)   E (right)   S (bottom)

As illustrated in Figure 19.3, each section contains one square mile, or *640 acres*, and is divided into quarters for reference purposes. One could refer to the *southeast quarter*, a 160-acre tract; this would be abbreviated as SE ¼. Quarter sections can be divided into quarters or halves, and such parts can be further divided by quarters. The SE ¼ of SE ¼ of SE ¼ of Section 1 would be a 10-acre square in the lower righthand corner of Section 1.

Figure 19.3: A Section

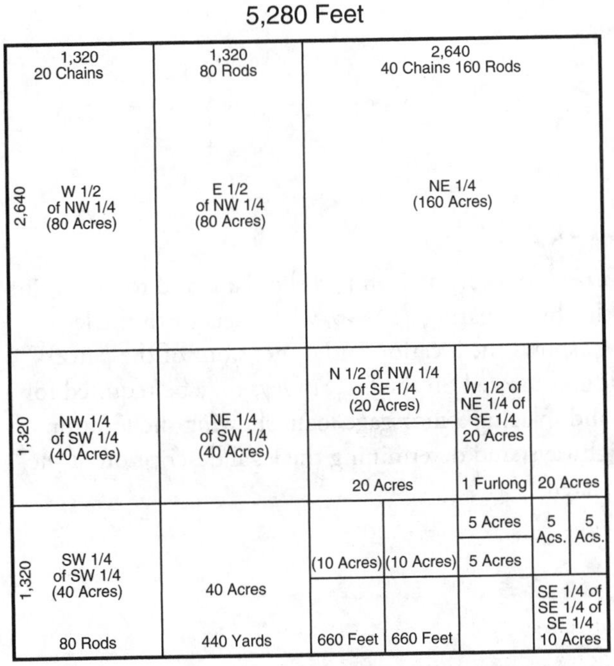

5,280 Feet

1,320 20 Chains	1,320 80 Rods	2,640 40 Chains 160 Rods
W 1/2 of NW 1/4 (80 Acres)	E 1/2 of NW 1/4 (80 Acres)	NE 1/4 (160 Acres)

2,640 (left vertical)

NW 1/4 of SW 1/4 (40 Acres)	NE 1/4 of SW 1/4 (40 Acres)	N 1/2 of NW 1/4 of SE 1/4 (20 Acres)	W 1/2 of NE 1/4 of SE 1/4 20 Acres	
		20 Acres	1 Furlong	20 Acres

1,320 (left vertical)

SW 1/4 of SW 1/4 (40 Acres)	40 Acres	(10 Acres)	(10 Acres)	5 Acres 5 Acres	5 Acs.	5 Acs.
80 Rods	440 Yards	660 Feet	660 Feet		SE 1/4 of SE 1/4 of SE 1/4 10 Acres	

1,320 (left vertical)

Recorded Plat of Subdivision

The third method of land description is by lot and map number, referring to a *plat of subdivision* filed with the clerk of the county in which the land is located.

The first step in subdividing land is the preparation of a *plat* (map) *of survey* by a licensed surveyor or engineer, as illustrated in Figure 19.4. On this plat the land is divided into blocks and lots, and streets or access roads for public use are indicated. The lots are assigned numbers or letters. Lot sizes and street details must be indicated. When properly signed and approved, the subdivision plat may be recorded in the county in which the land is located; it thereby becomes part of the legal description. In describing a lot from a recorded subdivision plat, the lot number, name or number of the subdivision plat, and name of the county and state are used. For example:

> *KNOWN and designated as Lots 7, 8, 9, and 10 in Block 3 on a certain map entitled, Map of Oakbrook Terrace, Jefferson Township, Morris County, New Jersey, filed in Bergen County Clerk's Office on August 8, 1893, as Map 509.*

Figure 19.4: Plat of Survey

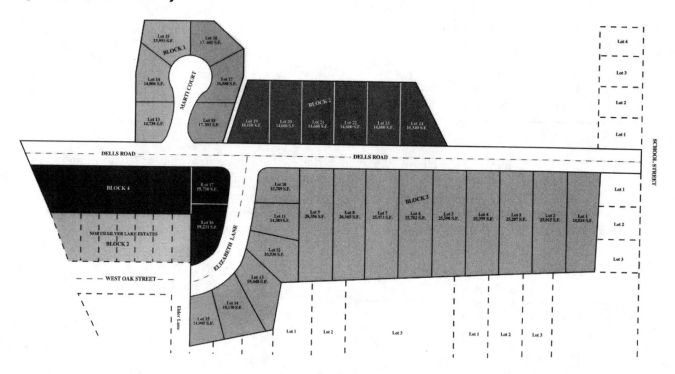

Preparation and Use of a Survey

A licensed surveyor is trained and authorized to locate a given parcel of land and to determine its legal description. The surveyor does this by preparing a *survey*, which sets forth the legal description of the property. A survey map shows the location and dimensions of the parcel and the location, size, and shape of buildings located on the lot. Surveys may be required for conveying a portion of a given tract of land, placing a mortgage loan, showing the location of new construction, locating roads and highways, and determining the legal description of the land on which a particular building is located.

Measuring Elevations

In preparing a subdivision plat for condominium use, where one unit is situated above another, a surveyor describes each condominium unit by reference to the elevation of the floors and ceilings above the city datum.

Datum

A point, line, or surface from which elevations are measured or indicated is a **datum**, defined by the United States Geological Survey as the mean sea level at New York harbor. A datum is of special significance to surveyors in determining the height of structures, establishing the grade of streets, and similar situations. Many large cities have established a local official datum.

Benchmarks

To aid surveyors, permanent reference points called **benchmarks** have been established throughout the United States. Local benchmarks simplify surveyors' work because measurements may be based on them rather than on the basic benchmark, which may be miles away.

Condominium Descriptions

A sufficient description of condominium property to be conveyed must include

■ a description of the land on which the building and improvements are located,

■ a designation of the unit conveyed as listed in the declaration, and

■ a description of the common interest conveyed with the unit.

DEEDS

A **deed** is a written instrument by which an owner of real estate intentionally conveys his or her right, title, or interest in a parcel of real estate. All deeds must be in writing, in accordance with the requirements of the statute of frauds. The owner (who sells or gives the land) is referred to as the **grantor**, and the new owner (who acquires the title) is called the **grantee**. A deed is *executed* (signed) by the grantor.

Types of Deeds

The most common forms of deed in New Jersey are

■ full covenant and warranty deed,

■ bargain and sale deed with covenants against grantor's acts,

■ bargain and sale deed (no covenants), and

■ quitclaim deed.

Warranty Deed

For a purchaser of real estate, a **warranty deed** (also known as a **general warranty deed or full covenant and warranty deed**) (shown in Figure 19.5) provides the greatest protection of any deed. It is referred to as a warranty deed because the grantor is legally bound by certain

covenants or warranties. The warranties usually are written into the deed itself. The basic warranties (guarantees) follow.

- Covenant of *seisin*—The grantor warrants that he or she is the owner of the property and has the right to convey title to it. The grantee may recover damages up to the full purchase price if this covenant is broken.

- Covenant against encumbrances—The grantor warrants that the property is free from any liens or encumbrances except those specifically stated in the deed. If this covenant is breached, the grantee may sue for expenses to remove the encumbrance or receive compensation.

- Covenant of quiet enjoyment—The grantor guarantees that the grantee's title is good against third parties who might bring court actions to establish superior title to the property.

- Covenant of further assurance—The grantor promises to obtain and deliver any instrument needed in order to make the title good.

- Covenant of warranty forever—The grantor guarantees that if at any time in the future the title fails, he or she will compensate the grantee for the loss sustained.

These covenants in a warranty deed are not limited to matters that occurred during the time the grantor owned the property; they extend back to all previous owners.

Bargain and Sale Deed With Covenants Against Grantor's Acts

Under a **bargain and sale deed with covenants** against grantor's acts (CAG), grantors covenant that they have done nothing to encumber the property while it was in their possession. This is the normal deed used in a transfer of property by sale in New Jersey, and this deed often is used by fiduciaries: executors, trustees, and corporations. The grantors are willing to warrant about the time they owned the property but not about previous owners (see Figure 19.6). This deed is also known as a bargain and sale deed with covenants *versus* grantors (bargain and sale [CVG]) or a *special warranty deed*.

Bargain and Sale Deed

A straight **bargain and sale deed** contains no express warranties. However, it does *imply* that the grantor holds title to the property. The grantee has little legal recourse if defects later appear in the title. The bargain and sale deed without covenants is used in foreclosure and tax sales.

Quitclaim Deed

A **quitclaim deed** provides the grantee with the least protection of any deed. It carries no covenants or warranties and conveys only such interest, if any, as the grantor may have when the deed is delivered. It does not imply that the grantor holds title. By a quitclaim deed the grantor only "remises, releases, and quitclaims" his or her interest in the property to the grantee.

If the grantor has no interest in the property, the grantee acquires nothing, nor does he or she acquire any claim against the grantor. A quitclaim deed can convey title as effectively as a warranty deed if the grantor has good title when he or she delivers the deed, but it provides no guarantees.

A quitclaim deed commonly is used for simple transfers within a family and for property transferred during divorce settlements. It also can be used to clear a cloud from the title.

Figure 19.5: Warranty Deed

𝕯𝖊𝖊𝖉

This Deed is made on   ,

BETWEEN

whose post office address is

referred to as the Grantor,

AND

whose post office address is

referred to as the Grantee.

The words "Grantor" and "Grantee" shall mean all Grantors and all Grantees listed above.

1. **Transfer of Ownership.**   The Grantor grants and conveys (transfers ownership of) the property (called the "Property") described below to the Grantee. This transfer is made for the sum of _____.

The Grantor acknowledges receipt of this money.

2. **Tax Map Reference.**   (N.J.S.A. 46:26A-3) Municipality of _____
    Block No. _____   Lot No. _____   Qualifier No. _____   Account No. _____ .
    ☐ No property tax identification number is available on the date of this Deed. (Check box if applicable.)

3. **Property.**   The Property consists of the land and all the buildings and structures on the land in the _____ of _____ , County of _____ and State of New Jersey. The legal description is:
    ☐ Please see attached Legal Description annexed hereto and made a part hereof. (Check box if applicable.)

Prepared by:	(For Recorder's Use Only)
_____	

107 - Deed - Warranty with Statutory Covenants
Ind. or Corp. Plain Language
Rev. 3/16   P3/21

Unit 19

Figure 19.5: Warranty Deed (continued)

The street address of the Property is:

4. **Promises by Grantor.** The Grantor's promises are listed below. Each promise is expressed in the language of a New Jersey law (with a reference to the law) and is followed by an explanation in plain language. The Grantor promises that:

    a. the Grantor is lawfully seized of the said land (N.J.S.A. 46:4-3) - the Grantor is the legal owner;

    b. the Grantor has the right to convey the said land to the Grantee (N.J.S.A. 46:4-4) - the Grantor has the right to convey (sell) this Property;

    c. the Grantee shall have quiet possession of the said land free from all encumbrances (N.J.S.A. 46:4-5) - the Grantee will not be disturbed by others with claims against this Property and the Property is free of all encumbrances;

    d. the Grantor will warrant generally the Property hereby conveyed (N.J.S.A. 46:4-7) - the Grantor guarantees the Grantee's ownership of the Property; and

    e. the Grantor will execute such further assurances of the said land as may be requisite (N.J.S.A. 46:4-10) - the Grantor will comply with the Grantee's reasonable requests to correct any title defect.

5. **Who Is Bound.** The promises made in this Deed are legally binding upon the Grantor and all who lawfully succeed to the Grantor's rights and responsibilities. These promises can be enforced by the Grantee and all future owners of the Property.

6. **Signatures.** The Grantor signs this Deed as of the date at the top of the first page. If the Grantor is a corporation, this Deed is signed and attested to by its proper corporate officers and its corporate seal is affixed. (Print name below signature).

Witnessed or Attested by:

    _____ (Seal)

    _____ (Seal)

STATE OF NEW JERSEY, COUNTY OF   SS:

I CERTIFY that on

personally came before me and stated to my satisfaction that this person (or if more than one, each person):

    (a) was the maker of this Deed;

    (b) executed this Deed as his or her own act; and

    (c) made this Deed for $_____ as the full and actual consideration paid or to be paid for the transfer of title. (Such consideration is defined in N.J.S.A. 46:15-5.)

    _____

Print name and title below signature

STATE OF NEW JERSEY, COUNTY OF   SS:

I CERTIFY that on

personally came before me and stated to my satisfaction that this person (or if more than one, each person):

    (a) was the maker of the attached Deed;

    (b) was authorized to and did execute this Deed as _____ of _____, the entity named in this Deed;

    (c) made this Deed for $_____ as the full and actual consideration paid or to be paid for the transfer of title. (Such consideration is defined in N.J.S.A. 46:15-5.); and

    (d) executed this Deed as the act of the entity.

RECORD AND RETURN TO:

    _____

Print name and title below signature

107 - Deed - Warranty with Statutory Covenants
Ind. or Corp. Plain Language
Rev. 3/16   P3/21

©2021 by ALL-STATE LEGAL®
A Division of All-STATE International, Inc.
www.aslegal.com   800.222.0510   Page 2

Figure 19.6: Bargain and Sale Deed With Covenant

Deed

This Deed is made on   ,
BETWEEN

whose post office address is

referred to as the Grantor,
AND

whose post office address is

referred to as the Grantee.

The words "Grantor" and "Grantee" shall mean all Grantors and all Grantees listed above.

1. **Transfer of Ownership.** The Grantor grants and conveys (transfers ownership of) the property (called the "Property") described below to the Grantee. This transfer is made for the sum of _____
_____ .

The Grantor acknowledges receipt of this money.

2. **Tax Map Reference.** (N.J.S.A. 46:26A-3) Municipality of _____

   Block No. _____, Lot No. _____, Qualifier No. _____ and Account No. _____ .

   ☐ No lot and block or account number is available on the date of this Deed. (Check box if applicable.)

3. **Property.** The Property consists of the land and all the buildings and structures on the land in the _____

   of _____, County of _____ and State of New Jersey.

   The legal description is:

   ☐ Please see attached Legal Description annexed hereto and made a part hereof. (Check box if applicable.)

SAMPLE

Prepared by:	(For Recorder's Use Only)
_____	

103 - Deed - Bargain and Sale Covenants to Grantor's
Act - Individual to Individual or Corporation
Rev. 3/16 P3/21

©2021 by ALL-STATE LEGAL®
A Division of ALL-STATE International, Inc.
www.aslegal.com 800.222.0510 Page 1

Figure 19.6: Bargain and Sale Deed With Covenant (continued)

The street address of the Property is:

4. **Promises by Grantor.** The Grantor promises that the Grantor has done no act to encumber the Property. This promise is called a "covenant as to grantor's acts" (N.J.S.A. 46:4-6). This promise means that the Grantor has not allowed anyone else to obtain any legal rights which affect the Property (such as by making a mortgage or allowing a judgment to be entered against the Grantor).

5. **Signatures.** The Grantor signs this Deed as of the date at the top of the first page. (Print name below each signature.)

Witnessed or Attested by:

_____ (Seal)

_____ (Seal)

STATE OF NEW JERSEY, COUNTY OF _____ SS:

I CERTIFY that on _____,

_____

personally came before me and stated to my satisfaction that this person (or if more than one, each person):

(a) was the maker of this Deed;

(b) executed this Deed as his or her own act; and

(c) made this Deed for $ _____ as the full and actual consideration paid or to be paid for the transfer of title. (Such consideration is defined in N.J.S.A. 46:15-5.)

┌─────────────────────────────┐
│ RECORD AND RETURN TO: │
│   │   _____
│   │
│   │   *Print name and title below signature*
└─────────────────────────────┘

103 - Deed - Bargain and Sale Covenants to Grantor's
Act - Individual to Individual or Corporation
Rev. 3/16   P3/21

©2021 by ALL-STATE LEGAL®
A Division of ALL-STATE International, Inc.
www.aslegal.com   800.222.0510   Page 2

Requirements for a Valid Conveyance

Although the formal requirements for a valid deed are not uniform in all states, certain requirements are basic. These are

■ a *grantor* having the legal capacity to execute (sign) the deed;

■ a *grantee* named with reasonable certainty, so that he or she can be identified;

■ a recital of *consideration*;

■ a *granting clause* (words of conveyance);

■ designation of any *limitations* on the conveyance of a full fee simple estate;

■ an *adequate description* of the property conveyed;

■ *exceptions and reservations* affecting the title;

■ the signature of the grantor; and

■ *delivery* of the deed and *acceptance* by the grantee to pass title.

Deeds do not have to be dated in order to be valid.

Grantor

In New Jersey a person must be of sound mind and have reached the age of 18 in order to effect a valid conveyance. A contract executed by an incompetent or a minor is *voidable* by the courts; that is, it may be set aside in a lawsuit conducted by a representative of the incompetent or minor. A minor may disaffirm a contract upon reaching the age of 18. A grantor generally is held to have sufficient mental capacity to execute a deed if he or she is capable of understanding the action.

Grantee

To be valid, a deed must name a grantee and do so in such a way that he or she is readily identifiable.

Consideration

To be valid, all deeds must contain a clause acknowledging the grantors receipt of something as consideration. Consideration is defined as *something of value offered by one party and accepted by another as an inducement to perform (or refrain from performing) some act.* Consideration must be "good and valuable" between the parties.

In many states a nominal consideration ("$1 and other valuable consideration") is customary. In New Jersey, however, a deed is not acceptable for recording unless it states the full sales price. If the deed does list "$1" or "love and affection" as consideration, it can be recorded if it is accompanied by an *affidavit* (sworn statement) explaining that the transaction is, for example, a gift.

Granting Clause (Words of Conveyance)

A deed must contain words in the **granting clause** that state the grantor's intention to convey the property. Depending on the type of deed and the obligations agreed to by the grantor, the wording generally is either convey and warrant (full warranty deed); "grant, bargain, and sell" (bargain and sale CAG deed); "bargain and sell" (bargain and sale), or "remise, release, and "quitclaim" (quitclaim deed).

If more than one grantee is involved, the granting clause should cover the creation of their specific rights in the property. The clause might state, for example, that the grantees take title as joint tenants or tenants in common. This is especially important in the case of joint tenants because specific wording is necessary to create a joint tenancy.

Deeds that convey the entire fee simple interest of the grantor usually contain wording such as "to Jacqueline Smith and to her heirs and assigns forever." If the grantor is conveying less than his or her complete interest, such as a life estate, the wording must indicate this limitation. A deed creating a life estate would convey property "to Jacqueline Smith for the duration of her natural life."

Habendum Clause

When it is necessary to define or explain the ownership to be enjoyed by the grantee, a **habendum clause** follows the granting clause. The habendum clause begins with the words *to have and to hold*. Its provisions must agree with those set down in the granting clause.

Description of Real Estate

For a deed to be valid it must contain an adequate description of the real estate conveyed. Land is considered adequately described if a competent surveyor can locate the property from the description used.

Exceptions and Reservations

A grantor may reserve some right in the land for his or her own use (an easement, for instance). A grantor also may place certain restrictions on a grantee's use of the property. A developer, for example, can restrict the number of houses that may be built on a one-acre lot in a subdivision. Such restrictions may be stated in the deed or contained in a previously recorded document (such as the subdivider's master deed) that is expressly cited in the deed.

Signature of Grantor

To be valid, a deed must be signed by *all grantors named in the deed*. A grantor's signature may be signed by an attorney-in-fact acting under a power of attorney (specific written authority). An *attorney-in-fact is any person who has been given power of attorney to execute and sign legal instruments for a grantor*. In such cases it usually is necessary for the power of attorney to be recorded in the county where the property is located. Because the power of attorney terminates on the death of the person granting such authority, evidence must be submitted that the grantor is alive at the time the attorney-in-fact signs the deed.

Acknowledgment

An **acknowledgment** is a declaration made by a person who is signing a document before a notary public or authorized public officer. This acknowledgment usually states that the person signing the deed or other document is known to the officer or has produced sufficient identification. The acknowledgment provides evidence that the signature is genuine.

Although an acknowledgment is usually made before a notary public, it can also be taken by a judge, attorney or other qualified person.

Although an acknowledgment is not required to make a deed valid, in New Jersey all deeds, mortgages, and similar documents must be acknowledged before they can be recorded. Each document must be signed before a notary public, other authorized public official, or before a witness, who must attest to the validity of the grantor's signature. The signature of the witness would then be acknowledged before an authorized public official.

From a purely practical point of view, a deed that is not acknowledged is not a satisfactory instrument. Although an unrecorded deed is valid between the grantor and the grantee, it does not protect against claims by subsequent innocent purchasers. To help assure good title a grantee should always require acknowledgment of the grantor's signature on a deed, so that it may be recorded. Further requirements before a deed may be recorded are detailed in Unit 21.

Delivery and Acceptance

Before a transfer of title by conveyance can take effect, **delivery and acceptance** must exist. There must be an actual *delivery* of the deed by the grantor and either actual or implied *acceptance* by the grantee. Title is said to pass when a deed is delivered. The effective date of the transfer of title from the grantor to the grantee is the date of delivery of the deed itself.

In England during the Middle Ages, when few people were literate, transfer of title occurred in the following manner: The seller took the buyer into the field in question and they walked the boundaries together ("beating the bounds"). Then the seller reached down, took up a clod of earth to represent the whole field and handed it to the buyer. At the moment when the buyer seized the clod, he became owner of the land. Today a document is used instead of a clod of earth, but title still transfers at the moment of delivery and acceptance, and the owner is still said to be *seized* of the property. The word *seisin* still denotes ownership and control.

Execution of Corporate Deeds

Under the law a corporation is considered to be a legal entity. Three basic rules must be followed when corporations are to convey real estate.

1. A corporation can convey real estate only upon a proper resolution passed by its board of directors.

2. If all or a substantial portion of a corporation's real estate is being conveyed, it is also usually required that a resolution authorizing the sale be secured from the stockholders.

3. Deeds to real estate can be signed only by an authorized officer. The authority of the officer must be granted by a resolution properly passed by the board of directors.

Note: The corporate seal need not be affixed to the conveyance unless the acknowledgment mentions the seal.

Rules pertaining to religious corporations and not-for-profit corporations vary widely. Because the legal requirements must be followed explicitly, it is advisable to consult an attorney for all corporate conveyances.

Unit 19

SUMMARY

Documents affecting or conveying interests in real estate must contain a *legal description* that accurately identifies the property involved. There are three methods of describing land in the United States.

1. Metes and bounds

2. fixed natural or manmade objects used to denote real estate boundaries in metes and bounds descriptions

3. Recorded plat of subdivision

In a *metes-and-bounds* description, the actual location of *monuments* is the most important consideration. When property is being described by metes and bounds, the description must always enclose a tract of land; the boundary line must end at the point at which it started.

The *rectangular survey system* is not used in New Jersey. It involves surveys based on principal meridians. Land is surveyed into squares 36 miles in area, called *townships*. Townships are divided into 36 *sections* of one square mile each. Each square mile contains 640 acres.

Land can be subdivided into lots by means of a recorded plat of subdivision. An approved plat of survey giving the size, location, and designation of lots, and specifying the location and size of streets to be dedicated for public use is filed in the recorder's office of the county in which the land is located.

A survey prepared by a surveyor is the usual method of certifying the legal description of a certain parcel of land. Surveys customarily are required when a mortgage or new construction is involved.

Measurements of vertical elevations may be computed from the U.S. Geodetic Survey *datum*, which is the mean sea level in New York harbor. Most large cities have established local survey datums for surveying within the area. Elevations from these datums are further supplemented by reference points, called *benchmarks*.

The voluntary transfer of an owner's title is made by a *deed*, executed (signed) by the owner as *grantor* to the purchaser or donee as *grantee*.

Among the most common requirements for a valid deed are a *grantor* with legal capacity to contract, a readily identifiable *grantee*, a *granting clause*, a *legal description* of the property, a *recital of consideration*, exceptions and reservations on the title, and the signature of the grantor. In addition, the deed should be acknowledged before a notary public or other officer to provide evidence that the signature is genuine and to allow recording. Title to the property passes when the grantor delivers a deed to the grantee and it is accepted.

The obligation of a grantor is determined by the form of the deed. A general *warranty deed* provides the greatest protection of any deed by binding the grantor to certain covenants or warranties. A *bargain and sale deed* carries with it no warranties but implies that the grantor holds title to the property. A *bargain and sale deed with covenant* warrants only that the real estate has not been encumbered by the grantor. A *quitclaim deed* carries with it no warranties whatsoever and conveys only the interest, if any, that the grantor possesses in the property.

KEY TERMS REVIEW

Match the number of each key term with the corresponding letter.

C	1. Acknowledgment
D	2. Bargain and sale deed
G	3. Bargain and sale CAG
N	4. Benchmark
M	5. Covenant
O	6. Datum
J	7. Deed
A	8. Delivery and acceptance
Q	9. Grantee
B	10. Granting clause
R	11. Grantor
U	12. Habendum clause
H	13. Legal description
I	14. Metes and bounds
L	15. Monuments
T	16. Point of beginning
F	17. Quitclaim deed
K	18. Rectangular survey system
P	19. Section
S	20. Township
E	21. Warranty deed

A.   actions that actually transfer title

B.   clause in a deed that makes the transfer

C.   declaration to notary or other official; to prevent forgeries

D.   deed implying that grantor owns the property

E.   deed providing grantee with the most protection

F.   deed releasing any interest grantor may have without claiming seisin

G.   deed stating grantor has not encumbered the property

H.   description sufficient to identify a parcel with certainty that is accepted by a court of law

I.   description using boundaries and directions

J.   document used to transfer title to a parcel of real property

K.   government system for land description; used in Western states

L.   fixed natural or man-made objects used to denote real estate boundaries in metes-and-bounds descriptions

M.   legal promise

N.   marker placed by U.S. Geological Survey, stating elevation

O.   mean sea level in New York harbor; also local zero-elevation point

P.   one mile square

Q.   one who receives property through a deed

R.   one who transfers title by signing a deed

S.   six mile square

T.   spot at which a metes-and-bounds description commences and ends

U.   "to have and to hold" clause that explains ownership being transferred

UNIT 19 REVIEW QUESTIONS

1. A person legally authorized to locate land and give a legal description of it is a(n)
   A. assessor.
   B. surveyor. ✓
   C. abstractor.
   D. recorder.

2. It is essential that every deed be signed by the
   A. grantor. ✓
   B. grantee.
   C. grantor and grantee.
   D. devisee.

3. Title to property transfers at the moment a deed is
   A. signed.
   B. acknowledged.
   C. delivered and accepted. ✓
   D. recorded.

4. Consideration in a deed refers to
   A. gentle handling of the document.
   B. something of value given by each party. ✓
   C. the habendum clause.
   D. the payment of transfer tax.

5. A declaration before a notary or other official providing evidence that a signature is genuine is an
   A. affidavit.
   B. acknowledgment. ✓
   C. affirmation.
   D. estoppel.

6. To be recorded, a document must be
   A. witnessed.
   B. sealed.
   C. acknowledged. ✓
   D. surveyed.

7. What is the purpose of an acknowledgment on the deed?
   A. To make the deed eligible for recording
   B. To assure that the title is good
   C. To provide a witness to the transfer
   D. To prove that the property has not been encumbered

8. Determination of the type of deed used in conveying title can be made by examining the
   A. grantor's name.
   B. grantee's name.
   C. granting clause.
   D. acknowledgment. ✗

9. In some areas, a bargain and sale deed with covenant against grantor is known as a
   A. trust deed.
   B. full covenant and warranty deed.
   C. special warranty deed.
   D. good deed.

10. A widower signs a deed giving the farm to his grandson but he tells no one and hides the deed. The widower later forgets and sells the farm to a banker who receives a deed and records it but tells no one. The widower dies leaving everything to his daughter in his will. The deed to his grandson is then discovered. Who owns the farm?
    A. The grandson
    B. The banker ✓
    C. The daughter
    D. The state

11. The covenant of quiet enjoyment promises that
    A. the grantor is seized of the property.
    B. the previous owner has not mortgaged the property.
    C. no one will question the buyer's full ownership.
    D. neighbors will turn stereos off after 11 pm.

12. A man executes a deed to a woman as grantee, has it acknowledged, and receives payment from the buyer. The man holds the deed, however, and arranges to meet the woman the next morning at the courthouse to deliver the deed to her. In this situation at this time,
    A. the woman owns the property because she has paid for it.
    B. title to the property does not officially pass until the woman is given the deed the next morning.
    C. title to the property does not pass until the woman has received the deed and recorded it the next morning.
    D. the woman owns the property when she signs the deed the next morning.

340

13. In New Jersey, deeds generally must
    A. be recorded to protect all tenants.
    B. state the actual sales price of the property being conveyed if they are to be recorded.
    C. include all outstanding mortgages.
    D. cite the appropriate datum.

14. The grantee receives greatest protection with what type of deed?
    A. Quitclaim
    B. Warranty
    C. Bargain and sale with covenant
    D. Executors

15. In New Jersey, a bargain and sale deed with covenant against grantor's acts is commonly used
    A. to transfer property after a sale.
    B. in tax sales.
    C. in divorce settlements.
    D. to clear cloud from a title.

16. The primary purpose of a deed is to
    A. establish chain of title.
    B. give constructive notice.
    C. transfer title rights.
    D. prove ownership.

17. Permanent reference points have been established throughout the United States to simplify surveyors' work. These reference points are called
    A. monuments.
    B. local official datums.
    C. sections.
    D. benchmarks.

18. What assists the surveyor to determine the height of structures and establishing the grade of streets?
    A. Benchmark
    B. Recorded plats
    C. Datum
    D. Monument

19. Which of the following methods of describing real property is NOT used in New Jersey?
    A. Government survey system
    B. Metes-and-bounds description
    C. Plat of survey
    D. Benchmarks

20. A plat of subdivision is filed with the
    A. chain of title.
    B. deed of the property that is being transferred.
    C. national records office in Washington, DC.
    D. clerk of the county in which the land is located.

21. A declaration before a notary or other official providing evidence that a signature is genuine is known as
    A. an affidavit.
    B. acknowledgment.
    C. affirmation.
    D. estoppel.

Answer questions 22 to 26 by referring to the Plat of Sea Pines Estates Subdivision (Figure 19.7).

22. Which of the following statements is TRUE?
    A. Lot 9, Block A, is larger than Lot 12 in the same block.
    B. The plat for the lots on the Southerly side of Wolf Road between Goodrich Boulevard and Carney Street is found on Sheet 4.
    C. The total subdivision is on five pages.
    D. Wolf Road is the most Northerly road on Sheet 3.

23. Which of the following lots has the *MOST* frontage on Jasmine Lane?
    A. Lot 10, Block B
    B. Lot 11, Block B
    C. Lot 7, Block A
    D. Lot 2, Block A

24. "Beginning at the intersection of the East line of Goodrich Boulevard and the South line of Jasmine Lane and running Southeasterly along the South line of Jasmine Lane a distance of 295 feet; thence Southwesterly on a course of N22E a distance of 135 feet; thence Westerly parallel to the North line of Wolf Road a distance of 195 feet; and thence North along the East line of Goodrich Boulevard to the point of beginning." Which lots are described here?
    A. Lots 13, 14, and 15, Block A
    B. Lots 9, 10, and 11, Block B
    C. Lots 1, 2, 3, and 15, Block A
    D. Lots 7, 8, and 9, Block A

25. On the plat, how many lots have easements?
    A. One
    B. Two
    C. Three
    D. Four

26. What is the ending point of a metes-and-bounds description?
    A. Point of beginning
    B. Point of closure
    C. References an iron rod in the ground
    D. References the nearest monument

Figure 19.7: Plat of Sea Pines Estates Subdivision

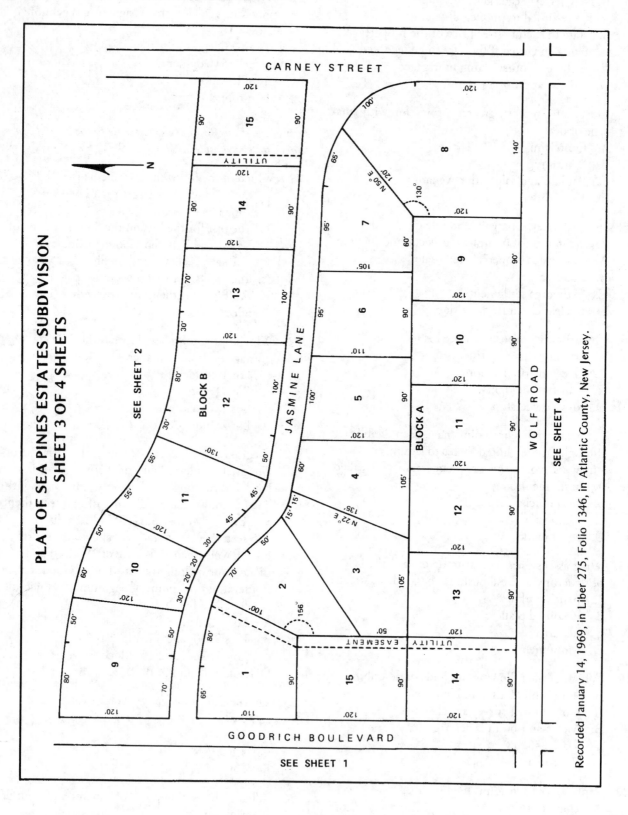

UNIT 20

Transfer of Title

LEARNING OBJECTIVES

When you have completed this unit, you will be able to accomplish the following.

› Describe four methods of title transfer.
› Explain the process of the transfer of title of a deceased person's property.

KEY TERMS

administrator	heir	probate
adverse possession	intestate	testate
descent	inverse condemnation	testator
devisee	involuntary alienation	voluntary alienation
executor	last will and testament	

TITLE

Title to real estate means the right to or ownership of the land.

A parcel of real estate may be transferred from one owner to another by the living or it may be transferred by will or descent after a person has died. In every instance, however, *alienation*, the transfer of title to a parcel of real estate, is a complex legal procedure, involving a number of laws and documents.

This unit discusses four methods of title transfer: Title can be transferred during a lifetime either voluntarily or involuntarily, and at death either voluntarily through a will or involuntarily if no will is left.

ALIENATION OF TITLE

Voluntary

Voluntary alienation (transfer) of title may be made by gift, sale, or exchange. To transfer title by voluntary alienation during his or her lifetime, an owner must use some form of deed of conveyance.

Title to land may be transferred voluntarily between an individual and the government through *dedication* or *public grant*. A developer passes ownership of subdivision lands earmarked for streets and roads to a municipality through the process of *dedication*. Lands owned by the government may be transferred to individuals through *public grant*.

Involuntary

Title to property can be transferred by **involuntary alienation**, that is, without the owner's consent (see Figure 20.1). Such transfers are usually carried out by operations of law, ranging from government condemnation of land for public use to the sale of property to satisfy delinquent tax or mortgage liens. When a person dies intestate and leaves no heirs, the title to his or her real estate passes to the state by *escheat*.

Figure 20.1: Involuntary Alienation

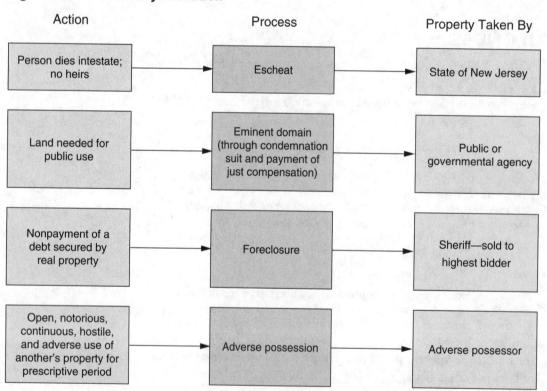

Federal, state, and local governments, school boards, some government agencies, and certain public and quasi-public corporations and utilities (railroads and gas and electric companies) have the power of *eminent domain*, as was explained in Unit 9.

Whenever private property is taken, the owner is given the opportunity to challenge in court the amount of money offered.

Land also may be transferred without an owner's consent to satisfy debts contracted by the owner. In such cases the debt is foreclosed, the property is sold, and the proceeds of the sale are applied to pay off the debt. Debts that can be foreclosed include mortgage loans, real estate taxes, construction liens, and general judgments against the property owner.

Involuntary alienation also may occur as a result of court action. In a *partition proceeding* one co-owner seeks to force another to divide or sell property. An *action to quiet title* requests that the court rule on a clouded or disputed title, canceling one claim in favor of another.

Land also may be transferred by the natural forces of water and wind, which either increase property by accretion or decrease it through erosion; the latter would result in involuntary alienation of land.

Adverse Possession

Adverse possession is another means of involuntary transfer. An owner may lose title to another person who has some claim to the land, takes possession, and most important, *uses* the land. In New Jersey a person may acquire title by adverse possession through the continuous, open, notorious, hostile, and exclusive occupation of another person's property for *30 years*, 60 if a woodland. After that time the user may perfect the claim of title to land through adverse possession by bringing a court suit to quiet title.

Through a process known as *tacking*, continuous periods of adverse possession may be combined by successive users, thus enabling a person who had not been in possession for the entire 30 years to establish a claim of adverse possession. The process is not automatic; legal action is necessary to *perfect the claim*. Adverse possession is not possible against publicly owned property.

Once an adverse user has established title, the former owner has no recourse. To prevent such loss of title, every person having a right or title to real estate must inspect the property at least once within a 30-year period and take action against any adverse claim. Property owners who feel that new governmental requirements have taken away rights to use and/or develop their property may seek damages under the concept of **inverse condemnation**. The burden is on owners who must prove that the governmental action has taken property rights without compensation.

TRANSFER OF A DECEASED PERSON'S PROPERTY

Every state has a law known as the *statute of descent and distribution*. When a person dies **intestate** *(without having left a will)*, the decedent's real estate and personal property pass to his or her heirs according to this statute. In contrast, a person who dies **testate** has prepared a will indicating the way to dispose of his or her property after death.

Legally, when a person dies, title to his or her real estate immediately passes either to the heirs by descent or to the persons named in the will. However, the will must be probated and all claims against the estate must be satisfied.

Probate Proceedings

Probate or administration is a legal process by which a court determines who inherits the property of a deceased person and what the assets of the estate are. Either an **executor** (or *executrix*), named in the will, or an **administrator**, named by the court (if no executor is named or there is no valid will), oversees the administration and distribution of the estate.

Transfer of Title by Will

A **last will and testament** is an instrument made by an owner to voluntarily convey title to the owner's property after his or her death. A will takes effect only after the death of the decedent; until that time, any property covered by the will can be conveyed by the owner.

A party who makes a will is known as a **testator**, or *testatrix* (female); the gift of real property by will is known as a *devise*, and a person who receives real property by will is known as a **devisee**. A gift of money or other personal property is a *legacy* or *bequest*; the person receiving the personal property is a *legatee*.

In New Jersey children can be disinherited, but a surviving spouse is entitled to at least one-third of the estate and the determination of the "augmented estate" is a complex calculation. In a case where a will does not provide the minimum statutory inheritance, the surviving spouse has the option of informing the court that he or she will take the statutory share rather than the lesser share provided in the will. This practice, called a right of election, is a right reserved only to a surviving spouse.

A will differs from a deed in that a deed conveys a present interest in real estate during the lifetime of the grantor, while a will conveys no interest in the property until after the death of the testator. To be valid a deed *must be delivered during the lifetime of the grantor*. The parties named in a will have no rights or interests as long as the party who has made the will is still alive; they acquire interest or title only after the owner's death.

Legal Requirements for Making a Will

A person must be of legal age and of sound mind when he or she executes the will. The drawing of the will must be a voluntary act, free of any undue influence by other people.

Any person of sound mind who is 18 years of age or older can make a will devising his or her real property. All wills must be in writing to be valid. The general rule is that a will must be witnessed by two persons; a beneficiary may serve as a witness in New Jersey. If the signatures of the witnesses are notarized within two days, probate proceedings are simplified. A *holographic will* (a handwritten will with no witnesses) is now legal in New Jersey.

For real property acquired by a married deceased person before May 28, 1980, the surviving spouse is still entitled to a life estate of one-half interest in all real estate owned by the deceased, no matter what other provisions are made in the will.

Transfer of Title by Descent

Title to real estate and personal property of a person who dies intestate passes to heirs. Under the **descent** statutes, the primary **heirs** of the deceased are his or her spouse, civil partner, or domestic partner, and close blood relatives. When children have been legally adopted, most states consider them to be heirs of the adopting parents but not heirs of ancestors of the adopting parents. In most states, illegitimate children inherit from the mother but do not inherit from the father, unless he has admitted parentage in writing or parentage has been established legally. If he legally adopts such a child, that child inherits as an adopted child.

Intestate real property is distributed according to the laws of the state in which the property is located. The New Jersey law of descent and distribution provides that real property belonging to an individual who has died intestate is distributed in the following order. This law and the estate discussed apply only to what remains of the estate after payment of all debts.

1. The laws of descent come into effect *only when the decedent leaves no will.* A surviving spouse or partner becomes sole heir if the decedent leaves no parents or children.

2. *If there is a child or children* (who are also children of the surviving spouse), the spouse or partner receives the first $50,000 plus one-half the remaining estate; the rest goes to the child or children.

3. *If the decedent leaves parent(s) and a spouse but no children,* the spouse or partner receives the first $50,000 plus one-half the remaining estate; the rest goes to the parent or parents.

4. *If there are children who are not the children of the surviving spouse,* the spouse or partner receives half the estate; the child or children the other half.

5. *Where no spouse or partner survives,* children become the sole natural heirs. *Where there is neither a surviving spouse nor children* or children's own heirs, the estate goes first to parents, and failing that, to brothers and sisters or their heirs.

6. *In default of any other natural heirs,* grandparents, aunts, uncles and first cousins may be considered heirs. Beyond that point, the entire estate goes to the State of New Jersey by escheat. The state treasurer sells such property at public sale, giving notice by publication in a newspaper in Trenton and in a newspaper in the county where the property is located. The proceeds of the sale are held for one year. If no claims are made within the year, the funds belong to the state.

SUMMARY

Title to real estate is the right to, and evidence of, ownership of the land. It may be transferred in four ways:

1. Voluntary alienation

2. Involuntary alienation

3. Will

4. Descent

An owner's title may be transferred without his or her permission by a court action such as a foreclosure or judgment sale, a tax sale, condemnation under the power of eminent domain, *adverse possession*, or escheat. Land also may be transferred by the natural forces of water and wind, which either increase property by accretion or decrease it through *erosion*.

The real estate of an owner who makes a valid will (who dies *testate*) passes to the devisees through the probating of the will. Generally, an *heir* or a devisee does not receive a deed, because title passes by the law or the will. The title of an owner who dies without a will *(intestate)* passes according to the provisions of the laws of *descent* of the state in which the real estate is located.

KEY TERMS REVIEW

Match the number of each key term with the corresponding letter.

_____ 1. Administrator

_____ 2. Adverse possession

_____ 3. Descent

_____ 4. Devisee

_____ 5. Executor

_____ 6. Heir

_____ 7. Intestate

_____ 8. Involuntary alienation

_____ 9. Last will and testament

_____ 10. Probate

_____ 11. Testate

_____ 12. Testator

_____ 13. Voluntary alienation

A. transfer of title with the grantor's consent

B. acquiring of property by natural heirs

C. court proceeding to establish validity of a will

D. document disposing of property after one's death

E. having made a will

F. one who makes a will

G. one who can inherit

H. one who receives real property through a will

I. person named in a will to administer decedent's estate

J. title acquired by usage

K. transfer of title without the grantor's consent

L. without a will

M. person named by the state to administer a decedent's will

UNIT 20 REVIEW QUESTIONS

1. Title to real estate may be transferred during a person's lifetime by
   A. devise.
   B. descent.
   C. involuntary alienation.
   D. escheat.

2. Title to an owner's real estate can be transferred at the death of the owner by which of the following documents?
   A. Warranty deed
   B. Quitclaim deed
   C. Referee's deed
   D. Last will and testament

3. A woman bought acreage in a distant county, never went to see the acreage, and did not use the ground. A man moved his mobile home onto the land, had a water well drilled, and lived there for 32 years. The man may become the owner of the land if he has complied with the state law regarding
   A. requirements for a valid conveyance.
   B. adverse possession.
   C. avulsion.
   D. voluntary alienation.

4. Which of the following is NOT one of the ways in which title to real estate may be transferred by involuntary alienation?
   A. Eminent domain
   B. Escheat
   C. Erosion
   D. Seisin

5. A person who has died leaving a valid will is called
   A. a devisee.
   B. a testator.
   C. a legatee.
   D. intestate.

6. The person whose land is taken for public use in New Jersey
   A. may or may not receive compensation.
   B. may refuse to give up the property.
   C. may still devise it by will.
   D. may challenge a money award in court.

7. Which of the following acquires title to real estate?
   A. Devisee
   B. Optionee
   C. Lessee
   D. Mortgagee

8. Condemnation of private property for public use is called the right of
   A. police power.
   B. acquisition.
   C. escheat.
   D. eminent domain.

9. The reversion of property to the state or county because of lack of heirs is called
   A. police power.
   B. acquisition.
   C. escheat.
   D. eminent domain.

10. A developer passes title of subdivision roads to the town by the process known as
    A. public grant.
    B. derivation.
    C. seisin.
    D. dedication.

11. An owner of real estate who was adjudged legally incompetent made a will during his stay at a nursing home. He later died and was survived by a wife and three children. His real estate will pass
    A. to his wife.
    B. to the heirs mentioned in his will.
    C. according to the state laws of descent.
    D. to the state.

12. Voluntary transfer of property includes the process of
    A. adverse possession.
    B. sale.
    C. foreclosure.
    D. escheat.

13. Involuntary transfer includes the process of
    A. gift.
    B. public grant.
    C. dedication.
    D. adverse possession.

14. A man bought an apartment house as a joint tenant with his business partner. He died ten years later, leaving a wife and two children. He left no will, so his widow
    A. owns half that apartment house as long as she lives, but cannot devise it in her will.
    B. owns the apartment house completely and can leave it in her will to anyone she wishes.
    C. owns half the apartment house completely.
    D. has no claim on that apartment house.

15. Land that the state of New Jersey acquires by escheat is then
    A. used for public purposes.
    B. vulnerable to adverse possessors.
    C. devised.
    D. sold at a public sale.

UNIT 21

Public Records, Titles, and Closings

LEARNING OBJECTIVES

When you have completed this unit, you will be able to accomplish the following.

- › Explain New Jersey recording acts that establish a chain of title, evidence of title, and marketable title.
- › Summarize the components of the closing process.

KEY TERMS

abstract of title	constructive notice	Real Estate Settlement
actual notice	credit	Procedures Act (RESPA)
affidavit	debit	realty transfer fee
arrears	escrow closing	suit to quiet title
attorney's opinion of title	evidence of title	title insurance policy
caveat emptor	marketable title	Uniform Settlement
chain of title	proration	Statement (HUD-1)
Closing Disclosure	public records	

PUBLIC RECORDS AND RECORDING

Before an individual purchases a parcel of real estate, he or she wants to be sure that the seller can convey good title to the property. The present owner of the real estate probably purchased from the previous owner, with the same question of kind and condition of title having been inquired into many times in the past.

Recording Acts

The state legislature has passed laws that allow owners or parties interested in real estate to record, or file, in the **public records** all documents affecting their interest in real estate to give *legal, public, and constructive notice* to the world of their interest.

In most counties, the county clerk is the recorder. A separate registrar of deeds handles public records in Camden, Essex, Hudson, Passaic, and Union counties.

Necessity for Recording

A deed or mortgage may not be effective as far as later purchasers are concerned *unless the document has been recorded.* Thus the public records should reveal the condition of the title, and a purchaser should be able to rely on a search of such public records. From a practical point of view, the recording acts give *priority* to those interests that are recorded first.

All written instruments affecting the title to real property may be recorded in the public record of the county in which the real estate is located, which then gives *constructive notice* to the world of their existence.

To be eligible for recording, an instrument must be *acknowledged,* notarized, or proved to be authentic before an authorized official. In addition, the words "prepared by" followed by the name of the person who prepared the document must be included on the document or following the acknowledgment. If the instrument is a deed, it must also state the exact consideration paid for the property and the proper amount of realty transfer fee must be paid.

Notice

Relying on the maxim of **caveat emptor** ("let the buyer beware"), the courts charge a prospective real estate buyer or mortgagee (lender) with the responsibility of inspecting the property and searching the public records to ascertain the interests of other parties. *Constructive notice* assumes that the information is available, therefore the buyer or lender is responsible for learning it.

Constructive notice, or what a buyer could find out, is distinguished from **actual notice**, or what the person actually knows (see Figure 21.1). After an individual has searched the public records and inspected the property, he or she has actual notice, or knowledge, of the information learned.

Figure 21.1: Notice

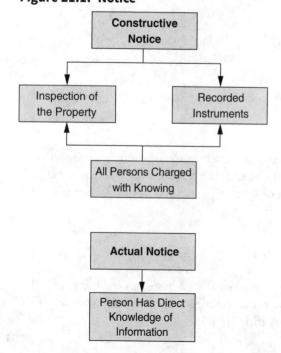

An individual is said to have actual notice of any information of which he or she has *direct knowledge.*

In New Jersey it is the *duty of the purchaser* to investigate the title of property to be conveyed. The purchaser is held to constructive notice of any outstanding rights on the title that could be discovered by a diligent search, including possible rights of persons in physical possession of the property.

Real estate taxes and special assessments automatically are direct liens on specific parcels of real estate and need not be recorded. Other liens such as inheritance taxes and franchise taxes are placed by statutory authority against all real estate owned either by a decedent at the time of death or by a corporation at the time the franchise tax became a lien; these liens also are not recorded.

Recording Sales Contracts

It can occasionally be desirable to enter a contract for the sale of real property in the public records. Any document to be filed must be acknowledged. If neither buyer nor seller can be reached for an acknowledgment, it is sufficient if a witness to their signatures appears before a notary.

CHAIN OF TITLE

The **chain of title** shows the record of ownership of the property over a period of time. An *abstract of title* is a condensed history of all instruments affecting a particular parcel of land.

Through the chain of title, the ownership of the property can be traced from its origin to its present owner. If this cannot be done, it is said that there is a *gap in the chain.* A quitclaim deed is commonly used to bridge such gaps. Sometimes, however, it is necessary to establish ownership by a court action called a **suit to quiet title**.

EVIDENCE OF TITLE

When dealing with an owner of real estate, a purchaser or lender requires satisfactory proof that the seller is the owner and has good title to the property. This documentary proof is called **evidence of title**.

There are four generally used forms of title evidence:

1. Abstract of title and attorney's opinion
2. Title insurance policy
3. Torrens certificate
4. Certificate of title

A *deed is not proof of title*; it proves the grantor transferred the property but does not prove the grantor had good title in the first place. The only effective proof must be one of the evidences of title, based on an adequate search of the public records.

Abstract of Title and Attorney's Opinion

An **abstract of title** is a brief history of the instruments appearing in the county record that affect title to the parcel in question. The legal description of the property is in the abstract's caption. Abstracts usually consist of several sections, or continuations. It is necessary for each section of the abstract to begin with a search of the public record from a date immediately following the date of the previous section. If this were not done, there would be a gap in the abstract.

When an abstract is first prepared or is continued, the abstractor lists and summarizes each instrument in chronological order, along with information relative to taxes, judgments, special assessments, and the like. The abstractor concludes with a certificate indicating which records were examined and when, and then he or she signs the abstract. Abstractors must exercise due care, because they can be liable for negligence for any failure to include or accurately record all pertinent data. An abstractor *does not*, however, *pass judgment on* or *guarantee* the condition of the title.

Local practice determines how far back an abstract is researched. Unless a title problem is discovered, in many parts of New Jersey the abstractor goes back only to the purchase by the present owner, or no more than 60 years.

For attorney's opinion of title, which is not used as extensively as in the past, the seller's attorney usually orders the abstract continued to cover the current date. It is then submitted to the buyer's attorney, who must examine the *entire abstract*. Following his or her detailed examination, the attorney must evaluate all the facts and material to prepare a written report for the purchaser on the condition of the ownership; this report is called an **attorney's opinion of title**.

To protect purchasers, title insurance is used increasingly. It is usually required by the lending institution when a new mortgage is to be placed.

Title Insurance

A buyer or seller seeking to obtain a **title insurance policy** as evidence of ownership makes an application to the title insurance company. The company examines the title records and agrees to insure against certain undiscovered defects. Exactly which defects the company insures against depends on the type of policy it issues. A policy usually insures against defects that may be found in the public records and such items as forged documents, documents of incompetent grantors, incorrect marital statements, and improperly delivered deeds. The company does not agree to insure against any defects in or liens against the title that are specifically listed in the policy as exceptions.

On completion of the examination, the title company usually issues a report of title or a commitment to issue a title policy. This describes the policy being issued. An owner's policy usually *excludes coverage* against the following exceptions: unrecorded documents, unrecorded defects of which the policyholder has knowledge, rights of parties in possession, and facts discoverable by survey. The title insurance company agrees to defend the title at its own expense and to reimburse the policyholder up to the amount of the policy for damages sustained by reason of any defect not excepted.

Title companies issue various forms of title insurance policies, the most common of which are the *owner's* title insurance policy (a *fee policy*), the *mortgage* title insurance policy, and the *leasehold* title insurance policy. As the names indicate, each of these policies is issued to insure specific interests. A mortgage title insurance policy ensures a lender that it has a valid first lien against the property.

The title policy required by lenders insures the lender's interest but does not protect the owner (borrower), and is always only for the remaining amount due on the mortgage. New Jersey law requires lenders to inform borrowers of this fact. When purchasing a mortgage title insurance policy, the owner can, for an additional charge, also purchase an owner's title insurance policy to protect his or her own interest in the property. The State of New Jersey regulates the rates that may be charged for title insurance, both original policies and reissues.

Torrens Certificate

In some other states the *Torrens system* of land registration is used to prove title. Once an applicant has proved that he or she is the owner, title is registered and a certificate of title is issued. At any given time, the certificate in the registrar's office reveals the owner of the land and all mortgages, judgments, and similar liens. It does not reveal unpaid federal or state taxes.

The Torrens system is not used in New Jersey.

Certificate of Title

In some rural localities a *certificate of title* prepared by an attorney is used, and no abstract is prepared. The attorney examines the public records and issues a certificate of title that expresses his or her opinion of the title's status. It is not, however, a title insurance policy and does not carry the full protection of such a policy. A lawyer's opinion of title is often oral, or implied, representation; the person who sustains damages by relying on it may look to the lawyer for satisfaction.

MARKETABLE TITLE

Under the terms of the usual real estate sales contract, the seller is required to deliver marketable or insurable title to the buyer at the closing. Generally, a **marketable** (or *merchantable*) **title** is one that is so free from significant defects (other than those the buyer has agreed to accept) that the purchaser can be assured against having to defend the title. Proper evidence of title is proof that the title is, in fact, marketable.

A buyer cannot be forced to accept a conveyance that is materially different from the one bargained for in the sales contract; he or she cannot be forced to buy a lawsuit. Questions of marketable title must be raised by a purchaser (or his or her broker or attorney) before acceptance of the deed. If a buyer accepts a deed with unmarketable title, the only available legal recourse is to sue the seller under the covenants of warranty (if any) contained in the deed.

CLOSING THE TRANSACTION

Although salespeople usually are not burdened with the technicalities of closing, they must clearly understand what takes place. A real estate specialist should be able to assist in preclosing arrangements and advise the parties in estimating their expenses and the approximate amounts the buyer needs and the seller receives at the closing.

Generally, the closing of a real estate transaction involves a gathering of interested parties at which the promises made in the *real estate sales contract* are carried out; that is, a deed is delivered in exchange for the purchase price. In many sales transactions two closings actually take place at this time:

1. The closing of the buyer's loan—the disbursal of mortgage funds in exchange for the note and mortgage

2. The closing of the sale

As discussed in Unit 11, a sales contract is the blueprint for the completion of a real estate transaction. The buyer wants to be sure that the seller is delivering good title and that the property is in the promised condition. This involves inspecting the title evidence; the deed the seller gives; any documents representing the removal of undesired liens and encumbrances; any survey; termite report; and leases, if there are tenants on the premises. The seller wants to be sure that the buyer has obtained the stipulated financing and has sufficient funds to complete the sale. Both parties wish to inspect the closing statement to make sure that all monies involved in the transaction have been properly accounted for. When the parties are satisfied that everything is in order, the exchange is made and all pertinent documents are then recorded.

Lender's Interest in Closing

When a buyer is obtaining a new loan, the lender wants to protect its security interest in the property—to make sure that the buyer is getting good, marketable title and that tax and insurance payments are maintained so that there are no liens with greater priority than the mortgage lien, and the insurance is paid up if the property is damaged or destroyed. For this reason the lender frequently requires the following items at or before the closing:

- A insurance policy or abstract of title
- A fire and hazard insurance policy with receipt for the premium
- Additional information such as survey, termite, or other inspection report
- Certificate of occupancy (if required)
- Establishment of reserve, or escrow, account for tax and insurance payments
- Representation by its own attorney at the closing

Homeowner's Insurance

When mortgaging is involved, the buyer must bring to the closing proof of insurance on the property and, when required, proof of flood insurance. The insurance policy or binder usually names the lender as lienholder who may also be paid in case of loss under the policy. (See CLUE report, Unit 3.)

New Jersey Requirements

Before the closing on any one- or two-family house (technically, at change of occupancy), the local government must certify that the building contains at least one properly installed carbon monoxide detector, as well as the smoke alarms and fire extinguisher described in Unit 18.

Federal Flood Insurance Program

Homeowners insurance does not cover damage caused by flooding, (i.e., rising water). For example, a sewer backup will only be covered by flood insurance *if* the sewer backup is caused by a flood, not if the backup is caused by some other problem.

The Federal Emergency Management Agency (FEMA), which is now part of the Department of Homeland Security, continually updates its maps that identify areas most likely to flood. Special flood hazard areas (SFHA) are those that have at least a one percent chance of being flooded in any given year.

By federal law, federally regulated or insured lenders must require flood insurance on any property secured by a mortgage in areas of high risk for flooding. However, since about 20 percent of flood claims come from owners whose properties are not located within a flood hazard zone, a lender may require flood insurance as a condition for mortgage approval even if the property is not located in an area of high risk.

Rates may be lower if the local community participates in the Community Rating System (CRS).

Generally, there is a 30-day waiting period before the flood insurance is in effect *unless* the lender requires the flood insurance as a condition of the loan. In order to have immediate coverage, a cash buyer may elect to take a mortgage loan that requires flood insurance so that coverage is immediately effective. The buyer can pay off the loan after closing.

RESPA Requirements

The federal **Real Estate Settlement Procedures Act (RESPA)**, formerly administered by HUD, is now administered by the Consumer Financial Protection Bureau (CFPB). It was created to ensure that the buyer and seller in a *residential* real estate transaction have knowledge of all settlement costs. RESPA requirements apply when the *purchase is financed by a federally related mortgage loan*. Federally related loans include those

- made by banks or other lenders whose deposits are insured by federal agencies (FDIC or FSLIC);

- insured by the FHA or guaranteed by the VA;

- made by RECD (the former Farmer's Home Administration);

- administered by the U.S. Department of Housing and Urban Development; or

- intended to be sold by the lender to Fannie Mae, Ginnie Mae or Freddie Mac.

RESPA regulations apply only to transactions involving new first mortgage loans. A transaction financed solely by a purchase-money mortgage taken back by the seller, land contract, or the buyer's assumption of the seller's existing loan would not be covered by RESPA, unless the terms of the assumed loan are modified or the lender charges more than $50 for the assumption. When a transaction is covered by RESPA, the following requirements must be met:

- *Section 8, prohibition against kickbacks:* RESPA explicitly prohibits the payment of kickbacks, or unearned fees; for example, when an insurance agency pays a kickback to a lender for referring one of the lender's recent customers to the agency. This prohibition does not include fee splitting between cooperating brokers or members of multiple listing services, brokerage referral arrangements, or the division of a commission between a broker and his or her salespeople.

- *Section 9:* Prohibits lenders and sellers from requiring that buyers use a particular title insurance provider; buyers may choose their own.

- *Section 10:* Lenders are not required to maintain escrow accounts to fund property taxes and insurance. However, if the lender does require an escrow account, RESPA limits the amount of escrow reserves required by a lender to pay property taxes, hazard insurance, and other charges. At least once a year, lenders must return overages of $50 or more.

TILA-RESPA Integrated Disclosures (TRID)

The CFPB merged forms that previously required by RESPA and the Truth in Lending Act (TILA) into the TILA-RESPA Integrated Disclosures (TRID). TRID requirements apply to most federally related first and second mortgages used to buy residential property.

They do not apply to the following:

- Home equity lines of credit (HELOCs)
- Mortgage secured by mobile homes or other "movable" dwellings that are not permanently attached to real estate
- Reverse mortgages
- Cash transactions
- Loans for commercial purposes

The settlement statement (HUD-1), the Good Faith Estimate (GFE,) and Truth in Lending (TIL) disclosures are still applicable to most HELOCs and reverse mortgages.

Under TRID rules, the lender is required to provide the five-page Closing Disclosure (CD) at least three business days before closing, with a minimum of seven business days between the issuance of the Loan Estimate (LE) and closing. See Figure 21.2 for a sample CD.

When borrowers receive the CD, they should compare the first three pages of the CD to the LE that they received shortly after signing their intent to proceed. There should be no changes.

Here are the highlights of the CD:

- Page 1: Costs to close: Note closing costs as well as cash to close, either by a cashier or certified check (not a personal check or cash).
- Page 2: Closing costs are itemized, including the origination fees, the costs of services that the borrower could and could not shop for. The escrow account requirements are explained if the lender requires an escrow account for the borrower's homeowner's insurance and some taxes. Lenders are not permitted to build up large amounts in the escrow account nor allow shortages.
- Page 3: A brief analysis of whether an item has changed or not from the original LE. The Summary of Transactions is nearly identical to the previous HUD-1.
- Page 4: More disclosures about the loan: assumption rights, demand feature, late payments, negative amortization, partial payments, security interests, details of the escrow account, and disclosure that escrow account payments may increase.
- Page 5: The last page is a final summary of loan payments and notes about liability after foreclosure as well as contact information for parties involved in the transaction: lender, mortgage broker, real estate broker(s), and settlement agent.

Figure 21.2: Closing Disclosure

Closing Disclosure

This form is a statement of final loan terms and closing costs. Compare this document with your Loan Estimate.

Closing Information

Date Issued	4/15/2013
Closing Date	4/15/2013
Disbursement Date	4/15/2013
Settlement Agent	Epsilon Title Co.
File #	12-3456
Property	456 Somewhere Ave
	Anytown, ST 12345
Sale Price	$180,000

Transaction Information

Borrower	Michael Jones and Mary Stone
	123 Anywhere Street
	Anytown, ST 12345
Seller	Steve Cole and Amy Doe
	321 Somewhere Drive
	Anytown, ST 12345
Lender	Ficus Bank

Loan Information

Loan Term	30 years
Purpose	Purchase
Product	Fixed Rate
Loan Type	☒ Conventional ☐ FHA
	☐ VA ☐ _____
Loan ID #	123456789
MIC #	000654321

Loan Terms

Loan Terms		Can this amount increase after closing?
Loan Amount	$162,000	**NO**
Interest Rate	3.875%	**NO**
Monthly Principal & Interest *See Projected Payments below for your Estimated Total Monthly Payment*	$761.78	**NO**
		Does the loan have these features?
Prepayment Penalty	**YES**	• **As high as $3,240** if you pay off the loan during the first 2 years
Balloon Payment	**NO**	

Projected Payments

Payment Calculation	Years 1-7		Years 8-30	
Principal & Interest		$761.78		$761.78
Mortgage Insurance	+	82.35	+	—
Estimated Escrow *Amount can increase over time*	+	206.13	+	206.13
Estimated Total Monthly Payment		**$1,050.26**		**$967.91**

Estimated Taxes, Insurance & Assessments *Amount can increase over time* *See page 4 for details*	$356.13 a month	This estimate includes	In escrow?
		☒ Property Taxes	**YES**
		☒ Homeowner's Insurance	**YES**
		☒ Other: Homeowner's Association Dues	**NO**
		See Escrow Account on page 4 for details. You must pay for other property costs separately.	

Costs at Closing

Closing Costs	$9,712.10	Includes $4,694.05 in Loan Costs + $5,018.05 in Other Costs – $0 in Lender Credits. *See page 2 for details.*
Cash to Close	$14,147.26	Includes Closing Costs. *See Calculating Cash to Close on page 3 for details.*

Figure 21.2: Closing Disclosure (continued)

Closing Cost Details

Loan Costs		Borrower-Paid		Seller-Paid		Paid by Others
		At Closing	Before Closing	At Closing	Before Closing	
A. Origination Charges		**$1,802.00**				
01 0.25 % of Loan Amount (Points)		$405.00				
02 Application Fee		$300.00				
03 Underwriting Fee		$1,097.00				
04						
05						
06						
07						
08						
B. Services Borrower Did Not Shop For		**$236.55**				
01 Appraisal Fee	to John Smith Appraisers Inc.					$405.00
02 Credit Report Fee	to Information Inc.		$29.80			
03 Flood Determination Fee	to Info Co.	$20.00				
04 Flood Monitoring Fee	to Info Co.	$31.75				
05 Tax Monitoring Fee	to Info Co.	$75.00				
06 Tax Status Research Fee	to Info Co.	$80.00				
07						
08						
09						
10						
C. Services Borrower Did Shop For		**$2,655.50**				
01 Pest Inspection Fee	to Pests Co.	$120.50				
02 Survey Fee	to Surveys Co.	$85.00				
03 Title – Insurance Binder	to Epsilon Title Co.	$650.00				
04 Title – Lender's Title Insurance	to Epsilon Title Co.	$500.00				
05 Title – Settlement Agent Fee	to Epsilon Title Co.	$500.00				
06 Title – Title Search	to Epsilon Title Co.	$800.00				
07						
08						
D. TOTAL LOAN COSTS (Borrower-Paid)		**$4,694.05**				
Loan Costs Subtotals (A + B + C)		$4,664.25	$29.80			

Other Costs						
E. Taxes and Other Government Fees		**$85.00**				
01 Recording Fees	Deed: $40.00 Mortgage: $45.00	$85.00				
02 Transfer Tax	to Any State			$950.00		
F. Prepaids		**$2,120.80**				
01 Homeowner's Insurance Premium (12 mo.) to Insurance Co.		$1,209.96				
02 Mortgage Insurance Premium (mo.)						
03 Prepaid Interest ($17.44 per day from 4/15/13 to 5/1/13)		$279.04				
04 Property Taxes (6 mo.) to Any County USA		$631.80				
05						
G. Initial Escrow Payment at Closing		**$412.25**				
01 Homeowner's Insurance $100.83 per month for 2 mo.		$201.66				
02 Mortgage Insurance per month for mo.						
03 Property Taxes $105.30 per month for 2 mo.		$210.60				
04						
05						
06						
07						
08 Aggregate Adjustment		– 0.01				
H. Other		**$2,400.00**				
01 HOA Capital Contribution	to HOA Acre Inc.	$500.00				
02 HOA Processing Fee	to HOA Acre Inc.	$150.00				
03 Home Inspection Fee	to Engineers Inc.	$750.00			$750.00	
04 Home Warranty Fee	to XYZ Warranty Inc.			$450.00		
05 Real Estate Commission	to Alpha Real Estate Broker			$5,700.00		
06 Real Estate Commission	to Omega Real Estate Broker			$5,700.00		
07 Title – Owner's Title Insurance (optional) to Epsilon Title Co.		$1,000.00				
08						
I. TOTAL OTHER COSTS (Borrower-Paid)		**$5,018.05**				
Other Costs Subtotals (E + F + G + H)		$5,018.05				
J. TOTAL CLOSING COSTS (Borrower-Paid)		**$9,712.10**				
Closing Costs Subtotals (D + I)		$9,682.30	$29.80	$12,800.00	$750.00	$405.00
Lender Credits						

Figure 21.2: Closing Disclosure (continued)

Calculating Cash to Close

Use this table to see what has changed from your Loan Estimate.

	Loan Estimate	Final	Did this change?
Total Closing Costs (J)	$8,054.00	$9,712.10	YES • See **Total Loan Costs (D)** and **Total Other Costs (I)**
Closing Costs Paid Before Closing	$0	– $29.80	YES • You paid these Closing Costs **before closing**
Closing Costs Financed (Paid from your Loan Amount)	$0	$0	NO
Down Payment/Funds from Borrower	$18,000.00	$18,000.00	NO
Deposit	– $10,000.00	– $10,000.00	NO
Funds for Borrower	$0	$0	NO
Seller Credits	$0	– $2,500.00	YES • See Seller Credits in **Section L**
Adjustments and Other Credits	$0	– $1,035.04	YES • See details in **Sections K and L**
Cash to Close	$16,054.00	$14,147.26	

Summaries of Transactions

Use this table to see a summary of your transaction.

BORROWER'S TRANSACTION

K. Due from Borrower at Closing	$189,762.30
01 Sale Price of Property	$180,000.00
02 Sale Price of Any Personal Property Included in Sale	
03 Closing Costs Paid at Closing (J)	$9,682.30
04	
Adjustments	
05	
06	
07	
Adjustments for Items Paid by Seller in Advance	
08 City/Town Taxes to	
09 County Taxes to	
10 Assessments to	
11 HOA Dues 4/15/13 to 4/30/13	$80.00
12	
13	
14	
15	

L. Paid Already by or on Behalf of Borrower at Closing	$175,615.04
01 Deposit	$10,000.00
02 Loan Amount	$162,000.00
03 Existing Loan(s) Assumed or Taken Subject to	
04	
05 Seller Credit	$2,500.00
Other Credits	
06 Rebate from Epsilon Title Co.	$750.00
07	
Adjustments	
08	
09	
10	
11	
Adjustments for Items Unpaid by Seller	
12 City/Town Taxes 1/1/13 to 4/14/13	$365.04
13 County Taxes to	
14 Assessments to	
15	
16	
17	

CALCULATION	
Total Due from Borrower at Closing (K)	$189,762.30
Total Paid Already by or on Behalf of Borrower at Closing (L)	– $175,615.04
Cash to Close ☒ **From** ☐ **To Borrower**	**$14,147.26**

SELLER'S TRANSACTION

M. Due to Seller at Closing	$180,080.00
01 Sale Price of Property	$180,000.00
02 Sale Price of Any Personal Property Included in Sale	
03	
04	
05	
06	
07	
08	
Adjustments for Items Paid by Seller in Advance	
09 City/Town Taxes to	
10 County Taxes to	
11 Assessments to	
12 HOA Dues 4/15/13 to 4/30/13	$80.00
13	
14	
15	
16	

N. Due from Seller at Closing	$115,665.04
01 Excess Deposit	
02 Closing Costs Paid at Closing (J)	$12,800.00
03 Existing Loan(s) Assumed or Taken Subject to	
04 Payoff of First Mortgage Loan	$100,000.00
05 Payoff of Second Mortgage Loan	
06	
07	
08 Seller Credit	$2,500.00
09	
10	
11	
12	
13	
Adjustments for Items Unpaid by Seller	
14 City/Town Taxes 1/1/13 to 4/14/13	$365.04
15 County Taxes to	
16 Assessments to	
17	
18	
19	

CALCULATION	
Total Due to Seller at Closing (M)	$180,080.00
Total Due from Seller at Closing (N)	– $115,665.04
Cash ☐ **From** ☒ **To Seller**	**$64,414.96**

Figure 21.2: Closing Disclosure (continued)

Additional Information About This Loan

Loan Disclosures

Assumption

If you sell or transfer this property to another person, your lender

☐ will allow, under certain conditions, this person to assume this loan on the original terms.

☒ will not allow assumption of this loan on the original terms.

Demand Feature

Your loan

☐ has a demand feature, which permits your lender to require early repayment of the loan. You should review your note for details.

☒ does not have a demand feature.

Late Payment

If your payment is more than *15* days late, your lender will charge a late fee of *5% of the monthly principal and interest payment.*

Negative Amortization (Increase in Loan Amount)

Under your loan terms, you

☐ are scheduled to make monthly payments that do not pay all of the interest due that month. As a result, your loan amount will increase (negatively amortize), and your loan amount will likely become larger than your original loan amount. Increases in your loan amount lower the equity you have in this property.

☐ may have monthly payments that do not pay all of the interest due that month. If you do, your loan amount will increase (negatively amortize), and, as a result, your loan amount may become larger than your original loan amount. Increases in your loan amount lower the equity you have in this property.

☒ do not have a negative amortization feature.

Partial Payments

Your lender

☒ may accept payments that are less than the full amount due (partial payments) and apply them to your loan.

☐ may hold them in a separate account until you pay the rest of the payment, and then apply the full payment to your loan.

☐ does not accept any partial payments.

If this loan is sold, your new lender may have a different policy.

Security Interest

You are granting a security interest in

456 Somewhere Ave., Anytown, ST 12345

You may lose this property if you do not make your payments or satisfy other obligations for this loan.

Escrow Account

For now, your loan

☒ will have an escrow account (also called an "impound" or "trust" account) to pay the property costs listed below. Without an escrow account, you would pay them directly, possibly in one or two large payments a year. Your lender may be liable for penalties and interest for failing to make a payment.

Escrow		
Escrowed Property Costs over Year 1	$2,473.56	Estimated total amount over year 1 for your escrowed property costs: *Homeowner's Insurance Property Taxes*
Non-Escrowed Property Costs over Year 1	$1,800.00	Estimated total amount over year 1 for your non-escrowed property costs: *Homeowner's Association Dues* You may have other property costs.
Initial Escrow Payment	$412.25	A cushion for the escrow account you pay at closing. See Section G on page 2.
Monthly Escrow Payment	$206.13	The amount included in your total monthly payment.

☐ will not have an escrow account because ☐ you declined it ☐ your lender does not offer one. You must directly pay your property costs, such as taxes and homeowner's insurance. Contact your lender to ask if your loan can have an escrow account.

No Escrow		
Estimated Property Costs over Year 1		Estimated total amount over year 1. You must pay these costs directly, possibly in one or two large payments a year.
Escrow Waiver Fee		

In the future,

Your property costs may change and, as a result, your escrow payment may change. You may be able to cancel your escrow account, but if you do, you must pay your property costs directly. If you fail to pay your property taxes, your state or local government may (1) impose fines and penalties or (2) place a tax lien on this property. If you fail to pay any of your property costs, your lender may (1) add the amounts to your loan balance, (2) add an escrow account to your loan, or (3) require you to pay for property insurance that the lender buys on your behalf, which likely would cost more and provide fewer benefits than what you could buy on your own.

Figure 21.2: Closing Disclosure (continued)

Loan Calculations

Total of Payments. Total you will have paid after you make all payments of principal, interest, mortgage insurance, and loan costs, as scheduled.	$285,803.36
Finance Charge. The dollar amount the loan will cost you.	$118,830.27
Amount Financed. The loan amount available after paying your upfront finance charge.	$162,000.00
Annual Percentage Rate (APR). Your costs over the loan term expressed as a rate. This is not your interest rate.	4.174%
Total Interest Percentage (TIP). The total amount of interest that you will pay over the loan term as a percentage of your loan amount.	69.46%

? **Questions?** If you have questions about the loan terms or costs on this form, use the contact information below. To get more information or make a complaint, contact the Consumer Financial Protection Bureau at **www.consumerfinance.gov/mortgage-closing**

Other Disclosures

Appraisal

If the property was appraised for your loan, your lender is required to give you a copy at no additional cost at least 3 days before closing. If you have not yet received it, please contact your lender at the information listed below.

Contract Details

See your note and security instrument for information about
- what happens if you fail to make your payments,
- what is a default on the loan,
- situations in which your lender can require early repayment of the loan, and
- the rules for making payments before they are due.

Liability after Foreclosure

If your lender forecloses on this property and the foreclosure does not cover the amount of unpaid balance on this loan,

☒ state law may protect you from liability for the unpaid balance. If you refinance or take on any additional debt on this property, you may lose this protection and have to pay any debt remaining even after foreclosure. You may want to consult a lawyer for more information.

☐ state law does not protect you from liability for the unpaid balance.

Refinance

Refinancing this loan will depend on your future financial situation, the property value, and market conditions. You may not be able to refinance this loan.

Tax Deductions

If you borrow more than this property is worth, the interest on the loan amount above this property's fair market value is not deductible from your federal income taxes. You should consult a tax advisor for more information.

Contact Information

	Lender	Mortgage Broker	Real Estate Broker (B)	Real Estate Broker (S)	Settlement Agent
Name	Ficus Bank		Omega Real Estate Broker Inc.	Alpha Real Estate Broker Co.	Epsilon Title Co.
Address	4321 Random Blvd. Somecity, ST 12340		789 Local Lane Sometown, ST 12345	987 Suburb Ct. Someplace, ST 12340	123 Commerce Pl. Somecity, ST 12344
NMLS ID					
ST License ID			Z765416	Z61456	Z61616
Contact	Joe Smith		Samuel Green	Joseph Cain	Sarah Arnold
Contact NMLS ID	12345				
Contact ST License ID			P16415	P51461	PT1234
Email	joesmith@ ficusbank.com		sam@omegare.biz	joe@alphare.biz	sarah@ epsilontitle.com
Phone	123-456-7890		123-555-1717	321-555-7171	987-555-4321

Confirm Receipt

By signing, you are only confirming that you have received this form. You do not have to accept this loan because you have signed or received this form.

_____ _____ _____ _____
Applicant Signature   Date   Co-Applicant Signature   Date

CLOSING DISCLOSURE

The Title Procedure

On the date when the sale is actually completed—the date of delivery of the deed—the buyer has a title commitment or an abstract that was issued several days or weeks before the closing. For this reason the title or abstract company is usually required to make a second search of the public records. A supplemental telephone search by the abstracting company is often made at the moment of closing.

The seller is usually required to execute an **affidavit** of title. This is a *sworn statement* in which the seller assures the title company (and the buyer) that since the date of the title examination there have been no judgments, bankruptcies, or divorces involving the seller; no repairs or improvements that have not been paid for; and that he or she is in possession of the premises. Through this affidavit the title company obtains the right to sue the seller if his or her statements in the affidavit prove incorrect.

Checking the Premises

It is important for the buyer to inspect the property to determine the interests of any parties in possession or other interests that cannot be determined from inspecting the public record. For example, a party in possession is considered as giving *constructive notice*, even if that person took possession under a deed that was never recorded. A survey is frequently required so that the purchaser knows the location, size, and legal description of the property. The contract should specify which party (usually the buyer) is to pay for this. It is usual for the survey to spot the location of buildings, driveways, fences, and other improvements on the premises being purchased, as well as any improvements on adjoining property that may encroach upon the premises. The survey also sets out in full any existing easements and encroachments. So that the survey clearly identifies the location of the property, the house number, if any, should be stated.

The buyer should also make a last-minute inspection before closing to check that the house remains in the condition originally presented and that the seller is leaving behind any appliances or other personal property stipulated in the written sales contract.

Releasing Existing Liens

When the purchaser is paying cash or is obtaining a new mortgage in order to purchase the property, the seller's existing mortgage usually is paid in full and released in the public record. To know the exact amount required to pay the existing mortgage, the seller secures a current *payoff statement* from the mortgagee. This payoff statement sets forth the unpaid amount of principal, interest due through the date of payment, any fee for issuing the release; credits, if any, for tax and insurance reserves; and any penalties that may be due because the loan is being prepaid before its maturity. The same procedure is followed for any other liens that must be released before the buyer takes title.

When the buyer is assuming the seller's existing mortgage loan, the buyer wants to know the exact balance of the loan as of the closing date. In some areas it is customary for the buyer to obtain a *mortgage reduction certificate* (sometimes inaccurately referred to as an estoppel certificate) from the lender, stating the exact balance due and the last interest payment made.

CLOSING IN ESCROW

In states in the western section of the country, the majority of transactions are closed in escrow, but the system is seldom used in New Jersey.

In an **escrow closing** a disinterested third party authorized to act as escrow agent coordinates the closing activities. The escrow agent may be an attorney, a title company, a trust company, an escrow company, or the escrow department of a lending institution. Buyer and seller choose an escrow agent and execute an escrow agreement after the sales contract is signed. This agreement sets forth the details of the transaction and the instructions to the escrow agent. Buyer and seller deposit all pertinent documents and other items with the escrow agent before the specified date of closing.

When all other conditions of the escrow agreement have been met, the agent is authorized to disburse the purchase price to the seller and to record the deed and mortgage (if a new mortgage has been executed by the purchaser).

PREPARATION OF CLOSING STATEMENTS

A typical real estate sales transaction involves numerous expenses for both parties in addition to the purchase price. There are a number of property expenses that the seller pays in advance for a set period of time or that the buyer pays in the future. The financial responsibility for these items must be *prorated* (adjusted proportionately) between the buyer and the seller. In closing a transaction it is customary to account for all these items by preparing a written statement to determine how much money the buyer needs and how much the seller will net after the broker's commission and expenses. There are many different formats of closing, or settlement, statements, but all are designed to achieve the same results.

Closing statements are prepared by the buyer's and seller's attorneys, title officers, or bank representatives. The broker should, however, possess the necessary knowledge to prepare statements so as to give the seller an accurate estimate of sale costs. In addition, the buyer must be prepared with the proper amount of money to complete the purchase and, again, the broker should be able to assist by making a reasonably accurate estimate.

How the Closing Statement Works

The completion of a **closing statement** involves an accounting of the parties' debits and credits. A **debit** is a charge, an amount that the party being debited owes and must pay at the closing. A **credit** is an amount entered in a person's favor—either an amount that the party already has paid, an amount that the party must be reimbursed for, or an amount the buyer promises to pay in the form of a loan.

To determine the amount the buyer needs at the closing, the buyer's debits are totaled. Any expenses and prorated amounts for items prepaid by the seller are added to the purchase price. Then the buyer's credits are totaled. These would include the earnest money (already paid), the balance of the loan the buyer is obtaining or assuming, and the seller's share of any prorated items that the buyer will pay in the future. Finally, the total of the buyer's credits is subtracted from the total amount the buyer owes (debits) to arrive at the actual amount of cash the buyer must bring to the closing. The buyer usually brings a bank cashier's check or a certified personal check.

A similar procedure is followed to determine how much money the seller actually receives.

The seller's debits and credits are each totaled. The credits would include the purchase price plus the buyer's share of any prorated items that the seller has prepaid.

The seller's debits would include expenses, the seller's share of prorated items to be paid later by the buyer, and the balance of any mortgage loan or other lien that the seller is paying off. Finally, the total of the seller's charges is subtracted from the total credits to arrive at the amount the seller will receive.

Expenses

In addition to the payment of the sales price and the proration of taxes, interest, and the like, a number of other expenses and charges may be involved in a real estate transaction. The following items are among those that are commonly included.

Broker's Commission

Where no buyer's broker is involved, the commission is paid by the seller. When the buyer has specifically hired his or her own broker, that agent's commission is sometimes paid by the buyer. In many cases, however, the seller has already agreed to pay the buyer's broker.

Attorney's Fees

If either of the parties' attorneys is to be paid from the closing proceeds, that party is charged with the expense in the closing statement.

Recording Expenses

The *seller* usually pays for recording charges (filing fees) that are necessary to clear all defects and furnish the purchaser with a clear title in accordance with the terms of the contract. Items usually charged to the seller include the recording of satisfaction of mortgages, quitclaim deeds, affidavits, and satisfaction of construction lien claims.

The *purchaser* pays for recording charges incident to the actual transfer of title. Items usually charged to the purchaser include recording the deed that conveys title to the purchaser and a mortgage executed by the purchaser.

Transfer Tax

New Jersey taxes the sale price at the rates shown in Figure 21.3.

The **realty transfer fee** is always charged to the seller in a real estate transaction. The deed is taken to the county clerk's office for recording, the proper tax is paid, and the document is stamped or imprinted to indicate that the tax has been paid. Persons claiming the reduced tax rate must attach a separate affidavit to the deed at the time of recording.

Certain transfers, including gifts, are exempt from the transfer fee. Lower fees apply to sales by seniors, the blind or disabled, and sales of low-income to moderate-income housing. For more information, visit http://www.state.nj.us/treasury/taxation/lpt/rtffaqs.shtml.

Figure 21.3: New Jersey Realty Transfer Fees

Paid by the Seller			
Standard Transactions and New Construction:			
Sales Price up to and including $350,000		**Sales Price over $350,000**	
Up to first $150,000	$2.00 per $500	Up to first $150,000	$2.90 per $500
$150,000.01–$200,000	$3.35 per $500	$150,000.01–$200,000	$4.25 per $500
$200,000.01–$350,000	$3.90 per $500	$200,000.01–$550,000	$4.80 per $500
		$550,000.01–$850,000	$5.30 per $500
		$850,000.01–$1,000,000	$5.80 per $500
		Over $1,000,000	$6.05 per $500
Senior Citizens, Blind Persons, Disabled Persons & Low- and Moderate-Income Property:			
Sales Price up to and including $350,000		**Sales Price over $350,000**	
Up to first $150,000	$0.50 per $500	Up to first $150,000	$1.40 per $500
$150,000.01–$350,000	$1.25 per $500	$150,000.01–$550,000	$2.15 per $500
		$550,000.01–$850,000	$2.65 per $500
		$850,000.01–$1,000,000	$3.15 per $500
		Over $1,000,000	$3.40 per $500
Paid by the Buyer			
For real properties zoned for residential use, whether improved or not, if the purchase price is equal to or greater than $1,000,000, the buyer will pay a fee of 1.0% of the purchase price.			

Title Expenses

The responsibility for title expenses varies according to the contract, which usually follows local custom. If the buyer's attorney inspects the evidence or if the buyer purchases title insurance policies, the buyer is charged for these expenses. In some situations the title or abstract company is required to make two searches of the public records: the first showing the status of the seller's title on the date of the sales contract and the second continuing after the closing and through the date the purchaser's deed is recorded. In some areas the seller pays for the initial search and the purchaser pays for the "redate" charge. Elsewhere, the buyer pays for the full search.

Loan Fees

When the purchaser is securing a mortgage to finance the purchase, the lender (mortgage company or bank) usually charges a service charge or *origination fee*. The fee is a flat charge and is usually paid by the purchaser at the time the transaction is closed. Also, the buyer may be charged an *assumption fee* if he or she assumes the seller's existing financing and in some cases may pay discount points. The seller also may be charged discount points, as discussed in Unit 14.

Tax Reserves and Insurance Reserves (Escrows)

A *reserve* is a sum of money set aside to be used later for a particular purpose. The mortgage lender usually requires the borrower to establish and maintain a reserve so that the borrower has sufficient funds to pay general taxes and renew insurance when these items become due. To set up the reserve, the borrower is required to make a lump-sum payment to the lender when the mortgage money is paid out (usually at the time of closing). Thereafter, the borrower is required to pay into the reserve an amount equal to one month's portion of the *estimated* general tax and insurance premium as part of the monthly payment made to the mortgage company.

Additional Mortgage-Related Fees

An FHA borrower owes a lump sum for prepayment of the mortgage insurance premium (MIP) if it is not being financed as part of the loan. A VA mortgagor pays a 1.25% fee directly to the VA at closing. If a conventional loan carries private mortgage insurance, the buyer prepays one year's insurance premium at closing.

Appraisal Fees

When the buyer obtains a mortgage, it is customary for the lender to require an appraisal, for which the buyer pays.

Survey Fees

If the purchaser obtains new mortgage financing, he or she customarily pays the *survey fees*. In some cases the sales contract may require the seller to furnish a survey.

Prorations

Most closings involve the dividing of financial responsibility between the buyer and seller for such items as loan interest, taxes, rents, and fuel and utility bills. These allowances are called **prorations** or *adjustments*. Prorations are necessary to ensure that expenses are fairly divided between the seller and the buyer. For example, when taxes have been paid in advance, the seller is entitled to reimbursement at the closing. If the buyer assumes the seller's existing mortgage, the seller usually owes the buyer an allowance for accrued interest through the date of closing.

As interest is usually paid in **arrears** (at the *end* of the period for which it is due), each payment covers interest for the preceding month. At a mid-month closing, the seller who has not made the current month's payment might owe six weeks' back interest on a mortgage.

Accrued items are items to be prorated (such as water bills and interest on an assumed mortgage) that are owed by the seller but eventually will be paid by the buyer. The seller therefore gives the buyer credit for these items at closing.

Prepaid items are items to be prorated (such as taxes or fuel oil left in the tank) that have been prepaid by the seller but not fully earned (not fully used up). They are, therefore, credits to the seller.

General Rules for Prorating

The rules or customs governing the computation of prorations for the closing of a real estate sale vary.

- It is generally provided that the buyer owns the property on the closing date. In practice, however, *either buyer or seller may be charged with that day's expenses.*

- Mortgage interest, general real estate taxes, water taxes, and similar expenses are computed in some areas *by using 360 days in a year and 30 days in a month*. However, the rules in other areas provide for computing prorations *on the basis of the actual number of days in the calendar month of closing.*

■ *Special assessments* for such municipal improvements as sewers, water mains, or streets *are usually paid in annual installments over several years.* Sellers are sometimes required to pay off special assessments entirely. In other cases, buyers may agree to assume future installments.

■ *Rents* are usually adjusted on the basis of the *actual number of days in the month of closing.* It is customary for the seller to receive the rents for the day of closing and to pay all expenses for that day. If any rents for the current month are uncollected when the sale is closed, the buyer often agrees in the contract or by a separate letter to collect the rents if possible and remit a share to the seller.

■ *Security deposits* are generally *transferred by the seller to the buyer*; the tenant must be notified of the transfer of deposit.

■ Unpaid wages of building employees are *prorated if the sale is closed between wage payment dates.*

Accounting for Credits and Charges

The items that must be accounted for in the closing statement fall into two general categories.

1. Prorations or other amounts due to either the buyer or seller (credit to) and paid for by the other party (debit to)

2. Expenses or items paid by the seller or buyer (debit only)

Items Credited to Buyer (Most Are Debited to Seller)

■ Unpaid principal balance of outstanding mortgage being assumed by buyer*

■ Interest on existing assumed mortgage not yet paid (accrued)

■ Buyer's earnest money (not debited to seller)

■ Unearned portion of current rent collected in advance

■ Earned janitor's salary (and sometimes vacation allowance)

■ Tenants' security deposits*

■ Purchase-money mortgage if seller is financing

■ Unpaid water bills

■ Real estate taxes in arrears

Items Credited to Seller (Debited to Buyer)

■ Sales price*

■ Fuel oil on hand, usually figured at current market price (prepaid)

■ Insurance and tax reserve (if any) when outstanding mortgage is being assumed by buyer (prepaid)

■ Refund to seller of prepaid water charge and similar expenses

■ Portion of real estate tax paid in advance

Items marked by an asterisk (*) are not prorated; they are entered in full as listed.

The buyer's earnest money, while credited to the buyer, is not usually debited to the seller. The buyer receives a credit because he or she has already paid that amount toward the purchase price. Under the usual sales contract the money is held by the broker or attorney until the settlement, when it is included as part of the total amount due the seller. If the seller is paying off an existing loan and the buyer is obtaining a new one, these two items are accounted for with a debit only to the seller for the amount of the payoff and a credit only to the buyer for the amount of the new loan.

Accounting for Expenses

Expenses paid out of the closing proceeds are usually debited only to the party making the payment.

THE ARITHMETIC OF PRORATIONS

There are three basic methods of calculating prorations:

1.   The yearly charge is *divided by a 360-day year*, or 12 months of 30 days each.

2.   The monthly charge is *divided by the actual number of days in the month of closing* to determine the amount.

3.   The yearly charge is *divided by 365* to determine the daily charge. Then the actual number of days in the proration period is determined and this number is multiplied by the daily charge.

In some cases, when a sale is closed on the fifteenth of the month, the one-half-month's charge is computed by simply dividing the monthly charge in two.

The final proration figure varies slightly, depending on which computation method is used.

CLOSING

The seller's attorney is responsible for all details of the transaction that concern the title to the property, such as preparing the deed and making sure that any prior liens have been repaid. The buyer's attorney prepares the settlement statements and makes the necessary disbursements of the buyer's checks. It is usually the broker's responsibility to ensure that the parties appear at the designated time and place with the appropriate documents and that arrangements have been made for any special factors, such as a measurement of the seller's existing supply of heating fuel. Normally, the broker collects his or her commission at the closing.

In some areas of southern New Jersey buyers and sellers do not use attorneys, and real estate licensees take a more active role in closings. Title officers prepare the settlement sheet and conduct the closing.

OTHER DOCUMENTS AT CLOSING

Every real estate sale must be reported to the Internal Revenue Service by one of the following: the person conducting the closing, the seller's attorney, the buyer's attorney, the title company, or the real estate broker involved. The report must include the seller's name, address, and tax identification number, and the full sales price. The seller furnishes to the individual making the report a certificate showing his or her correct Social Security number or other tax identification number.

SUMMARY

The purpose of the recording acts is to give legal, public, and *constructive notice* to the world of parties' interests in real estate. Possession of real estate is generally interpreted as notice of the rights of the person in possession. *Actual notice* is knowledge acquired directly and personally.

Four forms of title evidence are commonly in use throughout the United States:

1. Abstract of title and lawyer's opinion
2. Owner's title insurance policy
3. Torrens certificate
4. Certificate of title

A deed is evidence that a grantor has conveyed his or her interest, but it does not prove that the grantor had any interest at all. Each of the forms of title evidence bears a date and is evidence up to and including that date. All forms of title evidence show the previous actions that affect the title. Each must be redated or continued or reissued to cover a more recent date. Title evidence shows whether a seller is conveying *marketable title*. Marketable title is generally one that is so free from significant defects that the purchaser can be assured against having to defend the title.

Closing a sale involves both title procedures and financial matters. The broker, as agent of the seller, is often present at the closing to see that the sale is actually concluded and to account for the earnest money deposit.

At the closing a buyer may be required to prove hazard insurance coverage to a lender. A standard *homeowner's insurance policy* covers fire, theft, and liability and can be extended to cover many types of less common risks. Another type of insurance, which covers personal property only, is available to those in apartments and condominiums. In addition to homeowner's insurance, the federal government makes flood insurance mandatory for people living in flood-prone areas who wish to obtain federally regulated or federally insured mortgage loans. Many homeowner's policies contain a *coinsurance clause* that requires the policyholder to maintain fire insurance in an amount equal to 80% of the replacement cost of the home. If this percentage is not met, the policyholder may not be reimbursed for the full repair costs in case of loss.

The federal *Real Estate Settlement Procedures Act (RESPA)* requires disclosure of all settlement costs when a residential real estate purchase is financed by a federally related mortgage loan. Three sections of RESPA are important to real estate licensees: Section 8 prohibits kickbacks, Section 9 prohibits lenders and sellers from requiring that the buyer/borrower use a particular title insurance company, and Section 10 limits the amount of money held in escrow to be used to pay property taxes, hazard insurance and other charges.

Usually the title company or buyer's attorney examines the title evidence to ensure that the seller's title is acceptable. The sale may be closed **in escrow** by a neutral third party or escrow agent. The actual amount to be paid by the buyer at the closing is computed by preparation of a *closing*, or settlement, *statement*. This lists the sales price, earnest money deposit, and all adjustments and *prorations* due between buyer and seller. The purpose of this statement is to determine the net amount due the seller at closing. The buyer reimburses the seller for *prepaid items* such as unused taxes or fuel oil. The seller credits the buyer for bills the seller owes that will be paid by the buyer (accrued items), such as unpaid water bills. The TILA-RESPA Integrated Disclosures (TRID) merged previous forms into two new required documents for home loans provided by federally-related first and second mortgages used to buy residential property: the Loan Estimate (LE) and the Closing Disclosure (CD).

USEFUL WEBSITES

U.S. HUD Settlement Statement: www.hud.gov/content/releases/hud-1.pdf

Closing Disclosure: http://files.consumerfinance.gov/f/201311_cfpb_kbyo_closing-disclosure.pdf

Loan Estimate: http://www.consumerfinance.gov/owning-a-home/loan-estimate/

KEY TERMS REVIEW

Match the number of each key term with the corresponding letter.

_____ 1. Abstract of title

_____ 2. Actual notice

_____ 3. Affidavit

_____ 4. Arrears

_____ 5. Attorney's opinion of title

_____ 6. Caveat emptor

_____ 7. Chain of title

_____ 8. Closing Disclosure

_____ 9. Constructive notice

_____ 10. Credit

_____ 11. Debit

_____ 12. Escrow closing

_____ 13. Evidence of title

_____ 14. Marketable title

_____ 15. Proration

_____ 16. Public records

_____ 17. TRID

_____ 18. Realty transfer fee

_____ 19. Suit to quiet title

_____ 20. Title insurance policy

_____ 21. Section 8

A. abstract, lawyer's opinion, Torrens certificate, or title insurance

B. an account of what the borrower paid and what the seller paid, or what was paid by others

C. after the end of period for which the payment is due

D. closing handled by a neutral third party

E. condensed history of all documents affecting a parcel of real estate

F. information one actually knows

G. information one could know by investigating

H. lawyer's statement after studying an abstract

I. let the buyer beware

J. money due and payable to one party at closing

K. money to be paid by one party at closing

L. sworn statement

M. title traced from each owner to the following one

N. county's collection of documents relating to real estate

O. court action to remove cloud on title

P. title company's guarantee of clear title

Q. federal law ensuring that buyer and seller receive a detailed accounting of funds at closing

R. tax due the State of New Jersey at closing

S. good or clear title reasonably free from defects

T. corrective distribution of future expenses

U. prohibits kickbacks

UNIT 21 REVIEW QUESTIONS

1. Public records may be inspected by
   A. anyone.
   B. New Jersey attorneys and abstractors only.
   C. attorneys, abstractors, and real estate licensees only.
   D. anyone who obtains a court order under the Freedom of Information Act.

2. The date and time a document was recorded establish which of the following?
   A. Priority
   B. Chain of title
   C. Subrogation
   D. Marketable title

3. An instrument affecting title to a parcel of real estate gives constructive notice to the world when it is filed with the
   A. city clerk.
   B. county recorder.
   C. secretary of state.
   D. title insurance company.

4. In New Jersey no deed may be recorded unless
   A. it has been acknowledged.
   B. the transfer fee has been paid.
   C. full consideration is stated.
   D. all of the above occur.

5. The principle of caveat emptor states that if the buyer buys into a title problem, the fault lies with the
   A. buyer.
   B. seller.
   C. broker.
   D. lender.

6. Which of the following is NOT acceptable proof of ownership?
   A. A Torrens certificate
   B. A title insurance policy
   C. An abstract and lawyer's opinion
   D. A deed signed by the last seller

7. In locations where the abstract system is used, an abstract is usually examined by the
   A. broker.
   B. abstract company.
   C. seller.
   D. attorney for the purchaser.

8. Proof of the kind of estate and liens against a parcel of real estate can usually be found through
   A. a recorded deed.
   B. a court suit for specific performance.
   C. one of the four evidences of title.
   D. a foreclosure suit.

9. A fee title insurance policy generally defends the property owner against problems arising from
   A. unrecorded documents.
   B. facts discoverable by survey.
   C. forged documents.
   D. all of the above.

10. If a property has encumbrances, it
    A. cannot be sold.
    B. can be sold only if title insurance is provided.
    C. cannot have a deed recorded without a survey.
    D. can be sold if a buyer agrees to take it subject to the encumbrances.

11. Mortgage title policies protect which parties against loss?
    A. Buyers
    B. Sellers
    C. Lenders
    D. Real estate licensees

12. A seller is frantic because she cannot find her deed and now wants to sell the property. The seller
    A. may need a suit to quiet title.
    B. will have to buy title insurance.
    C. does not need the deed if it had been recorded.
    D. should execute a replacement deed to herself.

13. Flood insurance is required for mortgaging property if it is
    A. a multiple dwelling.
    B. on a flood-prone area on a special map.
    C. owned by HUD.
    D. going to have title insurance.

14. Identify one of the RESPA requirements.
    A. Real estate agents must give borrowers the *Your Home Loan Toolkit* booklet within three days of the loan application.
    B. Lenders must give borrowers a good-faith estimate of the closing costs within three days of the loan date.
    C. The closing agent must allow the purchaser to inspect the Closing Disclosure at least two business days before closing.
    D. RESPA prohibits kickbacks or unearned fees but does not include fee splitting between cooperating brokers.

15. A mortgage reduction certificate is executed by a(n)
    A. abstract company.
    B. attorney.
    C. lending institution.
    D. grantor.

16. A buyer of a $150,000 home has paid $2,000 as earnest money and has a loan commitment for 70% of the purchase price. How much more cash does the buyer need?
    A. $35,000
    B. $43,000
    C. $45,000
    D. $47,000

17. At the closing, the seller's attorney gave credit to the buyer for certain accrued items. These items were
    A. bills relating to the property that have already been paid by the seller.
    B. bills relating to the property that the buyer will pay.
    C. the real estate broker's commission.
    D. costs of recording the deed.

18. The earnest money left on deposit with the broker is a
    A. credit to the seller.
    B. credit to the buyer.
    C. debit to the seller.
    D. debit to the buyer.

19. A building was purchased for $285,000, with 10% down and a loan for the balance. If the lender charged the buyer two discount points, how much cash did the buyer need to come up with at closing if the buyer incurred no other costs?
    A. $31,700
    B. $28,500
    C. $33,630
    D. $30,200

20. The year's town, county, and state taxes amount to $3,600 and have been paid ahead for the calendar year. If closing is set for June 15, which of the following is TRUE?
    A. Credit seller $1,640; debit buyer $1,960
    B. Credit seller $3,600; debit buyer $1,640
    C. Credit buyer $1,960; debit seller $1,960
    D. Credit seller $1,960; debit buyer $1,960

21. Under TRID rules, what is the time frame for the lender to provide the Closing Disclosure (CD) to the borrower/buyer?
    A. Three business days before closing
    B. Five business days before closing
    C. Five calendar days before closing
    D. At closing

22. The seller collected rent of $1,000, payable in advance, from the attic tenant on June 1. At the closing on June 15,
    A. the seller owes the buyer $1,000.
    B. the buyer owes the seller $1,500.
    C. the seller owes the buyer $500.
    D. the buyer owes the seller $500.

23. Security deposits should be listed on a closing statement as a credit to the
    A. buyer.
    B. seller.
    C. lender.
    D. broker.

24. An amount that one party owes to another and must pay at the closing is a(n)
    A. expense.
    B. debit.
    C. credit.
    D. fee.

25. An amount entered in a person's favor is referred to as a(n)
    A. expense.
    B. debit.
    C. credit.
    D. fee.

26. When a realty transfer fee is involved, who of the following is responsible for the payment?
    A. All-cash buyer
    B. A VA buyer
    C. Seller
    D. Split equally between seller and buyer

UNIT 22

Real Estate Mathematics

This review is designed to familiarize the student with some basic mathematical formulas that are most frequently used in the computations required on state licensing examinations. These same computations are also important in day-to-day real estate transactions. If you need additional help in working these problems, you may want to consult *Mastering Real Estate Math* (Dearborn).

LEARNING OBJECTIVES

When you have completed this unit, you will be able to accomplish the following.

> Solve common percentage problems.
> Calculate area and volume problems.

PERCENTAGES

Many real estate computations are based on the calculation of percentages. *Percent* means *per 100* or *per 100 parts*. For example, 50% means 50 parts of the possible 100 parts that make up the whole. Percentages greater than 100% contain more than one whole unit. Thus 163% is one whole and 63 parts of another whole. A whole is always expressed as 100%.

Unless a calculator with a percent key is being used, the percentage *must be converted either to a decimal or to a fraction*. To convert a percentage to a decimal, move the decimal two places to the left and drop the percent sign.

$$60\% = 0.60 \quad 175\% = 1.75$$

To change a percentage to a fraction, place the percentage over 100. For example:

$$50\% = \frac{50}{100}$$

These fractions may then be reduced to make it easier to work the problem. To reduce a fraction, determine the largest number by which both the numerator (the top number) and the denominator (the bottom number) can be evenly divided. For example:

$$\frac{50}{100} = \frac{1}{2} \text{ (both numbers divided by 50)}$$

Percentage problems contain three elements: *percentage, total,* and *part*. To determine a specific percentage of a whole, multiply the percentage by the whole.

percent × whole = part

5% × 200 = 10

EXAMPLE

A broker is to receive a 7% commission on the sale of a $100,000 house. What is the broker's commission?

0.07 × $100,000 = $7,000 broker's commission

This formula is used in calculating mortgage loan interests, broker's commissions, loan origination fees, discount points, amount of earnest money deposits, and income on capital investments.

A variation of the percentage formula is used to find the total amount when the part and percentage are known.

total = part ÷ percent

EXAMPLE

A realty company received a $4,500 commission for the sale of a house. The broker's commission was 6% of the total sales price. What was the total sales price of this house?

$4,500 ÷ 0.06 = $75,000 total sales price

This formula is used in computing the total mortgage loan principal still due if the monthly payment and interest rate are known. It is also used to calculate the total sales price when the amount and percentage of commission are known, and the market value of property if the assessed value and the ratio (percentage) of assessed value to market value are known.

The formula may be used by a real estate salesperson thus: a buyer has $30,000 available for a down payment, and she must make a 20% down payment. How expensive a home can she purchase? The question is: $30,000 is 20% of what figure?

$30,000 ÷ 0.20 = $150,000

One type of percentage problem, which may take several forms, is often found on licensing examinations.

EXAMPLE

A man sold property for $180,000. This represents a 20% loss from his original cost. What was his cost?

In this problem the student must resist the impulse to multiply everything in sight. Taking 20% of $180,000 yields nothing significant. The $180,000 figure represents 80% of the original cost and the question resolves itself into $180,000 is 80% of what figure?

$180,000 ÷ 0.80 = $225,000

EXAMPLE

A seller clears $160,200 from the sale of her property after paying a 10% commission. How much did the property sell for? Taking 10% of $160,200 is an incorrect approach to the problem, because the commission was based not on the seller's net but on the full, unknown sales figure; $160,200 represents 90% of the sales price.

$160,200 ÷ 0.90 = $178,000
$160,200 = $178,000 × 0.90

To determine the percentage when the amounts of the part and the total are known:

percent = part ÷ total

This formula may be used to find the tax rate when taxes and assessed value are known or the commission rate if sales price and commission amount are known.

RATES

Property taxes, transfer taxes, and insurance premiums are usually expressed as rates. A rate is the cost expressed as the amount of cost per unit. For example, tax might be computed at the rate of $5 per $100 assessed value. The formula for computing rates is:

value ÷ unit × rate per unit = total

EXAMPLE

A house has been assessed at $90,000 and is taxed at an annual rate of $2.50 per $100 assessed valuation. What is the yearly tax?

_____ × $2.50 = total annual tax

$90,000 ÷ $100 = 900 (increments of $100)

900 × $2.50 = $2,250 total annual tax

Helpful Hint: Any problem that has either a rate or a percentage as one of its elements can be solved using the following formula:

part = rate × base

The **PRB** circle can help you remember this:

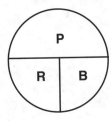 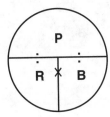

To solve for an unknown element in the circle, multiply sideways for the top number; divide the top number by one of the bottom ones for the other bottom number. When figuring out what to put where in the circle, it is always easiest to first identify **R**, which is always a percentage or identified by the word *rate*. Once this is done, decide whether the missing number is going to be the larger or the smaller of the two remaining sums: in most cases, if it is *bigger*, it is the *base* and goes on the *bottom*; if is *smaller*, it is the *part* and goes on *top*. An exception to this rule is in the calculation of *depreciation*; in that case, remember that the base is the starting value and that amount is higher than the depreciated final dollar amount. A second exception to this rule is in the calculation of *profit*; in that case, remember that the base is the original amount invested and that amount is lower than the final part.

EXAMPLE

A home was purchased a year ago for $172,300. Property in the neighborhood is said to be increasing in value at a rate of 3% annually. What is the current market value of the real estate?

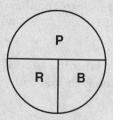

In this case, the base is the original purchase price of the home, $172,300. The increase of 3% is not the rate (it would be if the question asked how much the house appreciated); the rate we need to use is what the house is now worth, which is 103% of the original value.

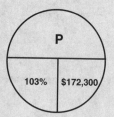

Because the rule is to multiply sideways,

1.03 × $172,300 = $177,469 present value

EXAMPLE

A home was purchased a year ago for $98,500. Property in the neighborhood is said to be decreasing in value at a rate of 5% annually. What is the current market value of the real estate?

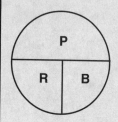

In this case, the base is the original purchase price of the home, $98,500. The decrease of 5% is not the rate (it would be if the question asked how much the house depreciated); the rate we need to use is what the house is now worth, which is 95% of the original value.

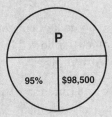

Because the rule is to multiply sideways,

0.95 × $98,500 = $93,575 present value

If the same house had increased in value 5%, our rate in the circle would be 105%, and the solution would be:

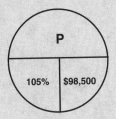

1.05 × $98,500 = $103,425 present value

The **IRV** formula, presented in Unit 16, is basic to investment problems. It is really the same as the **PRB** formula:

income = rate × value

It, too, can be expressed as a circle:

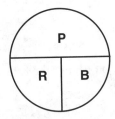 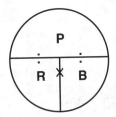

EXAMPLE

An investor wants to make an offer on an apartment building whose annual income is $225,000 after deducting for expenses. To go through with the purchase, the investor insists on a 10% capitalization rate. What is the most she would pay for the property?

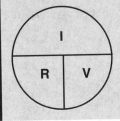 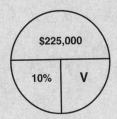

> Because we divide top by bottom:
>
> $225,000 ÷ 0.10 = $2,250,000

Helpful Hint: These problems are especially easy to do on a calculator. In the last example, enter 225000 then hit the divide key ÷ and then enter 10 followed by the percent key %, the calculator reads 2250000 and the decimal is in the correct place.

Important Point: In any IRV or PRB problem, the rate (interest, appreciation, etc.) is usually an *annual rate*, and income is annual income. If monthly income is given, multiply it by 12 before using it in the circle.

EXAMPLE

A woman owns a four-family home. Rents are $525, $575, $600, and $650 a month. Her operating expenses average $375 a month. If investors expect a cap rate of 11%, what should she expect to receive for the property?

First, add all the rents and subtract the expenses:

$525 + $575 + $600 + $650 − $375 = $1,975

Then multiply by 12 to calculate *I*, which is the *annual net operating income*:

$1,975 × 12 = $23,700

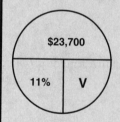

$23,700 ÷ 0.11 = $215,454.54

AREA AND VOLUME

To compute the area of a square or rectangular parcel, use the formula:

width × length = area

The area of a rectangular lot that measures 100 feet wide by 200 feet deep is:

100' × 200' = 20,000 square feet

The first figure given always represents *front feet*; a lot described as "80' × 150'" is 80 feet across and 150 feet deep. *Area is always expressed in square units.*

To compute the amount of surface in a triangular-shaped area, use the formula:

area = base × height ÷ 2

The base of a triangle is the bottom, on which the triangle rests. The height is an imaginary straight line extending from the point of the uppermost angle straight down to the base:

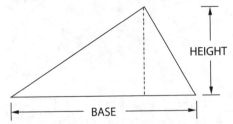

EXAMPLE

A triangle's base is 50 feet, and its height is 30 feet. What is its area?

50' × 30' ÷ 2 = area in square feet

1,500 × 2 = 750 square feet

To compute the area of an irregular room or parcel of land, divide the shape into regular rectangles, squares, or triangles. Next, compute the area of each regular figure and add the areas together to obtain the total area.

EXAMPLE

Compute the area of the hallway shown in the next column.

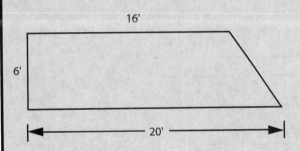

Make a rectangle and a triangle by drawing a single line through the figure.

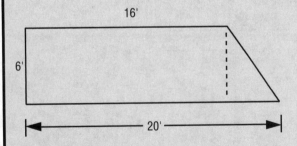

Compute the area of the rectangle.

area = length × width

16' × 6' = 96 square feet

Compute the area of the triangle.

area = ½ (base × height)

½ (4' × 6') = ½ (24) = 12 square feet

Total the two areas.

96 + 12 = 108 square feet total area

EXAMPLE

Compute the area of the following figure.

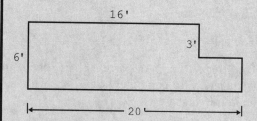

Make two rectangles by drawing a single line through the figure.

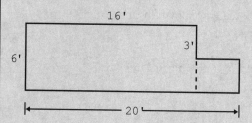

Now you can fill in the missing dimensions.

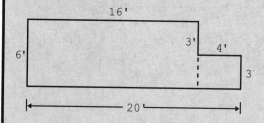

Compute the area of the 2 rectangles:

area = length × width

16' × 6' = 96 square feet

4' × 3' = 12 square feet

Total the two areas.

96 + 12 = 108 square feet total area

The cubic capacity of an enclosed space is expressed as volume, which is used to describe the amount of space in any three-dimensional area, for example, an ice *cube*, or in measuring the interior airspace of a room to determine what capacity heating unit is required. The formula for computing cubic or rectangular volume is:

volume = length × width × height

Volume is always expressed in cubic units.

EXAMPLE

The bedroom of a house is 12 feet long, 8 feet wide, and has a ceiling height of 8 feet. How many cubic feet does the room enclose?

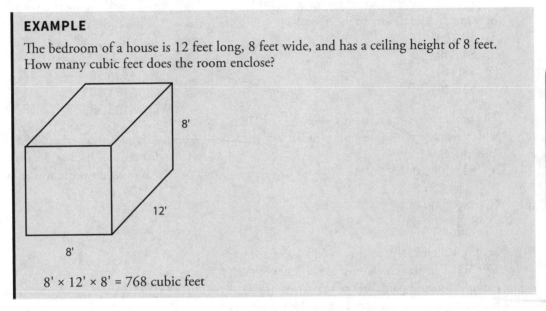

8' × 12' × 8' = 768 cubic feet

Cubic measurements of volume are used to compute the construction costs per cubic foot of a building, the amount of airspace being sold in a condominium unit, or the heating and cooling requirements for a building. When either area or volume is computed, *all dimensions used must be given in the same unit of measure.* For example, one may not multiply two feet by six inches to get the area; two feet must be multiplied by ½ foot, or 24 inches by 6 inches. Thus it is important to remember that:

12 inches = 1 foot

3 feet = 1 yard

1 square yard = 3 × 3 = 9 square feet

cubic yard = 3 × 3 × 3 = 27 cubic feet

LAND UNITS AND MEASUREMENTS

Some commonly used land units and measurements follow.

- A *rod* is 16½ feet.
- A *chain* is 66 feet, or 100 links.
- A *mile* is 5,280 feet.
- An *acre* contains 43,560 square feet. **Memorize this one**.
- A *section* of land (in the government survey method) is one square mile and contains 640 acres; a *quarter section* contains 160 acres; a *quarter of a quarter section* contains 40 acres.
- A circle contains 360 degrees; a *quarter segment* of a circle contains 90 degrees; a *half segment* of a circle contains 180 degrees. One *degree* (1°) can be subdivided into *60 minutes* (60'), each of which contains 60 *seconds* (60"). One-and-a-half degrees would be written 1°30'0".

UNIT 22 REVIEW QUESTIONS

Commissions

1. A salesperson works on a 50/50 commission split with her broker. If she lists a house at $146,000 for 6% commission and sells it for $144,000, how much does the salesperson receive?
   A. $8,760
   B. $4,380
   C. $8,340
   D. $4,320

2. The broker's commission on a sale was $14,100, which was 6% of the sales price. What was the sales price?
   A. $235,000.00
   B. $154,255.31
   C. $846,000.00
   D. $234,500.00

3. Happy Valley Realty recently sold a home for $79,500. The broker charged the sellers a 6½% commission and paid 30% of that amount to the listing salesperson and 25% to the selling salesperson. What amount of commission did the listing salesperson receive from the sale of this home?
   A. $5,167.50
   B. $1,550.25
   C. $3,617.25
   D. $1,291.87

4. A salesperson receives a monthly salary of $500 plus 3% commission on all of his listings that sell and 2.5% on all his sales. None of the listings that the salesperson took sold last month, but he received $3,675 in salary and commission. What was the value of the property sold by this salesperson?
   A. $147,000
   B. $127,000
   C. $122,500
   D. $105,833

Insurance and Taxes

5. The home on Dove Street is valued at $95,000. Property in the area is assessed at 60% of its value and the local tax rate is $2.85 per hundred. What is the amount of the monthly taxes for this home?
   A. $1,111.50
   B. $926.30
   C. $111.15
   D. $135.38

6. A house is valued at $98,000. It is to be insured for 80% of its cost. Insurance costs $0.60 per $100. What is the annual insurance premium?
   A. $470.40
   B. $47.04
   C. $588.00
   D. $58.80

Investment

7. Four investors pooled their savings and purchased a vacation home for $125,000. If one person invested $30,000 and two others each contributed $35,000, what percentage of ownership was left for the fourth investor?
   A. 20%
   B. 24%
   C. 28%
   D. 30%

8. An investor bought a building lot for $45,000 and sold it two years later for a 15% profit. How much did it sell for?
   A. $51,750
   B. $52,941
   C. $54,450
   D. $58,500

9. A house was listed for $249,999. The buyers offered $225,000, the sellers countered with $235,000, which the buyers accepted. The buyers are making a down payment of 20% and financing the rest at 5.25% for 30 years. How much will their monthly principal and interest payment be? (For reference, see Figure 14.4.)
   A. $1,039.64
   B. $1,106.99
   C. $1,244.50
   D. $1,299.50

10. The landlord leases the 13 apartments in the Overton Arms for a total monthly rental of $4,500. If this figure represents an 8% annual return on the landlord's investment, what was the original cost of the property?
    A. $675,000
    B. $450,000
    C. $54,000
    D. $56,250

Seller's Net

11. The seller received a net amount of $168,000 from the sale of his house after paying $1,200 in legal and other fees and 6% sales commission. What was the selling price of the house?
    A. $180,000
    B. $178,080
    C. $179,200
    D. $179,280

12. The sellers receive two offers for their property at the same time. The first buyers offer $95,000 all cash. The second buyers offer $100,000 subject to obtaining a conventional mortgage loan with 20% down payment and ask the sellers to pay three points to their lending institution. The sellers decide to accept the all-cash offer. If they had accepted the second buyers' offer instead, they would have received
    A. $2,600 more at closing.
    B. $2,000 more at closing.
    C. $2,400 less at closing.
    D. $3,000 less at closing.

Financing

13. An FHA loan on a house priced between $50,000 and $100,000 requires a loan-to-value ratio of no more than 97.76%. If the buyer is financing the purchase of a $95,000 house with an FHA loan, how much cash must she have for a down payment?
    A. $976.60
    B. $2,128
    C. $2,240
    D. $9,766

14. A lending institution allows its borrowers to spend 25% of their income for housing expense. What is the maximum monthly payment allowed for a family with an annual income of $37,000 and no other debts?
    A. $9,250
    B. $770.83
    C. $925
    D. None of the above

15. A man's monthly mortgage payment for principal and interest is $628.12. His property taxes are $1,800 a year, and his annual insurance premium is $365. What is his total monthly payment of PITI (principal, interest, taxes, and insurance)?
    A. $808.54
    B. $1,921.24
    C. $778.12
    D. None of the above

16. A first-time buyer is purchasing a home for $129,500. His lender requires a 20% down payment and 2 points at closing. In addition, the buyer has $750 in closing costs. What is the total amount he needs to close?
    A. $25,900
    B. $28,490
    C. $28,722
    D. $29,240

17. The buyers offer to buy a house for $120,000 and seek a fixed-rate loan of $90,000 for 25 years. One lender offers them a 10% loan with no points, monthly payments of $817.85. A second lender requires two points for a 9.5% loan, with monthly payments of $786.35. If the buyers decide to pay the points and take the lower-interest loan, how long will it take before the savings on their lower payments have made up for that extra cost at closing?
    A. Two years, eight months
    B. Three years, two months
    C. Four years, nine months
    D. Seven years, four months

18. A father is curious to know how much money his son and daughter-in-law still owe on their mortgage loan. He knows that the interest portion of their last monthly payment was $391.42. If the owners are paying interest at the rate of 7%, what was the outstanding balance of their loan before that last payment was made?
    A. $46,970.50
    B. $67,100.57
    C. $135,640.02
    D. $273,994.00

19. A 30-year fixed-rate amortized mortgage for $100,000 at 7% interest requires monthly payments of $665.30. What is the total amount of interest paid on this loan during the life of the mortgage?
    A. $139,508
    B. $239,508
    C. $258,106
    D. $665,300

20. In a sale of residential property, real estate taxes for the current year amounted to $975 and have already been paid by the seller. The sale is to be closed on October 27. What is the amount of real estate proration to be credited the seller?
    A. $173.33
    B. $162.50
    C. $798.96
    D. $83.96

21. The buyer is assuming the seller's mortgage with an interest rate of 5%. The unpaid balance after the most recent payment was $161,550. The seller made the payment due September 1 and the sale is to be closed on September 23. What is the amount of mortgage interest proration to be credited to the buyer at the closing?
    A. $113.08
    B. $493.64
    C. $807.75
    D. None, the buyer owes the seller.

Area

22. If the frontage of a half-acre lot is 75 feet, how deep is it?
    A. 189 feet
    B. 272 feet
    C. 290 feet
    D. 346 feet

23. A rectangular lot measures 60 feet wide and has an area of 1,200 square yards. What is the length of the lot?
    A. 20 feet
    B. 180 feet
    C. 20 yards
    D. 90 yards

24. A five-acre lot has front footage of 300 feet. How long is it?
    A. 145.2 feet
    B. 726 feet
    C. 88 feet
    D. 160 feet

25. A buyer signed an agreement to purchase a condominium apartment. The contract stipulated that the sellers replace the damaged bedroom carpet. The carpet the buyer has chosen costs $16.95 per square yard plus $2.50 per square yard for installation. If the bedroom dimensions are as illustrated, how much will the sellers have to pay for the job?

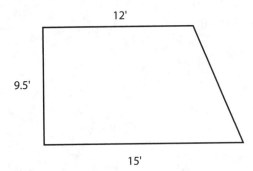

A. $241.54
B. $189.20
C. $277.16
D. $2,494.46

26. A lot measuring 120' × 200' is selling for $300 a front foot. What is its price?
A. $720,000
B. $60,000
C. $36,000
D. $800,000

27. A 100-acre farm is divided into house lots. The streets require one-eighth of the whole farm, and there are 140 lots. How many square feet are there in each lot?
A. 35,004
B. 31,114
C. 27,225
D. 43,560

28. If building requirements call for a 25' setback for a building, 10' on each side, and 15' from the rear property line, what is the buildable area in square feet for a lot that is 150' × 200'?
A. 3,000
B. 18,000
C. 20,800
D. 30,000

29. The property owner intends to put up a fence between his lot and his neighbor's. The fencing comes in six-foot sections. For a fence 120 feet long, how many fence posts are required?
A. 19
B. 20
C. 21
D. 22

30. When a residence has proved difficult to sell, the salesperson suggests it might sell faster if they enclose a portion of the backyard with a privacy fence. If the area to be enclosed is as illustrated, how much would the fence cost at $6.95 per linear foot?

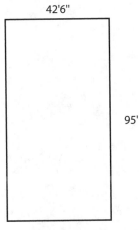

A. $1,911.25
B. $1,654.10
C. $1,615.88
D. $955.63

Miscellaneous

31. The buyers agree to a purchase price of $200,000 and make a 5% earnest money deposit. Ten days later the buyers give an additional $20,000 toward the purchase price. What is their balance due in cash at closing if they are securing an 80% loan-to-value mortgage?
A. $5,000
B. $10,000
C. $20,000
D. $25,000

32. A property closes on June 7. The annual taxes of $775 and a special assessment of $86 for the current calendar year had been paid in full on January 1. If these payments are prorated, what amount is returned to the seller?
    A. $373
    B. $416
    C. $488
    D. $508

33. A percentage lease calls for $460 a month rent, plus 4.5% of the annual gross over $100,000. If the business paid $7,780 last year, what was the gross income of the business?
    A. $110,170
    B. $150,222
    C. $262,207
    D. $272,889

34. An investor buys a small rental property on January 1 for $300,000, with the land accounting for 20% of its value. The IRS allows him to depreciate the building over a period of 27½ years. How much can the investor charge on his tax return as an expense?
    A. $6,000
    B. $8,727.27
    C. $10,909.09
    D. $24,000

CUMULATIVE REVIEW QUIZZES

Units 1 through 8

1. Someone who lives outside of New Jersey can be licensed as a nonresident broker if he or she
   A. posts a bond of $5,000.
   B. is a citizen of the United States.
   C. finds a New Jersey sponsor.
   D. consents to being sued in New Jersey.

2. By the time she received her broker's license, the licensee had studied real estate for at LEAST
   A. 75 hours.
   B. 90 hours.
   C. 165 hours.
   D. 225 hours.

3. In New Jersey, real estate licenses are administered by the
   A. local board of REALTORS®.
   B. Real Estate Commission.
   C. Department of Commerce.
   D. Bureau of Subdivided Land Control.

4. The authorized broker for a real estate company is officially called the
   A. broker-salesperson.
   B. Realtor®.
   C. supervisor.
   D. broker of record.

5. Licensing fee for a beginning salesperson, including application fee, criminal history check, and Guaranty Fund fee, is
   A. $75.
   B. $160.
   C. $270.
   D. $288.

6. A broker may agree to share commission with
   A. any licensed salesperson.
   B. a mortgage broker.
   C. a friend who refers a seller.
   D. any licensed broker.

7. A broker must deposit clients' or customers' deposits in
   A. a separate bank account for each person's money.
   B. the broker's business account, not a personal account.
   C. a trust or escrow account.
   D. the broker's file with the Real Estate Commission.

8. A licensed salesperson is allowed to prepare a sales contract for
   A. a shopping plaza.
   B. one-family to four-family residences.
   C. any real estate.
   D. single houses only.

9. Continuing education requires how many classroom hours?
   A. 12
   B. 14
   C. 16 for salespeople and 4 for brokers
   D. None for longtime brokers, who are exempted

10. A broker who mixes personal money with funds in the trust account is guilty of
    A. revocation.
    B. guilty knowledge.
    C. escrow.
    D. commingling.

11. All sales contracts prepared by licensees must
    A. contain the Attorney General's memorandum against discrimination.
    B. contain the Notice to Buyer and Seller.
    C. contain the Waiver of Broker Cooperation form.
    D. mention the buyer's purchase of insurance.

12. Any changes to a document after the initial signing should be
    A. initialed by all parties.
    B. filed in the public records.
    C. okayed by the broker of record.
    D. submitted to the parties' attorneys.

13. A licensee working as a transaction broker serves as agent for
    A. the buyer.
    B. the seller.
    C. the Real Estate Commission.
    D. no one. ✓

14. A broker-salesperson may
    A. sponsor an applicant for a salesperson's license.
    B. work as a salesperson under the supervision of a broker of record. ✓
    C. collect his or her own real estate fees.
    D. act as a broker of record.

15. Losing land by erosion is the opposite of gaining land through
    A. avulsion.
    B. accretion. ✓
    C. reliction.
    D. hereditament.

16. Personalty is also known as
    A. real property.
    B. littoral rights.
    C. trade fixtures.
    D. chattels. ✓

17. Real property can be changed to personal property through the process known as
    A. severance.
    B. accession.
    C. conversion.
    D. alluvion.

18. Intent of the parties and method of attachment are two of the tests of a(n)
    A. chattel.
    B. fixture.
    C. trade fixture.
    D. improvement.

19. Trade fixtures differ from regular fixtures in that they are
    A. removable. ✓
    B. permanently affixed.
    C. the property of the landowner.
    D. considered part of the real estate.

20. The attorney assures her client that no one else has a claim to the real estate she is buying and that she has a complete bundle of rights in the property. The client is receiving a
    A. fee simple estate. ✓
    B. leasehold estate.
    C. life estate.
    D. fee determinable estate.

21. A woman deeds her vacation cottage to her elderly uncle, with the provision that at his death, she will automatically become the owner again. During his lifetime, the woman owns a
    A. remainder interest.
    B. reversionary interest.
    C. life estate. ✓
    D. dower estate.

22. A mortgage is a type of
    A. general lien.
    B. encroachment.
    C. voluntary lien.
    D. license.

23. If a husband owns the family home in his own name, he can sell it without his wife's signature if
    A. he bought it before they were married.
    B. he bought it before May 28, 1980. ✓
    C. his wife owns property of equal value in her own name.
    D. they live in some other state, but not in New Jersey.

24. If a parcel of real estate has two mortgages on it, priority is given to the one first
    A. drawn up.
    B. signed.
    C. notarized.
    D. recorded. ✓

25. The term "conveying" property means
    A. having it surveyed.
    B. transferring ownership. ✓
    C. mortgaging it.
    D. tacking usage.

26. Ownership of real estate by one person alone is known as
    A. severalty. ✓
    B. tenancy in common.
    C. survivorship.
    D. sole proprietorship.

27. The buyer of a condominium apartment receives
    A. a proprietary lease.
    B. an individual property tax bill.
    C. stock that is considered personal property.
    D. a life estate.

28. A New Jersey couple buys a home together soon after they are married, with nothing specific stated in the deed about their ownership. The husband, who paid for the house, is killed in a car crash. His widow now owns
    A. the whole house only if he left his half to her in his will.
    B. nothing because she furnished none of the purchase price herself.
    C. the whole house in severalty.
    D. half, with their children owning the other half.

29. Either co-owner may go to court and ask that property be divided EXCEPT in the case of
    A. tenants in common.
    B. joint tenants.
    C. life tenants.
    D. tenants by the entirety.

30. A couple bought their oceanfront home in 1954 for $17,000. This year they decided to move to Florida, and they sold the house for $325,000. The IRS says their profit will be
    A. taxed as ordinary income.
    B. taxed at favorable capital gains rates.
    C. subject to tax on only $75,000.
    D. completely free from any federal tax.

31. New Jersey offers partial exemptions from property taxes to eligible
    A. veterans.
    B. single mothers.
    C. government employees.
    D. widows.

32. A special assessment is a form of property tax used to pay for a(n)
    A. deficit in a town or county's budget.
    B. one-time tax on the transfer of real estate.
    C. building fund for a school or library.
    D. improvement like sidewalks in a certain area.

33. A home is worth $160,000 and the town assessments run at 60% of market value. If the tax rate is 37 mills, how much is the property tax bill?
    A. $592
    B. $2,368
    C. $3,552
    D. $5,920

34. The lien with priority on a given parcel of real estate would usually be
    A. a mortgage recorded five years ago.
    B. a mortgage recorded this year.
    C. the current year's property taxes.
    D. a judgment filed four years ago.

35. *Redlining* is defined as
    A. steering home seekers to a particular neighborhood.
    B. drawing red lines on a local map indicating where the agent wants to look for listings.
    C. denying or restricting loans in a certain neighborhood.
    D. a zoning procedure.

36. The provisions of the Civil Rights Act of 1866
    A. prohibit any type of discrimination based on race and color.
    B. prohibit discrimination in federally funded housing.
    C. allow an exception for an owner-occupied two-family house.
    D. do not apply to nonlicensed persons.

37. Federal civil rights legislation forbids housing discrimination based on
    A. political affiliation.
    B. source of income.
    C. country of origin.
    D. pet ownership.

38. Although a property owner may be exempted sometimes from discrimination laws, a real estate licensee
    A. is exempt only if he or she is also the owner.
    B. can list the property for sale noting the exemption.
    C. can advertise the noted exemption.
    D. may not participate in the transaction in any way.

39. Using scare tactics regarding the possible change in the makeup of a neighborhood while soliciting for listings is called
    A. redlining.
    B. steering.
    C. blockbusting.
    D. harassment.

40. A woman is advertising for a tenant for the other half of her home. Which of these ads would violate fair housing laws?
    A. No pets
    B. No smokers
    C. No children
    D. None of the above

41. Which of the following is permitted under the federal Fair Housing Act?
    A. Advertising property for sale "suitable for" a special ethnic group
    B. Altering the terms of a loan for a member of a minority race
    C. Refusing to sell a home to a foreign-born homeseeker because of a poor credit history
    D. Telling nervous owners in a changing neighborhood to sell before their houses lose value

42. The New Jersey Law Against Discrimination adds to the protected classes under federal fair housing law
    A. members of political parties.
    B. people with prison records.
    C. welfare recipients.
    D. marital status.

43. For someone specifically retained as a buyer's broker, sellers would be in the position of
    A. clients.
    B. principals.
    C. customers.
    D. employers.

44. A broker's principal is the one who
    A. pays the commission.
    B. is the seller.
    C. hires the agent.
    D. brings about the meeting of the minds.

45. In New Jersey, the broker who wishes to offer services without owing fiduciary duties to either buyer or seller is allowed to function as a(n)
    A. transaction broker.
    B. broker's agent.
    C. independent contractor.
    D. attorney-in-fact.

46. A seller's broker is legally bound to disclose information to a potential buyer about a latent defect such as
    A. a previous suicide on the property.
    B. a rock band that rents the neighboring house.
    C. the fact that the seller has AIDS.
    D. an unused buried oil tank in the back yard.

47. The listing broker must advise a seller about the firm's plan to
    A. hold open houses.
    B. share or not share the commission with another broker who produces the buyer.
    C. reveal confidential information to other brokers.
    D. withhold information about felonies committed on the premises.

48. Which of these comments would be a breach of fiduciary duties?
    A. "Most beautiful house in town."
    B. "Handyman special."
    C. "Just listed."
    D. "Try bidding low."

49. If the buyers confide to a listing agent that "we'll offer $250,000, but if they don't take that we're prepared to go higher," the agent's duty is to
    A. remind the buyers that a seller's agent owes them no duty of confidentiality.
    B. keep the information to himself or herself.
    C. help persuade the seller to accept the offer.
    D. refuse to draw up the purchase offer.

50. The listing agent who tells sellers that "commission rates are standard in this community" is in violation of the
    A. New Jersey Real Estate Licensing Law.
    B. NAR Code of Ethics.
    C. Sherman Antitrust Act.
    D. Off-Site Conditions Disclosure Act.

Units 9 through 15

1. The Environmental Protection Agency requires that buyers of homes built before 1978 receive warnings about possible dangers of
   A. radon.
   B. electromagnetic fields.
   C. groundwater contamination.
   D. lead paint.

2. It is relatively easy to solve problems caused by the presence of
   A. asbestos.
   B. underground storage tanks.
   C. lead paint.
   D. radon.

3. Condemnation is the court process by which the state enforces its power of
   A. master planning.
   B. eminent domain.
   C. escheat.
   D. exclusionary zoning.

4. When someone dies without a will or any natural heirs, the state acquires his or her property through the power of
   A. eminent domain.
   B. condemnation.
   C. taxation.
   D. escheat.

5. New Jersey's Mt. Laurel decisions were concerned with
   A. exclusionary zoning.
   B. urea-formaldehyde foam insulation.
   C. eminent domain.
   D. certificates of occupancy.

6. A certificate of occupancy is issued by
   A. a zoning board of appeals.
   B. the Department of Environmental Protection.
   C. a building inspector.
   D. the Board of Adjustment.

7. It is important to remember that deed restrictions are placed on property by the
   A. zoning board.
   B. seller.
   C. state.
   D. municipal government.

8. A subdivision has deed restrictions stating that homes can be built only on five-acre lots, although the town itself requires only one-third acre lots. A man buys one acre in the subdivision. Can he obtain a building permit from the town?
   A. Yes, and his neighbors in the subdivision cannot do anything to stop his building.
   B. No, because the building department must observe the deed restriction.
   C. Yes, but the neighbors can ask a court to enforce the restriction and order his house torn down.
   D. No, because his lot is larger than the legal one-third acre.

9. The seller who wishes to cancel a listing
   A. must cite a legally acceptable reason.
   B. may not cancel without the agent's agreement.
   C. may be held liable for money the agent spent advertising the listing.
   D. may not sell the property for six months afterward.

10. All listing agreements are made between the homeseller and the
    A. salesperson who deals directly with the seller.
    B. firm's broker of record.
    C. local multiple listing service.
    D. transaction broker.

11. The seller owes a commission only to whichever broker produces an acceptable buyer with what type of listing?
    A. Open
    B. Exclusive-agency
    C. Net
    D. Exclusive-right-to-sell

12. The owner retains the right to sell without paying a commission to the one agent hired, with what type of listing?
    A. Open
    B. Exclusive-agency
    C. Net
    D. Exclusive-right-to-sell

13. The seller's agreement with her agent is that she receives $300,000 when her house is sold, and the agent can keep anything more that he can get. This owner has signed what type of illegal listing?
    A. Open
    B. Exclusive-agency
    C. Net
    D. Exclusive-right-to-sell

14. A comparative market analysis is used to
    A. aid the seller in setting the listing price.
    B. inform clients about local commission rates.
    C. submit a listing to the multiple listing service.
    D. determine the true tax figure.

15. The seller owes a commission to the listing agent no matter who sells the property with what type of listing?
    A. Open
    B. Exclusive-agency
    C. Net
    D. Exclusive-right-to-sell

16. The term "liquidated damages" refers to
    A. money that can be retained by the seller if the buyer defaults for no good reason.
    B. the consideration necessary for a valid contract.
    C. equitable title.
    D. novation.

17. The real estate broker is MOST motivated to invest time and effort on a(n)
    A. open listing.
    B. exclusive-agency listing.
    C. exclusive-right-to-sell listing.
    D. comparative market analysis.

18. The amount of commission split that the listing broker intends to offer a cooperating broker who finds a successful buyer must be revealed to
    A. no one except the cooperating broker.
    B. the seller.
    C. the Justice Department.
    D. the Real Estate Commission.

19. A comparative market analysis should take into consideration the
    A. seller's original cost.
    B. tax assessment figure.
    C. amount the seller has invested in improvements.
    D. recent sale prices of nearby homes.

20. If a sales contract is prepared by a salesperson or broker, the buyer and the seller each have how long in which to obtain review by their attorneys?
    A. 24 hours
    B. 3 business days
    C. 7 calendar days
    D. 10 calendar days

21. A binder and deposit receipt is one form of
    A. listing contract.
    B. sales contract.
    C. independent contractor agreement.
    D. buyer-broker agreement.

22. If the sales contract becomes legally enforceable only after the buyer receives a satisfactory report from a home inspector, that requirement is known as a(n)
    A. consideration.
    B. contingency.
    C. encumbrance.
    D. warranty.

23. An offer is NOT legally considered accepted until
    A. earnest money has been deposited.
    B. the other party has been notified of the acceptance.
    C. the parties have shaken hands.
    D. all inspections and appraisals have been completed.

24. A man takes out a mortgage loan to buy his first home, then discovers the next day that he could find a loan with a more favorable rate at another lending institution. He has how long to cancel the first loan?
    A. Three days
    B. Seven days
    C. Ten days
    D. He may not rescind the mortgage.

25. In a contract, whatever the parties promise to give to each other is known as
    A. consideration.
    B. novation.
    C. liquidated damages.
    D. assignment.

26. The word "executed," when applied to a contract, means "fulfilled," but is also used to mean
    A. voided.
    B. signed.
    C. assigned.
    D. expressed.

27. A man signs a contract to sell his house to a woman. Before closing, the man later changes his mind and refuses to sell. He offers the woman a few thousand dollars to void the contract, but because she wants that particular house she sues for
    A. liquidated damages.
    B. time being of the essence.
    C. rescission.
    D. specific performance.

28. A land contract is sometimes known as a(n)
    A. option agreement.
    B. contract for deed.
    C. purchase-money mortgage.
    D. counteroffer.

29. Real estate licensees are allowed to fill out sales contracts for the purchase of
    A. duplexes.
    B. option agreements.
    C. tracts of vacant land.
    D. all real estate.

30. In order to be legally enforceable, which contracts must be in writing according to the statute of frauds?
    A. Independent contractor agreements
    B. All contracts
    C. Leases for more than three years
    D. Management agreements

31. The tenant who is renting from month to month and wants to move out usually owes how much notice to the landlord?
    A. None
    B. 60 days
    C. 30 days, from a date the rent is due
    D. Two full months

32. A security deposit, minus itemized deductions for damages, must be returned to the departing tenant
    A. as the tenant moves out.
    B. within one week of the end of the lease.
    C. no more than 30 days after the end of the lease.
    D. within two months.

33. If rental property is sold, the tenant's security deposits must be
    A. returned.
    B. turned over to the new landlord.
    C. placed in a non-interest-bearing account.
    D. doubled.

34. A lease cannot become binding until the tenant has received a lead paint disclosure statement for any
    A. commercial property.
    B. shopping plaza.
    C. apartment house.
    D. residential property built before 1978.

35. In MOST cases, the store that rents space in a shopping mall is on what type of lease?
    A. Gross
    B. Ground
    C. Percentage
    D. Periodic

36. In some states, instead of mortgages borrowers sign
    A. reduction certificates.
    B. trust deeds.
    C. defeasance clauses.
    D. estoppel certificates.

37. If a mortgage pledges the property as security for the loan, what document serves as a personal promise to repay the debt?
    A. The note or bond
    B. A trust deed
    C. An estoppel certificate
    D. A subordination agreement

38. The buyer who takes over a mortgage already on the property is NOT personally responsible for the debt if he or she
    A. assumes the loan.
    B. takes title subject to the loan.
    C. receives a reduction certificate.
    D. signs a satisfaction certificate.

39. The buyer of foreclosed real estate at a public auction receives the property free of
    A. all liens.
    B. everything except unpaid property taxes.
    C. any liens junior to the one being foreclosed.
    D. any liens except those on record.

40. The mortgage lender may also be known as a
    A. payor.
    B. hypothecator.
    C. mortgagor.
    D. mortgagee.

41. When a couple divorces, the husband signs a deed turning over his share of the house to his former wife. A few years later she is unable to make the mortgage payments. The bank may try to collect the unpaid debt from
    A. no one, after the property is sold at a foreclosure sale.
    B. the ex-wife, because she is still in the house.
    C. the ex-husband, because he was the primary wage earner.
    D. both the ex-wife and the ex-husband.

42. Prepayment penalties for those who want to pay their mortgage loans off earlier than scheduled are limited in New Jersey to
    A. no charge.
    B. 1% of the outstanding debt.
    C. 2% of the debt, but only within the first year of the loan.
    D. Prepayments are not allowed in New Jersey.

43. The illegal charging of unreasonably high interest is known as
    A. default.
    B. estoppel.
    C. usury.
    D. hypothecation.

44. The seller has agreed to pay two points to the bank in return for the buyer's securing a mortgage loan on a house worth $225,000, with a 10% down payment. How much will this cost the seller?
    A. $4,500
    B. $2,250
    C. $2,500
    D. $4,050

45. In the preceding question (44), any points paid are income-tax-deductible by the
    A. buyer only.
    B. seller only.
    C. buyer and seller, each in full.
    D. buyer and seller, half by each.

46. If a mortgage debt grows gradually larger instead of being paid down, the borrower has
    A. a buydown.
    B. a straight loan.
    C. negative amortization.
    D. an adjustable interest rate.

47. Below-market interest rates are offered to qualified borrowers by
    A. NJHMFA.
    B. HUD-FHA.
    C. VA.
    D. PITI.

48. Artificially low "teaser" rates are a feature of
    A. VA mortgages.
    B. FHA mortgages.
    C. conventional mortgages.
    D. adjustable-rate mortgages.

49. What is the primary function of mortgage brokers?
    A. Handle only FHA mortgages
    B. Sell packages of loans on the secondary market
    C. Refer borrowers to mortgage lenders
    D. Keep certain loans in their own portfolios

50. A home equity loan is really a form of
    A. interim financing.
    B. reverse mortgage.
    C. open-end mortgage.
    D. second mortgage.

Units 16 through 22

1. Which of these appraisal methods uses a rate of investment return?
   A. Sales comparison approach
   B. Cost approach
   C. Income approach
   D. Gross income multiplier method

2. The amount of money a property is MOST likely to bring if widely advertised for sale is its
   A. intrinsic value.
   B. market value.
   C. subjective value.
   D. book value.

3. A homeowner constructs an eight-bedroom brick house with a tennis court in a neighborhood of modest two-bedroom frame houses. The value of this homeowner's house is likely to be affected by the principle of
   A. progression.
   B. regression.
   C. highest and best use.
   D. substitution.

4. For appraisal purposes, depreciation is related to
   A. capitalization.
   B. substitution.
   C. obsolescence.
   D. comparison.

5. A stadium would be best appraised using the
   A. cost approach.
   B. income approach.
   C. sales comparison approach.
   D. reconciliation approach.

6. The comparative market analysis that a broker furnishes to a homeseller is somewhat similar to a
   A. cost approach appraisal.
   B. income approach appraisal.
   C. sales comparison appraisal.
   D. certified appraisal.

7. The IRV formula is particularly useful in calculating
   A. depreciation.
   B. rent loss.
   C. external obsolescence.
   D. a capitalization rate.

8. The location of property and the public's preference for certain locations is known as
   A. external obsolescence.
   B. the substitution principal.
   C. highest and best use.
   D. situs.

9. When one investor manages a real estate partnership and takes on full liability for any losses, while the other investors are silent partners who cannot lose more than their investment, the enterprise is organized as a
   A. general partnership.
   B. real estate investment trust.
   C. limited partnership.
   D. pyramid.

10. Personal property is transferred using the regulations of the
    A. Real Estate Commission.
    B. Statute of Frauds.
    C. Securities and Exchange Commission.
    D. Uniform Commercial Code.

11. A real estate license is required for business brokerage
    A. in no case.
    B. when any real estate is involved.
    C. only when more than half the value of the business is in real estate.
    D. even when no real estate is involved.

12. When property is exchanged, any cash given to even out the exchange is known as
    A. marginal tax.
    B. appreciation.
    C. boot.
    D. bulk transfer.

13. The owner of a shopping plaza trades it for an apartment house, which is of equal value. In this transaction, the tax on the accumulated gain on the plaza is
    A. eliminated.
    B. deferred.
    C. calculated at alternative minimum tax rates.
    D. figured at favorable capital gains rates.

14. The IRS allows up to $25,000 in losses from rental property to offset other types of income only if the
    A. investor actively participates in the management of the property.
    B. investor's other income is more than $100,000.
    C. other income is in the form of wages.
    D. investor is a limited partner.

15. Original cost of investment property, plus cost of improvements, minus depreciation, yields a figure known as
    A. adjusted basis.
    B. salvage value.
    C. capital gain.
    D. marginal rate.

16. The term "cash flow" refers to
    A. the same thing as "operating expenses."
    B. spendable income left after expenses.
    C. borrowed money used to finance investment.
    D. accrued depreciation.

17. Master plans are usually adopted by
    A. the federal government.
    B. the state of New Jersey.
    C. boards of REALTORS.
    D. local communities.

18. The word "plat" means basically the same thing as
    A. subdivision.
    B. map.
    C. disclosure.
    D. PUD.

19. Installation of septic systems usually requires a(n)
    A. environmental impact study.
    B. zoning permit.
    C. utility easement.
    D. percolation test.

20. Oceanfront construction is regulated by the
    A. Environmental Protection Agency.
    B. Department of Environmental Protection.
    C. local zoning board.
    D. Department of Housing and Urban Development.

21. The buyer of new home construction receives a warranty on any type of defect for at LEAST
    A. one year.
    B. two years.
    C. five years.
    D. ten years.

22. No new building may be used for human habitation until it has received a(n)
    A. plat of subdivision.
    B. percolation test.
    C. environmental impact study.
    D. certificate of occupancy.

23. A typical developed lot sells for roughly how many times the cost of the raw land?
    A. Two
    B. Five
    C. Seven
    D. Ten

24. Simple transfers within a family are often made through use of a
    A. warranty deed.
    B. trust deed.
    C. full covenant deed.
    D. quitclaim deed.

25. Monuments are used in the legal description known as
    A. metes and bounds.
    B. plat of subdivision.
    C. rectangular survey system.
    D. datum.

26. The rectangular survey system is used in
    A. New Jersey only.
    B. all 13 original states.
    C. areas where usual surveying is difficult.
    D. Midwest and Western states.

27. The government has established benchmarks to aid
    A. land developers.
    B. title companies.
    C. surveyors.
    D. grantees.

28. The covenants in a deed are essentially
    A. legal descriptions.
    B. habendums.
    C. limitations.
    D. guarantees.

29. When people speak of having a signature "notarized," they mean it is
    A. acknowledged.
    B. executed.
    C. granted.
    D. warrantied.

30. A deed must be acknowledged before it can be
    A. effective in transferring property.
    B. recorded.
    C. executed.
    D. delivered.

31. A legal description can be determined by a title attorney or
    A. the owner.
    B. the United States Geological Survey.
    C. an attorney-in-fact.
    D. a surveyor.

32. Voluntary alienation includes transfer of real property by
    A. sale or gift.
    B. foreclosure or adverse possession.
    C. descent.
    D. eminent domain.

33. The landowner who dies without leaving a will is said to have been
    A. a devisee.
    B. alienated.
    C. a testator.
    D. intestate.

34. For the past 30 years a property owner has mowed a ten-foot strip at the edge of his lawn that really belongs to his neighbor. The neighbor never commented, protested, or gave the property owner permission to care for the strip. At this point the property owner
    A. has no claim on the neighbor's land.
    B. could go to court to claim the neighbor's land.
    C. has already been the owner for the past ten years.
    D. can ask the local zoning board for title to the land.

35. All metes-and-bounds descriptions begin and end with
    A. the surveyor's notes.
    B. lot and block descriptions.
    C. point of beginning.
    D. recorded plats of subdivision.

36. A partition proceeding is an example of
    A. involuntary alienation.
    B. public grant.
    C. tacking.
    D. adverse possession.

37. Which federal agency administers the NFIP?
    A. FDIC
    B. VA
    C. RESPA
    D. FEMA

38. Within three days of loan application, the borrower must receive a(n)
    A. Uniform Settlement Statement.
    B. abstract.
    C. title insurance policy.
    D. good-faith estimate of settlement costs.

39. An affidavit of title is signed at closing by the
    A. lending institution.
    B. buyer's attorney.
    C. seller.
    D. mortgagor.

40. The State of New Jersey requires the borrower to be notified that
    A. the property may be located in a flood plain.
    B. the title policy required by a lender does not protect the owner.
    C. someone other than the owner may be in physical possession of the property.
    D. abstractors usually go back no more than 60 years.

41. New Jersey public records are maintained by the
    A. local Bar Association.
    B. title insurance company.
    C. secretary of state's office.
    D. county clerk.

42. Any document to be recorded must be
    A. acknowledged.
    B. prorated.
    C. prepared.
    D. searched.

43. This year's taxes on the property, $2,400, have not been paid. At the August 1 closing, how are they accounted for?
    A. Debit buyer $1,200; debit seller $1,200
    B. Credit buyer $1,400; debit seller $1,000
    C. Credit buyer $1,400; debit seller $1,400
    D. Debit buyer $1,000; credit seller $1,400

44. The term *proration* refers to
    A. tax due the state of New Jersey at closing.
    B. the costs that are divided between buyer and seller.
    C. a lawyer's statement after studying an abstract.
    D. debits and credits to buyer and seller.

45. If information about property is in the public records, a potential buyer is assumed to know all about it through the principle of
    A. constructive notice.
    B. evidence of title.
    C. proration.
    D. RESPA.

46. A salesperson lists a house for $200,000 with a 7% commission. The seller accepts an offer of $185,000 from a buyer produced by a cooperating firm. The listing salesperson's broker splits the commission 50/50 with the other company. If the listing salesperson receives 60% of commissions and his company keeps 40%, how much does he receive?
    A. $2,590
    B. $2,800
    C. $3,885
    D. $4,200

47. A seller receives $100,000 cash from the sale of her house, after paying off a $120,000 mortgage, $5,600 in closing costs, and a 6% broker's commission. The house sold for
    A. $225,600.
    B. $239,136.
    C. $240,000.
    D. $254,400.

48. A house with replacement cost of $170,000 is insured for 80% of its value. Insurance costs $0.75 per $100. How much is the annual premium?
    A. $136
    B. $1,020
    C. $1,275
    D. $1,360

49. The prospective buyers tell their broker they have $60,000 a year income and no debts. If the mortgage plan they are considering uses a qualifying ratio of 28/36, what is the highest monthly payment they qualify for?
    A. $1,400
    B. $1,680
    C. $1,800
    D. $2,160

50. A three-acre lot on a lake is priced at $200 per front foot. If it is 1,000 feet deep, what is the asking price?
    A. $13,068
    B. $19,666
    C. $26,136
    D. $43,560

PRACTICE LICENSE EXAMINATIONS

THE NEW JERSEY LICENSE EXAMINATION

The license examination can be taken only after successful completion of the prelicense-qualifying course(s). The candidate for a salespersons license need not have a sponsoring broker before taking the examination. Broker candidates must have the Real Estate Commission's approval of their three-year apprenticeship before taking the broker examination.

PREPARING FOR THE EXAMINATION

Self-testing with the questions at the end of each unit in the book is probably the best preparation. Any question that is missed should send you back to the unit. Knowledge of Key Terms can be tested with the Key Terms Reviews.

Unit summaries are excellent for reviewing the main points; any one that is not understood should, again, send you back to the body of the unit. After separate unit review, each of the tests in this unit should be taken, with up to three hours allowed for each. Any wrong answers help identify weak spots for further review.

PRACTICE EXAMINATIONS

Practice examinations A and B are each set up like the state's licensing examination, with 80 multiple-choice, general real estate questions, followed by 30 questions specific to New Jersey.

Use 30-day months, 360-day years, and 43,560 square feet in an acre. Round off where applicable. Take your time—three hours are allowed for each test.

PRACTICE TEST A

1. Which of the following is considered personal property?
   A. Sewers
   B. Roads
   C. Building
   D. Crops

2. To the seller's agent, the buyer is properly described as a
   A. client.
   B. customer.
   C. principal.
   D. fiduciary.

3. Which appraisal approach computes the value of the land separately from the buildings?
   A. Cost
   B. Income capitalization
   C. Market data
   D. Market analysis

4. A person who has absolute control of a parcel of real estate is said to own a
   A. leasehold estate.
   B. fee determinable.
   C. life estate.
   D. fee simple.

5. A property owner lets his neighbor store her camper in his yard for a few weeks. He does not charge her rent. He has given the neighbor a(n)
   A. easement.
   B. encroachment.
   C. estate in land.
   D. license.

6. The HUD-1 statement will still be used for a mortgage secured by a
   A. conventional loan used to purchase a single-family dwelling.
   B. single-family dwelling financed by an FHA-insured loan.
   C. a duplex, in which the purchaser will live, financed by a VA-guaranteed loan.
   D. reverse mortgage.

7. A legal description that defines the boundary lines is called
   A. a geodetic survey.
   B. metes and bounds.
   C. a rectangular survey.
   D. a recorded plat.

8. Which of the following is considered dual agency?
   A. Broker acting for both buyer and seller
   B. Brokers cooperating in a multiple listing service
   C. Broker listing and selling to the same person
   D. Salesperson listing two houses on the same street

9. Which of the following is a lien that does NOT need to be recorded?
   A. Money judgment
   B. Real estate taxes
   C. A tax deed
   D. A voluntary lien

10. The term *depreciation* refers to
    A. the value of real estate after the expiration of its useful life.
    B. a loss of value due to any cause.
    C. costs incurred to modernize a building.
    D. capitalized value of rental losses.

11. Whether a salesperson is associated with a broker as an employee or as an independent contractor is important
    A. for income tax purposes.
    B. when applying for a license.
    C. when listing property, because an independent contractor may list in her own name.
    D. when establishing the escrow account.

12. A township contains
    A. 6 square miles.
    B. 36 sections.
    C. 18 sections.
    D. 640 acres.

13. A merchant signs a lease for $800 a month or 6% of gross sales, whichever is more. In July gross sales were $14,000. How much is the rent for July?
    A. $480
    B. $800
    C. $840 ⟵ circled
    D. $2,800

14. A property owner gave the hospital a vacant lot for "as long as it is used for hospital purposes." The hospital owns a
    A. fee determinable. ⟵ circled
    B. remainder interest.
    C. homestead.
    D. leasehold estate.

15. The buyer moves in and pays expenses and loan payments but the seller retains title in a
    A. lease-option. ⟵ circled
    B. purchase-money sale.
    C. land contract.
    D. sale and leaseback.

16. A tenant's written, one-year lease expires on May 1. To obtain possession on May 1, the landlord must give the tenant
    A. notice by April 30.
    B. 60 days' notice.
    C. one month's notice.
    D. no notice. ⟵ circled

17. Which of the following situations will NOT delay closing under the TRID rules?
    A. Escrow amount for taxes and insurance was changed
    B. Lender could not document applicant's overtime ⟵ circled
    C. Applicant decided on a different loan program
    D. Prepayment penalty added

18. A couple owns property that the city wants to use to extend the airport runway. The couple refuses to sell. The city may acquire this property by its right of
    A. eminent domain. ⟵ circled
    B. easement.
    C. accession.
    D. recapture.

19. When an owner sold her listed home herself, she didn't owe anyone a commission. The listing she had signed was probably a(n)
    A. multiple listing.
    B. net listing.
    C. exclusive-right-to-sell listing.
    D. exclusive-agency listing. ⟵ circled

20. Federal income tax regulations allow a homeowner to reduce taxable income by amounts paid for
    A. interest and property tax.
    B. repairs and maintenance.
    C. insurance premiums.
    D. all of the above. ⟵ circled

21. A grantor becomes a lessee, and the grantee becomes the lessor, in a
    A. land contract.
    B. lease-option.
    C. sale and leaseback. ⟵ circled
    D. wraparound mortgage.

22. A person has defaulted in payment of several debts, and a court has ordered his property sold to satisfy them. Which of the following would be considered the prior lien?
    A. The outstanding mortgage dated and recorded one year ago
    B. Current real estate taxes ⟵ circled
    C. A mechanic's lien for work that was started two months before the mortgage was recorded
    D. A court judgment rendered and recorded last month

23. A guarantee that the lender will commit to a certain percentage for the cost of the loan is called
    A. tariff security.
    B. requirement for a prepayment penalty.
    C. balloon payment.
    D. rate lock. ⟵ circled

24. What is the function of Fannie Mae?
    A. Buys FHA loans
    B. Insures FHA loans
    C. Makes FHA loans ⟵ circled
    D. Reviews FHA loans

25. Continuing education courses may be taken
    A. in a classroom only.
    B. exclusively over the internet.
    C. entirely by mail.
    D. by mail, internet, or classroom. ⟵ circled

26. As agent for a seller, a real estate broker may
    A. promise that the seller will accept any offer that meets the terms of the listing contract.
    B. solicit the buyer for an offer to purchase.
    C. sign an acceptance to a bona fide purchase offer.
    D. refuse to forward a ridiculously low offer.

27. One of the requirements of the federal TRID
    A. requires a lender to provide a Loan Estimate within three business days of completed loan application.
    B. forbids use of the term annual percentage rate.
    C. prevents a broker from saying "FHA financing available" in a classified ad.
    D. requires all mortgage loan applications to be made on standard government forms.

28. The amount of money that would be paid by a buyer to a seller, both well-informed and neither under duress, is real property's
    A. exchange value.
    B. market value.
    C. appraised value.
    D. salvage value.

29. Property is listed for $160,000 and sells for $150,000, in a town that reassesses at sales price on transfer. The tax rate is $1.93 per $100. How much is the tax bill?
    A. $289.50
    B. $308.80
    C. $2,895
    D. $3,088

30. A real estate broker who received a commission for the sale of a home in a transaction in which neither the buyer nor the seller was a principal acted as a
    A. transaction broker.
    B. seller's agent.
    C. buyer's broker.
    D. dual agent.

31. Which of the following is NOT essential to an enforceable real estate sales contract?
    A. Earnest money
    B. Writing
    C. Offer and acceptance
    D. Consideration

32. The lender has agreed to finance furnished condominium units. The lender has agreed to a
    A. package mortgage.
    B. blanket mortgage.
    C. shared equity mortgage.
    D. wraparound mortgage.

33. A married couple who meet the ownership and occupancy requirements may sell a principal residence with no federal capital gains tax on profit of up to
    A. $125,000.
    B. $250,000.
    C. $500,000.
    D. any amount.

34. The amount of commission due a salesperson is determined by
    A. agreement between broker and seller.
    B. agreement between broker and salesperson.
    C. the local association of REALTORS®.
    D. state law.

35. The practice of refusing to lend mortgage money in certain neighborhoods is called
    A. blockbusting.
    B. redlining.
    C. bird-dogging.
    D. steering.

36. In a real estate sale, transfer tax fees are usually paid by the
    A. seller.
    B. state.
    C. buyer.
    D. broker.

37. Which of the following is most acceptable as evidence or proof of ownership of an estate in land?
    A. Quitclaim deed
    B. Title insurance policy
    C. Warranty deed
    D. Affidavit

38. An appraiser would NOT generally use which of these items to determine the replacement cost of a building?
    A. Square footage
    B. Unit in place
    C. Original cost
    D. Quantity survey

39. Which of the following hazards requires a federal disclosure form in a residential purchase?
    A. Radon
    B. Lead-based paint
    C. Formaldehyde
    D. Asbestos

40. A tenant rents an apartment under a two-year written lease. After one year, the building is sold. Which statement is TRUE?
    A. The sale has no effect on the tenant's tenancy.
    B. The tenant must renegotiate with the new owner.
    C. The tenant must leave after 60 days' notice by the owner.
    D. The new owner is free to increase the rent immediately.

41. In 1977 a couple purchased their house and lot for $53,000. They made no major improvements. They recently sold it for $122,550. How much do they owe on their gain?
    A. Nothing
    B. Nothing, if they purchase another home within 24 months
    C. 15%
    D. 20%

42. A REALTOR® is
    A. any active broker.
    B. an attorney-in-fact.
    C. any licensed agent.
    D. a member of a trade association.

43. A broker received two offers at once, one through a salesperson in his office and one from a competitor. The broker should
    A. submit the salesperson's offer first because he is the lister.
    B. submit both offers at the same time.
    C. submit the competitor's first as a matter of courtesy.
    D. reject both offers and tell the seller to try for a higher price.

44. The act by which all parties agree to the terms of a contract is known as
    A. legality of object.
    B. consideration.
    C. meeting of the minds.
    D. informed consent.

45. A refusal to rent to a couple because they are unmarried violates
    A. no law.
    B. New Jersey law.
    C. the Civil Rights Act of 1866.
    D. the Fair Housing Act of 1968.

46. Exemption from a portion of property taxes is available to
    A. qualified veterans.
    B. qualified senior citizens.
    C. qualified nonprofit organizations.
    D. all of the above.

47. Those who are entitled to inspect all documents recorded in the county clerk's office include
    A. bank employees.
    B. private individuals.
    C. tax assessors.
    D. all of the above.

48. Seller lists a home for $400,000 and the listing broker tells a prospective buyer to submit a low offer because the seller is desperate. The buyer offers $320,000, which the seller accepts. In this instance,
    A. the broker violated the agency relationship.
    B. the broker did not act improperly, because no one was hurt.
    C. the action was proper because it obtained a quick offer.
    D. the broker was properly looking out for buyer's interests.

49. When real property is sold at a foreclosure sale and not enough money is realized to pay the mortgage, the lender may
    A. seek a deficiency judgment.
    B. foreclose on other real estate owned in that county.
    C. file a garnishment of the borrower's wages.
    D. ask a court to seize the borrower's bank accounts.

50. Which of the following is an example of economic obsolescence?
    A. Rusted boiler
    B. Poor floor plan
    C. Outmoded plumbing
    D. Car lot next door

51. The law that requires MOST real estate contracts to be in writing is known as the statute of
    A. descent.
    B. estoppel.
    C. frauds.
    D. limitations.

52. A licensed salesperson completed a difficult transaction. This salesperson may accept a bonus from
    A. the grateful seller.
    B. the buyer.
    C. his own broker.
    D. any of the above.

53. A custom-built house containing 2,320 square feet has been constructed on a $28,000 lot. Construction costs are $50.25 per square foot. Other fees and costs total $2,780. What is the total cost of the property?
    A. $116,580
    B. $144,000
    C. $144,580
    D. $147,360

54. From which of the following does one obtain an FHA loan?
    A. Federal Housing Authority
    B. Federal Home Loan Board
    C. Local FHA lender
    D. Farmers Home Agency

55. A broker may not act for both buyer and seller without
    A. notifying both of this fact after the sale is closed.
    B. having both sign a sales contract.
    C. having exclusive agreements signed by each.
    D. obtaining prior written consent of both parties.

56. A building sold for $949,000. The total commission was $56,940. What was the rate of commission?
    A. 5%
    B. 6%
    C. 6.5%
    D. None of the above

57. In the purchase of real estate, the buyer is held responsible for facts and information obtainable through actual notice and also through
    A. caveat emptor.
    B. incorporeal interest.
    C. eminent domain.
    D. constructive notice.

58. The power of eminent domain is exercised through the court proceeding known as
    A. specific performance.
    B. condemnation.
    C. escheat.
    D. adverse possession.

59. The gross income from a small office building is $73,500 and the annual expense total is $52,300. If the owner expects to receive an 11% return on her investment, what should she be willing to pay for the building?
    A. $192,727
    B. $212,000
    C. $475,455
    D. $668,182

60. A homeseller may avoid federal capital gains tax on profit from the sale of a principal residence only if
    A. the property has been owned and occupied as a principal residence for two of the preceding five years.
    B. either the seller or seller's spouse is over the age of 55.
    C. a replacement residence of equal or greater value is purchased within two years of the sale.
    D. fix-up expenses were paid within 90 days of the sale.

61. The selling landlord has collected the September rents from all five tenants: two at $345 and three at $425. The sale is closed on September 20. How much credit should the buyer be allowed?
    A. $720.50
    B. $690
    C. $1,275
    D. $1,965

62. Real estate brokers may protect themselves in case of professional lawsuits through a special type of insurance known as
    A. malpractice.
    B. errors and omissions.
    C. inland marine.
    D. floaters.

63. The amount of commission due on a sale is determined by
    A. state law.
    B. local custom.
    C. court decisions.
    D. agreement between broker and client.

64. No exceptions are permitted by federal law when the discrimination is based on
    A. race.
    B. marital status.
    C. sex.
    D. disability.

65. Regulation Z would require full disclosure of all financing terms if an advertisement mentioned
    A. "payment $1,500 a month."
    B. "terms negotiable."
    C. "$200,000 mortgage available."
    D. "owner will finance."

66. A purchaser in a cooperative usually receives
    A. title to the land on which the unit stands.
    B. a proprietary lease to one living unit.
    C. ownership and use for a certain portion of each year.
    D. a life estate.

67. What is the purpose of a comparative market analysis?
    A. Helps an investor determine feasibility of a proposal
    B. Is intended for use as evidence in a court proceeding
    C. Is often used in condemnations
    D. Helps a seller establish the right listing price

68. A developer is planning a building containing 103,000 square feet. Construction costs are estimated at $42 per square foot; 90% financing is available. How much money must the developer put up to complete the project?
    A. $432,600
    B. $3,684,000
    C. $3,893,400
    D. $428,600

69. Which of the following is an example of functional obsolescence?
    A. Used-car lot next door
    B. Outmoded plumbing
    C. Change in zoning
    D. Leaky roof

70. An investor purchased a duplex for $300,000, paying $37,500 down and financing the balance. About two years later he sold the property for $345,000. He has realized
    A. plottage.
    B. capital gain.
    C. escalation.
    D. highest and best use.

71. The real estate is operated by a general partner who is fully liable for operating losses and is owned jointly with several passive partners who are liable only to the extent of their investment. This form of ownership is called a
    A. joint partnership.
    B. real estate investment trust.
    C. general partnership.
    D. limited partnership.

72. Every deed in the subdivision has a restriction forbidding toolsheds or doghouses. One property owner erects both in his backyard. His neighbors may
    A. do nothing because they have no authority.
    B. go to court and obtain injunctive relief.
    C. call the local police.
    D. borrow his tools and his dog.

73. Estimating market value by considering sales of similar properties is used in which appraisal approach?
    A. Cost
    B. Income
    C. Market data
    D. Capitalization

74. In a new subdivision, streets, sidewalks, and curbs are usually provided by the
    A. municipality.
    B. county.
    C. property owners.
    D. developer.

75. A couple holds a proprietary lease on their apartment and directs that shares of stock in the corporation that owns the building. The couple owns a
    A. condominium.
    B. real estate investment trust.
    C. cooperative.
    D. syndicated venture.

76. The appraiser estimates the replacement cost of a building at $560,000. The building has an estimated life of 40 years and a current estimated remaining life of 30 years. What is the current value of the building?
    A. $140,000
    B. $420,000
    C. $475,000
    D. $560,000

77. The term condominium refers to a(n)
    A. apartment.
    B. type of ownership.
    C. type of building.
    D. PUD.

78. What is radon?
    A. A foul-smelling gas
    B. A colorless, odorless gas
    C. A hazardous mineral
    D. A valuable mineral

79. What is the purpose of a perc test?
    A. It determines the suitability of soil for installing a septic system.
    B. It is necessary if a house will be hooked up to a sewer system.
    C. It determines how much coffee a restaurant is allowed to brew.
    D. It is an unnecessary test when buying vacant land on which the buyer wants to build a house.

80. The current value of a piece of property is $350,000 and the assessed value is 40% of its current value. The tax rate is $4 per $100. What is the amount of the tax?
    A. $1,400
    B. $1,470
    C. $3,333
    D. $5,600

81. In New Jersey, a lease for four years
    A. may be recorded.
    B. is invalid.
    C. is not legal.
    D. involves an option.

82. A broker's license is suspended by the Real Estate Commission. His salespeople must immediately
    A. find a new broker to associate with.
    B. carry on the business until he regains his license.
    C. stop listing and selling.
    D. obtain broker's licenses.

83. Although federal law does not mention it, New Jersey law forbids discrimination on the grounds of
    A. political affiliation.
    B. pet ownership.
    C. sexual orientation.
    D. race.

84. The Real Estate Commission prohibits
    A. listing a home phone number on business cards.
    B. vague "vicinity" advertisements.
    C. real estate advertisements on cable television.
    D. puffery ads with words like "superb" or "terrific."

85. A man bought acreage in a distant county, never went to see it, and did not use it. A local person moved his mobile home onto the land, had a well drilled, and lived there for the past 32 years. A court might find the local person has become the owner of the land through
    A. adverse possession.
    B. Statute of Frauds.
    C. prescription.
    D. accretion.

86. The term *commingling* refers to
    A. mixing the broker's funds with escrow deposits.
    B. soliciting the services of another broker's salespersons.
    C. failing to deliver copies of contracts.
    D. promoting business at social gatherings.

87. A real estate broker must keep all documents relating to a real estate transaction for how long?
    A. Two years
    B. Four years
    C. Six years
    D. Indefinitely

88. A duly licensed salesperson may accept a bonus from
    A. a grateful seller.
    B. a grateful buyer.
    C. another salesperson. ✓
    D. her broker of record.

89. The New Jersey Real Estate Commission
    A. is funded from the general treasury.
    B. is under the Department of Banking and Insurance.
    C. sets commission rates.
    D. controls the Truth-in-Renting Law.

90. The Multiple Dwelling Reporting Rule is required by the
    A. New Jersey Real Estate Commission.
    B. public advocate.
    C. attorney general of New Jersey.
    D. Department of Community Affairs.

91. A New Jersey real estate licensee may NOT
    A. sell vacant land.
    B. sell mobile homes.
    C. negotiate rental contracts.
    D. draw up a sales contract for an eight-unit apartment complex.

92. If the Real Estate Commission wants to inspect a broker's office, how much notice must be given?
    A. 30 days
    B. 10 days
    C. 24 hours ✓
    D. None

93. The New Jersey Real Estate Commission includes
    A. three members at large.
    B. at least two lawyers.
    C. at least one minority member.
    D. eight members.

94. Which of the following words must be conspicuously displayed by brokers?
    A. Licensed real estate broker
    B. REALTOR®
    C. Licensed REALTOR®
    D. Licensed real estate agent

95. The real estate broker who also holds an insurance license is NOT allowed to
    A. sell insurance and real estate to the same person.
    B. operate the insurance business from a real estate office.
    C. include insurance placement in a real estate sales contract.
    D. discuss insurance with the seller who lists property.

96. A salesperson sold a house. When her broker received the commission check, he asked her to wait for her share until the check had cleared the bank. The broker must pay her the agreed-on split within
    A. three days.
    B. one week.
    C. ten days.
    D. one month.

97. A salesperson left a real estate firm to work at a bank. The broker must account for all commissions due the former salesperson within
    A. 3 days.
    B. 1 week.
    C. 10 days.
    D. 30 days.

98. The Real Estate Guaranty Fund
    A. pays commissions due if the broker's client fails to pay them.
    B. is administered by the salesperson's sponsoring broker.
    C. receives funding from license applicants.
    D. sets minimum wages for licensees.

99. The Real Estate Commission does NOT allow brokers to cooperate on
    A. multiple listings.
    B. price fixing.
    C. referral fees.
    D. fee splitting.

100. When the broker of record dies, a temporary broker's license to carry on the work of the office may be granted to
    A. the broker's widow.
    B. the broker's attorney.
    C. a salesperson who could qualify to be a broker.
    D. a salesperson with one year of experience.

101. In New Jersey, a landlord places tenants' security deposits in an interest-bearing bank account. The landlord must give his tenants
    A. all the interest earned.
    B. half the interest earned.
    C. all but 1% of the interest earned.
    D. none of the interest earned.

102. Someone whose license is suspended may receive a fine for a first offense of up to
    A. $10,000.
    B. $30,000.
    C. $40,000.
    D. $50,000.

103. The New Jersey Real Estate Commission was established to
    A. raise money for the public treasury.
    B. settle disputes between real estate agents.
    C. ensure equitable payment of brokers' commissions.
    D. protect the interests of the public.

104. An applicant for a broker's license who claims full-time experience in real estate should be able to show at LEAST how many transactions per category a year?
    A. 6
    B. 10
    C. 12
    D. Not specified

105. Who of the following is required to take the 75-hour course before applying for a real estate license?
    A. Attorney
    B. College graduate with a real estate major
    C. Licensed insurance broker
    D. Broker from another state

106. Any advertisement placed by a salesperson must also include the
    A. salesperson's home telephone number.
    B. name of the brokerage firm.
    C. exact listing price of the property.
    D. exact term "free appraisal" if one is being offered.

107. Any later change in a signed contract must be
    A. made only by an attorney.
    B. retyped and distributed to all the parties.
    C. initialed by all the parties.
    D. renegotiated with a new contract by novation.

108. A real estate licensee has his license revoked because he lied on his license application. His broker also loses his license
    A. automatically.
    B. if he knew at the time what the salesperson was doing.
    C. if the broker has any previous offense on his record.
    D. if the salesperson broke any rules while associated with the broker of record.

109. Real estate licenses must be renewed
    A. every July 1.
    B. only after completion of continuing education.
    C. on or before the licensee's birthday.
    D. every five years.

110. A fully qualified broker who chooses to remain in the role of a salesperson under another broker's supervision is known as a(n)
    A. licensed salesperson.
    B. broker-salesperson.
    C. REALTOR-ASSOCIATE.
    D. adjunct broker.

PRACTICE TEST B

This test contains 80 multiple-choice questions on general real estate topics, and 30 that are specific to New Jersey. Three hours are allowed.

1. A house contains screens, smoke alarms, and a crystal chandelier. The contract of sale mentions none of the items specifically. Before final closing, the seller has the right to remove
   A. the screens, because they are trade fixtures.
   B. the smoke alarms, which are personal property.
   C. the chandelier, because it is an appurtenance.
   D. none of these items.

2. The amount of earnest money deposit is determined by
   A. state law.
   B. the broker.
   C. agreement of the parties.
   D. the local association of REALTORS®.

3. An owner sold his house on his own and still owed a broker a commission. He must have signed a(n)
   A. open listing.
   B. net listing.
   C. exclusive-right-to-sell listing.
   D. exclusive-agency listing.

4. Which can be executed without subjecting the signers to further responsibility for title?
   A. Quitclaim deed
   B. Special warranty deed
   C. Warranty deed
   D. Bargain and sale deed

5. The utility company dug up a garden to lay gas lines. The company had an easement, recorded at the county clerk's office. The owner claimed the easement was invalid because she was never told about it. The easement
   A. was valid even if she had never heard of it.
   B. was valid only if the company could prove she knew about it when she bought.
   C. was appurtenant.
   D. had expired if it had not been used for ten years.

6. When a court orders real property sold to satisfy an unpaid lien, the process is known as a(n)
   A. easement.
   B. encumbrance.
   C. attachment.
   D. foreclosure.

7. The tax rate is $7.80 per $100 assessment. If property is valued at $87,500 and assessed for 50% of its value, what is the total property tax?
   A. $682.50
   B. $3,412.50
   C. $6,825
   D. $13,650

8. When appraising an office building, the appraiser is MOST concerned with
   A. accrued depreciation.
   B. annual mortgage payments.
   C. comparable sales.
   D. net annual income.

9. A borrower obtained a second mortgage loan for $20,000 at 10%. It called for payments of $175 a month over a period of five years. The final installment would be a balloon payment. This loan is a
   A. fully amortized loan.
   B. partially amortized loan.
   C. straight loan.
   D. blanket loan.

10. If the interest rate is 5% and the monthly interest payment is $650, the principal sum would be
    A. $130,000.
    B. $156,000.
    C. $84,000.
    D. $325,000.

11. A man dies and devises his real property to his second wife for her lifetime, after which the property will pass to his children. The man's children own a(n)
    A. life estate.
    B. reversion.
    C. remainder interest.
    D. estate for years.

12. The prospective borrower decided to change the loan from FHA-insured to a conventional loan. In this situation, the lender
    A. must issue a new Loan Estimate.
    B. does not have to issue a new Loan Estimate.
    C. has to meet the original closing date.
    D. is responsible for any delays caused by the change.

13. The market data approach is MOST important in appraising a(n)
    A. church.
    B. older residence.
    C. apartment building.
    D. newly constructed residence.

14. Among the several pieces of information that the lender must gather before issuing a Loan Estimate (LE) is the applicant's
    A. signed affidavit that borrower has complied with fair housing guidelines.
    B. statement of religious beliefs.
    C. social security number.
    D. estimated earnings statement.

15. A broker listed a property. His salesman accepted a check for $5,000 earnest money with an offer. The salesperson should take the check and
    A. give it to the sellers.
    B. hold it until closing.
    C. give it to the broker.
    D. deposit it in the salesperson's special escrow account.

16. An owner signed a 30-day listing with a broker. The next day the owner was killed in an accident. The listing was then
    A. invalid unless the owner's husband ratified it.
    B. still in effect for 29 more days.
    C. binding upon the owner's heirs if services had been performed.
    D. terminated.

17. A widow received ownership of the family home for the rest of her life, with title going to her children on her death. She owns a(n)
    A. life estate.
    B. leasehold.
    C. remainder.
    D. easement.

18. Under the common law of agency, the real estate broker has a fiduciary relationship with
    A. the client.
    B. other brokers only.
    C. the seller's attorney.
    D. both buyer and seller.

19. Title to real property is passed when a valid deed is
    A. escrowed.
    B. signed.
    C. delivered.
    D. witnessed.

20. A lot 80 feet wide and 200 feet deep is sold at $500 per front foot. Commission is 10% of sales price, and the selling salesperson receives 60% of the commission. What does the salesperson receive?
    A. $1,600
    B. $2,400
    C. $4,000
    D. $6,000

21. Restrictive covenants that "run with the land"
    A. are established by local municipalities.
    B. are binding on future owners of the property.
    C. must be approved by a court.
    D. may not be more restrictive than building codes.

22. VA and FHA mortgages are notable for their
    A. subsidized payments.
    B. prepayment penalties.
    C. adjustable rates.
    D. low down payments.

23. Who is uniquely in a position to provide the *Your Home Loan Toolkit* to a buyer, but not required to?
    A. Lender
    B. Buyer's agent
    C. Closing agent
    D. Insurance agent

24. Private restrictions on land use may be created by
    A. zoning regulations.
    B. building codes.
    C. deed.
    D. any of the above.

25. The use of subtle means to induce buyers to settle in neighborhoods the broker thinks appropriate is known as
    A. blockbusting.
    B. redlining.
    C. bird-dogging.
    D. steering.

26. A mortgage broker usually offers what service?
    A. Handles closing procedures
    B. Brings borrower and lender together
    C. Provides initial funding
    D. Sells mortgages on the secondary market

27. A broker receives a commission only if she produces a buyer before someone else sells the property. She is probably working under what type of listing?
    A. Open listing
    B. Net listing
    C. Exclusive-right-to-sell listing
    D. Exclusive-agency listing

28. Investors will sometimes borrow money to make a real estate purchase. This practice is called
    A. a bulk transfer.
    B. an exchange.
    C. leverage.
    D. pyramiding.

29. A broker listing a house may be guilty of discrimination for purposely not mentioning the house to
    A. qualified Hispanic homebuyers.
    B. qualified black homebuyers.
    C. qualified white homebuyers.
    D. any of the above.

30. Deed restrictions are a method by which
    A. local zoning ordinances are enforced.
    B. the planning commission makes its work effective.
    C. cities can control construction details.
    D. the seller can limit the buyer's use.

31. Which of the following exceptions is NOT allowed under New Jersey's fair housing law?
    A. Certain types of housing may be restricted to members of one sex.
    B. Homeowners may discriminate when selling their own homes.
    C. Religious organizations may discriminate on the basis of religion.
    D. When renting a duplex or up/down two-family dwelling, an owner-occupant may discriminate except for race.

32. The primary purpose of a deed is to
    A. furnish security.
    B. give notice.
    C. transfer title rights.
    D. prove ownership.

33. A summary of the history of all conveyances and legal proceedings affecting a specific parcel of real estate is called a(n)
    A. chain of title.
    B. title insurance policy.
    C. certificate of title.
    D. abstract of title.

34. At the closing, the cost of filing the deed in the public records usually appears as a
    A. credit to the buyer.
    B. credit to the seller.
    C. debit to the buyer.
    D. debit to the seller.

35. A person cannot successfully claim that he or she did not know about the contents of any recorded document. This legal principle is known as
    A. statute of frauds.
    B. actual notice.
    C. eminent domain.
    D. constructive notice.

36. The purpose of TRID's Loan Estimate is to ensure
    A. buyers do not borrow more than they can repay.
    B. real estate brokers are responsive to buyers' needs.
    C. buyers know how much money is required.
    D. buyers are aware of all costs relating to their mortgage loan.

37. A building was bought for $250,000, with 10% down and a loan for the balance. If the lender charged the buyer two points, how much cash did the buyer need?
    A. $20,000
    B. $22,500
    C. $25,000
    D. $29,500

38. A mortgage loan payable in installments sufficient to pay the principal off by the end of the term is called a
    A. fully amortized loan.
    B. partly amortized loan.
    C. straight loan.
    D. blanket loan.

39. Which of the following deeds contains no express or implied warranties?
    A. Bargain and sale deed
    B. Quitclaim deed
    C. Grant deed
    D. Warranty deed

40. The disclosures required by TRID apply to
    A. brokers selling office buildings.
    B. security salespersons with limited partnerships.
    C. Ginnie Mae when purchasing mortgages.
    D. lenders financing purchase of a residence.

41. A comparative market analysis is usually provided by the
    A. appraiser.
    B. listing agent.
    C. lender.
    D. closing agent.

42. A legal action brought by either buyer or seller to enforce the terms of the contract is known as
    A. an injunction.
    B. specific performance.
    C. lis pendens.
    D. an attachment.

43. To avoid possible violation of antitrust regulations, one should avoid any discussion of commissions with
    A. a competitor.
    B. other associates in the office.
    C. potential listers.
    D. anyone.

44. What is cash flow?
    A. The amount of money flowing into and out of a property
    B. A bookkeeping function accounting for each day's money
    C. Total remaining money after expenses have been paid
    D. Taxes, mortgage payment, and operating costs

45. The town allows construction on quarter-acre lots. One subdivision has a restriction for at least one-acre lots. In this situation,
    A. if the town issues a building permit for a quarter-acre lot, no one can block construction.
    B. neighbors in the subdivision may enforce the one-acre restriction by calling on local police.
    C. the town will not issue a permit for less than one-acre lots in that subdivision.
    D. neighbors may enforce the one-acre limit but only through a court order.

46. The owner lives in one side of a duplex. He refuses to rent the other side to a single black woman with good credit and income. He tells her he wants to choose his neighbors. The woman may have a remedy under which of the following acts?
    A. Fair Housing Act of 1968
    B. Civil Rights Act of 1866
    C. New Jersey Law Against Discrimination
    D. None of the above

47. In the valuation of a large office building, which approach is given MOST weight?
    A. Cost
    B. Income capitalization
    C. Market data
    D. All equal weight

48. A broker must pay Social Security taxes, workers' compensation, and unemployment insurance for all
    A. associates.
    B. part-time salespersons.
    C. independent contractors.
    D. employees.

49. The fiduciary duty forbids a listing broker
    A. advising a seller that list price is too high.
    B. negotiating for an offer if it is below listed price.
    C. advertising property at less than the listed price.
    D. relisting property at a lower price.

50. Which of the following represents a voluntary lien?
    A. Mortgage
    B. Special assessment
    C. Estate tax
    D. Ad valorem tax

51. A house sold for $157,000. The broker charged a 6% commission and divided it as follows: 10% to his salesperson who took the listing, and the rest divided equally between another salesperson who made the sale and the broker's office. What was the listing agent's commission?
    A. $942
    B. $4,710
    C. $9,420
    D. $15,700

52. A company constructed a swimming pool. On completion, the company filed a lien for nonpayment. This was MOST likely a
    A. general lien.
    B. special lien.
    C. construction lien.
    D. voluntary lien.

53. The term leverage refers to
    A. the movement of people that enhances value in the area.
    B. the use of borrowed money to finance most of an investment.
    C. using influence at the bank to make a loan.
    D. measuring the impact of the cash flow.

54. The illegal practice of inducing panic selling in a neighborhood for financial gain is called
    A. steering.
    B. redlining.
    C. blockbusting.
    D. canvassing.

55. A broker must obey a seller's instructions to
    A. avoid all mention of the septic system.
    B. show the property only to white couples.
    C. refuse low offers without presenting them.
    D. be present personally at all showings of the property.

56. A document that transfers possession but does not transfer ownership is a
    A. warranty deed.
    B. deed with restriction.
    C. will.
    D. lease.

57. "Triggering terms" are phrases in an advertisement that
    A. move the buyer to action.
    B. first catch the reader's attention.
    C. mislead the reader as to geographic location.
    D. require full disclosure of financing details.

58. The term depreciation refers to
    A. the value of real estate after its useful life.
    B. loss of value in real estate due to any cause.
    C. costs incurred to modernize a building.
    D. the capitalized value of rent losses.

59. How many lots, each measuring 72.5 feet wide by 100 feet deep, could be created from a two-acre block of land?
    A. 3
    B. 6
    C. 9
    D. 12

60. The amount of money that would be paid for property by a buyer to a seller, both being ready, willing, and able to act and both being fully informed, represents that property's
    A. exchange value.
    B. market value.
    C. appraised value.
    D. equalized value.

61. The owner sold a duplex for a profit of $50,000 and took back a mortgage. The seller
    A. owes income tax on the entire gain in the year the property is sold.
    B. pays income tax year by year as payment is received.
    C. postpones tax if he purchases a vacation cottage within two years.
    D. collects interest in the first years, principal later.

62. A subdivider/developer, would like to control the types of vehicles that can be parked in front of homes in his classy subdivision. He can accomplish this with
    A. deed restrictions.
    B. enforcement of zoning.
    C. a reverter clause.
    D. eminent domain.

63. One way an investor in real estate may defer capital gain taxes is by
    A. exchanging for like property.
    B. obtaining maximum leverage.
    C. selling for cash.
    D. building reserves.

64. In the valuation of a hospital, which approach is given MOST weight?
    A. Cost
    B. Income capitalization
    C. Market data
    D. All equal weight

65. The sale of time-sharing units
    A. does not require a real estate license.
    B. allows buyers the right of rescission for seven days.
    C. is forbidden to individual owners.
    D. is usually on a flat-fee basis.

66. Covenants, conditions, and restrictions are placed on a condominium or cooperative development by the
    A. homeowners' association.
    B. attorney general's office.
    C. developer.
    D. present tenants.

67. The primary objective of a property manager should be to provide the owner with
    A. a low vacancy rate.
    B. the highest return on the property value.
    C. complete monthly reports of income and expense.
    D. allocated costs.

68. If a radon test on a home reveals a reading of 14 picocuries per liter, a prospective purchaser should probably
    A. not worry about it.
    B. report it to the local health department.
    C. ask to see a survey.
    D. request remediation.

69. A house sells for $102,000 and is appraised at $100,000 by a lender who is willing to make a 75% loan-to-value ratio loan. How much down payment does this house require?
    A. $25,000
    B. $25,500
    C. $27,000
    D. $75,000

70. Under the provisions of the ordinary store lease, trade fixtures that remain in the store after the expiration of the lease become the property of the
    A. lessee.
    B. new tenant.
    C. lessor.
    D. chattel mortgagee.

71. Which of the following obligates the broker to distribute the listing to other brokers?
    A. Open listing
    B. Option
    C. Multiple listing
    D. Friendly listing

72. A void contract is one that is
    A. not in writing.
    B. rescindable by agreement.
    C. missing an essential element.
    D. executory.

73. If there is an incident of discrimination, the complainant has to prove that
    A. the act was intentional.
    B. the offense was repeated.
    C. discrimination occurred.
    D. the act caused a loss.

74. An option is a contract that
    A. requires the buyer to complete the purchase.
    B. keeps an offer open for a specified time.
    C. gives the buyer an easement on the property.
    D. allows the buyer to occupy the property.

75. In the cost approach, the appraiser makes use of the
    A. owner's cost of the original building.
    B. estimate of the replacement cost of the building.
    C. sales prices of similar buildings.
    D. depreciated value used for income tax purposes.

76. A lease that requires the lessee to pay taxes, operating expenses, and insurance is called a
    A. gross lease.
    B. net lease.
    C. percentage lease.
    D. recorded lease.

77. The tenant with a month-to-month tenancy must give the landlord how much notice of intention to vacate?
    A. One week
    B. Two months
    C. One month
    D. No notice

78. When recorded in the county where real property of the defendant is located, a judgment becomes a(n)
    A. voluntary lien.
    B. attachment lien.
    C. involuntary lien.
    D. equitable lien.

79. Zoning ordinances are usually established by
    A. the federal government.
    B. local authorities.
    C. the state of New Jersey.
    D. court order.

80. A woman sold to a man an acre of land but reserved the right to cross the man's acre to reach the public road. The man's new property is called the
    A. dominant tenement.
    B. servient tenement.
    C. homestead.
    D. leasehold.

81. If a broker's license is suspended, the licenses of his or her salespersons are
    A. also suspended automatically.
    B. not affected.
    C. suspended for any salesperson who was aware of the offense at the time.
    D. allowed to continue for a six-month temporary period.

82. A broker-salesperson must
    A. maintain a separate escrow account.
    B. meet all broker qualifications.
    C. use only the designation "salesperson" on business cards.
    D. obtain a branch office license.

83. In New Jersey, an oral listing agreement
    A. is never legally enforceable.
    B. is enforceable if it is for less than one year.
    C. must be confirmed in writing within five days.
    D. is the most commonly used form of listing.

84. In New Jersey, a licensed broker must have
    A. a $50,000 bond.
    B. a separate escrow bank account.
    C. a college degree.
    D. all of the above.

85. A salesperson or broker may have to start all over again with classes and examination if a license is not renewed for
    A. one year.
    B. two years.
    C. three years.
    D. four years.

86. New Jersey's laws allow a landlord to refuse to rent to
    A. anyone on welfare.
    B. people with children.
    C. people with dogs.
    D. any of the above.

87. Which type of listing is illegal in New Jersey?
    A. Open listing
    B. Net listing
    C. Exclusive-right-to-sell listing
    D. Exclusive-agency listing

88. Every listing must include
    A. the broker's home phone number.
    B. square-foot measurement of the property.
    C. notice that commissions are negotiable.
    D. broker's promise to advertise the property.

89. In New Jersey, a landlord may not refuse a tenant solely because of
    A. political affiliation.
    B. children in the family.
    C. pet ownership.
    D. car ownership.

90. In New Jersey, continuous, open, notorious, hostile, and exclusive occupation of another's real property may lead to acquisition through adverse possession after a period of
    A. 5 years.
    B. 10 years.
    C. 20 years.
    D. 30 years.

91. After the 75-hour course is successfully completed, license application must be made within
    A. 30 days.
    B. 6 months.
    C. 1 year.
    D. 2 years.

92. The salesperson's license examination can be taken only by
    A. anyone who walks in.
    B. anyone enrolled in an approved prelicensing course.
    C. anyone who has successfully completed an approved prelicensing course.
    D. someone who has a sponsoring broker.

93. Unless the experience requirement is waived, the applicant for a broker's license must have served a full-time apprenticeship as a licensed salesperson for at LEAST
    A. 6 months.
    B. 1 year.
    C. 18 months.
    D. 3 years.

94. Records of all contracts of sale and listing agreements must be kept by a broker for at LEAST
    A. four years.
    B. five years.
    C. six years.
    D. seven years.

95. The Real Estate Commission is composed of how many members?
    A. Three
    B. Five
    C. Eight
    D. Ten

96. Educational requirements for a broker's license can be waived for certain
    A. brokers licensed in other states.
    B. spouses of recently deceased brokers.
    C. salespersons with ten years of full-time experience.
    D. college graduates who hold a doctorate.

97. A New Jersey real estate salesperson must be
    A. a citizen of the United States.
    B. at least 21 years old.
    C. a college graduate.
    D. sponsored by a supervising broker.

98. The Guaranty Fund is used to
    A. pay a broker commission unlawfully withheld by a seller.
    B. protect a salesperson if a broker refuses to split a commission as previously agreed.
    C. reimburse the public for losses arising from licensees' wrongdoing.
    D. compensate buyers who have suffered from unlawful discrimination.

99. A broker could lose his or her license for sharing a commission with
    A. another broker's salesperson.
    B. a broker in another state.
    C. a former salesperson who listed the house while in that broker's employ.
    D. another New Jersey broker.

100. With certain restrictions, a commission may be shared with an unlicensed person in the form of a rebate to the
    A. seller.
    B. buyer.
    C. broker's assistant.
    D. office secretary.

101. When a new building is considered safe for human habitation, a building inspector can issue a
    A. certificate of occupancy.
    B. restrictive covenant.
    C. special-use permit.
    D. building permit.

102. The largest fine that may be charged as a penalty for a violation of the New Jersey license law is
    A. $500.
    B. $5,000.
    C. $10,000.
    D. $50,000.

103. The New Jersey Real Estate Commission is part of the
    A. Department of Banking and Insurance.
    B. Attorney General's office.
    C. Education Department.
    D. Secretary of State's office.

104. Which of the following needs a real estate license when involved in handling a real estate transaction?
    A. An executor
    B. A bank
    C. A developer selling homes in her subdivision
    D. An auctioneer

105. The deed known in New Jersey as a bargain and sale deed with covenants against grantors acts is also known as a
    A. quitclaim deed.
    B. fiduciary deed.
    C. warranty deed.
    D. special warranty deed.

106. A man dies suddenly, leaving a wife and two minor children but no will. The New Jersey law of descent provides that his wife is entitled to
    A. his entire estate.
    B. half of his estate.
    C. $50,000 plus half the remaining estate.
    D. the entire remaining estate after the children reach 21.

107. New Jersey's Consumer Information Statement lists
    A. both obvious and latent defects in the property.
    B. protected classes under the state's fair housing laws.
    C. the licensees agency relationship to each party.
    D. current mortgage plans available from local lenders.

108. In New Jersey, Megan's Law requires that
    A. a community be alerted to the presence of convicted sex offenders.
    B. buyers be given three days after signing in which to void a purchase contract.
    C. in the absence of a will, surviving children are entitled to half an estate.
    D. tenants aged 62 or older may not be evicted.

109. The Mt. Laurel lawsuits were concerned with
    A. blockbusting.
    B. redlining.
    C. stigmatized property.
    D. exclusionary zoning.

110. In New Jersey, a residential lease for one year or more is subject to review and possible cancellation by the tenant's attorney
    A. but not by the landlord's attorney.
    B. any time during the first month of tenancy.
    C. within three business days of signing.
    D. only if the attorney's notice is given by certified mail.

APPENDIX A: NEW JERSEY REAL ESTATE LICENSE ACT—STATUTE AND RULES*

THE NEW JERSEY

REAL ESTATE LICENSE ACT

STATUTE AND RULES

Phil Murphy, Governor

Sheila Oliver, Lt. Governor

Marlene Caride, Commissioner
Department of Banking and Insurance

Aurelio Romero, Executive Director
NJ Real Estate Commission

REVISED 11/2019

STATE OF NEW JERSEY
REAL ESTATE COMMISSION MANUAL

FOREWORD

This Reference Manual contains the entire New Jersey Real Estate License Law, N.J.S.A. 45:15-1 et seq., as amended through P.L. 2019 Chapter 266 and J.R. 22 of the Second Annual Session of the New Jersey 218th Legislature, and all rules issued under the statute through the New Jersey Register, Vol. 51, No. 21, November 4, 2019. The text of the statute is an exact duplication of the official text of the law. The text of the rules is an exact duplication of the official text found in Title 11, Chapter 5 of the New Jersey Administrative Code.

Please direct any questions regarding this manual to: New Jersey Real Estate Commission, P.O. Box 328, Trenton, New Jersey 08625-0328.

Please direct any questions regarding the New Jersey Administrative Code and/or New Jersey Register to: Office of Administrative Law, P.O. Box 049, Trenton, New Jersey 08625.

PREFACE

This reference manual is being furnished to real estate licensees. It is being provided so that licensees may have the benefit of a current publication of the New Jersey License Law and the Rules promulgated thereunder.

The Real Estate Commission urges all brokers to make this manual part of their office library, conveniently available to all licensees.

This reference manual project was authorized pursuant to N.J.S.A. 45:15-16.2 as an educational and informational project. The Commission gratefully acknowledges the cooperation of the Commissioner of Banking and Insurance in releasing earnings from the New Jersey Guaranty Fund to enable this project to be accomplished at no cost to New Jersey taxpayers. Thus, all licensees can see tangible evidence of the benefits which accrue to them by their contributions to the Real Estate Guaranty Fund.

The New Jersey Real Estate Commission was created in 1921 by an act of the Legislature, N.J.S.A. 45:15-1 et. seq., entitled "An Act to define, regulate and license real estate brokers and salesmen, to create a State Real Estate Commission and to provide penalties for the violation of the provisions hereof." Five members of the Commission must be real estate brokers, licensed for a period of at least ten years; two members are public members and one member is a representative of an appropriate department of state government. All members of the Commission serve for a term of three years except the government representative who serves at the pleasure of the Governor.

CURRENT COMMISSIONERS – 2019

Linda Stefanik, President, Broker Member, since 2010 (Seaside Park)

Eugenia K. Bonilla, Vice-President, Broker Member, since 2012 (Mount Laurel)

Denise Illes, Department Representative, since 2015 (Trenton)

Christina Banasiak, Broker Member, since 2017 (Manalapan)

Darlene Bandazian, Broker Member, since 2018 (Ramsey)

Jacob Elkes, Public Member, since 2016 (Freehold)

Kathryn Godby Oram, Broker Member, since 2016 (Morristown)

Carlos Lejnieks, Public Member, since 2018 (Newark)

REVISED 11/2019

REAL ESTATE COMMISSION PERSONNEL AND PHONE NUMBERS

General Phone Numbers	
Licensing	**(609) 292-7272**
Administration	**(609) 292-7272**
Fax Number	**(609) 292-0944**
E-mail	**(General)** realestate@dobi.nj.gov
	(Licensing) relic@dobi.nj.gov
Website	www.dobi.nj.gov
Executive Director	**(609) 292-7272**
Aurelio Romero	
Licensing and Education Bureau	**(609) 292-7272**
Gwendolyn T. Cobb, Supervisor	Ext. 50536
Investigations Bureau	**(609) 292-7272**
Lauren Glantzberg, Supervisor	Ext. 50145
Bureau of Subdivided Land Sales Control	**(609) 940-7396**
Jaqueline Ferri	

REVISED 11/2019

CONTENTS

PROFESSIONS AND OCCUPATIONS
TITLE 45, CHAPTER 15
REAL ESTATE BROKERS, BROKER-SALESPERSONS, AND SALESPERSONS

Section

Page

ARTICLE 1. GENERAL PROVISIONS

ARTICLE 2. REAL ESTATE AUCTIONEERS [REPEALED]

ARTICLE 3. REAL ESTATE GUARANTY FUND

SUBCHAPTER 8. DISCIPLINARY ACTIONS/ CONDITIONS FOR RESTORATION OF LICENSE/ REAL ESTATE GUARANTY FUND CLAIMS

SUBCHAPTER 9. RULES INTERPRETING AND IMPLEMENTING THE REAL ESTATE SALES FULL DISCLOSURE ACT, N.J.S.A. 45:15-16.27 ET SEQ.

SUBCHAPTER 9A. RULES INTERPRETING AND IMPLEMENTING THE NEW JERSEY REAL ESTATE TIMESHARE ACT, N.J.S.A. 45:15-16.50 ET SEQ.

REAL ESTATE BROKERS, BROKER-SALESPERSONS, AND SALESPERSONS

N.J.S.A. 45:15-1 ET SEQ.

TITLE 45. PROFESSIONS AND OCCUPATIONS

SUBTITLE 1. PROFESSIONS AND OCCUPATIONS
SUBJECT TO STATE BOARDS OF REGISTRATION
AND EXAMINATION

CHAPTER 15.

Phil Murphy, Governor
State of New Jersey

Sheila Oliver, Lt. Governor
State of New Jersey

Marlene Caride, Commissioner
Department of Banking and Insurance

Aurelio Romero, Executive Director
NJ Real Estate Commission

TITLE 45. PROFESSIONS AND OCCUPATIONS

SUBTITLE 1. PROFESSIONS AND OCCUPATIONS SUBJECT TO STATE BOARDS OF REGISTRATION AND EXAMINATION

CHAPTER 15. REAL ESTATE BROKERS, BROKER-SALESPERSONS, AND SALESPERSONS

ARTICLE 1. GENERAL PROVISIONS

45:15-1.   License required

No person shall engage either directly or indirectly in the business of a real estate broker, broker-salesperson, or salesperson, temporarily or otherwise, and no person shall advertise or represent himself as being authorized to act as a real estate broker, broker-salesperson, or salesperson, or to engage in any of the activities described in R.S.45:15-3, without being licensed so to do as hereinafter provided.

45:15-1.1.   Role of housing referral aide

A person employed in a participant position as a housing referral aide under any program established and funded pursuant to the Comprehensive Employment and Training Act of 1973, Pub.L. 93-203, 29 U.S.C. 801 et seq., while performing his duties in such position, shall not be deemed to be engaged in the business of a real estate broker, broker-salesperson or salesperson under the provisions of chapter 15 of Title 45 of the Revised Statutes.

45:15-1.2.   License required for acceptance of compensation for providing assistance in locating rental housing

Any person who, before a lease has been fully executed or, where no lease is drawn, before possession is taken by the tenant, charges or accepts any fee, commission or compensation in exchange for providing assistance in locating rental housing, including providing written lists or telephone information on purportedly available rental units, without being licensed pursuant to this act shall be a disorderly person and shall be subject to a fine of not less than $200 or to imprisonment for not more than 30 days or both.

The provisions of this section shall not be construed to prohibit a licensed real estate broker, or an owner of rental properties or his agents and employees, from requiring the payment of a deposit to reserve a particular unit or from charging and accepting a fee for processing an application to rent an apartment or for performing a credit check or other investigation upon prospective tenants prior to the execution of a lease or the taking of possession of a rental unit by a prospective tenant.

45:15-2.   "Engaging in business" defined

Any single act, transaction or sale shall constitute engaging in business within the meaning of this article.

45:15-3.   Terms defined, license required for bringing action for compensation

A real estate broker, for the purposes of R.S.45:15-1 et seq., is defined to be a person, firm or corporation who, for a fee, commission or other valuable consideration, or by reason of a promise or reasonable expectation thereof, lists for sale, sells, exchanges, buys or rents, or offers or attempts to negotiate a sale, exchange, purchase or rental of real estate or an interest therein, or collects or offers or attempts to collect rent for the use of real estate or solicits for prospective purchasers or assists or directs in the procuring of prospects or the negotiation or closing of any transaction which does or is contemplated to result in the sale, exchange, leasing, renting or auctioning of any real estate or negotiates, or offers or attempts or agrees to negotiate a loan secured or to be secured by mortgage or other encumbrance upon or transfer of any real estate for others, or any person who, for pecuniary gain or expectation of pecuniary gain conducts a public or private competitive sale of lands or any interest in lands. In the sale of lots pursuant to the provisions of R.S.45:15-1 et seq., the term "real estate broker" shall also include any person, partnership, association or corporation employed or contracted by or on behalf of the owner or owners of lots or other parcels of real estate, at a stated salary, or upon a commission, or upon a salary and commission, or otherwise, to sell such real estate, or any parts thereof, in lots or other parcels, and who shall sell or exchange, or offer or attempt or agree to negotiate the sale or exchange, of any such lot or parcel of real estate. A real estate broker shall also include any person, firm, or corporation who supervises a real estate referral company.

A real estate salesperson, for the purposes of R.S.45:15-1 et seq., is defined to be any natural person who, for compensation, valuable consideration or commission, or other thing of value, or by reason of a promise or reasonable expectation thereof, is employed or contracted by and operates under the supervision of a licensed real estate broker to sell or offer to sell, buy or offer to buy or negotiate the purchase, sale or exchange of real estate, or offers or attempts to negotiate a loan secured or to be secured by a mortgage or other encumbrance upon or transfer of real estate, or to lease or rent, or offer to lease or rent any real estate for others, or to collect rents for the use of real estate, or to solicit for prospective purchasers or lessees of real estate, or who is employed or contracted by a licensed real estate broker to sell or offer to sell lots or other parcels of real estate, at a stated salary, or upon a commission, or upon a salary and commission, or otherwise to sell real estate, or any parts thereof, in lots or other parcels, or in the case of a salesperson licensed with a real estate referral company refers prospective consumers of real estate brokerage services to a particular broker. For the purposes of R.S.45:15-1 et seq., the definition of real estate salesperson

45:15-3.1

shall include a salesperson licensed with a real estate referral company unless otherwise indicated.

A real estate broker-salesperson, for the purposes of R.S.45:15-1 et seq., is defined to be any natural person who is qualified to be licensed as a real estate broker but who, for compensation, valuable consideration or commission, or other thing of value, or by reason of a promise or reasonable expectation thereof, is employed or contracted by and operates under the supervision of a licensed real estate broker to perform the functions of a real estate salesperson as defined herein.

A real estate salesperson licensed with a real estate referral company, for the purposes of R.S.45:15-1 et seq., is defined to be any natural person employed or contracted by and operating under the supervision of a licensed real estate broker through a real estate referral company whose real estate brokerage-related activities are limited to referring prospects for the sale, purchase, exchange, leasing or rental of real estate or an interest therein. Salespersons licensed with a real estate referral company shall only refer such prospects to the real estate broker who supervises the real estate referral company through whom they are licensed and shall only accept compensation for their activity from that broker. A salesperson licensed with a real estate referral company shall not be employed or contracted by or licensed with more than one real estate broker or real estate referral company at any given time. No salesperson licensed with a real estate referral company may simultaneously be licensed as a real estate broker or broker-salesperson and no salesperson licensed with a real estate referral company may engage in the business of a real estate broker or broker-salesperson to an extent beyond that authorized by their status as a licensed salesperson.

A real estate referral company, for the purposes of R.S.45:15-1 et seq., is defined to be a business entity established and supervised by a licensed real estate broker, separate and apart from any business entity maintained by the licensed real estate broker to conduct real estate brokerage-related activities other than the referral of prospective consumers of real estate brokerage services to that broker, for the purpose of employing or contracting licensed salespersons who strictly engage in the referral of prospects for the sale, purchase, exchange, leasing or rental of real estate or an interest therein solely on behalf of the supervising real estate broker.

No person, firm, partnership, association or corporation shall bring or maintain any action in the courts of this State for the collection of compensation for the performance of any of the acts mentioned in R.S.45:15-1 et seq. without alleging and proving that he was a duly licensed real estate broker at the time the alleged cause of action arose.

No person claiming to be entitled to compensation as a salesperson or broker-salesperson for the performance of any of the acts mentioned in R.S.45:15-1 et seq. shall bring or maintain any action in the courts of this State for the collection of compensation against any person, firm, partnership or corporation other than the licensed broker with whom the salesperson or broker-salesperson was employed or contracted at the time the alleged cause of action arose and no action shall be brought or maintained without the claimant alleging and proving that he was a duly licensed real estate salesperson or broker-salesperson at the time the alleged cause of action arose.

45:15-3.1.   Payment of referral fee, commission to person licensed in another jurisdiction

A duly licensed real estate broker of this State may pay a referral fee or referral commission to a person not licensed if the person is a licensed real estate broker of another jurisdiction in which the licensed broker maintains a bona fide office. A licensed real estate broker of another jurisdiction may make a referral, receive a referral fee or referral commission, and bring or maintain an action in the courts of this State against a duly licensed real estate broker of this State for the collection of the fee or commission.

For the purposes of this section, "referral" means the introduction, assisting, or directing of a person by one broker to another broker for real estate brokerage services, aid, or information; "referral fee" or "referral commission" means the compensation paid or received for the referral.

45:15-3.2.   Written agreement

a. No broker-salesperson or salesperson shall commence business activity for a broker and no broker shall authorize a broker-salesperson or salesperson to act on the broker's behalf until a written agreement, as provided in this subsection, has been signed by the broker and broker-salesperson or salesperson. Prior to an individual's commencement of business activity as a broker-salesperson or salesperson under the authority of a broker, the broker and broker-salesperson or salesperson shall both sign a written agreement which recites the terms under which the services of the broker-salesperson or salesperson have been retained by the broker.

b. Notwithstanding any provision of R.S.45:15-1 et seq. or any other law, rule, or regulation to the contrary, a business affiliation between a broker and a broker-salesperson or salesperson may be that of an employment relationship or the provision of services by an independent contractor. The nature of the business affiliation shall be defined in the written agreement required pursuant to subsection a. of this section.

45:15-4.   Application of provisions of article limited

The provisions of this article shall not apply to any person, firm, partnership, association or corporation who, as a bona fide owner or lessor, shall perform any of the aforesaid acts with reference to property owned by him, nor shall they apply to or be construed to include attorneys at law, receivers, trustees in bankruptcy, executors, administrators or persons selling real estate under the order of any court or the terms of a deed of trust, state banks, federal banks, savings banks and trust companies located within the state, or to insurance companies incorporated under the insurance laws of this state.

45:15-5.   New Jersey Real Estate Commission continued

The New Jersey Real Estate Commission, hereinafter in this article designated as the "commission," created and established by an act entitled "An act to define, regulate and license real estate brokers and salesmen, to create a State real estate commission and to provide penalties for the violation of the provisions hereof," approved April 5, 1921 (P.L.1921, c. 141, s. 370), as amended by an act approved April 23, 1929 (P.L.1929, c. 168, s. 310), is continued. The commission shall constitute the division of the New Jersey Real Estate Commission in the Department of Insurance. The commission shall consist of eight members, appointed by the Governor pursuant to the provisions of P.L.1971, c. 60 (C. 45:1-2.1 et seq.), each of whom shall have been a resident of this State for a period of at least 10 years. Five members shall have been real estate brokers for a period of at least 10 years; two members shall be public members; and one member shall be a representative of an appropriate department. The department representative shall serve at the pleasure of the Governor. Upon the expiration of the term of office of any other member, his successor shall be appointed by the Governor for a term of three years. A majority of the voting members of the commission shall constitute a quorum thereof. Each member shall hold his office until his successor has qualified. Members to fill vacancies shall be appointed by the Governor for the unexpired term. The Governor may remove any commissioner for cause, upon notice and opportunity to be heard.

45:15-6.   Commission salaries

The commission shall select from its members a president, and may do all things necessary and convenient for carrying into effect the provisions of this article, and may promulgate necessary rules and regulations pursuant to the "Administrative Procedure Act," P.L. 1968, c. 410 (C. 52:14B-1 et seq.) The president shall receive a salary of $15,000.00 per year and each other member of the commission shall receive a salary of $10,000.00 per year, except the department representative who serves without compensation pursuant to section 2 of P.L. 1971, c. 60 (C. 45:1-2.2). No commissioner shall receive any other compensation, either directly or indirectly, for his services.

45:15-7.   Provision, duties of personnel

The Commissioner of Insurance shall provide the commission with such personnel as he shall deem necessary, after consulta-

tion with the commission, for the proper discharge of the duties imposed by the provisions of this article. The Commissioner of Insurance shall prescribe the duties of persons thus assigned to the commission, and shall fix their compensation, within the limits of available appropriations therefor. The Commissioner of Insurance shall provide the commission with such office space, furniture and stationery as he shall determine, after consultation with the commission, to be reasonably necessary for carrying out the provisions of this article.

45:15-8.   Seal; certified copies of records as evidence; public inspection of records

The commission shall adopt a common seal by which it shall authenticate its proceedings. Copies of all records and papers in the office of the commission, duly certified and authenticated by its seal, shall be received in evidence in all courts with like effect as the original. All records kept in the office of the commission under the authority of this article shall be open to public inspection under regulations prescribed by the commission.

45:15-9.   Real estate licenses

a. All persons desiring to become real estate brokers, broker-salespersons, or salespersons shall apply to the commission for a license under the provisions of R.S.45:15-1 et seq. Every applicant for a license as a broker, broker-salesperson, or salesperson shall be of the age of 18 years or over, and in the case of an association or a corporation the directors thereof shall be of the age of 18 years or over. Application for a license, whether as a real estate broker, broker-salesperson, or salesperson, shall be made to the commission upon forms prescribed by it and shall be accompanied by an application fee of $50 which fee shall not be refundable. Every applicant for a license whether as a real estate broker, broker-salesperson, or salesperson shall have the equivalent of a high school education. The issuance of a license to an applicant who is a nonresident of this State shall be deemed to be his irrevocable consent that service of process upon him as a licensee in any action or proceeding may be made upon him by service upon the secretary of the commission or the person in charge of the office of the commission. The applicant shall furnish evidence of good moral character, and in the case of an association, partnership or corporation, the members, officers or directors thereof shall furnish evidence of good moral character. The commission may make such investigation and require such proof as it deems proper and in the public interest as to the honesty, trustworthiness, character and integrity of an applicant. Any applicant for licensure pursuant to this section and any officer, director, partner or owner of a controlling interest of a corporation or partnership filing for licensure pursuant to this section shall submit to the commission the applicant's name, address, fingerprints and written consent for a criminal history record background check to be performed. The commission is hereby authorized to exchange fingerprint data with and receive criminal history record information from the State Bureau of Identification in the Division of State Police and

45:15-9

the Federal Bureau of Investigation consistent with applicable State and federal laws, rules and regulations, for the purposes of facilitating determinations concerning licensure eligibility. The applicant shall bear the cost for the criminal history record background check, including all costs of administering and processing the check. The Division of State Police shall promptly notify the commissioner in the event a current holder of a license or prospective applicant, who was the subject of a criminal history record background check pursuant to this section, is arrested for a crime or offense in this State after the date the background check was performed. Every applicant for a license as a broker or broker-salesperson shall have first been the holder of a New Jersey real estate salesperson's license and have been actively engaged on a full-time basis in the real estate brokerage business in this State as a real estate salesperson for three years immediately preceding the date of application, which requirement may be waived by the commission where the applicant has been the holder of a broker's license in another state and actively engaged in the real estate brokerage business for at least three years immediately preceding the date of his application, meets the educational requirements and qualifies by examination. No license as a broker shall be granted to a general partnership or corporation unless at least one of the partners or officers of said general partnership or corporation qualifies as and holds a license as a broker to transact business in the name and on behalf of said general partnership or corporation as its authorized broker and no such authorized broker shall act as a broker on his own individual account unless he is also licensed as a broker in his individual name; the license of said general partnership or corporation shall cease if at least one partner or officer does not hold a license as its authorized broker at all times. A change in the status of the license of an authorized broker to an individual capacity or vice versa shall be effected by application to the commission accompanied by a fee of $50. No license as a broker shall be granted to a limited partnership unless its general partner qualifies as and holds a license as a broker to transact business in the name of and on behalf of the limited partnership. In the event that a corporation is a general partner of a limited partnership, no license as a broker shall be granted to the limited partnership unless the corporation is licensed as a broker and one of the officers of the corporation qualifies as and holds a license as the corporation's authorized broker.

b. An application for licensure as a salesperson licensed with a real estate referral company and for any renewal thereof shall include a certification signed by the licensed real estate broker by whom the applicant is or will be employed or contracted, on a form and in a manner prescribed by the commission, which certification shall confirm that: the broker and the applicant or renewing salesperson licensed with a real estate referral company have reviewed the restrictions imposed by law upon the activities of a salesperson licensed with a real estate referral company; and the applicant or salesperson licensed with a real estate referral company has acknowledged that he is aware that such activity is limited to referring prospective consumers of real estate brokerage services to that broker.

c. In the event that a person who held a broker, broker-salesperson or salesperson license fails to renew that license and then, in the two years immediately following the expiration date of the last license held, seeks to reinstate such license, the commission shall require, as a condition to such reinstatement during that two-year period, that the applicant submit proof of having completed the continuing education requirement applicable to that license type in the preceding license term.

d. In the event that any person to whom a broker's or broker-salesperson's license has been or shall have been issued shall fail to renew such license or obtain a new license for a period of more than two but less than five consecutive years after the expiration of the last license held, prior to issuing another broker or broker-salesperson license to the person, the commission shall require such person to complete the continuing education requirements applicable to salesperson licensees in the preceding license term, to work as a licensed salesperson on a full-time basis for one full year, to pass the broker's license examination, and to successfully complete a 90-hour general broker's pre-licensure course at a licensed real estate school, as the commission shall prescribe by regulation. In the event that any person to whom a broker's or broker-salesperson's license has been or shall have been issued fails to maintain or renew the license or obtain a new license for a period of more than five consecutive years after the expiration of the last license held, prior to issuing another broker or broker-salesperson license to the person the commission shall require the person to pass the salesperson's license examination and then to work as a licensed salesperson on a full-time basis for three years, to fulfill all of the educational requirements applicable to first time applicants for a broker or broker-salesperson license and to pass the broker's license examination. The commission may, in its discretion, approve for relicensure the former holder of a broker or broker-salesperson license who has not renewed the license or obtained a new license for two or more consecutive years upon a sufficient showing that the applicant was medically unable to do so. All applicants so approved shall pass the broker's license examination and complete the continuing education requirements applicable to broker licensees in the preceding licensure term prior to being relicensed. This subsection shall not apply to a person reapplying for a broker's or broker-salesperson's license who was licensed as a broker or broker-salesperson and who allowed his license to expire due to subsequent employment in a public agency in this State with responsibility for dealing with matters relating to real estate if the person reapplying does so within one year of termination of that employment.

e. In the event that any person to whom a salesperson's license, including a salesperson's license with a real estate referral company, has been or shall have been issued shall fail to maintain or renew such license or obtain a new license for a period of two consecutive years or more after the expiration of the last license held, the commission shall require such person to attend a licensed school and pass the State examination prior to issuance of a further license. The commission may, in its discretion, approve for relicensure a salesperson applicant, including a salesperson applicant licensed with a real estate referral company, who has not renewed his license or obtained a new license for two or more consecutive years upon a sufficient showing that the applicant was medically unable to do so. All salesperson applicants, including salesperson applicants licensed with a real estate referral company, so approved shall pass the salesperson's license examination and, with respect to salespersons, except those salespersons licensed with a real estate referral company, complete the continuing education requirements applicable to salesperson licensees in the preceding licensure term prior to being relicensed. Nothing in this section shall be construed to require a salesperson licensed with a real estate referral company to complete the continuing education requirements applicable to salesperson licensees as a condition of license renewal under this section or section 23 of P.L.2009, c.238 (C.45:15-16.2a). This subsection shall not apply to a person reapplying for a salesperson's license, including a salesperson reapplying for licensure with a real estate referral company, who was a licensed salesperson, including a salesperson licensed with a real estate referral company, and who allowed his license to expire due to subsequent employment in a public agency in this State with responsibility for dealing with matters relating to real estate if the person reapplying does so within one year of termination of that employment.

f. A salesperson licensed with a real estate referral company who was not previously licensed as a broker, broker-salesperson, or salesperson and who has been a salesperson licensed with a real estate referral company for the six immediately preceding years or any lesser period of time shall, in order to qualify for licensure as a salesperson, complete up to 30 hours of continuing education as prescribed by commission rule.

g. A salesperson licensed with a real estate referral company who was not previously licensed as a broker, broker-salesperson or salesperson and who has been a salesperson licensed with a real estate referral company for more than the six immediately preceding years shall, in order to qualify for licensure as a salesperson, be required to complete the pre-licensure education requirement applicable to candidates for licensure as a salesperson and pass the State license examination. A person who was previously licensed as a broker, broker-salesperson or salesperson and who has been a salesperson licensed with a real estate referral company shall, in order to qualify for relicensure as a broker, broker-salesperson or salesperson, as applicable, complete up to 30 hours of continuing education as prescribed by commission rule.

h. Any salesperson licensed with a real estate referral company seeking licensure as a real estate broker, broker-salesperson or salesperson shall make application for such license on a form as prescribed by the commission, pay all application and licensure fees as set forth herein, furnish to the commission evidence of the salesperson's good moral character, and be subject to investigation by and required to produce to the commission such proof of the salesperson's honesty, trustworthiness and integrity as the commission deems proper and in the public interest.

i. Upon the effective date of P.L.2018, c.71 (C.45:15-3.2 et al.), any person licensed as a referral agent through a real estate referral company shall be deemed to be a salesperson licensed with a real estate referral company until the next renewal of licenses by the commission. All requirements set forth in subsections f., g., and h. of this section with respect to licensure and length of experience as a salesperson licensed with a real estate referral company shall include licensure and length of experience as a referral agent licensed with a real estate referral company.

45:15-10.   Examination required for initial licensure; term, renewal

Before any such license shall be granted, the applicant, and in the case of a partnership, association or corporation, the partners, directors or officers thereof actually engaged in the real estate business as a broker, broker-salesperson, or salesperson, shall submit to an examination to be conducted under the supervision of the commission which examination shall test the applicant's general knowledge of the statutes of New Jersey concerning real property, conveyancing, mortgages, agreements of sale, leases and of the provisions of R.S.45:15-1 et seq., the rules and regulations of the commission and such other subjects as the commission may direct. The commission may make rules and regulations for the conduct of such examinations. Upon satisfactorily passing such examination and fulfilling all other qualifications a license shall be granted by the commission to the successful applicant therefor as a real estate broker, broker-salesperson, or salesperson, and the applicant upon receiving the license is authorized to conduct in this State the business of a real estate broker, broker-salesperson, or salesperson, as the case may be. Such license shall expire on the last day of a two-year license term as established by the commission; such license shall be renewed, without examination, biennially thereafter, upon the payment of the fee fixed by R.S.45:15-15, and in the case of a broker, broker-salesperson or salesperson license, upon completion of the continuing education requirements applicable to the holders of such licenses, except that a salesperson licensed with a real estate referral company shall not be required to complete the continuing education requirements as a condition of license renewal under this section or section 23 of P.L.2009, c.238 (C.45:15-16.2a).

45:15-10.1.   Educational requirements

a. As a prerequisite to admission to an examination, every individual applicant for licensure as a real estate salesperson shall give evidence of satisfactory completion of 75 hours in the aggregate of such courses of education in real estate subjects at

45:15-10.2

a school licensed by the commission as the commission shall by regulation prescribe. At least three hours of that course of study shall be on the subject of ethics and ethical conduct in the profession of a real estate salesperson, and at least one hour of that course of study shall be on the subject of fair housing and housing discrimination.

b. As a prerequisite to admission to an examination, every individual applicant for licensure as a real estate broker or broker-salesperson shall give evidence of satisfactory completion of 150 hours in the aggregate of such courses of education in real estate and related subjects at a school licensed by the commission as the commission shall by regulation prescribe. Thirty hours of that course of study shall be on the subject of ethics and ethical conduct in the profession of a real estate broker, and at least one hour of that course of study shall be on the subject of fair housing and housing discrimination.

The commission may approve courses in specialized aspects of the real estate brokerage business offered by providers who are not the holders of a real estate school license pursuant to section 47 of P.L.1993, c.51 (C.45:15-10.4), the completion of which may be recognized as fulfilling a portion of the total broker pre-licensure education requirements.

45:15-10.2.   Waiver of educational requirements for licensure

The commission may waive some or all of the educational requirements for licensure established pursuant to subsection a. of section 1 of P.L.1966, c. 227 (C. 45:15-10.1) in the case of an applicant whose education or experience is in the judgment of the commission substantially equivalent to those educational requirements. The commission shall prescribe by regulation the requirements which an applicant shall meet in order to qualify for the waiver of educational requirements pursuant to this section.

45:15-10.3.   Bureau of Real Estate Education

There is established within the Division of the New Jersey Real Estate Commission in the Department of Insurance a Bureau of Real Estate Education which shall be responsible for the licensure of real estate pre-licensure schools and instructors.

45:15-10.4.   Licensure of real estate school

a. No school shall conduct real estate education courses, the attendance and successful completion of which shall constitute the fulfillment of the educational prerequisites for licensure established pursuant to section 1 of P.L.1966, c. 227 (C.

45:15-10.1) unless licensed as a real estate school pursuant to P.L.1993, c. 51 (C. 45:15-12.3 et al.).

b. A school shall not be licensed as a real estate school unless its owners, management and facilities meet all of the qualifications for licensure established pursuant to this amendatory and supplementary act and which the commission may by regulation prescribe. An applicant for a license to operate a real estate school, and in the case of a partnership or corporation the members, officers, directors and owners of a controlling interest thereof, shall affirmatively demonstrate their good moral character to the commission. The commission may make such investigation and require such proof as it deems proper and in the public interest as to the honesty, trustworthiness, character and integrity of an applicant.

45:15-10.5.   Licensure as real estate instructor

a. No person, with the exception of a guest lecturer, may teach real estate education courses, the attendance and successful completion of which shall constitute the fulfillment of the educational prerequisites for licensure established pursuant to section 1 of P.L.1966, c. 227 (C. 45:15-10.1) unless licensed as a real estate instructor pursuant to this amendatory and supplementary act.

b. A person shall not be licensed as a real estate instructor unless the person affirmatively demonstrates to the commission his good moral character, successfully completes a real estate instructor course approved by the commission, successfully completes a written examination conducted under the auspices of the commission, and meets all other qualifications as the commission may prescribe by regulation.

45:15-10.6.   Application for, issuance of license as real estate school, fees

a. Every application for licensure as a real estate school shall be accompanied by an application fee of $100 and a criminal history record check fee for all individual owners, members of a partnership, or officers, directors and owners of a controlling interest in a corporation, which fees shall be non-refundable. Any applicant filing for licensure pursuant to this section and any officer, director, partner or owner of a controlling interest of a corporation or partnership filing for licensure pursuant to this section shall submit to the commission, the applicant's name, address, fingerprints and written consent for a criminal history record background check to be performed. The commission is hereby authorized to exchange fingerprint data with and receive criminal history record information from the State Bureau of Identification in the Division of State Police and the Federal Bureau of Investigation consistent with applicable State and federal laws, rules and regulations, for the purposes of facilitating determinations concerning licensure eligibility. The applicant shall bear the cost for the criminal history record background check, including all costs of administering and processing the check. The Division of State Police shall promptly notify the commissioner in the event a current holder of a license or prospective applicant, who was the subject of a criminal history record background check pursuant to this section, is arrested for a crime or offense in this State after the date the background was performed.

b. All licenses issued to real estate schools shall expire on a date fixed by the commission which date shall not be more than two years from the date of issuance of the license. The license fee for each real estate school license issued in the first 12 months of any two-year real estate school license term established by the commission shall be $400 for the first location and $200 for each additional location licensed. The license fee for each real estate school license issued in the second 12 months of any two-year real estate school license term established by the commission shall be $200 for the first location and $100 for each additional location licensed. The fee for the renewal of each real estate school license for an additional two-year license term shall be $400 for the first location and $200 for each additional location.

c. Any accredited college or university located in this State or any public adult education program conducted by a board of education in this State which otherwise qualifies for licensure as a real estate school shall be issued a license without the payment of any license or license renewal fee.

45:15-10.7.   Application for, issuance of license as real estate instructor; fees

Every application for licensure as a real estate instructor shall be accompanied by an application fee of $50 and a criminal history record check fee, which fees shall be non-refundable. Any applicant filing for licensure pursuant to this section and any officer, director, partner or owner of a controlling interest of a corporation or partnership filing for licensure pursuant to this section shall submit to the commission the applicant's name, address, fingerprints and written consent for a criminal history record background check to be performed. The commission is hereby authorized to exchange fingerprint data with and receive criminal history record information from the State Bureau of Identification in the Division of State Police and the Federal Bureau of Investigation consistent with applicable State and federal laws, rules and regulations, for the purposes of facilitating determinations concerning licensure eligibility. The applicant shall bear the cost for the criminal history record background check, including all costs of administering and processing the check. The Division of State Police shall promptly notify the commissioner in the event a current holder of a license or prospective applicant, who was the subject of a criminal history record background check pursuant to this section, is arrested for a crime or offense in this State after the date the background was performed. All licenses issued to real estate instructors

shall expire on a date fixed by the commission which shall be no more than two years from the date of issuance of the license. The license fee for each real estate instructor license issued in the first 12 months of any two-year real estate instructor license term established by the commission shall be $200 and the fee for an instructor license issued in the second 12 months of the cycle shall be $100. The fee for the renewal of each real estate instructor license for an additional two-year license term shall be $100. Upon payment of the renewal fee and the submission of evidence of satisfactory completion of any continuing education requirements which the commission may by regulation prescribe, the commission shall renew the license of a real estate instructor for a two-year period.

45:15-10.8.   Director of real estate school

A school shall not be licensed as a real estate school unless it is under the management and supervision of a director who is approved by the commission and who is licensed as a real estate instructor in accordance with the provisions of this act. In the event of the death or mental or physical incapacity of the director of a licensed real estate school, which leaves no other owner or employee of the school licensed as a real estate instructor and willing to assume the responsibilities of the director on an interim or permanent basis, the commission may issue temporary authorization to another person to enable that person to carry on the duties of the director until such time as either another licensed instructor is designated by the school and approved by the commission as the director, or until such time as the real estate courses in progress at the time of the former director's death or incapacity are completed. A school shall not commence any new real estate courses until a qualified licensee is designated and approved as the school's director.

The provisions of this section shall not apply to any public adult education program conducted under the auspices of a board of education in this State or any accredited college or university licensed as real estate schools.

45:15-10.9.   Director of public adult education program

No public adult education program conducted under the auspices of a board of education in this State and no accredited college or university in this State shall be licensed as a real estate school unless its real estate pre-licensure education program is under the supervision of a director who is a licensed real estate instructor or an individual who has affirmatively demonstrated to the commission his good moral character and has attended a real estate instructor course approved by the commission within two years of applying to the commission for approval as the director of the real estate program. In the event of the death or physical or mental incapacity of the director of a public adult education program or the director of a college or university licensed as a

45:15-10.10

real estate school, which leaves no other employee licensed as a real estate instructor or otherwise qualified to be the director of the program and willing to assume the responsibilities of the director on an interim or permanent basis, the commission may issue a temporary authorization to another person to enable that person to carry on the duties of the director until such time as either another licensed instructor or qualified person is designated by the school and approved by the commission as the director, or until such time as the real estate courses in progress at the time of the former director's death or incapacity are completed. New courses shall not be commenced by the school until a qualified person is designated and approved as the director of the school.

45:15-10.10. Real estate school, instructor license

Upon application to the commission and payment of the prescribed license fee no later than January 1, 1994, any school and instructor then designated by the commission as an approved school or instructor shall, subject to the results of the commission's investigation into the good moral character of the applicant, be issued a real estate school or instructor license.

45:15-10.11. Grounds for suspension, revocation of real estate school instructor license

The commission may suspend or revoke the license of any real estate school or instructor or impose fines as provided in R.S.45:15-17 upon satisfactory proof that the licensee is guilty of:

a. Making any false promise or substantial misrepresentation;

b. Pursuing a flagrant and continued course of misrepresentation or making false promises through agents, advertisements or otherwise;

c. Engaging in any conduct which demonstrates unworthiness, incompetency, bad faith or dishonesty;

d. Failing to provide a student with a copy of a written agreement which designates the total tuition charges for attendance at a real estate pre-licensure or continuing education course offered by a licensed school, or other charges imposed upon students who enroll in the course, and the refund policy of the school in regard to tuition and other charges;

e. Using any plan, scheme or method of attracting students to enroll in a real estate pre-licensure or continuing education course which involves a lottery, contest, game, prize or drawing;

f. Being convicted of a crime, knowledge of which the commission did not have at the time of last issuing a license to the licensee;

g. Procuring a real estate license for himself or anyone else by fraud, misrepresentation or deceit;

h. Making any verbal or written statement which falsely indicates that a person attended or successfully completed any real estate pre-licensure or continuing education course conducted by the licensee; or

i. Any other conduct whether of the same or of a different character than specified in this section which constitutes fraud or dishonest dealing.

45:15-10.12. Restrictions on persons with revoked license

A person whose license has been revoked pursuant to section 54 of P.L.1993, c. 51 (C. 45:15-10.11) shall not be a general partner, officer, director or owner, either directly or indirectly, of a controlling interest in any licensed school, nor shall the person be retained or employed in any capacity, or compensated in any manner by a licensed school, nor shall the person occupy or share office space in a licensed school location for any purpose during the period of revocation.

45:15-10.13. Revocation of license of school; exceptions

Upon the revocation of the instructor license issued to any partner, officer, director or owner of a controlling interest in any licensed school, the commission shall revoke the license of the school unless, within a period of time fixed by the commission, the following conditions are fulfilled: a. in the case of a licensed school owned by a partnership, the connection of the partner whose instructor license has been revoked to the school shall be severed and his interest in the school shall be divested; or b. in the case of a licensed school owned by a corporation, the officer, director or owner of a controlling interest whose instructor license has been revoked shall be terminated from the position and, where an owner of a controlling interest, his ownership of the interest shall be divested; or c. in the case of a limited partnership, if the person whose instructor license has been revoked was a general partner, his interest in the school shall be divested or, if the person whose instructor license was revoked was a limited partner, his interest in the school shall be divested if it constituted a controlling interest as defined herein. For the purposes of this section, the term "controlling interest" means 5% or more of the equity of a licensed corporation or of the ownership of a partnership.

45:15-10.14. Power, authority of commission

The commission is expressly vested with the power and authority to promulgate and enforce all necessary rules and regulations for the conduct of the business of real estate schools offering pre-licensure and continuing education courses consistent with the provisions of this amendatory and supplementary act.

45:15-11.   Disabled war veterans; granting of licenses

Any citizen of New Jersey who has served in the armed forces of the United States or who served as a member of the American Merchant Marine during World War II and is declared by the United States Department of Defense to be eligible for federal veterans' benefits, who has been honorably discharged, and who, having been wounded or disabled in the line of duty, has completed a program of courses in real estate approved by the New Jersey Real Estate Commission, and who has successfully passed an examination conducted by said commission qualifying him to operate as a real estate broker, broker-salesperson, or salesperson, may, upon presentation of a certificate certifying that he has completed such program of courses as aforesaid, obtain without cost from the commission and without qualification through experience as a salesperson, a license to operate as a real estate broker, broker-salesperson, or a real estate salesperson, as the case may be, which licenses shall be the same as other licenses issued under R.S.45:15-1 et seq. Renewal of licenses may be granted under this section for each ensuing license term, upon request, without fees therefor.

45:15-11.1, 45:15-11.2.   Repealed by L. 1970, c. 255, § 2, eff. Nov. 2, 1970

45:15-11.3.   Issuance of temporary broker's license

In the event of the death or mental or physical incapacity of a licensed real estate broker where no other member or officer in the agency, copartnership, association or corporation of which he was a member or officer is the holder of a broker-salesperson's license or where an individual broker operating as a sole proprietor dies or is mentally or physically incapacitated leaving no employee holding a real estate broker-salesperson's license, then the Real Estate Commission may issue a temporary broker's license on a special form to another person for the purpose of enabling such other person to continue the real estate activities on behalf of and under the same designation of said agency, copartnership, association, corporation or individual, as the case may be, upon the filing of an application and a certified copy of the death certificate or a certification of mental or physical incapacity executed by a duly licensed physician or officer of a medical institution, together with payment of the regular license fee; provided such other person has been the holder of a real estate salesperson's license for at least three years immediately preceding the date of the application and provided that said application shall have been made within 30 days from date of the demise or incapacity of said broker.

Such temporary license shall continue only until the licensee is afforded an opportunity of pursuing the approved broker's course in accordance with the provisions of subsection b. of section 1 of P.L.1966, c. 227 (C. 45:15-10.1) and qualifying by examination. Such license may be issued and effective for a period of one year from the date of issuance. Such temporary license shall not be extended or renewed.

45:15-12.   Broker to maintain office

Every real estate broker shall maintain a designated main office open to the public. A real estate broker's main office shall have prominently displayed therein the license certificate of the broker and all licensed persons in his employ and shall be deemed the business address of all licensed persons for all purposes under chapter 15 of Title 45 of the Revised Statutes. In case a real estate broker maintains more than one place of business, a branch office license shall be issued to such broker for each branch office so maintained in this State; provided, however, that the said branch office or offices are under the direct supervision of a broker-salesperson. The branch office license or licenses shall be issued upon the payment of a fee of $50 for each license so issued. Every place of business maintained by a real estate broker shall have conspicuously displayed on the exterior thereof the name in which the broker is authorized to operate and, in the case of a corporation or partnership, the name of the individual licensed as its authorized broker, and the words Licensed Real Estate Broker. A real estate broker whose main office is located in another state shall maintain a valid real estate broker's license in good standing in the state where the office is located.

The provisions of this section shall apply to any real estate broker who supervises a real estate referral company as defined under R.S.45:15-3.

45:15-12.1.   Bars to issuance of license

No license shall be issued by the commission to any person known by it to have been, within five years theretofore, convicted of forgery, burglary, robbery, any theft offense other than shoplifting, criminal conspiracy to defraud, or other like offense or offenses, or to any copartnership of which such person is a member, or to any association or corporation of which said person is an officer, director, or employee, or in which as a stockholder such person has or exercises a controlling interest either directly or indirectly. No license shall be issued or renewed by the commission to any person known by it to have been convicted of any sex offense that would qualify the person for registration pursuant to section 2 of P.L.1994, c.133 (C.2C:7-2) or under an equivalent statute of another state or jurisdiction.

45:15-12.2.   Repeal

Sections 45:15-30 to 45:15-33, inclusive, of the Revised Statutes are repealed.

45:15-12.3

45:15-12.3. Revoked license, disability to act

A person whose license has been revoked pursuant to R.S. 45:15-17 or section 6 of P.L. 1953, c. 229 (C. 45:15-19.1) shall not be a general partner, officer, director or owner, either directly or indirectly, of a controlling interest in a licensed partnership, limited partnership or corporation, nor shall the person be retained or employed in any capacity, or compensated in any manner by a licensee, nor shall the person occupy or share office space in a licensed office location for any purpose during the period of revocation.

45:15-12.4. Revocation of partnership, corporate license

Upon the revocation of the license issued to any partner, officer, director or owner of a controlling interest in any licensed partnership, limited partnership or corporation, the commission shall revoke the license of the partnership or corporation unless, within a period fixed by the commission, the following conditions are fulfilled: a. in the case of a partnership, the connection of the partner whose license has been revoked to the licensee shall be severed and his interest in the licensee shall be divested; b. in the case of a corporation, the officer, director or owner of a controlling interest whose license has been revoked shall be terminated from the position and, where an owner of a controlling interest, his ownership of the interest shall be divested; or c. in the case of a limited partnership, if the person whose license has been revoked is the general partner, the connection of that person to the licensee shall be severed and his interest in the licensee shall be divested or, if the person whose license was revoked is a limited partner, his interest in the licensee shall be divested if it constituted a controlling interest as defined herein. For the purposes of this section, the term "controlling interest" means 5% or more of the equity of a licensed corporation or of the ownership of a partnership.

45:15-12.5. Maintenance of special account required

a. Every individual, partnership or corporation licensed as a real estate broker shall maintain in a State or federally chartered bank, savings bank, savings and loan association or other depository institution physically located and authorized to transact business in this State and approved by the commission a special account into which the broker shall deposit and maintain all monies received while acting in the capacity of a real estate broker, or as escrow agent, or as the temporary custodian of funds of others in real estate transactions in this State. The account shall be maintained in the name in which the individual, partnership or corporation is licensed to do business as a broker and shall be designated as either the broker's "trust account" or "escrow account" and shall be maintained separate and apart from all other personal and business accounts. All checks and deposit slips produced as a result of the establishment of the account shall contain the words "trust account" or "escrow account." The provisions of this subsection shall not apply to an individual licensed as a broker-salesperson.

b. A real estate broker may establish a special interest bearing escrow account under the broker's control in a depository institution approved by the commission for the deposit of monies from a specific transaction provided the account is clearly identified as pertaining to that transaction. Such accounts shall be maintained separate and apart from all other escrow, business and personal funds.

45:15-12.6. Approval of depository institution

The commission shall approve a depository institution as required pursuant to section 42 [C.45:15-12.5] of this amendatory and supplementary act upon the institution providing written confirmation to the commission that it shall immediately notify the commission of any issuance of a notice to a licensed broker that a check or other instrument written upon the broker's escrow or trust account has been dishonored or returned for insufficient funds.

45:15-12.7. Agent, custodian may not use interest on escrow funds

A real estate broker acting in the capacity of an escrow agent or as the temporary custodian of the funds of others in any real estate transaction shall not receive, obtain or use any interest earned on the funds for the broker's own personal or business use.

45:15-12.8. Acceptance of monies

Every real estate licensee who, in the performance of any of the activities described in R.S. 45:15-3, receives any monies of others as a representative of a broker acting as an escrow agent or as the temporary custodian of the funds of others in a real estate transaction, shall only accept the monies if they are in the form of cash or a negotiable instrument payable to the broker through whom the individual is licensed, or such other form as the commission may prescribe by rule. The licensee shall, immediately upon receipt of the funds, account for and deliver the funds to the broker for deposit into the escrow or trust account maintained by the broker, or for such other disposition as is required by the escrow agreement under the terms of which the funds were provided to the licensee.

45:15-13. Form of license; change of broker's address

All licenses shall be issued by the commission in such form as it shall prescribe. Each license shall show the name and address of the licensee and shall have imprinted thereon the seal of the commission. Notice in writing shall be given to the commission by each licensed broker of any change of business address, whereupon the commission shall issue new licenses to the broker and to all persons licensed through the broker for the unexpired period, upon the payment of a fee of $50 for the issuance of the new broker license and a fee of $10 for each additional new license certificate so issued. A change of business address without notification to the commission, and without the issuance of a new broker's license, shall automatically cancel the license theretofore issued.

45:15-14.   License kept by employing broker

All licenses issued to real estate brokers, broker-salespersons, and salespersons shall be kept by the broker by whom such real estate licensee is employed or contracted, and the pocket card accompanying the same shall be delivered by the broker to the licensee who shall have the card in his possession at all times when engaged in the business of a real estate broker, broker-salesperson, or salesperson. When any real estate licensee is terminated or resigns his employment with the real estate broker by whom he was employed or contracted at the time of the issuing of such license to him, notice of the termination shall be given in writing by the broker to the terminated licensee with the effective date of the termination reflected thereon, or notice of the resignation shall be given in writing by the resigning licensee to the broker with the effective date of the resignation reflected thereon. Upon the issuance of a written notice of termination by a broker or his authorized representative, or upon receipt of a written resignation by a broker or his authorized representative, such employer or contracting broker shall within five business days of the effective date of the termination or resignation, either: a. deliver, or send by registered mail, to the commission, such real estate licensee's license and, at the same time, send a written communication to such real estate licensee at his last known residence, advising him that his license has been delivered or mailed to the commission. A copy of such communication to the licensee shall accompany the license when mailed or delivered to the commission; or, b. deliver to the departing licensee and to the commission any other materials as the commission may prescribe by regulation to accomplish the transfer of the licensee to another employing or contracting broker. No real estate licensee shall perform any of the acts contemplated by R.S.45:15-1 et seq., either directly or indirectly, under the authority of such license, from and after the effective date of the licensee's termination or resignation until authorized to do so by the commission. A new license may be issued to such licensee, upon the payment of a fee of $25, and upon the submission of satisfactory proof that he has obtained employment or contracted with another licensed broker. A broker-salesperson or salesperson shall be licensed under a broker; he cannot be licensed with more than one broker at the same time.

45:15-15.   License fees

The biennial fee for each real estate broker's license shall be $200, the biennial fee for each real estate broker-salesperson's license shall be $200 and the biennial fee for each real estate salesperson's license shall be $100. The biennial fee for a branch office license shall be $100. Each license granted under R.S.45:15-1 et seq. shall entitle the licensee to perform all of the acts contemplated herein during the period for which the license is issued, as prescribed by R.S.45:15-1 et seq. If a licensee fails to apply for a renewal of his license prior to the date of expiration of such license, the commission may refuse to issue a renewal license except upon the payment of a late renewal fee in the amount of $20 for a salesperson or broker-salesperson and $40 for a broker; provided, however, the commission may, in its discretion, refuse to renew any license upon sufficient cause being shown. The commission shall refuse to renew the license of any licensee convicted of any offense enumerated in section 6 of P.L.1953, c.229 (C.45:15-19.1) during the term of the last license issued by the commission unless the conviction was previously the subject of a revocation proceeding. Renewed licenses may be granted for each ensuing two years upon request of licensees and the payment of the full fee therefor as herein required. Upon application and payment of the fees provided herein, initial licenses and licenses reinstated pursuant to R.S.45:15-9 may be issued, but the commission may, in its discretion, refuse to grant or reinstate any license upon sufficient cause being shown. The license fees for initial or reinstated licenses shall be determined based upon the biennial fees established herein, with a full biennial fee payable for the license term in which application is received. The revocation or suspension of a broker's license shall automatically suspend every real estate broker-salesperson's and salesperson's license granted to employees or contractors of the broker whose license has been revoked or suspended, pending a change of employer or contracting broker and the issuance of a new license. The new license shall be issued without additional charge, if the same is granted during the license term in which the original license was granted. Any renewal fee in this section shall be billed by the commission at or before the time of the submission of a renewal application by a licensee.

A real estate broker who maintains a main office or branch office licensed by the commission which is located in another state shall maintain a valid real estate broker's license in good standing in the state where the office is located and shall maintain a real estate license in that other state for each office licensed by the commission. Upon request, the real estate broker shall provide a certification of his license status in the other state to the commission. Any license issued by the commission to a real estate broker for a main or branch office located outside this State shall be automatically suspended upon the revocation, suspension or refusal to renew the real estate broker's license issued by the state where the office is located. The licenses issued by the commission to every broker-salesperson and salesperson

45:15-16

employed or contracted by the broker shall be automatically suspended pending a change of employer or contracting broker and the issuance of a new license. The new license shall be issued without additional charge if granted during the license term in which the original license was granted.

███████████████████████

45:15-16.   Acceptance of commission, valuable consideration

No real estate salesperson or broker-salesperson shall accept a commission or valuable consideration for the performance of any of the acts herein specified, from any person except his employer or contracting broker, who must be a licensed real estate broker.

███████████████████████

45:15-16a.   Rebate paid by broker to purchaser

a. Any rebate paid by a broker to a purchaser of residential real property pursuant to paragraph (2) of subsection k. of R.S.45:15-17 shall be:

(1) Calculated after the purchaser negotiates the rebate commission rate;

(2) Memorialized in a written document, electronic document or a buyer agency agreement provided by the broker to the purchaser at the outset of the broker relationship, which document or agreement shall provide the terms of any rebate credited or paid by the broker to the purchaser; and

(3) Disclosed to all parties involved in the transaction, including, but not limited to, any mortgage lender.

b. A rebate shall not be:

(1) Paid to a person not licensed as a real estate broker for any act that requires licensure;

(2) Contingent upon the use of other services or products being offered by a broker or an affiliate of a broker; or

(3) Based on the use of a lottery, contest or game.

███████████████████████

45:15-16b.   Advertisement for rebate

a. Any advertisement for a rebate allowed pursuant to paragraph (2) of subsection k. of R.S.45:15-17 shall include:

(1) A disclosure concerning the purchaser's obligation to pay any applicable taxes for receipt of the rebate; and

(2) A notice that the purchaser should contact a tax professional concerning the tax implications of receiving the rebate.

b. The disclosure and notice required pursuant to subsection a. of this section shall be clearly and conspicuously displayed in the advertisement and the size of the text in the notice and disclosure shall be equal to or larger than the size of the text used for the advertisement.

███████████████████████

45:15-16c.   Regulations

The New Jersey Real Estate Commission may promulgate regulations pursuant to the "Administrative Procedure Act," P.L.1968, c.410 (C.52:14B-1 et seq.), necessary to effectuate the provisions of this act [C.45:15-16a et al.].

███████████████████████

45:15-16.1.   Repealed by L. 1975, c. 235, § 25, eff. Dec. 23, 1975

45:15-16.2.   Educational and information programs

The Division of the New Jersey Real Estate Commission in the State Department of Insurance, within the limits of appropriations available or to be made available to it for the purpose, may conduct educational and information programs relating to the real estate brokerage business and real estate brokers, broker-salespersons and salespersons for the information, education, guidance and protection of the general public, licensees, and applicants for licensure. The educational and information programs may include preparation, printing and distribution of publications and articles and the conduct of conferences, forums, lectures, and a public information service.

███████████████████████

45:15-16.2a.   Continuing education required; exceptions

a. The New Jersey Real Estate Commission shall require each natural person licensed as a real estate broker, broker-salesperson or salesperson, as a condition of biennial license renewal pursuant to R.S.45:15-10, to complete not more than 16 hours of continuing education requirements imposed by the commission pursuant to this section and sections 24 through 28 of P.L.2009, c.238 (C.45:15-16.2a through 45:15-16.2f), except that a salesperson licensed with a real estate referral company shall not be required to complete the continuing education requirements as a condition of biennial license renewal. This subsection shall not apply to any real estate broker or broker-salesperson who has been a real estate broker or broker-salesperson for 40 years or more, which shall include any equivalent experience in any other jurisdiction as determined by the commission.

b. The commission shall:

(1) (a) Approve continuing education courses, course providers, and instructors recommended to the commission by the Volunteer Advisory Committee created pursuant to subparagraph (b) of this paragraph. Schools licensed by the commission as real estate schools pursuant to section 47 of P.L.1993, c.51

(C.45:15-10.4) shall be deemed approved providers of continuing education courses. Persons licensed by the commission as real estate instructors pursuant to section 48 of P.L.1993, c.51 (C.45:15-10.5) shall be deemed approved instructors of continuing education courses in core topics as set forth in section 27 of P.L.2009, c.238 (C.45:15-16.2e). Real estate trade associations that qualify under the standards to be established by commission rule as approved providers may offer approved continuing education courses.

(b) There is hereby created a Volunteer Advisory Committee which shall consist of 14 members to be comprised of real estate licensees and other subject matter experts, whose members shall be appointed by and serve at the pleasure of the Commissioner of Banking and Insurance. One real estate licensee shall be selected upon the recommendation of the President of the Senate and one real estate licensee shall be selected upon the recommendation of the Speaker of the General Assembly. Three members of the advisory committee shall be members of the commission or their designees, and not less than eight of the members, other than the commission members, shall be real estate licensees. Members shall be appointed to effect balanced geographic representation from the central, northern and southern areas of the State, with not less than three members serving from each of these areas at any time on the advisory committee.

Members shall be appointed by the Commissioner of Banking and Insurance no later than 60 days following the enactment date of this act. The first meeting of the advisory committee shall be held no later than 30 days from the date the commission adopts initial regulations for the effectuation of this act.

(2) Confer continuing education credits for courses completed in other states on topics approved by the commission as appropriate for elective courses, provided that such courses have been approved as continuing education courses by the agency exercising regulatory authority over the real estate licensees of another state and that satisfactory evidence of licensees' attendance at and completion of such courses is provided to the commission by the course provider.

(3) Confer continuing education credits for courses completed and offered in this State on topics deemed of a timely nature which have not been granted prior approval by the advisory committee, provided that such courses are advertised prior to the time of offering as not having been approved; that the course provider shall submit such course offering for approval and the course is subsequently approved as provided in subparagraph (a) of paragraph (1) of this subsection; and that satisfactory evidence of licensees' attendance at and completion of such courses is provided to the commission by the course provider.

(4) Set parameters for the auditing and monitoring of course providers.

(5) Establish, by regulation, the amounts of application fees payable by persons seeking approval as continuing education course providers, persons seeking approval of continuing educa-

tion courses, and persons other than instructors of pre-licensure real estate education courses licensed by the commission pursuant to section 48 of P.L.1993, c.51 (C.45:15-10.5), seeking approval as instructors of continuing education courses. These fees shall be non-refundable and shall be in amounts which do not exceed the costs incurred by the commission to review these applications.

(6) Have the authority to waive continuing education requirements, in whole or in part, on the grounds of illness, emergency, hardship or active duty military service.

(7) Confer continuing education credits upon a person who is licensed by the commission as a real estate instructor or as a broker, broker-salesperson or salesperson for teaching an approved continuing education course offered by an approved provider. Regardless of the number of times during a biennial license term that the same approved course is taught by that person, the person shall receive credit toward the continuing education requirement for the renewal of the person's broker, broker-salesperson or salesperson license, as applicable, only in the number of credit hours conferred upon licensees who attend and complete that course one time during that biennial license term.

45:15-16.2b.   Delivery of continuing education courses

Continuing education courses may be delivered in a classroom setting or via the Internet or video modalities, subject to the approval by the New Jersey Real Estate Commission of the providers and the content of such courses and of the measures utilized to ensure the security and integrity of the course delivery process. The commission may approve continuing education courses which include periodic progress assessments and the achievement of a satisfactory level of performance by the licensee on such progress assessments as a condition to continuing to a succeeding segment of the course. The commission shall not require, as a condition of the receipt of credit for attendance at any continuing education course, that a licensee pass a comprehensive examination testing the licensee's knowledge of the entire course content.

45:15-16.2c.   Completion of continuing education requirements

Continuing education requirements, as set forth by the New Jersey Real Estate Commission, shall be completed on or before April 30 of the year in which the biennial license expires. Any licensee required to complete continuing education requirements who fails to do so prior to May 1 of the second year of a biennial license term shall be subject to a reasonable processing fee, as determined by the commission, of not more than $200.

45:15-16.2d

45:15-16.2d. Fulfillment of continuing education requirement

A person who, during a biennial licensing term, successfully completes one or more broker pre-licensure education courses as prescribed by the New Jersey Real Estate Commission shall be deemed to have fulfilled the continuing education requirement applicable to the license that such a person may seek to renew upon the conclusion of that license term. A person who is initially licensed as a salesperson during the first year of a two-year license term shall complete all applicable continuing education requirements in order to renew that license upon the conclusion of that license term. A person who is initially licensed as a salesperson in the second year of the two-year license term shall not be required to fulfill any continuing education requirements in order to renew that license at the conclusion of that license term.

45:15-16.2e. Core topics for continuing education courses

a. Not less than 50 percent of the continuing education courses of study that a broker, broker-salesperson or salesperson are required to complete as a condition for license renewal shall be comprised of one or more of the following core topics:

(1) Agency;

(2) Disclosure;

(3) Legal issues;

(4) Ethics, which shall not be less than two hours;

(5) Fair housing;

(6) Rules and regulations;

(7) Real estate licensee safety;

(8) Financial literacy and planning; and

(9) Any other core topics that the New Jersey Real Estate Commission may prescribe by rule.

In no event shall the commission require that courses in these core topics comprise more than 60 percent of the total continuing education hours required for the renewal of any license.

b. In the case of continuing education courses and programs, each hour of instruction shall be equivalent to one credit.

c. Notwithstanding the provisions of subsection a. of this section, the commission shall require that the continuing education courses of study that a broker, broker-salesperson or salesperson are required to complete as a condition for license renewal shall be comprised of at least one hour on the core topic of fair housing and housing discrimination during each biennial license term.

45:15-16.2f. Maintenance of records by course providers

Course providers shall maintain records of the successful completion of continuing education courses by licensees and shall transmit this data to the New Jersey Real Estate Commission or its designee in a manner as directed by the commission.

45:15-16.2g. Rules, regulations

The New Jersey Real Estate Commission shall adopt rules and regulations pursuant to the "Administrative Procedure Act," P.L. 1968, c.410 (C.52:14B-1 et seq.), necessary to effectuate the purposes of this act.

45:15-16.3 to 45:15-16.26. Repealed by L. 1989, c. 239, § 24, eff. Jan. 2, 1990

45:15-16.27. Short title [Real Estate Sales Full Disclosure Act]

This act shall be known and may be cited as the "Real Estate Sales Full Disclosure Act."

45:15-16.28. Definitions

As used in this act [C.45:15-16.27 et seq.]:

"Advertising" means the publication, or causing to be published, of any information offering for sale, or for the purpose of causing or inducing any other person to purchase or acquire, an interest in the title to subdivided lands, including the land sales contract to be used and any photographs or drawings or artist's representation of physical conditions or facilities on the property existing or to exist by means of any:

(1) Newspaper or periodical;

(2) Radio or television broadcast;

(3) Written or printed or photographic matter produced by any duplicating process producing 10 copies or more;

(4) Billboards or signs;

(5) Display of model homes or units;

(6) Material used in connection with the disposition or offer of subdivided lands by radio, television, telephone or any other electronic means; or

(7) Material used by subdividers or their agents to induce prospective purchasers to visit the subdivision; particularly va-

cation certificates which require the holders of those certificates to attend or submit to a sales presentation by a subdivider or its agents.

"Advertising" does not mean: stockholder communications such as annual reports and interim financial reports, proxy materials, registration statements, securities prospectuses, applications for listing securities on stock exchanges, or similar documents; prospectuses, property reports, offering statements, or other documents required to be delivered to a prospective purchaser by an agency of any other state or the federal government; all communications addressed to and relating to the account of any person who has previously executed a contract for the purchase of the subdivider's lands except when directed to the sale of additional lands.

"Blanket encumbrance" means a trust deed, mortgage, judgment, or any other lien or encumbrance, including an option or contract to sell or a trust agreement, affecting a subdivision or affecting more than one lot offered within a subdivision, except that term shall not include any lien or other encumbrance arising as the result of the imposition of any tax assessment by any public authority.

"Broker" or "salesperson" means any person who performs within this State as an agent or employee of a subdivider any one or more of the services or acts as set forth in this act, and includes any real estate broker or salesperson licensed pursuant to R.S.45:15-1 et seq. or any person who purports to act in any such capacity.

"Commission" means the New Jersey Real Estate Commission.

"Common promotional plan" means any offer for the disposition of lots, parcels, units or interests of real property by a single person or group of persons acting in concert, where those lots, parcels, units or interests are contiguous, or are known, designated or advertised as a common entity or by a common name regardless of the number of lots, parcels, units or interests covered by each individual offering.

"Disposition" means the sale, lease, assignment, award by lottery, or any other transaction concerning a subdivision if undertaken for gain or profit.

"Notice" means a communication by mail from the commission executed by its secretary or other duly authorized officer. Notice to subdividers shall be deemed complete when mailed to the subdivider's address currently on file with the commission.

"Offer" means every inducement, solicitation or attempt to encourage a person to acquire an interest in a subdivision if undertaken for gain or profit.

"Person" means an individual, corporation, government or governmental subdivision or agency, business trust, estate, trust, partnership, unincorporated association, two or more of any of the foregoing having a joint or common interest, or any other legal or commercial entity.

"Purchaser" means a person who acquires or attempts to acquire or succeeds to an interest in a subdivision.

"Subdivider" or "developer" means any owner of subdivided lands or the agent of that owner who offers the subdivided lands for disposition.

"Subdivision" and "subdivided lands" mean any land situated outside the State of New Jersey whether contiguous or not, if one or more lots, parcels, units or interests are offered as a part of a common promotional plan of advertising and sale and expressly means and includes such units or interests commonly referred to as a "condominium," defined in the "Condominium Act," P.L.1969, c.257 (C.46:8B-1 et seq.). In addition to condominiums, this definition shall also specifically include, but shall not be limited to, any form of homeowners association, any housing cooperative and any community trust or other trust device.

45:15-16.29. Bureau of Subdivided Land Sales Control continued

The Bureau of Subdivided Land Sales Control within the Division of the New Jersey Real Estate Commission in the Department of Insurance, established pursuant to section 3 of P.L.1975, c.235 (C.45:15-16.5), shall continue.

45:15-16.30. Conditions for disposition of subdivided lands

Unless the subdivided lands or the transaction is exempt pursuant to section 6 [C.45:15-16.32] of this act:

a. No person may offer, dispose or participate in this State in the disposition of subdivided lands or of any interest in subdivided lands unless in accordance with the provisions of this act.

b. No person may dispose or participate in the disposition of any interest in subdivided lands unless a current public offering statement, disclosing fully all information required in section 12 [C.45:15-16.38] of this act, is delivered to the purchaser and the purchaser is afforded a reasonable opportunity to examine the public offering statement prior to the disposition.

45:15-16.30a. Registration as secondary registration subdivider

a. A subdivider or developer who owns subdivided land upon which there is a completed residential unit, or for which there is a contract to construct and deliver a completed residential unit by the subdivider or developer or an affiliated or related entity

45:15-16.30a

within two years from the date of the offer or disposition, may register as a secondary registration subdivider under this section provided that:

(1) the registration is made prior to execution of a contract with, or acceptance of any deposit from, a purchaser of an interest in those lands who is a New Jersey resident;

(2) the subdivider is not already registered pursuant to P.L. 1989, c.239 (C.45:15-16.27 et seq.); and

(3) the subdivision does not qualify for an exemption pursuant to subsection a. of section 6 of P.L. 1989, c.239 (C.45:15-16.32).

b. The commission shall establish the format and forms for registration pursuant to this section. The application form shall require at a minimum:

(1) the name and address of the property;

(2) the name and address of the secondary registration subdivider;

(3) a description of the particulars of the offering, and a certification by the secondary registration subdivider that: (a) the offering is in compliance with all applicable requirements of governmental agencies having jurisdiction over the offering; (b) the deposit moneys of purchasers who are New Jersey residents will be held in an escrow account, or protected in some other manner acceptable to the commission, until closing of title and delivery of the residential unit; and (c) the secondary registration subdivider can convey, or cause to be conveyed, title to the interest in the offering;

(4) copies of all forms of conveyance to be used in selling the property to the purchaser, which forms shall include a seven day right of rescission as required by subsection g. of this section;

(5) unless included as part of the forms of conveyance provided pursuant to paragraph (4) of this subsection, a disclosure statement detailing the common property, if any, of the community, obligations of the owners and the assessments of a homeowners' association formed to manage common property, if any, mandatory club membership, and special taxing district affecting the property being offered. The commission may accept disclosure statements approved for use in the jurisdiction where the property is located;

(6) a certification that the secondary registration subdivider has not, or if a corporation, its officers, directors, and principals have not, been convicted of a crime or civil offense involving land dispositions or any aspect of the land sales business in this State, the United States, or any other state or foreign country; and that the secondary registration subdivider has not been subject to any permanent injunction or final administrative order restraining a false and misleading promotional plan involving real property dispositions, the seriousness of which in the opinion of the commission warrants the denial of secondary registration;

(7) a consent to service of process and jurisdiction of the Courts of the State of New Jersey as provided in section 19 of P.L. 1989, c.239 (C.45:15-16.45); and

(8) a filing fee as prescribed in section 8 of P.L. 1989, c.239 (C.45:15-16.34).

c. The commission shall, within 30 days of receipt of a substantially completed application, including all filing fees, provide the secondary registration subdivider with a notice of completion of the secondary registration or a notice of deficiency. If the commission does not provide a notice of completion or deficiency within 30 days, the secondary registration shall be deemed complete.

d. A secondary registration subdivider who files an application for secondary registration under this section shall immediately report any material changes in the application or the offering, but shall be exempt from the annual reporting requirements under section 14 of P.L. 1989, c.239 (C.45:15-16.40).

e. Prior to filing an application for secondary registration under this section and up to the time of the issuance of a notice of completion or the secondary registration is deemed complete pursuant to subsection c. of this section, a secondary registration subdivider with an interest in subdivided lands described in subsection a. of this section, may respond to inquiries initiated by New Jersey residents in response to the secondary registration subdivider's website or multi-state advertising by providing general information about the subdivided lands being offered, including sales prices, and by forwarding advertising materials. However, until a notice of completion for the subdivided land is issued, or the secondary registration is deemed complete pursuant to subsection c. of this section, a secondary registration subdivider shall not engage in the following acts in this State concerning the subdivided lands: (1) offer a contract; (2) collect deposit moneys; or (3) subsidize travel to the subdivided property. Except as permitted by this section, a secondary registration subdivider shall not otherwise offer, dispose, or participate in this State in the disposition, of subdivided land or of any interest in subdivided land and shall not direct such an offer or disposition into the State.

f. Prior to the execution of a contract for sale of subdivided lands described in subsection a. of this section, a secondary registration subdivider shall, unless included as part of the forms of conveyance provided pursuant to paragraph (4) of subsection b. of this section, provide to a purchaser a copy of the disclosure statement described in paragraph (5) of subsection b. of this section, and obtain a signed receipt from the purchaser stating that the disclosure statement has been received.

g. A contract for the purchase of subdivided lands described in subsection a. of this section may be rescinded by the purchaser without cause of any kind by sending or delivering written notice of cancellation by midnight of the seventh calendar day following the day on which the purchaser has executed the contract, or the day the purchaser receives notification from the secondary registration subdivider that the secondary registration subdivider has completed secondary registration in accordance with this section, whichever is later.

h. Any person who violates any provision of this section or who, in the application for secondary registration, makes any untrue statement of a material fact or omits to state a material fact, shall be fined as provided in section 20 of P.L. 1989, c.239 (C.45:15-16.46).

i. The provisions of this section shall not apply to the offering of subdivided lands in situations in which registration is required by the "Interstate Land Sales Full Disclosure Act," Pub.L. 90-448 (15 U.S.C. § 1701 et seq.) with the Office of Interstate Land Sales Registration, in the Department of Housing and Urban Development.

45:15-16.31.   Subdivisions, subdivided lands subject to this act

Disposition of subdivision or subdivided lands are subject to this act if:

a. Any offer or disposition of subdivided lands is made in this State; or

b. Any offer of subdivided land originating outside this State is directed by the subdivider or his agent to a person or resident within this State.

45:15-16.32.   Inapplicability to offers, dispositions of an interest in a subdivision

a. Unless the method of disposition is adopted for the purpose of evasion of this act [C.45:15-16.27 et seq.], the provisions of this act are not applicable to offers or dispositions of an interest in a subdivision:

(1) By an owner for his own account in a single or isolated transaction;

(2) Wholly for industrial or commercial purposes;

(3) Pursuant to court order;

(4) By any governmental agency;

(5) As cemetery lots or interests;

(6) Of less than 100 lots, parcels, units or interests;

(7) Where the common elements or interests, which would otherwise subject the offering to this act, are limited to the provision of unimproved, unencumbered open space, except where registration is required by the "Interstate Land Sales Full Disclosure Act," Pub.L.90-448 (15 U.S.C. § 1701 et seq.)

with the Office of Interstate Land Sales Registration, in the Department of Housing and Urban Development; or

(8) In a development comprised wholly of rental units, where the relationship created is one of landlord and tenant.

b. Unless the method of disposition is adopted for the purpose of evasion of this act, the provisions of this act are not applicable to:

(1) Offers or dispositions of evidences of indebtedness secured by a mortgage or deed of trust of real estate;

(2) Offers or dispositions of securities or units of interest issued by a real estate investment trust regulated under any State or federal statute;

(3) Offers or dispositions of securities currently registered with the Bureau of Securities in the Department of Law and Public Safety; or

(4) Offers or dispositions of any interest in oil, gas or other minerals or any royalty interest therein if the offers or dispositions of such interests are regulated as securities by federal law or by the State Bureau of Securities.

c. The commission may, from time to time, pursuant to any rules and regulations promulgated pursuant to this act, exempt from any of the provisions of this act any subdivision or any lots in a subdivision, if it finds that the enforcement of this act with respect to that subdivision or the lots therein, is not necessary in the public interest, or required for the protection of purchasers, by reason of the small amount involved or the limited character of the offering.

d. A subdivider or developer who qualifies for and completes secondary registration pursuant to section 2 of P.L.2007, c.292 (C.45:15-16.30a) shall be exempt from the registration requirements of section 4 of P.L.1989, c.239 (C.45:15-16.30).

45:15-16.33.   Notice of filing; registration; rejection

a. Upon the filing of an application for registration at the offices of the commission, naming the brokers licensed as real estate brokers pursuant to R.S. 45:15-1 et seq. who are the authorized representatives of the subdivider, and accompanied by the proper registration fee in the proper form, and a statement of record as provided for in section 10 [C.45:15-16.36] of this act, and the proposed public offering statement, the commission shall issue a notice of filing to the applicant. Within 90 days from the date of the notice of filing, the commission shall enter an order registering the subdivision or subdivided lands or rejecting the registration. If no order of rejection is entered within 90 days from the date of notice of filing, the subdivisions or subdivided lands shall be deemed registered unless the applicant has consented in writing to a delay.

b. If the commission affirmatively determines upon inquiry and examination that the requirements of section 9 [C.45:15-16.35] of this act have been met, it shall enter an order registering the subdivision or subdivided lands and shall designate the form of the public offering statement.

c. If the commission determines upon inquiry and examination that any of the requirements of section 9 of this act have not been met, the commission shall notify the applicant that the application for registration must be corrected in the particulars specified within 30 days from the date the notice is received by the applicant. These findings shall be the result of the commission's preliminary inquiry and examination and no hearing shall be required as the basis for those findings. The receipt of a written request for a hearing shall stay the order of rejection until a hearing has been held and a determination has been made.

45:15-16.34. Initial registration fee; inspection fee; consolidated filing fee

a. (1) The fee for an initial registration shall be $500.00 plus $35.00 for each lot, parcel, unit or interest which fee shall not exceed $3,000.00. The initial registration shall be valid for a period of one year from the date of approval of the registration. If the fees are insufficient to defray the cost of rendering services required by the provisions of this act, the commission may, by regulation, establish a revised fee schedule. Any revised fee schedule shall assure that the fees collected reasonably cover, but do not exceed, the expenses of administering the provisions of this act.

(2) Annual renewal of registration shall be made in accordance with the provisions of section 14 [C.45:15-16.40] of this act.

(3) Any current registration filed with and approved by the commission pursuant to the provisions of P.L. 1975, c. 235 (C. 45:15-16.3 et seq.) prior to the date of enactment of this act shall be exempt from initial registration under this act.

b. The application for registration shall be made on forms prescribed by the commission and shall be accompanied by the appropriate filing fee. As provided in subsection f. of section 15 [C.45:15-16.41] of this act, the commission may determine, at its discretion, that an onsite investigation or inspection is required. The commission shall advise the registrant of the amount of the cost of travel from New Jersey to the location of the subdivided lands and return and any additional expenses of an inspection, which shall be the amount of the inspection fee. All inspection fees shall be accounted for to the applicant.

c. The fee for a consolidated filing, filed pursuant to section 13 [C.45:15-16.39] of this act, shall be the same as set forth in subsection a. of this section.

45:15-16.35. Examination by commission

Upon receipt of an application for registration in proper form, accompanied by a statement of record, the commission shall initiate an examination to determine that:

a. The subdivider can convey or cause to be conveyed the interest in subdivided lands offered for disposition if the purchaser complies with the terms of the offer, and when appropriate, that release clauses, conveyances in trust or other safeguards have been provided;

b. There is reasonable assurance that all proposed improvements will be completed as represented;

c. The advertising material and the general promotional plan are not false, misleading, or discriminatory and comply with the standards prescribed by the commission in its rules and regulations and afford full and fair disclosure;

d. The subdivider has not, or if a corporation, its officers, directors, and principals have not, been convicted of a crime or civil offense involving land dispositions or any aspect of the land sales business in this State, the United States, or any other state or foreign country; and that the developer has not been subject to any permanent injunction or final administrative order restraining a false or misleading promotional plan involving real property dispositions, the seriousness of which in the opinion of the commission warrants the denial of registration; and

e. The public offering statement requirements of section 12 [C.45:15-16.38] of this act have been satisfied.

45:15-16.36. Contents of statement of record

The statement of record shall contain the information and be accompanied by the documents specified as follows:

a. The name and address of each person having an interest in the lots in the subdivision to be covered by the statement of record and the extent of that interest;

b. A legal description of, and a statement of the total area included in, the subdivision and a statement of the topography, together with a map showing the subdivision proposed and the dimensions of the lots, parcels, units, or interests to be covered by the statement of record and their relation to existing streets, roads and other improvements. The map shall be drawn to scale, signed and sealed, by a licensed professional engineer or land surveyor;

c. A statement of the condition of the title to the land comprising the subdivision, including all encumbrances and deed restrictions and covenants applicable thereto;

d. A statement of the general terms and conditions proposed to dispose of the lots in the subdivision;

e. A statement of the present condition of access to the subdivision, the existence of any unusual conditions relating to noise or safety, which affect the subdivision and are known or should reasonably be known to the developer, the availability of sewage disposal facilities and other public utilities, including water, electricity, gas, and telephone facilities, in the subdivision to nearby municipalities, and the nature of any improvements to be installed by the developer and his estimated schedule for completion;

f. A statement as to whether the property or any portion thereof is regularly or periodically subject to natural forces that would tend to adversely affect the use or enjoyment of the property and whether the property or any portion thereof is located in a federally designated flood hazard area;

g. In the case of any subdivision or portion thereof against which there exists a blanket encumbrance, a statement of the consequences for an individual purchaser of a failure, by the persons bound, to fulfill obligations under the instruments creating such encumbrances and the steps, if any, taken to protect the purchaser in such eventuality;

h. (1) Copy of its articles of incorporation, with all amendments thereto, if the developer is a corporation; (2) copies of all instruments by which the trust is created or declared, if the developer is a trust; (3) copies of its articles of partnership or association and all other papers pertaining to its organization, if the developer is a partnership, unincorporated association, joint stock company, or any other form of organization; and (4) if the purported holder of legal title is a person other than the developer, copies of the appropriate documents required pursuant to this subsection for that person;

i. Copies of the deed or other instrument establishing title to the subdivision in the developer or other person and copies of any instrument creating a lien or encumbrance upon the title of developer or other person or copies of the opinion of counsel in respect to the title to the subdivision in the developer or other person or companies of the title insurance policy guaranteeing that title;

j. Copies of all forms of conveyance to be used in selling or leasing lots to purchasers;

k. Copies of instruments creating easements or other restrictions;

l. Certified and uncertified financial statements of the developer as required by the commission;

m. Copies of any management contract, lease of recreational areas, or similar contract or agreement affecting the use, maintenance, or access of all or any part of the subdivision;

n. A statement of the status of compliance with the requirements of all laws, ordinances, regulations, and other requirements of governmental agencies, including the federal government, having jurisdiction over the premises;

o. The developer shall immediately report any material changes in the information contained in an application for registration. The term "material changes" shall be further defined by the commission in its regulations; and

p. Any other information and any other documents and certification as the commission may require as being reasonably necessary for the protection of purchasers.

45:15-16.37.   Information available to public

The information contained in any statement of record and any additions or corrections required by section 10 [C.45:15-16.36] of this act shall be made available to the public under regulations promulgated by the commission pursuant to this act and copies shall be furnished to every applicant at a reasonable charge prescribed by the commission.

45:15-16.38.   Public offering statement; not to be used for promotional purposes; amendments to; right to cancel

a. A public offering statement shall disclose fully and accurately the physical characteristics of the subdivided lands offered and shall make known to prospective purchasers all unusual and material circumstances or features affecting those lands. The proposed public offering statement submitted to the commission shall be in a form prescribed by the rules and regulations promulgated pursuant to this act and shall include the following:

(1) The name and principal address of the developer and his authorized New Jersey representative who shall be a licensed real estate broker licensed to maintain offices within this State;

(2) A general description of the subdivision or subdivided lands stating the total number of lots, parcels, units or interests in the offering;

(3) A summary of the terms and conditions of any management contract, lease of recreational areas, or similar contract or agreement affecting the use, maintenance, or access of all or any part of the subdivision or subdivided lands, the effect of each agreement upon a purchaser, and a statement of the relationship, if any, between the developer or subdivider and the managing agent or firm;

(4) The significant terms of any encumbrances, easements, liens and restrictions, including zoning and other regulations affecting the lands and each unit or lot, and a statement of all existing taxes and existing or proposed special taxes or assessments which affect the lands;

45:15-16.39

(5) A statement of the use for which the property is offered, including, but not limited to:

(a) Information concerning improvements, including hospitals, health and recreational facilities of any kind, streets, water supply, levees, drainage control systems, irrigation systems, sewage disposal facilities and customary utilities; and

(b) The estimated cost, date of completion and responsibility for construction and maintenance of existing and proposed improvements which are referred to in connection with the offering or disposition of any interest in the subdivision or subdivided lands;

(6) The notice, as required in subsection d. of this section, shall, in addition to being contained in all contracts or agreements, be conspicuously located and simply stated in the public offering statement; and

(7) Additional information required by the commission to assure full and fair disclosure to prospective purchasers.

b. The public offering statement shall not be used for any promotional purposes before registration of the subdivided lands and afterwards only if it is used in its entirety. No person may advertise or represent that the commission approves or recommends the subdivided lands or the disposition thereof. No portion of the public offering statement may be underscored, italicized, or printed in larger or heavier or different color type than the remainder of the statement unless the commission requires or permits it.

c. The commission may require the subdivider to alter or amend the proposed public offering statement in order to assure full and fair disclosure to prospective purchasers, and no change in the substance of the promotional plan or plan of disposition or development of the subdivision may be made after registration without notifying the commission and without making an appropriate amendment to the public offering statement. A public offering statement is not current unless all amendments or consolidations are incorporated.

d. Any contract or agreement for the purchase or the leasing of a lot may be rescinded by the purchaser or lessee without cause of any kind by sending or delivering written notice of cancellation by midnight of the seventh calendar day following the day on which the purchaser has executed the contract or agreement. Every contract or agreement shall be in writing and shall contain the following notice in 10-point bold type or larger, directly above the space provided for the signature of the purchaser or lessee:

NOTICE to PURCHASER or LESSEE: You are entitled to the right to cancel this contract by midnight of the seventh calendar day following the day on which you have executed this contract or agreement.

e. The subdivider shall make copies of the public offering statement available to prospective purchasers prior to their signing any contract or agreement.

45:15-16.39.   Consolidated filing

A subdivider may register additional subdivided lands pursuant to the same common promotional plan as those previously registered by submitting an additional filing providing the additional information necessary to register the additional lots, parcels, units or interests which shall be designated as "a consolidated filing."

45:15-16.40.   Report by subdivider

a. Within 30 days after each annual anniversary date of an order registering the subdivided lands, or on or before a date set by the commission, and while the subdivider retains any interest therein, the subdivider of these lands shall file a report in the form prescribed by the rules and regulations promulgated by the commission. The report shall reflect any material changes in the information contained in the original application for registration; except that, with respect to any registration filed with and approved by the commission prior to the date of enactment of this act, no additional information shall be required on the subdivided land covered by such registration other than that necessary to indicate any material changes in information contained in the original application for registration.

b. The commission shall process and review requests for amendments to a registration in accordance with the standards and procedures established in this act for review of applications for registration. Requests for amendment, other than price changes and advertising, shall be accompanied by a fee as the commission may prescribe by rule.

c. Upon a determination by the commission that an annual report is no longer necessary for the protection of the public interest or that the developer no longer retains any interest and no longer has any contractual, bond or other obligations in the subdivision, the commission shall issue an order terminating the responsibilities of the developer under this act.

45:15-16.41.   Powers of commission

The commission may:

a. Accept registrations filed in this State, in other states or with the federal government;

b. Contract with similar agencies in this State or other jurisdictions to perform investigative functions;

c. Accept grants in aid from any governmental or other source;

d. Cooperate with similar agencies or commissions in this State or other jurisdictions to establish uniform filing procedures and forms, uniform public offering statements, advertising standards, rules and common administrative practices;

e. Grant exemptions pursuant to the rules and regulations adopted pursuant to section 23 [C.45:15-16.49] of this act;

f. Make any necessary public or private investigations within or outside of this State to determine whether any person has violated or is about to violate any provision of this act, or to aid in the enforcement of this act or in the prescribing of rules and regulations and forms hereunder;

g. Require or permit any person to file a statement in writing, under oath or otherwise, as the commission determines, as to all the facts and circumstances concerning the matter to be investigated;

h. For the purpose of any investigation or proceeding under this act, the commission or any officer designated by rule, may administer oaths, or affirmations, and upon its own motion or upon request of any party may subpoena witnesses and compel their attendance, take evidence, and require the production of any matter which is relevant to the investigation, including the existence, description, nature, custody, condition and location of any books, documents, or other tangible things and the identity and location of persons having knowledge of relevant facts or any other matter reasonably calculated to lead to the discovery of material evidence; and

i. Upon failure to obey a subpoena or to answer questions propounded by the investigating officer and upon reasonable notice to all persons affected thereby, the commission may apply to the Superior Court for an order compelling compliance.

45:15-16.42. Commission empowered to issue cease and desist orders

a. If the commission determines after notice and hearing that a person has:

(1) Violated any provision of this act;

(2) Directly or through an agent or employee engaged in any false, deceptive, or misleading advertising, promotional or sales methods in the State of New Jersey to offer or dispose of an interest in the subdivision or subdivided lands;

(3) Made any material change in the plan of disposition and development of the subdivision or subdivided lands subsequent to the order of registration without first complying with the provisions of subsection o. of section 10 [C.45:15-16.36] of this act;

(4) Disposed of any subdivision or subdivided lands which have not been registered with the commission; or

(5) Violated any lawful order or rule or regulation of the commission;

the commission may issue an order requiring the person to cease and desist from the unlawful practice and to take such affirmative action as in the judgment of the commission will carry out the purposes of this act.

b. If the commission makes a finding of fact in writing that the public interest will be irreparably harmed by delay in issuing an order, it may issue a temporary cease and desist order. Every temporary cease and desist order shall include in its terms a provision that upon request a hearing will be held within 15 days of the receipt of the request.

45:15-16.43. Conditions for revocation of registration

a. A registration may be revoked after notice and hearing upon a written finding of fact that the subdivider has:

(1) Failed to comply with the terms of a cease and desist order issued pursuant to subsection a. of section 16 [C.45:15-16.42] of this act;

(2) Been convicted in any court for a crime or civil offense involving fraud, deception, false pretenses, misrepresentation, false advertising, dishonest dealing, or other like offense subsequent to the filing of the application for registration;

(3) Disposed of, concealed, or diverted any funds or assets of any person so as to defeat the rights of subdivision purchasers;

(4) Failed faithfully to perform any stipulation or agreement made with the commission as an inducement to grant any registration, to reinstate any registration, or to approve any promotional plan or public offering statement;

(5) Advertised his subdivision or responded to applications for his subdivision in a manner which was discriminatory on the basis of marital status, sex, race, creed, color, religion or national origin;

(6) Willfully violated any provision of this act or of a rule or regulation promulgated pursuant to section 23 [C.45:15-16.49] of this act; or

(7) Made intentional misrepresentation or concealed material facts in the documents and information submitted in the application filed for registration. Findings of fact, if set forth in statutory language, shall be accompanied by a concise and explicit statement of the underlying facts supporting the findings.

b. If the commission finds, after notice and hearing, that the subdivider has been guilty of a violation for which revocation could be ordered, it may, in lieu thereof, issue a cease and desist

45:15-16.44

order pursuant to subsection a. of section 16 [C.45:15-16.42] of this act.

45:15-16.44.   Commission empowered to bring action in Superior Court; intervene in suits

a. If it appears that a person has engaged, or is about to engage, in an act or practice constituting a violation of a provision of this act, the commission, with or without prior administrative proceedings, may bring an action in the Superior Court to enjoin the acts or practices and to enforce compliance with this act or any rule, regulation or order hereunder. Upon proper showing, injunctive relief or temporary restraining orders shall be granted, and a receiver may be appointed. The commission shall not be required to post a bond in any court proceeding.

b. The commission may intervene in a suit involving any subdivision. In any such suit, by or against the developer or subdivider, the developer or subdivider shall promptly furnish the commission with notice of the suit and copies of all pleadings.

45:15-16.45.   Submission of applicant to the courts; methods of service

a. For purposes of this act, an applicant for registration submitted to the commission shall be deemed as submission, by the applicant, to the jurisdiction of the Courts of the State of New Jersey.

b. In addition to the methods of service provided for in the Rules Governing the Courts of the State of New Jersey, service may be made by delivering a copy of the process to the person in charge of the office of the commission at its office, but that service shall not be effective unless the plaintiff, which may be the commission in a proceeding instituted by it:

(1) Sends a copy of the process and the pleading by certified mail to the defendant or respondent at his last known address; and

(2) The plaintiff's affidavit of compliance with this section is filed in the case on or before the return day of the process, if any, or within the time as the court allows.

c. If any person, including any nonresident of this State, engaged in conduct prohibited by this act and has not filed a consent of service of process and personal jurisdiction over him cannot otherwise be obtained in this State, that conduct authorizes the commission to receive service of process in any non-criminal proceedings against him or his successor which grows out of that conduct and which is brought under this act with the same force and validity as if served on him personally. Notice shall be given as provided in subsection a. of this section.

45:15-16.46.   Violations by brokers, salespeople; fines, penalties

a. Any broker or salesperson who violates any of the provisions of this act shall, in addition to the penalties set forth herein, be subject to the penalties as set forth in R.S. 45:15-17.

b. Any person who violates any provision of this act or any person who, in an application for registration filed with the commission, makes any untrue statement of a material fact or omits to state a material fact shall be fined not less than $250, nor more than $50,000, per violation.

c. The commission may levy and collect the penalties set forth in subsection b. of this section after affording the person alleged to be in violation of this act an opportunity to appear before the commission and to be heard personally or through counsel on the alleged violations and a finding by the commission that said person is guilty of the violation. When a penalty levied by the commission has not been satisfied within 30 days of the levy, the penalty may be sued for and recovered by, and in the name of, the commission in a summary proceeding pursuant to "the penalty enforcement law" (N.J.S. 2A:58-1 et seq.).

d. The commission may, in the interest of justice, compromise any civil penalty, if in its determination the gravity of the offense or offenses does not warrant the assessment of the full fine.

45:15-16.47.   Actions, counterclaims permitted against non-compliers

a. Any person who suffers any ascertainable loss of moneys as a result of the failure of another to comply fully with the provisions of this act may bring an action or assert a counterclaim in any court of competent jurisdiction. In any action filed under this section in which a defendant is found to have knowingly engaged in any false, deceptive, misleading promotional or sales methods or discriminatory advertising on the basis of race, sex, creed, color, marital status, national origin or religion, concealed or fraudulently diverted any funds or assets so as to defeat the rights of subdivision purchasers, made an intentional misrepresentation or concealed a material fact in an application for registration, or disposed of any subdivision or subdivided lands required to be registered under section 7 [C.45:15-16.33] of this act which are not so registered, the court shall, in addition to any other appropriate legal or equitable remedy, award double the damages suffered, and court costs expended, including reasonable attorney's fees. In the case of an untruth, omission, or misleading statement the developer sustains the burden of proving that the purchaser knew of the untruth, omission or misleading statement, or that he did not rely on such information, or that the developer did not know, and in the exercise of reasonable care could not have known, of the untruth, omission, or misleading statement.

b. The court may, in addition to the remedies provided in this act, frame any other relief that may be appropriate under the circumstances including, in the court's discretion, restitution of all monies paid and, where a subdivider has failed to provide to a purchaser a copy of the current public offering statement approved by the commission prior to execution of the contract or agreement, rescission of the contract. If the purchaser fails to establish a cause of action, and the court further determines that the action was wholly without merit, the court may award attorney's fees to the developer or subdivider.

c. Every person who directly or indirectly controls a subdivision or developer and violates the provisions of subsection a. of this section, every general partner, officer, or director of a developer, and every person occupying a similar status or performing a similar function, shall be jointly and severally liable with and to the same extent as the developer. The person otherwise liable pursuant to this subsection sustains the burden of proof that he did not know, and in the exercise of reasonable care could not have known, of the existence of the facts by reason of which the liability is alleged to exist. There is a right to contribution among persons found liable.

d. Any stipulation or provision purporting to bind any purchaser acquiring a parcel, lot, unit, or interest in any development subject to the provisions of this act to a waiver of compliance with the provisions of this act, shall be void.

e. Any party to an action asserting a claim, counterclaim or defense based upon any violation of this act shall mail a copy of the initial or responsive pleading containing the claim, counterclaim or defense to the commission within 10 days of the filing of the pleading with court. Upon application to the court where the matter is pending, the commission shall be permitted to intervene or to appear in any status appropriate to the matter.

45:15-16.48.   Existing registrations deemed in force and effect

Any registration of a subdivision or amendment thereto, or consolidation, or renewal thereof approved by the commission prior to August 2, 1989, under the "Land Sales Full Disclosure Act," P.L.1975, c. 235 (C. 45:15-16.3 et seq.) shall, upon the enactment of this act, be deemed in force and effect for the remainder of the 12-month period for which it was issued.

45:15-16.49.   Rules and regulations

The commission shall, pursuant to the provisions of the "Administrative Procedure Act," P.L.1968, c. 410 (C. 52:14B-1 et seq.), promulgate rules and regulations necessary to effectuate the provisions of this act. The rules may include, but shall not be limited to: a. provisions for advertising standards to insure full and fair disclosure; b. provisions for adequate bondings or access to some escrow or trust fund not otherwise required by

the municipal governing body to be located within this State, or the state or country where the property is located, so as to insure compliance with the provisions of this act, and to compensate purchasers for failure of the registrant to perform in accordance with the terms of any contract or public statement; c. provisions that require a registrant to deposit purchaser down payments, security deposits or other funds in an escrow account, or with an attorney licensed to practice law in this State, or the state or country where the property is located, until such time as the commission by its rules and regulations deems it appropriate to permit such funds to be released; d. provisions to insure that all contracts between developer and purchaser are fair and reasonable; e. provisions that the developer must give a fair and reasonable warranty on construction of any improvements; f. provisions that the budget for the operation and maintenance of the common or shared elements or interest shall provide for adequate reserves for depreciation and replacement of the improvements; g. provisions for operating procedures; and h. other rules and regulations necessary to effectuate the purposes of this act, and taking into account and providing for, the broad range of development plans and devises, management mechanisms, and methods of ownership, permitted under the provisions of this act.

45:15-16.50.   Short title [New Jersey Real Estate Timeshare Act]

Sections 1 through 36 [C.45:15-16.50 through C.45:15-16.85] of this act shall be known and may be cited as the "New Jersey Real Estate Timeshare Act."

45:15-16.51.   Definitions relative to timeshares

As used in sections 1 through 36 [C.45:15-16.50 through C.45:15-16.85] of this act:

"Accommodation" means any apartment, condominium or cooperative unit, cabin, lodge, hotel or motel room, or other private or commercial structure containing toilet facilities therein that is designed and available, pursuant to applicable law, for use and occupancy as a residence by one or more individuals which is a part of the timeshare property.

"Advertisement" means any written, oral or electronic communication that is directed to or targeted to persons within the State and contains a promotion, inducement or offer to sell a timeshare plan, including but not limited to brochures, pamphlets, radio and television scripts, electronic media, telephone and direct mail solicitations and other means of promotion.

"Advertisement" does not mean:

(1) Any stockholder communication such as an annual report or interim financial report, proxy material, a registration statement, a securities prospectus, a registration, a property report

45:15-16.51

or other material required to be delivered to a prospective purchaser by an agency of any state or federal government;

(2) Any oral or written statement disseminated by a developer to broadcast or print media, other than paid advertising or promotional material, regarding plans for the acquisition or development of timeshare property. However, any rebroadcast or any other dissemination of such oral statements to prospective purchasers by a seller in any manner, or any distribution of copies of newspaper magazine articles or press releases, or any other dissemination of such written statement to a prospective purchaser by a seller in any manner, shall constitute an advertisement; or

(3) Any communication addressed to and relating to the account of any person who has previously executed a contract for the sale or purchase of a timeshare period in a timeshare plan to which the communication relates shall not be considered advertising under this act, provided they are delivered to any person who has previously executed a contract for the purchase of a timeshare interest or is an existing owner of a timeshare interest in a timeshare plan.

"Assessment" means the share of funds required for the payment of common expenses which is assessed from time to time against each timeshare interest by the association.

"Association" means the organized body consisting of the purchasers of interests in a timeshare property.

"Commission" means the New Jersey Real Estate Commission.

"Common expense" means casualty and liability insurance, and those expenses properly incurred for the maintenance, operation, and repair of all accommodations constituting the timeshare plan and any other expenses designated as common expenses by the timeshare instrument.

"Component site" means a specific geographic location where accommodations which are part of a multi-site timeshare plan are located. Separate phases of a single timeshare property in a specific geographic location and under common management shall be deemed a single component site.

"Department" means the Department of Banking and Insurance.

"Developer" means and includes any person or entity, who creates a timeshare plan or is in the business of selling timeshare interests, or employs agents or brokers to do the same, or any person or entity who succeeds to the interest of a developer by sale, lease, assignment, mortgage or other transfer, except that the term shall include only those persons who offer timeshare interests for disposition in the ordinary course of business.

"Dispose" or "disposition" means a voluntary transfer or assignment of any legal or equitable interest in a timeshare plan, other than the transfer, assignment or release of a security interest.

"Escrow agent" means an independent person, including an independent bonded escrow company, an independent financial institution whose accounts are insured by a governmental agency or instrumentality, or an independent licensed title insurance agent who is responsible for the receipt and disbursement of funds in accordance with this act. If the escrow agent is not located in the State of New Jersey, then this person shall subject themselves to the jurisdiction of the commission with respect to disputes that arise out of the provisions of this act.

"Incidental benefit" means an accommodation, product, service, discount, or other benefit which is offered to a prospective purchaser of a timeshare plan or to a purchaser of a timeshare plan prior to the expiration of his or her rescission period pursuant to section 18 [C.45:15-16.67] of this act and which is not an exchange program, provided that:

(1) use or participation in the incidental benefit is completely voluntary;

(2) no costs of the incidental benefit are included as common expenses of the timeshare plan;

(3) the good faith represented aggregate value of all incidental benefits offered by a developer to a purchaser may not exceed 20 percent of the actual price paid by the purchaser for his or her timeshare interest; and

(4) the purchaser is provided a disclosure that fairly describes the material terms of the incidental benefit. The term shall not include an offer of the use of the accommodations of the timeshare plan on a free or discounted one-time basis.

"Managing entity" means the person who undertakes the duties, responsibilities and obligations of the management of the timeshare property.

"Offer" means any inducement, solicitation, or other attempt, whether by marketing, advertisement, oral or written presentation or any other means, to encourage a person to acquire a timeshare interest in a timeshare plan, for gain or profit.

"Person" means a natural person, corporation, limited liability company, partnership, joint venture, association, estate, trust, government, governmental subdivision or agency, or other legal entity or any combination thereof.

"Promotion" means a plan or device, including one involving the possibility of a prospective purchaser receiving a vacation, discount vacation, gift, or prize, used by a developer, or an agent, independent contractor, or employee of a developer, agent or independent contractor on behalf of the developer, in connection with the offering and sale of timeshare interests in a timeshare plan.

"Purchaser" means any person, other than a developer, who by means of a voluntary transfer acquires a legal or equitable interest in a timeshare plan other than as security for an obligation.

"Purchase contract" means a document pursuant to which a person becomes legally obligated to sell, and a purchaser becomes legally obligated to buy, a timeshare interest.

"Reservation system" means the method, arrangement or procedure by which a purchaser, in order to reserve the use or occupancy of any accommodation of a multi-site timeshare plan for one or more timeshare periods, is required to compete with other purchasers in the same multi-site timeshare plan, regardless of whether the reservation system is operated and maintained by the multi-site timeshare plan managing entity or any other person.

"Sales agent" means any person who performs within this State as an agent or employee of a developer any one or more of the services or acts as set forth in this act, and includes any real estate broker, broker salesperson or salesperson licensed pursuant to R.S. 45:15-1 et seq., or any person who purports to act in any such capacity.

"Timeshare instrument" means one or more documents, by whatever name denominated, creating or governing the operation of a timeshare plan.

"Timeshare interest" means and includes either:

(1) A "timeshare estate," which is the right to occupy a timeshare property, coupled with a freehold estate or an estate for years with a future interest in a timeshare property or a specified portion thereof; or

(2) A "timeshare use," which is the right to occupy a timeshare property, which right is neither coupled with a freehold interest, nor coupled with an estate for years with a future interest, in a timeshare property.

"Timeshare period" means the period or periods of time when the purchaser of a timeshare plan is afforded the opportunity to use the accommodations of a timeshare plan.

"Timeshare plan" means any arrangement, plan, scheme, or similar device, whether by membership agreement, sale, lease, deed, license, or right to use agreement or by any other means, whereby a purchaser, in exchange for consideration, receives ownership rights in or the right to use accommodations for a period of time less than a full year during any given year on a recurring basis, but not necessarily for consecutive years. A timeshare plan may be:

(1) A "single-site timeshare plan," which is the right to use accommodations at a single timeshare property; or

(2) A "multi-site timeshare plan," which includes:

(a) A "specific timeshare interest," which means an interest wherein a purchaser has, only through a reservation system:

(i) a priority right to reserve accommodations at a specific timeshare property without competing with owners of timeshare interests at other component sites that are part of the multi-site timeshare plan, which priority right extends for at least 60 days; and

(ii) the right to reserve accommodations on a non-priority basis at other component sites that are part of the multi-site timeshare plan; or

(b) A "non-specific timeshare interest", which means an interest wherein a purchaser has, only through a reservation system, the right to reserve accommodations at any component site of the multi-site timeshare plan, with no priority right to reserve accommodations at any specific component site.

"Timeshare property" means one or more accommodations subject to the same timeshare instrument, together with any other property or rights to property appurtenant to those accommodations.

45:15-16.52. Applicability of act

This act shall apply to the following:

a. Timeshare plans with an accommodation or component site in the State; and

b. Timeshare plans without an accommodation or component site in this State if those timeshare plans are offered to be sold within this State, regardless of whether the offer originates from within or outside of this State.

45:15-16.53. Inapplicability of act

a. This act shall not apply to any of the following:

(1) Timeshare plans, whether or not an accommodation or component site is located in the State, consisting of 10 or fewer timeshare interests;

(2) Timeshare plans, whether or not an accommodation or component site is located in this State, the use of which extends over any period of three years or less. For purposes of determining the term of a timeshare plan, the period of any automatic renewal shall be included, unless a purchaser has the right to terminate the purchaser's participation in the timeshare plan at any time and receive a pro rata refund, or the purchaser receives a notice, not less than 30 days, but not more than 60 days, prior to the date of renewal, informing the purchaser of the right to terminate at any time prior to the date of automatic renewal;

45:15-16.54

(3) Timeshare plans, whether or not an accommodation or component site is located in the State, under which the prospective purchaser's total financial obligation will be equal to or less than $3,000 during the entire term of the timeshare plan;

(4) Component sites of specific timeshare interest multi-site timeshare plans that are neither located in nor offered for sale in this State, except that these component sites are still subject to the disclosure requirements of section 10 [C.45:15-16.59] of this act;

(5) Offers or dispositions of securities or units of interest issued by a real estate investment trust regulated under any State or federal statute;

(6) Offers or dispositions of securities currently registered with the Bureau of Securities within the Division of Consumer Affairs in the Department of Law and Public Safety.

b. A person shall not be required to register as a developer under this act if:

(1) The person is an owner of a timeshare interest who has acquired the timeshare interest for the person's own use and occupancy and who later offers it for resale in a single or isolated transaction; or

(2) The person is a managing entity or an association that is not otherwise a developer of a timeshare plan in its own right, solely while acting as an association or under a contract with an association to offer or sell a timeshare interest transferred to the association through foreclosure, deed in lieu of foreclosure, or gratuitous transfer, if such acts are performed in the regular course of, or as an incident to, the management of the association for its own account in the timeshare plan.

c. If a developer has already registered a timeshare plan under this act, the developer may offer or dispose of an interest in a timeshare plan that is not registered under this act if the developer is offering a timeshare interest in the additional timeshare plan to a current timeshare interest owner of a timeshare interest in a timeshare plan created or operated by that same developer subject to the rules and regulations adopted by the commission.

d. The commission may, from time to time, pursuant to any rules and regulations adopted pursuant to this act, exempt from any of the provisions of this act any timeshare plan, if it finds that the enforcement of this act with respect to that plan is not necessary in the public interest, or required for the protection of purchasers, by reason of the small amount of the purchase price or the limited character of the offering.

45:15-16.54.   Administration by Real Estate Commission

This act shall be administered by the New Jersey Real Estate Commission in the Department of Banking and Insurance.

45:15-16.55.   Nonpreemption of local codes; supersedure of other regulation of timeshares

Except as provided in this section, no provision of this act shall invalidate or modify any provision of any zoning, subdivision, or building code, law, ordinance or regulation. In case of conflict between the provisions of this act and the provisions of any other law, ordinance or regulation governing or purporting to govern the creation, registration, disclosure requirements or sale of timeshare interests in a component site, the provisions of this act shall control.

45:15-16.56.   Creation of timeshare plan

A timeshare plan may be created in any accommodation unless otherwise prohibited. A timeshare plan shall maintain a one-to-one purchaser-to-accommodation ratio, which means the ratio of the number of purchasers eligible to use the accommodations of a timeshare plan on a given day to the number of accommodations available for use within the plan on that day, such that the total number of purchasers eligible to use the accommodations of the timeshare plan during a given consecutive 12-month period never exceeds the total number of accommodations available for use in the timeshare plan during that consecutive 12-month period. For purposes of the calculation under this section, each purchaser shall be counted at least once, and an individual accommodation shall not be counted more than one time per day per year. An owner of a timeshare interest who is delinquent in the payment of a timeshare plan assessment shall continue to be considered eligible to use the accommodations of the timeshare plan for purposes of calculating the one-to-one purchaser-to-accommodation ratio.

45:15-16.57.   Requirements for developers of timeshares; application, registration

a. A developer who sells, offers to sell, or attempts to solicit prospective purchasers in this State to purchase a timeshare interest, or any person who creates a timeshare plan with an accommodation in the State, shall register with the commission, on forms provided by the commission or in electronic formats authorized by the commission, all timeshare plans which have accommodations located in the State or which are sold or offered for sale to any individual located in the State.

b. Upon the submission of an application approved by the commission, the commission may grant a 90-day preliminary registration to allow the developer to begin offering and selling timeshare interests in a timeshare plan regardless of whether the accommodations of the timeshare plan are located within or outside of the State. Upon submission of a substantially complete application for an abbreviated or comprehensive registration under this act, including all appropriate fees, to the commission prior to the expiration date of the preliminary registration, the preliminary registration will be automatically extended during the registration review period provided that the developer is actively and diligently pursuing registration under this act. The preliminary registration shall automatically terminate with respect to those timeshare interests covered by a final public offering statement that is issued before the scheduled termination date of the preliminary registration. The preliminary registration shall also terminate upon the issuance of any notice of rejection due to the developer's failure to comply with the provisions of this act.

To obtain a preliminary registration, the developer shall provide all of the following:

(1) Submit the reservation instrument to be used in a form previously approved by the department with at least the following provisions:

(a) The right of both the developer and the potential purchaser to unilaterally cancel the reservation at any time;

(b) The payment to the potential purchaser of his or her total deposit following cancellation of the reservation by either party;

(c) The placing of the deposit into an escrow account; and

(d) A statement to the effect that the offering has not yet received final approval from the commission, and that no offering can be made until an offering plan has been filed with, and accepted by, the commission;

(2) Agree to provide each potential purchaser with a copy of the preliminary public offering statement and an executed receipt for a copy before any money or other thing of value has been accepted by or on behalf of the developer in connection with the reservation;

(3) Agree to provide a copy of the reservation instrument signed by the potential purchaser and by or on behalf of the developer to the potential purchaser;

(4) Provide evidence acceptable to the commission that all funds received by the developer will be placed into an independent escrow account with instructions that no funds will be released until a final order of registration has been granted;

(5) Submit the filing fee for a preliminary registration as provided for by regulation. The filing fee shall be in addition to the filing fees for an abbreviated or comprehensive registration as established by this act;

(6) File all advertisements to be utilized by the developer under the preliminary registration with the commission before use.

All advertisements and advertising literature shall contain the following, or substantially similar, disclaimer:

"This advertising material is being used for the purpose of soliciting sales of timeshare interests.";

(7) Such other information as the commission may require in order to further the provisions of this act, to assure full and fair disclosure and for the protection of purchaser interests.

c. Prior to the issuance of an order of registration for an abbreviated or comprehensive registration, the commission may issue a conditional registration approval for a timeshare plan if the filing is deemed to be substantially complete by the commission and the commission determines that the deficiencies are likely to be corrected by the applicant in a reasonable time and manner. Once the commission issues a conditional registration approval, the applicant may begin entering into purchase contracts with the purchaser and provide the purchaser with the most current version of the public offering statement; however, no rescission period may begin to run until the final approved public offering statement is delivered to the purchaser. If there is no material difference between the documents provided to the purchaser pursuant to the conditional registration and the documents approved as part of the final order of approval, then those documents need not be delivered again to the purchaser. All purchase contracts that are executed under the authority of a conditional registration approval shall contain the following provisions:

(1) No escrow will close, funds will not be released from escrow, and the interest contracted for will not be conveyed until a final approved public offering statement for the timeshare plan is furnished to the purchaser.

(2) The contract may be rescinded, in which event the entire sum of money paid or advanced by the purchaser shall be returned if the purchaser or lessee is dissatisfied with the final public offering statement.

(3) The term for a conditional registration approval shall be six months from the date of approval by the commission, and may be extended upon application to the commission for an additional six month period.

d. A developer shall include in its application for registration with the commission, the following information:

(1) The developer's legal name, any assumed names used by the developer, and the developer's principal office location, mailing address, primary contact person and telephone number;

(2) The name, location, mailing address, primary contact person and telephone number of the timeshare plan;

(3) The name and principal address of the developer's authorized New Jersey representative who shall be a licensed real estate broker licensed to maintain offices within this State;

(4) A declaration as to whether the timeshare plan is a single-site timeshare plan or a multi-site timeshare plan and, if a multi-

45:15-16.57

site timeshare plan, whether it consists of specific timeshare interests or non-specific timeshare interests;

(5) The name and principal address of all brokers within New Jersey who sell or offer to sell any timeshare interests in any timeshare plan offered by the developer to any person in this State, who shall be licensed as a real estate broker pursuant to R.S.45:15-1 et seq., and who are the authorized representatives of the developer;

(6) The name and principal address of all non-affiliated marketing entities who, by means of inducement, promotion or advertisement, attempt to encourage or procure prospective purchasers located in the State to attend a sales presentation for any timeshare plan offered by the developer or authorized broker;

(7) The name and principal address of all managing entities who manage the timeshare plan;

(8) A public offering statement which complies with the requirements of this act; and

(9) Any other information regarding the developer, timeshare plan, brokers, marketing entities or managing entities as required by the commission and established by the commission by regulation.

e. The developer shall comply with the following escrow requirements:

(1) A developer of a timeshare plan shall deposit with an escrow agent all funds which are received during the purchaser's cancellation period set forth in section 18 [C.45:15-16.67] of this act, into an escrow account in a federally insured depository or a depository acceptable to the commission. The deposit of such funds shall be evidenced by an executed escrow agreement between the escrow agent and the developer. The escrow agreement shall include provisions that funds may be disbursed to the developer by the escrow agent from the escrow account only after expiration of the purchaser's cancellation period and in accordance with the purchase contract, subject to paragraph (2) of this subsection.

(2) If a developer contracts to sell a timeshare interest and the construction of any property in which the timeshare interest is located has not been completed, the developer, upon expiration of the cancellation period set forth in section 18 [C.45:15-16.67] of this act, shall continue to maintain in an escrow account all funds received by or on behalf of the developer from the purchaser under the purchase contract. The commission shall establish by rule the type of documentation which shall be required for evidence of completion, including but not limited to a certificate of occupancy, a certificate of substantial completion, or equivalent certificate from a public safety inspection agency in the applicable jurisdiction. Funds shall be released from escrow as follows:

(a) If a purchaser properly cancels the purchase contract pursuant to its terms, the funds shall be paid to the purchaser or paid to the developer if the purchaser's funds have been previously refunded by the developer.

(b) If a purchaser defaults in the performance of the purchaser's obligations under the purchase contract, the funds shall be paid to the developer.

(c) If the funds of a purchaser have not been previously disbursed in accordance with the provisions of this paragraph, they may be disbursed to the developer by the escrow agent upon the issuance of acceptable evidence of completion of construction as provided herein.

(3) In lieu of the provisions in paragraphs (1) and (2) of this subsection, the commission may accept from the developer a surety bond, bond in lieu of escrow, irrevocable letter of credit or other financial assurance acceptable to the commission. Any acceptable financial assurance shall be in an amount equal to or in excess of the lesser of the funds which would otherwise be placed in escrow in accordance with the provisions of paragraph (1) of this subsection, or in an amount equal to the cost to complete the incomplete property in which the timeshare interest is located. However, in no event shall the amount be less than the amount of funds that would otherwise be placed in escrow pursuant to paragraph (1) of this subsection.

(4) The developer shall provide escrow account information to the commission and shall execute in writing an authorization consenting to an audit or examination of the account by the commission on forms provided by the commission. The developer shall comply with the reconciliation and records requirements established by rule by the commission. The developer shall make documents related to the escrow account or escrow obligation available to the commission upon the commission's request. The escrow agent shall maintain any disputed funds in the escrow account until either:

(a) Receipt of written direction agreed to by signature of all parties, or

(b) Deposit of the funds with a court of competent jurisdiction in which a civil action regarding the funds has been filed.

f. The commission may accept, as provided by regulation, an abbreviated registration application of a developer of a timeshare plan in which all accommodations are located outside of the State. The developer shall provide evidence that the timeshare plan is registered with the applicable regulatory agency in a state or jurisdiction where the timeshare plan is offered or sold, or that the timeshare plan is in compliance with the laws and regulations of the applicable state jurisdiction in which some or all of the accommodations are located, which state or jurisdiction shall have disclosure requirements that are substantially equivalent to or greater than the information required to be disclosed pursuant to subsections b. and c. of this section to purchasers in this State. A developer filing an abbreviated registration application shall provide the following:

(1) The developer's legal name, any assumed names used by the developer, and the developer's principal office location, mailing address, primary contact person and telephone number;

(2) The name, location, mailing address, primary contact person and telephone number of the timeshare plan;

(3) The name and principal address of the developer's authorized New Jersey representative who shall be a licensed real estate broker licensed to maintain offices within this State;

(4) The name and principal address of all brokers within New Jersey who sell or offer to sell any timeshare interests in any timeshare plan offered by the developer to any person in this State, who shall be licensed as a real estate broker pursuant to R.S. 45:15-1 et seq., and who are the authorized representatives of the developer;

(5) The name and principal address of all non-affiliated marketing entities who, by means of inducement, promotion or advertisement, attempt to encourage or procure prospective purchasers located in the State to attend a sales presentation for any timeshare plan offered by the developer or authorized broker;

(6) The name and principal address of all managing entities who manage the timeshare plan;

(7) Evidence of registration or compliance with the laws and regulations of the jurisdiction in which the timeshare plan is located, approved or accepted;

(8) A declaration as to whether the timeshare plan is a single-site timeshare plan or a multi-site timeshare plan and, if a multi-site timeshare plan, whether it consists of specific timeshare interests or non-specific timeshare interests;

(9) Disclosure of each jurisdiction in which the developer has applied for registration of the timeshare plan, and whether the timeshare plan or its developer were denied registration or were the subject of any disciplinary proceeding;

(10) Copies of any disclosure documents required to be given to purchasers or required to be filed with the jurisdiction in which the timeshare plan is located, approved or accepted as may be requested by the commission;

(11) The appropriate fee; and

(12) Any other information regarding the developer, timeshare plan, brokers, marketing entities or managing entities as required by the commission and established by the commission by regulation.

A developer of a timeshare plan with any accommodation located in this State may not file an abbreviated filing with regard to such timeshare plan, with the exception of a succeeding developer after a merger or acquisition when the developer's timeshare plan was registered in this State prior to the merger or acquisition.

45:15-16.58.   Responsibilities of timeshare developer for offering, marketing violations

The developer shall have responsibility for each timeshare plan registered with the commission and for the actions of any sales agent, managing entity or marketing entity utilized by the developer in the offering or promotional selling of any registered timeshare plan. Any violation of this act which occurs during the offering activities shall be a violation by the developer as well as by the sales agent, marketing entity or managing entity who actually committed the violation. Notwithstanding anything to the contrary in this act, the developer shall be responsible for the actions of the association and managing entity only while they are subject to the developer's control.

45:15-16.59.   Public offering, disclosure statements; requirements

a. A developer shall: (1) prepare a public offering statement; (2) provide the statement to each purchaser of a timeshare interest in any timeshare plan at the time of purchase; and (3) fully and accurately disclose those facts concerning the timeshare developer and timeshare plan that are required by this act or by regulations promulgated by the commission.

The public offering statement shall be in writing and dated and shall require the purchaser to certify in writing that the purchaser received the statement. Upon approval of the commission, the developer may offer to deliver the public offering statement and other documents on CD-ROM format, Internet website or other electronic media if the purchaser consents.

b. The public offering disclosure statement for a single-site timeshare plan shall include:

(1) The name and address of the developer;

(2) A description of the duration and operation of the timeshare plan;

(3) A description of the existing or proposed accommodations, including the type and number of timeshare interests in the accommodations expressed in periods of seven-day use availability or other time increments applicable to the timeshare plan. The description of each type of accommodation included in the timeshare plan shall be categorized by the number of bedrooms, the number of bathrooms, and sleeping capacity, and shall include a statement indicating whether the accommodation contains a full kitchen, which means a kitchen that has a minimum of a dishwasher, range, sink, oven, and refrigerator. If the accommodations are proposed or incomplete, a schedule

45:15-16.59

for commencement, completion, and availability of the accommodations shall be provided;

(4) A description of any existing or proposed amenities of the timeshare plan and, if the amenities are proposed or incomplete, a schedule for commencement, completion, and availability of the amenities;

(5) The extent to which financial arrangements have been provided for the completion of all promised accommodations and amenities that are committed to be built;

(6) A description of the method and timing for performing maintenance of the accommodations;

(7) A statement indicating that, on an annual basis, the sum of the nights that purchasers are entitled to use the accommodations does not exceed the number of nights the accommodations are available for use by the purchasers;

(8) A description of the method by which purchasers' use of the accommodations is scheduled;

(9) A statement that an association exists or is expected to be created or that such an association does not exist and is not expected to be created and, if such an association exists or is reasonably contemplated, a description of its powers and responsibilities;

(10) A statement that within seven days after receipt of the public offering statement or after execution of the purchase contract, whichever is later, a purchaser may cancel any purchase contract for a timeshare interest from a developer together with a statement providing the name and street address to which the purchaser should mail any notice of cancellation. However, if by agreement of the parties by and through the purchase contract, the purchase contract allows for cancellation of the purchase contract for a period of time exceeding seven days, then the public offering statement shall include a statement that the cancellation of the purchase contract is allowed for that period of time exceeding seven days;

(11) Copies of the following documents, if applicable, including any amendments to the documents, unless separately provided to the purchaser simultaneously with the public offering statement:

(a) the timeshare instrument;

(b) the association articles of incorporation;

(c) the association bylaws;

(d) the association rules; and

(e) any lease or contract, excluding the purchase contract and other loan documents required to be signed by the purchaser at closing;

(12) The name and principal address of the managing entity and a description of the procedures, if any, for altering the powers and responsibilities of the managing entity and for removing or replacing it;

(13) The current annual budget, if available, or the projected annual budget for the timeshare plan. The budget shall include:

(a) a statement of the amount reserved or budgeted for repairs or replacements, if any;

(b) the projected common expense liability, if any, by category of expenditure for the timeshare plan; and

(c) a statement of any services or expenses not reflected in the budget that the developer provides or pays;

(14) The projected assessments and a description of the method for calculating and apportioning those assessments among purchasers;

(15) Any initial or special fee due from the purchaser at closing, together with a description of the purpose and method of calculating the fee;

(16) A description of any lien, defect, or encumbrance on or affecting title to the timeshare interest and, if applicable, a copy of each written warranty provided by the developer;

(17) A description of any bankruptcy that is pending or which has occurred within the past five years, pending civil or criminal proceeding, adjudication, or disciplinary action material to the timeshare plan of which the developer has knowledge;

(18) A description of any financing offered by or available through the developer;

(19) Any current or anticipated fees or charges to be paid by timeshare purchasers for the use of any accommodations or amenities related to the timeshare plan, and a statement that the fees or charges are subject to change;

(20) A description and amount of insurance coverage provided for the protection of the purchaser;

(21) The extent to which a timeshare interest may become subject to a tax lien or other lien arising out of claims against purchasers of different timeshare interests;

(22) A description of those matters required by section 18 [C.45:15-16.67] of this act;

(23) A statement disclosing any right of first refusal or other restraint on the transfer of all or any portion of a timeshare interest;

(24) A statement disclosing that any deposit made in connection with the purchase of a timeshare interest shall be held by an escrow agent until expiration of any right to cancel the contract and that any deposit shall be returned to the purchaser if the pur-

chaser elects to exercise the right of cancellation; or, if the commission accepts from the developer a surety bond, irrevocable letter of credit, or other form of financial assurance instead of an escrow deposit, a statement disclosing that the developer has provided a surety bond, irrevocable letter of credit, or other form of financial assurance in an amount equal to or in excess of the funds that would otherwise be held by an escrow agent and that the deposit shall be returned if the purchaser elects to exercise the right of cancellation;

(25) A description of the name and address of the exchange company and the method by which a purchaser accesses the exchange program, if the timeshare plan provides purchasers with the opportunity to participate in an exchange program; and

(26) Any other information the commission determines is necessary to protect prospective purchasers or to implement the purpose of this act.

The developer may also include any other information in the timeshare disclosure statement following approval by the commission.

c. The disclosure statement for a specific timeshare interest multi-site timeshare plan shall include:

(1) With regard to the timeshare property in which the purchaser will receive a specific timeshare interest that includes a reservation priority right, all of the applicable information related to that timeshare property as required under subsection b. of this section;

(2) With regard to the component site in which the purchaser does not receive a specific timeshare interest, the following information:

(a) a description of each component site, including the name and address of each component site;

(b) a description of each type of accommodation in each component site, categorized by the number of bedrooms, the number of bathrooms, and sleeping capacity, and a statement indicating whether the accommodation contains a full kitchen, which means a kitchen that has a minimum of a dishwater, range, sink, oven, and refrigerator;

(c) a description of the amenities at each component site available for use by the purchaser;

(d) a description of the reservation system, which shall include:

(i) the entity responsible for operating the reservation system, its relationship to the developer, and the duration of any agreement for operation of the reservation system;

(ii) a summary or the rules governing access to and use of the reservation system; and

(iii) the existence of and explanation regarding any priority reservation features that affect a purchaser's ability to make reservations for the use of a given accommodation on a first-come, first-served basis;

(e) The name and principal address of the managing entity for the multi-site timeshare plan and a description of the procedures, if any, for altering the powers and responsibilities of the managing entity and for removing or replacing it;

(f) A description of any right to make additions to, substitutions in, or deletions from accommodations, amenities, or component sites, and a description of the basis on which accommodations, amenities, or component sites may be added to, substituted in, or deleted from the multi-site timeshare plan;

(g) A description of the purchaser's liability for any fees associated with the multi-site timeshare plan;

(h) The location of each component site of the multi-site timeshare plan, as well as any periodic adjustment or amendment to the reservation system that may be needed in order to respond to actual purchaser use patterns and changes in purchaser use demand for the accommodations existing at the time within the multi-site timeshare plan; and

(i) Any other information the commission determines is necessary to protect prospective purchasers or to implement the purpose of this act.

d. The public offering statement for a non-specific timeshare interest multi-site timeshare plan shall include:

(1) The name and address of the developer;

(2) A description of the type of interest and usage rights the purchaser will receive;

(3) A description of the duration and operation of the timeshare plan;

(4) A description of the type of insurance coverage provided for each component site;

(5) An explanation of who holds title to the accommodations of each component site;

(6) A description of each component site, including the name and address of each component site;

(7) A description of the existing or proposed accommodations expressed in periods of seven-day use availability or other time increments applicable to the timeshare plan. The description of each type of accommodation included in the timeshare plan shall be categorized by the number of bedrooms, the number of bathrooms, and sleeping capacity, and shall include a statement indicating whether the accommodation contains a full kitchen, which means a kitchen that has a minimum of a dishwasher, range, sink, oven, and refrigerator. If the accommodations are

45:15-16.59

proposed or incomplete, a schedule for commencement, completion and availability of the accommodations shall be provided;

(8) A statement that an association for the multi-site timeshare plan exists or is expected to be created or that such an association does not exist and is not expected to be created and, if such an association exists or is reasonably contemplated, a description of its powers and responsibilities;

(9) If applicable, copies of the following documents applicable to the multi-site timeshare plan, including any amendments to such documents, unless separately provided to the purchaser simultaneously with the timeshare disclosure statement:

(a) the timeshare instrument;

(b) the association articles of incorporation;

(c) the association bylaws; and

(d) the association rules;

(10) A description of the method and timing for performing maintenance of the accommodations;

(11) A statement indicating that, on an annual basis, the total number of purchasers eligible to use the accommodations of the timeshare plan during a given consecutive 12-month period never exceeds the total number of accommodations available for use in the timeshare plan during that consecutive 12-month period;

(12) A description of amenities available for use by the purchaser at each component site;

(13) The location of each component site of the multi-site timeshare plan, as well as any periodic adjustment or amendment to the reservation system that may be needed in order to respond to actual purchaser use patterns and changes in purchaser use demand for the accommodations existing at the time within the multi-site timeshare plan;

(14) A description of any right to make any additions, substitutions, or deletions of accommodations, amenities, or component sites, and a description of the basis upon which accommodations, amenities, or component sites may be added to, substituted in, or deleted from the multi-site timeshare plan;

(15) A description of the reservation system that shall include all of the following:

(a) the entity responsible for operating the reservation system, its relationship to the developer, and the duration of any agreement for operation of the reservation system;

(b) a summary of the rules governing access to and use of the reservation system; and

(c) the existence of and an explanation regarding any priority reservation features that affect a purchaser's ability to make res-

ervations for the use of a given accommodation on a first-come, first-served basis;

(16) The name and principal address of the managing entity for the multi-site timeshare plan and a description of the procedures, if any, for altering the powers and responsibilities of the managing entity and for removing or replacing it, and a description of the relationship between the multi-site timeshare plan managing entity and the managing entity of the component sites of the multi-site timeshare plan, if different from the multi-site timeshare plan managing entity;

(17) A statement that within seven days after receipt of the public offering statement or after execution of the purchase contract, whichever is later, a purchaser may cancel any purchase contract for a timeshare interest from a developer together with a statement providing the name and street address to which the purchaser should mail any notice of cancellation. However, if by agreement of the parties by and through the purchase contract, the purchase contract allows for cancellation of the purchase contract for a period of time exceeding seven days, then the public offering statement shall include a statement that the cancellation of the purchase contract is allowed for that period of time exceeding seven days;

(18) The current annual budget of the multi-site timeshare plan, if available, or the projected annual budget for the multi-site timeshare plan, which shall include:

(a) a statement of the amount reserved or budgeted, if any, for repairs, replacements, and refurbishment;

(b) the projected common expense liability, if any, by category of expenditure for the multi-site timeshare plan; and

(c) a statement of any services or expenses not reflected in the budget that the developer provides or pays;

(19) The projected assessments and a description of the method for calculating and apportioning those assessments among purchasers of the multi-site timeshare plan;

(20) Any current fees or charges to be paid by purchasers for the use of any amenities related to the timeshare plan and a statement that the fees or charges are subject to change;

(21) Any initial or special fee due from the purchaser at closing, together with a description of the purpose and method of calculating the fee;

(22) A description of the purchaser's liability for any fees associated with the multi-site timeshare plan;

(23) A description of any lien, defect, or encumbrance on or affecting title to the timeshare interest and, if applicable, a copy of each written warranty provided by the developer;

(24) The extent to which a timeshare interest may become subject to a tax lien or other lien arising out of claims against purchasers of different timeshare interests;

(25) A description of those matters required by section 18 [C.45:15-16.67] of this act;

(26) A description of any financing offered by or available through the developer;

(27) A description of any bankruptcy that is pending or which has occurred within the past five years, pending civil or criminal proceeding, adjudication, or disciplinary action material to the timeshare plan of which the developer has knowledge;

(28) A statement disclosing any right of first refusal or other restraint on the transfer of all or a portion of a timeshare interest;

(29) A statement disclosing that any deposit made in connection with the purchase of a timeshare interest shall be held by an escrow agent until expiration of any right to cancel the contract and that any deposit shall be returned to the purchaser if the purchaser elects to exercise the right of cancellation; or, if the commission accepts from the developer a surety bond, irrevocable letter of credit, or other form of financial assurance instead of an escrow deposit, a statement disclosing that the developer has provided a surety bond, irrevocable letter of credit, or other form of financial assurance in an amount equal to or in excess of the funds that would otherwise be held by an escrow agent and that the deposit shall be returned if the purchaser elects to exercise the right of cancellation;

(30) A description of the name and address of the exchange company and the method by which a purchaser accesses the exchange program, if the timeshare plan provides purchasers with the opportunity to participate in an exchange program;

(31) Any other information the commission determines is necessary to protect prospective purchasers or to implement the purpose of this act. The developer may also include any other information in the timeshare disclosure statement following approval by the commission.

e. The developer shall also distribute to the purchaser any additional documents as the commission may require for accommodations in this State as provided by regulation, including such additional documentation as may be required under the "Condominium Act," P.L.1969, c.257 (C.46:8B-1 et seq.).

regulations promulgated by the commission. The report shall reflect any material changes in the information contained in the original or subsequently submitted applications or documents.

b. (1) The developer shall file amendments to its registration to reflect any material change in any information set forth in the project and disclosure documents. The developer shall notify the commission of the material change prior to implementation of the change, unless the change is beyond the control of the developer, in which event, the developer shall provide written notice to the commission as soon as reasonably practicable after the occurrence of the event. All amendments, supplements, and facts relevant to the material change shall be filed with the commission within 20 calendar days of the material change.

(2) The developer may continue to sell timeshare interests in the timeshare plan so long as, prior to closing, the developer provides a notice to each purchaser that describes the material change and provides to each purchaser the previously approved public offering statement. If the change is material and adverse to the purchasers of the timeshare plan as a whole, as determined by the commission, no closing shall occur until the amendment relating to the material and adverse change has been approved by the commission. After the amendment relating to the material and adverse change has been approved and the amended public offering statement has been issued, the amended public offering statement shall be provided to the purchaser, and an additional seven-day rescission period shall commence. The developer shall be required to maintain evidence of the receipt by each purchaser of the amended public offering statement. If the commission refuses to approve the amendment relating to the material and adverse change, all sales made using the notice shall be subject to rescission and all funds returned.

(3) The developer shall update the public offering statement to reflect any changes to the timeshare plan that are not material and adverse, including the addition of any component sites, within a reasonable time as determined by the commission pursuant to regulation.

c. Upon a determination by the commission that an annual report is no longer necessary for the protection of the public interest or that the developer no longer retains any interest and no longer has any contractual, bond or other obligations in the subdivision, the commission shall issue an order terminating the responsibilities of the developer under this act.

45:15-16.60. Filing of annual reports by developer of timeshare

a. Within 30 days after each annual anniversary date of an order registering the timeshare, or on or before a date set by the commission, and while the developer continues to offer any timeshare interests in the timeshare plan in this State, the developer shall file a report in the form prescribed by the rules and

45:15-16.61. Issuance of notice of filing of registration

Upon receipt of a substantially complete application for registration, in proper form and accompanied by the appropriate filing fees, the commission shall, within 10 business days of receipt of the registration, issue a notice of filing. The notice shall not be construed as an approval of the registration, or any portion thereof.

45:15-16.62

45:15-16.62.   Review of registration; orders, schedule

Every registration required to be filed with the commission under this act shall be reviewed by the commission and the commission shall issue an order of registration in accordance with the following schedule:

a. As to comprehensive registrations, registrations shall be effective upon the issuance of an order of registration by the commission within 60 days after receipt and issuance of a notice of filing. The commission shall provide a list of deficiencies in the application, if any, within 60 days of the issuance of the notice of filing. If a list of deficiencies is not provided to the applicant within 60 days of issuance of the notice of filing, the timeshare plan shall be deemed registered unless the applicant has consented in writing to a delay.

b. As to abbreviated registrations, registration shall be effective upon the issuance of an order of registration by the commission 30 days after receipt and issuance of a notice of filing. The commission shall provide a list of deficiencies in the application, if any, within 30 days of the issuance of the notice of filing. If a list of deficiencies is not provided to the applicant within 30 days of the issuance of the notice of filing, the timeshare plan shall be deemed registered unless the applicant has consented in writing to a delay.

c. A preliminary registration shall be effective within 20 days of receipt, unless the commission provides to the applicant a written list of deficiencies in the application, if any, within 20 days of receipt of a completed application and fee. If a list of deficiencies is not provided to the applicant within 20 days of receipt of the application for a preliminary registration, the preliminary registration shall be deemed approved unless the applicant has consented in writing to a delay.

45:15-16.63.   Deficiency notice, appeal

a. If the commission determines upon inquiry and examination that any of the requirements of this act have not been met, the commission shall notify the applicant that the application for registration shall be corrected as specified in writing within 30 days from the date the notice is received by the applicant. These findings shall be the result of the commission's preliminary inquiry and examination and no hearing shall be required as the basis for those findings.

b. In the event that the requirements of the deficiency notice are not met within the time frame provided in subsection a. of this section, and the applicant has not demonstrated a good faith effort to correct the deficiencies, the commission may enter an order rejecting the filing. The order shall include the factual and legal basis for the rejection and shall provide that, unless appealed as provided for in subsection c. of this section, the terms of the order shall become final after 45 days of delivery to the applicant.

c. Upon the applicant's receipt of an order of rejection, the applicant shall have the right to file an appeal with the commission and shall be entitled to a hearing thereon provided that the appeal is filed within 45 days of the applicant's receipt of the order of rejection. In the event that an appeal is filed by the applicant, the order of rejection shall not take effect until such time as a determination has been rendered on the appeal. While an appeal of an order of rejection remains pending, a timeshare plan which is the subject of the notice of filing referenced in the order of rejection shall not be considered registered.

45:15-16.64.   Fee for initial registration

a. The fee for an initial registration shall be $1,000 plus $50 per timeshare interest, which fee shall not exceed $7,500, unless otherwise provided by the commission pursuant to regulation to defray the cost of rendering the services required by the provisions of this act.

b. The commission may also provide, by regulation, for fees to cover the reasonable expenses of carrying out other responsibilities established under this act, including, but not limited to, fees for the processing of amendments, exemption applications and preliminary registrations.

45:15-16.65.   Registrations required for sale

Unless otherwise provided by regulation, a developer, or any of its agents, shall not sell, offer, or dispose of a timeshare interest in this State unless all necessary registrations are filed and approved by the commission, or while an order revoking or suspending a registration is in effect.

45:15-16.66.   Creation of provision for managing entity, duties

a. Before the first sale of a timeshare interest, the developer shall create or provide for a managing entity, which shall be either the developer, a separate manager or management firm, the board of directors of an owners' association, or some combination thereof.

b. The duties of the managing entity shall include, but not be limited to:

(1) Management and maintenance of all accommodations constituting the timeshare plan;

(2) Collection of all assessments as provided in the timeshare instrument;

(3) Providing to all purchasers each year an itemized annual budget, which shall include all estimated revenues and expenses;

(4) Maintenance of all books and records concerning the timeshare plan;

(5) Scheduling occupancy of accommodations, when purchasers are not entitled to use specific timeshare periods, so that all purchasers will be provided the opportunity to possess and use the accommodations of the timeshare plan which they have purchased; and

(6) Performing any other functions and duties that are necessary and proper to maintain the accommodations or that are required by the timeshare instrument.

c. In the event a developer, managing entity or association files a complaint in a foreclosure proceeding involving timeshare interests, the developer, managing entity or association may join in the same action multiple defendant obligers and junior interest holders of separate timeshare interests, provided:

(1) The foreclosure proceeding involves a single timeshare plan;

(2) The foreclosure proceeding is filed by a single plaintiff;

(3) The default and remedy provisions in the written instruments on which the foreclosure proceeding is based are substantially the same for each defendant; and

(4) The nature of the defaults alleged is the same for each defendant.

d. In any foreclosure proceeding involving multiple defendants filed under subsection c. of this section, the court shall, if appropriate, sever for separate trial any count of the complaint in which a defense or counterclaim is timely raised by a defendant.

45:15-16.67.   Voidability of purchase contract

Any purchase contract entered into by a purchaser of a timeshare interest under this act shall be voidable by the purchaser, without penalty, within seven calendar days after the receipt of the public offering statement or the execution of the purchase contract, whichever date is later. The purchase contract shall provide notice of the seven-day cancellation period, together with the name and mailing address to which any notice of cancellation shall be delivered. Notice of cancellation shall be timely if the notice is deposited with the United States Postal Service not later than midnight of the seventh day. Upon such cancellation, the developer shall refund to the purchaser all payments made by the purchaser, less the amount of any benefits actually received pursuant to the purchase contract. The refund shall be made within 30 days after the receipt of the notice of cancellation, or receipt of funds from the purchaser's cleared check, whichever occurs later. If a purchaser elects to cancel a purchase contract pursuant to this section, the purchaser may do so by hand delivering a written notice of cancellation or by mailing a notice of cancellation by certified mail, return receipt

requested, to the developer, as applicable, at an address set forth in the purchase contract.

45:15-16.68.   Conditions for release of escrow funds to the developer

Excluding any encumbrance placed against the purchaser's timeshare interest securing the purchaser's payment of purchase money financing for the purchase, the developer shall not be entitled to the release of any funds escrowed with respect to each timeshare interest and any other property or rights to property appurtenant to the timeshare interest, including any amenities represented to the purchaser as being part of the timeshare plan, until the developer has provided satisfactory evidence to the commission of one of the following:

a. The timeshare interest together with any other property or rights to property appurtenant to the timeshare interest, including any amenities represented to the purchaser as being part of the timeshare plan, are free and clear of any of the claims of the developer, any owner of the underlying fee, a mortgagee, judgment creditor, or other lienor or any other person having an interest in or lien or encumbrance against the timeshare interest or appurtenant property or property rights;

b. The developer, any owner of the underlying fee, a mortgagee, judgment creditor, or other lienor, or any other person having an interest in or lien or encumbrance against the timeshare interest or appurtenant property or property rights, including any amenities represented to the purchaser as being part of the timeshare plan, has recorded a subordination and notice to creditors document in the jurisdiction in which the timeshare interest is located. The subordination document shall expressly and effectively provide that the interest holder's right, lien or encumbrance shall not adversely affect, and shall be subordinate to, the rights of the owners of the timeshare interests in the timeshare plan regardless of the date of purchase, from and after the effective date of the subordination document;

c. The developer, any owner of the underlying fee, a mortgagee, judgment creditor, or other lienor, or any other person having an interest in or lien or encumbrance against the timeshare interest or appurtenant property or property rights, including any amenities represented to the purchaser as being part of the timeshare plan, has transferred the subject accommodations or amenities or all use rights therein to a nonprofit organization or owners' association to be held for the use and benefit of the purchasers of the timeshare plan, which entity shall act as a fiduciary to the purchasers, provided that the developer has transferred control of that entity to the purchasers or does not exercise its voting rights in that entity with respect to the subject accommodations or amenities. Prior to the transfer, any lien or other encumbrance against the accommodation or facility shall be made subject to a subordination and notice to creditors instrument pursuant to subsection b. of this section; or

45:15-16.69

d. Alternative arrangements have been made which are adequate to protect the rights of the purchasers of the timeshare interests and are approved by the commission.

45:15-16.69. Compliance by sales agents; non-monetary compensation

a. A sales agent in New Jersey shall comply with the provisions of R.S.45:15-1 et seq., and the regulations adopted pursuant thereto, including licensure requirements, unless otherwise exempt by law.

b. A timeshare interest owner, who, for non-monetary compensation, as provided for in this act and by regulation, refers in a calendar year no more than 12 prospective purchasers of timeshare interests in the timeshare plan shall not be required to be licensed pursuant to R.S.45:15-1 et seq., provided the referring timeshare interest owner does not show, discuss terms or conditions of purchase or otherwise participate in negotiations with regard to the timeshare purchase. Examples of non-monetary compensation shall include, but shall not be limited to, the following:

(1) Waiver of association maintenance fees;

(2) Free meals at a restaurant or rounds of golf at a golf course;

(3) Points or other non-monetary currency associated with hotel, timeshare or other loyalty programs; or

(4) Other benefits specifically associated with the timeshare plan.

c. A person licensed under R.S.45:15-1 et seq., who also is a bona fide owner of a timeshare property, shall be entitled to receive non-monetary compensation as defined in subsection b. of this section on the same basis as any other owner of a timeshare property. The non-monetary compensation or referral pursuant to subsection b. of this section shall not fall within the scope of R.S.45:15-1 et seq. or the rules and regulations implementing R.S.45:15-1 et seq.

45:15-16.70. Prohibitions relative to developers of timeshares

a. A developer or other person offering a timeshare plan shall not:

(1) Misrepresent a fact material to a purchaser's decision to buy a timeshare interest;

(2) Predict any increase in the value of a timeshare interest represented over a period of time, excluding bona fide pending price increases by the developer;

(3) Materially misrepresent the qualities or characteristics of accommodations or the amenities available to the occupant of those accommodations;

(4) Misrepresent the length of time accommodations or amenities will be available to the purchaser of a timeshare interest; or

(5) Misrepresent the conditions under which a purchaser of a timeshare interest may exchange the right of the purchaser's occupancy for the right to occupy other accommodations.

b. A developer or other person using a promotion in connection with the offering of a timeshare interest shall clearly disclose all of the following:

(1) That the purpose of the promotion is to sell timeshare interests, which shall appear in bold face or other conspicuous type on all promotional materials;

(2) That any person whose name or address is obtained during the promotion may be solicited to purchase a timeshare interest;

(3) The name of each developer or other person trying to sell a timeshare interest through the promotion, and the name of each person paying for the promotion if different from the developer;

(4) The complete details of participation in the promotion;

(5) The method of awarding premiums or other benefits under the promotion;

(6) A complete and fully detailed description, including approximate retail value of each premium or benefit under the promotion if the retail value of the premium or benefit is over $50;

(7) The quantity of each premium to be awarded or conferred;

(8) The date by which each premium or benefit will be awarded or conferred; and

(9) Any other disclosures required by the commission pursuant to regulation.

c. The required disclosures for an advertisement that contains a promotion in connection with the offering of a timeshare interest shall be provided or otherwise made available to prospective purchasers in writing or electronically at least once prior to any scheduled sales presentation and received by the prospective purchasers prior to their leaving to attend the sales presentation. The required disclosures need not be included in every written, oral or electronic communication to the prospective purchaser prior to the sales presentation.

d. If a person represents that a premium or benefit will be awarded in connection with a promotion, the premium or benefit shall be awarded or conferred in the manner represented, and on or before the date represented for awarding or conferring the premium or benefit.

45:15-16.71.   Detailed financial records

The managing entity shall keep detailed financial records directly related to the operation of the timeshare plan. All financial and other records shall be made reasonably available for examination by any purchaser, or the authorized agent of the purchaser, and the commission. The managing entity may charge the purchaser a reasonable fee for copying any requested information.

45:15-16.72.   Maintenance of employee records

Every developer shall maintain, for a period of two years, records of any real estate brokers, broker-salespersons or salespersons licensed in the State and employed by the developer, as well as all other managerial employees located in the State and employed by the developer, including the last known address of each of those individuals.

45:15-16.73.   Permitted action for partition

No action for partition of a timeshare interest may be initiated except as permitted by the timeshare instrument.

45:15-16.74.   Refusal to issue, renew; revocation, suspension of registration; penalties

The commission may refuse to issue or renew any registration, or revoke or suspend any registration or place on probation or administrative supervision, or reprimand any registrant, or impose an administrative penalty not to exceed $50,000, in a summary proceeding pursuant to the "Penalty Enforcement Law of 1999," P.L. 1999, c.274 (C.2A:58-10 et seq.), after notice and an opportunity to be heard, for any of the following causes:

a. A registrant's violation of any provision of this act or of the regulations adopted by the commission to enforce this act.

b. A conviction of the registrant or any principal of the registrant of:

(1) A felony that is punishable by death or imprisonment for a term exceeding one year under the laws of any state or federal jurisdiction;

(2) A misdemeanor under the laws of any state or federal jurisdiction if an essential element of the offense is dishonesty; or

(3) Any crime under the laws of any state or federal jurisdiction if the crime relates directly to the practice of the profession regulated by this act.

c. A registrant's making any misrepresentation for the purpose of obtaining an order of registration or exemption.

d. A registrant's discipline in another state or federal jurisdiction, State agency, or foreign country regarding the practice of the profession regulated by this act, if at least one of the grounds for the discipline is the same as or substantially equivalent to one of those set forth in this act.

e. A finding by the commission that the registrant, after having his registration placed on probationary status, has violated the terms of probation.

f. A registrant's practicing or attempting to practice under a name other than the name as shown on his registration or any other legally authorized name.

g. A registrant's failure to file a return, or to pay the tax, penalty, or interest shown in a filed return, or to pay any final assessment of tax, penalty, or interest, as required by any tax law administered by the State Department of the Treasury or any local government entity, until the requirements of any tax are satisfied.

h. A registrant's engaging in any conduct likely to deceive, defraud or harm the public.

i. A registrant's aiding or abetting another person in violating any provision of this act or of the regulations adopted by the commission to enforce this act.

j. Any representation in any document or information filed with the commission that is materially false or misleading.

k. A registrant's disseminating or causing to be disseminated any materially false or misleading promotional materials or advertisements in connection with a timeshare plan.

l. A registrant's concealing, diverting, or disposing of any funds or assets of any person in a manner that impairs the rights of purchasers of timeshare interests in the timeshare plan.

m. A registrant's failure to perform any stipulation or agreement made to induce the commission to issue an order relating to the timeshare plan.

n. A registrant's, or its agents or brokers engaging in any act that constitutes a violation of the "Law Against Discrimination," P.L. 1945, c.169 (C.10:5-1 et seq.).

o. A registrant's, or its agent's or broker's failure to provide information requested in writing by the commission, either as the result of a complaint to the commission or as a result of a random audit conducted by the commission, which would indicate a violation of this act.

p. A registrant's, or its agent's or broker's, failure to account for or remit any escrow funds coming into his possession which belonged to others.

45:15-16.75

q. A registrant's, or its agent's or broker's, failure to make available to commission personnel during normal business hours all escrow records and related documents maintained in connection therewith, within a reasonable period of time after a request from the commission personnel, but in no event later than five business days from the request.

45:15-16.75.   Powers of commission

The commission may:

a. Accept registrations filed in this State, in other states, or with the federal government;

b. Contract with similar agencies in this State or other jurisdictions to perform investigative functions;

c. Accept grants-in-aid from any governmental or other source;

d. Cooperate with similar agencies or commissions in this State or other jurisdictions to establish uniform filing procedures and forms, uniform public offering statements, advertising standards, rules and common administrative practices;

e. Grant exemptions pursuant to the rules and regulations adopted pursuant to this act;

f. Make any necessary public or private investigations within or outside of this State to determine whether any person has violated or is about to violate any provision of this act, or to aid in the enforcement of this act or in the prescribing of rules and regulations and forms hereunder;

g. Require or permit any person to file a statement in writing, under oath or otherwise, as the commission determines, as to all the facts and circumstances concerning any matter to be investigated;

h. For the purpose of any investigation or proceeding under this act, the commission or any officer designated by regulation, may administer oaths, or affirmations, and upon its own motion or upon request of any party may subpoena witnesses and compel their attendance, take evidence, and require the production of any matter which is relevant to the investigation, including the existence, description, nature, custody, condition and location of any books, documents, or other tangible things and the identity and location of persons having knowledge of relevant facts or any other matter reasonably calculated to lead to the discovery of material evidence; and

i. Upon failure to obey a subpoena or to answer questions propounded by the investigating officer and upon reasonable notice to all persons affected thereby, the commission may apply to the Superior Court for an order compelling compliance with the subpoena.

45:15-16.76.   Determinations by commission; cease and desist order

a. If the commission determines after notice and hearing that a person has:

(1) Violated any provision of this act;

(2) Directly or through an agent or employee engaged in any false, deceptive, or misleading advertising, promotional or sales methods in the State to offer or dispose of an interest in the timeshare plan;

(3) Made any material change in the plan of disposition and development of the timeshare plan subsequent to the order of registration without first complying with the provisions of section 11 [C.45:15-16.60] of this act;

(4) Disposed of any timeshare plan which have not been registered with the commission; or

(5) Violated any lawful order or rule or regulation of the commission;

The commission may issue an order requiring the person to cease and desist from the unlawful practice and to take such affirmative action as in the judgment of the commission will carry out the purposes of this act.

b. If the commission makes a finding of fact in writing that the public interest will be irreparably harmed by delay in issuing an order, the commission may issue a temporary cease and desist order. Every temporary cease and desist order shall include in its terms a provision that upon request a hearing will be held within 15 days of the receipt of the request.

45:15-16.77.   Violations

a. If it appears that a person has engaged, or is about to engage, in an act or practice constituting a violation of a provision of this act, the commission, with or without prior administrative proceedings, may bring an action in the Superior Court to enjoin the acts or practices and to enforce compliance with this act or any rule, regulation or order hereunder. Upon proper showing, injunctive relief or a temporary restraining order shall be granted, and a receiver may be appointed. The commission shall not be required to post a bond in any court proceeding.

b. The commission may intervene in any suit relating to this act. Each developer registered pursuant to this act shall provide the commission with notice of any lawsuit that is filed against the developer or the registered timeshare plan that relates to rights, duties, or responsibilities of the developer or timeshare plan as set forth in this act.

45:15-16.78.   Application for registration deemed submission to jurisdiction of courts

a. For purposes of this act, an application for registration submitted to the commission shall be deemed a submission, by the applicant, to the jurisdiction of the courts of the State of New Jersey.

b. In addition to the methods of service provided for in the Rules of Court, service may be made by delivering a copy of the process to a person designated by the commission to receive the process at its office, but that service shall not be effective unless the plaintiff, which may be the commission, in a proceeding instituted by it:

(1) Sends a copy of the process and the pleading by certified mail to the defendant or respondent at his last known address; and

(2) The plaintiff's affidavit of compliance with this section is filed in the case on or before the return day of the process, if any, or within the time as the court allows.

c. If any person, including any nonresident of this State, engages in conduct prohibited by this act and has not filed a consent to service of process, and personal jurisdiction over him cannot otherwise be obtained in this State, that conduct authorizes the commission to receive service of process, in any noncriminal proceedings against him or his successor which arises from that conduct and which is brought under this act with the same force as if served on him personally. Notice shall be given as provided in subsection b. of this section.

45:15-16.79.   Additional penalties

a. Any broker, broker-salesperson or salesperson who violates the provisions of this act shall, in addition to the penalties set forth herein, be subject to the penalties as set forth in R.S.45:15-17.

b. Any person who violates any provision of this act or any person who, in an application for registration filed with the commission, makes any untrue statement of a material fact or omits to state a material fact shall be fined not less than $250, nor more than $50,000, per violation.

c. The commission may levy and collect the penalties set forth in subsection b. of this section after affording the person alleged to be in violation of this act an opportunity for a hearing in accordance with the "Administrative Procedure Act," P.L.1968, c.410 (C.52:14B-1 et seq.) on the alleged violations and a finding by the commission that the person is guilty of the violation. When a penalty levied by the commission has not been satisfied within 30 days of the levy, the penalty may be sued for and recovered by, and in the name of, the commission in a summary proceeding pursuant to the "Penalty Enforcement Law of 1999," P.L. 1999, c.274 (C.2A:58-10 et seq.).

d. The commission may, in the interest of justice, compromise any civil penalty, if in its determination the gravity of the offense does not warrant the assessment of the full fine.

45:15-16.80.   Actions, counterclaims, remedies

a. Any person who suffers any ascertainable loss of moneys as a result of the failure of another to comply fully with the provisions of this act may bring an action or assert a counterclaim in any court of competent jurisdiction. In any action filed under this section in which a defendant is found to have knowingly engaged in any false, deceptive, misleading promotional or sales methods or discriminatory advertising on the basis of race, sex, creed, color, marital status, national origin or religion, concealed or fraudulently diverted any funds or assets so as to defeat the rights of timeshare plan purchasers, made an intentional misrepresentation or concealed a material fact in an application for registration, or disposed of any timeshare plan required to be registered under this act, which are not so registered, the court shall, in addition to any other appropriate legal or equitable remedy, award double the damages suffered, and court costs, including reasonable attorney's fees. In the case of an untruth, omission, or misleading statement the developer sustains the burden of proving that the purchaser knew of the untruth, omission or misleading statement, or that he did not rely on such information, or that the developer did not know, and in the exercise of reasonable care could not have known of the untruth, omission, or misleading statement.

b. The court, in addition to the remedies provided in this act, may award any other relief appropriate under the circumstances including, in the court's discretion, restitution of all monies paid and, where a developer has failed to provide to a purchaser a copy of the current public offering statement approved by the commission prior to execution of the contract or agreement, rescission of the contract. If the purchaser fails to establish a cause of action, and the court further determines that the action was wholly without merit, the court shall award attorney's fees to the developer.

c. Any stipulation or provision purporting to bind a purchaser acquiring an interest in a timeshare plan subject to the provisions of this act to a waiver of compliance with the provisions of this act shall be void.

45:15-16.81.   Valid registration required for action

a. An action shall not be maintained by any developer in any court in this State with respect to any agreement, contract, or services for which registration is required by this act, or to recover the agreed price or any consideration under any agreement, or to recover for services for which a registration is required by this act, without proving that the developer had a valid order of

45:15-16.82

registration at the time of making the agreement or performing the work.

b. A person licensed in this State as a real estate broker pursuant to R.S.45:15-1 et seq. shall not represent any unregistered timeshare plan and shall not accept or collect any commission or other form of consideration from any developer unless the timeshare plan is registered pursuant to the requirements of this act.

45:15-16.82. Rules

The commission shall adopt rules for the implementation and enforcement of this act in accordance with the "Administrative Procedure Act," P.L.1968, c.410 (C.52:14B-1 et seq.).

45:15-16.83. Forms, procedures

The commission may prescribe forms and procedures for submitting information to the commission.

45:15-16.84. Investigation of matters relative to application for registration

The commission shall thoroughly investigate all matters relating to an application for registration under this act and may require a personal inspection of any timeshare plan, accommodation, and any offices where any of the foregoing may transact business. All reasonable expenses incurred by the commission in investigating such matters shall be paid by the registrant. The commission may require a deposit sufficient to cover the expenses prior to incurring the expenses.

45:15-16.85. Existing timeshare plans remain in full force and effect

All timeshare plans that were registered and approved pursuant to the provisions of the "Real Estate Sales Full Disclosure Act," P.L.1989, c.239 (C.45:15-16.27 et seq.) and "The Planned Real Estate Development Full Disclosure Act," P.L.1977, c.419 (C.45:22A-21 et seq.) in effect on the effective date [Oct. 31, 2006] of this act shall remain in full force and effect after the effective date of this act and shall be considered registered under this act and shall not be required to file any further documentation under this act, except as to comply with the requirements of section 11 [C.45:15-16.60].

Developers who have filed timeshare plans that were exempt from the requirements of the "Real Estate Sales Full Disclosure Act," P.L.1989, c.239 (C.45:15-16.27 et seq.) and "The Planned Real Estate Development Full Disclosure Act," P.L.1977, c.419 (C.45:22A-21 et seq.) shall be required to file a registration application with the commission within 90 days from the effective date [Oct. 31, 2006] of this act unless they are otherwise exempt under this act. These developers and timeshare plans shall be allowed to continue operating as long as a registration application is filed with the commission within the timeframe stated above and as long as they, in good faith, continue to work with the commission to correct any and all deficiencies in the registration application.

Any existing injunction or temporary restraining order validly obtained under the "Real Estate Sales Full Disclosure Act," P.L.1989, c.239 (C.45:15-16.27 et seq.) or "The Planned Real Estate Development Full Disclosure Act," P.L.1977, c.419 (C.45:22A-21 et seq.) which prohibits unregistered practice of timeshare developers, timeshare plans, and their agents shall not be invalidated by the enactment of this act and shall continue to have full force and effect on and after the effective date of this act. Any existing disciplinary action or investigation pursuant to a violation under the "Real Estate Sales Full Disclosure Act," P.L.1989, c.239 (C.45:15-16.27 et seq.) or "The Planned Real Estate Development Full Disclosure Act," P.L.1977, c.419 (C.45:22A-21 et seq.) shall not be invalidated by the enactment of this act and shall continue to have full force and effect on and after the effective date of this act.

45:15-17. Investigation of actions of licensees; suspension or revocation of licenses and causes therefor

The commission may, upon its own motion, and shall, upon the verified complaint in writing of any person, investigate the actions of any real estate broker, broker-salesperson, or salesperson, or any person who assumes, advertises or represents himself as being authorized to act as a real estate broker, broker-salesperson, or salesperson or engages in any of the activities described in R.S.45:15-3 without being licensed so to do. The lapse or suspension of a license by operation of law or the voluntary surrender of a license by a licensee shall not deprive the commission of jurisdiction to proceed with any investigation as herein provided or prevent the commission from taking any regulatory action against such licensee, provided, however, that the alleged charges arose while said licensee was duly licensed. Each transaction shall be construed as a separate offense.

In conducting investigations, the commission may take testimony by deposition as provided in R.S.45:15-18, require or permit any person to file a statement in writing, under oath or otherwise as the commission determines, as to all the facts and circumstances concerning the matter under investigation, and, upon its own motion or upon the request of any party, subpoena witnesses, compel their attendance, take evidence, and require the production of any material which is relevant to the investigation, including any and all records of a licensee pertaining to his activities as a real estate broker, broker-salesperson, or salesperson. The commission may also require the provision of any information concerning the existence, description, nature, custody, condition and location of any books, documents, or other tangible material and the identity and location of persons having knowledge of relevant facts of any other matter reasonably calculated to lead to the discovery of material evidence. Upon failure to obey a subpoena or to answer questions posed by an investigator or legal representative of the commission and upon reasonable notice to all affected persons, the commission may commence an administrative action as provided below or apply to the Superior Court for an order compelling compliance.

The commission may place on probation, suspend for a period less than the unexpired portion of the license period, or may revoke any license issued under the provisions of R.S.45:15-1 et seq., or the right of licensure when such person is no longer the holder of a license at the time of hearing, or may impose, in addition or as an alternative to such probation, revocation or suspension, a penalty of not more than $5,000 for the first violation, and a penalty of not more than $10,000 for any subsequent violation, which penalty shall be sued for and recovered by and in the name of the commission and shall be collected and enforced by summary proceedings pursuant to the "Penalty Enforcement Law of 1999," P.L.1999, c.274 (C.2A:58-10 et seq.), where the licensee or any person, in performing or attempting to perform any of the acts mentioned herein, is deemed to be guilty of:

a. Making any false promises or any substantial misrepresentation; or

b. Acting for more than one party in a transaction without the knowledge of all parties thereto; or

c. Pursuing a flagrant and continued course of misrepresentation or making of false promises through agents, broker-salespersons, or salespersons, advertisements or otherwise; or

d. Failure to account for or to pay over any moneys belonging to others, coming into the possession of the licensee; or

e. Any conduct which demonstrates unworthiness, incompetency, bad faith or dishonesty. The failure of any person to cooperate with the commission in the performance of its duties or to comply with a subpoena issued by the commission compelling the production of materials in the course of an investigation, or the failure to give a verbal or written statement concerning a matter under investigation may be construed as conduct demonstrating unworthiness; or

f. Failure to provide his client with a fully executed copy of any sale or exclusive sales or rental listing contract at the time of execution thereof, or failure to specify therein a definite terminal date which terminal date shall not be subject to any qualifying terms or conditions; or

g. Using any plan, scheme or method for the sale or promotion of the sale of real estate which involves a lottery, a contest, a game, a prize, a drawing, or the offering of a lot or parcel or lots or parcels for advertising purposes, provided, however, that a promotion or offer of free, discounted or other services or products which does not require that the recipient of any free, discounted or other services or products enter into a sale, listing or other real estate contract as a condition of the promotion or offer shall not constitute a violation of this subsection if that promotion or offering does not involve a lottery, a contest, a game, a drawing or the offering of a lot or parcel or lots or parcels for advertising purposes. A broker shall disclose in writing any compensation received for such promotion or offer in the form and substance as required by the federal "Real Estate Settlement Procedures Act of 1974," 12 U.S.C. ss.2601 et seq., except that, notwithstanding the provisions of that federal act, written disclosure shall be provided no later than when the promotion or offer is extended by the broker to the consumer; or

h. Being convicted of a crime, knowledge of which the commission did not have at the time of last issuing a real estate license to the licensee; or

i. Collecting a commission as a real estate broker in a transaction, when at the same time representing either party in a transaction in a different capacity for a consideration; or

j. Using any trade name or insignia of membership in any real estate organization of which the licensee is not a member; or

k. Paying any rebate, profit, compensation or commission to anyone not possessed of a real estate license, except that: (1) free, discounted or other services or products provided for in subsection g. of this section shall not constitute a violation of this subsection; and (2) a real estate broker may provide a purchaser of residential real property, but no other third party a rebate of a portion of the commission paid to the broker in a transaction, so long as: the broker and the purchaser contract for such a rebate at the onset of the broker relationship in a written document, electronic document or a buyer agency agreement; the broker complies with any State or federal requirements with respect to the disclosure of the payment of the rebate; and the broker recommends to the purchaser that the purchaser contact a tax professional concerning the tax implications of receiving that rebate. The rebate paid to the purchaser shall be in the form of a credit, reducing the amount of the commission payable to the broker, or a check paid by the closing agent and shall be made at the time of closing; or

l. Any other conduct, whether of the same or a different character than specified in this section, which constitutes fraud or dishonest dealing; or

m. Accepting a commission or valuable consideration as a real estate broker-salesperson or salesperson for the performance of any of the acts specified in this act, from any person, except his employing or contracting broker, who must be a licensed broker; or

n. Procuring a real estate license, for himself or anyone else, by fraud, misrepresentation or deceit; or

45:15-17.1

o. Commingling the money or other property of his princi-pals with his own or failure to maintain and deposit in a special account, separate and apart from personal or other business ac-counts, all moneys received by a real estate broker, acting in said capacity, or as escrow agent, or the temporary custodian of the funds of others, in a real estate transaction; or

p. Selling property in the ownership of which he is interested in any manner whatsoever, unless he first discloses to the pur-chaser in the contract of sale his interest therein and his status as a real estate broker, broker-salesperson, or salesperson; or

q. Purchasing any property unless he first discloses to the seller in the contract of sale his status as a real estate broker, broker-salesperson, or salesperson; or

r. Charging or accepting any fee, commission or compen-sation in exchange for providing information on purportedly available rental housing, including lists of such units supplied verbally or in written form, before a lease has been executed or, where no lease is drawn, before the tenant has taken posses-sion of the premises without complying with all applicable rules promulgated by the commission regulating these practices; or

s. Failing to notify the commission within 30 days of hav-ing been convicted of any crime, including any sex offense that would qualify the licensee for registration pursuant to section 2 of P.L.1994, c.133 (C.2C:7-2) or under an equivalent statute of another state or jurisdiction, misdemeanor or disorderly persons offense, or of having been indicted, or of the filing of any formal criminal charges, or of the suspension or revocation of any real estate license issued by another state, or of the initiation of for-mal disciplinary proceedings in another state affecting any real estate license held, or failing to supply any documentation avail-able to the licensee that the commission may request in connec-tion with such matter; or

t. The violation of any of the provisions of R.S.45:15-1 et seq. or of the administrative rules adopted by the commission pursuant to the provisions of R.S.45:15-1 et seq. The commis-sion is expressly vested with the power and authority to make, prescribe and enforce any and all rules and regulations for the conduct of the real estate brokerage business consistent with the provisions of chapter 15 of Title 45 of the Revised Statutes.

If a licensee is deemed to be guilty of a third violation of any of the provisions of this section, whether of the same provision or of separate provisions, the commission may deem that person a repeat offender, in which event the commission may direct that no license as a real estate broker, broker-salesperson, or sales-person shall henceforth be issued to that person.

45:15-17.1.   Temporary suspension of license

The commission may, on its own motion, enter an order temporarily suspending the license of any licensee upon mak-ing a finding that prima facie evidence exists that the licensee has violated subsection d. or subsection o. of R.S. 45:15-17. At least 24 hours prior to entering the order, the commission shall give notice to the licensee of the application for the order and shall provide the licensee with an opportunity to be heard. The notice may be given either by telephone or in writing and may be served personally or sent by certified mail to the last known business address of the licensee.

When the commission orders the temporary suspension of a license, it shall advise the licensee of the date upon which the commission shall hold an evidentiary hearing on the violations upon which the temporary suspension is based, which date shall be no more than 30 days following the date of the order entering the temporary suspension.

45:15-17.2.   Freezing accounts during suspension of broker's license

Upon entering an order temporarily suspending the license of any broker, the commission may also enter an order direct-ing that some or all of the accounts maintained by the broker in any depository institution in the State be temporarily frozen. The commission shall serve copies of the order upon the institution either in person or by certified mail within ten days and, where a broker's trust or escrow account is frozen, upon all persons known to the commission for whom the broker was acting as es-crow agent or trustee. In the event the commission subsequently determines that the suspension shall not be continued, it shall immediately notify the depository institution and other inter-ested parties that the temporary freeze order is dissolved. If the commission orders that the license suspension shall continue for more than 30 days or that a license revocation shall be imposed, the commission shall, within 10 days of that ruling, make appli-cation to Superior Court for payment into the court of all funds in the accounts temporarily frozen by order of the commission. The commission shall provide notice of the application to the broker and all known interested parties. Following payment into court, the monies or any portion of them shall thereafter only be released upon court order obtained by the broker or other inter-ested party, upon notice to the commission and in compliance with court rules.

45:15-17.3.   Sanctions for noncomplying sales of mobile homes

A real estate licensee who acts as an agent or broker in the sale of a mobile or manufactured home, as defined in subsection a. of R.S. 39:10-19, in a manner which does not comply with all requirements of R.S. 39:10-1 et seq. applicable to the sale of any such mobile or manufactured home, shall, pursuant to

R.S. 45:15-17, be subject to sanctions by the New Jersey Real Estate Commission for engaging in conduct which demonstrates incompetency.

45:15-17.4.   Rules, regulations

The New Jersey Real Estate Commission, after consultation with the Director of the Division of Motor Vehicles, shall, pursuant to the provisions of the "Administrative Procedure Act," P.L.1968, c. 410 (C. 52:14B-1 et seq.), promulgate rules and regulations to effectuate the provisions of this act.

45:15-18.   Notification to licensee of charges made in license suspension, revocation

With the exception of a temporary suspension imposed by the commission pursuant to section 23 of P.L.1993, c.51 (C.45:15-17.1), the commission shall, before suspending or revoking any license, and at least ten days prior to the date set for the hearing, notify in writing the licensee of any charges made, and afford him an opportunity to be heard in person or by counsel. Such written notice may be served either personally or sent by certified mail to the last known business address of the licensee. If the licensee is a broker-salesperson or salesperson, the commission shall also notify the broker employing or contracting with him, specifying the charges made against such licensee, by sending a notice thereof by certified mail to the broker's last known business address. The commission shall have power to bring before it any licensee or any person in this State pursuant to subpoena served personally or by certified mail, or the commission may take testimony by deposition in the same manner as prescribed by law in judicial proceedings in the courts of this State. Any final decision or determination of the commission shall be reviewable by the Appellate Division of the Superior Court.

45:15-19.   Cause for revocation of license

Any unlawful act or violation of any of the provisions of R.S.45:15-1 et seq., by any real estate broker-salesperson or salesperson, shall not be cause for the revocation of any real estate broker's license, unless it shall appear to the satisfaction of the commission that the real estate broker employing or contracting with such licensee had guilty knowledge thereof.

45:15-19.1.   License revoked upon conviction

When, during the term of any license issued by the commission, the licensee shall be convicted in a court of competent jurisdiction in the State of New Jersey or any state (including federal courts) of forgery, burglary, robbery, any theft or related offense with the exception of shoplifting, criminal conspiracy to defraud, or other like offense or offenses, or any crime involving, related to or arising out of the licensee's activities as a real estate broker, broker-salesperson, or salesperson, and a duly certified or exemplified copy of the judgment of conviction shall be obtained by the commission, the commission shall revoke forthwith the license by it theretofore issued to the licensee so convicted. The commission shall revoke the license of any licensee convicted of any sex offense that would qualify the licensee for registration pursuant to section 2 of P.L.1994, c.133 (C.2C:7-2) or under an equivalent statute of another state or jurisdiction.

45:15-19.2.   License suspended when licensee is indicted

In the event that any licensee shall be indicted in the State of New Jersey or any state or territory (including federal courts) for murder, kidnapping, aggravated sexual assault or any sex offense that would qualify the licensee for registration pursuant to section 2 of P.L.1994, c.133 (C.2C:7-2) or under an equivalent statute of another state or jurisdiction, robbery, burglary, arson, any theft offense, bribery, racketeering, distribution of a controlled dangerous substance or conspiracy to distribute a controlled dangerous substance, forgery, criminal conspiracy to defraud, or other like offense or offenses, or any crime involving, related to or arising out of the licensee's activities as a real estate broker, broker-salesperson, or salesperson, and a certified copy of the indictment is obtained by the commission, or other proper evidence thereof be to it given, the commission shall have authority, in its discretion, to suspend the license issued to such licensee pending trial upon such indictment.

45:15-19.3.   No supercedure

No provision of R.S.45:15-1 et seq., or any amendment or supplement thereof, shall be deemed to supersede P.L.1968, c.282 (C.2A:168A-1 et seq.).

45:15-20.   Nonresident licenses

A nonresident may become a real estate broker, broker-salesperson, or salesperson by conforming to all of the provisions of R.S.45:15-1 et seq. All nonresident licenses issued by the commission prior to July 1, 1994 may be renewed upon payment of the renewal fees established pursuant to R.S.45:15-15. All nonresident licenses so renewed shall be issued by the commission in the same form as a resident license. In the event that any person to whom a nonresident license is issued fails to maintain or renew the license or to obtain a new license from the commission for a period of two or more consecutive years, the person shall be required to fulfill the requirements for initial licensure

45:15-21

established pursuant to R.S.45:15-9 prior to the issuance of any further license.

A licensed broker whose main office is not located within this State shall only provide brokerage services concerning real estate located within this State either personally or through persons in the broker's employ or with whom the broker has contracted who are the holders of real estate broker-salesperson or salesperson licenses issued by the commission. In the event that a broker maintains one or more branch offices in this State, no person shall engage in the business of a real estate broker, broker-salesperson, or salesperson at those offices unless the person is a holder of a license issued by the commission authorizing him to do so.

45:15-21.   Filing of irrevocable consent to service

Every applicant for a license whose business address is outside this State shall file an irrevocable consent that suits and actions may be commenced against such applicant by the commission or by any person in any of the courts of record of this State, by the service of any process or pleading authorized by the laws of this State, in any county in which the plaintiff may reside, by serving the same on the secretary of the commission, said consent stipulating and agreeing that such service of such process or pleadings on said secretary shall be taken and held in all courts to be as valid and binding as if due service had been made personally upon the applicant in this State. This consent shall be duly acknowledged, and, if made by a corporation, shall be authenticated by its seal. The consent from a corporation shall be accompanied by a duly certified copy of the resolution of the board of directors, authorizing the proper officers to execute it. In all cases where process or pleadings shall be served, under the provisions of this article, upon the secretary of the commission, such process or pleadings shall be served in duplicate, one of which shall be filed in the office of the commission and the other shall be forwarded immediately by the secretary of the commission, by registered mail, to the last known business address of the licensee against which such process or pleadings are directed.

Every licensee whose business address is outside this State shall, by acceptance of a license for that out-of-state address, automatically and irrevocably consent to the commission's jurisdiction over and investigative authority regarding the licensed business premises, and all records and conduct of the licensee both within and outside of the State. The licensee shall also automatically and irrevocably consent that service of any pleading or subpoena issued by the secretary of the commission pursuant to R.S. 45:15-17 or R.S. 45:15-18 which is delivered by certified mail to the licensee's last known address, shall constitute valid and binding service of the subpoena or pleading upon the licensee as if service had been made personally upon the licensee in this State.

45:15-22.   Repealed by L. 1993, c. 51, § 58, eff. May 20, 1993

45:15-23.   Repealed by L. 1989, c. 126, § 7, eff. July 3, 1989

45:15-24.   Commitment for nonpayment of judgment

The trial shall be with a jury upon the demand of any party to the action. The court shall, if judgment be rendered for the plaintiff, cause any such defendant, who refuses or neglects to pay forthwith the amount of the judgment rendered against him and all costs and charges incident thereto, to be committed to the county jail for a period not exceeding thirty days.

45:15-25, 45:15-26. Repealed by L. 1953, c. 43, §§ 76, 77

45:15-27.   Disposition of penalties

Any penalty recovered for any violation of this article shall be applied by the commission to the same purpose as other funds of the commission collected in accordance with the provisions of this article.

45:15-28.   Repealed by L. 1953, c. 43, § 79

45:15-29.   Payment of fines, penalties; funding of commission's expenses

a. All fines and penalties received by the commission pursuant to the provisions of this article shall be paid by it into the State treasury monthly. The payments shall be made on or before the tenth day of each month following their receipt, and at the time of payment a statement thereof shall be filed with the Director of the Division of Budget and Accounting.

b. All expenses incurred by the commission shall be paid from fees collected by the commission pursuant to the provisions of article I of chapter 15 of Title 45 of the Revised Statutes. Monies collected annually pursuant to this subsection shall be dedicated to the commission for the purposes of funding its incurred expenses for the current fiscal year, which expenses shall include, in addition to the direct cost of personal service, the cost of maintenance and operation, the cost of employee benefits and the workers' compensation paid for and on account of personnel, rentals for space occupied in State-owned or State-leased buildings and all other direct and indirect costs of the administration thereof.

45:15-29.1.   Employees transferred

Such employees of the New Jersey Real Estate Commission, as the Commissioner of Insurance may determine are needed for the proper performance of the work of the division of the New Jersey Real Estate Commission in the Department of Insurance, are hereby transferred to the Department of Insurance. Persons so transferred shall be assigned to such duties as the Commissioner of Insurance shall determine.

45:15-29.2.   Rights under Title 11 and under pension laws not affected

Nothing in this act shall be construed to deprive any person of any right or protection provided him by Title 11 of the Revised Statutes, Civil Service, or under any pension law or retirement system.

45:15-29.3.   Orders, rules, regulations continued

The orders, rules and regulations heretofore made or promulgated by the New Jersey Real Estate Commission shall continue with full force and effect until amended or repealed by the New Jersey Real Estate Commission constituted hereunder as the Division of the New Jersey Real Estate Commission in the Department of Insurance.

45:15-29.4.   "New Jersey Real Estate Commission," reference

Whenever the term "New Jersey Real Estate Commission" occurs or any reference is made thereto, in any law, contract or document, the same shall be deemed to mean or refer to the New Jersey Real Estate Commission constituted hereunder as the Division of the New Jersey Real Estate Commission in the Department of Insurance.

45:15-29.5.   Actions, proceedings not affected

This act shall not affect actions or proceedings, civil or criminal, brought by or against the New Jersey Real Estate Commission and pending on the effective date of this act, and such actions or proceedings may be prosecuted or defended in the same manner and to the same effect by the New Jersey Real Estate Commission constituted hereunder as the Division of the New Jersey Real Estate Commission in the Department of Insurance as if the foregoing provisions had not taken effect; nor shall any of the foregoing provisions affect any order or recommendation made by, or other matters or proceedings before, the New Jersey Real Estate Commission; and all such matters or proceedings pending before the New Jersey Real Estate Commission on the effective date of this act shall be continued by the New Jersey Real Estate Commission constituted hereunder as the Division of the New Jersey Real Estate Commission in the Department of Insurance.

ARTICLE 2. REAL ESTATE AUCTIONEERS [REPEALED]

45:15-30 to 45:15-33.   Repealed by L. 1953, c. 229, § 9

ARTICLE 3. REAL ESTATE GUARANTY FUND

45:15-34.   Real estate guaranty fund established

A real estate guaranty fund is established as a special trust fund to be maintained by the State Treasurer and administered by the New Jersey Real Estate Commission in accordance with the provisions of this act to provide a fund from which recovery may be obtained by any person aggrieved by the embezzlement, conversion or unlawful obtaining of money or property in a real estate brokerage transaction by a licensed real estate broker, broker-salesperson, or salesperson or an unlicensed employee of a real estate broker; provided, however, that the amount of such recovery shall not exceed in the aggregate the sum of $10,000 in connection with any one transaction regardless of the number of claims, persons aggrieved, or parcels of, or interests in real estate involved in the transaction. The maximum amount recoverable per transaction shall be increased to $20,000 for claims filed on the basis of causes of action which accrue after the effective date of P.L.1993, c.51 (C.45:15-12.3 et al.).

45:15-35.   Additional amount payable upon initial issuance of license

Upon the initial issuance of a biennial license as a real estate broker, broker-salesperson, or salesperson the licensee shall pay to the commission, in addition to the license fee fixed by R.S.45:15-15, an additional amount to be forwarded by the commission to the State Treasurer and accounted for and credited by him to the real estate guaranty fund. The additional amount payable by a broker or broker-salesperson shall be $20 and by a salesperson, $10.

45:15-36.   Management and investment of funds

The State Treasurer shall hold, manage and through the Division of Investment, invest and reinvest funds of the real estate guaranty fund and credit all interest and other income earned thereon to the real estate guaranty fund in the same manner as provided by law with respect to investment of pension and retirement funds administered by the State. The Real Estate Commission shall keep the State Treasurer advised of the anticipated cash demands for payment of claims against the fund.

45:15-37.   Payments from real estate guaranty fund

No claim shall be made for payment from the real estate guaranty fund except upon the reduction to final judgment, which shall include reasonable attorney fees and costs, of a civil action

45:15-38

against the broker, broker-salesperson, or salesperson or unlicensed employee of a broker, and, where the judgment creditor has pursued all available remedies, made all reasonable searches, and has been unable to satisfy the judgment from the licensee's assets, the entry of a court order which directs the New Jersey Real Estate Commission to make payment from the fund. No such order shall authorize a payment to the spouse or personal representative of the spouse of the judgment debtor.

No order shall be entered unless the claimant, either at the time of filing the civil action or thereafter, files a certification affirming that a criminal complaint alleging the misappropriation of funds by the broker, broker-salesperson, or salesperson or unlicensed employee has been filed with a law enforcement agency of this State or of a county or municipality in this State. The criminal complaint shall refer to the same conduct to which reference is made in the civil action as forming the basis for a claim against the real estate guaranty fund. The certification shall specify the date on which the criminal complaint was filed and the law enforcement agency with which it was filed. A copy of the certification shall be provided to the New Jersey Real Estate Commission upon its being filed. The requirement to file a certification shall apply prospectively only to claims seeking reimbursement from the fund filed on the basis of causes of action which accrue after the effective date of P.L.1993, c.51 (C.45:15-12.3 et al.).

Upon delivery by the New Jersey Real Estate Commission to the State Treasurer of a certified copy of the court order together with an assignment to the New Jersey Real Estate Commission of the judgment creditor's right, title and interest in the judgment to the extent of the amount of the court order, the State Treasurer shall make payment to the claimant from the real estate guaranty fund.

45:15-38.   **Civil action which may result in court order for payment; limitations of action; joinder of commission**

Any civil action which may result in a court order for payment from the real estate guaranty fund shall be instituted within six years of the accrual of the cause of action and the New Jersey Real Estate Commission shall be joined as a necessary party to any such civil action. Nothing in this section shall affect the right of any aggrieved person to pursue other rights or remedies authorized by law.

45:15-39.   **Secretary of commission constituted as agent**

Any person to whom is issued a license to be a real estate broker, broker-salesperson, or salesperson shall, by the securing of said license, make and constitute the secretary of the commission or the person in charge of the office of the commission as agent for the acceptance of process in any civil proceeding hereunder.

45:15-40.   **Insufficiency of funds; replenishment; excess amounts**

a. If at any time the funds available in the real estate guaranty fund are insufficient to satisfy in full court orders for payment therefrom, payment shall be made in the order in which such court orders were issued; and the New Jersey Real Estate Commission shall by regulation impose further additional amounts to be paid by brokers, broker-salespersons, or salespersons to replenish the guaranty fund. No such additional amount assessed at any one time shall exceed the amounts specified in section 2 of P.L.1976, c.112 (C.45:15-35).

b. If at any time the funds available in the real estate guaranty fund are, in the opinion of the New Jersey Real Estate Commission, in excess of amounts anticipated to be necessary to meet claims for a period of at least two years, the commission may, with the approval of the Commissioner of Banking and Insurance, allocate and receive from the guaranty fund a specified amount thereof for research and educational projects to increase the proficiency and competency of real estate licensees.

45:15-41.   **Revocation of license upon issuance of court order for payment from fund**

Upon the issuance of a court order for payment from the real estate guaranty fund the license of the broker, broker-salesperson, or salesperson, whose acts gave rise to the claim, shall be revoked and no such broker, broker-salesperson, or salesperson shall be eligible for reinstatement of his license until he shall have satisfied the judgment in full including reimbursement of the real estate guaranty fund together with interest.

45:15-42.   **Rules and regulations**

The Real Estate Commission is authorized to issue rules and regulations to implement the provisions of this act.

REGULATIONS
FOR
THE NEW JERSEY
REAL ESTATE COMMISSION

N.J.A.C. 11:5-1.1 et seq.

Phil Murphy, Governor
State of New Jersey

Sheila Oliver, Lt. Governor
State of New Jersey

Marlene Caride, Commissioner
Department of Banking and Insurance

Aurelio Romero, Executive Director
NJ Real Estate Commission

REAL ESTATE COMMISSION

TITLE 11. INSURANCE

CHAPTER 5. REAL ESTATE COMMISSION

Chapter Authority

N.J.S.A. 45:15-6, 45:15-10.4, 45:15-16.2g, 45:15-16.49, 45:15-16.82, 45:15-17.t, 45:15-17.4, and 45:15-42.

Chapter Source and Effective Date

Effective: February 24, 2016.

See: 48 N.J.R. 493(b).

Chapter Expiration Date

Chapter 5, Real Estate Commission, expires on February 24, 2023.

Chapter Historical Note

Chapter 5, Real Estate Commission, was filed and became effective prior to September 1, 1969. Pursuant to Executive Order No. 66(1978), Chapter 5 expired on August 2, 1983.

Chapter 5, Real Estate Commission, was adopted as new rules by R.1983 d.471, effective November 7, 1983. See: 15 N.J.R. 1343(a), 15 N.J.R. 1865(c).

Pursuant to Executive Order No. 66(1978), Chapter 5, Real Estate Commission, was readopted as R.1988 d.555, effective October 28, 1988. See: 20 N.J.R. 2184(a), 20 N.J.R. 3019(a).

Subchapter 2, Organizational Rules, was adopted as R.1989 d.258, effective April 19, 1989. See: 21 N.J.R. 1364(a).

Subchapter 3, Petitions for Rulemaking, Subchapter 4, Proceedings before the Commission, and Subchapter 5, Appeals of Initial Denials of Licensing Applications, were adopted as R.1989 d.429, effective August 21, 1989. See: 21 N.J.R. 1315(a), 21 N.J.R. 2524(a).

Subchapter 6, Rules Interpreting and Implementing the Real Estate Sales Full Disclosure Act, N.J.S.A. 45:15-16.27 et seq., was adopted as R.1990 d.455, effective September 17, 1990. See: 22 N.J.R. 1421(a), 22 N.J.R. 2969(d).

Pursuant to Executive Order No. 66(1978), Chapter 5, Real Estate Commission, was readopted as R.1993 d.552, effective October 15, 1993. See: 25 N.J.R. 3597(b), 25 N.J.R. 5229(a).

Pursuant to Executive Order No. 66(1978), Chapter 5, Real Estate Commission, was readopted as R.1998 d.497, effective September 14, 1998. As a part of R.1998 d.497, effective October 5, 1998, sections 1.1 through 1.44 of Subchapter 1, Rules and Regulations, were recodified as Subchapter 2, Education; Subchapter 3, Licensing; Subchapter 4, Employment Practices/Office and Licensee Supervision; Subchapter 5, Trust Accounts/Records of Brokerage Activity; Subchapter 6, Conduct of Business; Subchapter 7, Prohibited Activities; and Subchapter 8, Disciplinary Actions/Conditions for Restoration of License/Real Estate Guaranty Fund Claims. Also as a part of R.1998 d.497, effective October 5, 1998, Subchapter 2, Organizational Rules, was recodified as Subchapter 1; Subchapter 6, Rules Interpreting and Implementing the Real Estate Sales Full Disclosure Act, N.J.S.A. 45:15-16.27 et seq., was recodified as Subchapter 9; Subchapter 3, Petitions for Rulemaking, was recodified as Subchapter 10; Subchapter 4, Proceedings before the Commission,

was recodified as Subchapter 11, Procedures on Disciplinary Actions, Contested Applications, Declaratory Ruling Requests; and Subchapter 5, Appeals of Initial Denials of Licensing Applications, was recodified as section 11.10. See: 30 N.J.R. 2333(a), 30 N.J.R. 3646(a).

Chapter 5, Real Estate Commission, was readopted as R.2004 d.130, effective March 5, 2004. See: 35 N.J.R. 4812(a), 36 N.J.R. 1780(a).

Subchapter 9A, Rules Interpreting and Implementing the New Jersey Real Estate Timeshare Act, N.J.S.A. 45:15-16.50 et seq., was adopted as new rules by R.2009 d.222, effective July 6, 2009. See: 40 N.J.R. 3944(a), 41 N.J.R. 2663(a).

Chapter 5, Real Estate Commission, was readopted as R.2009 d.287, effective August 27, 2009. See: 41 N.J.R. 1381(a), 41 N.J.R. 3440(a).

Subchapter 12, Continuing Education, was adopted as new rules by R.2011 d.184, effective July 18, 2011. See: 43 N.J.R. 369(a), 43 N.J.R. 1592(a).

In accordance with N.J.S.A. 52:14B-5.1b, Chapter 5, Real Estate Commission, was scheduled to expire on August 27, 2016. See: 43 N.J.R. 1203(a).

Chapter 5, Real Estate Commission, was readopted, effective February 24, 2016. See: Source and Effective Date.

SUBCHAPTER 1. ORGANIZATIONAL RULES

11:5-1.1   Commission responsibilities

The Real Estate Commission is responsible for the supervision and regulation of the education, examination and licensing of real estate brokers, broker-salespersons, salespersons, and referral agents; the regulation of the sale or lease of out-of-State properties to New Jersey residents through promotional activities in New Jersey; the investigation and adjudication of disciplinary actions against licensees; and the administration of the Real Estate Guaranty Fund.

11:5-1.2   Organization of the Commission

The organizational chart of the Division of the Real Estate Commission is as follows:

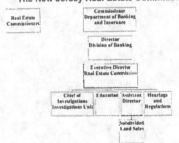

Organizational Chart of
The New Jersey Real Estate Commission

11:5-1.3   Functions of the Commission

(a) The Commission is comprised of four sections whose functions are as follows:

1. The Investigations Section is responsible for investigating the qualifications of applicants for licensure, and for investigating complaints against licensed brokers, broker-salespersons, salespersons or referral agents or individuals who have allegedly engaged in the business of a real estate broker, salesperson or referral agent without being licensed to do so.

2. The Real Estate Education Section is responsible for reviewing the qualifications of real estate school and instructor applicants and for regulating their activities as such through the Education Subsection.

3. The Bureau of Subdivided Land Sales Control is responsible for enforcing the provisions of the New Jersey Real Estate Sales Full Disclosure Act, N.J.S.A. 45:15-16.27 et seq. Its duties include, but are not limited to, reviewing applications for the registration of new projects, conducting inspections of conditionally registered projects, and reviewing applications for the renewal of projects.

4. The Hearings and Regulatory Affairs Section is responsible for processing the rulemaking activity of the Commission, the scheduling and processing of contested cases, the prosecution of certain contested matters, and other functions.

11:5-1.4   Information available to the public

With the exception of the records designated as non-public in N.J.A.C. 11:5-1.5(g), the public may obtain information or make submissions or requests concerning any Commission functions by contacting the Real Estate Commission, Department of Banking and Insurance, PO Box 328, Trenton, New Jersey 08625-0328.

11:5-1.5   Commission records open to public inspection; investigative files not open to the public

(a) The New Jersey Real Estate Commission makes, maintains and keeps records as listed in (b) through (g) below.

(b) Current and computerized public licensing records are available at the Commission's office for inspection and copying during normal business hours upon sufficient notice to the Commission staff. The Commission staff may require several weeks notice to locate records other than computerized records. Except as otherwise noted in this section, records are maintained for a minimum of three years. Older records may be unavailable. Copies of records can be purchased from the Commission at the fees established in the Right to Know Law, N.J.S.A. 47:1A-2.

(c) Requests for certified copies of the Commission's public licensing records (or for a certificate of the absence of a public record) shall be submitted in writing and must specify which records are requested and the time period covered by the request. The Commission staff requires at least 10 working days to provide certified copies of public records.

(d) The following records are maintained pursuant to the Real Estate Licensing Act:

1. Certifications of license history and status based upon computerized licensing records;

2. Real estate broker, broker-salesperson, salesperson, referral agent, school and instructor license applications, and materials submitted therewith to obtain, transfer, reinstate or renew such licenses, and the final disposition of such applications. However, criminal history information obtained by the Commission pursuant to N.J.A.C. 11:5-3.3 and personal data on a licensee such as home address, home telephone number and date of birth are considered confidential;

3. Real Estate Commission meeting minutes;

4. Orders to Show Cause and complaints issued by the Attorney General's office charging that a licensee or an unlicensed person has violated provisions of the Real Estate License Act or the Commission's administrative rules; documents accepted into the agency record in any such proceeding; and the final disposition of such proceedings including settlements; and

5. Notices, proposals and other records concerning rulemaking required to be kept or distributed to the public by the Commission pursuant to the Administrative Procedure Act, N.J.S.A. 52:14B-1 et seq. and N.J.A.C. 1:30-3 and 4 et seq. Complete records of unadopted proposals are available for one year after publication of the proposal. Complete records of adopted rules are available for three years after each rule's effective date.

(e) The following records are maintained by the Bureau of Subdivided Land Sales Control, pursuant to the Real Estate Full Disclosure Act, N.J.S.A. 45:15-16.27 et seq.:

1. Statements of record and additions or corrections thereto filed with the Bureau pursuant to N.J.S.A. 45:15-16.33, 16.36, 16.39 and 16.41(a);

2. Annual reports submitted by a subdivider pursuant to N.J.S.A. 45:15-16.40;

3. Public offering statements and amended public offering statements prepared pursuant to N.J.S.A. 45:15-16.38;

4. Orders to Show Cause and other pleadings charging violations of N.J.S.A. 45:15-16.27 et seq. and the final disposition of such orders, including Orders to Cease and Desist and/or imposing penalties or sanctions; documents accepted into the agency record in any such proceedings; and

5. Applications for exemption of a subdivision filed with the Bureau pursuant to N.J.S.A. 45:15-16.32(c) and N.J.A.C. 11:5-9.18 and the final disposition of any such exemption application.

(f) The following records are maintained pursuant to the Real Estate Guaranty Fund Act, N.J.S.A. 45:15-34 et seq.:

1. Court orders for payment from the Real Estate Guaranty Fund; and

2. Pleadings served upon the Commissioner of Insurance or any duly authorized agent or employee of the Department of Insurance pursuant to N.J.S.A. 45:15-39.

(g) The following licensee records are nonpublic in accordance with N.J.S.A. 47:1A-1 et seq.:

1. Criminal complaints, indictments, judgments of conviction and other separate documents submitted in connection with a license application concerning whether an applicant is disqualified by reason of indictment for or conviction of a crime;

2. Criminal history records obtained as the result of any criminal history check;

3. Petitions or discharges in bankruptcy, complaints, orders or other pleadings in actions for assignment to creditors and other separate documents submitted in connection with a license application concerning whether the applicant is disqualified by reason of unworthiness;

4. Copies of orders of suspension or revocation issued by professional or occupational licensing authorities, and other separate documents submitted in connection with a license application concerning whether the applicant is disqualified from licensure;

5. Records concerning the medical disability of any licensee;

6. Investigative files in any matter pending investigation, or in any completed investigation in which no formal disciplinary action was taken;

7. Personal data on a licensee such as home address, home telephone number and date of birth;

8. The Social Security numbers of any applicants or licensees which were submitted to the Commission on a license application or otherwise obtained by the Commission; and

9. Purchaser information submitted pursuant to N.J.S.A. 45:15-16.38.

SUBCHAPTER 2. EDUCATION

11:5-2.1   **Educational requirements for salespersons, referral agents and brokers in making application for licensure examination**

(a) All applicants for a salesperson's, referral agent's or broker's license shall present with their license application evidence of their satisfactory completion of a course of education in real estate subjects taught in accordance with N.J.S.A. 45:15-10.1 and as required by this section.

1. This requirement shall also apply to disabled veterans making application for licensure pursuant to N.J.S.A. 45:15-11. However, the Commission shall approve a program of studies in real estate completed by such a veteran offered by a provider other than a licensed school if the program consisted of at least 75 hours in the case of an applicant for a salesperson's or referral agent's license, or 225 hours in the case of an applicant for a broker's license and the program was offered by an accredited college or university for credit.

2. No person shall receive credit toward the fulfillment of the salesperson or referral agent prelicensure education requirement for attendance at a broker's prelicensure course and no person shall receive credit toward the fulfillment of the broker's prelicensure education requirements for attendance at a salesperson's or referral agent's prelicensure course.

(b) To qualify to challenge the examination for licensure as a real estate salesperson or referral agent, a candidate must first successfully complete a course of study in real estate at a school licensed by the Commission pursuant to N.J.S.A. 45:15-10.4 consisting of a minimum of 75 hours as specified in (f) below. To qualify to challenge the real estate broker's license exam, a candidate must first successfully complete courses of study in real estate consisting of a minimum of 150 hours as specified in (g) below, offered by a licensed school or, with respect to those certain courses specified in (g)5 below, offered by some other Commission-approved provider.

(c) No person with the exception of qualified disabled veterans shall receive credit for satisfactory completion of the prescribed 150 hours of broker's courses unless that person was the holder of a salesperson's license at the time of enrollment in said course.

(d) The time allotted by any school for a final examination covering real estate subjects shall be applicable toward the minimum hours of course study. No more than five minutes of each course hour may be utilized for breaks in the actual classroom instruction being conducted at any given session of a pre-licensure course. During the time in which actual classroom instruction is conducted, in addition to covering the substantive material mandated by (f) and (g) below, instructors are to provide thorough instruction on the State license examination and license issuance procedures for salesperson, referral agent and broker license candidates, as applicable, and to perform all reasonably required administrative functions such as taking attendance and making announcements of general interest.

(e) The requirements that broker license candidates complete the general 90 hour broker prelicensure education course and that salesperson or referral agent license candidates complete the 75 hour salesperson prelicensure education course shall not apply to:

1. Applicants for licensure as a broker, salesperson or referral agent who have held a real estate broker's license issued by another state and who were actively engaged in the real estate brokerage business for three years or more immediately preceding the date of application;

2. Applicants for licensure as a broker who are attorneys at law admitted to the practice in the State of New Jersey and applicants for licensure as a salesperson or referral agent who are attorneys at law admitted to practice in New Jersey or in any other state at the time of making application;

3. Applicants for licensure as a salesperson or referral agent who have earned a college degree from any accredited institution of higher education, provided that:

i. The total number of college level classroom hours devoted to real estate and related subjects was 75 or more, and such courses were completed within three years of making application;

ii. The applicant received a bachelor or associate degree in real estate regardless of how long prior to their application for a waiver they received that degree; or

iii. The applicant satisfactorily completed 75 or more classroom hours of course work in real estate or related subjects, at least 45 hours of which consisted of instruction on real estate conducted as part of a post-graduate program and that such post-graduate studies were completed within three years of making application.

4. Applicants for licensure as a salesperson or referral agent who hold or held a real estate license issued by another state, provided that:

i. The applicant has satisfactorily completed a prelicensure course of real estate education at a proprietary school, college or university in that other state;

ii. The prelicensure course was sanctioned by the real estate licensing authority of that state;

iii. The total number of classroom hours included in the course was 75 or more;

iv. The applicant qualified for licensure in that state by examination; and

v. The applicant was actively licensed in that state within three years of applying for the waiver.

5. Applicants for licensure as a salesperson or referral agent who previously held a license as a New Jersey real estate broker and whose last license expired more than two but less than five years prior to making application.

(f) The salesperson's prelicensure course shall consist of 75 hours of education. Subject to (e) above, applicants for licensure as a salesperson or referral agent shall complete the 75 hour salesperson prelicensure course that shall include:

1. Property rights (9 hours);

2. Contracts and other property instruments (12 hours);

3. Leases and landlord-tenant relations (6 hours);

4. Mortgages and other liens (12 hours);

5. Business opportunity sales (2 hours);

6. The laws of agency (12 hours);

7. Appraising (2 hours);

8. License Act and regulations (9 hours);

9. Other state, Federal and municipal laws and regulations, including N.J.S.A. 17:16C-1 et seq., 39:1-1 et seq., 46:8-43 et seq. and 46:8C-1 et seq. as they pertain to the resale of mobile and manufactured housing units which bear or are required to bear motor vehicle titles (5 hours);

10. Salesperson duties and pitfalls in the real estate business (3 hours);

11. Quizzes and final examination (3 hours).

(g) The 150 hours of prelicensure education required of candidates for licensure as a broker or broker-salesperson by N.J.S.A. 45:15-10 shall be acquired as provided in this subsection. A 90 hour general broker's prelicensure course shall first be completed in accordance with the following syllabus and directives. Thereafter, two 30 hour broker courses as described in (g)5, 6 and 7 below shall be completed. All three courses, totaling 150 hours of instruction, must be successfully completed within a period of two years. Where the three courses are not so completed, a candidate must again successfully complete any previously taken course and all courses not previously taken within the two year time frame, and again fulfill the experience requirement established at N.J.S.A. 45:15-9 and N.J.A.C. 11:5-3.8 in order to qualify to challenge the broker license examination.

1. The 90 hour general broker's prelicensure course may be taught in blocks or modules of material. The maximum number of modules into which the course may be divided is 23, with their content corresponding to the 23 subject matter areas identi-

fied in the syllabus below. Schools offering courses in modules may include more than one subject matter in a given module. No student may commence a course which is offered in modules on a date other than the starting date of any module. No student shall be given credit for the successful completion of a 90 hour general broker's prelicensure course unless and until they have received instruction in all of the subject matter areas identified below for approximately the number of hours indicated, and passed a comprehensive final examination. The 90 hour general broker's prelicensure course shall be conducted in accordance with the following syllabus and directives. Substantive instruction shall be provided on the following topics for approximately the number of hours indicated:

i. Review license laws and regulations including provisions of the Real Estate Sales Full Disclosure Act and N.J.A.C. 11:5-9 (six hours);

ii. Listing contracts—sales and rentals (three hours);

iii. Sale contracts (three hours);

iv. Deeds and real property rights and interests including nature of ownership, legal description, chain of title, restrictions, consideration, various types, acknowledgments and recording, land and land elements, water rights (including riparian rights), state claims regarding tidelands estates and other interests, methods of ownership, dower and curtesy, wills and descent, adverse possession and fixtures (three hours);

v. Advanced financing techniques including qualification formulae, various types, typical prerequisites (insurance, flood insurance, if applicable, certificate of occupancy, etc.) and income tax ramifications (six hours);

vi. Liens, foreclosures and redemptions (one hour);

vii. Easements, restrictions, etc. (one hour);

viii. Condemnation (one hour);

ix. Zoning, including non-conforming uses, variances, subdivisions, planning, zoning issues raised by condominium construction or conversion and other types of real estate development (five hours);

x. Surveys (non-government type) and legal descriptions (one hour);

xi. Property taxes, assessment, re-valuations, assessment appeals and special appeals (three hours);

xii. Real estate valuation including techniques and distinctions between comparative market analyses and formal appraisals (three hours);

xiii. Settlement/closing procedures, RESPA forms (six hours);

xiv. Mathematics relative to real estate (six hours);

xv. Laws: Federal Fair Housing and the New Jersey Law Against Discrimination, New Jersey "Mount Laurel" requirements, RESPA, Truth in Lending, rent control, New Jersey Land Use Law, New Jersey's Truth in Renting Law, and the provisions in that law, in N.J.S.A. 17:16C-1 et seq., in N.J.S.A. 39.1-1 et seq. and in N.J.S.A. 46:8C-1 et seq. which pertain to the resale of mobile and manufactured housing units which bear or are required to bear motor vehicle titles (total three hours);

xvi. Business and management practices (total of six hours for (g)1xvi(1) through (6) below), including:

(1) Company structure including single ownership, partnership, corporate, requirements to establish, employees vs. independent contractors;

(2) Office management including bookkeeping and accounting relative to real estate, escrow responsibilities, company dollars, ledgers, records and computers;

(3) Personnel management including recruiting, hiring, training, supervising, compensation and termination;

(4) Advertising and promotions;

(5) Community involvement by the company, broker, salespersons and referral agents; and

(6) Insurance including errors and omissions, etc.

xvii. Principles of agency including ethics and legal liability, disclosure requirements and case studies (six hours);

xviii. Commercial and industrial real estate including small scale, large scale, leasing, financing, site analysis, advertising, remuneration, bulk sales, U.C.C., considerations in franchise transactions, E.C.R.A., BOCA Code, construction financing and other commercial construction concerns (three hours);

xix. Property management including responsibilities and information regarding repairs and maintenance, public relations, collection of rents, government regulations, business trends, personnel, recordkeeping, advertising, etc. (three hours);

xx. Residential real estate development including requirements of New Jersey's Planned Real Estate Development Act including time-sharing, the Home Owner's Warranty program and other concerns regarding single-family and condo/co-op development, conversion, marketing and financing (two hours);

xxi. Leases and landlord/tenant laws including Truth in Renting Law (four hours);

xxii. Real estate investments, syndications, REIT's, limited partnerships and S.E.C. licensing requirements (two hours); and

xxiii. Income tax considerations and ramifications of various real estate transactions (three hours).

2. Within the 90 hour general broker prelicensure course instruction will also be provided on the following topics for the hours indicated. These topics shall be taught in such a manner as to familiarize students with the basic elements of the listed topics and to impart to students an awareness of their scope and effect. The coverage on these topics will also inform students of the sources which can be contacted in order to obtain additional general information and/or specific data concerning the topics' applicability to or impact upon particular locations, and to educate students on their obligations and responsibilities as licensees to ascertain and disclose such information. The topics to be taught are:

i. Radon contamination, which instruction shall also include testing techniques, remediation techniques and the New Jersey DEP confidentiality statute (one hour);

ii. Ground water contamination, which instruction shall also include testing and remediation techniques (one hour);

iii. Problems posed by a property's proximity to solid waste disposal and/or toxic waste sites (one hour);

iv. Ground water percolation and private sewage disposal systems, which instruction shall also include testing methods (one hour);

v. Problems posed by lands officially designed as Wetlands, Pinelands, or within any other special classifications (one hour); and

vi. New Jersey's Coastal Areas Facilities Review Act (one hour).

3. Instructors conducting 90 hour general broker prelicensure courses shall provide general information to their students concerning the procedures through which students can arrange to sit for the State license examination and through which licenses are issued by the Commission, and shall give at least two spot quizzes and a comprehensive final exam on the material covered in the course (four hours).

4. In addition to classroom instruction and assigned reading from a general textbook, in the 90 hour broker course students shall also be assigned additional outside reading on various topics which shall include, but not be limited to, informational publications of the New Jersey Department of Environmental Protection on the various environmental topics covered, those sections of the New Jersey Law Against Discrimination

REAL ESTATE COMMISSION

which directly relate to the activities of real estate professionals, and other topics as directed by the New Jersey Real Estate Commission.

5. After having successfully completed the 90 hour broker course, all candidates for licensure as a broker or broker-salesperson must successfully complete a 30 hour prelicensure course on brokers' ethics and agency law and relationships, and a second 30 hour prelicensure course on office management and related topics.

i. All such agency/ethics and office management courses shall be taught by licensed instructors at licensed schools.

ii. All such agency/ethics courses shall be taught utilizing methods which maximize the use of case studies of recent Commission decisions in disciplinary actions, demonstration models and other non-lecture techniques.

iii. A final examination of not less than one hour shall be administered in all such courses on which students must receive a passing grade in order to be deemed to have successfully completed such courses.

iv. No school shall allow students to commence any 30 hour agency/ethics course or office management course at a time other than the starting date of such courses.

6. The 30 hours of instruction in the ethics/agency course shall be devoted to:

i. The fiduciary duties owed by agents to their principals;

ii. Disclosed and undisclosed dual agency;

iii. Conflicts of interest and self-dealing;

iv. The risks and benefits of sub-agency to the principal and the agent;

v. Restrictions on and disclosure requirements regarding acting for more than one party to a transaction, including those pertaining to licensees providing mortgage services;

vi. Disclosure requirements to non-principals;

vii. Issues raised by licensees involved in transactions as non-agents; and

viii. The obligations to properly qualify or pre-qualify prospective purchasers and related issues.

7. The 30 hours of instruction in the office management and related topics course shall be devoted to:

i. Office management requirements imposed upon supervising brokers of main and branch offices;

ii. Recordkeeping requirements, with particular emphasis upon and extensive coverage of escrow account records;

iii. The importance of adequate supervision and training of other licensees to assure their compliance with the license law and the rules of the Commission;

iv. Instruction on proper qualification and pre-qualification techniques, including requiring demonstrations by the students, and with emphasis upon the significance of training and oversight of other licensees;

v. Statutory and rule requirements pertaining to contracts, leases and listing agreements and to broker advertising;

vi. Closings;

vii. Environmental concerns; and

viii. Instruction on licensure requirements and procedures applicable to license applications, transfers, changes of broker address, branch offices, etc., and office closing requirements.

(h) A complete syllabus for the salesperson and broker courses shall be maintained at the offices of the Real Estate Commission and be open to the public for inspection.

(i) All course hours are suggested and may be modified at the discretion of the director of the approved school subject to written notice to and written approval by the Real Estate Commission.

11:5-2.2   Licensed schools and instructors; requirements

(a) The following regulations are applicable to schools and instructors licensed to conduct prelicensure courses of education in real estate subjects pursuant to N.J.S.A. 45:15-10.4 and 10.5, to applicants for such licenses and, as applicable, to the conducting of continuing education courses by such schools and instructors pursuant to N.J.A.C. 11:5-12.1.

1. The original license term for pre-licensure course instructors and schools shall begin on July 1, 1994 and terminate on February 28, 1997. Thereafter, each two-year license term for school and instructor licenses shall run from March 1 to the last day of February of the second following year.

(b) The Commission shall require any school or instructor in making application for licensure to submit certain documents, statements and forms which shall form the basis for the Commission's judgment whether to grant a license. Where the Commission initially denies an application for a school or instructor license, it shall provide to the applicant notification in writing with reasons for such action. The applicant may appeal such a decision to the full Commission. N.J.A.C. 11:5-11.10 shall be applicable to all such appeals.

(c) Public adult education programs conducted under the auspices of a board of education in this State and any college or

university accredited as such by the State Department of Higher Education shall be presumed to be qualified providers of real estate courses, so long as their real estate prelicensure education program is under the direction of a licensed instructor or other qualified individual who has affirmatively demonstrated to the Commission his or her good moral character and has met the other requirements of N.J.S.A. 45:15-10.9.

(d) Except as provided in (c) above, all other applicants for a license to operate a real estate prelicensure school, and in the case of a corporation, or limited or general partnership, the members, officers, directors and owners of a controlling interest thereof, shall demonstrate their good moral character, including the absence of any conviction for the crimes or other offenses specified under the provisions of N.J.S.A. 45:15-12.1. The Commission may make such further investigation and require such proof as it deems proper as to the honesty, trustworthiness, character and integrity of an applicant.

(e) When a school is to be conducted in the name of a corporation, a certified copy of its certificate of incorporation shall accompany the application for licensure. When a school is to be conducted under a trade name, whether a sole proprietorship, firm, general partnership, or limited partnership, a true copy of the certificate of trade name or articles of the general or limited partnership as filed in the office of the county clerk shall accompany the application. A school shall not use the designation of "College" or "University," as part of its name or in any other manner, unless it, in fact, meets the standards and qualifications of the State agency having jurisdiction and has been approved by that agency.

(f) Every school licensed by the Commission shall maintain a bona fide office open to the public during normal business hours for the purpose of assisting former and current students. Schools shall provide adequate space, seating, equipment and instructional materials for their students. The premises, equipment and facilities of the school shall comply with all local, city, county and State regulations, such as fire codes, building and sanitation codes. A certificate from a proper authority evidencing compliance with these requirements shall accompany an application for school licensure. The Commission may require proof of ownership or a copy of the lease if the facility is rented. Public adult education programs conducted under the auspices of a board of education in this State and any college or university accredited as such by the New Jersey Commission on Higher Education, the facilities of which have been approved by a State agency, shall be presumed to have met the requirements of this paragraph, so long as the real estate courses offered are held at the approved facility.

1. Any additional teaching locations must be licensed by the Commission and must comply with all the requirements appli-

cable to licensed schools, their directors and instructors as set forth in the Act and this rule. School directors shall have oversight responsibility for these locations. All prelicensure courses conducted at such locations must be taught by licensed instructors or guest lecturers, pursuant to N.J.S.A. 45:15-10.5 and this rule. All continuing education courses conducted at such locations shall be taught by licensed instructors or by individuals approved as continuing education instructors pursuant to N.J.A.C. 11:5-12.10.

(g) All schools shall furnish to the Commission at the time of application for initial licensure the school policy and regulations pertaining to standards for satisfactory completion of the courses offered at the school and the issuance of a Certificate, conditions for dismissal of a student and conditions for reinstatement.

1. Any changes in school policy and regulations, as set forth in (g) above, from the information submitted with the original application for school licensure or as otherwise previously supplied, shall be disclosed to the Commission within 10 business days in writing, or on a form which the Commission prescribes.

(h) When a school fulfills all of the requirements for licensure, then a license shall be executed by the President of the Commission as attested by the Executive Director. School licensure shall be limited to the specific ownership and school locations identified on the license document(s).

(i) An individual seeking approval as a director of a licensed real estate school administered by a public adult education program or an accredited college or university who is not licensed as a real estate instructor may nevertheless qualify as the director of such a school, so long as he or she is at least 18 years of age; has a background of good moral character, including the absence of any conviction for the crimes or other offenses specified under the provisions of N.J.S.A. 45:15-12.1; and has fulfilled all of the education requirements imposed upon candidates for licensure as real estate instructors within two years of applying to the Commission for approval to be the director of such a school.

(j) In order to enable the Commission to confirm that courses offered by real estate schools include the required number of hours of instruction as prescribed in N.J.S.A. 45:15-10.1(a) and (b) and N.J.A.C. 11:5-2.1, every six months, each school director shall submit data on courses to be offered by their school in the forthcoming six month period, the starting and ending dates of the courses, the days and hours of class sessions and teaching locations. Such course information shall be provided on forms prescribed by the Commission and shall be retained as permanent records for not less than three years after submission.

(k) No person, other than a guest lecturer, shall teach real estate education courses, the attendance and successful completion of which shall constitute the fulfillment of the educational

prerequisites for licensure established under N.J.S.A. 45:15-10.1, unless that person is licensed as an instructor pursuant to N.J.S.A. 45:15-10.5 and this section.

1. Each applicant for licensure as a real estate instructor shall be 18 years of age or older and shall have a background of good moral character, including the absence of any conviction for those certain crimes or other like offenses referred to in N.J.S.A. 45:15-12.1, subject to the applicant's ability to affirmatively demonstrate his or her rehabilitation from such conviction. In order to confirm the absence of any such conviction, the Commission shall require all non-attorney applicants to submit with their application for instructor licensure a New Jersey State Police Request for Criminal History Record Information Form and a certified check or money order in the amount established by the New Jersey State Police as the processing fee for such forms.

2. Each applicant for licensure must hold a bachelor's degree from an accredited college or university, except for the following applicants:

i. New Jersey licensed brokers who have been continuously licensed as such for the two years immediately preceding their application; and

ii. Licensed brokers from other states who have been continuously licensed as such for the three years immediately preceding their application.

3. Except as provided in (*l*)3i and ii below, all instructor license applicants must successfully complete all of the education requirements for licensure as a New Jersey broker established at N.J.A.C. 11:5-2.1, totaling 150 hours, not more than one year prior to passing the instructor license examination and applying for an instructor license.

i. New Jersey broker licensees who have been licensed as such for at least the two years immediately preceding the application and who have completed the full 150 hours of broker prelicensure courses established at N.J.A.C. 11:5-2.1 shall be deemed to have fulfilled the education requirements for licensure as an instructor.

ii. The following individuals will not be required to take the 90-hour general broker course but must successfully complete the two 30-hour broker prelicensure courses referred to in N.J.A.C. 11:5-2.1 in order to fulfill the instructor prelicensure education requirements:

(1) New Jersey broker licensees who have been licensed as such for the two years preceding their application for an instructor license but who have not previously completed those two courses; and

(2) Licensed brokers from other states who have been licensed as such for the three years immediately preceding application.

4. All instructor license applicants shall successfully complete an instructor license examination as established by the Commission. The examination shall extensively test the applicant's general real estate knowledge and shall include questions on teaching methods. Applicants are advised to engage in independent study and/or to take courses offered by independent providers on teaching methods.

5. Subsequent to passing the instructor license examination, as a prerequisite to being issued an instructor license, all applicants must attend a seminar conducted by or under the direction of the Commission staff covering Commission and licensing procedures. Such seminars shall not exceed one day in length.

(*l*) Regulations applicable to the renewal of school and instruction licenses are as follows:

1. Pursuant to N.J.S.A. 45:15-10.7, the fee for the renewal of a real estate instructor license for an additional two-year license term shall be $ 100.00. The fee for the renewal of a real estate school license shall be $ 400.00 for the first teaching location licensed and $ 200.00 for each additional licensed location to be renewed.

2. As a prerequisite for the renewal of an instructor license, an instructor must attend a Commission-sponsored seminar updating them on recent developments affecting the real estate brokerage business in New Jersey. Such seminars shall be offered on a minimum of two dates, each in a different location throughout the state, during the second year of each two-year license term. Persons initially licensed as instructors in the last six months of the two-year license term are exempt from this seminar attendance requirement for the first renewal of their instructor license.

3. In the event that any person to whom an instructor's license has been or shall have been issued shall fail to renew such license or obtain a new license for a period of two consecutive years or more after the expiration of the last license held, the Commission shall require such person to again fulfill all the qualifications for initial licensure as an instructor prior to issuance of a further instructor's license. This requirement shall not apply to a person reapplying for an instructor's license who was a licensed instructor and who allowed their license to expire due to subsequent employment in a public agency in this State with responsibility for dealing with matters relating to real estate if the person reapplying does so within one year of termination of that employment.

(m) For real estate prelicensure courses, the maximum teaching load per instructor or guest lecturer shall not exceed the ratio of one instructor or guest lecturer to 60 students per class. Each prelicensure course offered by a licensed school shall be under the supervision of an instructor licensed pursuant to N.J.S.A. 45:15-10.5 and N.J.A.C. 11:5-2.2(k). At least one licensed instructor shall be present in the classroom at all sessions. However, additional instructors or guest lecturers may be utilized for instruction so long as not more than 25 percent of the required instruction is done by guest lecturers. Broker prelicensure courses may be taught by up to three instructors, provided that one licensed instructor is designated as having the responsibility for the quality of instruction in that course. School directors shall maintain as a business record the names of any persons teaching as guest lecturers or as a group of instructors, with an indication of the designated supervising instructor.

(n) All tuition charged by a school shall be specified separately. If additional fees are to be charged for supplies, materials or books needed in course of work, they shall be itemized by the school prior to the payment of any fees and such items shall become the property of the student upon payment.

(o) The tuition and fees shall be specifically set forth in a student contract. The contract shall expressly state the school's policy regarding the return of unearned tuition when a student is dismissed or withdraws voluntarily or because of hardship.

(p) Any person who has a permanent disability or physical handicap which precludes that person from attending regular scheduled classes at a licensed school may request Commission approval to receive special instruction through a licensed school provided this request is supported by sworn statements of doctors or other persons having knowledge of the facts and provided a licensed school is willing to undertake such an agreement.

(q) No school shall, without the approval of the Commission, accept for enrollment as a transfer student any person concurrently enrolled with any other licensed school, unless upon the showing of good cause by said student to the Commission in writing.

(r) Any school that offers real estate continuing education courses shall maintain records of licensees' attendance at such courses as prescribed by N.J.A.C. 11:5-12.8. Every school shall permanently establish and maintain for each student enrolled in a prelicensure education course, complete, accurate and detailed records for a period of not less than three years after student matriculation. Such records shall be available for inspection during regular school hours by the Commission and shall contain the following information:

1. The total number of hours of instruction undertaken by the student;

2. Completed areas of study in real estate subjects prescribed by the Act and these regulations;

3. The student's attendance record; and

4. The names of all supervising instructors and guest lecturers.

(s) To satisfactorily complete any prelicensure course, a student must receive a passing grade and attend at least 80 percent of the class session hours required for the course by N.J.A.C. 11:5-2.1.

(t) Upon a student's satisfactory completion of a prelicensure course in real estate, the school shall issue to the student a Course Completion Certificate.

(u) The director of a real estate school shall be responsible for properly closing the school in compliance with this subsection.

1. No later than 10 days after the date on which the school ceases operations, the director shall return the school license, stamp, and all education certificates to the Commission and shall advise the Commission in writing of the date on which the school closed.

2. Within 30 days of the date on which the school ceases operations, the director shall submit an affidavit to the Commission certifying the following:

i. The location where student records are to be kept in compliance with (r) above and the name of the person who is to act as custodian of the records. The Commission shall be notified immediately of any change in such information. Records shall be kept for a period of not less than three years;

ii. The name of the owner or authorized representative of the school and the address where he or she may be contacted by the Commission;

iii. That the school license and school stamp have been returned to the Commission;

iv. That all students have been timely notified of the school closing, and any tuition received by the school for future courses or courses which were not completed has been returned to the students;

v. That all signs have been removed, and all advertisements and trade materials which refer to the school have been recalled;

vi. That the appropriate telephone services have been advised that the school is closed and that future telephone directories should not contain the name of the school; and

vii. That there are no outstanding fees, fines or penalties due and owing the Commission.

(v) No school shall use any name other than the name in which it is licensed for advertising or publicity purposes; nor shall any school advertise or imply that it is "recommended," "endorsed," "accredited," or "approved" by the Commission, but a licensed school may indicate that it has been "licensed" to conduct courses of education in real estate subjects to qualify applicants for licensure examination. No school shall make any warranties or guarantees that a student will pass the State license examination as a result of taking its course.

(w) (Reserved)

(x) The purpose of this subsection is to assure that there is a total separation between instructional activity conducted by licensed schools and any solicitation of students, which, as defined in (x)2ii below, means any recruiting efforts or brokerage activity directed at students. These provisions will be construed in a manner consistent with that regulatory objective. A violation of any of these provisions will be considered by the Commission as conduct demonstrating unworthiness for licensure, thereby subjecting the offending licensee to sanctions pursuant to N.J.S.A. 45:15-17(e) and (t). The Commission may also impose sanctions for a violation of these provisions pursuant to N.J.S.A. 45:15-10.11 and N.J.A.C. 11:5-12.15. Requirements regulating the involvement of licensed schools in soliciting students to become salespersons or referral agents for particular real estate brokers are as follows:

1. At the beginning of the first class session of all salesperson or referral agent prelicensure courses, all licensed schools shall distribute to all students in writing the following:

NOTICE

TO: ALL SALESPERSON/REFERRAL AGENT COURSE STUDENTS

FROM: NEW JERSEY REAL ESTATE COMMISSION

RE: SOLICITATION OF SALESPERSON OR REFERRAL AGENT LICENSE CANDIDATES AT PRELICENSURE SCHOOLS

It is the policy of the New Jersey Real Estate Commission that there be a complete and total separation between the instruction you receive in your prelicensure education course and any efforts by brokers to recruit you to join their firm and/or to secure listings or offers on listed properties from you. This policy is reflected in Commission rule N.J.A.C. 11:5-2.2(x), which is reproduced in its entirety below.

If you are subjected to any recruitment efforts or are solicited for listings or offers during class time you should immediately notify your instructor, the Director of your school, and the New Jersey Real Estate Commission by writing to:

New Jersey Real Estate Commission
20 West State Street
PO Box 328
Trenton, New Jersey 08625-0328
Attn: Director, Real Estate Education

You are free to negotiate the terms of your employment with any broker. It is in your own best interest to talk to several prospective employing brokers before deciding which offers the best compensation plan, including post-termination payment provisions, and support package for you. You should also consider a prospective employer's professionalism and reputation for honesty and integrity when deciding which broker to work for.

In the event an enrolled student does not attend the first session of a salespersons/referral agents course, a copy of the foregoing notice shall be delivered to that student at the commencement of the first class session which that student does attend.

2. For the purposes of this subsection, the following definitions shall apply:

i. The phrase "brokerage activity" means any activity which, pursuant to N.J.S.A. 45:15-1 and 45:15-3 would require the person engaging in such activity to hold a license as a real estate broker, real estate salesperson or referral agent;

ii. The term "solicit" means to recruit, invite or urge a student to seek employment with a particular broker, or to list, purchase or lease through, or to make referrals of listing, purchaser or lessee prospects to a particular broker; and

iii. The phrase "successful completion" means the receipt by the student of a Real Estate Commission school certificate form, duly signed by the instructor and the school director and stamped by the licensed school, certifying to the student's having completed and passed a prelicensure course conducted by that school.

3. With the exception of posting, distributing or displaying written materials as provided in (x)5 below, no school director, instructor, guest lecturer or staff member shall, prior to, nor within seven days following, a student's successful completion of a course, solicit a student to become a salesperson or referral agent for any particular real estate broker, nor shall any such person at any time accept any fee or other compensation for soliciting or recruiting students attending their school to apply for employment with a particular real estate broker.

4. No in-person or electronic solicitation of students to apply for employment as salespersons or referral agents with a particu-

lar real estate broker shall be permitted at a licensed school location during the prescribed class hours, nor in the breaks between such class hours. Such soliciting may be scheduled and held at licensed schools before, after or separate from the prescribed class hours, for example as a "career night" for students, provided that students are notified in writing in advance that their attendance at such recruitment functions is completely voluntary. However, no school director, instructor, guest lecturer or staff member shall engage in such activity at any time prior to, nor within seven days following, a student's successful completion of a course. Licensed instructors who are also licensed brokers, salespersons or referral agents may conduct prelicensure courses, and licensees who are not licensed instructors may appear as guest lecturers in such courses, so long as their presentations do not include the solicitation of students.

5. Any licensed school which posts, distributes or displays written material which solicits students to inquire about employment as a salesperson or referral agent with a particular broker must similarly post, distribute or display comparable written material from any real estate broker who requests the school to do so. However, no written material soliciting students to apply for employment with a particular real estate broker or any referral program shall be distributed during the prescribed class hours.

6. No licensed school may offer a reduced tuition rate to students where eligibility for the lower tuition is contingent upon a student making a commitment to becoming licensed through a particular broker subsequent to their qualifying for licensure and no licensed school may otherwise make or imply any promise or guarantee of employment to any student.

7. No oral statements or written text referring to a licensed school may be included or contained in any advertisement by a real estate licensee, and no advertisement of a licensed school may refer to the brokerage operation or include the telephone number of any licensee except that a school which is owned by a real estate licensee or franchisor may use that name in its school name.

i. Any advertisement by a school whose name includes the name of an affiliated licensed real estate broker or franchisor shall include the following disclosure legend:

Attending this school will not obligate you to become employed with our affiliated real estate broker(s), nor guarantee you an interview or a job with our affiliated real estate broker(s).

ii. No advertisement referring to a licensed school may be placed in the Help Wanted classified section of any newspaper or periodical.

8. No licensed school shall conduct prelicensure course sessions in any area which is part of a location which is licensed as a main or branch office of a real estate broker. For the purposes of this paragraph, an area will be considered as part of a licensed office location if any brokerage activity is conducted in that area at any time.

i. Where space on two or more floors in a multi-story building is licensed as a main or branch office location, it is permissible for prelicensure courses to be conducted in such a building, provided that the primary means of access to and egress from the floor where the courses are conducted does not require the students to walk through any area of the licensed office location wherein brokerage activity occurs.

ii. Where only one floor in a building is licensed as a main or branch office, it is permissible for prelicensure courses to be conducted in another area on that floor, provided that there is a separate entrance to that area either from the exterior of the building or from a common foyer or lobby and provided that the primary means of access to and egress from the area wherein the courses will be conducted does not require students to walk through a portion of the licensed premises wherein brokerage activity takes place.

iii. In all situations where prelicensure courses are conducted in the same building in which brokerage activity occurs under the authority of a broker in any way affiliated with the licensed school conducting such courses, the broker shall post signs either on the exterior of the building or in any common foyer or lobby, directing students either to the separate exterior entrance to the school location or to the primary route of access to the school location from such foyer or lobby.

9. No licensed school shall allow any person to solicit students enrolled in, or considering enrolling in, a prelicensure or continuing education course to list, purchase or lease any property; or for referrals of prospective sellers, purchasers or lessees at any time while such students are on school premises.

(y) Licensed schools providing continuing education courses shall comply with all requirements imposed upon the providers of such courses as set forth in N.J.A.C. 11:5-12.

11:5-2.3   **Applications processed by the Education Bureau of the Real Estate Commission**

(a) Applications for the following licenses and approvals are processed by the Education Bureau of the Real Estate Commission:

1. Real Estate Instructor license;

2. Real Estate School license;

11:5-2.4   **INSURANCE**

3. License for additional teaching location of a licensed real estate school;

4. Approval of Real Estate School Director;

5. Approval of experience report for broker license applicant;

6. Approval of real estate continuing education provider;

7. Approval of real estate continuing education instructor; and

8. Approval of real estate continuing education course.

(b) Applications for the following waivers are processed by the Education Bureau of the Real Estate Commission:

1. Waiver of salesperson or referral agent prelicensure education requirement;

2. Partial waiver of broker prelicensure education requirement and/or complete waiver of broker experience requirement;

3. Waiver of broker experience and certain prelicensure education requirements based upon status of applicant as a qualifying disabled veteran pursuant to N.J.S.A. 45:15-11; and

4. Waiver of continuing education requirement pursuant to N.J.A.C. 11:5-12.5.

11:5-2.4   **Examination eligibility certificates**

(a) The Education Bureau issues Certificates of Examination Eligibility to:

1. Broker license candidates who have fulfilled or, to the extent permitted by N.J.A.C. 11:5-3.8 and 2.1(e), had waived the broker license experience and/or education requirements;

2. Instructor license candidates who have fulfilled or, to the extent permitted by N.J.A.C. 11:5-2.2(k), had waived the instructor license education requirement; and

3. Salesperson or referral agent license candidates who, as provided in N.J.A.C. 11:5-2.1(e), have had the salesperson's or referral agent's license education requirement waived.

11:5-2.5   **Education Bureau forms and processing times**

(a) The following forms are utilized by the Education Bureau of the Real Estate Commission:

1. Application for real estate school license for non-public school;

2. Application for licensure of additional teaching location for a non-public real estate school;

3. Application for real estate school license for public college, university or adult education program;

4. Application for real estate instructor license;

5. Application for change in address of administrative office or primary teaching location of non-public real estate prelicensure school;

6. Application for relicensure of public college, university or adult education program with new director;

7. Application for relicensure of non-public school with new director or with new partner(s) (partnership) or new owner(s) of a controlling interest (corporation) or school name change;

8. Application for waiver of salesperson or referral agent prelicensure education requirement;

9. Application for partial waiver of broker prelicensure education requirement and/or complete waiver of experience requirements;

10. Experience report for Broker License Applicant;

11. New Jersey State Police, State Bureau of Identification Request for Criminal History Record Information Form;

12. Application for approval of real estate continuing education provider;

13. Application for approval of real estate continuing education instructor; and

14. Application for approval of real estate continuing education course.

(b) Following the receipt by the Commission of complete and accurate application forms with the required fee(s) in the correct form, the applications specified below are generally processed by the Education Bureau within the time frames indicated:

1. Applications for real estate instructor licenses, school licenses, and additional teaching location licenses—three weeks;

REAL ESTATE COMMISSION   11:5-2.6

2. Applications for a change of address of a licensed school—three weeks;

3. Applications for relicensure of schools with new directors or new owners of a controlling interest—three weeks;

4. Applications for renewal of instructor licenses, school licenses, and additional teaching location licenses—four weeks;

5. Applications for waivers of the prelicensure education requirements and/or the broker experience requirement which do not require the review of additional information—four weeks;

6. Applications for the approval of experience as a real estate salesperson to fulfill the experience requirement for licensure as a broker (see N.J.S.A. 45:15-9 and N.J.A.C. 11:5-3.8)—four weeks;

7. Applications for approval of real estate continuing education provider—three weeks after recommendation by the Voluntary Advisory Committee is considered by the Real Estate Commission;

8. Applications for approval of real estate continuing education instructor—three weeks after recommendation by the Voluntary Advisory Committee is considered by the Real Estate Commission;

9. Applications for approval of real estate continuing education course—three weeks after recommendation by the Voluntary Advisory Committee is considered by the Real Estate Commission; and

10. Applications for the issuance of a waiver of the continuing education requirement—three weeks after receipt of a complete waiver application.

11:5-2.6   Education Bureau transaction fees

The fees applicable to transactions processed by the Education Bureau of the Real Estate Commission that are unrelated to real estate continuing education are listed in the table below. Fees applicable to applications for approval of real estate continuing education providers, instructors and courses are listed in N.J.A.C. 11:5-12.17.

EDUCATION BUREAU TRANSACTION FEES	
Description	Amount
Criminal history check and electronic fingerprint scan	State-contracted vendor fee (paid directly to vendor)
Application fee, school license	$ 100.00
Application fee, instructor license	$ 50.00
Application fee, waiver of salesperson or referral agent education	$ 25.00
Initial license fee, non-public school	$ 400.00 for licenses issued in the first year of a two-year license term;
	$ 200.00 for licenses issued in the second year of a two-year term.
Renewal fee, non-public school	$ 400.00 plus $ 200.00 for each additional licensed location
License fee, additional teaching location	$ 200.00 for licenses issued in the first year of a two-year license term;
	$ 100.00 for licenses issued in the second year of a two-year term.
Change of address (school)	$ 50.00
License fee, instructor	$ 200.00 for licenses issued in the first year of a two-year license term;
	$ 100.00 for licenses issued in the second year of a two-year term.
Renewal fee, instructor	$ 100.00
Change of name (school)	$ 100.00
Change of name for individual	$ 50.00
Change of school director	$ 50.00
Application fee, waiver of salesperson education	$ 25.00
Application fee, waiver of broker education or experience	$ 25.00
Application fee, approval of experience report for broker license applicant	$ 25.00

SUBCHAPTER 3. LICENSING

11:5-3.1   Terms of real estate licenses

Commencing July 1, 1997, broker, broker-salesperson, salesperson, referral agent and branch office licenses shall be issued on the basis of two year license terms. All licenses issued during each biennial term shall run from the date of issuance to the end of the biennial term. All licenses shall expire on June 30 of the second year following the year in which the license term commenced.

11:5-3.2   Payment of fees as prescribed by statute

With the exception of fees paid to the State-contracted fingerprint scanning vendor, fees paid to the license examination administration vendor and fees paid to accomplish an online transfer or termination as set forth in N.J.A.C. 11:5-3.11, any and all fees prescribed by the Real Estate License Act shall be paid by broker's business account check, certified or bank check or money order payable to the State Treasurer of New Jersey. No cash or currency shall be accepted.

11:5-3.3   Criminal history record check

(a) The Commission shall require an individual licensee or any officer, director, partner or owner of a controlling interest of a licensed corporation or partnership to complete an electronic fingerprint scan through the State-contracted vendor, pay the fees required for its processing and submit proof of completion of the fingerprint process with their licensing application.

(b) Evidence of completion of the fingerprint scanning process shall include the applicant's copy of the completed fingerprint scanning vendor's form and a copy of the payment receipt issued by the fingerprint scanning vendor at the time of the completion of the fingerprint scanning process.

(c) The applicant, if a natural person, shall submit with his or her license application the evidence of completion of the fingerprint scanning process set forth in (b) above.

(d) The applicant, if a corporation or partnership, shall submit with its application for license evidence of completion of the fingerprint scanning process as set forth in (b) above for each officer, director, partner, or owner of a controlling interest.

11:5-3.4   Examination rules

(a) In the administration of examinations for licensure as a real estate broker, broker-salesperson, salesperson or referral agent, the following examination rules shall apply:

1. Examinees shall not be permitted to refer to any notes, books, or memoranda.

2. The copying of questions or making of notes for personal use is strictly prohibited.

3. No examinee shall leave the examining room except at the discretion of the examiner.

4. The real estate broker license, salesperson and referral agent license examinations, required by N.J.S.A. 45:15-10 to be taken and successfully passed by all applicants for a real estate broker, broker-salesperson, salesperson or referral agent license before said license may be issued, shall be in the form of a multiple choice examination prepared by a testing service as designated by the Commission. Fees charged applicants to take the real estate examinations and for fingerprinting scanning shall be considered service fees to be paid directly to the testing service and fingerprint scanning vendor separate and apart from any fee required by N.J.S.A. 45:15-9 to be paid to the Commission at the time of the license application.

(b) A request for special accommodations may be made if the applicant qualifies for such accommodations as provided in the Americans With Disabilities Act or any other applicable law. Such requests shall initially be made to the firm administering the licensing examinations. The Commission shall retain final authority to determine whether such requests shall be granted.

11:5-3.6   **Salesperson's and referral agent's licenses; age requirement**

(a) No salesperson's or referral agent's license shall be issued to any person who has not attained the age of 18 years.

(b) Every applicant for licensure as a salesperson or referral agent shall present with his or her application for licensure a certificate of satisfactory completion of a course of education in real estate subjects at a school licensed by the Commission pursuant to N.J.S.A. 45:15-10.1(a) and 10.4 and N.J.A.C. 11:5-2.2, unless waived by the Commission in accordance with the provisions of N.J.S.A. 45:15-10.2.

(c) An applicant must pass the State salesperson or referral agent examination and apply for and request the issuance of a salesperson's or referral agent's license not later than one year after the date of successful completion of the course prescribed at N.J.A.C. 11:5-2.1. Any person who fails to apply for the issuance of a salesperson's or referral agent's license within the one year period shall be required to retake and successfully complete the prescribed course in real estate and the examination.

(d) All applicants for licensure as a salesperson or referral agent shall certify that they possess a high school education or equivalency. The Commission may require the production of evidence of such education or equivalency as a condition to issuing a license to any applicant.

11:5-3.5   **Requests for disclosure of social security numbers and electronic mailing addresses**

(a) The Commission may request that licensees and license applicants, including registrants for license examinations, submit their social security numbers to the Commission. All such requests shall either include or be accompanied by a notice stating:

1. The purpose or purposes for which the Commission intends to use the social security numbers;

2. That disclosure made pursuant to the request is either voluntary or mandatory; and

3. That the request is authorized by this section and by such other law as may be applicable.

(b) Business entity and sole proprietor broker licensees ("brokers") shall establish an official e-mail address. Brokers shall provide to the Commission their current official e-mail address at the time of applying for license renewal through the on-line renewal system. Upon the establishment by the Commission of an Internet-based system for updating brokers' official e-mail addresses, brokers shall, within 30 days of being advised of the availability of that system, enter their current official e-mail address on that system. Subsequent to the implementation of the Internet-based system for updating the official e-mail addresses of brokers, the Commission shall, at its discretion, transmit all general orders, bulletins and public notices to brokers either through e-mail or regular mail.

(c) Upon making any subsequent change to their official e-mail address, the broker shall update the information on the on-line broker e-mail address notification system within 10 days of making such a change.

11:5-3.7   Employment of salesperson or referral agent sponsored by broker

(a) No broker shall knowingly sponsor an applicant for licensure as a real estate salesperson or referral agent who does not bear a good reputation for honesty and fair dealings.

(b) An application for licensure or renewal of licensure as a referral agent shall include a certification signed by the licensed real estate broker by whom the applicant is or will be employed confirming:

1. The broker and the applicant have reviewed the restrictions imposed by law upon the activities of a referral agent; and

2. The applicant or referral agent has acknowledged that he or she is aware that the activities of a referral agent are limited to referring prospective consumers of real estate brokerage services only as set forth in N.J.A.C. 11:5-6.10(a)2.

(c) Applications for licensure as a referral agent other than renewal applications shall also contain a certification signed by the applicant confirming the statements in (b)1 and 2 above.

11:5-3.8   Qualifications for licensing; broker and broker-salesperson

(a) All references in this section to "brokers" shall include broker-salespersons. The experience requirement for licensure as a broker imposed by N.J.S.A. 45:15-9 is construed to require a demonstration by the applicant of their commitment to real estate brokerage as their primary vocation, as evidenced by their involvement in the real estate brokerage business on a full-time basis.

1. A person who is presently licensed as a broker in another state and who has been actively licensed and engaged in the real estate brokerage business on a full time basis as a broker, broker-salesperson or salesperson for at least three years immediately preceding the date of application shall qualify for a waiver of the experience requirement for licensure as a New Jersey real estate broker.

2. With the exception of persons licensed as brokers in other states, all applicants for licensure as a broker must have been continuously licensed and employed on a full-time basis as a real estate salesperson during the three years immediately preceding their application. Such full-time employment shall be demonstrated by a showing that:

i. The applicant has worked as a salesperson under the authority of the broker(s) with whom they were licensed for at least 40 hours per week and during the hours of approximately 10:00 A.M. to 8:00 P.M.;

ii. Such work in (a)2i above was performed during any five days in each week of the three-year period; and

iii. If the applicant was employed in any other occupation during the three year period, such other employment was on a part-time basis and did not exceed 25 hours per calendar week.

3. No applications for approval of an applicant's experience to qualify for licensure as a broker shall be made until an applicant:

i. Has been continuously licensed as a salesperson for at least the three years immediately preceding such application;

ii. Has completed the 90-hour general broker's prelicensure course and the two 30-hour courses referred to in N.J.A.C. 11:5-2.1(g).

(b) The Commission shall give due consideration to the following in reviewing the experience of an applicant:

1. Evidence of having been actively involved in the real estate brokerage business as a real estate salesperson on a full-time basis during each year of the three year period. Written statements by the brokers with whom the applicant was licensed during the three year period which certify the applicant's activity as a salesperson while licensed through those brokers must be submitted.

2. Applicants and/or brokers may also be required to submit supporting documentation relating to the closed transactions on which the applicant received compensation as a salesperson from the broker, or to supply other evidence of full-time activity, such as extensive involvement in a specialized field of real estate brokerage.

3. In no event will an applicant whose brokerage activity was limited to solely making referrals to other licensees be deemed to have fulfilled the full-time, active involvement in the brokerage business requirement for licensure.

(c) Broker-salespersons shall meet the same qualifications as brokers, including the qualifications as set forth in (a) and (b) above. A person licensed as a broker-salesperson must be employed by and act under the supervision of a duly licensed real estate broker and shall not independently maintain an office or escrow account. A broker-salesperson may be authorized to serve as an office supervisor or a branch office in accordance with the provisions of N.J.S.A. 45:15-12.

(d) Every applicant for licensure as a broker or broker-salesperson shall present with his or her application for licensure examination a certificate of satisfactory completion of courses in real estate and related subjects at a school licensed by the Commission or offered by another approved provider pursuant to N.J.S.A. 45:15-10.1(b) and N.J.A.C. 11:5-2.1 and 2.2, unless waived by the Commission in accordance with the provisions of N.J.S.A. 45:15-10.2 and N.J.A.C. 11:5-2.1.

(e) An applicant must pass the State broker license examination and apply for and request the issuance of a license as a broker or broker-salesperson not later than one year after successful completion of the 150-hour broker prelicensure education requirements. Any person who fails to apply for the issuance of a license as a broker or broker-salesperson within the said one year time period shall be required to retake and successfully complete all prescribed courses and the examination and must submit evidence of having again fulfilled the experience requirement during the three years immediately preceding the new application.

11:5-3.9 **Return of license when broker ceases to be active; office closing; change of broker of record**

(a) Each broker who ceases to be active shall within five business days of the cessation of business return to the Commission his license, and the licenses of all salespersons, broker-salespersons and referral agents for cancellation.

(b) Each employee's license must be accompanied by a letter terminating employment in compliance with N.J.S.A. 45:15-14.

(c) No broker engaging in the real estate brokerage business as a sole proprietor, as a broker of record of a partnership or as a broker of record of a corporation shall be relicensed by the Commission unless within 30 days of the date of which the broker ceases engaging in the real estate brokerage business he or she shall complete and submit an affidavit to the Commission certifying that:

1. The broker's license, the corporate or partnership license, and the licenses of all referral agents, salespersons and broker-salespersons have been returned to the Commission for cancellation;

2. The broker's trust account has been closed and that all funds held in trust for others have been disbursed to proper parties;

3. All commissions and other compensation owed to salespersons, referral agents and broker-salespersons have been paid, or, if not yet received by the broker, will be paid upon receipt;

4. No further commissions are due the broker except that any commissions for services previously rendered and payable in the future upon the occurrence of specified events are described on a list attached to the affidavit. The list shall describe the nature and amounts of such outstanding commissions with sufficient information to identify each transaction;

5. The broker has notified all principals in ongoing transactions, in writing, that the broker has ceased engaging in the real

estate brokerage business or that the broker will hereinafter engage in the real estate brokerage business in another capacity. The notice shall describe the disposition of pending transactions and the name of custodian and place of deposit of any funds received from principals;

6. The broker has removed from the licensed premises all signs indicating that the premises contains the office of a licensed real estate broker;

7. The broker has recalled all signs and other advertisements or trade materials indicating that the broker is engaged in the real estate brokerage business;

8. The broker has advised the appropriate telephone services that the firm is no longer engaged in the real estate brokerage business, and that further telephone directories should not contain the name of the individual or firm as licensed brokers;

9. There are no outstanding fines or penalties due and owing the Real Estate Commission;

10. The broker acknowledges his or her responsibility to maintain records as required in N.J.A.C. 11:5-5.4. The broker must provide the address of the place of depository of such records and acknowledge responsibility to advise the Commission of any change in the name of the custodian or place of depository for a period of six years.

(d) When a new broker of record of a corporation or partnership is being substituted for the existing broker of record, the existing broker of record satisfies the certification requirements of (c) above when in compliance with the substitution procedures of (e) below.

(e) No new broker of record of a corporation or partnership shall be substituted unless the new broker of record and the former broker of record prepare and submit a joint affidavit to the Commission certifying that:

1. Custody of all funds held in trust for principals has been assumed by the new broker of record;

2. The new broker of record has reviewed all pending transactions and is satisfied that all funds held in trust have been accounted for;

3. All salespersons', broker-salespersons' and referral agents' commissions and other compensation are paid to date;

4. The new broker acknowledges responsibility to pay salespersons', broker-salespersons' and referral agents' commissions in accordance with the policy for payment existing on the date of substitution;

5. No fines are presently owed to the Real Estate Commission, and if any fines are assessed after the date of substitution for actions occurring prior to substitution, both the former broker and new broker are jointly and severally responsible for payment;

6. All signs and advertisements have been changed to reflect the broker now authorized to transact business in the name of the firm;

7. All records required to be maintained pursuant to N.J.A.C. 11:5-5.4 have been turned over to the new broker, and the new broker acknowledges responsibility to maintain such records for a period of six years;

8. The new broker acknowledges that he or she will be responsible to transact business in the name and on behalf of the firm.

11:5-3.10   Sponsoring of license applications or transfers of license

(a) The New Jersey Real Estate Commission, Department of Banking and Insurance, hereby grants to brokers of record or employing brokers the right to have initial applications for licenses of referral agents, salespersons or broker-salespersons who will be in their employ authorized by one other person, other than the broker of record or employing broker. This other person must be the holder of a broker's license and an officer of the broker of record's corporation or a member of his or her partnership, as the case may be. In the event the employing broker is a sole proprietor, such a designee shall be licensed as a broker-salesperson in the employ of the employing broker. The broker of record or employing broker, as applicable, shall file with the New Jersey Real Estate Commission a power of attorney granting this authority to the designated person at least 10 days prior to delegating performance of the function of that person.

REAL ESTATE COMMISSION

(b) Any employing broker or broker of record may authorize one individual in their employ to sign and surrender to the Real Estate Commission, in accordance with the requirements of N.J.S.A. 45:15-14, the real estate referral agent, salesperson or broker-salesperson license of any licensee whose employment relationship with that employing broker or broker of record is terminated. The employing broker or broker of record shall, on a form to be provided by the Commission, notify the Commission in writing of the designation of the employee so authorized, which person need not be the holder of a real estate license. The form designating the authorized person shall be filed with the Real Estate Commission at least 10 days prior to delegating performance of the function of that person. The employing broker or broker of record shall immediately notify the Real Estate Commission in writing in the event that, for any reason, the authority of the person so designated to perform that function is revoked, and shall indicate whether a new designee is to be named. Only the employing broker or broker of record and one other person duly designated and identified to the Real Estate Commission as provided in this section may perform the said license transfer functions at any one time.

11:5-3.11   License transfer and termination procedures

(a) For the purpose of expediting the right of licensees to engage in real estate activities, where license certificates cannot be issued without delay after all conditions have been fulfilled, the Commission directs that a certificate of authority in the form of a letter to the licensee be sent to serve as a temporary license for a limited period of time.

(b) In cases where a licensee who is transferring from one broker to another requests that their current broker deliver their license to them, rather than return it to the Commission, so as to personally facilitate the transfer process, the license shall be so delivered, provided that:

1. The rear of the license certificate is signed and dated by the terminating broker in the appropriate location prior to the delivery of the license to the departing licensee;

2. At the time of the delivery of the license to the departing licensee, the termination confirmation section of the license, reflecting the effective date of the licensee's separation from that broker, has been completed, signed and retained by the terminating broker; and

3. Within five business days of the delivery of the license to the departing licensee, the terminating broker shall either:

i. Mail to the Commission the completed and signed termination confirmation section of the license and send a copy of it to the departing licensee at their last known residence address; or

ii. Process the termination online at http://www.state.nj.us/dobi and send a copy of the completed and signed termination confirmation section of the license to the departing licensee at their last known residence address.

(c) A transferring licensee who receives their license from the terminating broker after that broker has signed the license and entered the date of termination on it may then take that license to their new employing broker. Prior to the transferring person commencing work as a licensee for the new employing broker, that broker shall:

1. Enter on the license in the appropriate location the effective date of the individual's employment with that broker and sign the license as the new employing broker;

2. Detach the temporary license stub portion from the main license document and place it with the licenses of the other persons licensed with that broker; and

3. Either mail to the Commission the dated and signed license of the transferring individual with the required transfer fee (see N.J.S.A. 45:15-14) in the form of a certified or cashier's check or money order or broker's business account check (See N.J.A.C. 11:5-3.2) or process the transfer online at http://www.state.nj.us/dobi and pay the required transfer fee in the form of an electronic check or credit card and retain the paper license signed by the broker, with the effective date of the transferring individual's employment with their firm entered thereon, as a business record as set forth in (f) below.

(d) In cases where a broker terminates the employment of a broker-salesperson, salesperson or referral agent with his or her firm or where a broker-salesperson, salesperson or referral agent resigns such employment, written notice specifying the effective date of the termination or resignation shall be provided by the terminating broker or by the resigning licensee, as applicable. Within five business days of the broker's issuance of a notice of termination or receipt of a resignation, if the licensee has not requested the delivery of the license to them so as to personally

11:5-3.12   **INSURANCE**

facilitate a transfer of their license to another broker, the broker shall either:

1. Deliver or mail to the Commission the licensee's license; or

2. Process the termination online at http://www.state.nj.us/dobi; and

3. Regardless of whether the procedure in (d)1 or 2 above is utilized, contemporaneously send to the licensee at their last known residence address written notice of the license having been returned to the Commission or of the termination of the licensee's employment with the broker having been processed online.

(e) The following regulations pertain to online transfers and terminations:

1. Only referral agent, salesperson or broker-salesperson licenses can be transferred or terminated online;

2. All terminations and transfers shall be completed by an active broker of record or an active employing broker;

3. A broker of record or employing broker shall not process an online termination or transfer on their own license; and

4. Online transfers are not allowed unless the license of a referral agent, salesperson or broker-salesperson has been terminated by the broker of record or employing broker under whose supervision the transferring individual was licensed to engage in brokerage activity prior to the termination.

(f) Brokers who terminate licensees or accomplish the transfer of licensees to their firms as set forth in this section shall maintain records of such terminations and transfers for six years.

11:5-3.12   License applications processed by the Real Estate Section of the Department of Banking and Insurance Licensing Services Bureau

(a) Applications for the following license types are processed by the Department of Banking and Insurance Licensing Services Bureau, Real Estate Section:

1. Real Estate Salesperson;

2. Real Estate Referral Agent;

3. Real Estate Broker—Salesperson;

4. Real Estate Broker—Sole Proprietor;

5. Real Estate Broker—Business entity;

6. Real Estate Broker—Broker of Record of a licensed business entity; and

7. Branch office.

11:5-3.13   Licensing Services Bureau, Real Estate Section forms, instructions, processing times, deadlines

(a) The following forms are utilized by the Real Estate Section of the Department of Banking and Insurance Licensing Services Bureau:

1. Original salesperson or referral agent license application;

2. Original broker/broker-salesperson application;

3. Name change (by license or application);

4. Broker status change;

5. Referral agent, salesperson or broker-salesperson transfer of license (on rear of license document);

6. Broker's Authorized Designee or Power of Attorney;

7. Change of business address;

8. Application for broker license for business entity (includes application for broker of record license);

9. Application for sole proprietor broker license;

10. Application for reactivation within current license term or for reinstatement of referral agent or salesperson license;

11. Application for reactivation within current license term or for reinstatement of broker-salesperson license;

12. Office Closing affidavit;

13. Application for branch office license;

14. Change of branch office supervisor;

15. Initial Application for Renewal of Broker License and of all related licenses;

16. First Supplemental Renewal Application (lists licensees who became licensed with the broker between the date on which the Initial Renewal Application form was generated and the date on which the First Supplemental Renewal Application form was generated);

17. Second Supplemental Renewal Application (lists licensees who became licensed with the broker between the date on which the First Supplemental Renewal Application form was generated and the expiration date of the license term in which the renewal forms are generated);

18. Change of corporate representative and multiple license;

19. Change of broker of record;

20. Change of corporate title;

21. Corporate license and multiple broker license;

22. Reinstatement of business entity broker license;

23. Reinstatement of sole proprietor broker license;

24. Additional broker of record license to sole proprietor broker;

25. Change of tradename or new tradename;

26. Multiple broker of record license;

27. Temporary broker's license;

28. Change of Broker of Record Affidavit;

29. Individual irrevocable consent to service of process;

30. Corporate irrevocable consent to service of process;

31. Partnership/LLC/other irrevocable consent to service of process;

32. The form to request fingerprint scan processing utilized by the State-contracted fingerprint scanning vendor; and

33. Change of license type.

(b) In addition to the instructions that are contained on the forms themselves, separate instructions for the licensing forms related to broker licenses and branch offices are available from the Licensing Services Bureau, Real Estate Section.

(c) License applications are normally processed within 15 business days from the date a complete and accurate application with all required fees in the correct form is received. Processing times during the biennial renewal of licenses may vary. License certifications are normally processed within 15 business days from receipt of the written request and correct fee.

(d) Deadlines for the submission of license applications and other required forms are as follows:

1. Original salesperson, referral agent, broker-salesperson or broker: one year from date on which prelicensure course and education requirements were completed (see N.J.A.C. 11:5-3.6(c) for salespersons and referral agents and 11:5-3.8(e) for brokers and broker-salespersons);

2. Applications for the reinstatement of a salesperson, referral agent, broker-salesperson or brokers license: two years from the expiration date of the last license held unless exempted as provided in N.J.S.A. 45:15-9;

3. Brokerage firm office closing affidavit: within 30 business days from date of closing (see N.J.A.C. 11:5-3.9(c));

4. Brokerage firm change of address: prior to or immediately upon move to new address (see N.J.S.A. 45:15-12 and 45:15-13);

5. Temporary broker license: within 30 business days from date of death or of incapacity of sole proprietor broker or broker of record (see N.J.S.A. 45:15-11.3); and

6. License renewals:

i. Initial renewal application: by June 30 of the year in which the license is due to expire (see N.J.A.C. 11:5-3.1);

ii. First supplemental renewal application: 45 days from date application issued; and

iii. Second supplemental renewal application: 30 days from date application issued.

(e) Late fees are assessed for license renewals postmarked and received by the Commission after the deadlines referenced in (d)6 above. Those fees are set forth in N.J.A.C. 11:5-3.14.

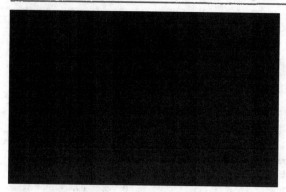

11:5-3.14   Licensing fees

The fees applicable to transactions processed by the Department of Banking and Insurance Licensing Services Bureau, Real Estate Section are listed in the table below. Renewal fees are assessed biennially for the renewal of licenses for a two-year term pursuant to N.J.S.A. 45:15-15. All other fees are payable in full regardless of when during a license term the application to which the fee pertains is submitted.

LICENSE FEES

Initial License Fees (amounts include $ 50.00 application fee and, where applicable, Real Estate Guaranty Fund fees of $ 10.00 for salespersons and referral agents and $ 20.00 for brokers and broker-salespersons. See N.J.S.A. 45:15-35. Amounts do not include the processing fee for fingerprint scanning payable directly to the State-contracted vendor):

License	Fee
Corporations, partnerships and other business entities	$ 270.00
Broker of record	$ 270.00
Sole proprietor broker	$ 270.00
Broker-salesperson	$ 270.00
Salesperson	$ 160.00
Referral agents	$ 160.00
Branch office	$ 150.00
Temporary broker license	$ 300.00

Renewal Fees:

License	Fee
Corporations, partnerships and other business entities	$ 200.00
Broker of record	$ 200.00
Sole proprietor broker	$ 200.00
Broker-salesperson	$ 200.00
Salesperson	$ 100.00
Referral agents	$ 100.00
Branch office	$ 100.00

Late Renewal Fees:

License	Fee
Corporations, partnerships and other business entities	$ 40.00
Broker	$ 40.00
Broker-salesperson	$ 20.00
Salesperson	$ 20.00
Referral agents	$ 20.00

Transfers:

License	Fee
Broker-salesperson	$ 25.00
Salesperson	$ 25.00
Referral agents	$ 25.00

Reinstatements of unrenewed licenses (amounts include $ 50.00 application fee):

License	Fee
Corporations, partnerships and other business entities	$ 250.00
Broker of record	$ 250.00
Sole proprietor broker	$ 250.00
Broker-salesperson	$ 250.00
Salesperson	$ 150.00
Referral agent	$ 150.00
Branch office	$ 150.00

Changes:

Type	Fee
Name change	$ 50.00
Change of business address: sole proprietor brokers and corporations, partnerships or other business entities (plus $ 10.00 for each individual licensee)	$ 50.00
Change of status—sole proprietor, broker, broker of record, broker-salesperson, salesperson or referral agent	$ 50.00
Change of branch office supervisor	$ 50.00

11:5-3.15   Change of status from referral agent to salesperson or broker-salesperson

(a) A licensed referral agent who was not previously licensed as a broker, broker-salesperson or salesperson and who has been licensed as a referral agent for less than one year shall be eligible for licensure as a salesperson without being required to complete any continuing education.

(b) A licensed referral agent who was not previously licensed as a broker, broker-salesperson or salesperson and who has been licensed as a referral agent for between one and six years immediately preceding making application for a change of status to that of a licensed salesperson shall, in order to qualify for licensure as a salesperson, complete 24 hours of continuing education, all of which shall be in core topics as set forth in N.J.A.C. 11:5-12.4. The 24 hours of continuing education shall be completed within the two years immediately preceding application for licensure as a salesperson.

(c) A licensed referral agent who was not previously licensed as a broker, broker-salesperson of salesperson and who has been licensed as a referral agent for more than the six immediately preceding years shall, in order to qualify for licensure as a salesperson, be required to complete the prelicensure education requirement applicable to salespersons and to pass the State license examination for salespersons.

(d) A licensed referral agent who was previously licensed as a broker, broker-salesperson or salesperson who has been licensed as a referral agent for the six immediately preceding years or any lesser period shall, in order to qualify for reissuance of a broker, broker-salesperson or salesperson license, complete the hours of continuing education as set forth below:

1. To qualify for relicensure as a salesperson, a person who has been licensed as a referral agent for less than three years shall complete 12 hours of continuing education, all of which shall be in core topics as set forth in N.J.A.C. 11:5-12.4 within the two years immediately preceding application.

2. To qualify for relicensure as a salesperson, a person who has been licensed as a referral agent three years or more, but less than six years, shall complete 18 hours of continuing education, all of which shall be in core topics as set forth in N.J.A.C. 11:5-12.4 within the two years immediately preceding application.

3. To qualify for relicensure as a broker or broker-salesperson, a person who has been licensed as a referral agent for less than three years shall complete 18 hours of continuing education within two years immediately preceding application, all of which shall be in core topics as set forth in N.J.A.C. 11:5-12.4.

4. To qualify for relicensure as a broker or broker-salesperson, a person who has been licensed as a referral agent for three years or more, but less than six years, shall complete 24 hours of continuing education within the two years immediately preceding application, all of which shall be in core topics as set forth in N.J.A.C. 11:5-12.4.

(e) A licensed referral agent who was previously licensed as a broker, broker-salesperson or salesperson who has been licensed as a referral agent for more than the six immediately preceding years shall, in order to qualify for re-licensure as a broker, broker-salesperson or salesperson, complete 30 hours of continuing education, 24 hours of which shall be in core topics as set forth in N.J.A.C. 11:5-12.4, and shall pass the broker's license examination or the salesperson's license examination, as applicable.

SUBCHAPTER 4. EMPLOYMENT PRACTICES/OFFICE AND LICENSEE SUPERVISION

11:5-4.1   Licensee business relationship agreements; commissions; accounting to salespersons and referral agents; actions for collection of compensation

(a) Prior to a salesperson or referral agent engaging in any real estate brokerage activity, a broker and the salesperson or referral agent must enter into and sign a written agreement that contains the terms of their business relationship. Such agreement shall contain terms including, but not limited to, the following:

1. The rate of compensation to be paid to the salesperson or referral agent during his or her affiliation with the broker;

2. A promise by the broker to pay to the salesperson or referral agent his or her portion of commissions earned within 10 business days of their receipt by the broker or as soon thereafter as such funds have cleared the broker's bank, or in accordance with another payment schedule explicitly set forth in the written agreement;

3. The rate of compensation payable to the salesperson or referral agent on transactions which close and, if applicable, on renewals which occur subsequent to the termination of the salesperson's or referral agent's affiliation with the broker; and

4. A provision that any future changes to the agreement will not be binding unless the changes are contained in a writing signed by both parties.

(b) A copy of the fully executed agreement shall be provided to the salesperson or referral agent upon the commencement of his or her affiliation with the broker, and the original thereof shall be maintained by the broker as a business record in accordance with N.J.A.C. 11:5-5.5.

(c) All compensation paid to brokers shall, unless debited from funds held in escrow in accordance with N.J.A.C. 11:5-5.1(d), be deposited into the general business account of the broker within five business days of their receipt by the broker.

(d) If any monies due a salesperson or referral agent under the terms of the written agreement with their broker are not paid within 10 business days of the broker's receipt of such funds or promptly thereafter upon their having cleared the broker's account, the broker shall provide to the salesperson or referral agent a complete written explanation of the failure to pay such monies.

(e) Within 30 days of the termination of the affiliation of a salesperson or referral agent with a broker, the broker shall provide a complete written accounting of all monies due the salesperson or referral agent as of the date of termination and/or which may become due in the future. If any sums so accounted for are not in accord with the terms of the post-termination compensation clause in the written agreement between the broker and the salesperson or referral agent, the broker shall give a complete written explanation of any difference to the salesperson or referral agent with the accounting.

(f) A broker must maintain copies of the following documents and proof of delivery of the document to the salesperson or referral agent for six years: agreements as described in (a) above; explanations of the failure to pay compensation due a salesperson or referral agent on a timely basis as described in (d) above; and accountings and explanations regarding compensation due a salesperson or referral agent subsequent to the termination of their affiliation with a broker as described in (e) above.

(g) If the Commission confirms that a broker has complied with the requirements imposed by this section, the Commission will not further investigate a complaint alleging the non-payment of a commission by a broker to a salesperson or referral agent unless such complaint is accompanied by a copy of an arbitration decision or the equivalent, or a copy of a judgment of a court of competent jurisdiction secured by the salesperson or referral agent against the broker. Unless appealed, the failure by a broker to pay monies awarded to a salesperson or referral agent under the terms of any such decision or judgment within 30 days of its effective date shall subject the broker to sanctions pursuant to N.J.S.A. 45:15-17.

(h) Broker, salesperson and referral agent licensees may only bring or maintain actions in the courts of New Jersey for the payment of compensation due them for brokerage services performed as provided in N.J.S.A. 45:15-3.

1. The Commission interprets the language "at the time the alleged cause of action arose" as used in N.J.S.A. 45:15-3 to mean at the time that the brokerage services which form the basis for the alleged claim to compensation were rendered. For example, at the time when a property was listed for sale or rental by a licensee.

2. The Commission does not interpret the language "at the time the alleged cause or action arose" as requiring that the licensee must have been actively licensed at the time that the compensation allegedly due was to have been paid. For example, the Commission does not construe this language as requiring licensure at the time of the renewal of a lease to enable a claimant to sue for compensation based upon a promise, made or in effect when the lease was originally executed, to pay additional consideration to the claimant in the event that the lease was renewed.

(i) All references to "salesperson" in this section include individuals licensed as broker-salespersons. All references to "non-payment of a commission" in this section shall be construed to include the non-payment of other forms of compensation.

(j) The Commission interprets "employment agreement," "employ," and "employing broker" in N.J.S.A. 45:15-1 et seq., and this section to permit an employment relationship or an independent contractor relationship between a broker and a broker-salesperson, salesperson, or referral agent.

REAL ESTATE COMMISSION 11:5-4.3

11:5-4.2 Broker supervision and oversight of individual licensees, office operations and escrowed monies

(a) The following apply to individual broker licensees operating as sole proprietors (employing brokers) or as the authorized broker (broker of record) of a corporation or other entity licensed as a New Jersey real estate broker. As used in this section, the term "individual broker" shall refer to employing brokers and brokers of record and the term "broker licensee" shall refer to sole proprietors and corporations or other entities licensed as brokers.

1. The Commission will hold responsible individual brokers for any actions of the broker licensee or any person employed by or licensed through the broker licensee taken in the pursuit of its real estate brokerage business which violate any of the provisions of the real estate license law, N.J.S.A. 45:15-1 et seq., or the regulations promulgated thereunder.

i. This responsibility shall apply regardless of where the persons licensed through the broker licensee engage in actions in pursuit of the broker licensee's real estate brokerage business.

2. Every real estate transaction in which a broker licensee participates as a broker shall be under the ultimate supervision of the individual broker.

3. The individual broker shall, in addition to ascertaining that a separate account is maintained for the funds of others coming into the possession of the broker licensee, make certain that no such funds of others are disbursed or utilized without his or her express authorization and knowledge.

4. The provisions of this subsection do not apply to brokers licensed as broker-salespersons.

11:5-4.3 Use of license for the benefit of others

(a) No arrangement, direct or indirect, shall be entered into by any licensee whereby an individual licensee lends his name or license for the benefit of another person, firm or corporation, or whereby the provisions of the real estate statute and rules relating to licensing are circumvented.

(b) Lending a broker's license for the benefit of another person, firm or corporation shall be construed as including any arrangement whereby a broker fails to personally oversee and direct the operations of the business of which he or she is licensed as broker of record or employing broker. For the purposes of this section, personal oversight and direction of the business shall be construed as requiring the broker to be physically present in the main office or branch office locations of the business at least one day each week (excluding vacations and emergencies). Communication via telephone and/or mail alone for an extended period of time may be considered by the Commission as evidence of prohibited license lending.

(c) Nothing in this section shall be construed to limit a broker's responsibility to insure the adequate supervision of all offices in accordance with the requirements of N.J.A.C. 11:5-4.4 and 4.5.

11:5-4.4   Maintained offices

(a) Every resident real estate broker not licensed as a broker-salesperson shall maintain a main office for the transaction of business in the State of New Jersey, which shall be open to the public during usual business hours. This main office and the activities of the licensees working from it shall be under the direct supervision of either the broker himself or herself, or of a person licensed as a broker-salesperson. Such supervision shall be maintained on a full time basis. Maintaining full-time supervision shall not be construed as requiring the person performing the supervisory functions to be present at the office location continuously during usual business hours. However, the person performing the supervisory functions shall provide sufficient information so as to allow the personnel at the main office to make communication with that person at all times. Further, the licensee supervising the main office shall be so employed on a full-time basis and, when not required to be away from the office for reasons related to the business of the office, shall be physically present at that office during usual business hours at least five days per calendar week (excluding vacations and emergencies) and shall not be otherwise employed during such time.

1. In the event the main office of a broker is under the direct supervision of a broker-salesperson, the broker who maintains such a main office shall be ultimately responsible for all activities conducted by licensees and employees. Such a broker shall also provide sufficient information to the personnel at such offices so as to allow them to make communication with such broker at all times. Nothing in this section shall be construed to limit a broker's responsibility to comply with the requirements of N.J.A.C. 11:5-4.3.

(b) If such office is located in a residence, it shall be independent of living quarters and shall have a separate exterior entrance plainly visible from the street upon which the licensed premises shall have frontage. This subsection shall not apply to offices in existence prior to December 1, 1963.

(c) No broker's maintained place or places of business shall be in the dwelling premises of any salesperson or referral agent in that broker's employ.

(d) Sole proprietor employing brokers and persons licensed as a broker of record for a licensed entity are responsible to supervise, track and oversee the brokerage activity of persons licensed under their authority regardless of where such activity takes place.

11:5-4.5   Branch office compliance with N.J.A.C. 11:5-4.4 (Maintained offices)

(a) In the event a real estate broker maintains a branch office or offices, every such place of business shall comply with the provisions of N.J.A.C. 11:5-4.4 (Maintained offices).

(b) No license shall be issued for a branch office situated in the dwelling premises of a referral agent, a salesperson or a broker-salesperson.

(c) Any branch office shall be under the direct supervision of a licensed broker employed as a broker salesperson by the broker maintaining the branch office.

(d) Such individual shall devote his or her full time to management of said office during the usual business hours.

(e) The name of the individual responsible for the supervision of the branch office shall be recorded at all times with the Commission.

(f) When a branch office license is issued to a broker it shall specifically set forth the name of the broker and the address of the branch office, and shall be conspicuously displayed at all times in the branch office. The branch office shall also prominently display the name of the broker-salesperson licensee in charge as "office supervisor" and the names of all other licensees doing business at that branch office.

(g) The said branch office license shall be returned for cancellation or correction upon the change of an "office supervisor".

SUBCHAPTER 5. TRUST ACCOUNTS/RECORDS OF BROKERAGE ACTIVITY

11:5-5.1   Special accounts for funds of others; commingling

(a) Every resident real estate broker shall establish and maintain, in an authorized financial institution in New Jersey, and every reciprocally licensed Real Estate broker shall establish and maintain in an authorized financial institution in New Jersey or the State wherein he has a resident real estate broker's license, a special account or special accounts, separate and apart from other business or personal accounts, for the deposit of all moneys or others received by the broker acting in said capacity, or as escrow agent, or as temporary custodian, in a real estate transaction.

(b) Every real estate broker shall file with the broker's application for licensure or license renewal an affidavit or certificate setting forth the name or names of the financial institution or institutions where said special account or accounts have been established and shall identify any and all account numbers. Any change in an existing account or the establishment of any new account shall be immediately reported to the Real Estate Commission in the form of an affidavit or certification.

(c) In construing N.J.S.A. 45:15-17(o), the following shall be considered to constitute commingling by a licensee:

1. Mingling the money of his principals with his own;

2. Failure to maintain and deposit promptly in a special account in an authorized financial institution, separate and apart from personal or other business accounts, all moneys received

by a real estate broker acting in said capacity, or as escrow agent, or as the temporary custodian of the funds of others in a real estate transaction; or

3. Failure to promptly segregate any moneys received which are to be held for the benefit of others.

(d) Where the nature of a given real estate transaction is such that the commissions earned by a broker in connection with services rendered in said transaction are included among the funds deposited to the broker's trust account, the portion of such funds deposited to the broker's trust account which constitute the broker's commission shall be promptly paid from the trust account, with appropriate annotations to the broker's business records to indicate the amount and source of such commissions; provided, however, that such broker shall have been previously authorized to make such disbursement.

(e) Within the meaning of this section, the word "promptly" means not more than five business days next following the receipt of the money or property of another. However, where monies are received by a licensee as provided in (c)2 above as a good faith or earnest money deposit accompanying an offer to buy or lease property, if during the five business day period next following the date of the licensee's receipt of those funds the offer is withdrawn prior to acceptance by the offeree or is rejected with no counteroffer made by the offeree, the licensee need not deposit those funds into an escrow or trust account but may, upon the request of the offerer, return them in the same form in which they were received to the offerer. In all other cases, the licensee must deposit such monies within five business days of receipt. Examples of such cases include transactions where negotiations are ongoing, or if a contract or lease is being reviewed by an attorney, or if subsequently to the rejection of an offer the offerer has requested the licensee to retain the monies in the event that the offerer determines to submit another offer on the same or a different property.

(f) The maintenance of clearly nominal amounts of the licensee's funds in trust accounts solely to provide continuity in such account or to meet bank service charges shall not be construed to be commingling.

(g) Where any law or governmental regulation compels maintenance of a fixed amount of the funds of a licensee is a trust account for the purpose of providing a safety factor, the maintenance of such fixed amount shall not be construed to be commingling.

(h) Every person licensed as a broker of record or as a sole proprietor broker shall be a signatory on the escrow or trust account(s) of their brokerage firm. Only individuals who are actively licensed by the Commission as a real estate broker-salesperson or salesperson may be additional signatories on escrow or trust accounts.

(i) Brokers may accept payments to be held in trust or in escrow, or as the temporary custodian of the funds of others in any real estate transaction, in the following forms: cash; a negotiable instrument payable to the broker's firm; a charge against a check debit card resulting in a credit to the broker's trust or escrow account; or a wire transfer of funds directly from an account of the payor to the trust or escrow account of the broker. As provided in this subsection, brokers may also accept deposit and rent payments to be held by them in trust or in escrow or as a temporary custodian in the form of charges made upon the credit cards of tenants in short term rental transactions.

1. All payments to be held by a broker in trust or in escrow, or as the temporary custodian of monies in a real estate transaction, made in the form of cash, negotiable instruments, wire transfers or by charges made upon credit cards or check debit cards shall be recorded in the broker's trust or escrow account ledger and as otherwise required by N.J.A.C. 11:5-5.4.

2. Brokers shall not accept payments made through credit card charges in any real estate transaction other than a short term rental. For the purposes of this subsection, a "short term rental" is a rental of a residential property for not more than 125 consecutive days with a specific termination date.

3. Brokers who accept payments in the form of credit card charges in short term rentals shall cause those payments to be credited to a special trust or escrow account, distinct from the escrow or trust account(s) maintained by the broker for other purposes. Brokers who accept such payments shall also maintain a business account, separate and apart from all trust or escrow accounts including the account to which the credit card charges shall be credited. The said business account may be the same business account maintained by the broker for general purposes.

4. Before accepting any payment in the form of a credit card charge on a short term rental, a broker shall inform the owner in writing of the potential for such payments to be "charged-back" by the tenant and obtain written authorization signed by the owner for the broker to accept such payments.

i. For the purposes of this subsection, "charged-back" means the recrediting of a previously charged payment to the account of a cardholder through the electronic debiting of an account of the broker.

ii. Where an owner's written authorization is secured by the listing broker, it shall be made a part of or an addendum to a listing agreement.

iii. In all cases, the owner's written authorization shall be retained by the broker to whom it was given as a business record in accordance with N.J.A.C. 11:5-5.4.

5. In the event that a dispute concerning a charged-back payment arises between a broker and a consumer, under no circumstances may the broker apply or set-off against the disputed amount any monies paid to the broker on another transaction in which the same consumer is a party.

6. Brokers who accept credit card charges in payment of deposits or rent on short term rentals shall formulate a written statement of their policy on credit card payment cancellations. All such cancellation policies shall include:

i. An indication of the time period during which the cardholder may cancel the charged payment made to the broker; and

ii. A statement that, in the event a cancellation request is not received by the broker within the specified cancellation time period, the request will not be honored and the disposition of the monies credited to the broker will be governed by the terms of the lease or rental agreement between the landlord and the cardholder.

7. In no event shall the cancellation period terminate prior to the delivery to the cardholder of a fully executed written lease containing the final terms of the rental agreement, or the full acceptance by the parties of the final terms of a verbal rental agreement.

8. Brokers shall provide copies of the written cancellation policy in the following manner:

i. To property owners upon the earlier of the broker obtaining a listing on the rental property or presenting an offer to rent the property; and

ii. To prospective tenants at the time of first accepting a payment in the form of a credit card charge. In the event that the same tenant makes subsequent payments on the same rental transaction through charges against a credit card, the broker accepting such payments shall not be required to provide additional copies of the written cancellation policy.

9. Except as otherwise provided in (j) below, brokers who accept payments in the form of credit card charges shall comply with all restrictions and requirements imposed by N.J.S.A. 45:15-17(o) and this section with regard to the deposit and maintenance of such funds.

(j) In all cases, the amount credited to a broker's special escrow or trust account as a result of a charged payment on a short term rental transaction shall be the full amount of the payment made by the tenant to the broker. All transaction fees payable by the broker to the company which issued the credit card shall not be paid before the full amount of the charged payment is credited to the broker's special escrow or trust account. Brokers who accept payments through charges on credit cards shall also comply with one of the procedures specified in (j)1 and 2 below.

1. A business account of the broker shall be designated in the contract between the broker and any company whose credit card charges the broker shall accept as the sole source of funds for the payment by the broker of all credit card transaction fees due to the company, and the sole source of funds for all charge-backs which may be assessed against the broker by the company; or

2. The broker shall maintain a reserve amount of the broker's funds in the special escrow or trust account to which charged payments will be credited. The said reserve shall be sufficient to cover all transaction fees incurred by the broker on charged transactions and all estimated charge-backs of payments by cardholders. The maintenance of such reserve funds in the said special escrow or trust account shall not be construed as commingling. In all cases where brokers utilize this procedure:

i. Transaction fees debited from the said reserve amount shall be replenished by the broker on at least a monthly basis;

ii. In the event that a broker is notified that a charge-back has occurred after some or all of the funds received through the charged-back payment have been disbursed, the broker shall, within one business day of receipt of such notice, replenish the reserve funds in the special escrow or trust account in an amount equal to the amount debited from the reserve through the charge-back; and

iii. Brokers may replenish or increase the said reserve amount as often as necessary. Brokers may only reduce the said reserve amount on an annual basis. All credits to and debits from the special escrow or trust account made by the broker to replenish, increase or decrease the reserve amount shall be duly noted in the business records of the broker and maintained as such as required by N.J.A.C. 11:5-5.4.

11:5-5.2   Funds of others; safeguards

(a) No licensee shall accept funds or deposits from a prospective purchaser without ascertaining that there have been established by escrow, or otherwise, adequate precautions to safeguard such funds or deposits where the licensee knows, or conditions are such as to palpably give him reason to know, any facts which would tend to reasonably create a doubt:

1. As to the ability of the seller to perform his contractual obligations; or

2. As to the ability of the seller to return such funds or deposits in the event of the failure of a contingency contained in a real estate contract.

(b) The provisions of subsection (a) shall not apply to a licensee who, before accepting such funds or deposits, has adequately informed the prospective purchaser of any risk entailed and has secured from him a separate signed writing in which the purchaser has acknowledged:

1. His awareness of any risk or contingency;

2. The disposition of his funds or deposits; and

3. The absence of any representations by the licensee as to the solvency of the seller and his ability to return such funds.

(c) Funds or deposits placed in escrow pursuant to this regulation may be held by any person or entity legally authorized to hold funds in that capacity, such as, but not limited to, the real estate broker himself, lawyers or banks.

11:5-5.3   Advance fees; accounting

(a) Any broker who charges or collects an advance fee in excess of $ 25.00 for services to be rendered, such as, but not limited to advertising costs, under an advance fee agreement, shall within 90 days after such charge or collection furnish his principal with an accounting as to the use of such moneys.

(b) Such accounting shall set forth the actual amount of each individual expenditure, including date of insertion and name of newspaper or periodical, and similarly detail any other type of promotional expenditure if the funds are spent for other than newspaper or periodical advertising.

11:5-5.4   Records to be maintained by broker

(a) Every broker shall keep records as prescribed herein of all funds of others received by him or her for not less than six years from the date of receipt of any such funds. All such funds shall be deposited by the broker in accordance with the requirements of N.J.A.C. 11:5-5.1.

1. Whenever a broker receives funds to be held in trust in cash, a written receipt signed by the licensee to whom the funds were paid and specifying the date, amount, purpose and from whom those funds were received shall be issued to the payor of the funds. A copy of that receipt shall be retained by the broker as prescribed in this section.

(b) The records required to be kept pursuant to (a) above shall include:

1. Written references on the checkbook stubs or checkbook ledger pages to all deposits into and withdrawals from the account(s) maintained by the broker in accordance with N.J.A.C. 11:5-5.1, which shall specifically identify the date, amount and payor of each item deposited, the property to which the monies pertain and the reason for their being held by the broker. Such records shall also specify the date, amount, payee and purpose of each disbursement. All trust or escrow account withdrawals shall be only by authorized intrastate or interstate bank transfer or by check payable to a named payee and not to cash;

2. In appropriate ledger book for all trustee accounts or escrow accounts showing, in one location in that ledger book for each separate trust transaction, the payor of all funds deposited in such accounts, the date of deposit, the names of all persons for whom the funds are or were held, the amount of such funds, the amounts and dates of all disbursements of such moneys, and the names of all persons to whom such funds were disbursed. The Commission will not deem a regular checkbook ledger as sufficient to constitute an appropriate ledger book. Such a ledger book may be maintained in a computer or similar device, so long as it is capable of reproducing the electronically stored data on paper so as to depict the complete history of all activity in each separate trust transaction, and the data can be maintained in an easily accessible form for the required six year period. A regular running balance of the individual transaction ledger sheets shall be maintained. The total of the running balance must agree with the control figure computed by taking the beginning balance, adding the total of moneys received in trust on that transaction, and deducting the total of all moneys disbursed;

i. Brokers who accept credit card charges on short term rental transactions and who maintain a reserve in their special trust or escrow account to which funds received through such charges are credited as provided in N.J.A.C. 11:5-5.1(j) shall record in one location in their ledger book, entries specifying deposits

REAL ESTATE COMMISSION

made to establish, replenish, and increase the reserve amount and all withdrawals made to reduce the reserve amount. Brokers who maintain reserves in such special escrow or trust accounts shall not be required to make an entry in their ledger for each transaction fee debited from the said account as a result of their acceptance of a payment through a charge on a credit card.

3. Copies of all records, showing that at least quarterly a reconciliation has been made of the checkbook balance, the bank statement balance and the client trust ledger sheet balances;

4. All bank statements, cancelled checks, duplicate deposit slips and, if the broker accepts credit card charges on short term rental transactions as provided in N.J.A.C. 11:5-5.1, all confirmation slips or other written material reflecting the broker's acceptance of such payments;

5. Copies of all offers, contracts of sale and sale or rental listing agreements;

6. Copies of all leases and property management agreements;

7. Copies of all statements to owners, sellers, purchasers and tenants showing the disbursement of funds to them or on their behalf, which statements shall identify the property and unit, if applicable, for which the disbursement was made and the reason for the disbursement;

8. Copies of all bills paid for owners, sellers, purchasers or tenants by the broker from escrowed funds, which payments may only be made pursuant to written authorization;

9. Copies of all records showing payments to persons licensed with the paying broker and to cooperating brokers, which records shall contain all information required by N.J.A.C. 11:5-5.1(d); and

10. Copies of all receipts issued for all security deposits accepted from tenants, and of checks for and letters accompanying the release of such funds, and/or the duplicate deposit slips evidencing the deposit of such funds by the broker.

(c) With the exception of the materials described in (d) below, on transactions where a broker has not received the property or funds of others, the following records shall be maintained for six years from the earlier of the date of the listing or property management agreement or of the contract or lease:

1. Copies of all fully executed leases, contracts of sale, property management and listing agreements;

2. Copies of bills for brokerage services rendered in such transactions;

3. Copies of all records showing payments to persons licensed with the paying broker and to co-operating brokers; and

4. Copies of all bank statements, cancelled checks and duplicate deposit slips pertaining to the broker's general business account.

(d) Unaccepted offers and expired listing agreements during the term of which no contract of sale was executed or no tenancy was entered into shall be maintained for six months from the date of the offer or the expiration date of the listing agreement.

(e) The financial books and other records as described in (a), (b), (c) and (d) above shall be maintained in accordance with generally accepted accounting practice. They shall be located at the main New Jersey office of each broker or, in situations where separate general business and/or trust or escrow accounts are maintained at licensed branch offices, either at that branch office or at the main office of the broker. Copies of all items designated as records in (a) through (d) above shall be maintained by brokers as provided in this section. Items may be maintained either on paper or stored electronically in a computer or similar device, so long as the electronically stored data can be readily reproduced on paper so as to depict the complete history of all activity and the data can be maintained in an easily accessible form for the required six-year period. This requirement shall apply to all such records, including any items generated through e-mail or any other means which does not require the creation of a paper document. All such records shall be available for inspections, checks for compliance with this section and copying by a duly authorized representative of the New Jersey Real Estate Commission. Licensees may be required to certify to the accuracy of the reproduced data.

11:5-5.5   Inspection of records

(a) Every licensee shall make available for inspection by the Commission or its designated representatives all records of transactions, books of account, instruments, documents and

11:5-6.1

forms utilized or maintained by such licensee in the conduct of the licensed business, which may be pertinent to the conduct of the investigation of any specific complaint.

(b) To accomplish the objectives and carry out the duties prescribed by this Act, especially the provisions of N.J.S.A. 45:15-17, the Commission may issue subpoenas to any person, administer an oath or affirmation to any person, and conduct hearings in aid of any investigation or inquiry.

(c) All files on pending and closed sale, exchange or lease transactions, all files on listings for sales or rentals, and all property management files shall be maintained or stored at the offices of brokers licensed as employing brokers or corporate or partnership brokers. Upon terminating their employment with such a broker, and/or transferring to the employ of another such broker, no referral agent, salesperson or broker-salesperson shall remove or cause to be removed any of the contents of such files from the offices of the broker. The term "files" as used herein shall be construed to mean all transaction records required to be kept by brokers pursuant to N.J.A.C. 11:5-5.4.

SUBCHAPTER 6. CONDUCT OF BUSINESS

11:5-6.1   Advertising rules

(a) Unless otherwise set forth herein, subsections (b) through (o) below shall apply to all categories of advertising including all publications, radio or television broadcasts, all electronic media including E-mail and the Internet, business stationery, busi-

ness cards, business and legal forms and documents, and signs and billboards.

1. Individuals operating as sole proprietors and licensed as employing brokers shall conspicuously display on the exterior of their maintained place of business their name and the words "Licensed Real Estate Broker".

2. Firms licensed as corporate or partnership brokers shall conspicuously display on the exterior of their maintained place of business their regular business name and the name of the individual licensed as their broker of record and the words "Licensed Real Estate Broker".

(b) All advertising of any licensed individual, partnership, firm, or corporate broker shall include their regular business name which for the purposes of these rules, shall mean the name in which that individual, partnership, firm or corporation is on record with the Commission as doing business as a real estate broker. All advertising by a referral agent, a salesperson or a broker-salesperson shall include the name in which they are licensed and the regular business name of the individual, partnership, firm or corporate broker through whom they are licensed. If such advertisements contain a reference to the licensed status of the person placing the ad, their status as a referral agent, a salesperson or a broker-salesperson must be indicated through inclusion of a descriptive term as provided in (e) below. A referral agent or salesperson may not indicate in any advertisement or otherwise that he or she is licensed as a broker-salesperson.

1. In all advertisements which contain the name of a referral agent, a salesperson or a broker-salesperson, the regular business name of the individual, partnership, firm or corporate broker through whom that person is licensed shall appear in larger print or be displayed in a more prominent manner than the name of the referral agent, salesperson or broker-salesperson.

2. Where a webpage on the worldwide web established by a referral agent, a salesperson, a broker-salesperson, or a team of such licensees is not linked electronically to the webpage of the broker through whom the person or team is licensed, the webpage shall display the telephone number and may display the street address of the licensed brokerage office from which the individual or team operates as real estate licensees. That information shall appear in wording as large as the predominant size wording on the webpage.

3. Where a webpage of an individual or team is linked electronically to the webpage of the broker through whom such person or persons are licensed, the webpage of the nonbroker licensee(s) shall display information which clearly indicates how to link to the broker. That information shall appear in wording as large as the predominant size wording on the webpage.

(c) All advertising, with the exception of lawn signs placed on residential properties containing four or fewer units, shall clearly indicate after the licensee's regular business name that the advertising licensee is engaged in the real estate brokerage business. Except as prescribed by N.J.S.A. 45:15-17(j), examples of permissible language shall include, but are not limited to, "Realtor," "Realtist," "real estate broker," "broker," or "real estate agency". Examples of prohibited language when used alone shall include, but are not limited to, "realty," "real estate," "land sales," and "land investments." This provision shall not apply when the word "agency" appears in the advertisement as part of the licensee's regular business name or when the licensee has legal or equitable ownership of the property.

(d) Any advertising which contains a home telephone number, cell-phone number, beeper or pager number, home fax number, or e-mail address of an individual referral agent, salesperson or broker-salesperson, or a team of such licensees, shall also include the telephone number and may include the street address of the licensed brokerage office from which the advertising licensee(s) operate. All such advertising shall also contain language identifying each number included in the advertising. For example, a home telephone number may be followed or preceded by the word "home" or the abbreviation "res."

1. No advertising shall represent that a location is a place at which the business of a real estate licensee is conducted unless that location is the licensed main office or a licensed branch office of the broker through whom the advertising licensee is licensed. Referral agents, salespersons and broker-salespersons shall not include in their advertisements any reference to a "home office."

(e) The business card of any licensed referral agent shall indicate that this licensee is a referral agent by the use of the words referral agent or referral associate. The business card of any licensed salesperson shall indicate that this licensee is a salesperson by the use of the words salesperson or sales representative, or sales associate, or where permitted by law, realtor-associate or realtist associate. The business card of any licensed broker-salesperson shall indicate that this licensee is a broker-salesperson by the use of the words broker-associate, associate broker, realtor-associate or broker-salespersons. The business card of any licensed broker shall indicate that this licensee is a broker by use of the word broker or, where permitted by law, Realtor or Realtist.

(f) Any advertising which refers to amounts of down payment, monthly payment, or carrying charges, or which indicates that a mortgage is obtainable (where the mortgage referred to is not already a lien against the premises advertised), shall contain the words "to a qualified buyer".

(g) Any advertisement which sets forth amounts of down payment, monthly payment, carrying charges, taxes or mortgage money obtainable shall contain appropriate qualifying words such as "approximate" or "estimated," which qualifying words shall be clearly associated with the amounts set forth. If such amounts are mentioned the broker shall maintain written proof of the validity of these statements in the broker's files. Such written proof shall be maintained for a period of 12 months from the date upon which an advertisement containing such references shall have last appeared in any publication.

(h) With the exception of magazine or newspaper advertisements published under municipality headings, any advertisement for the sale, exchange or rental of real property, or any interest therein, shall designate the geographical area containing that property by specifying the municipality within which that property is located.

(i) No licensed individual, limited or general partnership, firm or corporation shall advertise or use any form of application or make any inquiry which expresses directly or indirectly any limitation, specification or discrimination as to race, religion, creed, color, sex, affectional or sexual orientation, marital status, national origin, ancestry or as to whether a person has a disability as that term is defined in N.J.A.C. 11:5-6.4(k).

(j) Any use of an insignia, emblem, logo, trade name or other form of identification in any advertising or other public utterance, either by a single licensee or any group of licensees, which suggests or otherwise implies common ownership or common management among such licensees, shall be prohibited except in the case of branch offices controlled by a single broker or licensee and duly licensed as branch offices pursuant to the provision of N.J.S.A. 45:1-1 et seq. Nothing herein provided is intended to preclude or inhibit the use, advertising or display of any insignia, emblem, logo or trade name of any bona fide trade association by any licensee provided that such licensee is a member of such trade association.

1. Any franchised licensee using in any advertising the trade name of a franchisor shall include in such advertising in a manner reasonably calculated to attract the attention of the public the franchised licensee's regular business name.

2. Any licensee including the franchisor using the trade name of franchisor in any advertising shall also include in a manner reasonably calculated to attract the attention of the public the following legend or a substantially similar legend: "each office is independently owned and operated", except in the following categories of advertising:

i. "For sale" signs located on the premises of specific properties for sale;

11:5-6.1

ii. Small "spot" classified advertising by a licensee in newspapers, magazines or other publications advertising properties. A small spot classified advertisement is defined as an advertisement which is no more than one column wide and 20 lines long and which describes no more than two properties; a line is defined as a standard newspaper classified advertising line of the newspaper, magazine or other publication in which the advertisement is published;

iii. Business cards; and

iv. Advertising placed or distributed by offices which are wholly owned by the franchisor, which contains the office address and contains language which identifies the office as being wholly owned or the franchisor.

3. The intent of this subsection is to further promote the general purpose of the Real Estate License Act of ensuring that all individuals, firms or corporations are clearly identifiable to the public as the licensed brokers who are financially and otherwise responsible to the consuming public for their real estate brokerage activities. It is not the intent of this subsection to limit or otherwise inhibit the operation of branch offices as set forth in N.J.S.A. 45:15-12 and sections 18 and 19 of this subchapter, nor is it the intent of this subsection to prevent the franchising of any group of licensees provided such franchising or other association is not inconsistent with the purpose of the Real Estate License Act as expressed herein.

(k) Any advertising by any licensed individual, partnership, firm or corporation referring generally to membership in any real estate multiple listing service operation shall specify the complete name of the listing service in which membership is held, except in the following categories of advertising:

1. "For sale" signs and small "spot" classified advertising of any licensee as described in (j) above;

2. Business cards;

3. All business signs.

(*l*) Any home warranty offer contained in any advertisement shall comply with all Federal and State warranty legislation, including the New Home Warranty and Builder's Registration Act, P.L. 1977, c.467, N.J.S.A. 46:3B-1 et seq., and the Magnuson-Moss Warranty Act, P.L. 93-637, 15 U.S.C. §§ 2301 et seq. Such advertising shall specify clearly whether the warranty is by inspection or non-inspection of the premises, whether the warranty is mandatory, and who is responsible for payment for the warranty. No advertisement shall contain an offer for a warranty unless a warranty may be secured for the property being advertised.

(m) Except as herein provided, licensees may include offers of free, discounted or other services or products in advertisements or promotional material. No offering of free, discounted or other services or products, including the offering of a free appraisal, shall be made by a real estate licensee in any advertisement or promotional material or otherwise where the promotion or offering involves a lottery, a contest, a game or a drawing, or the offering of a lot or parcel or lots or parcels, or where the consumer is required to enter into a sale, listing or other real estate contract as a condition of the promotion or offer.

1. Nothing herein shall be construed as prohibiting the use of such words as "included" or "included in the purchase price" in reference to items included by the owner in the sale of any real property or interest therein.

2. The prohibition upon licensees making offerings of free, discounted or other services or products as set forth in (m) above applies to all such offerings which confer a monetary benefit upon consumers. Examples of free or discounted products or services which would be prohibited if offered in a manner proscribed by (m) above include free or subsidized homeowners warranties, property, radon and pest inspections, surveys, mortgage fees, offers to pay other costs typically incurred by parties to real estate transactions, and coupons offering discounts on commissions charged by brokerage firms.

3. "Appraisal" as used herein is given its technical meaning as a study and analysis by an appraiser authorized by law to perform appraisals of New Jersey real estate to ascertain fair market value by using a process in which all factors that would fix price in the market place must be considered. A comparative market analysis or study is not an appraisal as herein defined. Any written comparative market study or analysis (CMA) provided by a licensee to a consumer shall include a statement indicating that the CMA is not an appraisal and should not be considered the equivalent of an appraisal. The said statement shall appear in print as large as the predominant size print in any writing reporting the results of the CMA.

4. Subject to (m) above, whenever a licensee participates in a promotion or offering of free, discounted, or other services or products which confers upon the recipient a monetary benefit of greater than token value, which for the purposes of this rule shall mean a value of more than $ 5.00 retail, the licensee shall provide written disclosure to the recipient of the promotional material or offering. The disclosure shall state in a clear and conspicuous manner:

i. That a consumer is not required to enter into any sale, listing or other real estate contract as a condition of their receipt and use of the free, discounted or other services or products included in the promotion or offer;

ii. Whether the consumer is required to perform any action to qualify to receive the free, discounted or other services or products offered and, if so, what specific action(s) the consumer must perform in order to do so. For the purposes of this paragraph, a consumer's attendance at any listing presentation, informational session or other meeting is considered to be an action by the consumer; and

iii. In the event that delivery of the offered services or products does not occur at the time that the disclosure is provided to the consumer, the date by which the services or products will be delivered to the consumer if the offer is accepted. If the delivery date is unknown to the licensee at the time the offer or promotion is extended to the consumer, the written disclosure to be provided by the licensee to the consumer shall so state.

5. In the event that a licensee has received, or will receive, compensation for participating in a promotion or offering of free, discounted, or other services or products, the disclosure required under (m)4 above shall also state the compensation the licensee has received or will receive. Should the Real Estate Settlement Procedures Act of 1974, 12 U.S.C. §§ 2601 et seq., be applicable to the arrangement between the broker and the person paying the compensation to the broker, the disclosure shall be in the form and substance required by that Act.

6. The written disclosure referenced in (m)4 and 5 above shall be provided to consumers no later than when the promotion or offer is extended by the licensee to the consumer.

i. For the purposes of this subsection, an offer or promotion is extended to a consumer when the free or discounted product or service is delivered to the consumer, or when written confirmation of the consumer's right to receive the free or discounted product or service at some future time is delivered to the consumer.

7. No licensee may utilize a marketing or promotional program which requires, as a condition of the consumer's receipt of a free or discounted product or service, the taking of any action by the consumer prior to the delivery of the disclosure(s) referenced in (m)4 and 5 above other than an action necessary to accomplish the delivery of the disclosure to the consumer.

(n) No licensee shall publish or cause to be published any advertisement or place any sign which makes reference to the availability of a specific property which is exclusively listed for sale by another broker unless the licensee obtains the prior written consent of the broker with whom the property is exclusively listed. Such consent shall not be given or withheld by the listing broker without the knowledge of the owner.

1. With regard to information on listings disseminated through the Internet by licensees other than the listing broker,

listing brokers shall be deemed to have given the consent referred to in (n) above with the knowledge of the owner where:

i. A written listing agreement contains the seller's authorization for information on the listing to be posted on the website of the broker, or of a multiple listing service to which the broker belongs, or of another party to which the broker or such an MLS submits information on listings; and

ii. The website on which the listing information shall initially appear has instituted no measures to prevent other parties with websites from utilizing an electronic link to enable consumers to view that information while remaining in the website of the other party.

(o) No licensee shall indicate in any advertisement that a property has been sold, or that they participated in the sale of a property, until a closing has occurred at which title to the property was transferred from the seller to the buyer.

1. For the purposes of this subsection, the term "advertisement" shall include communications to other licensees through notices submitted to a multiple listing service or otherwise.

2. In the time period after a contract prepared by a licensee emerges from Attorney Review or a contract not subject to Attorney Review is fully executed and delivered to all parties, but before a closing occurs at which title is transferred, unless such a contract is canceled and the seller authorizes the listing broker to renew efforts to market the property, any advertisement of the property which is the subject of the contract shall include the term "under contract."

(p) Advertisements by licensees may, but are not required to, include a statement indicating that the advertiser is licensed by the New Jersey Real Estate Commission. Any advertisement by a licensee that includes a reference to licensure by the New Jersey Real Estate Commission shall immediately thereafter also include the following statement: "Licensure does not imply endorsement," which statement shall be included in the advertisement in a clear and conspicuous manner.

1. The foregoing shall not apply to the displays which, pursuant to N.J.S.A. 45:15-12, are required to conspicuously appear on the exterior of every place of business maintained by New Jersey real estate brokers and to include the name of the broker and, in the case of business entities licensed as brokers, the name of the individual licensed as its authorized broker, and the words "Licensed Real Estate Broker."

(q) Any advertisement which includes any reference to a commission rate or compensation amount charged by the advertising licensee's brokerage firm or by one or more other brokerage firms shall also include the following statement: "In New

Jersey commissions are negotiable." The said statement shall be included in the advertisement in a clear and conspicuous manner.

(r) No advertisement shall contain false, misleading or deceptive claims or misrepresentations. In all advertisements which make express or implied claims that are likely to be misleading in the absence of certain qualifying information such qualifying information shall be disclosed in the advertisement in a clear and conspicuous manner.

(s) No person licensed as a referral agent shall include in any advertisement any content stating or implying that he or she is authorized to engage in real estate brokerage activity beyond that which he or she is permitted under N.J.S.A. 45:15-3 or N.J.A.C. 11:5-6.10.

(t) On all advertisements, except business cards, referral agents shall include the following statement in a clear and conspicuous manner: Services limited to referring prospects to broker.

11:5-6.2   Contracts of sale, leases and listing agreements

(a) The following paragraphs specify licensees' obligations to obtain written confirmation of the intentions of, and to deliver copies of documents to, parties to a real estate transaction.

1. Where a licensee memorializes the terms of an offer or counter-offer on a writing which will itself become an "instrument" as defined in (a)3 below, the licensee shall deliver to the maker of such an offer or counter-offer a clear copy of the executed offer or counter-offer immediately upon its being signed, and initialed if necessary as provided in this section, by the maker of the offer or counter-offer. Any addition, deletion, or other change in any such offer or counter-offer shall be initialed by the party proposing such a revision and, if accepted, by the other party to the transaction.

2. Where a licensee records the terms of an offer or counter-offer on a writing which is not intended to be binding upon either party, and which so states on its face, in the event that the licensee secures the signature and/or initials of any party on such a writing, the licensee shall provide to the signing and/or initialing party a clear copy of the writing as signed and/or initialed by them.

3. As used in this subsection, the term "instrument" means any complete and fully executed written contract of sale, lease, option agreement, or other writing affecting an interest in real estate, or any complete and fully executed addendum or amendment to any such contract, lease, option agreement or writing. The term instrument as used in this subsection does not include listing agreements and buyer brokerage agreements.

4. Licensees shall immediately deliver to all parties to any fully executed instrument a clear copy with original signatures of any such fully executed instrument. Licensees shall provide their clients with a fully executed copy of any sale or exclusive sale or rental listing contract at the time of execution thereof.

5. Licensee-prepared revisions or additions reflected on the instrument itself shall be initialed by all parties to the transaction. Licensee-prepared revisions or additions to an instrument not memorialized by changes on the instrument itself shall be reflected on amendments or addenda to the instrument signed by all parties to the transaction.

i. Licensees shall immediately deliver to the party proposing a revision or addition to an instrument a clear copy of any proposed revised instrument initialed by that party and a clear copy of any proposed amendment or addendum signed by that party.

ii. All revisions, amendments and addenda to any fully executed instrument which are prepared by licensees must comply with New Jersey law as it pertains to the attorney review of contract and lease documents prepared by real estate licensees.

6. This rule is to ensure prompt communication of the executed evidence of a transaction to all interested parties.

(b) No listing agreement or contract for the sale of real property, or any interest therein, shall contain a prescribed or predetermined fee, commission rate, or commission amount; nor shall any such writing contain a commission clause or provision which suggests (such as with a small blank space and percent sign) to a seller that the commission is a prescribed rate or amount.

(c) The commission clause or provision in all listing agreements for the sale of one to four family dwelling units or interest therein, or in all contracts for such sale, if there is no listing agreement, shall contain in print larger than the predominant size print in the writing, the language: "As seller you have the right to individually reach an agreement on any fee, commission, or other valuable consideration with any broker. No fee, commission or other consideration has been fixed by any governmental authority or by any trade association or multiple listing service." Nothing herein is intended to prohibit an individual broker from independently establishing a policy regarding the amount of fee, commission or other value consideration to be charged in transaction by the broker.

(d) Upon request, the listing broker shall advise the seller of the rate or amount of any commission split or distribution.

(e) All listing agreements of any licensed individual, partnership, firm or corporation which provide for the listing of property with any real estate multiple listing service operation shall specify the complete name of that listing service.

(f) No licensed individual, partnership, firm or corporation shall enter into a "net listing" contract for the sale of real property, or any interest therein. A "net listing" is defined as an agency agreement in which a prospective seller lists real estate for sale with an authorization to a broker to sell at a specified net dollar return to the seller, and which provides that the broker may retain as commission the difference between the specified dollar return to the seller and the actual sales price.

(g) Licensees shall comply with the following provisions:

1. All contracts prepared by licensees for the sale of residential real estate containing one to four dwelling units and for the sale of vacant one-family lots in transactions in which the licensee has a commission or fee interest shall contain, at the top of the first page and in print larger than the predominant size print in the writing, the following language:

THIS IS A LEGALLY BINDING CONTRACT THAT WILL BECOME FINAL WITHIN THREE BUSINESS DAYS. DURING THIS PERIOD YOU MAY CHOOSE TO CONSULT AN ATTORNEY WHO CAN REVIEW AND CANCEL THE CONTRACT. SEE SECTION ON ATTORNEY REVIEW FOR DETAILS.

2. The contract shall also contain the following language within the text of every such contract.

ATTORNEY REVIEW:

1. Study by Attorney

The Buyer or the Seller may choose to have an attorney study this contract. If an attorney is consulted, the attorney must complete his or her review of the contract within a three-day period. This contract will be legally binding at the end of this three-day period unless an attorney for the Buyer or Seller reviews and disapproves of the contract.

2. Counting the Time

You count the three days from the date of delivery of the signed contract to the Buyer and the Seller. You do not count Saturdays, Sundays or legal holidays. The Buyer and the Seller may agree in writing to extend the three-day period for attorney review.

3. Notice of Disapproval

If an attorney for the Buyer or the Seller reviews and disapproves of this contract, the attorney must notify the Broker(s) and the other party named in this contract within the three-day period. Otherwise this contract will be legally binding as written. The attorney must send the notice of disapproval to the Broker(s) by certified mail, by telegram, or by delivering it personally. The telegram or certified letter will be effective upon sending. The personal delivery will be effective upon delivery to the Broker's office. The attorney may but need not also in-

form the Broker(s) of any suggested revisions in the contract that would make it satisfactory.

3. The contract shall also contain the names and full addresses of all persons to whom a Notice of Disapproval must be sent in order to be effective as provided in item three of the Attorney Review Provision.

4. All leases prepared by licensees for a term of one year or more for residential dwelling units in transactions in which they have a commission or fee interest shall, at the top of the first page and in print larger than the predominant size print of the writing, contain the following language:

THIS IS A LEGALLY BINDING LEASE THAT WILL BECOME FINAL WITHIN THREE BUSINESS DAYS. DURING THIS PERIOD YOU MAY CHOOSE TO CONSULT AN ATTORNEY WHO CAN REVIEW AND CANCEL THE LEASE. SEE SECTION ON ATTORNEY REVIEW FOR DETAILS.

5. The lease shall also contain the following language within the text of every such lease.

ATTORNEY REVIEW:

1. Study by Attorney

The Tenant or the Landlord may choose to have an attorney study this lease. If an attorney is consulted, the attorney must complete his or her review of the lease within a three-day period. This lease will be legally binding at the end of this three-day period unless an attorney for the Tenant or the Landlord reviews and disapproves of the lease.

2. Counting the Time

You count the three days from the date of delivery of the signed lease to the Tenant and the Landlord. You do not count Saturdays, Sundays or legal holidays. The Tenant and the Landlord may agree in writing to extend the three-day period for attorney review.

3. Notice of Disapproval

If an attorney for the Tenant or the Landlord reviews and disapproves of this lease, the attorney must notify the Broker(s) and the other party named in the lease within the three-day period. Otherwise this lease will be legally binding as written. The attorney must send the notice of disapproval to the Broker(s) by certified mail, by telegram, or by delivering it personally. The telegram or certified letter will be effective upon sending. The personal delivery will be effective upon delivery to the Broker's office. The attorney may but need not also inform the Broker(s)

REAL ESTATE COMMISSION 11:5-6.4

of any suggested revisions in the lease that would make it satisfactory.

6. The lease shall also contain the names and full addresses of all persons to whom a Notice of Disapproval must be sent in order to be effective, as provided in item three of the Attorney Review Provision.

7. The failure of any licensee to include such language in any such contract of sale or lease agreement prepared by the licensee shall be construed by the Commission as engaging in the unauthorized practice of law and shall be considered by the Commission as conduct which demonstrates the licensee's unworthiness and incompetency, thereby subjecting the licensee to sanctions pursuant to N.J.S.A. 45:15-17(e).

11:5-6.3 **Broker insurance placement provision**

Where a contract provided by a real estate broker contains a provision to the effect that such broker, in his capacity as a licensed insurance agent or broker, is authorized to place or procure insurance on the property being sold, the licensee benefitting by such a provision shall obtain separate written reaffirmation of such provision by the prospective insured not less than five days prior to the closing of title.

11:5-6.4 **Obligations of licensees to public and to each other**

(a) All licensees are subject to and shall strictly comply with the laws of agency and the principles governing fiduciary relationships. In accepting employment as an agent, the licensee pledges himself to protect and promote, as he would his own, the interests of the client or principal he has undertaken to represent;

11:5-6.4

this obligation of absolute fidelity to the client's or principal's interest is primary but does not relieve the licensee from the obligation of dealing fairly with all parties to the transaction.

(b) Every licensee shall make reasonable effort to ascertain all material information concerning the physical condition of every property for which he or she accepts an agency or which he or she is retained to market as a transaction broker, and concerning the financial qualifications of every person for whom he or she submits an offer to his or her client or principal. Information about social conditions and psychological impairments as defined in (d) below is not considered to be information which concerns the physical condition of a property.

1. A reasonable effort to ascertain material information shall include at least:

i. Inquiries to the seller or seller's agent about any physical conditions that may affect the property; and

ii. A visual inspection of the property to determine if there are any readily observable physical conditions affecting the property.

2. As used in this section, information is "material" if a reasonable person would attach importance to its existence or nonexistence in deciding whether or how to proceed in the transaction, or if the licensee knows or has reason to know that the recipient of the information regards, or is likely to regard it as important in deciding whether or how to proceed, although a reasonable person would not so regard it.

(c) Licensees shall disclose all information material to the physical condition of any property which they know or which a reasonable effort to ascertain such information would have revealed to their client or principal and when appropriate to any other party to a transaction. Licensees shall also disclose any actual or potential conflicts of interest which the licensee may reasonably anticipate.

1. With respect to off-site conditions which may materially affect the value of the residential real estate, in all sales contracts involving newly constructed residential real estate they prepare, licensees shall include a statement as set forth below. By including this statement in a contract of sale prepared by the licensee, the licensee shall be deemed to have fulfilled his or her disclosure obligations under (c) above with respect to such off-site conditions. The statement shall be in print as large as the predominant size print in the document and shall read as follows:

"NOTIFICATION REGARDING OFF-SITE CONDITIONS

Pursuant to the New Residential Construction Off-Site Conditions Disclosure Act, P.L. 1995, c.253 (C.46:3C-1 et seq.), sellers of newly constructed residential real estate are required

to notify purchasers of the availability of lists disclosing the existence and location of off-site conditions which may affect the value of the residential real estate being sold. The lists are to be made available by the municipal clerk of the municipality within which the residential real estate is located and in other municipalities which are within one-half mile of the residential real estate. The address(es) and telephone number(s) of the municipalities relevant to this project and the appropriate municipal offices where the lists are made available are listed below. Purchasers are encouraged to exercise all due diligence in order to obtain any additional or more recent information that they believe may be relevant to their decision to purchase the residential real estate. Purchasers are also encouraged to undertake an independent examination of the general area within which the residential real estate is located in order to become familiar with any and all conditions which may affect the value of the residential real estate.

The purchaser has five (5) business days from the date the contract is executed by the purchaser and the seller to send notice of cancellation of the contract to the seller. The notice of cancellation shall be sent by certified mail. The cancellation will be effective upon the notice of cancellation being mailed. If the purchaser does not send a notice of cancellation to the seller in the time or manner described above, the purchaser will lose the right to cancel the contract as provided in this notice.

Municipality_____

Address_____

Telephone Number_____"

The statement shall either be included in the text of the contract itself or attached to the contract as an Addendum.

2. In all residential real estate sale contracts they prepare except contracts for newly constructed residential real estate, licensees shall include a statement as set forth below. The statement shall be in print as large as the predominant size print in the document and shall read as follows:

"NOTICE ON OFF-SITE CONDITIONS

Pursuant to the New Residential Construction Off-site Conditions Disclosure Act, P.L. 1995, c.253 the clerks of municipalities in New Jersey maintain lists of off-site conditions which may affect the value of residential properties in the vicinity of the off-site condition. Purchasers may examine the lists and are encouraged to independently investigate the area surrounding this property in order to become familiar with any off-site conditions which may affect the value of the property. In cases where a property is located near the border of a municipality, purchasers may wish to also examine the list maintained by the neighboring municipality."

The statement shall either be included in the text of the contract itself or attached to the contract as an Addendum.

i. Licensees who possess actual knowledge of an off-site condition which may materially affect the value of residential real estate other than newly constructed properties shall disclose that information to prospective purchasers of such residential real estate affected by the condition. That disclosure shall be made prior to the signing of the contract by a prospective purchaser.

ii. In cases where the licensee did not possess actual knowledge of the presence of an off-site condition which might materially affect the value of the residential real estate, by virtue of including the foregoing statement in a contract of sale prepared by him or her, the licensee shall be deemed to have fulfilled his or her disclosure obligations under (c) above with respect to such off-site conditions.

3. As used in this subsection, the following words and terms shall have the following meanings:

i. "Newly constructed" means any dwelling unit not previously occupied, excluding dwelling units constructed solely for lease and units governed by the National Manufactured Housing Construction and Safety Standards Act of 1974, 42 U.S.C. §§ 5402 et seq.

ii. "Off-site conditions" refers to the following conditions as set forth in the New Residential Construction Off-Site Conditions Disclosure Act, N.J.S.A. 46:3C-3 (P.L. 1995 c.253), or as amended:

(1) The latest Department of Environmental Protection listing of sites included on the National Priorities List pursuant to the "Comprehensive Environmental Response, Compensation and Liability Act of 1980," 42 U.S.C. §§ 9601 et seq.;

(2) The latest sites known to and confirmed by the Department of Environmental Protection and included on the New Jersey master list of known hazardous discharge sites, prepared pursuant to P.L. 1982, c.202 (N.J.S.A. 58.10-23.15 et seq.);

(3) Overhead electric utility transmission lines conducting 240,000 volts or more;

(4) Electrical transformer substations;

(5) Underground gas transmission lines as defined in 49 C.F.R. 192.3;

(6) Sewer pump stations of a capacity equal to, or in excess of 0.5 million gallons per day and sewer trunk lines in excess of 15 inches in diameter;

(7) Sanitary landfill facilities as defined pursuant to section 3 of P.L. 1970, c.39 (N.J.S.A. 13:1E-3);

(8) Public wastewater treatment facilities; and

(9) Airport safety zones as defined pursuant to section 3 of P.L. 1983, c.260 (N.J.S.A. 6:1-82).

iii. "Residential real estate" means a property or structure or both which will serve as a residence for the purchaser.

(d) Information about social conditions or psychological impairments of a property is not considered information which affects the physical condition of a property. Subject to (d)3 below, licensees are not required by (c) above to disclose such information.

1. As used in this section, the term "social conditions" includes, but is not limited to, neighborhood conditions such as barking dogs, boisterous neighbors, and other conditions which do not impact upon or adversely affect the physical condition of the property.

2. As used in this section, the term "psychological impairments" includes, but is not limited to, a murder or suicide which occurred on a property, or a property purportedly being haunted.

3. Except as provided below, upon receipt of an inquiry from a prospective purchaser or tenant about whether a particular property may be affected by a social condition or psychological impairment, licensees shall provide whatever information they know about the social conditions or psychological impairments that might affect the property.

i. In accordance with N.J.S.A. 10:5-1 et seq. (the "Law Against Discrimination"), licensees shall make no inquiry and provide no information on the racial composition of, or the presence of a group home in, a neighborhood. In response to requests for such information, licensees shall inform the persons making the inquiry that they may conduct their own investigation. This paragraph does not apply to the owner of a multiple dwelling or his agent to the extent that such inquiries are necessary for compliance with N.J.A.C. 13:10.

ii. In accordance with N.J.S.A. 2C:7-6 through 11 ("Megan's Law") and the guidelines promulgated thereunder, licensees shall make no inquiry about and provide no information on notifications from a county prosecutor issued pursuant to that law. In response to requests for such information, licensees shall inform the person making the inquiry that information about registered sex offenders is maintained by the county prosecutor.

11:5-6.4

(e) In all contracts and leases on residential real estate they prepare, licensees shall include the following statement in print as large as the predominant size print in the document:

MEGAN'S LAW STATEMENT—Under New Jersey law, the county prosecutor determines whether and how to provide notice of the presence of convicted sex offenders in an area.

In their professional capacity, real estate licensees are not entitled to notification by the county prosecutor under Megan's Law and are unable to obtain such information for you. Upon closing the county prosecutor may be contacted for such further information as may be disclosable to you.

(f) Unless directed not to do so in writing by an owner as provided herein, every licensee shall fully cooperate with all other New Jersey licensees utilizing cooperation arrangements which shall protect and promote the interests of the licensee's client or principal. Collusion and discrimination with respect to commission rates and splits are prohibited as provided in N.J.A.C. 11:5-7.5 and 7.6.

1. The obligation to fully cooperate with all other licensees includes the requirements that listing brokers:

i. Notify any Multiple Listing System to which a listing is to be submitted of having acquired the listing within 48 hours of the effective date of the listing;

ii. Transmit to their principal(s) all written offers on their listings submitted by licensees with other firms within 24 hours of receipt of the written offer by their firm; and

iii. Place no unreasonable restrictions upon the showing of properties listed with them to prospective purchasers who are working through cooperating brokers. A requirement that all appointments for showings must be made through the listing broker's office is not considered an unreasonable restriction upon showings.

2. All requirements imposed by the obligation to fully cooperate shall be complied with on all listings unless the client or principal, with full knowledge of all relevant facts, expressly relieves the listing broker from one or more of those requirements in writing. Such a writing shall be signed by the owner and made an attachment to the listing agreement. Such a writing shall be made available for inspection by other brokers upon request.

3. All written listing agreements prepared by licensees shall include a provision as set forth below, which provision shall be in print larger than the predominant size print in the agreement. The provision may be included within the body of the listing agreement or attached to the listing as an addendum to it. Where the provision is made an addendum to the listing agreement it shall be signed by the owner at the same time that the owner

signs the listing agreement. Prior to securing the owner's signature on the listing agreement, the listing broker shall specify the complete formula for determining the commission split in the indicated location in the provision.

COMMISSION SPLITS

LISTING BROKERS USUALLY COOPERATE WITH OTHER BROKERAGE FIRMS BY SHARING INFORMATION ABOUT THEIR LISTINGS AND OFFERING TO PAY PART OF THEIR COMMISSION TO THE FIRM THAT PRODUCES A BUYER. THIS IS GENERALLY REFERRED TO AS THE "COMMISSION SPLIT."

SOME LISTING BROKERS OFFER TO PAY COMMISSION SPLITS OF A PORTION OF THE GROSS COMMISSION, USUALLY EXPRESSED AS A PERCENTAGE OF THE SELLING PRICE, LESS A SIGNIFICANT DOLLAR AMOUNT. OTHER LISTING BROKERS OFFER A PORTION OF THE GROSS COMMISSION LESS ONLY A MINIMAL LISTING FEE OR LESS ZERO.

THE AMOUNT OF COMMISSION SPLIT YOUR BROKER OFFERS CAN AFFECT THE EXTENT TO WHICH YOUR PROPERTY IS EXPOSED TO PROSPECTIVE BUYERS WORKING WITH LICENSEES FROM OTHER BROKERAGE FIRMS.

ON THIS LISTING, THE BROKER IS OFFERING A COMMISSION SPLIT OF ...... MINUS ...... TO POTENTIAL COOPERATING BROKERS.

IF YOU FEEL THAT THIS MAY RESULT IN YOUR PROPERTY RECEIVING LESS THAN MAXIMUM EXPOSURE TO BUYERS, YOU SHOULD DISCUSS THOSE CONCERNS WITH THE LISTING SALESPERSON OR HIS/HER SUPERVISING BROKER.

BY SIGNING THIS LISTING AGREEMENT THE OWNER(S) ACKNOWLEDGE HAVING READ THIS STATEMENT ON COMMISSION SPLITS.

4. Should the client or principal direct the listing broker not to cooperate at all with all other licensees, evidence of this intent shall be in writing in the form of a WAIVER OF BROKER COOPERATION as set forth below and signed by the client or principal. Copies of this WAIVER OF BROKER COOPERATION and the listing agreement to which it relates shall be provided to the client or principal and to their authorized representative by the broker. This waiver shall become a part of the listing agreement at the time it is signed, and shall be made available for inspection by other brokers upon request. However, no direction or inducement from the client or principal shall relieve the list-

REAL ESTATE COMMISSION   **11:5-6.4**

ing broker of his responsibility of dealing fairly and exercising integrity with all other licensees.

WAIVER OF BROKER COOPERATION

I UNDERSTAND THAT COOPERATION AMONGST BROKERS PRODUCES WIDER EXPOSURE OF MY PROPERTY AND MAY RESULT IN IT BEING SOLD OR LEASED SOONER AND AT A HIGHER PRICE THAN WOULD BE THE CASE WERE MY BROKER NOT TO COOPERATE WITH OTHER BROKERS. I FURTHER UNDERSTAND THAT WHEN MY BROKER COOPERATES WITH OTHER BROKERS, I CAN STILL HAVE THE ARRANGEMENTS FOR THE SHOWING OF THE PROPERTY AND ALL NEGOTIATIONS WITH ME OR MY ATTORNEY MADE ONLY THROUGH MY LISTING BROKER'S OFFICE, SHOULD I SO DESIRE.

However, despite my awareness of these factors, I direct that this property is to be marketed only through the efforts of the listing broker. This listing is not to be published in any multiple listing service. I will only consider offers on this property which are obtained by, and I will only allow showings of this property to be conducted by the listing broker or his or her duly authorized representatives. THE LISTING BROKER IS HEREBY DIRECTED NOT TO COOPERATE WITH ANY OTHER BROKER.

By signing below, the parties hereto confirm that no pressure or undue influence has been exerted upon the owners as to how this property is to be marketed by the Listing Broker.

The owner(s) further confirm receipt of fully executed copies of the listing agreement on this property and of this Waiver of Broker Cooperation form.

Dated: ....   Owner ....
                           Owner ....
                           Listing Broker ....
           By: Authorized Licensee or Broker ....

(g) If any offer on any real property or interest therein is made orally, the licensee shall advise the offeror that he is not obligated to present to the owner or his authorized representative any offer unless the offer is in writing. Unless a writing containing or confirming the terms of the listing agreement otherwise provides, the licensee shall transmit every written offer on any real property or interest therein presented to or obtained by the licensee during the term of the listing to the owner or his authorized representative within 24 hours of receipt of the written offer by their firm. For the purposes of this section, the term of a listing shall be deemed to expire either on the termination date established in the listing agreement, or upon the closing of a pending sale or lease. If any acceptance of an offer is given

orally, the licensee shall secure the acceptance in writing within 24 hours.

(h) Back-up offers shall be handled as follows:

1. As used in this subsection, the term "back-up offer" shall mean a written and signed offer to purchase or lease an interest in real estate which is received by a licensee at a time when a previously executed contract or lease pertaining to the same interest in real estate is pending and in effect, having survived attorney review if it was subject to such review. Offers obtained while a previously executed contract or lease is still pending attorney review are not considered back-up offers and must be presented as provided in (g) above.

2. Whenever a licensee transmits a back-up offer to an owner, the licensee shall advise the owner in writing to consult an attorney before taking any action on the back-up offer, and shall retain a copy of such written notice as a business record in accordance with N.J.A.C. 11:5-5.4.

3. Whenever a licensee receives a back-up offer, the licensee shall notify the offeror in writing that the property to which the offer pertains is the subject of a pending contract of sale or lease and, in the event that the licensee receiving the back-up offer is not licensed with the listing broker, a copy of that notice shall be delivered to the listing broker at the time the offer is presented. The said notice shall not disclose the price and terms of the pending contract or lease. A copy of such written notice shall be retained by the licensee as a business record in accordance with N.J.A.C. 11:5-5.4.

(i) It shall be the duty of a licensee to recommend that legal counsel be obtained whenever the interests of any party to a transaction seem to require it.

(j) At the time of the taking of any listing of residential property, a licensee shall furnish to the owner a copy of a summary of the New Jersey Law Against Discrimination N.J.S.A. 10:5-1 et seq. which summary shall have been prepared and furnished by the Attorney General of the State of New Jersey, shall state the provisions of the Law Against Discrimination, and shall state which properties are covered by this law and which properties are exempt from this law. Should the owner profess an unwillingness to abide by or an intention to violate this law then the licensee shall not accept these listings.

(k) No licensee shall deny real estate brokerage services to any person for reasons of race, creed, color, national origin, ancestry, marital status, civil union status, domestic partnership status, familial status, sex, gender identity or expression, affectional or sexual orientation, disability, nationality, or source of lawful income used for rental or mortgage payments, and no licensee shall participate or otherwise be a party to any plan, scheme or agreement to discriminate against any person on the basis of race, creed, color, national origin, ancestry, marital status, civil union status, domestic partnership status, familial status, sex, gender identity or expression, affectional or sexual orientation, disability, nationality, or source of lawful income used for rental or mortgage payments. For the purposes of this subsection, the term "disability" shall have the same meaning as the definition of "disability" codified at N.J.S.A. 10:5-5q.

(*l*) Licensees may engage in brokerage activity in transactions involving the resale of mobile and manufactured homes as provided in N.J.S.A. 39:10-19. Licensees who do so shall be familiar with all laws applicable to such transactions. These laws include N.J.S.A. 39:1-1 et seq. as it applies to the resale of and the transfer of the titles to such motor vehicle units, N.J.S.A. 46:8C-1 et seq., as it applies to the resale of such units when situated in Mobile Home Parks, N.J.S.A. 17:16C-1 et seq., as it applies to the financing of purchases of personal property and New Jersey's Truth in Renting Act, N.J.S.A. 46:8-43 et seq. Licensees who, when involved in transactions of this type, evidence a lack of familiarity with these laws either through acts of omission or commission shall be subject to sanctions by the Commission for having engaged in conduct demonstrating incompetency, in violation of N.J.S.A. 45:15-17(e).

11:5-6.5   Residential rental referral agencies

(a) Every person engaged in the business of referring, for a fee, prospective residential tenants to possible rental units shall be licensed in accordance with the New Jersey Real Estate License Act, N.J.S.A. 45:15-1 et seq., and shall comply with the provisions of this section in addition to the obligations imposed by the Act, and other rules contained in this chapter.

(b) Every licensee subject to this section shall enter into a written contract with the prospective tenant and give such person a copy of the contract. The contract shall accurately state:

1. The services to be performed by the agency;

2. The fee charged;

3. The date and duration of the contract;

4. The affirmative actions required of the prospective tenant to utilize the service;

5. The refund policy; and

6. A statement that the business is licensed by the New Jersey Real Estate Commission.

(c) No licensee shall advertise or refer to a prospective residential tenant to:

1. A non-existent address;

2. A property not verified as available as provided in (e) below;

3. A possible rental unit or location for which the licensee does not have the lessor's, or the duly authorized agent of the lessor's, oral or written consent to refer prospective tenants.

(d) Oral consent of the lessor or his duly authorized agent to refer prospective tenants to a possible rental unit or location shall be confirmed by the licensee in writing within 24 hours of the licensee's receipt of such consent.

(e) Every licensee subject to this section shall verify the continuing availability of the rental unit with the lessor or agent as follows:

1. All units advertised in media shall be verified each day the advertisement appears; and

2. All units to which prospective tenants are referred shall be verified as available every three working days.

(f) In the event a diligent effort by the licensee to verify availability of the rental unit is unsuccessful because of a failure of a lessor or agent to respond, the prospective tenant shall be specifically advised of the date and time the unit was last verified as available.

1. Every prospective tenant shall upon request be advised of the date and time any particular unit was last verified as available.

2. No licensee subject to this section shall refer a prospective tenant to any rental unit not verified as available within the previous seven calendar days.

(g) Every licensee subject to this section shall maintain sufficient telephone lines and staff to receive and answer inquiries from contract consumers.

(h) Prior to the prospective tenant obtaining rental property through the services of the licensee, no licensee shall charge or accept a fee in excess of $ 25.00 unless:

1. Any fee charged, collected or received in excess of $ 25.00 is deposited promptly in the broker's escrow account until the services described by the contract are fully performed; or

2. The licensee posts with an approved escrow agent cash security in an amount approved by the Commission, based upon the following criteria:

i. The rental referral fees;

ii. The volume of rental referral business of the licensee;

iii. The duration of the rental referral contract; and

iv. The prior performance of the licensee or its principals in the rental referral business.

(i) Any licensee subject to this section shall maintain for one year the following records:

1. Written consent or written confirmation of oral consent of a lessor or agent to refer prospective tenants;

2. Records of the verification of availability of rental units as set forth in (e) above; and

11:5-6.6

3. Copies of contracts with prospective tenants.

(j) Every licensee subject to this section shall prominently post a copy of this regulation in its office for the information of its customers, and provide customers a copy upon request.

11:5-6.6   Participation in trade associations or listing services

(a) No licensed individual, partnership, firm or corporation shall become a member of or otherwise participate in the activities or operation of any trade association or organization or of any multiple listing service operation which engages in the following policies and practices:

1. Places requirements, obligations, or standards upon licensed members or participants which conflict with the Real Estate License Act, N.J.S.A. 45:15-1 et seq., the Real Estate Sales Full Disclosure Act, N.J.S.A. 45:15-16.27 et seq., the New Jersey Antitrust Act, N.J.S.A. 56:9-1 et seq., or the New Jersey Law Against Discrimination, N.J.S.A. 10:5-1 et seq., or which otherwise relate to the comprehensive scheme of regulation already preempted by the State of New Jersey.

2. Interferes with the licensee's obligation of fidelity to his client's interests, his obligation of dealing fairly with all other parties in a transaction, or his obligation of fully cooperating with any other New Jersey licensee, as more fully set forth in N.J.A.C. 11:5-6.4;

3. Directly or indirectly imposes or attempts to impose prescribed or predetermined fees or commission rates or commission amounts, or prescribed or predetermined commission splits, between the listing broker and the selling broker.

11:5-6.7   Disclosures by licensees providing mortgage financing services to buyers for a fee

(a) Every real estate licensee who provides mortgage financing services to buyers must provide written disclosure to the buyer/borrower and to the seller as required in this rule as a condition to receiving, in addition to a share of the brokerage commission on the sale, any compensation, reimbursement or thing of value from the buyer, or any other source. These disclosures are required whenever the real estate brokerage agency, any division therein, or any individual licensed or employed by the agency will receive compensation or reimbursement for providing mortgage financing services related to the sales transaction, even if that particular division or individual will not share in the sales commission. Copies of all written disclosures required by this rule must be retained by the broker as business records pursuant to N.J.A.C. 11:5-5.4. The broker shall maintain records of such related mortgage transactions which shall be available to the Commission for inspection pursuant to N.J.A.C. 11:5-5.5.

(b) The licensee must provide written disclosure as required by (a) above to the buyer/borrower before charging or accepting or contracting for any fees for mortgage financing services and providing such services other than prequalification. The written disclosure to the buyer must include the following information:

1. The amount of all fees which the buyer will be expected to pay to the licensee for mortgage services, and whether and under what circumstances such fees are refundable;

2. The amount and source of any compensation or reimbursement which the licensee will receive for providing mortgage financing services to the buyer;

3. Where the licensee takes applications for or places loans exclusively with any three or fewer lenders, or is affiliated with any lender or mortgage broker as defined in N.J.A.C. 11:5-6.8, the disclosure must advise the buyer of that fact, give the names of such lenders and state:

YOU ARE UNDER NO OBLIGATION TO USE THE MORTGAGE SERVICES OFFERED BY THIS REAL ESTATE LICENSE. YOU MAY OBTAIN YOUR MORTGAGE LOAN FROM ANOTHER SOURCE.

4. Where the licensee or agency is also representing the seller in the sales transaction, the disclosure to the buyer/borrower must include the statement set forth in (e) below.

(c) Real estate licensees who are dually licensed as mortgage bankers or brokers may combine the disclosures to buyers required in this rule with the written disclosure to borrowers required by the Department of Banking and Insurance pursuant to its rules mandating such disclosures.

REAL ESTATE COMMISSION   **11:5-6.8**

(d) A listing broker who represents only the seller and who offers to provide mortgage financing services to buyers for compensation or reimbursement shall provide written disclosure to the seller by including the following statement in the listing agreement. A selling broker who represents only the seller as subagent of the listing broker, and who offers to provide mortgage financing services to buyers for compensation or reimbursement, shall provide the following disclosure statement to the seller, with a copy to the listing broker, at the time any written offer is presented.

THIS REAL ESTATE AGENCY MAY OFFER TO PROVIDE MORTGAGE FINANCING SERVICES TO THE BUYER FOR A FEE IN ADDITION TO THE SALES COMMISSION. AS AGENT OF THE SELLER, THIS REAL ESTATE AGENCY HAS A FIDUCIARY DUTY TO YOU, THE SELLER, WHICH WILL NOT CHANGE SHOULD MORTGAGE FINANCING SERVICES BE PROVIDED. IN THE EVENT THAT MORTGAGE FINANCING SERVICES ARE PROVIDED TO THE BUYER, THIS AGENCY SHALL NOT UNDERTAKE REPRESENTATION OF THE BUYER IN THIS REAL ESTATE SALE.

(e) Where the licensee or agency does provide mortgage financing services to the buyer for compensation or reimbursement and also represents only the seller in the sales transaction, the following statement must be included in the written disclosure to the buyer required by (b) or (c) above. The licensee or agency must also promptly send or deliver the following written disclosure statement to the seller, with a copy to the listing broker, at the time a mortgage application is submitted on behalf of the buyer/ borrower.

....
(name of licensee and brokerage agency)

REPRESENTS THE SELLER IN THE REAL ESTATE SALES TRANSACTION. UPON CLOSING OF TITLE, THIS REAL ESTATE AGENCY WILL RECEIVE A SALES COMMISSION FOR REPRESENTING THE SELLER. THIS REAL ESTATE AGENCY ALSO PROVIDES MORTGAGE FINANCING SERVICES TO THE BUYER FOR A FEE IN THE AMOUNT OF .. AS AGENT OF THE SELLER, THIS REAL ESTATE AGENCY HAS A FIDUCIARY DUTY TO THE SELLER WHICH IS NOT CHANGED BY PROVIDING MORTGAGE SERVICES TO THE BUYER. THIS AGENCY DOES NOT REPRESENT THE BUYER IN THIS REAL ESTATE SALE.

Where the precise amount of the compensation to the licensee or agency for providing mortgage services has not yet been established, the maximum estimated amount of compensation should be included in this disclosure. The compensation received by the licensee may not be increased above the amount disclosed here without written notice to both parties, with a copy to the listing broker.

11:5-6.8   **Disclosure of licensee's affiliation with a mortgage lender or mortgage broker to whom the licensee refers buyers**

(a) Whenever a real estate licensee refers a buyer/borrower to a mortgage lender or mortgage broker with whom the licensee is affiliated, the licensee must provide written disclosure of the affiliation to the buyer. This disclosure must be made even though the licensee will receive no fees or compensation for the referral, see N.J.A.C. 11:5-7.2, and even though the licensee also refers the buyer to other, unaffiliated sources of mortgage financing. The disclosure must include the following statement:

YOU ARE UNDER NO OBLIGATION TO USE THE MORTGAGE SERVICES OF _____ WHO/WHICH IS AFFILIATED WITH THIS REAL ESTATE LICENSEE. YOU MAY OBTAIN YOUR MORTGAGE LOAN FROM ANOTHER SOURCE.

(b) For the purposes of this rule, a real estate licensee is considered to be affiliated with a mortgage lender or mortgage broker when:

1. The licensee, or the licensee's spouse, parent or child, is an officer, director or employee of the lender or mortgage broker, or works as a solicitor for the lender or mortgage broker;

2. The licensee, either alone or with spouse, parent or child, owns more than one percent of the lender or mortgage broker; the licensee is more than one percent owned by the lender or mortgage broker, or the licensee owns more than one percent or is more than one percent owned by a corporate parent, holding company or other business entity which is a majority shareholder in the lender or mortgage broker;

3. The licensee is a franchisee of a franchiser which owns more than one percent of the lender or mortgage broker or the licensee itself is the franchiser or franchisee of a mortgage lending franchise; or

4. The licensee shares office space or other facilities, or staff, with the lender or mortgage broker.

(c) Where an employing broker or broker of record of a real estate agency has an individual or corporate affiliation with a lender or mortgage broker, all licensees licensed with that real estate broker must provide the required disclosures to buyers referred to the affiliate.

1. Where an office manager has such an individual affiliation, the manager and all licensees working under his or her supervision must provide the disclosure to all buyers referred to the affiliate by that office.

2. Where a referral agent, a salesperson or a broker-salesperson has such an individual affiliation, he or she must provide the disclosure to all buyers he or she refers to the affiliate.

(d) The disclosure required by this section may be combined with the disclosure of affiliation required under RESPA, 12 U.S.C. §§ 2601 et seq. Copies of all written disclosures required by this rule must be retained by the broker as business records available for inspection pursuant to N.J.A.C. 11:5-5.4 and 5.5.

11:5-6.9   Consumer Information Statement

(a) When applied to rental transactions which are not exempt from this rule, references to sellers and buyers, and to the various types of brokerage agreements and business relationships mentioned throughout this rule should be construed as indicating their appropriate counterparts in rental transactions. For example, references to sellers should be read as lessors or owners and references to buyers should be read as lessees or tenants, etc. As used in this rule, the following terms or phrases shall have the following meanings:

1. "Brokerage agreement" means a written agreement between a brokerage firm and a party describing the terms under which that firm will perform brokerage services as specified in N.J.S.A. 45:15-3. Brokerage agreements include, but are not limited to, sale and rental listing agreements, buyer-broker, lessee-broker, transaction broker, and dual agency agreements.

2. "Brokerage firm" means a licensed corporate, partnership or sole proprietor broker, and all individuals licensed with that broker.

3. Consumer Information Statement" means the Consumer Information Statement on New Jersey Real Estate Relationships as prescribed in (h) below.

4. "Informed consent to dual agency" means the written authorization by a party for the brokerage firm which represents them as their agent in a real estate transaction to also represent the other party to that transaction as an agent. Informed consent can only be obtained after the brokerage firm has disclosed to the consenting party all material facts which might reasonably impact on that party's decision to authorize dual agency, including the extent of the conflicts of interests involved and the specific ways in which each consenting party will receive less than full agency representation from the dual agent. In order to obtain informed consent it is also necessary for the licensee to first advise the consenting party of the other business relationships offered by that licensee and of those not offered by that licensee, and of that party's right to consult an attorney.

5. "Party" shall mean actual or prospective sellers, lessors, buyers or lessees of an interest in real estate.

6. "Short term rental" shall mean the rental of a residential property for not more than the 125 consecutive day time period specified in N.J.S.A. 46:8-19 as constituting the "seasonal use or rental" of real property, under the terms of an oral rental agreement or written lease which contains a specific termination date. Month-to-month tenancies are not considered short term rentals.

7. "Transaction broker" shall mean a brokerage firm which works with both parties in an effort to arrive at an agreement on the sale or rental of real estate and facilitates the closing of a transaction, but does not represent either party, and has no agency relationship with either party to the transaction. The New Jersey Real Estate License Law, N.J.S.A. 45:15-1 et seq., and the administrative rules promulgated thereunder do not mandate that licensees must act as agents when rendering real estate brokerage services.

8. "Business relationship(s)" means real estate licensees working as a seller's agent; a buyer's agent; a disclosed dual agent; or a transaction broker.

(b) Prior to acting as a dual agent, a brokerage firm must have the written informed consent of the parties to the transaction. Informed consent is not acquired through distribution of the Consumer Information Statement on New Jersey Real Estate

REAL ESTATE COMMISSION

Relationships as required by (e) and (k) below alone. At a minimum, licensees must also secure the signature of the party on a separate writing which confirms the party's informed consent to the licensee acting as a Disclosed Dual Agent for that party. Such a writing may be part of, or an attachment to a brokerage agreement.

(c) Licensees shall supply information with regard to their working relationship with parties to real estate transactions as provided in this section.

(d) Licensees shall comply with all requirements of this section when involved in:

1. Transactions which involve the sale of residential real estate containing one to four dwelling units or the sale of vacant one-family lots;

2. Residential lease transactions other than short term rentals. However, in short-term rental transactions, licensees shall include in all leases prepared by them a statement indicating that they are acting in the transaction either as an agent of the landlord, an agent of the tenant, a disclosed dual agent or a transaction broker; and

3. The securing of brokerage agreements on residential properties, including rental listing agreements on residential properties to be offered for short term rentals.

(e) All licensees shall supply information on business relationships to buyers and sellers in accordance with the following:

1. With respect to buyers:

i. All licensees shall verbally inform buyers of the four business relationships described in this section prior to the first discussion at which a buyer's motivation or financial ability to buy is discussed.

ii. If the first such discussion occurs during a business meeting on the buyer's real estate needs, licensees shall deliver the written Consumer Information Statement to the buyers prior to such a discussion. If the first such discussion is telephonic or in a social setting, licensees shall, after having verbally informed the buyer of the four business relationships, deliver the written Consumer Information Statement to the buyer at their next meeting. However, if prior to their first business meeting after such a discussion, any material is mailed, faxed or delivered by the licensee to the buyer, the Consumer Information Statement shall be included with such material.

iii. Where the written Consumer Information Statement has not been delivered to buyers as provided in (e)1ii above, licensees shall deliver the written statement to buyers no later than the

first showing and, if no showing is conducted, no later than the preparation of an initial offer or contract.

iv. Those licensees who intend to enter into a buyer-brokerage relationship with such persons shall deliver the Consumer Information Statement no later than the commencement of their buyer-brokerage agreement presentation.

2. With respect to sellers:

i. All licensees shall verbally inform sellers of the four business relationships described in this section prior to the first discussion at which the seller's motivation or desired selling price is discussed.

ii. If the first such discussion occurs during a business meeting on the seller's real estate needs, licensees shall deliver the written Consumer Information Statement to the sellers prior to such a discussion. If the first such discussion is telephonic or in a social setting, licensees shall, after having verbally informed the seller of the four business relationships, deliver the written Consumer Information Statement to the seller at their next meeting. However, if prior to their first business meeting after such a discussion, any material is mailed, faxed or delivered by the licensee to the seller, the Consumer Information Statement shall be included with such material.

iii. On unlisted properties where the written Consumer Information Statement has not been delivered to sellers as provided in (e)2ii above, licensees shall deliver the written statement to sellers no later than their first showing of the property, and if no showing is conducted, no later than the presentation of an initial offer or contract.

iv. Those licensees who intend to enter into a listing or transaction brokerage agreement with a seller shall deliver the Consumer Information Statement no later than the commencement of their listing or transaction brokerage agreement presentation.

(f) The purpose of (e) above and (h) below is to require licensees to provide basic and introductory information to the public in a convenient and consistent manner, rather than a comprehensive explanation of agency law.

(g) The statement as supplied by the Commission shall be reproduced and delivered by licensees as required in this section as a separate item, with no deletions or additions, other than the optional additional text referred to in (g)1 and 2 below, and recited in (h) below.

1. Brokerage firms may acknowledge delivery of the Statement by procuring the signature of the party to whom it was delivered and the date of delivery in the appropriate place at the bottom of the Statement.

i. On transactions which result in fully executed contracts of sale or consummated rental transactions, copies of Consumer Information Statements on which receipt has been acknowledged as set forth in (g)1 above, shall be maintained as business records for six years in accordance with N.J.A.C. 11:5-5.4(c).

2. Brokerage firms may also indicate on the Statement the capacity in which they intend to work with the party to whom they deliver the Statement.

3. Regardless of whether brokerage firms choose to include on the Statement the additional information referred to in (g)1 and 2 above, all brokerage firms, as is required by (i) and (j) below, shall:

i. Indicate in all brokerage agreements the business relationship they intend to have with the other party to the agreement; and

ii. Indicate in all offers, contracts, or leases prepared by licensees the business relationship the firm has with respect to the parties named in those documents.

(h) The mandatory text of the Consumer Information Statement to be delivered by licensees as provided in (e) above is as follows:

CONSUMER INFORMATION STATEMENT ON NEW JERSEY REAL ESTATE RELATIONSHIPS

In New Jersey, real estate licensees are required to disclose how they intend to work with buyers and sellers in a real estate transaction. (In rental transactions, the terms "buyers" and "sellers" should be read as "tenants" and "landlords," respectively.)

1. AS A SELLER'S AGENT OR SUBAGENT, I, AS A LICENSEE, REPRESENT THE SELLER AND ALL MATERIAL INFORMATION SUPPLIED TO ME BY THE BUYER WILL BE TOLD TO THE SELLER.

2. AS A BUYER'S AGENT, I, AS A LICENSEE, REPRESENT THE BUYER AND ALL MATERIAL INFORMATION SUPPLIED TO ME BY THE SELLER WILL BE TOLD TO THE BUYER.

3. AS A DISCLOSED DUAL AGENT, I, AS A LICENSEE, REPRESENT BOTH PARTIES. HOWEVER, I MAY NOT, WITHOUT EXPRESS PERMISSION, DISCLOSE THAT THE SELLER WILL ACCEPT A PRICE LESS THAN THE LISTING PRICE OR THAT THE BUYER WILL PAY A PRICE GREATER THAN THE OFFERED PRICE.

4. AS A TRANSACTION BROKER, I, AS A LICENSEE, DO NOT REPRESENT EITHER THE BUYER OR THE SELLER. ALL INFORMATION I ACQUIRE FROM ONE PARTY MAY BE TOLD TO THE OTHER PARTY.

Before you disclose confidential information to a real estate licensee regarding a real estate transaction, you should understand what type of business relationship you have with that licensee.

There are four business relationships: (1) seller's agent; (2) buyer's agent; (3) disclosed dual agent; and (4) transaction broker. Each of these relationships imposes certain legal duties and responsibilities on the licensee as well as on the seller or buyer represented. These four relationships are defined in greater detail below. Please read carefully before making your choice.

SELLER'S AGENT

A seller's agent WORKS ONLY FOR THE SELLER and has legal obligations, called fiduciary duties, to the seller. These include reasonable care, undivided loyalty, confidentiality and full disclosure. Seller's agents often work with buyers, but do not represent the buyers. However, in working with buyers a seller's agent must act honestly. In dealing with both parties, a seller's agent may not make any misrepresentation to either party on matters material to the transaction, such as the buyer's financial ability to pay, and must disclose defects of a material nature affecting the physical condition of the property which a reasonable inspection by the licensee would disclose.

Seller's agents include all persons licensed with the brokerage firm which has been authorized through a listing agreement to work as the seller's agent. In addition, other brokerage firms may accept an offer to work with the listing broker's firm as the seller's agents. In such cases, those firms and all persons licensed with such firms are called "sub-agents." Sellers who do not desire to have their property marketed through sub-agents should so inform the seller's agent.

BUYER'S AGENT

A buyer's agent WORKS ONLY FOR THE BUYER. A buyer's agent has fiduciary duties to the buyer which include reasonable care, undivided loyalty, confidentiality and full disclosure. However, in dealing with sellers a buyer's agent must act honestly. In dealing with both parties, a buyer's agent may not make any misrepresentations on matters material to the transaction, such as the buyer's financial ability to pay, and must disclose defects of a material nature affecting the physical condition of the property which a reasonable inspection by the licensee would disclose.

A buyer wishing to be represented by a buyer's agent is advised to enter into a separate written buyer agency contract with the brokerage firm which is to work as their agent.

DISCLOSED DUAL AGENT

A disclosed dual agent WORKS FOR BOTH THE BUYER AND THE SELLER. To work as a dual agent, a firm must first obtain the informed written consent of the buyer and the seller. Therefore, before acting as a disclosed dual agent, brokerage firms must make written disclosure to both parties. Disclosed dual agency is most likely to occur when a licensee with a real estate firm working as a buyer's agent shows the buyer properties owned by sellers for whom that firm is also working as a seller's agent or subagent.

A real estate licensee working as a disclosed dual agent must carefully explain to each party that, in addition to working as their agent, their firm will also work as the agent for the other party. They must also explain what effect their working as a disclosed dual agent will have on the fiduciary duties their firm owes to the buyer and to the seller. When working as a disclosed dual agent, a brokerage firm must have the express permission of a party prior to disclosing confidential information to the other party. Such information includes the highest price a buyer can afford to pay and the lowest price a seller will accept and the parties' motivation to buy or sell. Remember, a brokerage firm acting as a disclosed dual agent will not be able to put one party's interests ahead of those of the other party and cannot advise or counsel either party on how to gain an advantage at the expense of the other party on the basis of confidential information obtained from or about the other party.

If you decide to enter into an agency relationship with a firm which is to work as a disclosed dual agent, you are advised to sign a written agreement with that firm.

TRANSACTION BROKER

The New Jersey Real Estate Licensing Law does not require licensees to work in the capacity of an "agent" when providing brokerage services. A transaction broker works with a buyer or a seller or both in the sales transaction without representing anyone. A TRANSACTION BROKER DOES NOT PROMOTE THE INTERESTS OF ONE PARTY OVER THOSE OF THE OTHER PARTY TO THE TRANSACTION. Licensees with such a firm would be required to treat all parties honestly and to act in a competent manner, but they would not be required to keep confidential any information. A transaction broker can locate qualified buyers for a seller or suitable properties for a buyer. They can then work with both parties in an effort to arrive at an agreement on the sale or rental of real estate and perform tasks to facilitate the closing of a transaction. A transaction broker primarily serves as a manager of the transaction, communicating information between the parties to assist them in arriving at a mutually acceptable agreement and in closing the transaction, but cannot advise or counsel either party on how to gain an

advantage at the expense of the other party. Owners considering working with transaction brokers are advised to sign a written agreement with that firm which clearly states what services that firm will perform and how it will be paid. In addition, any transaction brokerage agreement with a seller or landlord should specifically state whether a notice on the property to be rented or sold will or will not be circulated in any or all Multiple Listing System(s) of which that firm is a member.

YOU MAY OBTAIN LEGAL ADVICE ABOUT THESE BUSINESS RELATIONSHIPS FROM YOUR OWN LAWYER.

THIS STATEMENT IS NOT A CONTRACT AND IS PROVIDED FOR INFORMATIONAL PURPOSES ONLY.

(END OF MANDATORY CONSUMER INFORMATION STATEMENT TEXT)

(OPTIONAL ACKNOWLEDGEMENT OF RECEIPT AFTER TEXT OF CONSUMER INFORMATION STATEMENT.)

FOR SELLERS AND LANDLORDS

"By signing this Consumer Information Statement, I acknowledge that I received this Statement from (Name of Brokerage Firm) prior to discussing my motivation to sell or lease or my desired selling or leasing price with one of its representatives."

FOR BUYERS AND TENANTS

"By signing this Consumer Information Statement, I acknowledge that I received this Statement from (Name of Brokerage Firm) prior to discussing my motivation or financial ability to buy or lease with one of its representatives."

(OPTIONAL INDICATION OF IN WHAT CAPACITY FIRM INTENDS TO WORK WITH RECIPIENT OF CONSUMER INFORMATION STATEMENT AS PERMITTED BY (g)2 ABOVE):

I, ..., as an authorized representative of ...., intend, as of this time, to work with you as a
(indicate one of the following):
seller's agent only
buyer's agent only
seller's agent and disclosed dual agent if the opportunity arises
buyer's agent and disclosed dual agent if the opportunity arises
transaction broker only
seller's agent on properties on which this firm is acting as the seller's

agent and transaction broker on other properties

(i) In all brokerage agreements, brokerage firms must include the following:

1. A statement acknowledging receipt of the Consumer Information Statement; and

2. A declaration of business relationship indicating the regular business name of the broker and in what capacity the licensee servicing the agreement and their firm will operate as real estate licensees with respect to the other party to the brokerage agreement. The declaration of business relationship in all brokerage agreements shall contain, in print larger than the predominant size print in the writing, the following language:

I, ..., as an authorized representative of ...., intend, as of this time, to work with you as a

    (indicate one of the following):
    seller's agent only
    buyer's agent only
    seller's agent and disclosed dual agent if the opportunity arises
    buyer's agent and disclosed dual agent if the opportunity arises
    transaction broker only
    seller's agent on properties on which this firm is acting as the seller's agent and transaction broker on other properties

3. Where brokerage firms secure a written acknowledgement of receipt of the Consumer Information Statement on the Statement itself as provided in (g)1 above and include on the Consumer Information Statement a declaration of the business relationship they intend to have with the other party to the brokerage agreement as provided in (g)2 above, the attachment of a copy of the Consumer Information Statement to the brokerage agreement and the inclusion of a reference to the receipt of the Consumer Information Statement in the brokerage agreement shall constitute compliance with this section.

(j) Licensees shall disclose to consumers what type of brokerage services they will provide in the following manner:

1. Buyer-brokers shall verbally disclose to sellers that they are acting on behalf of a buyer prior to their first communication with the seller during which the seller's motivation to sell or desired price is discussed.

2. All offers, contracts or leases not exempt by this rule which are prepared by licensees shall include the following statements:

"By signing below the sellers (or landlords as applicable) and purchasers (or tenants as applicable) acknowledge they received the Consumer Information Statement on New Jersey Real Estate Relationships from the brokerage firms involved in this transaction prior to the first showing of the property."

3. In all offers, contracts, or leases, including leases for short-term rentals, prepared by licensees as permitted by N.J.A.C. 11:5-6.2(g), licensees shall include the regular business name of the broker with whom they are licensed and a declaration of business relationship indicating in what capacity they and their firm are operating as real estate licensees in that real estate transaction. The declaration of business relationship in all offers to purchase or to lease property, including those made on contracts of sale or lease documents prepared by licensees, shall contain, in print as large as the predominant size print in the writing, the following language: .... and .... as its authorized

(Name of firm) (Name(s) of licensee(s)) representative(s) are working in this transaction as .... (indicate one of the following):

    seller's agents

    buyer's agents

    disclosed dual agents

    transaction brokers

i. In transactions in which more than one firm is involved, all licensee-prepared offers, contracts and leases, including leases on short-term rentals, shall contain, in the same size type and immediately following the declaration of business relationship set forth above, the following clause:

Information supplied by.(Name of firm) ....

  (Name of firm)

has indicated that it is operating in this transaction as a __ (indicate one of the following):

    seller's agent only

    buyer's agent only

    transaction broker

ii. The requirement to include the clause cited in (j)3i above in licensee-prepared offers, contracts and leases shall not apply with respect to firms whose involvement in a transaction was limited to merely referring a party to another firm.

(k) Licensees shall disclose to other licensees what type of business relationship they have with the party with whom they have a brokerage agreement, and with any other parties with whom they may be working, in the following manner:

1. In all written or computer generated notices directed to other brokerage firms through a Multiple Listing Service or otherwise, the listing broker shall indicate whether they are working as a seller's agent or as a transaction broker. On listings where the listing broker is operating as a seller's agent, such notices shall also state:

i. Whether subagency is offered;

ii. Whether the seller has authorized the sharing of the listing broker's compensation with cooperating subagents and/or transaction brokers and/or buyer brokers; and

iii. The amount of compensation offered to cooperating subagents and/or transaction brokers and/or buyer brokers.

2. When a licensee with a listing broker receives an inquiry about a particular property from any other licensee, the licensee with the broker shall, before providing any information to the inquiring licensee beyond general information previously circulated about the listing, verbally ascertain from the inquiring licensee the capacity in which that licensee is operating or intends to operate (buyer-broker, subagent, disclosed dual agent or transaction broker). Inquiries from other licensees in the listing broker's firm shall also be responded to as set forth in this subsection.

(*l*) In transactions where brokers seek compensation for their brokerage services from a party to the transaction whom they are not representing or working with, the business relationship with the party they are representing or working with and the compensation arrangement shall also be disclosed to both parties as required by N.J.A.C. 11:5-7.1.

(m) Notwithstanding anything appearing in (g) and (h) above to the contrary, where a brokerage firm is itself the owner of the property being sold by individuals licensed through the broker-owner of the property, a Consumer Information Statement, revised as provided in this section, shall be delivered to prospective purchasers in accordance with the provisions of this rule.

1. On the line immediately below the title of the Consumer Information Statement, the following text shall appear in print larger than the predominant size print in the writing:

As the holder of a New Jersey real estate license, I am required by law to inform you how I will operate in this transaction, should you pursue it, and to provide this statement to you.

My employer is the owner of the property(s) in which you have expressed an interest. For the purposes of its business relationship disclosure rules, the New Jersey Real Estate Commission deems brokers selling property they own and licensees employed or retained by such broker-owners to be operating as seller's agents when they sell property owned by the broker. The statements which follow with regard to licensees who act as sellers' agents apply to me and other persons employed or retained by the owner, particularly those statements concerning the obligation of sellers' agents to pass on to the sellers all material information they obtain with regard to the buyers' ability to pay.

11:5-6.10   Referral agents

(a) A licensed referral agent's real estate brokerage-related activities shall be limited to:

1. Directing prospects to websites and other sources of information on real estate matters generally available to the general public; and

2. Referring prospects for the sale, purchase, exchange, leasing or rental of real estate to the real estate broker through whom they are licensed as a referral agent or, should that broker autho-

rize the referral agent to do so, to another real estate licensee. In all cases where referrals are made pursuant to such an authorization, the referral agent shall provide written or electronic notice to his or her broker or to that broker's designee, who shall be a broker-salesperson or salesperson licensee, at the time the referral is made. In accordance with N.J.S.A. 45:15-16, all compensation payable to a referral agent for any referral shall be paid by the broker through whom the referral agent is licensed.

(b) A referral agent shall not be employed by or licensed with more than one real estate broker at any given time.

(c) No person shall be simultaneously licensed as a referral agent and a real estate broker, broker-salesperson or a salesperson in this State.

(d) Referral agents shall not engage in prohibited brokerage activity for their broker or for others, and shall not receive compensation from their broker or any other person for engaging in prohibited brokerage activity. For the purposes of this section, prohibited brokerage activity includes, but is not limited to, the following:

1. Negotiating the purchase, sale, or exchange of an interest in real estate;

2. Leasing or renting or offering to lease or rent any interest in real estate;

3. Collecting rents for the use of real estate or any other monies;

4. Negotiating commissions or compensation rates and otherwise negotiating or signing listing or buyer-brokerage agreements;

5. Negotiating or signing contracts of sale or leases of real estate;

6. Accepting any funds of others to be held by a real estate broker acting in that capacity or as escrow agent or as the temporary custodian of the funds of others in a real estate transaction;

7. Conducting a public or private competitive sale of land or any interest in lands;

8. Negotiating, assisting in, or directing, the closing of any transaction which results or is contemplated to result in the sale, exchange, leasing, renting or auctioning of any real estate;

9. Negotiating, offering, attempting to, or agreeing to negotiate a loan secured or to be secured by a mortgage or other encumbrance upon or transfer of any real estate;

10. Conducting showings or open house presentations of properties;

11. Participating in expositions, marketing shows or other presentations where information on specific properties or real estate interests marketed through a common promotional plan, including but not limited to planned unit developments, is provided to the public;

12. Providing information on listings, either in person, or through electronic communication including telephone and the internet, beyond the information which referral agents are permitted to provide with respect to websites and other sources of information as referenced in (a) above; and

13. Producing or presenting comparative market analyses or similar studies of real estate.

SUBCHAPTER 7. PROHIBITED ACTIVITIES

11:5-7.1   Prohibition against licensees receiving dual compensation for dual representation in the sale or rental transaction

(a) Real estate licensees are prohibited from receiving compensation from both a seller and a buyer for representing both seller and buyer in the same real estate sales transaction. This prohibition applies even when the dual agency has been fully disclosed by the licensee to both parties.

(b) Real estate licensees are prohibited from receiving compensation from both a landlord and a tenant for representing both the landlord and the tenant in the same rental transaction. This prohibition applies even when the dual agency has been fully disclosed by the licensee to both parties.

(c) Within the meaning of this section, the phrases "sales transaction" and "rental transaction" do not include any related transactions whether or not they are contingencies in the contract or lease. For example, where there is a mortgage contingency in a contract of sale, the mortgage loan is a related transaction between the buyer and lender; it is not the same transaction as the sale.

(d) A licensee who represents only one party to a sale or rental transaction may receive the entire compensation for such representation from either party or a portion of that compensation from both parties to the transaction, provided that where a licensee prepares a contract or lease full written disclosure of the agency relationship and of the compensation arrangement is made to both parties to the transaction in the contract or lease. Where a licensee does not prepare the contract or lease, but seeks compensation from a party whom he or she does not represent, that licensee's agency relationship and proposed compensation

REAL ESTATE COMMISSION 11:5-7.2

arrangement shall be disclosed to all parties in a separate writing prior to execution of the contract or lease.

(e) A licensee who represents any party to a sale or rental transaction may receive compensation from either party for providing actual services in related transactions, provided that the licensee discloses the related services, sources and amounts of compensation in writing to the parties to the sale or rental transaction. Where the related services to be provided by the licensee are mortgage financing services provided to the buyer for compensation or reimbursement, the written disclosures must comply with N.J.A.C. 11:5-6.7. The broker shall maintain records of such related transactions including all required written disclosures, which records shall be available to the Commission for inspection pursuant to N.J.A.C. 11:5-5.5.

(f) Except as provided in (g) below, when providing mortgage financing services related to the purchase or sale of a one to six family residential dwelling, a portion of which may be used for non-residential purposes, located in New Jersey:

1. A real estate broker shall not solicit or receive compensation or reimbursement pursuant to (e) above greater than the expense amount permitted at closing by rule of the Department of Banking and Insurance unless licensed as a mortgage broker or mortgage banker by the Department of Banking and Insurance pursuant to the New Jersey Licensed Lenders Act, N.J.S.A. 17:11C-1 et seq.; and

2. A real estate referral agent, salesperson or broker-salesperson shall not solicit or receive any compensation or reimbursement pursuant to (e) above from any person other than his or her employing real estate broker unless licensed as a residential mortgage broker or mortgage banker or a mortgage loan originator by the Department of Banking and Insurance pursuant to the New Jersey Residential Mortgage Lending Act, N.J.S.A. 17:11C-51 et seq.

(g) Any real estate licensee who is individually employed as a mortgage solicitor by a licensed mortgage banker or mortgage broker and registered in compliance with applicable law and the rules of the Department of Banking and Insurance may solicit and accept compensation from his or her licensed mortgage employer for providing mortgage services in residential mortgage transactions.

11:5-7.2   Prohibition against kickbacks for related business referrals

(a) Any real estate licensee who solicits or accepts any fee, kickback, compensation or thing of value merely for referring a customer or client to a lender, mortgage broker, or other provider of related services, shall be subject to sanction by the Commission for engaging in conduct demonstrating unworthiness, bad faith and dishonesty. Any compensation received by a real estate licensee, pursuant to N.J.A.C. 11:5-7.1(e), for services in related transactions must be for services actually performed by the licensee beyond mere referral. Compliance with the anti-kickback provisions of the Federal Real Estate Settlement Procedures Act ("RESPA"), 12 U.S.C. § 2607, the regulations thereunder, or any opinion regarding RESPA issued by the Federal Department of Housing and Urban Development will be considered to be in compliance with this subsection.

(b) Any compensation paid by a real estate broker to a referral agent shall be limited to compensation for referring prospective consumers of real estate brokerage services to the broker. Real estate brokers are prohibited from offering incentives to the referral agents, salespersons or broker-salespersons licensed under them for merely referring clients or customers to a particular lender, mortgage broker or other provider of related services. Any compensation paid by a real estate broker to a salesperson or broker-salesperson for services in transactions related to a sale or rental transaction must be for services actually performed by the salesperson beyond mere referral to a mortgage lender, mortgage broker or other provider of related services. For example, a real estate broker who provides in-house mortgage services may compensate a salesperson licensed with that broker who performs actual mortgage services. However, the broker is prohibited from offering bonuses or any extra consideration of any kind to licensees of his or her firm for merely referring buyers to the in-house mortgage service or any particular lender or mortgage broker. For example, a real estate broker shall not offer or pay a salesperson a higher commission rate on a real estate transaction because the mortgage is placed through the in-house mortgage service or affiliated lender. A broker shall not award prizes or bonuses to salespersons based upon the number of customer referrals made to the in-house mortgage service or to a particular lender.

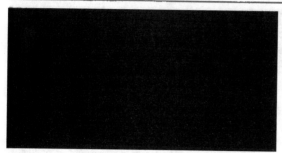

11:5-7.3 **Licensees with in-house mortgage services prohibited from excluding all outside mortgage solicitors**

Real estate brokers who provide mortgage financing services to buyer/borrowers in-house, whether through computerized loan origination systems, or affiliated lenders or affiliated mortgage brokers, etc., are prohibited from limiting buyer's choices by denying outside lenders reasonable access to solicit mortgage loans in their real estate offices. Reasonable access will be presumed where three or more outside, non-affiliated lenders are permitted to send solicitors into the real estate office during business hours to contact salespersons. The reasonableness of the broker's overall office policy concerning rate sheets, and access by outside lenders, other visitors and solicitors, will also be considered. In no event shall this rule be interpreted to require any real estate broker to permit any one specific lender to solicit loans inside the real estate office or to require the real estate broker to set aside any particular space or facilities inside the real estate office for the use of outside mortgage solicitors.

11:5-7.4 **Blockbusting; solicitation**

(a) No licensee shall affirmatively solicit the sale, lease or the listing for sale or lease of residential property on the grounds of alleged change of value due to the presence or prospective entry into the neighborhood of a person or persons of another race, religion or ethnic origin, nor shall distribute, or cause to be distributed, material, or make statements designed to include a residential property owner to sell or lease his property due to such change in the neighborhood.

(b) Every real estate broker who, in a personal meeting, solicits the sale, lease or the listing for sale or lease of three or more residential properties fronting on either side of any street between intersecting or cross streets or between a cul-de-sac or other like termination point and an intersecting or cross street within the same month, whether directly or through personal meetings attended by his or her firm's licensees, shall maintain a permanent record for at least one year from the date of said solicitation, which shall be available for inspection by the Commission or any representative thereof upon request, setting forth the name and address of each person so solicited, the address of the property involved, the name of the licensee actually making such solicitation, and the date upon which the solicitation took place. At the request of the Commission or any representative thereof, any such broker shall file with the Commission a copy of the permanent record, or a statement containing the same information as set forth in the permanent record. Such filing shall be made with the Commission no later than 10 days following the request therefore.

11:5-7.5 **Proscription of price-fixing and agreements in regard to methods of arriving at commission**

(a) No licensee shall combine, conspire, suggest, or recommend to, or with any other licensee(s) that any rate, commission or fee to be charged by them, or any division of such commission by them be fixed, established, maintained, suggested or stabilized. Nothing in this section shall prohibit any intra-office communications with regard to the establishment of commissions or division of commissions.

(b) No licensee shall directly or indirectly recommend or suggest to any other licensee(s) that such person(s) adhere to any schedule or recommendation of another concerning the rates, commissions or fees to be charged or the methodology or approach by which a commission, rate or fee is arrived at, or division of fees to be made, in the conduct of business. Nothing in this section shall prohibit any intra-office communications with regard to the establishment of commissions or division of commissions. Information imparted solely for the purposes of instruction, and not for the purpose of recommending guidelines or a preferred method of pricing, at any bona fide trade association seminar or educational courses shall be excepted from the proscription set forth in this section.

11:5-7.6   Proscription of certain discriminatory commission splits

No licensee shall directly or indirectly take any punitive or retaliatory action against any other licensee(s) where such action is based upon the failure or refusal to adhere or to adopt any commission. No licensee shall adopt a discriminatory commission split against another broker because of such other broker's failure or refusal to adhere to or adopt any commission; if a listing broker varies his commission split policy with any selling broker on a cooperative sale, the listing broker shall maintain a file at his place of business which shall contain in writing an explanation for the variation and which reflects who made the decision and why it was made. Nothing in this section shall prohibit a listing broker from varying his commission split policy with respect to any one or more selling brokers in order to achieve equality of commission splits with such other selling broker or brokers in connection with their commission split policy with such listing broker.

11:5-7.7   Proscription on pressuring media

No licensee shall agree, combine or conspire with another to boycott, or threaten to boycott, or refuse to do business with any promotional medium where such refusal or boycott is based on the acceptance by any medium of advertising of price or commissions of a competitive or discount nature.

SUBCHAPTER 8. DISCIPLINARY ACTIONS/CONDITIONS FOR RESTORATION OF LICENSE/REAL ESTATE GUARANTY FUND CLAIMS

11:5-8.1   Disciplinary action; restitution

(a) Violation of any of these rules and regulations, or of any real estate statute, shall be sufficient cause for any disciplinary action permitted by statute.

(b) In accordance with the provisions of N.J.S.A. 45:15-9 and N.J.S.A. 45:15-17, the Commission, in appropriate circumstances, will exercise its authority to impose restitution of moneys owed others as a condition to the issuance of a license or to the reinstatement of a license after revocation or suspension.

(c) The Commission may, where the nature of the offense so warrants, impose as a condition to any future license restoration, the successful accomplishment of a written examination of the same type normally given to applicants for initial licenses.

11:5-8.2

<header>INSURANCE</header>

11:5-8.2   Real estate guaranty fund

(a) Every real estate licensee shall pay an additional amount as specified in N.J.S.A. 45:15-35 with their application for a license.

1. Said fees shall be paid into the real estate guaranty fund and be utilized in accordance with N.J.S.A. 45:15-34 et seq.

(b) Before making a request for the entry of a court order directing payment from the real estate guaranty fund, a judgment credit shall have a writ of execution issued and prior to its return shall make a bona fide effort to examine the judgment debtor under oath and make any and all other reasonable searches and inquiries to ascertain whether the judgment debtor possesses real or personal property or other assets, liable to be sold or applied in satisfaction of the judgment in whole or in part. Information regarding any personal or real property or other assets liable to be sold or applied in satisfaction of the judgment which are discovered must be reported in writing to the officer to whom the writ of execution is directed.

SUBCHAPTER 9. RULES INTERPRETING AND IMPLEMENTING THE REAL ESTATE SALES FULL DISCLOSURE ACT, N.J.S.A. 45:15-16.27 ET SEQ.

11:5-9.1   Applicability and scope

(a) The rules in this subchapter are promulgated by the New Jersey Real Estate Commission (hereinafter, the Commission) to implement the provisions of the Real Estate Sales Full Disclosure Act (hereinafter, the Act), N.J.S.A. 45:15-16.27 et seq. These rules are applicable to all applications and matters pertaining to and/or effected by the provisions of this Act.

(b) All registration and exemption applications and all correspondence and inquiries should be directed to: New Jersey Real Estate Commission, Bureau of Subdivided Land Sales Control, 20 West State Street, PO Box 328, Trenton, New Jersey 08625-0328.

REAL ESTATE COMMISSION   11:5-9.2

11:5-9.2　　Definitions

The following words and terms, as used in this subchapter, shall have the following meanings, unless the context clearly indicates otherwise.

"Advertising" means the publication or causing to be published, of any information offering for sale or for the purpose of causing or inducing any other person to purchase or acquire, an interest in the title to subdivided lands, including the sales contract to be used and any photographs or drawings or artist's representation of physical conditions or facilities on the property existing or to exist by means of any:

    1. Newspaper or periodical;

    2. Radio or television broadcast;

    3. Written or printed or photographic matter produced by any duplicating process producing 10 copies or more;

    4. Billboards or signs;

    5. Display of model homes or units;

    6. Material used in connection with the disposition or offer of subdivided lands by radio, television, telephone or any other electronic means; or

    7. Material used by subdividers or their agents to induce prospective purchasers to visit the subdivision; particularly vacation certificates which require the holders of those certificates to attend or submit to a sales presentation by a subdivider or its agents.

"Advertising" does not mean: stockholder communications such as annual reports and interim financial reports, proxy materials, registration statements, securities prospectuses, applications for listing securities on stock exchanges, or similar documents, prospectuses, property reports, offering statements or other documents required to be delivered to a prospective purchaser by an agency of any other state or the Federal Government, all communications addressed to and relating to the account of any person who has previously executed a contract for the purchase of the subdivider's lands except when directed to the sale of additional lands.

"Applicant" means a person who or entity which has applied for the registration of real property of interests therein with the Commission pursuant to the Act or for a total or limited exemption from those registration requirements.

"Blanket encumbrance" means a trust deed, mortgage, judgment, or any other lien or encumbrance, including an option or contract to sell, or a trust agreement affecting a subdivision or affecting more than one lot offered within a subdivision, except that term shall not include any lien or other encumbrance arising as the result of the imposition of any tax assessment by any public authority.

"Broker" or "salesperson" means any person who performs within this State as an agent or employee of a subdivider any one or more of the services or acts as set forth in this Act, and includes any real estate broker or salesperson licensed pursuant to N.J.S.A. 45:15-1 et seq. or any person who purports to act in any such capacity.

"Broker's Release" means the document issued by the Commission affirming that the broker to whom it is issued has been approved by the Commission as the designated New Jersey broker of record or as a supplemental broker of a registrant, and has been authorized by the Commission to commence solicitation and sales efforts on behalf of that registrant in New Jersey.

"Commission" means the New Jersey Real Estate Commission.

"Common promotional plan" means any offer for the disposition of lots, parcels, units or interests of real property by a single person or group of persons acting in concert, where those lots, parcels, units or interests are contiguous, or are known, designated or advertised as a common entity or by a common name regardless of the number of lots, parcels, units or interests covered by each individual offering.

"Deed in trust" means a written instrument, in recordable form and conforming to all applicable laws of the situs state, under the terms of which title to a property passes to a trustee who is independent of and unaffiliated with the applicant/registrant, and which title is to be held by that trustee on behalf of the purchaser pursuant to a trust agreement or equivalent instrument between the registrant and the trustee obligating the trustee to convey title to the purchaser promptly upon the purchaser's fulfillment of their obligations under an installment contract for the purchase of such property by the purchaser from the registrant.

"Disposition" means the sale, lease, assignment, award by lottery, or any other transaction concerning a subdivision if undertaken for gain or profit.

"Notice" means a communication by mail from the Commission executed by its secretary or other duly authorized officer. Notice to subdividers shall be deemed complete when mailed to the subdivider's address currently on file with the Commission.

"Offer" means every inducement, solicitation or attempt to encourage a person to acquire an interest in a subdivision if undertaken for gain or profit.

"Person" means an individual, corporation, government or governmental subdivision or agency, business trust, estate, trust, partnership, unincorporated association, two or more of any of the foregoing having a joint or common interest, or any other legal or commercial entity.

"Principal" means all individual applicants or subdividers; all general partners of applicants or subdividers that are partnerships; all officers, directors and shareholders of corporate applicants or subdividers who are actively involved in the planning, management or promotion of the offering; and all other individuals who either own or control an interest of 10 percent or more in an applicant or subdivider, or who will actively participate in the planning, management or promotion of the offering, regardless of the form of organization of the applicant or subdivider.

"Purchaser" means a person who acquires or attempts to acquire or succeeds to an interest in a subdivision.

"Situs state" means the state, province, territory, protectorate, country or other jurisdiction situated outside of the State of New Jersey within which a subdivision is located.

"Subdivider" or "developer" means any owner of subdivided lands or the agent of that owner who offers the subdivided lands for disposition.

"Subdivision" and "subdivided lands" mean any land situated outside the State of New Jersey whether contiguous or not, if one or more lots, parcels, units or interests are offered as part of a common promotional plan of advertising and sale and expressly means and includes such units or interests commonly referred to as a "condominium" defined in the "Condominium Act" P.L. 1969, c. 257 (N.J.S.A. 46:8B-1 et seq.). In addition to condominiums, this definition shall also specifically include, but shall not be limited to, any form of homeowners association, any housing cooperative, and any community trust or other trust device.

11:5-9.3   Forms of documents

(a) Rules concerning documents with respect to the registration of subdivisions with the Commission and to the sale of interests in out-of-State subdivisions pursuant to the Act are as follows:

1. All statements of record submitted to the Commission shall be bound, referenced and properly indexed with the ex-

ception of those received from the Office of Interstate Land Sales Registration, U.S. Department of Housing and Urban Development.

2. With the exception of the affidavits and affirmations referenced in (a)5 below, documents submitted to the Commission may be filed on a properly bookmarked and indexed computer disc (CD ROM) or other electronic medium acceptable to the Commission. All paper documents submitted to the Commission for filing shall, wherever possible, be typewritten on one side of the paper only. One copy of each exhibit or document shall be submitted, unless the Commission requests more than one copy. All documents submitted to the Commission shall not exceed 8 1/2 x 14 inches. The Commission will make exceptions for documents which an applicant for registration cannot reasonably reduce, such as topographical maps, plat maps and surveys, if such documents can be folded to 8 1/2 x 14 inches. Where the Commission requires certified documents and the applicant cannot obtain reduced certified documents, the applicant may reduce such documents and submit therewith an affidavit verifying such document. All documents submitted pursuant to these rules shall become part of the Commission's public records.

3. An applicant may submit photographs as part of the application for registration. Photographs shall not be used in lieu of the legal description of the registered property or any other required written documents.

4. An applicant may submit verified copies of original documents.

5. An affidavit or affirmation as prescribed in the Commission's forms shall be executed for each of the following documents:

i. Statement of record, partial statement of record;

ii. Application for consolidated registration;

iii. Application for amendment to Order of Registration;

iv. Annual report of registered properties;

v. Statement of Non-conviction and partner, officer, director or principal disclosure;

vi. Consent(s) to service of process; and

vii. Broker's Affidavit and application for release.

6. A certified property report and statement of record of the Office of Interstate Land Sales Registration, Department of Housing and Urban Development, may be filed as a statement of record conforming to the requirements of the Act, provided the following documentation shall also be submitted:

i. Consent(s) to service of process;

ii. Audited financial statement(s) as provided in N.J.A.C. 11:5-6.4(a)15;

iii. A statement detailing any bonding or security agreements entered into;

iv. Broker's Affidavit and application for release;

v. A copy of each contract to be used in the sale of property in the development to New Jersey purchasers;

vi. Statement of Non-conviction and partner, officer, director or principal disclosure;

vii. A copy of the articles or certificate of incorporation;

viii. Application/affidavit of developer; and

ix. Such other additional documents or proofs that may be requested.

7. The acceptance of the certified report and statement of record of the Office of Interstate Land Sales Registration may be conditioned upon an acceptable on-site inspection by the Commission or its designee. No marketing or sales activity will be permitted in New Jersey until all the proper authorizations have been received by the applicant and broker from the Commission.

8. Any applicant who wishes to register a subdivision which has been similarly registered in this State or any other state where the requirements of that registration are substantially similar to those imposed by this subchapter, may submit a certified copy of the approved application for registration filed in such other jurisdictions. In the event the Commission finds upon review that such an application substantially conforms to the standards and requirements imposed by the Act and this subchapter, the Commission may register such property; provided, however, that prior to such registration, the Commission may require submission of such supplemental documents and information as it may deem necessary.

9. Nothing herein, or in the Act, shall be construed to require an applicant to whom an Order of Registration has previously been issued to file any additional documents or affidavits with the Commission other than notices of amendments or requests for approval of material change(s) and annual reports prior to the expiration of that Order of Registration.

(b) The forms used by the Bureau of Subdivided Land Sales Control in the New Jersey Real Estate Commission are listed in the table below.

BUREAU OF SUBDIVIDED LAND SALES FORMS

1. Broker-Developer application/affidavit

2. Statement of Non-conviction and partner, officer, director or principal disclosure

3. Consent to Service of Process

4. Annual report of registered properties

5. Application for limited exemption or complete exemption

6. New Jersey Public Offering Statement—Timeshare (may not be required where situs state Public Offering Statement is deemed acceptable)

7. New Jersey Public Offering Statement—Non-timeshare (may not be required where situs state Public Offering Statement is deemed acceptable)

8. Application for Registration Questionnaire

11:5-9.4   Contents of application for registration

(a) All applications for registration shall contain the following documents and information:

1. A form application provided by the Commission in which the applicant identifies the specific lots, parcels, units or interests to be registered. The application shall be accompanied by an affidavit, on a form provided by the Commission, signed by the applicant which affirms and attests that the applicant is familiar with the project being registered, the nature and content of the application for registration, the Act and the rules promulgated thereunder, and that the contents of the application are true and correct and conform with those requirements. A second affidavit to be completed by the designated New Jersey broker of record shall accompany the application. The broker's affidavit shall state that he is familiar with the registration and its contents or has physically inspected the property, or both, that he is familiar with the Act and the rules promulgated thereunder, and with the Real Estate Brokers and Salesmen Act, and that he is not aware of any information that would lead him to believe that the information in the registration application does not provide full and fair disclosure of the offering;

2. One copy of the proposed New Jersey Public Offering Statement;

3. A statement by the applicant confirming that all monies paid by New Jersey residents to the applicant or his agents prior to closing will be held in an escrow account, or in trust by an attorney licensed to practice law in this State or the state or country where the property is located, or be guaranteed by some means acceptable to the Commission. The statement shall specify the name and location of the institution where the escrow account is maintained as well as the name and address of any trustee or escrow agent. The statement shall include the applicant's acknowledgement that he shall hold all funds in escrow or in trust until the closing and delivery of the deed or until the applicant posts a bond or some other guarantee acceptable to the Commission to ensure New Jersey purchaser deposits, which bond shall be separate from and in addition to any bond or assurance for the completion of infrastructure and promised improvements. In the event that interests in the subdivision, are offered through installment sale contracts where closing and delivery of deed or deed in trust are postponed until three or more installment payments, including, but not limited to, monthly payments for licenses, memberships or other non-fee interests in the subdivision, have been paid, the statement shall confirm:

i. That all monies paid by New Jersey purchasers shall be escrowed until:

(1) The statutory seven-day rescission period has expired;

(2) A deed in trust memorializing the transaction has been offered to the purchaser, which offer shall be made within 180 days of the date on which the first installment payment was made, presuming that all payments are current as of that time, and which deed in trust will, presuming that the purchaser has performed all acts required to enable the subdivider to do so, be recorded within the said 180 day period with the appropriate recording authority in the situs state;

(3) All statutory and other rescission periods have passed; and

(4) All contingencies other than the completion of secured promised improvements have been fulfilled; or

ii. By means of evidence acceptable to the Commission, that a bond, irrevocable bank letter of credit, or other financial assurances acceptable to the Commission, but in no event bonds issued by the applicant or any affiliated company, in an amount sufficient to ensure all monies paid by New Jersey purchasers prior to the delivery of a deed or deed in trust has been posted by an acceptable third party surety or entity on behalf of the applicant. In order for a surety or entity to be deemed acceptable, it shall be authorized to do business in the situs state and engaged in the general business of providing financial assurances on the open market. Such a bond or other financial assurance shall provide that the New Jersey Real Estate Commission on behalf of all New Jersey purchasers, or the appropriate regulatory agency of the situs state on behalf of all purchasers, is the insured and shall ensure all purchasers' deposits paid and/or all installment payment made prior to the delivery of a deed in recordable form to the purchaser or trustee. Whether the amount of such instruments is acceptable shall be determined based upon past and projected sales, purchase price and other contract terms and shall be reviewed annually by the Commission if it is a named insured;

4. An irrevocable appointment of the Commission to accept, on behalf of the applicant, service of any lawful process in any proceeding arising under the Act against the applicant or his agents;

5. A statement as to the states or other jurisdictions, including the Federal government, in which an application for registration, or similar documents, have been filed, and copies of any adverse orders, judgments or decrees by any regulatory agency, court, or administrative body, with the exception of orders approving advertising, entered against the applicant, any parent or subsidiary of the applicant, or any company related to or affiliated with the applicant with respect to the property for which the application for registration is being filed;

6. The name, address and principal occupation for the past five years of every principal officer and director of the applicant, and of every partner who owns a 10 percent or greater interest in the applicant, and of every shareholder who owns 10 percent or more of the stock of the applicant as of 30 days prior to the filing of the application for registration, with an indication of the nature and extent of their interest in the applicant;

7. Copies of the certificate or articles of incorporation, with all amendments thereto, if the applicant is a corporation; copies of all instruments by which the trust is created or declared, if the developer is a trust; copies of the articles of partnership or association and all other organization papers if the applicant is organized under another form. In the event the applicant is not the legal title holder to the property being registered, the above documents shall be submitted for both the applicant and the legal title holder;

8. A legal description by metes and bounds or by lot and block numbers, section, township and range designation, or other acceptable means of the lands to be registered, together with a map showing the proposed or actual subdivision and showing the dimensions of the lots, parcels, units or interests, as available, and the relation of such lands to existing streets, roads and other improvements. The aforesaid map or plat shall be drawn to scale, signed and sealed by a licensed professional engineer or land surveyor;

9. Copies of the deed or other instruments establishing title in the developer or other record owner and any escrow agreement required pursuant to (a)3 above, and a current title search, title report, title insurance policy, title opinion from an independent attorney, or certificate or binder issued by a licensed title insurance company. The Commission may also require a copy of any agreement which grants the applicant the rights to dispose of the property interest on behalf of the title holder;

10. A statement or listing of any pending litigation, court orders, judgments or decrees which materially affect the sale or development of the offering or the financial stability of the applicant;

11. A statement that the lots, parcels, units or interests in the development will be offered to the public and sold or alienated without regard to marital status, sex, race, handicap, religion, familial status, color, ancestry, creed or national origin;

12. A statement of the present condition of access to the development and of the existence of any adverse conditions that affect the development, or unusual conditions relating to noise or safety which affect the development that are known to the applicant, or should reasonably be known, or are readily ascertainable;

13. Copies of all contracts, agreements and acknowledgements which a purchaser or lessee may be required to execute in connection with this offering;

14. In the event there is, or will be, a blanket encumbrance affecting the development or a portion thereof, a copy of the document creating it and a statement of the consequences to a purchaser of a failure of the person bound to fulfill the obligations under the instrument, and of the manner in which the interest of the purchaser is to be protected in the event of such eventuality;

15. The audited financial statements of the applicant for the fiscal year. The term "financial statements" includes, but is not limited to, the following statements: auditor's report, balance sheet, statement of income, statement of changes in retained earnings, statement of changes in financial position, statement of changes in owner's equity, notes to financial statements and current profit and loss statement. The filing of the audited consolidated financial statements of a parent company of an applicant may be permitted if the parent company is the registrant, applicant, co-registrant or guarantor. In the discretion of the Commission, it may accept or require alternative information evidencing the applicant's ability to complete the promised improvements to the development in lieu of the audited financial statements;

16. A statement concerning any filing for or adjudication of bankruptcy during the last five years by or with regard to the ap-

plicant, its predecessor, parent or subsidiary company and any principal owning more than a 10 percent interest in the subdivision at the time of the filing of the application for registration. These requirements shall not extend to limited partners or those whose interests are solely those of passive investors;

17. Copies of all easements and restrictions of record and any easements or restrictions not of record which are within the applicant's knowledge;

18. A statement as to the status of all applications for permits and/or compliance with any permits required or issued by any Federal, state, or local agencies or similar organizations which have the authority to regulate development or issue permits, approvals or licenses which may be material to the development, sale or other disposition of the lots, units, parcels or interests to be registered and the existing or proposed facilities, common areas or improvements thereof;

19. A statement indicating whether the applicant, or a parent or subsidiary of the applicant, or any of their current officers or principals have, during the past 10 years, or any of their former officers or principals have during the last two years been convicted of a crime involving any aspect of the real estate sales or real estate securities business in this State, the United States or any other state or foreign jurisdiction and whether the applicant has been subject to any permanent injunction or final administrative order restraining a false or misleading promotional plan involving real property disposition, or any final administrative order or judgement by any court finding that the applicant or any such persons have engaged in any unfair acts and/or fraudulent or deceptive practices involving the disposition of real property or of other products or services;

20. A copy of the proposed budget for the operation and maintenance of the common elements and facilities based upon full occupancy together with the estimated annual assessment and monthly charges to be assessed to each type of unit. If the proposed offering is a condominium or other interest in real estate that is subject to the authority of or to assessments by a homeowners association, or involves any common ownership interest, the budget shall specifically state the amount set aside as reserves for the replacement of the common elements and facilities, as certified by an independent public accountant, or property manager or other independent expert. The budget should also indicate whether the applicant is subsidizing the maintenance fee or plans to subsidize the maintenance fee during sales prior to transfer of control to any association, and if so, the amount of the subsidy and the probable effect of the applicant's discontinuing the making of such payments upon the maintenance fee payable by each owner. The budget shall be accompanied by a letter of adequacy issued by an independent public accountant, or certified property manager, attesting that

11:5-9.5

the budget was prepared in good faith and a letter from an independent insurance agent or broker confirming that the insurance coverage meets any standards required in the project documents and as required by situs state law;

21. A covering letter specifying the following information with regard to the project:

i. The nature of the project;

ii. Identifying to whom all correspondence should be directed, with an address; and

iii. Identifying to whom Annual Report Notices and forms should be sent, with an address and telephone number; and

22. Such other additional information as the Commission may require, after review of an application for registration, to assure full and fair disclosure.

11:5-9.5   Public Offering Statements

(a) No registrant may dispose of any lot, parcel, unit or interest in a registered subdivision unless said registrant delivers to the purchaser a current New Jersey Public Offering Statement or approved equivalent, and affords the purchaser a reasonable opportunity to read the same before the purchaser signs the contract or purchase agreement.

1. In all cases where a New Jersey purchaser has not had contact with an authorized New Jersey broker, registrants shall maintain the signed and dated receipt for the New Jersey Public Offering statement and a copy of the contract which the New Jersey purchaser signed for a period of seven years.

(b) The Public Offering Statement shall disclose fully and accurately the characteristics of the subdivision and the lots, parcels, units or interests offered and shall make known to prospective purchasers all unusual and material circumstances and features affecting the subdivision. The Public Offering Statement shall be in clear and concise language and combine simplicity and accuracy in order to fully advise purchasers of their rights, privileges, obligations and restrictions.

1. The Public Offering Statement shall be in a form designated by the Commission. No change in form may be made without the consent of the Commission.

(c) The Commission may require an applicant to alter or amend the proposed Public Offering Statement in order to assure full and fair disclosure to prospective purchasers and may require the revision of a Public Offering Statement which it finds to be unnecessarily complex, confusing, illegible or incomplete.

(d) A Public Offering Statement shall not be deemed current unless it contains all amendments approved by the Commission.

(e) The Public Offering Statement shall contain the following information:

1. The name and address of the subdivision being offered, the name and principal address of the applicant and the name and address of the New Jersey broker of record;

2. A narrative description of the interest to be offered including; but not limited to; the rights and obligations of purchasers in their lots, parcels, units or interests and in the common elements;

3. A narrative description of the subdivision including, but not limited to, specific designation of the total number of lots, parcels, units or interests contained in the offering, the total number of lots, parcels, units or interests which will or may be constructed in the entire project, the present and proposed access to the development and the promised completion date of the present offering for sale and the estimated completion date of the entire development;

4. Relevant community information including, but not limited to, the existence and location of hospitals, health and recreational facilities, schools, fire and police protection, places of worship, streets, water supplies, levees, drainage control systems, irrigation systems, customary utilities, etc.;

5. A statement of the nature, type and capacity of improvements to be installed by the developer and the proposed dates of completion for sections offered for sale and estimated dates of completion for sections not yet offered for sale. The developer may indicate that the estimated dates of completion of improvements in sections not yet offered for sale are subject to market conditions and other variables, or similar qualifying language. Also, a statement of any approvals not yet obtained, the acquisition of which is a precondition to the completion of such improvements, and whether the identified improvements will be dedicated to public use;

6. A statement of the proposed method of operation and management of the common elements and facilities, and of all fixed, estimated or proposed fees, assessments, and reserves for future replacement and repair of common elements. If there are no pro-

visions for reserves, a statement indicating same shall be included. If the proposed offering is a condominium or other interest in real estate that is subject to the authority of or to assessments by a homeowners association, or involves any common ownership interest, in addition to the amount set aside as reserves for the replacement or repair of the common elements and facilities, the risk to purchasers if the applicant fails to sell out shall also be stated. A statement indicating whether the applicant is subsidizing the maintenance fee or plans to subsidize the maintenance fee during sales prior to transfer of control to any association, and if so, the amount of the subsidy and the probable effect of the cessation of the payment of the subsidy upon the maintenance fee payable by each owner shall also be included;

7. A description of any management or service contract, lease or other contract or agreement affecting the use, maintenance or access from and to any and all of the common elements or community facilities, together with a statement as to the effect of each upon the purchaser;

8. A statement of the relationship, if any, between the applicant and any management or servicing agent or firm;

9. A statement explaining any restrictions on occupancy, on the right of alienation and on the right of alteration of the lot, parcel, unit or interest, and on the use of any common facilities or amenities;

10. The significant terms of any encumbrances, easements, liens and restrictions including, but not limited to, zoning regulations affecting such lands and each lot, parcel, unit or interest, as well as the uses on and the zoning classification of adjoining lands at the time of registration, consolidation or the last filed annual report;

11. A statement as to whether the property or any portion thereof is regularly or periodically subject to natural forces that would tend to adversely affect the use or enjoyment of the property and whether the property or any portion thereof is located in a Federally designated flood hazard area;

12. A statement as to whether the property or any portion thereof is subject to man-made forces that would tend to adversely affect the use or enjoyment of the property such as, but not limited to, the property's proximity to airports or flight paths, railroads, noisy or polluting industrial use, landfills, dumps, nuclear or toxic waste facilities or other similar forces;

13. A statement of all current or estimated taxes;

14. A statement of all existing or proposed special taxes and proposed assessments or assessments of record and identifying who shall be responsible for payment thereof;

15. A statement of all of the estimated title closing or settlement costs to be paid by the purchaser, including, but not limited to, all costs that are charged by the applicant and its agents and any person or entity controlled by the applicant;

16. A statement explaining the warranty or guarantee given by the applicant, if any, and the rights and remedies of the purchaser;

17. A statement by the applicant confirming that all monies paid by New Jersey residents to the applicant or his agents prior to closing will be held in escrow or in trust or guaranteed by some other means acceptable to the Commission, and which shall include all of the information required to be provided in applications for registration by N.J.A.C. 11:5-9.4(a)3.

18. A statement printed in 10-point boldface type or larger, conspicuously located, which states that the purchaser has the right to cancel any contract or agreement for the purchase of any lot, parcel, unit or interest in the development, without cause, by sending or delivering written notice of cancellation to the developer or his agent by midnight of the seventh calendar day following the day on which such contract or agreement was executed and that all monies paid will be promptly refunded, and further stating that the purchaser should read the Public Offering Statement in its entirety before signing any contracts or paying any monies;

19. A statement indicating that, regardless of whether the registrant offers or recommends financing the purchase of an interest in the subdivision through a particular lender or lenders, alternate sources of financing are available;

20. Where applicable, a statement explaining the nature, type and amount of hazard and liability insurance supplied or to be supplied by the applicant or association and what the insurance covers and an explanation of the nature and type of hazard and liability insurance available to the owner, and the necessity of flood or hazard insurance; and

21. Any additional information required by the Commission to assure full and fair disclosure to prospective purchasers.

(f) Applicants and registrants shall immediately report to the Commission any material change, as defined in N.J.A.C. 11:5-9.10(b), in the information contained in any proposed or approved Public Offering Statement and shall simultaneously submit a request for approval of the appropriate amendment.

(g) The Commission shall process and review requests for amendments to Public Offering Statements in accordance with the standards and procedures established in N.J.A.C. 11:5-9.10.

(h) The Public Offering Statement shall not be used for any promotional purposes before registration of the project, and thereafter only if used in its entirety.

1. No Public Offering Statement shall indicate, and no person shall represent or imply, that the Commission approves the merits of, or recommends the purchase of, an interest in the properties described in the offering.

(i) Prior to distributing a Public Offering Statement as required by N.J.A.C. 11:5-9.14(i) written in a language other than English, registrants who advertise in a language other than English shall file with the Commission copies of the Public Offering Statement approved by the Commission printed in both English and in the language in which the advertising appears. That filing shall be accompanied by a certification attesting to the accuracy of the translation of the text of the Public Offering Statement. The certification shall be in a form as specified by the Commission and signed by an authorized representative of the registrant and a qualified translator.

11:5-9.6   Representation of applicants and registrants by New Jersey real estate brokers

(a) The applicant shall designate a currently licensed New Jersey real estate broker as its original broker of record with the initial application for registration, and such broker and any substituted or supplemental brokers must comply with the New Jersey Real Estate Brokers and Salesmen Act, N.J.S.A. 45:15-1 et seq., and the rules promulgated thereunder. An applicant/registrant may substitute another broker for the one initially designated. The initially designated broker and all substituted brokers shall execute an affidavit in accordance with N.J.A.C. 11:5-9.4(a)1.

1. The applicant may designate, in addition to the broker of record, other brokers who may join in the disposition of the registered property subject to filing the proper application with the Commission. The additional brokers, known as supplemental brokers, shall also execute an affidavit as required by N.J.A.C. 11:5-9.4(a). Nothing herein shall prevent any New Jersey bro-

ker from cooperating with any other New Jersey broker in any transaction, in accordance with N.J.A.C. 11:5-6.4(c). For the purposes of this section, persons who are licensed as New Jersey real estate brokers, and who have been designated by the applicant/registrant and approved by the Commission as the broker of record or as a supplemental broker for a particular subdivision, and who have been issued a current brokers release for that subdivision, are considered authorized brokers.

(b) Only authorized brokers may receive commissions from the registrant for the sale of interests in registered properties within New Jersey.

(c) Only authorized brokers and persons licensed under them may distribute literature on, or personally or via telephone solicit for prospective purchasers and only persons licensed under such authorized brokers as broker-salespersons or salespersons may offer or attempt to negotiate the sale or rental of an interest in a registered property, or provide or prepare contracts in New Jersey pertaining to registered property.

1. Where permitted by local law, unlicensed employees of a registrant working in the situs state and/or from the offices of the registrant may mail to New Jersey purchasers promotional literature on registered properties and may make appointments for New Jersey purchasers to inspect registered properties, provided that such persons make no material representations about such properties.

2. An authorized broker and only persons licensed under such authorized brokers as broker-salespersons or salespersons shall be present at any promotional booth maintained by a registrant or an agent of a registrant at any trade show or similar exhibition in New Jersey, and at any seminar promoting the sale or rental of registered property conducted by a registrant or any agent of a registrant in this State.

(d) All authorized brokers shall:

1. Prominently display the current broker's release;

2. Provide a copy of the current New Jersey Public Offering Statement to all New Jersey purchasers with whom they have had contact prior to the signing of any contract;

3. Obtain a signed and dated receipt for the same from the purchaser in all cases where the broker provides the Public Offering Statement to the purchaser, which receipt shall be maintained as a business record by the broker in accordance with N.J.A.C. 11:5-5.4; and

4. In all cases where the broker provides or prepares a contract which is signed by a New Jersey purchaser, the broker shall maintain a copy of that contract as a business record in accordance with N.J.A.C. 11:5-5.4.

REAL ESTATE COMMISSION   **11:5-9.8**

(e) New Jersey brokers may not represent unregistered subdivisions or sections of unregistered subdivisions unless such projects are exempted from registration pursuant to N.J.S.A. 45:15-16.32 and N.J.A.C. 11:5-9.18.

11:5-9.7   Fees with respect to the registration of interstate properties

(a) All applicants for registration shall pay application fees as prescribed in N.J.S.A. 45:15-16.34 and in (f) below.

(b) All applicants for an exemption or a limited exemption shall pay application fees as prescribed in N.J.A.C. 11:5-9.18 and in (f) below.

(c) Any request for approval of a material change in, or an amendment to, an application for registration and/or an Order of Registration and/or a Public Offering Statement shall be accompanied by a fee of $ 250.00. No fee shall be charged for amendments to applications or proposed Public Offering Statements made prior to the issuance of an Order of Registration.

1. If applications for approval of a material change in and/or for an amendment to an Order of Registration and/or an amendment to a Public Offering Statement are made simultaneously, only one fee will be payable;

2. If applications are made for approval of multiple material changes, and/or multiple amendments to an Order of Registration, and/or multiple amendments to a Public Offering Statement simultaneously, only one fee will be payable.

(d) The Commission shall maintain a copy of every application for registration, together with all amendments thereto, that has been approved and shall make them reasonably available for public inspection during ordinary business hours at the Commission's office.

1. The Commission will furnish to the public, upon request, a copy of the statement of record of any registered subdivision at

a cost in accordance with the copying fees set forth in N.J.S.A. 47:1A-5(b).

(e) All fees paid are non-refundable.

(f) Fees charged by the Bureau of Subdivided Land Sales Control are listed in the table below.

BUREAU OF SUBDIVIDED LAND SALES CONTROL FEES

Description	Fee
Out-of-State Property Registration application fee	$ 500.00 plus $ 35.00 per unit fee up to a maximum of $ 3,000
Limited Exemption	$ 250.00
Complete Exemption	$ 80.00
Amendments to registrations	$ 250.00

11:5-9.8   Issuance by the Commission of a Notice of Filing, Order of Registration, Notice of Correction, or Order of Rejection; Petition for Reconsideration, Automatic Registration

(a) Upon receipt of an application for registration in proper form and accompanied by payment of the required filing fee in the correct amount as prescribed by N.J.S.A. 45:15-16.34, the Commission shall, within 10 business days of its receipt of the same, issue a Notice of Filing to the applicant. The notice of filing shall not be construed as an approval of the registration or any portion thereof.

1. The date of filing shall be considered as the date when all required documents have been submitted in proper form and all fees, including the inspection fee, if requested, have been paid.

(b) Within 90 days from the date of a notice of filing, the Commission shall either enter an Order of Rejection or, if the Commission affirmatively determines that the requirements of N.J.S.A. 45:15-16.27 et seq. and this subchapter have been met, an Order of Registration. If within the said 90-day time period, no Order of Rejection is entered and no Notice of Deficiency as set forth in (c) below is issued, the subdivision or subdivided lands shall be deemed registered unless the applicant has consented in writing to a delay.

(c) If, during the 90 days following the date of the Notice of Filing, the Commission determines that any of the requirements of N.J.S.A. 45:15-16.27 et seq. or of this subchapter have not been met, the Commission shall issue a Notice of Deficiency to the applicant. The Notice of Deficiency shall indicate that the properties referenced in the application for registration are not registered and that the application must be corrected in a manner specified in the notice within 30 days from the date that the Notice of Deficiency is received by the applicant.

1. In the event the requirements of the Notice of Deficiency are not met within the time allowed, the Commission may enter an order rejecting the registration. All such orders shall include the factual and legal basis for the rejection and shall provide that, unless appealed, as provided in (d) below the terms of the order shall become final after 45 days.

(d) Upon the issuance of an Order of Rejection, the applicant shall have the right to file an appeal with the Commission and shall be entitled to a hearing thereon, provided that the appeal shall be filed within 45 days of the date of the Order of Rejection.

1. In the event an appeal is filed by the applicant, the Order of Rejection shall not take effect until such time as a determination has been rendered on the appeal. While an appeal of an Order of Rejection remains pending, no property which was the subject of the Notice of Filing referenced in the Order of Rejection shall be considered registered.

11:5-9.9   Inspection of properties by the Commission

(a) As provided in N.J.S.A. 45:15-16.41, the Commission, at its discretion, may make on-site inspections of any subdivision which is the subject of an application for registration, either before an Order of Registration has been issued or thereafter. In any instance where an Order of Registration has been issued prior to the subdivision being inspected by the Commission, such Order shall be considered conditional and subject to the results of the Commission's inspection of the premises. The Commission may at its discretion conduct subsequent on-site inspections.

(b) The costs of inspections shall be paid by the applicant who shall provide a deposit when requested by the Commission. After the inspection the Commission shall provide the applicant/registrant with a statement of costs incurred and a refund of any portion of the deposit not expended or a request for additional funds if required.

11:5-9.10   Amendments to registration applications and Public Offering Statements

(a) The registrant shall immediately file with the Commission amendments to its registration application and/or Public Offering Statement reflecting any material change(s) in previously sup-

plied information or documents, in order that the information provided purchasers is current.

(b) Material change means, but is not limited to, any significant change in the size or character of the development or interest being offered or anything having a significant effect on the rights, duties or obligations of the developer or purchaser.

1. Changes in selling prices and advertising, the identity of the officers and directors of a registrant, and notice of the completion of improvements on a timely basis as represented in a previously approved Public Offering Statement are not considered material changes.

2. The transfer of control of any association responsible for the maintenance of common areas and/or the operation of common facilities or amenities by the registrant to the owners of interests in the subdivision is a material change.

(c) Subsequent to the Commission having approved a Public Offering Statement, no revised Public Offering Statement shall be given to prospective purchasers without the approval of the Commission.

1. Applications for approval of an amended or corrected Public Offerings Statement shall be made by filing a red-lined copy of the proposed Revised Public Offering Statement with the Commission and an application update.

(d) The Commission shall process and review requests for amendments to Orders of Registration and Public Offering Statements in accordance with the standards and procedures established in the Act and this subchapter for the review of applications for registration. Requests for amendments shall be accompanied by a fee of $ 250.00, as provided in N.J.A.C. 11:5-9.7.

11:5-9.11   Annual reporting upon and the termination of registrations

(a) No later than 30 days after the anniversary date of the latest Order of Registration, and while the registrant retains any interest in the subdivision, the registrant shall file, on a form designated by the Commission, an annual report reflecting any material changes in the information contained in the original application for registration or in the most recent Annual Report previously filed.

1. This requirement shall not diminish the obligation of the registrant to notify the Commission of material changes as they occur.

2. The annual report shall contain an audited financial statement or compilation prepared by an independent public accountant showing the receipts and expenditures of any association serving the project and under the control of the registrant, which financial statements shall be compiled on a yearly basis, and certified if required by the situs state.

3. The yearly audit submitted with the annual report shall be the most current audit available. In no event may the date of the yearly audit be earlier than 18 months prior to the date of the annual report. The registrant will not have to file a separate audit with the Commission for any association controlled by the owners of interests in the subdivision.

(b) The registrant may file an application for termination of its obligations with the Commission in which the registrant shall certify the grounds for termination.

1. Upon a determination by the Commission that an annual report is no longer necessary for the protection of the public interest or that the registrant no longer retains any interest and no longer has any contractual, bond or other obligations to New Jersey purchasers in the subdivision, including having fulfilled all undertakings referred to in the Public Offering Statement, and that the registrant has ceased all marketing activity in New Jersey, the Commission shall issue an order terminating the responsibilities of the registrant under the Act upon the registrant making application for the issuance of an Order of Termination, accompanied by acceptable proofs that the above requirements have been met.

11:5-9.12   Home builders

Unless exempt pursuant to N.J.S.A. 45:15-16.32, a home builder selling house and lot packages offered as part of a common promotional plan, regardless of whether the lots are contiguous, is a "subdivider" as defined in N.J.S.A. 45:15-16.28, and therefore such offerings are subject to the Act and to this subchapter.

11:5-9.13   Grounds for denial of registration applications and for the revocation of Orders of Registration

A finding that an applicant or registrant has previously been determined to have engaged in unfair acts and/or fraudulent or deceptive practices by the Federal Trade Commission, or as set forth in the Federal Interstate Land Sales Full Disclosure Act (82 Stat. 590; 15 U.S.C. § 1701 et seq.), or to have violated the Act and/or similar acts in other States, may constitute grounds for the Commission, after providing the applicant or registrant

with the opportunity for a hearing pursuant to the Administrative Procedure Act, N.J.S.A. 52:14B-1 et seq., and the Uniform Administrative Procedure Rules, N.J.A.C. 1:1, to refuse to issue or to revoke an Order of Registration.

11:5-9.14   Advertising and sales promotions with respect to the sale and marketing of registered properties

(a) Advertisements that refer to the purchase price of any lot, unit, parcel or interest in real estate shall state the full purchase price and shall disclose any known or estimated additional assessments or costs to the purchaser.

1. In order to eliminate fictitious pricing or illusionary discounts, no certificates shall be distributed indicating that a discount from the advertised price shall be given. This shall not preclude the giving of a discount on the basis of any reasonable criteria.

2. Advertising shall not refer to a price increase unless the amount and date of the increase are indicated.

(b) Advertising that contains statements regarding taxes shall not use terms such as "low" and "stable", but shall state what the current taxes are, or an accurate estimate of such taxes based on current tax rates or value ratios.

1. Any reference to proposed improvements for which the purchaser will be assessed shall clearly set forth the facts of the assessment and the estimated amount of the assessment.

2. Advertising shall not state that items or services are free when the cost thereof is included in the assessment.

(c) Advertising shall not refer to any common element or facility that does not presently exist unless that fact is prominently stated in the advertising, accompanied by the proposed date of completion, which shall also appear prominently in the advertising.

(d) Advertising shall not contain photographs, sketches or artist's conceptions unless the fact that these are conceptions are stated immediately adjacent to them in the advertisement.

(e) Advertising shall not refer in wording, photograph, sketch or conception to any recreation, medical, social, shopping or other facility that is not located within the subdivision unless it clearly states that the facilities are not located in the subdivision and states the approximate distance therefrom in miles via paved roads.

(f) Any model unit that is used as part of a promotional plan shall be in substantial conformity with the units that are subsequently constructed unless otherwise noted in the contract of sale. If changes are to be made in the units other than landscap-

11:5-9.15

ing, appliances, furnishings, heating, air conditioning, electrical or plumbing, a legible notice shall be conspicuously placed in the model, or picture photo or rendering of the model, advertising prospective purchasers of the change. In the event that there are items in the model that are available only at additional cost, legible notice informing purchasers that the items are available only at additional cost should be posted in a prominent place in the model.

(g) When properties or interests therein are not registered with the Commission, nor wholly or partially exempt from the Act, and advertisements regarding such properties or interests are placed in any media which is distributed in or broadcast into the State of New Jersey, a disclaimer shall be included, indicating that the properties or interests are not registered with the New Jersey Real Estate Commission, and that the advertisement is not an offer to New Jersey residents.

1. As a result of their failure to register such properties or interests pursuant to N.J.S.A. 45:15-16.27 et seq., the owners of such properties or interests may not make, or cause to be made, an offer or disposition of the properties or interests in this State, nor direct any offer of such properties or interests originating outside of this State to a person or resident within this State.

(h) Advertisements which contain offers of premiums or of reimbursement of travel expenses in cash or merchandise shall be subject to the following:

1. The promotional material shall clearly and conspicuously state the necessity of attendance at or submission to a sales promotion, the minimum length of time required to be spent at such sales promotion in order to qualify for reimbursement or other premium or inducement, the terms and conditions of the offer, and the retail value of any premiums offered;

i. Such advertisements shall also include a statement indicating that the promotion is a solicitation for the sale of condominiums, lots, or other interests in real estate as applicable, the name of the project and the registration number assigned to the project by the Commission preceded by: "N.J. Reg. No."

2. "Travel expenses" may be reimbursed in cash or by merchandise;

3. Any advertisements, including those which contain offers of reimbursement of travel expenses, offers of premiums, or other inducements must also comply with the provisions of the New Jersey Consumer Fraud Act (N.J.S.A. 56:8-1 et seq.).

(i) Registrants who advertise in a language other than English shall make available to prospective purchasers all disclosure documents, including, but not limited to, the Public Offering

Statement, and the sales contract written in the same language as that used in the registrant's advertisements.

11:5-9.15   Compliance with situs state requirements

Any instrument evidencing the sale or disposition of an interest in a registered property shall be executed in accordance with the laws of the situs state. An applicant/registrant may be required to submit proof of compliance.

11:5-9.16   Improvements to be made at registered properties

(a) A property in a subdivision, or any part thereof, on which construction of a promised improvement for public use, convenience or necessity has not been completed, shall not be registered for disposition unless completion of the improvement is assured by a court order, or government approved improvement district with sufficient taxing or other authority to raise adequate capital to assure completion, or a substantial completion bond or similar undertaking acceptable to the Commission as provided in (c) below, or by adequate reserves established and maintained in a trust or escrow account meeting the following criteria:

1. Such funds shall be kept and maintained in an escrow account separate and apart from the registrant's funds and from any other escrowed funds;

2. The account shall be established in a bank or trust company doing business in this State or the situs state, and approved by the Commission; and

3. The trust or escrow agreement shall have as its purpose the protection of the purchaser or prospective purchaser in the event of a failure to complete construction of promised improvements or a failure to satisfy any obligations or liens encumbering the purchaser's title by reason of the construction.

(b) A property in a subdivision, or a part thereof, on which construction of a promised improvement not for public use, convenience or necessity is represented or implied, shall not be registered for disposition to the public where such improvement has not been completed, unless completion is assured by:

1. An adequate plan of development, including financial resources committed to carry out the plan as provided in (c) below, which plan is subject to the Commission's continuing review and approval; or

2. Adequate funds maintained in a trust or escrow account, or an irrevocable bank letter of credit.

(c) The Commission may accept surety bonds, escrow accounts, irrevocable bank letters of credit, or any other financial security adequate to assure a plan of development. In determining the security required, the Commission shall examine the status of improvements, the overall cost of improvements, the terms of purchaser contracts, the financial condition of the subdivider and such other data as it considers necessary. The Commission may consider whatever financial security has been posted with other governmental authorities in making its determination.

11:5-9.17   Contracts for the purchase of an interest in a registered property

(a) All contracts or agreements for the disposition of a lot, parcel, unit or interest in a registered subdivision shall not impose undue restrictions or hardships upon the purchaser. All contracts shall be in accordance with the laws of the situs state, except that they shall conform to the Real Estate Sales Full Disclosure Act and to this subchapter, and all conflicts shall be resolved to the satisfaction of the Commission.

(b) Any contract or agreement for the purchase of any lot, parcel, unit or interest in a registered subdivision may be cancelled without cause, by the purchaser sending or delivering written notice of cancellation by midnight of the seventh calendar day following the date on which such contract or agreement was executed. Upon receipt of such a notice of cancellation, the developer or his agent shall promptly refund all monies to the purchaser.

(c) Every contract or agreement shall contain the following notice in 10-point boldfaced type or larger, directly above the space provided for the signature of the purchaser:

NOTICE to PURCHASER or LESSEE: You have the right to cancel this contract by midnight of the seventh calendar day following the day on which you have executed this contract or agreement. You should read this entire contract and the Public Offering Statement on this project before signing any documents or paying any monies.

(d) All contracts which contain provisions requiring the payment of deposit monies shall contain a statement describing how the deposit moneys will be maintained in escrow or otherwise secured as provided in N.J.A.C. 11:5-9.4(a)3.

(e) Prior to using a contract or an agreement for the disposition of a lot, parcel, unit or interest in a registered subdivision that is written in a language other than English, as required by N.J.A.C. 11:5-9.14(i), registrants who advertise in a language other than English shall file with the Commission copies of the contract accepted by the Commission that are printed in both English and in the language in which the advertising appears. That filing shall be accompanied by a certification attesting to the accuracy of the translation of the text of the contract. The certification shall be in a form as specified by the Commission and signed by an authorized representative of the registrant and a qualified translator.

11:5-9.18   Exemptions from the provisions of N.J.S.A. 45:15-16.27 et seq.

(a) Any person who believes that property may be exempt from the provisions of the Act, or who is contemplating marketing property in New Jersey which he believes may be exempt, may apply to the Commission for a Letter of Exemption. Such application shall be in written affidavit form and shall list the reasons why such property or proposed project may be exempt from the Act. Such an application for exemption shall be accompanied by a non-refundable fee of $ 80.00.

1. In the event the Commission shall determine that such property is exempt from the Act, it shall issue a Letter of Exemption setting forth the facts upon which the determination is based.

2. In the event the Commission shall determine that such property is not exempt from the provisions of the Act, it shall deny the request for exemption in writing, setting forth therein the facts upon which the determination is based, and shall send such writing to the applicant via certified mail, return receipt requested.

3. Any person who is aggrieved by such a determination is entitled to a hearing on such determination, provided said hearing is requested in writing no later than 30 days from the date of the applicant's receiving notice of such determination.

4. The Commission shall issue a determination as to whether a property is, or is not, exempt within 30 days of its receipt of a complete request for exemption, with the appropriate fee.

(b) If the nature of the property and/or of the proposed offering indicate that the applicant would be subject to the registration requirements of the Act, the applicant may apply to the Commission for a limited exemption. If the commission determines that enforcement of the entire Act and of all of these rules is not necessary in the public interest or for the protection of purchasers, due to the small amounts involved or the limited character of the offering, it may issue a "Limited Exemption" from registration to the applicant.

1. A limited exemption may be granted by reason of the small number of lots, parcels, units or interests to be offered only if all improvements necessary for the use of the property have been completed, or adequate surety and/or financial assurances for completion of promised improvements and amenities has been established. No limited exemption may be granted with regard to property contiguous or reasonably contiguous to property for which a limited exemption has previously been granted and which is being offered by the same applicant, or by a predecessor or successor in title to or an affiliate of that applicant.

2. A limited exemption may be granted by reason of the limited character of the offering where the nature of the property, or of the prospective purchasers to whom the property will be offered, is such that it is likely prospective purchasers will have expert advice concerning the purchase independent of that supplied by the applicant or his agents. An application for a limited exemption for this reason shall include a copy of any prospectus, offering statement or other such solicitation. A limited exemption granted for this reason shall be confined to the group of offerees specified in the application.

3. An application for a limited exemption shall specify the particular lots, parcels, units or interests for which exemption is sought. Any limited exemption granted shall be confined to those lots, parcels, units or interests so specified.

4. An application for a limited exemption shall include a narrative description that clearly describes the nature of the subdivision and the factual basis and reasons why the limited exemption should be granted.

5. The Commission shall assign a New Jersey exemption number beginning with the prefix "N.J.E." to each project to which a limited exemption is issued. This number shall thereafter appear on all publications or broadcasts of advertisements of the exempted project which include offers of a premium or to provide or reimburse the cost of travel which are directed to citizens of this State, or which appear in national or regional advertising circulated within this State.

6. Any limited exemption granted shall remain in effect for a period of two years from the date of issuance indicated in the Letter of Exemption, unless revoked as described below.

7. Any limited exemption granted shall permit the recipient to offer the property to New Jersey residents without obtaining an Order of Registration. A limited exemption shall not deprive the Commission of jurisdiction to enforce any other provision of the Act or this subchapter, or to revoke the limited exemption after notice and an opportunity to be heard.

8. A $ 250.00 non-refundable fee shall be tendered with any application for a limited exemption.

9. All applications for a limited exemption shall comply with the following minimum requirements:

i. The filing of an exemption application affidavit-questionnaire;

ii. The filing of proof of title and a plat map specifying the lots or units to be exempted, with colored shading;

iii. The requirements for the securing of all deposits, down payments, or funds of others as prescribed in this subchapter;

iv. The filing of satisfactory proof of surety and/or financial assurances for any promised improvements or amenities;

v. The advertisement standards and procedures established at N.J.A.C. 11:5-9.14; and

vi. The filing of any other documents that the Commission may deem necessary.

10. Any applicant granted a limited exemption by the Commission, pursuant to this subchapter, shall comply with the annual reporting requirements of N.J.S.A. 45:15-16.40 and N.J.A.C. 11:5-9.11.

11. No limited exemption granted hereunder shall be effective until a Letter of Limited Exemption is issued by the Commission to the applicant for the exemption.

12. A copy of the New Jersey Letter of Limited Exemption, or of a Public Offering Statement approved by the Commission, shall be provided to each New Jersey purchaser prior to their signing any contract for the purchase of an interest in property included within the limited exemption issued by the Commission, and a receipt obtained for the same shall be kept on file for seven years by the recipient of the limited exemption.

13. Any material change in the information reflected on the application for a limited exemption or on any documentation submitted in support of such application, shall immediately void any exemption issued based upon such application.

REAL ESTATE COMMISSION   **11:5-9A.2**

11:5-9.19   Imposition of regulatory sanctions; cease and desist orders; hearings

(a) Prior to issuing an Order revoking or suspending a registration and/or imposing any penalty authorized by the Act, and/or directing that a registrant permanently cease and desist from taking any action or continuing any course of conduct, the Commission shall provide written notice of the charges which allegedly support the entry of such an Order and afford the registrant to whom such notice is directed the opportunity for a hearing on the charges. All such hearings shall be conducted in accordance with the Administrative Procedures Act, N.J.S.A. 52:14B-1 et seq., and the Uniform Administrative Procedure Rules, N.J.A.C. 1:1, promulgated thereunder by the Office of Administrative Law, and any rules of the Commission applicable to such hearings.

1. If the Commission makes a finding of fact in writing that the public interest will be irreparably harmed by a delay in issuing an order, it may issue a temporary cease and desist order. Every temporary cease and desist order shall include in its terms a provision that upon written request of the party to whom the order was directed, a hearing will be held within 15 days of the Commission's receipt of the request.

SUBCHAPTER 9A. RULES INTERPRETING AND IMPLEMENTING THE NEW JERSEY REAL ESTATE TIMESHARE ACT, N.J.S.A. 45:15-16.50 ET SEQ.

11:5-9A.1   Purpose and scope

(a) The rules in this subchapter implement the provisions of the New Jersey Real Estate Timeshare Act, N.J.S.A. 45:15-16.50 et seq. These rules are applicable to:

1. Timeshare plans with an accommodation or component site in this State; and

2. Timeshare plans without an accommodation or component site in this State if these timeshare plans are offered to be sold within this State, regardless of whether the offer originates from within or outside of this State.

(b) This Act shall not apply to any of the following:

1. Timeshare plans, whether or not an accommodation or component site is located in the State, consisting of 10 or fewer timeshare interests;

2. Timeshare plans, whether or not an accommodation or component site is located in this State, the use of which extends over any period of three years or less. For purposes of determining the term of a timeshare plan, the period of any automatic renewal shall be included unless a purchaser has the right to terminate the purchaser's participation in the timeshare plan at any time and receive a pro rata refund, or the purchaser receives a notice, not less than 30 days, but not more than 60 days, prior to the date of renewal, informing the purchaser of the right to terminate at any time prior to the date of automatic renewal;

3. Timeshare plans, whether or not an accommodation or component site is located in the State, under which the prospective purchaser's total financial obligation shall be equal to or less than $ 3,000 during the entire term of the timeshare plan;

4. Component sites of specific timeshare interest multi-site timeshare plans that are neither located in nor offered for sale in this State, except that these component sites are still subject to the disclosure requirements of the Act;

5. Offers or dispositions of securities or units of interest issued by a real estate investment trust regulated under any State or Federal statute; and

6. Offers or dispositions of securities currently Registered with the Bureau of Securities within the Division of Consumer Affairs in the Department of Law and Public Safety.

(c) All correspondence and inquiries related to the Act should be directed to:

New Jersey Real Estate Commission
Bureau of Subdivided Land Sales Control
20 West State Street
P.O. Box 328
Trenton, NJ 08625-0328.

11:5-9A.2   Definitions

The following words and terms, as used in this subchapter, shall have the following meanings, unless the context clearly indicates otherwise.

"Abbreviated registration" means an expedited filing procedure for those out-of-State filings that are located in a state or jurisdiction where the disclosure requirements are substantially equivalent or greater than those required under the Act.

"Accommodation" means any apartment, condominium or cooperative unit, cabin, lodge, hotel or motel room, or other private or commercial structure containing toilet facilities therein that is designed and available, pursuant to applicable law, for use and occupancy as a residence by one or more individuals which is a part of the timeshare property.

"Act" means the New Jersey Real Estate Timeshare Act, N.J.S.A. 45:15-16.50 et seq.

"Advertisement" means any written, oral or electronic communication that is directed to or targeted to persons within the State and contains a promotion, inducement or offer to sell a timeshare plan, including, but not limited to, brochures, pamphlets, radio and television scripts, electronic media, telephone and direct mail solicitations and other means of promotion. "Advertisement" does not mean:

1. Any stockholder communication such as an annual report or interim financial report, proxy material, a registration statement, a securities prospectus, a registration, a property report or other material required to be delivered to a prospective purchaser by an agency of any local, state or Federal government;

2. Any oral or written statement disseminated by a developer to broadcast or print media, other than paid advertising or promotional material, regarding plans for the acquisition or development of timeshare property. However, any rebroadcast or any other dissemination of such oral statements to prospective purchasers by a seller in any manner, or any distribution of copies of newspaper or magazine articles or press releases, or any other dissemination of such written statements to a prospective purchaser by a seller in any manner, shall constitute an advertisement; or

3. Any communication addressed to and relating to the account of any person who has previously executed a contract for the sale or purchase of a timeshare interest in a timeshare plan to which the communication relates shall not be considered advertising under this Act, provided they are delivered to any person who has previously executed a contract for the purchase of a timeshare interest or is an existing owner of a timeshare interest in a timeshare plan.

"Assessment" means the share of funds required for the payment of common expenses which is assessed from time to time against each timeshare interest by the association.

"Association" means the organized body consisting of the purchasers of interests in a timeshare property.

"Commission" means the New Jersey Real Estate Commission.

"Common expense" means casualty and liability insurance, and those expenses properly incurred for the maintenance, operation, and repair of all accommodations and common areas and facilities constituting the timeshare plan and any other expenses designated as common expenses by the timeshare instrument.

"Component site" means a specific geographic location where accommodations which are part of a multi-site timeshare plan are located. Separate phases of a single timeshare property

in a specific geographic location and under common management shall be deemed a single component site.

"Concurrent preliminary registration" means a preliminary registration filed concurrently with a substantially complete comprehensive or abbreviated registration.

"Conditional order of registration" means the authorization to allow sales of interests in a timeshare plan where the comprehensive or abbreviated registration application is substantially complete and only minor deficiencies remain.

"Consolidated filing" means the registration of additional timeshare interests pursuant to a previously registered plan by the filing of the supplemental information necessary to register the additional interests and the payment of an additional comprehensive or abbreviated registration fee, as applicable.

"Department" means the Department of Banking and Insurance.

"Developer" means and includes any person or entity who creates a timeshare plan or is in the business of selling timeshare interests, or employs agents or brokers to do the same, or any person or entity who succeeds to the interest of a developer by sale, lease, assignment, mortgage or other transfer, except that the term shall include only those persons who offer timeshare interests for disposition in the ordinary course of business.

"Dispose" or "disposition" means a voluntary transfer or assignment of any legal or equitable interest in a timeshare plan, other than the transfer, assignment or release of a security interest.

"Escrow agent" means an independent person, including an independent bonded escrow company, an independent financial institution whose accounts are insured by a governmental agency or instrumentality, or an independent licensed title insurance agent who is responsible for the receipt and disbursement of funds in accordance with the Act. If the escrow agent is not located in the State of New Jersey, then this person shall subject himself or herself to the jurisdiction of the Commission with respect to disputes that arise out of the provisions of the Act.

"Incidental benefit" means an accommodation, product, service, discount, or other benefit which is offered to a prospective purchaser of a timeshare plan or to a purchaser of a timeshare plan prior to the expiration of his or her rescission period pursuant to the Act and which is not an exchange program, provided that:

1. Use or participation in the incidental benefit is completely voluntary;

2. No costs of the incidental benefit are included as common expenses of the timeshare plan;

3. The good faith represented aggregate value of all incidental benefits offered by a developer to a purchaser shall not exceed 20 percent of the actual price paid by the purchaser for his or her timeshare interest; and

4. The purchaser is provided a disclosure that fairly describes the material terms of the incidental benefit.

The term "incidental benefit" shall not include an offer of the use of the accommodations of the timeshare plan on a free or discounted one-time basis.

"Managing entity" means the person who undertakes the duties, responsibilities and obligations of the management of the timeshare property.

"Offer" means any inducement, solicitation, or other attempt, whether by marketing, advertisement, oral or written presentation or any other means, to encourage a person to acquire a timeshare interest in a timeshare plan, for gain or profit.

"Person" means a natural person, corporation, limited liability company, partnership, joint venture, association, estate, trust, government, governmental subdivision or agency, or other legal entity or any combination thereof.

"Preliminary registration" means a procedure by which any applicant may obtain an authorization to commence a limited marketing program for the purpose of soliciting non-binding reservations in a timeshare plan prior to completing an abbreviated or comprehensive registration.

"Promotion" means a plan or device, including one which creates the possibility of a prospective purchaser receiving a vacation, discount vacation, gift, or prize, that is used by a developer, or an employee of a developer, or an agent or independent contractor acting on behalf of the developer, in connection with the offering and sale of timeshare interests in a timeshare plan.

"Purchase contract" means a document pursuant to which a person becomes legally obligated to sell, and a purchaser becomes legally obligated to buy, a timeshare interest.

"Purchaser" means any person, other than a developer, who by means of a voluntary transfer acquires a legal or equitable interest in a timeshare plan other than as security for an obligation.

"Reservation system" means the method, arrangement or procedure by which a purchaser, in order to reserve the use or occupancy of any accommodation in a multi-site timeshare plan for one or more timeshare periods, is required to compete with other purchasers in the same multi-site timeshare plan, regardless of whether the reservation system is operated and maintained by the multi-site timeshare plan managing entity or any other person.

"Sales agent" means any person who performs within this State as an agent or employee of a developer any one or more of the services or acts as set forth in the Act, and includes any real estate broker, broker salesperson or salesperson licensed pursuant to N.J.S.A. 45:15-1 et seq., or any person who purports to act in any such capacity.

"Timeshare instrument" means one or more documents, by whatever name denominated, creating or governing the operation of a timeshare plan.

"Timeshare interest" means and includes either:

1. A "timeshare estate," which is the right to occupy a timeshare property, coupled with a freehold estate or an estate for years with a future interest in a timeshare property or a specified portion thereof; or

2. A "timeshare use," which is the right to occupy a timeshare property, which right is neither coupled with a freehold interest, nor coupled with an estate for years with a future interest, in a timeshare property.

"Timeshare period" means the period or periods of time when the purchaser of an interest in a timeshare plan is afforded the opportunity to use the accommodations of a timeshare plan.

"Timeshare plan" means any arrangement, plan, scheme, or similar device, whether by membership agreement, sale, lease, deed, license, or right to use agreement or by any other means, whereby a purchaser, in exchange for consideration, receives ownership rights in or the right to use accommodations for a period of time less than a full year during any given year on a recurring basis, but not necessarily for consecutive years. A timeshare plan may be:

1. A "single-site timeshare plan," which is the right to use accommodations at a single timeshare property; or

2. A "multi-site timeshare plan," which includes:

i. A "specific timeshare interest," which means an interest wherein a purchaser has, only through a reservation system:

(1) A priority right to reserve accommodations at a specific timeshare property without competing with owners of timeshare interests at other component sites that are part of the multi-site timeshare plan, which priority right extends for at least 60 days, and

(2) The right to reserve accommodations on a non-priority basis at other component sites that are part of the multi-site timeshare plan; or

ii. A "non-specific timeshare interest," which means an interest wherein a purchaser has, only through a reservation system, the right to reserve accommodations at any component site of the multi-site timeshare plan, with no priority right to reserve accommodations at any specific component site.

"Timeshare property" means one or more accommodations subject to the same timeshare instrument, together with any other property or rights to property appurtenant to those accommodations.

11:5-9A.3   Forms of documents

(a) Provisions concerning documents with respect to the registration of timeshare plans with the Commission are as follows. With the exception of the affidavits or affirmations referenced in (a)6 below, the documents may be filed on a properly bookmarked and indexed computer disc (CD-ROM) or other electronic medium acceptable to the Commission.

1. All registration statements of record submitted to the Commission shall be referenced and properly indexed and, if submitted on paper, properly bound.

2. All paper documents submitted to the Commission for filing shall, wherever possible, be typewritten on one side of the paper only.

3. One copy of each exhibit or document shall be submitted, unless the Commission requests more than one copy.

4. All paper documents submitted to the Commission shall not exceed 8 1/2 x 14 inches.

5. An applicant shall submit verified copies of original documents.

6. An affidavit or affirmation as prescribed in the Commission's forms shall be executed for each of the following documents:

i. An application for preliminary, comprehensive and abbreviated registrations;

ii. An annual report;

iii. A statement of non-conviction;

iv. A consent(s) to service of process; and

v. A broker's affidavit, including an application for a broker's release.

7. The acceptance of a registration and offering statement approved in another state may be conditioned upon an acceptable on-site inspection.

11:5-9A.4   Registration filings

(a) A developer who sells, offers to sell, or attempts to solicit prospective purchasers in this State to purchase a timeshare interest, or any person who creates a timeshare plan with an accommodation in this State, shall register with the Commission, on forms provided by the Commission or in electronic formats authorized by the Commission, all timeshare plans which have accommodations located in this State or which are sold or offered for sale to any individual located in this State.

(b) Preliminary registration requirements are as follows:

1. Upon the submission of an application approved by the Commission, the Commission may grant a 90-day preliminary registration to allow the developer to begin offering and selling timeshare interests in a timeshare plan regardless of whether the accommodations of the timeshare plan are located within or outside of the State. Upon submission to the Commission of a substantially complete application for an abbreviated or comprehensive registration under the Act, including all appropriate fees prior to the expiration date of the preliminary registration, the preliminary registration shall be automatically extended during the registration review period provided that the developer is actively and diligently pursuing registration under the Act. The preliminary registration shall automatically terminate with respect to those timeshare interests covered by an approved public offering statement and by a final order of registration that is issued before the scheduled termination date of the preliminary registration. The preliminary registration shall also terminate upon the issuance of any notice of rejection due to the developer's failure to comply with the provisions of the Act.

2. Upon termination of a preliminary registration order for any reason other than the issuance of a final order of registration and public offering statement, all reservations executed under the preliminary registration shall be null and void, and all funds obtained shall be refunded to the purchaser within 15 days of termination. Evidence of such refunds must be filed with the Commission within 30 days of the date of termination.

3. To obtain a preliminary registration, the developer shall provide all of the following:

i. The reservation instrument to be used, in a form previously approved by the Commission and supplied with the preliminary registration application, which shall, at a minimum, provide for the following:

(1) The right of both the developer and the potential purchaser to unilaterally cancel the reservation at any time;

(2) The placement by the developer of any deposit paid by the purchaser into an escrow account maintained in accordance with (b)3iv below;

(3) The repayment to the potential purchaser of his or her total deposit within 15 days following the receipt of a notice of cancellation of the reservation by either party; and

(4) A statement to the effect that the reservation concerns an offering plan that has not yet received final approval from the Commission, and that no offering of the timeshare interest referenced in the reservation instrument can be made by the developer until an offering plan has been filed with, and accepted by, the Commission;

ii. A preliminary public offering statement in a form approved by the Commission with an agreement to provide each potential purchaser with a copy of the preliminary public offering statement and an executed receipt for a copy before any money or other thing of value has been accepted by or on behalf of the developer in connection with the reservation;

iii. An agreement to provide a copy of the reservation instrument signed by the potential purchaser and by or on behalf of the developer to the potential purchaser;

iv. A fully executed escrow agreement, acceptable to the Commission, stating that all funds received by the developer shall be placed into an independent escrow account to be maintained in a financial institution located within the State of New Jersey under the control of an attorney, real estate broker or title company licensed to practice in New Jersey. This agreement must state that no funds shall be released until a final order of registration has been granted unless refunded to the purchaser upon cancellation of the reservation agreement or expiration of the preliminary registration. The name and address of the financial institution, and escrow account number must also be provided;

v. The filing fee for a preliminary registration, specified at N.J.A.C. 11:5-9A.10(e), which filing fee shall be in addition to the filing fees for an abbreviated or comprehensive registration as established in that subsection;

vi. Any advertisements to be utilized by the developer while the preliminary registration is in effect. All such advertisements shall be provided to the Commission before use;

vii. If the timeshare plan is located wholly or in part outside of the State of New Jersey, a fully executed consent to service of process, along with evidence of compliance with all laws governing the offering of a timeshare plan in that jurisdiction;

viii. A statement indicating whether the applicant, or a parent or a subsidiary of the applicant, or any of their current officers or principals have, during the past 10 years, or any of their former

officers or principals have during the last two years, been convicted of any criminal or disorderly persons offense involving any aspect of the real estate sales or real estate securities business; and

ix. Such other information as the Commission may require from a particular developer in order to further the provisions of the Act, to assure full and fair disclosure and protect the interests of purchasers.

(c) Comprehensive registration requirements are as follows:

1. In addition to the required documentation under N.J.S.A. 45:15-16.57(d), to obtain a comprehensive registration, the developer shall provide all of the following:

i. The developer's legal name, any alternate names or other names under which the developer has operated or is operating, and the developer's principal office location, mailing address, primary contact person and telephone number;

ii. The name, location, mailing address, primary contact person and telephone number of the timeshare plan;

iii. The name and principal address of the developer's authorized New Jersey representative who shall be a licensed real estate broker licensed to maintain offices within this State;

iv. A declaration as to whether the timeshare plan is a single-site timeshare plan or a multi-site timeshare plan and, if a multi-site timeshare plan, whether it consists of specific timeshare interests or non-specific timeshare interests;

v. The name and principal address of all brokers within New Jersey who sell or offer to sell any timeshare interests in any timeshare plan offered by the developer to any person in this State, who shall be licensed as a real estate broker pursuant to N.J.S.A. 45:15-1 et seq., and who are the authorized representatives of the developer;

vi. The name and principal address of all affiliated and non-affiliated marketing entities who, by means of inducement, promotion or advertisement, attempt to encourage or procure prospective purchasers located in this State to attend a sales presentation for any timeshare plan offered by the developer or authorized broker;

vii. The name and principal address of all managing entities who manage the timeshare plan;

viii. A public offering statement which complies with the requirements of the Act;

ix. A form application provided by the Commission in which the applicant identifies the timeshare plan and the timeshare in-

11:5-9A.4   **INSURANCE**

terests to be registered. The application shall be accompanied by an affidavit, on a form provided by the Commission and signed by the applicant, which affirms and attests that the applicant is familiar with the project being registered, the nature and content of the application for registration, the Act and the rules promulgated thereunder, and that the contents of the application are true and correct and conform with those requirements. A second affidavit, to be completed by the designated New Jersey broker of record, shall accompany the application. The broker's affidavit and application for a broker's release shall state that he or she is familiar with the registration and its contents or has physically inspected the property, or both, that he or she is familiar with the Act and the rules promulgated thereunder, and with the New Jersey Real Estate License Act, and that he or she is not aware of any information that would lead him or her to believe that the information in the registration application does not provide full and fair disclosure of the offering;

x. A statement by the applicant confirming that all monies paid by New Jersey residents to the applicant or his agents prior to closing shall be held in an escrow account pursuant to N.J.S.A. 45:15-16.57(e), or be guaranteed by some means acceptable to the Commission. The statement shall specify the name and location of the institution where the escrow account is maintained as well as the name and address of any trustee or escrow agent;

xi. An irrevocable appointment of the Commission to accept, on behalf of the applicant, service of any lawful process in any proceeding arising under the Act against the applicant or his agents;

xii. Copies of the developer's certificate or articles of incorporation, with all amendments thereto, if the applicant is a corporation; copies of all instruments by which the trust is created or declared, if the developer is a trust; copies of the articles of partnership or association and all other organization papers if the applicant is organized under another form. In the event the applicant is not the holder of the legal title to the property being registered, the above documents shall be submitted for both the applicant and the legal title holder;

xiii. Copies of the deed or other instruments establishing title in the developer or other record owner and any escrow agreement required pursuant to this section, and a current title search, title report, title insurance policy, title opinion from an independent attorney, or certificate or binder issued by a licensed title insurance company. The Commission may also require a copy of any agreement which grants the applicant the right to dispose of the timeshare interest on behalf of the title holder;

xiv. In the event there is, or shall be, a blanket encumbrance affecting the property or a portion thereof, a copy of the document creating it and a statement of the consequences to a purchaser of a failure of the person bound to fulfill the obligations under the instrument, and of the manner in which the interest of the purchaser is to be protected in the event of such failure;

xv. Copies of any association documents and instruments creating or affecting the timeshare plan;

xvi. A statement or listing of any pending administrative actions or litigation and pending or issued court orders, administrative orders, judgments or decrees which materially affect the sale or development of the offering or the financial stability of the applicant;

xvii. A statement that the interests in the timeshare plan shall be offered to the public and sold or alienated without regard to age, ancestry, color, creed (religion), disability (including AIDS and HIV infection), atypical hereditary cellular or blood trait, familial status, liability for military service, marital status, domestic partnership status, nationality, national origin, race, sex, and affectional or sexual orientation;

xviii. A statement of the present condition of access to the property and of the existence of any adverse conditions that affect the property, or unusual conditions relating to noise or safety which affect the property that are known to the applicant, or should reasonably be known, or are readily ascertainable;

xix. Copies of all contracts, agreements and acknowledgments which a purchaser or lessee may be required to execute in connection with this offering;

xx. The audited financial statements of the applicant for the immediately preceding fiscal year. The term "financial statements" includes, but is not limited to, the following statements: auditor's report, balance sheet, statement of income, statement of changes in retained earnings, statement of changes in financial position, statement of changes in owner's equity, notes to financial statements and current profit and loss statement. The filing of the audited consolidated financial statements of a parent company of an applicant may be permitted if the parent company is the registrant, applicant, co-registrant or guarantor. In the discretion of the Commission, it may accept or require alternative information evidencing the applicant's ability to complete the promised improvements to the development in lieu of the audited financial statements;

xxi. A statement concerning any filing for or adjudication of bankruptcy during the last five years by or with regard to the applicant, its predecessor, parent or subsidiary company and any principal owning more than a 10 percent interest in the timeshare plan at the time of the filing of the application for registration. These requirements shall not extend to limited partners or those whose interests are solely those of passive investors;

xxii. A statement as to the status of all applications for permits and/or compliance with any permits required or issued by any Federal, state, or local agencies or similar organizations which have the authority to regulate or issue permits, approvals or licenses which may be material to the development, sale or other disposition of the timeshare interests to be registered and the existing or proposed facilities, common areas or improvements thereof;

xxiii. A copy of the proposed budget for the operation and maintenance of the common elements and facilities based upon full occupancy together with the estimated annual assessment and monthly charges to be assessed to each type of unit. The budget shall specifically state the amount set aside as reserves for the replacement of the common elements and facilities, as certified by an independent public accountant or other independent expert. The budget should also indicate whether the applicant is subsidizing the maintenance fee or plans to subsidize the maintenance fee during sales prior to transfer of control to any association, and if so, the amount of the subsidy and the probable effect of the applicant's discontinuance of the subsidy payments upon the maintenance fee payable by each owner. The budget shall be accompanied by a letter of adequacy issued by an independent public accountant attesting that the budget was prepared in accordance with generally acceptable accounting principles and a letter from an independent insurance agent or broker confirming that the insurance coverage meets any standards required in the project documents and as required by situs state law;

xxiv. A covering letter specifying the following information with regard to the project:

(1) The nature of the project;

(2) The individual to whom all correspondence should be directed, with an address; and

(3) The individual to whom annual report notices and forms should be sent, with an address and telephone number;

xxv. Such additional information as the Commission may require, after review of an application for registration, to assure full and fair disclosure; and

xxvi. A statement indicating whether the applicant, or a parent or subsidiary of the applicant, or any of their current officers or principals have, during the past 10 years, or any of their former officers or principals have, during the last two years, been convicted of any criminal or disorderly persons offense involving any aspect of the real estate sales or real estate securities business in this State, the United States or any other state or foreign jurisdiction and whether the applicant has been subject to any permanent injunction or final administrative order re-

straining a false or misleading promotional plan involving real property disposition, or any final administrative order or judgment by any court finding that the applicant or any such persons have engaged in any unfair acts and/or fraudulent or deceptive practices involving the disposition of real property or of other products or services.

(d) Abbreviated registration requirements are as follows:

1. In addition to the required documentation under N.J.S.A. 45:15-16.57(f), to obtain an abbreviated registration, the developer shall provide all of the following:

i. A broker of record affidavit in which the broker states that he or she is familiar with the registration and its contents or has physically inspected the property, or both, that he or she is familiar with the Act and the rules promulgated thereunder and with the Real Estate Brokers and Salesmen Act, and that he or she is not aware of any information that would lead him or her to believe that the information in the abbreviated application does not permit full and fair disclosure of the offering;

ii. A statement confirming that all monies paid by New Jersey residents to the applicant or his agents prior to closing shall be held in an escrow account pursuant to N.J.S.A. 45:15-16.57(e) or be guaranteed by some other means acceptable to the Commission. The statement shall specify the name and location of the institution where the escrow account is maintained as well as the name and address of any trustee or escrow agent;

iii. An irrevocable appointment of the Commission to accept, on behalf of the developer, service of any lawful process in any proceeding arising under the Act against the applicant or his agents;

iv. A statement as to the status of all applications for permits and/or compliance with any permits required to be issued by any Federal, state or local agencies or similar organizations which have the authority to regulate or issue permits, approvals or licenses which may be material to the development, sale or other disposition of the timeshare interests to be registered and the existing or proposed facilities, common areas or improvements thereof;

v. Copies of all contracts, agreements and acknowledgements which a purchaser or lessee may be required to execute in connection with the offering. The Commission may require additional or supplemental documentation in order to resolve any discrepancies between local law and the requirements of the Act;

vi. A statement or listing of any pending administrative actions, litigation and pending or issued court orders, administrative orders, judgments or decrees which materially affect the sale or development of the offering or the financial stability of the applicant; and

vii. A statement indicating whether the applicant, or a parent or subsidiary of the applicant, or any of their current officers or principals have, during the past 10 years, or any of their former officers or principals have, during the last two years, been convicted of any criminal or disorderly persons offense involving any aspect of the real estate sales or real estate securities business in this State, the United States or any other state or foreign jurisdiction and whether the applicant has been subject to any permanent injunction or final administrative order restraining a false or misleading promotional plan involving real property disposition, or any final administrative order or judgment by any court finding that the applicant or any such persons have engaged in any unfair acts and/or fraudulent or deceptive practices involving the disposition of real property or of other products or services.

11:5-9A.5   Amendments to registrations and to public offering statements

(a) The registrant shall file with the Commission amendments to its registration application and/or public offering statement reflecting any material or adverse change(s) in previously supplied information or documents in accordance with N.J.S.A. 45:15-16.60b(1), in order to ensure that the information provided to purchasers is current.

(b) Material change means any significant change, whether beneficial or adverse, in the size or character of the interest being offered or anything having a significant affect on the regular duties or obligations of the registrant, developer or purchaser.

1. Material change includes, but is not limited to:

i. A change of the developer or registrant;

ii. A change of exchange company or association with an additional exchange company;

iii. Any substantial change in the accommodations and/or amenities that are part of the timeshare plan;

iv. An increase or decrease in the number of timeshare interests in the timeshare plan;

v. A change of escrow agent, type of escrow or alternative assurance, or a change in any substantive provisions of the escrow agreement between the registrant and escrow agent;

vi. An increase in assessments of 15 percent or more;

vii. A change in management company or a change to a substantive provision of the management agreement;

viii. The transfer of control of the association to the owners of interests in the timeshare plan by the registrant;

ix. A filing of bankruptcy on the part of the developer, registrant, or management entity;

x. Substantive changes in the procedures for obtaining reservations or access to the accommodations that are part of the timeshare plan;

xi. The refinancing of or the placing of any additional mortgages or blanket encumbrances on the timeshare property or interests subsequent to registration approval; and

xii. Any special assessments.

(c) Adverse changes include any material change to the timeshare plan that substantially reduces benefits or increases costs to purchasers.

1. If the change is determined by the Commission to be both material and adverse to the purchasers of the timeshare plan as a whole, no closing shall occur until the amendment relating to the material and adverse change has been approved by the Commission.

(d) "Material" or "adverse" changes do not include:

1. Correction of any typographical errors that do not affect the rights or obligations of purchasers;

2. Changes in selling prices or advertising materials;

3. Timely completion of promised improvements as represented in a previously approved public offering statement; and

4. With the exception of special assessments, any increase in fees payable by a purchaser of less than 15 percent.

(e) Unless otherwise permitted by the Act, no revised public offering statement shall be given to prospective purchasers without the approval of the Commission.

1. Applications for approval of an amended or corrected public offering statement shall be made by filing a red-lined copy or other submission utilizing a similar method of clearly showing the differences between the current and previously submitted drafts of the proposed revised public offering statement with the Commission and an application update.

(f) The Commission shall process and review requests for amendments to orders of registration and public offering statements in accordance with the standards and procedures established in the Act and this subchapter for the review of applications for registration. Requests for approval of amendments to orders of registration and revisions to public offering statements shall be accompanied by a fee of $ 300.00 as provided in N.J.A.C. 11:5-9A.10.

(g) The developer shall update the public offering statement to reflect any changes to the timeshare plan that are not material or adverse at the time of the filing of next annual report.

11:5-9A.6   Public offering statements

(a) No person shall dispose of any timeshare interest in a registered timeshare plan unless he or she delivers a current public offering statement and affords the purchaser a reasonable opportunity to read the same before the purchaser signs the contract or purchase agreement.

1. In all cases where a New Jersey purchaser has not had contact with an authorized New Jersey broker, registrants shall maintain the signed and dated receipt for the New Jersey public offering statement and a copy of the contract which the New Jersey purchaser signed for a period of seven years.

(b) The public offering statement shall disclose fully and accurately the characteristics of the timeshare plan offered and shall make known to prospective purchasers all unusual and material circumstances and features affecting the timeshare plan. The public offering statement shall be in clear and concise language and combine simplicity and accuracy in order to fully advise purchasers of their rights, privileges, obligations and restrictions.

1. The public offering statement shall be in a form authorized by the Commission. No change in form shall be made without the consent of the Commission.

2. The Commission may require an applicant to alter or amend the proposed public offering statement in order to assure full and fair disclosure to prospective purchasers.

3. A public offering statement shall not be deemed current unless it contains all amendments approved by the Commission.

4. Applicants and registrants shall report to the Commission any material change, as defined in N.J.A.C. 11:5-9A.5, in the information contained in any proposed or approved public offering statement in accordance with N.J.S.A. 45:15-16.60b(1) and shall simultaneously submit a request for approval of the appropriate amendments.

5. The Commission shall process and review requests for amendments to public offering statements in accordance with the standards and procedures established in N.J.A.C. 11:5-9A.5.

6. The public offering statement shall not be used for any promotional purposes before registration of the project, and thereafter only if used in its entirety.

7. No public offering statement shall indicate, and no person shall represent or imply, that the Commission approves the merits of, or recommends the purchase of, an interest in the properties described in the offering.

8. Prior to distributing a public offering statement as required under the Act in a language other than English, registrants who advertise in a language other than English shall file with the Commission copies of the public offering statement approved by the Commission printed in both English and in the language in which the advertising appears. The filing shall be accompanied by a certification attesting to the accuracy of the translation of the text of the public offering statement. The certification shall be in a form as specified by the Commission and signed by an authorized representative of the registrant and a qualified translator.

9. The public offering statement shall contain a statement, printed in 10 point type or larger and conspicuously located, indicating that within seven days after receipt of the public offering statement or execution of the purchase contract, whichever is later, a purchaser may cancel any purchase contract for a timeshare interest from the developer. The statement shall also contain the name and street address to which the purchaser shall mail any notice of cancellation. If by agreement of the parties in the contract, and/or if local law in the jurisdiction where the timeshare interest is located provides for a cancellation period of greater than seven days, then the longer cancellation period shall apply and the public offering statement shall so state.

10. All public offering statements shall contain a glossary defining the key terms in the offering statement and timeshare plan. This glossary shall be located prior to the narrative portion of the offering statement.

11. The following documents, if applicable, shall be contained in the public offering statement or simultaneously provided to the purchaser:

i. The timeshare instrument;

ii. The association articles of incorporation;

iii. The association bylaws;

iv. The association rules;

v. Copies of any leases or contracts, excluding the purchase contract and loan documents, required to be signed by the purchaser;

vi. The actual or estimated operating budget for the timeshare plan containing the information required under N.J.S.A. 45:15-16.59(b)13, and the schedule of purchaser's expenses,

vii. The form of any applicable agreement for the escrow of ad valorem tax escrow payments;

viii. Documents detailing the procedures and methods by which a purchaser's use and access to the accommodations is scheduled; and

ix. For accommodations located in New Jersey, all documentation required to be given to purchasers under the New Jersey Condominium Act, N.J.S.A. 46:8B-1 et seq., and any other laws governing the transfer of interests in real property, including interests in common interest ownership communities in New Jersey.

12. A signed and dated receipt for the public offering statement and required documents shall be maintained by the developer, along with an executed copy of the purchaser contract for a period of seven years. If the documents are delivered in an alternative format as permitted under N.J.S.A. 45:15-16.59(a), a signed receipt evidencing the purchaser's acceptance of the documents in the alternative format, shall also be maintained by the developer.

11:5-9A.7   Exemptions

(a) Any person who believes that an offering may be exempt from the provisions of the Act, or who is contemplating marketing property in New Jersey which he or she believes may be exempt, may apply to the Commission for a letter of exemption. Such application shall be in written affidavit form and shall list the reasons why the offering or proposed offering may be exempt from the Act. Such an application for exemption shall be accompanied by a non-refundable fee of $ 100.00.

1. In the event the Commission shall determine that the offering is exempt from the Act, it shall issue a letter of exemption setting forth the facts upon which the determination is based.

2. In the event the Commission shall determine that the offering is not exempt from the provisions of the Act, it shall deny the request for exemption in writing, setting forth therein the facts upon which the determination is based, and shall send such writing to the applicant via certified mail, return receipt requested.

3. The Commission shall issue a determination as to whether an offering is or is not exempt within 30 days of its receipt of a complete request for exemption, with the appropriate fee.

4. Any person who is aggrieved by such a determination is entitled to a hearing, in accordance with the Administrative Procedure Act, N.J.S.A. 52:14B-1 et seq., and the Uniform Administrative Procedure Rules, N.J.A.C. 1:1, on the determination, provided said hearing is requested in writing no later than 30 days from the date of the applicant's receipt of notice of such determination.

(b) If the nature of the proposed offering indicates that the applicant would be subject to the registration requirements of the Act, the applicant may apply to the Commission for a limited exemption. If the Commission determines that enforcement of the entire Act and all of these rules is not necessary in the public interest or for the protection of purchasers due to the small amounts involved or the limited character of the offering, it shall issue a limited exemption from registration to the applicant.

1. A limited exemption may be granted by reason of the limited character of the offering where the nature of the property, or of the prospective purchasers to whom the timeshare interest shall be offered, is such that it is likely prospective purchasers shall have expert advice concerning the purchase independent of that supplied by the applicant or his agents. An application for a limited exemption for this reason shall include a copy of any prospectus, offering statement or other such solicitation. A limited exemption granted for this reason shall be confined to the group of offerees specified in the application.

2. An application for a limited exemption shall specify the particular timeshare interests for which exemption is sought. Any limited exemption granted shall be confined to those timeshare interests so specified.

3. An application for a limited exemption shall include a narrative description that clearly describes the nature of the offering and the factual basis and reasons why the limited exemption should be granted.

4. Any limited exemption granted shall remain in effect for a period of two years from the date of issuance indicated in the letter of exemption, unless revoked as described below.

5. Any limited exemption granted shall permit the recipient to offer the timeshare interests covered by the limited exemption to New Jersey residents without obtaining an order of registration. A limited exemption shall not deprive the Commission of jurisdiction to enforce any other provision of the Act or this subchapter, or to revoke the limited exemption after notice and opportunity to be heard.

6. A $ 300.00 non-refundable fee shall be tendered with any application for a limited exemption.

7. All applications for a limited exemption shall comply with the following minimum requirements.

i. The filing of a limited exemption application affidavit-questionnaire;

ii. The filing of proof of title specifying the units or interests to be exempted;

REAL ESTATE COMMISSION   11:5-9A.9

iii. The filing of satisfactory proof of surety and/or financial assurances for any promised improvements or amenities;

iv. The advertisement standards and procedures established by this Act; and

v. The filing of any other documents that the Commission shall deem necessary.

8. No limited exemption granted hereunder shall be effective until a letter of limited exemption is issued by the Commission to the applicant for the exemption.

9. Any material change in the information reflected on the application for a limited exemption or on any documentation submitted in support of such application, shall immediately void any exemption issued based upon such application.

(c) Any offering under this subsection may only be made to those persons who are current bona fide owners of an interest in a timeshare plan currently registered under the Act or previously registered under the Act, or under N.J.S.A. 45:15-16.27 et seq. or the Planned Real Estate Development Full Disclosure Act, N.J.S.A. 45:22A-21 et seq., by the same developer making the offer. A developer of a timeshare plan that either is or was so registered may offer and dispose of an interest in another timeshare plan created by that developer that is located outside of this State and not registered under the Act to a person in this State who is a current owner of an interest in the currently or previously registered timeshare plan provided that:

1. The developer files a notice with the Commission identifying the timeshare plan that it intends to offer;

2. The developer certifies that all purchasers shall be provided with all disclosure documentation required by law to be provided in the jurisdiction in which the timeshare plan is located;

3. The developer certifies that New Jersey purchasers shall be provided with a right to rescind their purchase within seven days after the purchase contract is signed and all documents required under this Act and local and municipal law are delivered, whichever is later. If local or municipal law grants a longer rescission period, then the longer period would apply;

4. The developer submits a fee of $ 300.00 per notice filed in accordance with (c)1 above; and

5. If the offer is made to owners of interests in a previously registered timeshare plan, the registration of that plan was terminated in good standing as provided in N.J.S.A. 45:15-16.60c, 45:15-16.40c or 45:22A-31, as applicable.

11:5-9A.8   Advertising and sales promotions with respect to the sale and marketing of registered timeshare plans

(a) Advertisements that refer to the purchase price of a timeshare interest shall state the full purchase price and shall disclose any known or estimated additional assessments or costs to the purchaser.

1. No advertisement shall refer to a price increase unless the amount and date of the increase are indicated.

(b) No advertisement shall refer to any common element or facility that does not presently exist unless that fact is prominently stated in the advertisement, accompanied by the proposed date of completion, which shall also appear prominently in the advertisement.

(c) No advertisement shall contain photographs, sketches or artist's conceptions unless the fact that these are conceptions is stated immediately adjacent to them in the advertisement.

(d) Unless otherwise noted in the contract of sale, any model unit that is used as part of a promotional plan shall be in substantial conformity with the units that have been or are subsequently constructed.

(e) The owners of timeshare plans that are not registered with the Commission, nor wholly or partially exempt from the Act, shall not make or cause to be made an offer or disposition of any timeshare interest in such a plan to a person or resident within this State regardless of whether the offer or disposition originates within or outside of this State.

1. When advertisements for such properties or interests are placed in any media which is distributed in or broadcast into this State, a disclaimer shall be included indicating that the properties or interests are not registered with the New Jersey Real Estate Commission and that the advertisement is not an offer to New Jersey residents.

(f) Any advertisement, including those which contain offers of reimbursement of travel expenses and/or offers of premiums or other inducements, shall also comply with the provisions of the New Jersey Consumer Fraud Act, N.J.S.A. 56:8-1 et seq.

(g) Registrants who advertise in a language other than English shall make available to prospective purchasers all disclosure documents, including, but not limited to, the public offering statement, and the sales contract written in the same language as that used in the registrant's advertisements.

11:5-9A.9   Inspection of timeshare offerings

(a) As provided in N.J.S.A. 45:15-16.84, the Commission, at its discretion, may make on-site inspections of any timeshare

11:5-9A.10

plan which is the subject of an application for registration, either before an order of registration has been issued or thereafter. The Commission may in its discretion conduct subsequent on-site inspections.

(b) The costs of inspections shall be paid by the applicant who shall provide a deposit when requested by the Commission. After the inspection, the Commission shall provide the applicant/registrant with a statement of costs incurred and a refund of any portion of the deposit not expended or a request for additional funds if required.

11:5-9A.10   Fees

(a) All applicants for registration shall pay application fees as prescribed in N.J.S.A. 48:15-16.64 and in (e) below.

(b) Any request for approval of a material change in, or an amendment to, an application for registration on the basis of which an order of registration has been issued and/or an order of registration and/or a public offering statement shall be accompanied by a fee of $ 300.00. No fee shall be charged for amendments to applications or proposed public offering statements made prior to the issuance of an order of registration.

1. If applications are made simultaneously for approval of a material change and/or an amendment to an order of registration and/or an amendment to a previously approved public offering statement, only one fee shall be payable.

2. If applications are made for approval of multiple material changes, and/or multiple amendments to an order of registration, and/or multiple amendments to a public offering statement simultaneously, only one fee shall be payable.

(c) In accordance with the provisions of N.J.A.C. 15:3, the Commission shall maintain a copy of every application for registration of a timeshare plan that is currently registered together with all amendments thereto and shall make them reasonably available for public inspection during ordinary business hours at the Commission's office.

1. The Commission shall furnish to the public, upon request, a copy of the statement of record of any registered subdivision at a cost in accordance with the copying fees set forth in N.J.S.A. 47:1A-5(b).

(d) All fees paid are non-refundable.

(e) Fees charged pursuant to the Act are listed in the table below:

Description	Fee
Comprehensive registration	$ 1,000 plus $ 50.00 per timeshare interest, up to a maximum of $ 7,500

Description	Fee
Preliminary registration	$ 3,000 if filed separately
Concurrent preliminary registration	$ 500.00 in addition to comprehensive or abbreviated registration fee
Abbreviated registration	$ 1,000 plus $ 50.00 per timeshare interest, up to a maximum of $ 7,500
Amendments to registration	$ 300.00
Exemption to market to current owners	$ 300.00
Limited exemption	$ 300.00
Statutory exemption	$ 100.00

(f) The fee for a consolidation filing shall be the same as for a comprehensive or abbreviated registration as set forth in (e) above.

SUBCHAPTER 10. RULEMAKING AND PETITIONS FOR RULEMAKING

11:5-10.1   Rulemaking—scope

Unless otherwise specified in this subchapter, the procedures governing the promulgation of administrative rules by the New Jersey Real Estate Commission pursuant to the authority granted in N.J.S.A. 45:15-6, 45:15-10.14, 45:15-16.49, 45:15-17(t), 45:15-17.4 and 45:15-42 shall be those established in the Administrative Procedure Act, P.L. 1968, c.410 (N.J.S.A. 52:14B-1 et seq.) and the Rules for Agency Rulemaking, N.J.A.C. 1:30.

11:5-10.2   Notice of proposed adoption of new rule, or proposed amendment or repeal of existing rule

(a) The Commission shall provide primary notice of any proposal to adopt a new rule, or amend or repeal any existing rule, by filing such notice with the Office of Administrative Law for publication in the New Jersey Register through the procedures established in N.J.S.A. 52:14B-1 et seq. and N.J.A.C. 1:30.

(b) With the exception of rules which, pursuant to *N.J.S.A. 52:14B-4,* may be adopted without prior notice, in addition to the primary notice described in (a) above in all circumstances the Commission shall provide secondary notice of proposals to adopt a new rule, or amend or repeal an existing rule, through the following methods:

1. Notice to the news media maintaining a press office to cover the New Jersey State House complex;

REAL ESTATE COMMISSION   **11:5-10.4**

2. Notice posted on the bulletin board of the office of the New Jersey Real Estate Commission;

3. Notice posted on the website of the New Jersey Real Estate Commission at http://www.naic.org/nj/realcom.htm; and

4. Notice mailed to all persons who have submitted written or e-mail requests to the Commission for advance notice of its rulemaking proposals.

(c) In addition to the methods for providing secondary notice of proposed rulemaking specified in (b) above, the Commission may provide such notice in the text of a newsletter or similar publication mailed to all licensed offices of New Jersey real estate brokers and/or a written communication from the New Jersey Real Estate Commission mailed to all licensed offices of New Jersey real estate brokers.

(d) The Commission shall provide secondary notice under (b) above at least 30 days prior to its intended action of adopting a new rule, or amending or repealing any existing rule.

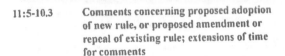

11:5-10.3   Comments concerning proposed adoption of new rule, or proposed amendment or repeal of existing rule; extensions of time for comments

(a) For a period of no less than 30 days following the publication of any proposal to adopt a new rule, or amend or repeal an existing rule, the Commission shall afford all interested persons reasonable opportunity to submit written comments on the proposal in accordance with the procedures established in N.J.S.A. 52:14B-1 et seq. and N.J.A.C. 1:30. Said period shall be deemed the "comment period."

(b) A written comment may be submitted via mail, delivery service, facsimile transmission, e-mail or any other means which results in the Commission's receipt of a writing containing the text of the comment.

(c) If, during the comment period, sufficient public interest is demonstrated in an extension of the time for the submission of comments, the Commission shall provide an additional 30-day period for the receipt of comments from interested persons. In determining whether sufficient public interest has been demonstrated for the purposes of extending the comment period pursuant to N.J.A.C. 1:30-5.4, the Commission shall consider the following criteria:

1. Whether comments received indicated a previously unrecognized impact on regulated entities or persons, or

2. Whether comments received raise unanticipated issues related to the notice of proposal.

(d) Where a 30-day extension of the comment period under (c) above is granted, the proposal shall not be adopted until the Commission has considered all comments received during the entire comment period as extended.

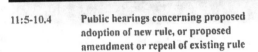

11:5-10.4   Public hearings concerning proposed adoption of new rule, or proposed amendment or repeal of existing rule

(a) The Commission may hold a public hearing to gather information concerning any proposed rule, amendment, or repeal.

(b) The Commission shall publish a notice of the place, date and time of the hearing at least 15 business days before the date of the hearing.

(c) If, during the comment period following the publication of any proposal to adopt a new rule, or amend or repeal any existing rule, sufficient public interest in holding a public hearing on the proposal is demonstrated, the Commission shall conduct such a hearing. The Commission shall provide at least 15 days notice of such a public hearing, which shall be conducted in accordance with the procedures established in N.J.S.A. 52:14B-1 et seq. and N.J.A.C. 1:30.

(d) In determining whether sufficient public interest has been demonstrated for purposes of conducting a public hearing pursuant to N.J.A.C. 1:30-5.5, the Commission shall consider a request for such a hearing that has been submitted on a form prescribed by the Department of Banking and Insurance. Such a request shall be submitted within 60 days following the publication of the notice of proposal in the New Jersey Register.

1. A person interested in having a public hearing held on a notice of proposal shall submit an application on a form prescribed by the Department of Banking and Insurance to New Jersey Real Estate Commission, Department of Banking and Insurance, PO Box 328, Trenton, NJ 08625-0328. The application shall contain the following information:

i. The person's name, address, telephone number, agency or association (if applicable);

ii. The citation and title of the proposed rule and the date the notice of proposal was published in the New Jersey Register; and

iii. The reasons a public hearing regarding the notice of proposal is considered necessary pursuant to (e) below.

(e) Sufficient public interest for the purpose of holding a public hearing pursuant to N.J.A.C. 1:30-5.5 shall be demonstrated if the Commission determines that the consideration of additional data, findings and/or analysis regarding the notice of proposal is necessary in order to ensure that the proposed rulemaking does not violate the intent of the statutory authority.

11:5-10.5   Petitions for rulemaking—scope

N.J.A.C. 11:5-10.5, 10.6 and 10.7 shall apply to all petitions made by interested persons for the adoption of a new rule, or the amendment or repeal of any existing rule by the New Jersey Real Estate Commission, in accordance with *N.J.S.A. 52:14B-4(f)*.

11:5-10.6   Procedure for the submission of petitions for rulemaking

(a) Any interested person may petition the Real Estate Commission to adopt a new rule, or amend or repeal an existing rule. Such interested person shall be deemed a "petitioner." The petitioner may include with any petition the text of the proposed new rule, amended rule or repealed rule. All petitions for rulemaking shall clearly and concisely state:

1. The full name and address of the petitioner;

2. The substance or nature of the rulemaking action which is requested;

3. The reasons for the request;

4. The petitioner's interest in the request, including, without limitation, any relevant organizational affiliation or economic interest; and

5. References to the Commission's authority to take the requested action.

(b) A petitioner shall submit a petition to the following address:

New Jersey Real Estate Commission
PO Box 328
Trenton, New Jersey 08625-0328

(c) A petitioner shall file a petition by forwarding an original and two copies to the Commission at the address indicated in (b) above.

(d) Any submission by a petitioner which is not in substantial compliance with the requirements specified above shall not be considered a petition for rulemaking requiring further Commission action pursuant to *N.J.S.A. 52:14B-4(f)*.

(e) Within 30 days of receiving a petition for rulemaking the Commission shall review the same to ascertain if the submission is in substantial compliance with the requirements set forth above. In the event that the Commission determines that the submission is not in substantial compliance with those requirements, the Commission shall notify the petitioner of such noncompliance and of the particular deficiency or deficiencies in the submission upon which the Commission's determination was based. The Commission shall also advise the petitioner that any deficiencies may be corrected and that the corrected petition may be resubmitted for further consideration.

11:5-10.7   Procedure for the consideration and disposition of rulemaking petitions

(a) Subsequent to making a determination that a petition is in substantial compliance with N.J.A.C. 11:5-10.6, the Commission shall file a notice of petition with the Office of Administrative Law for publication in the New Jersey Register. The Commission's notice shall include:

1. The name of the petitioner;

2. The substance or nature of the rulemaking action which is requested;

3. The problem or purpose which is the subject of the request; and

4. The date that the petition was received.

(b) Within 60 days of receiving a petition which is in substantial compliance with N.J.A.C. 11:5-10.6, the Commission shall consider the petition and decide upon an action to be taken on the petition. During that time period the petitioner may be requested to attend a public meeting of the Commission and answer questions concerning the petition. The Commission shall mail to the petitioner, and file with the Office of Administrative Law for publication in the New Jersey Register, a notice of action on the petition which shall include:

1. The name of the petitioner;

2. The New Jersey Register citation for the notice of petition, if that notice appeared in a previous Register;

3. Certification by the Commission that the petition was duly considered pursuant to law;

4. The nature or substance of the Commission's action upon the petition; and

5. A brief statement of reasons for the Commission's action.

(c) Commission action on a petition shall either:

1. Deny the petition, and give a written statement of the Commission's reasons for such denial;

2. Grant the petition and file a notice of proposed rule or a notice of preproposal with the Office of Administrative Law within 90 days of granting the petition; or

3. Refer the matter for further deliberations, the nature of which shall be specified to the petitioner and in the notice of action and which deliberations shall be concluded within 90 days of referring the matter for further deliberations. Upon conclusion of such further deliberations, the Commission shall either deny the petition and provide a written statement of its reasons for such denial or grant the petition and initiate a rulemaking proceeding within 90 days or such other time period as may be provided for in N.J.A.C. 1:30-4. The Commission shall mail the results of these further deliberations to the petitioner and submit the results to the Office of Administrative Law for publication in the New Jersey Register.

SUBCHAPTER 11. PROCEDURES ON DISCIPLINARY ACTIONS, CONTESTED APPLICATIONS, DECLARATORY RULING REQUESTS

11:5-11.1   Pleadings enumerated and defined

(a) Pleadings before the Commission shall be orders to show cause, complaints, answers, petitions, and motions, which for purposes of these rules are defined as follows:

1. "Orders to show cause" means orders issued by the Director on behalf of the New Jersey Real Estate Commission compelling the persons to whom the order is directed to appear and show cause before the Commission why certain actions, including but

not limited to the imposition of sanctions, should not be taken by the Commission pursuant to the Real Estate Licensing Act, N.J.S.A. 45:15-1 et seq. and the rules promulgated thereunder.

2. "Complaint" means a filing by the Office of the Attorney General of New Jersey alleging violations of one or more of the provisions of N.J.S.A. 45:15-1 et seq. and/or of the Commission's rules.

3. "Answer" means the pleading filed by a licensee or other party against whom an order to show cause or complaint is directed which sets forth the respondent's position with the respect to each factual and legal allegation in the order or complaint and specifies all affirmative defenses raised by the respondent.

4. "Petition" means the pleading filed by an interested person to request a rulemaking action or declaratory ruling by the Commission or the pleading filed by an interested person seeking to intervene in any rulemaking or declaratory ruling proceeding.

5. "Motion" means the application filed incidental to an action before the Commission for the purpose of obtaining a ruling or order directing that some action be taken in favor of the movant.

(b) Documents, affidavits or other evidentiary matter submitted with or attached to a pleading other than a motion shall not be deemed evidentiary. Such materials must be offered into evidence at a hearing and admitted as such in order to be considered as part of the evidentiary record.

11:5-11.2   Answers

(a) Any party against whom an order to show cause or complaint is directed and who desires to contest the same or make any representation to the Commission in connection therewith shall file an answer in writing with the Commission.

(b) The answer shall apprise the Commission fully and completely of the nature of all defenses and shall admit or deny specifically and in detail all material allegations of the order to show cause or complaint.

(c) Matters alleged by way of affirmative defense shall be separately stated and numbered in the answer.

(d) An Answer must be filed within 20 days after service of the Order to Show Cause or complaint unless the deputy attorney general or staff member who represents the complainant consents, or the Commission orders an extension of time to Answer.

(e) Filing of an Answer shall be made by forwarding an original and two copies to the Director of the Commission and a copy

11:5-11.3

to the deputy attorney general or staff member who is representing the complainant in the matter.

11:5-11.3   Adversary hearing determination by the Commission

(a) Promptly after the answer is filed, the Commission will review the pleadings at a Commission meeting and decide whether any material fact or issue of law is contested. If the Commission determines that a matter is contested, a hearing will be scheduled. On its own motion or at the request of either party, the Commission may, in its discretion, transmit the case to the Office of Administrative Law for hearing and initial decision.

(b) If, upon review of the pleadings, the Commission determines that no material facts or issues of law are contested, the Commission shall afford the respondent an opportunity to be heard and to present witnesses and documentary evidence, which presentation shall be limited to the issue of the severity of any sanction or penalty to be imposed. By stipulation or other means, the deputy attorney general or staff member representing the complainant shall present evidence sufficient to establish the factual basis for all alleged violations and may present documentary evidence or witnesses in rebuttal of any mitigation testimony or evidence presented by the respondent.

11:5-11.4   Motions

(a) In all matters heard by the Commission, motions and replies shall be made in the manner and form prescribed by the rules which establish the procedures for motion practice before the Office of Administrative Law, N.J.A.C. 1:1-12. In construing those rules, the terms "Executive Director" and "Commission" are substituted for the terms "Clerk" and "Judge", respectively.

(b) Filing of a motion or reply shall be made by forwarding an original and 15 copies to the Director of the Commission and a copy to all other attorneys and pro se parties, if any, in the matter.

(c) A motion shall be considered by the Commission at a regularly scheduled meeting pursuant to the requirements of N.J.A.C. 1:1-12.

(d) Oral argument on a motion when permitted or directed by the Commission shall be presented to the Commission by the parties or their representatives in person at a Commission meeting; motions will not be heard by telephone conference.

(e) Motions for the reconsideration of sanctions imposed by the Commission must be filed within 30 days of the date upon which notice of the decision imposing sanctions was provided to the movant. Such motions must be accompanied by a recitation of the particular facts and legal basis which purportedly support the application.

11:5-11.5   Hearing procedure

The Director may, on behalf of the Commission, issue an Order to Show Cause requiring a licensee or other person to appear before the Commission for a hearing, pursuant to the rules of the Office of Administrative Law, in circumstances where violations of N.J.S.A. 45:15-17d, 17n, 17o and/or 19.1 are alleged to have occurred or where there is danger of imminent harm to the public.

11:5-11.6   Sanctions: failure to answer or appear; default

(a) In all matters heard by the Commission, the imposition of sanctions for the failure to appear and/or to comply with any order of the Commission or the requirements of these procedural rules shall be governed by the procedures established for the imposition of sanctions in matters heard by the Office of Administrative Law at N.J.A.C. 1:1-14.4.

(b) The Commission shall have the discretionary authority to grant extensions of the time to file an answer or appear.

11:5-11.7   Settlements

(a) The parties to a proposed settlement shall present the settlement to the Commission pursuant to the requirements of N.J.A.C. 1:1-19.1.

(b) Such a settlement shall be presented to the Commission during the public session of a Commission meeting. Should a proposed settlement be rejected by the Commission, the proposal shall not be considered or used for any purpose in any subsequent hearing. Any settlement approved by the Commission shall be a public record.

11:5-11.8   Decisions in enforcement actions, motions for reconsideration

(a) All final decisions of the Real Estate Commission on contested and uncontested matters shall be reduced to writing, in

REAL ESTATE COMMISSION   **11:5-11.9**

the form of an Order of the Commission, which shall be served upon all parties to the matter either personally or by registered or certified mail sent to the last known business address of all parties. Unless otherwise ordered, all fines imposed by order of the Commission shall be payable within 30 days of the effective date of the order as established by the Administrative Procedure Act, N.J.S.A. 52:14B-1 et seq.

(b) Motions for reconsideration of final decisions of the Real Estate Commission shall be made within the time frame specified in N.J.A.C. 11:5-11.4. All such motions shall be considered on the papers unless oral argument is requested and that request is granted by the Commission or the Commission directs oral argument on the motion.

██

11:5-11.9   Applications for temporary suspension

(a) The Commission may on its own motion, and upon the terms and conditions as set forth in N.J.S.A. 45:15-17.1 and as the Commission deems appropriate, enter an order temporarily suspending the license of any licensee upon making a finding that prima facie evidence exists that:

1. The licensee has failed to account for or to pay over any moneys belonging to others that have come into the possession of the licensee, in violation of N.J.S.A. 45:15-17(d); or

2. The licensee has commingled his or her personal money or property with the money or property of others or has failed to maintain and deposit such moneys in a special account, separate and apart from personal or other business accounts, when acting in the capacity of a real estate broker, or escrow agent, or as the temporary custodian of the funds of others, in a real estate transaction, in violation of N.J.S.A. 45:15-17(o).

(b) At least 24 hours prior to ordering a temporary suspension, the Commission shall give notice to the licensee of the application for the order and provide the licensee an opportunity to appear before the Commission to show cause why the license should not be suspended pending a full hearing of the matter. Such notice shall be given in writing or telephonically.

1. Written notice shall be served personally or sent by certified mail to the last known business address of the licensee.

2. Telephonic notice shall be confirmed in a writing sent to the licensee's last known business address as soon as practicable after the delivery of the telephonic notice.

3. The person who personally or telephonically delivers notice of an application for a temporary suspension shall execute a certification confirming that he or she has provided the notice, which certification shall be submitted into the record of the proceeding on the application for the temporary suspension.

(c) At the hearing on the application for the temporary suspension, the Commission shall consider evidence presented by the licensee to explain, disprove or rebut the prima facie evidence upon which the application for the temporary suspension is based. Unless otherwise provided in N.J.S.A. 45:15-17.1, the provisions of N.J.A.C. 1:1-12.6(f) shall apply to proceedings on applications for temporary suspensions.

(d) Prior to entering any order imposing a temporary suspension as provided in (a) above, the Commission shall also make findings that:

1. An adequate good faith effort to provide notice to the licensee was made and that the licensee was afforded an opportunity to be heard. Submission of the certification referred to in (b) above shall be sufficient to establish that an adequate good faith effort was made to provide notice of the proceeding;

2. Based on the evidence presented, there is a substantial likelihood that the charging party will prevail on the merits when the matter is fully argued before the Commission; and

3. Immediate and irreparable harm will probably result before the licensee can be fully heard. Prima facie evidence of a violation of N.J.S.A. 45:15-17(d) or (o) shall be considered sufficient to satisfy this criterion.

(e) All orders imposing temporary suspensions shall advise the suspended licensee of the date upon which the Commission shall hold a full evidentiary hearing on the violations upon which the temporary suspension is based, which date shall be no more than 30 days following the effective date of the temporary suspension. Such a hearing shall be a plenary hearing, conducted in accordance with N.J.A.C. 1:1-14.1 through 14.7.

(f) The temporary suspension shall become effective upon issuance by the Commission, and the licensee and his or her broker shall promptly be notified of its issuance, whereupon the license of the suspended person shall immediately be returned to the Commission. The Commission shall confirm the suspension in a written order which shall be served upon the licensee and his or her broker via personal service or by certified mail, return receipt requested at the licensee's last known business address.

(g) In order to entertain applications for temporary suspensions made during time periods when the Commission is not scheduled to meet, or when a quorum cannot be obtained, the Commission may delegate to three commissioners, at least one

11:5-11.10   **INSURANCE**

of whom shall be either the President or Vice-President of the Commission and at least one of whom shall be a public member. the authority to temporarily suspend a license as provided in (a) through (f) above. In such circumstances, all references in these rules to the Commission shall be construed as referring to the three commissioners so designated by the Commission.

11:5-11.10   **Procedures applicable to appeals of initial denials of licensing applications**

(a) Initial denials of the following applications may be appealed to the Real Estate Commission through compliance with all of the requirements established in (b) below:

1. License applications;

2. Applications from disabled veterans for education waivers and/or broker experience requirement waivers;

3. Applications for the issuance of education waivers by persons other than disabled veterans;

4. Applications for the issuance of broker experience requirement waivers by broker licensees of other states; and

5. Applications by broker license candidates for the Commission's approval of their experience as a salesperson so as to qualify to challenge the broker license examination.

(b) All appeals to the Real Estate Commission provided for in (a) above shall be filed by the appealing applicant submitting to the Commission within 45 days of the date of the notice of denial an original and two copies of all of the documentation noted below:

1. A covering letter stating the factual and legal basis of the appeal, to which shall be attached a copy of the application and the denial letter which forms the basis of the appeal. The said covering letter shall also state whether the applicant desires to appear and present oral argument and/or testimony when the appeal is considered by the Commission;

2. Where the denial was based upon an applicant's prior criminal history and/or their loss of a professional license, all judgments of conviction on the convictions which form the basis of the denial and a letter from their probation or parole officer, if within one year of making the application they were under

such supervision, which letter shall state the extent of the applicant's compliance with the terms and conditions of his or her probationary sentence or parole supervision, and/or a copy of the order or memorandum of settlement evidencing the loss of the professional license;

3. On all applications as described in (b)2 above, a letter from the broker with whom the applicant intends to be licensed, evidencing that person's full knowledge of the factors which formed the basis of the initial denial;

4. Any other relevant documentation which the applicant desires the Commission to consider when hearing the appeal; and

5. Any other documentation which the Commission determines is required in order to allow it to make a fully informed decision on the appeal.

(c) Upon the proper filing of an appeal as described in (b) above, the appeal package shall be reviewed and the applicant advised of the following:

1. The date, time and place at which the appeal will be considered by the Real Estate Commission; or

2. That based upon the content of the appeal documents a determination has been made to approve the application; or

3. The appeal package is deficient in certain respects, which shall be specified to the applicant, with an indication that upon receipt of the missing documentation the appeal will be given further consideration.

(d) All applicants have the opportunity to be represented by counsel when submitting an appeal and/or appearing before the Real Estate Commission and to call witnesses to testify on their behalf at the time of its consideration of their appeal.

(e) Upon the conclusion of a hearing on an appeal, the Commission shall either render a decision or take the matter under advisement and render a decision at a future date. The ruling of the Commission shall be communicated to the applicant in written form promptly upon the decision being rendered.

REAL ESTATE COMMISSION   **11:5-12.3**

SUBCHAPTER 12. CONTINUING EDUCATION

11:5-12.1   Purpose and scope

(a) The purpose of this subchapter is to implement N.J.S.A. 45:15-16.2a et seq. by establishing continuing education requirements for real estate brokers, broker-salespersons and salespersons as a condition of biennial licensure renewal, and by establishing standards for the approval of continuing education courses, course providers and course instructors.

(b) This subchapter shall apply to all individuals licensed as real estate brokers, and to all broker-salespersons and salespersons licensed in this State, and to all applicants for the approval of continuing education courses or for approval as continuing education course instructors or providers.

11:5-12.2   Definitions

The following words and terms, as used in this subchapter, shall have the following meanings unless the context clearly indicates otherwise:

"ARELLO" means the Association of Real Estate License Law Officials, which may be contacted at 334-260-2928 and at mailbox@arello.org.

"Commission" means the New Jersey Real Estate Commission.

"Continuing education coordinator" means the individual designated by an approved continuing education provider as the person responsible for assuring compliance with the provisions of N.J.S.A. 45:15-16.2a et seq., and the rules in this chapter that are applicable to continuing education providers.

"Distance learning" means any educational process based on the geographical separation of instructor and learner (for example, CD-ROM, disk, on-line courses, correspondence courses, webinars or video conferencing).

"Real estate broker" or "broker" means a person, firm or corporation as defined at N.J.S.A. 45:15-3.

"Real estate broker-salesperson" or "broker-salesperson" means a person as defined at N.J.S.A. 45:15-3.

"Real estate salesperson" or "salesperson" means a person as defined at N.J.S.A. 45:15-3.

"Volunteer Advisory Committee" means the committee established pursuant to N.J.S.A. 45:15-16.2a.b(1)(b), which is responsible for recommending continuing education course providers, instructors and courses for approval by the Commission.

11:5-12.3   Continuing education requirements

(a) Unless granted a waiver pursuant to N.J.A.C. 11:5-12.5, commencing with the July 1, 2013 renewal and continuing for every renewal thereafter, in order to qualify for license renewal every individual licensed as a real estate broker and every licensed broker-salesperson or salesperson shall, during the 24-month period prior to that renewal, have completed 12 hours of approved continuing education as set forth in this subchapter, two hours of which shall have been on the topic of ethics, except that:

1. A Commission-licensed real estate instructor or Commission-approved continuing education course instructor shall earn credit for teaching an approved continuing education course offered by an approved provider. Notwithstanding the number of times the instructor teaches an approved course during a two-year license term, the instructor shall earn the number of continuing education credits granted to a licensee who attends and completes that course one time during that license term;

2. A person who successfully completes one or more broker pre-licensure education courses as set forth in N.J.A.C. 11:5-2.1 shall be deemed to have fulfilled the continuing education requirement applicable to the license that such person may seek to renew upon the conclusion of the license term during which the broker pre-licensure course was completed; and

3. A person who is initially licensed as a salesperson in the second year of a biennial license term shall not be required to fulfill any continuing education requirements in order to renew the salesperson's license upon the conclusion of that license term. A person who is initially licensed as a salesperson during the first year of a biennial license term shall complete all applicable continuing education requirements in order to renew the salesperson's license upon the conclusion of that license term.

(b) A licensee for whom a renewal application is timely submitted who completes the continuing education requirements between May 1 and June 30 of the second year in a biennial license term, and a licensee for whom a late renewal application as referenced in N.J.S.A. 45:15-15 is submitted who completes the continuing education requirements between May 1 of the second year of a biennial license term and the conclusion of the late renewal period, shall pay a processing fee of $ 200.00 in order to qualify for the renewal of his or her license. Renewing licensees who complete the continuing education requirements on or before April 30 of the second year of a biennial license term shall not be required to pay this processing fee.

(c) The successful completion of an approved continuing education course shall not be considered for continuing education credit more than once within a two-year license term.

11:5-12.4

(d) When applying to renew their licenses, licensees shall certify to the Commission, either directly or through their broker, that they have either complied with the continuing education requirement, were not required to do so for one of the reasons set forth in (a) above, or have received a waiver as set forth in N.J.A.C. 11:5-12.5.

███████████████████████

11:5-12.4   Curricula

(a) The continuing education requirement may be fulfilled by acquiring credits exclusively in the core topic areas listed below in this subsection. Licensees shall acquire at least six of the 12 continuing education credits required for license renewal pursuant to this subchapter in one or more of the following core topic areas:

1. Agency;

2. Disclosure;

3. Legal issues, for example, listing agreements, contracts of sale, leases, attorney review, forms of ownership and deed restrictions;

4. Ethics;

5. Fair housing and the New Jersey Law Against Discrimination;

6. New Jersey real estate brokers and salesmen statute and rules;

7. New Jersey and Federal environmental laws/rules pertinent to the practice of real estate brokerage; and

8. Legal requirements regarding escrow monies and financial recordkeeping.

(b) The remaining number of continuing education credits may be acquired through the acquisition of continuing education credits in excess of the core topic area minimum requirement referenced in (a) above through the completion of elective courses approved in accordance with this subchapter.

(c) All courses in core topics other than ethics shall include instruction on the manner in which ethics relates to the subject matter of the course.

11:5-12.5   Waiver of continuing education requirements

(a) An applicant for license renewal who was unable to fulfill the continuing education requirements imposed by N.J.S.A. 45:15-16.2a and this subchapter may request and be granted a waiver, in whole or part, of the continuing education requirement by the Commission.

(b) An applicant requesting a waiver of the continuing education requirement shall certify that the applicant was unable to fulfill the continuing education due to:

1. An incapacitating illness;

2. Active duty service in the armed forces of the United States for one year or more of the two-year licensure period;

3. Emergency; or

4. Other substantial and unavoidable hardship. Financial hardship, unreasonable delay, and conflicts with business or personal obligations shall not constitute a basis on which the continuing education requirement may be waived pursuant to this section.

(c) An applicant for a waiver of the continuing education requirements shall request the waiver in writing on a form prescribed by the Commission and provide documentation that corroborates the applicant's certification as to the basis upon which the waiver is sought.

(d) With the exception of requests based on an emergency, requests for a waiver shall be filed with the Commission on or before March 15 of the second year of a two-year license term. Requests for a waiver based on an emergency shall be filed within a reasonable time given the circumstances.

(e) The Commission may seek additional information regarding the basis of an applicant's request for a waiver of the continuing education requirement under this section, including, but not limited to, the provision of sworn statements or testimony under oath by the waiver applicant.

(f) With the exception of waivers granted to active duty military personnel, licensees who receive a waiver of any portion of the core course continuing education requirement shall make up the waived core course(s), in addition to all continuing education credits required for the current license term, as a condition of renewing their license for the license term immediately following the license term for which the waiver was issued. (For example, if a licensee receives a waiver of six core credits in the first licensing term, then the licensee must complete those six previously waived core credits and the full 12 continuing education credits, for a total of 18 credits, in the immediately following licensing term in order to be eligible for renewal upon the conclusion of that license term.)

REAL ESTATE COMMISSION   **11:5-12.7**

(g) Licensees who receive a waiver of the elective course requirement shall not be required to make up the waived elective course(s).

11:5-12.6   Continuing education providers; standards and application process

(a) An applicant seeking approval from the Commission to become an approved continuing education provider shall submit a completed application on forms provided by the Commission with the required fee. The application shall include the following:

1. A non-refundable application fee of $ 300.00;

2. The business name which the Commission is to record as the official business name of the provider and any trade name or alternate name under which the provider will operate;

3. A description of the type(s) of courses to be provided (in-person or distance learning, including the specific type(s) of distance learning course(s));

4. A designation of an individual, including their phone number and e-mail address, who will serve as the provider's primary contact person with the Commission for matters relating to continuing education and who shall be designated as the provider's New Jersey continuing education coordinator, and

5. If the provider will offer in-person courses, the address(es) and a description of the known location(s) where the course(s) will be offered.

(b) Upon the assignment to them of a New Jersey continuing education provider identification number, the following shall be deemed to be approved providers of real estate continuing education courses without being required to file an application for approval as a continuing education provider or pay the provider approval application fee specified at N.J.A.C. 11:5-12.17:

1. Real estate prelicensure schools licensed by the Commission pursuant to N.J.S.A. 45:15-10.4 and N.J.A.C. 11:5-2.2; and

2. The New Jersey Real Estate Commission.

(c) Public adult education programs and all accredited colleges and universities shall be deemed to be approved providers upon application. Public adult education programs and public accredited colleges and universities shall not be required to pay an application fee.

(d) If an applicant is disapproved, the reasons for disapproval shall be set forth in a written notice provided to the applicant by the Commission as set forth in N.J.A.C. 11:5-12.15.

(e) All approvals of providers that are conferred by the Commission prior to June 30, 2016 shall remain in effect until that date. Providers whose approval is expiring may seek re-approval by complying with all of the requirements set forth in this section, including payment of the non-refundable application fee. Applications for re-approval may be submitted commencing on January 1 of the year in which approval is scheduled to expire. Subsequent to June 30, 2016, approvals shall expire on June 30, 2020 and at four-year intervals thereafter.

11:5-12.7   Continuing education providers; responsibilities

(a) Providers' responsibilities shall include the following:

1. The general supervision of the continuing education courses;

2. Ensuring the offered course and instructor have been approved by the Commission;

3. Ensuring that the instructor is knowledgeable in the subject matter of each course offered by the provider that is taught by that instructor;

4. Securing, maintaining, and reporting upon evaluations of courses and instructors as set forth in N.J.A.C. 11:5-12.8(h) and (i);

5. All recordkeeping and supplying of information to the Commission or its designee in accordance with the provisions of this subchapter; and

6. Ensuring that all course offerings comply with the requirements imposed by this subchapter (for example, appropriate facilities).

(b) Providers shall notify the Commission in writing prior to any change in the provider's business name(s), its continuing education coordinator and the contact information for that individual, the provider's business telephone number, or any material change in its qualifications (for example, a change in the provider's location at which classroom-based courses are offered).

(c) Each non-distance learning course shall be conducted at a location and in such facilities as shall be appropriate to properly present the course. The providers of such courses shall ensure that they are conducted at times and in locations that are conducive to learning, free of excessive distractions and segregated from non-course related activity, including any solicitation activity directed to attendees of the course. The facilities at which such courses are offered shall comply with all local, state and Federal laws and regulations.

(d) Providers shall be responsible for verifying attendance at each continuing education course delivered in a classroom or conference room setting, or verifying completion of each continuing education course delivered via distance learning, by the licensee who, based upon information reported by the provider, will receive credit for having completed the course.

1. Providers of non-distance learning continuing education courses shall verify the identity of all individuals attending such courses. Providers may do so by requiring such individuals to present a driver's license or other form of photographic identification and their real estate license pocket card to a representative of the course provider at the location where the course is offered, or through other means that assure that the individual attending the course is the licensee who registered for the course.

(e) Prior to a student's completion of the process of registering for a continuing education course and a provider's acceptance of any fee related to such registration, the course provider shall provide prospective students with a notice which specifies the number of credits for which the course is approved and whether the course is on a core or elective topic. The notice shall also include information about course fees, refund policies, course subject matter and learning objectives, procedures and requirements for satisfactory course completion.

(f) Continuing education course providers shall enable representatives of the Commission to attend an in-person course or review a distance learning course in the form it is offered at no cost to the Commission.

11:5-12.8   Continuing education providers; reporting and recordkeeping requirements

(a) Providers shall provide to licensees who successfully complete an approved course a certificate of completion signed or affirmed by the provider, which shall include the licensee's name, the course name, date of completion, New Jersey continuing education course number, number of credits earned for the course and the provider's New Jersey continuing education provider identification number.

(b) For a period of six years, providers shall maintain and be capable of producing for inspection by a Commission representative the course and instructor evaluations referenced in (h) and (i) below and the information on the satisfactory completion of continuing education courses by licensees set forth in (d) below. In addition, providers shall maintain and be capable of producing for inspection copies of all course-specific written material provided to students who attend a course. Presuming there is no change in such written material, only one set of copies need be maintained, regardless of the number of times the provider offers the course.

(c) Providers shall use recordkeeping systems that are capable of producing written reports on attendance at approved continuing education courses which include all of the information set forth in (a) above.

(d) Providers shall electronically submit data to the Commission or its designee on a weekly basis identifying those licensees who have completed continuing education courses offered by the provider during the preceding reporting period and shall include, at a minimum, the following information in each record of the completion of a continuing education course by a licensee:

1. The licensee's name and license reference number;

2. The license term for which the licensee is seeking credit for having completed the continuing education course;

3. The provider's name and identification number; and

4. The continuing education course name, course number, course category (core or elective), completion date and number of credit hours.

(e) The data referenced in (d) above shall be submitted on forms or in a computer readable format provided by the Commission or its designee.

(f) Providers who offer distance learning courses shall utilize systems that assure that students have actually performed all tasks designated to assure student participation and otherwise comply with all applicable provisions of N.J.A.C. 11:5-12.12 and 12.14.

(g) An approved provider shall notify the Commission in the event that it intends to cease offering continuing education courses. Such notice shall be submitted in writing no later than 30 days prior to the provider's cessation of operations as a continuing education course provider and shall specify that the records required by this section will be maintained by the provider for the six-year period referenced in (b) above, and the location at which those records will be maintained.

(h) Providers shall request all students who complete the continuing education courses they provide to submit evaluations of the course(s) attended by the student and, for all courses except distance learning or correspondence courses that are not taught by an instructor, of the instructor of the course. All students who supply such evaluations shall remain anonymous. The evaluations shall provide for the students to indicate their favorable, neutral or negative assessments of the performance factors referenced in (h)4 and 5 below.

1. Providers of non-distance learning courses may request that students manually complete such evaluations during the

REAL ESTATE COMMISSION   **11:5-12.10**

concluding minutes of the course or electronically subsequent to the completion of the course.

2. Providers of distance learning courses shall request that students complete such evaluations electronically upon completing the course.

3. All evaluations shall specify the name and identification number of the provider and the name and identification number of the instructor and course being evaluated.

4. All evaluations of instructors shall include:

i. A question on the quality of the instructor's presentation of the material;

ii. A question on the level of knowledge of the subject matter of the course displayed by the instructor; and

iii. An opportunity for the licensee to comment upon the instructor's performance.

5. All evaluations of courses shall include:

i. A question on the quality of the materials and the content of the course;

ii. A question on the quality of the manner in which the information in the course is organized and presented; and

iii. An opportunity for the licensee to comment upon the course.

(i) Within 30 days after offering a course, providers shall report to the Commission's Education Bureau instances where more than 50 percent of the evaluations received on a course or instructor indicate negative assessments on one or more of the performance factors to be evaluated as referenced in (h)4 and 5 above for instructors and courses, respectively.

11:5-12.9   Continuing education providers; advertising

(a) Any advertisement or promotional material used by a provider shall include the provider's official name or trade or alternate name on file with the Commission.

(b) No advertisement shall contain false, misleading or deceptive claims or misrepresentations. In all advertisements which make express or implied claims that are likely to be misleading in the absence of certain qualifying information, such qualifying information shall be disclosed in the advertisement in a clear and conspicuous manner.

11:5-12.10   Continuing education instructors; standards and application process

(a) An applicant seeking approval from the Commission to become an approved continuing education instructor shall submit a completed application on forms provided by the Commission with the required fee. An application for approval as a continuing education instructor shall include:

1. A non-refundable application fee of $ 150.00;

2. An indication of the core and/or elective topics the applicant considers him or herself qualified to teach;

3. A resume and other material evidencing the applicant's qualifications for approval as an instructor in accordance with one or more of the criteria set forth in (d) below; and

4. Such additional information as the applicant may wish to provide in support of their application, for example, letters of professional reference.

(b) Real estate instructors licensed pursuant to N.J.S.A. 45:15-10.5 and N.J.A.C. 11:5-2.2 shall, upon the assignment to them of a continuing education instructor identification number, be deemed approved as continuing education instructors in core topics as defined in this subchapter.

(c) ARELLO-approved instructors of ARELLO-approved courses in elective topics shall, upon the assignment to them of a continuing education instructor identification number, be deemed approved as continuing education instructors in such courses.

(d) An individual applying to become an approved continuing education instructor shall meet at least one of the following criteria:

1. A college or university professor in real estate, finance, business, economics or a related field;

2. A specialist with a college degree or experience teaching one or more subjects in the topic(s) noted in their application for approval as an instructor;

3. Possess at least three years of experience in a profession, trade or technical occupation in the real estate field related to the subject matter of proposed instruction;

4. A real estate instructor licensed or otherwise authorized by the agency with regulatory authority over real estate licensees in another jurisdiction who can show subject matter expertise;

5. A member in good standing of the State Bar of New Jersey who is engaged in the field of real estate related law; or

6. Persons who otherwise evidence their teaching qualifications by education or experience or a combination of the two.

(e) If an applicant is disapproved, the reasons for disapproval shall be set forth in a written notice provided to the applicant by the Commission as set forth in N.J.A.C. 11:5-12.15.

(f) An approved instructor shall promptly notify the Commission in the event of a material change in his or her qualifications for continuing in the status of an approved instructor (for example, disbarment as an attorney).

(g) All approvals of instructors conferred by the Commission prior to June 30, 2016 shall remain in effect until that date. Instructors whose approval is expiring may seek re-approval by complying with all of the requirements set forth in N.J.A.C. 11:5-12.10, including payment of the non-refundable application fee. Applications for re-approval may be submitted commencing on January 1 of the year in which approval is scheduled to expire. Subsequent to June 30, 2016, approvals shall expire on June 30, 2020 and at four-year intervals thereafter.

11:5-12.11   Continuing education courses; application process

(a) Except as set forth in (b) below, all continuing education courses shall require approval by the Commission. An applicant seeking approval of a course by the Commission shall submit a complete application on a form provided by the Commission with the required fee. An application for approval of a continuing education course shall include:

1. A non-refundable application fee of $ 200.00;

2. The name, address and telephone number of the applicant;

3. The title of the course to be offered;

4. The number of hours required to complete the course, which shall be expressed in increments of entire hours;

5. A detailed outline of the subject matter of the course;

6. A description of the materials to be distributed to the participants; and

7. With respect to distance learning courses, such other information as is referenced in N.J.A.C. 11:5-12.14.

(b) All distance learning courses certified by the ARELLO that are of a duration of at least one hour and that provide instruction on one of the elective topic areas listed in N.J.A.C. 11:5-12.13 shall, upon payment of the required fee, submission of an application as set forth in (a) above, and approval of their content by the Voluntary Advisory Committee, be approved by the Commission. All distance learning courses certified by the

ARELLO shall be deemed to have fulfilled the criteria applicable to such courses set forth in N.J.A.C. 11:5-12.14(b)1, 3, 4 and 7.

(c) If an application for course approval is denied, written notice of such a denial shall be provided to the applicant, which notice shall include a statement of reasons for the denial in accordance with N.J.A.C. 11:5-12.15.

(d) All approvals of continuing education courses shall expire on December 31 of the fifth year following the year in which the course was approved by the Commission. Applications for re-approval of a course shall comply with all requirements set forth in (a) above.

11:5-12.12   Continuing education courses; standards and requirements

(a) All courses shall be instructional and contribute to the professional competence of individuals engaged in the practice of real estate brokerage.

(b) In order to qualify for approval, courses may but are not required to compel a licensee to pass a comprehensive examination testing the licensee's knowledge of the entire course content as a condition of the receipt of credit for the completion of the continuing education course.

(c) Approved continuing education courses may be offered in a traditional classroom setting or as distance learning courses.

(d) The following shall not qualify for approval as a continuing education course:

1. Real estate salesperson prelicensure courses offered pursuant to N.J.S.A. 45:15-10.1 and N.J.A.C. 11:5-2.1;

2. General education or review courses offered to prepare a student to take a real estate broker's or salesperson's examination;

3. Sales meetings;

4. Motivational classes or seminars; and

5. Offerings in mechanical office and business skills, such as typing, computer training, instructional navigation of the world wide web and internet, instructional use of generic computer software, speed reading, memory improvement, report writing, salesmanship and sales psychology.

(e) To qualify for approval, a continuing education course shall have a duration of at least one hour and be designed to confer credits in whole credit increments. All courses shall consist of no less than 50 minutes of actual instruction for each hour of the course's duration, with no more than 10 minutes of each hour utilized for attendance, the completion of or an explanation of the anonymous evaluations required pursuant to N.J.A.C. 11:5-12.8(h) and (i), and other administrative work.

(f) Material revisions in course content cannot be made without prior approval by the Commission, except that changes in course content made solely for the purpose of updating a course to reflect recent developments such as the enactment of new or amended laws or rules do not require prior approval. Any such non-approved changes shall be disclosed in any application for re-approval of the course submitted immediately subsequent to the making of such changes.

11:5-12.13   Continuing education courses; elective courses

(a) The following are approved topic areas for elective continuing education courses:

1. Commercial real estate;

2. Property management;

3. Seasonal rentals;

4. Requirements of and transactions subject to the Real Estate Sales Full Disclosure Act and the New Jersey Real Estate Timeshare Act;

5. Financing;

6. Land use;

7. Real estate valuation;

8. Foreclosures and short-sale transactions; and

9. Specific aspects of residential real estate transactions.

(b) Continuing education courses offered in the elective topics set forth in (a) above shall be deemed approved by the Commission upon application if they are:

1. Offered by a public adult education program or an accredited college or university that has obtained from the Commission a New Jersey real estate continuing education provider identification number;

2. Courses that are offered by providers who have obtained a New Jersey real estate continuing education provider identification number and that are approved as pre-licensure or continuing education courses in this State in professions related to real estate brokerage, for example, courses approved for prelicensure or continuing education under the New Jersey Residential Mortgage Lending Act, N.J.S.A. 17:11C-51 et seq. or the Real Estate Appraisers Act, N.J.S.A. 45:14F-1 et seq.; or

3. Courses for which continuing education credit is conferred for their completion upon real estate licensees by another state, provided that:

i. The course is approved as a continuing education course by the agency exercising regulatory authority over the real estate licensees of the other state;

ii. The course is instructional and contributes to the enhancement of the integrity and/or professional competence of the attending real estate licensees; and

iii. The course provider obtains a New Jersey course provider identification number and provides the Commission or its designee with satisfactory evidence of a licensee's participation in and completion of such course in accordance with N.J.A.C. 11:5-12.8.

(c) The Commission shall confer credit for the satisfactory completion of a continuing education course offered by an approved provider on a topic deemed of a timely nature which has not previously been approved by the Commission provided that:

1. The course is submitted for approval no later than March 1 of the second year in a biennial license term for real estate licensees and the course is subsequently approved prior to April 30 of that year;

2. The course provider delivers a written statement to licensees prior to their attendance at the course notifying them that the course is pending approval by the Real Estate Commission and, if the course is advertised prior to the time of offering, all advertisements state in a prominent manner that the course is pending approval by the Real Estate Commission; and

3. The course provider provides the Commission or its designee with satisfactory evidence of a licensee's attendance at and completion of such course in accordance with N.J.A.C. 11:5-12.8 and complies with all other requirements applicable to the providers of continuing education courses as set forth in this subchapter.

11:5-12.14   Distance learning continuing education courses; additional requirements

(a) The Commission may approve distance learning continuing education courses that include periodic progress assessments and the achievement of a satisfactory level of performance by the licensee on such progress assessments as a condition to continuing to a succeeding segment of the course.

(b) Except as limited in (b)1 below, distance learning courses shall meet the following criteria:

1. The course is designed to promote students' active participation in the instructional process by utilizing techniques

that provide for substantial student interaction with the instructor, other students or a computer program. However, upon the recommendation of the Voluntary Advisory Committee, the Commission may approve a correspondence course or a course offered through a video modality that does not provide for such substantial interaction but fulfills all other requirements for course approval as set forth in this section and in N.J.A.C. 11:5-12.12 and 12.13;

2. The course, when taken without interruption, consists of no less than one hour of distance learning education, in accordance with N.J.A.C. 11:5-12.12(e);

3. The time required for a student of average ability to complete the course shall be at least equal to the number of course credit hours to be assigned in accordance with N.J.A.C. 11:5-12.12(e), as verified by the results of studies or field tests or other means;

4. Providers of distance learning courses shall, in addition to providing to students the notice containing all of the information referenced in N.J.A.C. 11:5-12.7(e), include in that notice information on how interaction is accomplished in the course and on any special requirements related to computer hardware, software or any other equipment needed to complete the distance learning course;

5. Providers of distance learning courses shall make provisions for handling equipment failures, including hardware or software failures or transmission interruptions, and provide appropriate instructor and/or technical support, as necessary, to enable students to satisfactorily complete the course in the event of such a failure or interruption;

6. Providers of distance learning courses shall use procedures that provide reasonable assurance of student identity and verification that the student receiving the continuing education credit for completing the course is actually the individual who performed all of the work required to complete the course;

7. Distance learning courses shall be equipped with a time-default mechanism for inactivity so that a student is not credited when not actively participating in the program; and

8. The provider of a distance learning course shall obtain, electronically or through other means, a signed and dated statement from each student certifying that he or she personally completed the course.

11:5-12.15   Denials, suspension or revocation of approvals

(a) The Commission may conduct investigations as may be necessary to enforce the provisions of N.J.S.A. 45:15-16.2a et seq. and this subchapter and may deny an application for ap-

proval and issue a reprimand to or suspend or revoke the approval of a real estate continuing education provider, instructor, including an instructor otherwise deemed approved pursuant to N.J.A.C. 11:5-12.10, or course, as applicable, if it is determined that:

1. An applicant, an instructor or a provider, individually or through any of the provider's employees, has failed to comply with applicable law or this subchapter;

2. A course submitted for approval or previously approved does not adequately reflect and present current and accurate information;

3. The provider or instructor or applicant for approval has engaged in misrepresentation in advertising or otherwise;

4. The provider or instructor has failed to timely and accurately download data on course completion;

5. The provider or instructor or applicant for approval has included false information in an application or reported false data to the Commission or its designee;

6. The provider or instructor is affiliated with a real estate broker or broker-salesperson licensee that has used or threatened to use a penalty or other form of coercion to compel a licensee to take a continuing education course from the affiliated provider or instructor;

7. A payment to the Commission was dishonored or, if made by credit card, reversed;

8. The provider or instructor has been disciplined by the Commission or any other occupational licensing agency in New Jersey or another jurisdiction;

9. The provider has collected money from licensees for a continuing education course, but refused or failed to provide the promised instruction; or

10. The provider or instructor has provided to a licensee any false or misleading information related to real estate licensing or education matters or to the licensee's education needs or license status.

(b) In the event that a provider or instructor who is also a New Jersey real estate licensee is found to have engaged in any of the conduct set forth in (a) above, the provider or instructor shall also be subject to discipline pursuant to N.J.S.A. 45:15-17 or 45:15-10.11, as applicable.

(c) If an application for approval is denied or disciplinary action is initiated, written notice of the grounds for denial, suspension or revocation of approval shall be issued by the Commission to the affected party. The applicant or respondent shall thereafter have the opportunity to be heard by the Commission in accordance with the provisions of the Administrative Procedure Act, N.J.S.A. 52:14B-1 et seq.

11:5-12.16   Appeals of initial denials of applications for continuing education course, instructor and provider approval and of applications for a waiver of the continuing education requirement

(a) Complete applications for continuing education course, instructor and provider approval shall be reviewed by the Voluntary Advisory Committee. Should the Voluntary Advisory Committee recommend denial of the application, the Executive Director of the Commission shall so notify the applicant in writing, which notification shall include the specific grounds on the basis of which the Voluntary Advisory Committee determined to recommend the denial of the application. Such a notification shall constitute an initial denial of the application and shall advise the applicant of their opportunity to appeal the initial denial to the Real Estate Commission as set forth in this section.

(b) Applications for a waiver of the continuing education requirement shall be initially reviewed by the Commission staff. Should it be determined that an applicant does not qualify for such a waiver, the Executive Director of the Commission shall issue an initial denial in writing so notifying the applicant. The initial denial shall include the specific grounds on the basis of which it was determined that the applicant did not qualify for a waiver and shall advise the applicant of their opportunity to appeal the initial denial to the Real Estate Commission as set forth in this section.

(c) An applicant may appeal an initial denial as referenced in (a) or (b) above to the Commission by submitting an original and two copies of a written submission requesting such an appeal.

1. All appeal submissions shall include a copy of the initial denial of the Executive Director denying the application.

2. Appeal submissions may include any other relevant written material tending to support the appeal.

3. Appeals shall be filed within 30 days of the date of the initial denial issued by the Executive Director. A failure by the applicant to timely appeal an initial denial of an application shall result in the application being deemed withdrawn.

(d) Unless the Commission determines that there is a genuine issue of material fact in dispute, the Commission shall consider all appeals referenced in this section on the papers. Should the Commission determine that a genuine issue of material fact does exist, the applicant shall be notified of the date and place at which an evidentiary hearing, which shall include live testimony and which shall be conducted in accordance with N.J.A.C. 1:1-14, will be held.

(e) Upon the conclusion of a hearing on the papers or with live testimony on an appeal as referenced in this section, the Commission shall issue a written order, which may be in the form of a letter, either affirming the initial denial of the application or granting the application.

11:5-12.17   Fees

(a) The fees for applications related to the requirements imposed by this subchapter are as follows:

1. Application for approval as a continuing education provider - $ 300.00.

2. Application for approval as a continuing education instructor - $ 150.00.

3. Application for approval of a continuing education course - $ 200.00.

4. Fee to process completion of continuing education requirement subsequent to May 1 in the second year of a biennial license term - $ 200.00.

(b) All fees referenced in (a) above shall be payable in the form of a certified or bank check or money order or business account check until such time as an on-line or otherwise automated payment system is established. Upon the implementation of such a system, payment shall be made via credit or debit card or otherwise in accordance with the instructions for the use of such a system posted on the website of the Commission. Personal checks shall not be accepted.

11:5-12.18   Voluntary Advisory Committee

(a) The Voluntary Advisory Committee created pursuant to N.J.S.A. 45:15-16.2a.b(1)(b) shall elect a chairperson and a vice-chairperson from among its members. Any member of the Committee shall be eligible for election to either position.

(b) The Voluntary Advisory Committee shall form committees and subcommittees to review complete applications for the approval of courses in the various core and elective topics set forth in N.J.A.C. 11:5-12.4 and 12.13 and complete applications for approval as a continuing education instructor or provider.

(c) The Voluntary Advisory Committee shall promptly report to the Commission's Executive Director its recommendations to approve or disapprove all of the complete applications it reviews. Each subcommittee of the Voluntary Advisory Committee shall report the results of its reviews of applications to the Voluntary Advisory Committee promptly upon completing such reviews and shall provide to the Executive Director copies of all recommendations for approval or disapproval contained in such reports. In the event that the Voluntary Advisory Committee fails to recommend approval or disapproval of a continuing education course, instructor or provider within 30 days of the completion of a subcommittee's review of such a complete application, the Commission may take action based upon the recommendation of the subcommittee.

(d) A majority of the appointed members of the Committee shall constitute a quorum and a majority vote by the members taken when a quorum is present shall constitute an action taken by the Committee.

1. The Voluntary Advisory Committee may meet in person or via teleconference, video conference or through the use of similar technologies.

(e) Members of the Voluntary Advisory Committee shall recuse themselves from the consideration of any application for approval to be considered by the Committee where grounds for recusal as set forth in the New Jersey Uniform Code of Ethics are present.

ANSWER KEY

Unit 1: Real Estate Licensing

Key Terms Review

1.	D	4.	I	7.	F	10.	H
2.	C	5.	A	8.	J	11.	K
3.	L	6.	E	9.	G	12.	B

Review Questions

1.	C	7.	B	13.	C	19.	A
2.	C	8.	B	14.	A	20.	A
3.	C	9.	B	15.	D	21.	D
4.	A	10.	C	16.	D		
5.	C	11.	B	17.	C		
6.	B	12.	B	18.	D		

Unit 2: Commission Rules and Regulations

Key Terms Review

1.	A	4.	F	7.	E	10.	J
2.	D	5.	G	8.	H		
3.	B	6.	C	9.	I		

Review Questions

1.	B	6.	A	11.	C	16.	D
2.	A	7.	A	12.	B	17.	D
3.	D	8.	D	13.	C	18.	B
4.	D	9.	C	14.	A	19.	C
5.	A	10.	D	15.	D	20.	C

Unit 3: Agency, Brokerage, and Ethical Considerations

Key Terms Review 1

1.	G	6.	K	11.	E	16.	N
2.	A	7.	C	12.	F	17.	L
3.	H	8.	P	13.	I		
4.	O	9.	D	14.	M		
5.	B	10.	Q	15.	J		

Key Terms Review 2

1.	I	5.	C	9.	L	13.	H
2.	E	6.	B	10.	M	14.	F
3.	J	7.	P	11.	D	15.	A
4.	K	8.	N	12.	G	16.	O

Key Terms Review 3

1.	I	4.	C	7.	F	10.	D
2.	G	5.	E	8.	B	11.	A
3.	H	6.	K	9.	J		

Review Questions

1.	A	9.	C	17.	C	25.	B
2.	A	10.	D	18.	D	26.	B
3.	B	11.	D	19.	D	27.	B
4.	C	12.	C	20.	D	28.	C
5.	B	13.	B	21.	B	29.	C
6.	C	14.	C	22.	B		
7.	C	15.	A	23.	C		
8.	C	16.	A	24.	C		

Unit 4: Fair Housing

Key Terms Review

1. M	5. A	9. E	13. F
2. C	6. D	10. K	
3. B	7. H	11. I	
4. L	8. G	12. J	

Review Questions

1. C	8. C	15. D	22. C
2. C	9. A	16. B	23. B
3. D	10. A	17. D	24. C
4. B	11. C	18. D	25. D
5. C	12. A	19. A	
6. B	13. C	20. C	
7. C	14. D	21. B	

Unit 5: What Is Real Estate?

Key Terms Review 1

1. K	5. L	9. E	13. G
2. A	6. F	10. B	
3. M	7. D	11. H	
4. I	8. C	12. J	

Key Terms Review 2

1. H	4. D	7. F	10. G
2. I	5. C	8. J	11. K
3. L	6. B	9. A	12. E

Review Questions

1. B	6. C	11. A	16. A
2. A	7. A	12. B	17. A
3. B	8. C	13. B	18. C
4. B	9. C	14. B	19. C
5. C	10. C	15. D	20. D

Unit 6: Estates and Interests

Key Terms Review 1

1. J	5. P	9. A	13. D
2. N	6. L	10. O	14. K
3. H	7. M	11. E	15. G
4. F	8. C	12. B	16. I

Key Terms Review 2

1. M	5. I	9. O	13. B
2. K	6. G	10. E	14. D
3. F	7. N	11. H	15. A
4. C	8. J	12. P	16. L

Review Questions

1. B	6. D	11. C	16. B
2. A	7. A	12. C	17. A
3. A	8. D	13. C	18. D
4. B	9. D	14. B	19. C
5. D	10. A	15. D	20. D

Unit 7: Ownership of Real Estate

Key Terms Review 1

1. B	5. J	9. C	13. K
2. I	6. D	10. M	
3. F	7. G	11. A	
4. H	8. E	12. L	

Key Terms Review 2

1. **G**	4. **C**	7. **B**	10. **J**
2. **K**	5. **E**	8. **F**	11. **D**
3. **H**	6. **A**	9. **I**	

Review Questions

1. **B**	8. **C**	15. **D**	22. **B**
2. **B**	9. **C**	16. **B**	23. **D**
3. **B**	10. **B**	17. **D**	24. **A**
4. **B**	11. **D**	18. **C**	25. **B**
5. **B**	12. **B**	19. **A**	
6. **C**	13. **C**	20. **A**	
7. **A**	14. **D**	21. **A**	

Unit 8: Real Estate Taxes

Key Terms Review

1. **D**	5. **C**	9. **I**	13. **F**
2. **E**	6. **G**	10. **L**	
3. **B**	7. **K**	11. **H**	
4. **A**	8. **M**	12. **J**	

Review Questions

1. **B**	5. **B**	9. **B**	13. **D**
2. **B**	6. **C**	10. **A**	14. **C**
3. **D**	7. **D**	11. **C**	15. **B**
4. **C**	8. **C**	12. **B**	

Unit 9: Land-Use Regulations and Environmental Issues

Key Terms Review

1. **L**	6. **A**	11. **B**	16. **P**
2. **K**	7. **F**	12. **R**	17. **G**
3. **I**	8. **H**	13. **Q**	18. **O**
4. **C**	9. **D**	14. **N**	
5. **E**	10. **J**	15. **M**	

Review Questions

1. **D**	6. **B**	11. **B**	16. **B**
2. **C**	7. **C**	12. **A**	17. **A**
3. **A**	8. **D**	13. **C**	18. **C**
4. **D**	9. **A**	14. **B**	19. **B**
5. **C**	10. **A**	15. **D**	20. **D**

Unit 10: Listing Agreements

Key Terms Review

1. **F**	3. **D**	5. **A**
2. **C**	4. **E**	6. **B**

Review Questions

1. **A**	4. **B**	7. **D**	10. **B**
2. **B**	5. **A**	8. **D**	
3. **C**	6. **D**	9. **C**	

Unit 11: Real Estate Contracts

Key Terms Review 1

1. **O**	5. **M**	9. **C**	13. **H**
2. **I**	6. **D**	10. **J**	14. **F**
3. **B**	7. **A**	11. **L**	15. **E**
4. **N**	8. **K**	12. **G**	16. **P**

Key Terms Review 2

1. **N**	5. **L**	9. **I**	13. **G**
2. **M**	6. **D**	10. **C**	14. **E**
3. **O**	7. **H**	11. **B**	15. **F**
4. **A**	8. **J**	12. **K**	

Review Questions

1. **C**	6. **B**	11. **A**	16. **D**
2. **B**	7. **B**	12. **B**	17. **D**
3. **D**	8. **D**	13. **A**	18. **B**
4. **D**	9. **D**	14. **C**	19. **B**
5. **B**	10. **D**	15. **A**	20. **A**

Unit 12: Leases: Landlord and Tenant

Key Terms Review 1

1. **J**	4. **G**	7. **E**	10. **C**
2. **L**	5. **F**	8. **H**	11. **A**
3. **B**	6. **D**	9. **I**	12. **K**

Key Terms Review 2

1. **G**	4. **D**	7. **A**	10. **L**
2. **I**	5. **F**	8. **C**	11. **K**
3. **E**	6. **H**	9. **B**	12. **J**

Review Questions

1. **D**	8. **B**	15. **A**	22. **C**
2. **C**	9. **C**	16. **A**	23. **C**
3. **B**	10. **B**	17. **C**	24. **B**
4. **A**	11. **D**	18. **D**	25. **C**
5. **C**	12. **C**	19. **D**	
6. **D**	13. **B**	20. **A**	
7. **D**	14. **A**	21. **D**	

Unit 13: Mortgages

Key Terms Review

1. **H**	7. **B**	13. **O**	19. **T**
2. **F**	8. **R**	14. **M**	20. **C**
3. **P**	9. **G**	15. **U**	21. **D**
4. **K**	10. **S**	16. **N**	
5. **E**	11. **L**	17. **J**	
6. **I**	12. **A**	18. **Q**	

Review Questions

1. **B**	7. **D**	13. **A**	19. **C**
2. **B**	8. **B**	14. **B**	20. **D**
3. **B**	9. **A**	15. **A**	21. **D**
4. **A**	10. **C**	16. **A**	22. **B**
5. **B**	11. **A**	17. **A**	
6. **A**	12. **C**	18. **A**	

Unit 14: Financing I: Conventional, FHA, and VA Loans

Key Terms Review 1

1. **J**	5. **C**	9. **G**	13. **M**
2. **H**	6. **L**	10. **I**	14. **A**
3. **F**	7. **N**	11. **E**	
4. **K**	8. **B**	12. **D**	

Key Terms Review 2

1. **B**	5. **C**	9. **E**	13. **N**
2. **A**	6. **D**	10. **G**	14. **L**
3. **J**	7. **H**	11. **F**	
4. **I**	8. **K**	12. **M**	

Review Questions

1.	**B**	7.	**A**	13.	**C**	19.	**B**
2.	**B**	8.	**B**	14.	**C**	20.	**B**
3.	**C**	9.	**D**	15.	**B**	21.	**B**
4.	**B**	10.	**A**	16.	**D**	22.	**D**
5.	**D**	11.	**B**	17.	**C**	23.	**C**
6.	**C**	12.	**B**	18.	**B**	24.	**A**

Unit 15: Financing II: Primary and Secondary Markets

Key Terms Review 1

1.	**K**	5.	**D**	9.	**J**	13.	**H**
2.	**M**	6.	**F**	10.	**I**		
3.	**C**	7.	**L**	11.	**A**		
4.	**E**	8.	**B**	12.	**G**		

Key Terms Review 2

1.	**G**	5.	**K**	9.	**H**	13.	**N**
2.	**D**	6.	**I**	10.	**E**	14.	**O**
3.	**L**	7.	**B**	11.	**J**	15.	**M**
4.	**A**	8.	**F**	12.	**C**		

Review Questions

1.	**A**	7.	**D**	13.	**A**	19.	**D**
2.	**B**	8.	**D**	14.	**B**	20.	**C**
3.	**D**	9.	**B**	15.	**A**	21.	**B**
4.	**D**	10.	**B**	16.	**C**	22.	**C**
5.	**B**	11.	**A**	17.	**B**		
6.	**B**	12.	**C**	18.	**D**		

Unit 16: Appraisal

Key Terms Review 1

1.	**F**	5.	**L**	9.	**I**	13.	**E**
2.	**J**	6.	**D**	10.	**A**		
3.	**M**	7.	**G**	11.	**B**		
4.	**K**	8.	**H**	12.	**C**		

Key Terms Review 2

1.	**D**	4.	**A**	7.	**K**	10.	**J**
2.	**I**	5.	**C**	8.	**E**	11.	**H**
3.	**F**	6.	**B**	9.	**G**		

Review Questions

1.	**C**	8.	**B**	15.	**B**	22.	**C**
2.	**D**	9.	**D**	16.	**D**	23.	**A**
3.	**A**	10.	**A**	17.	**B**	24.	**C**
4.	**D**	11.	**D**	18.	**C**	25.	**D**
5.	**D**	12.	**D**	19.	**B**	26.	**B**
6.	**D**	13.	**C**	20.	**D**	27.	**A**
7.	**B**	14.	**C**	21.	**C**		

Unit 17: Investment and Business Brokerage

Key Terms Review 1

1.	**A**	4.	**B**	7.	**H**	10.	**J**
2.	**D**	5.	**C**	8.	**G**	11.	**I**
3.	**E**	6.	**F**	9.	**K**		

Key Terms Review 2

1.	**J**	4.	**I**	7.	**A**	10.	**G**
2.	**C**	5.	**E**	8.	**F**		
3.	**H**	6.	**D**	9.	**B**		

Review Questions

1.	C	6.	D	11.	A	16.	D
2.	B	7.	B	12.	C	17.	B
3.	B	8.	B	13.	C	18.	D
4.	D	9.	C	14.	D	19.	B
5.	A	10.	C	15.	C	20.	C

Unit 18: Subdivision and Development

Key Terms Review

1.	R	6.	E	11.	H	16.	L
2.	A	7.	B	12.	C	17.	J
3.	D	8.	K	13.	F	18.	N
4.	O	9.	M	14.	I		
5.	P	10.	G	15.	Q		

Review Questions

1.	D	8.	D	15.	C	22.	A
2.	B	9.	C	16.	A	23.	B
3.	A	10.	B	17.	A	24.	B
4.	D	11.	D	18.	C	25.	A
5.	C	12.	B	19.	C		
6.	D	13.	B	20.	A		
7.	C	14.	B	21.	C		

Unit 19: Legal Descriptions and Deeds

Key Terms Review

1.	C	7.	J	13.	H	19.	P
2.	D	8.	A	14.	I	20.	S
3.	G	9.	Q	15.	L	21.	E
4.	N	10.	B	16.	T		
5.	M	11.	R	17.	F		
6.	O	12.	U	18.	K		

Review Questions

1.	B	8.	C	15.	A	22.	B
2.	A	9.	C	16.	C	23.	C
3.	C	10.	B	17.	D	24.	C
4.	B	11.	C	18.	C	25.	D
5.	B	12.	B	19.	A	26.	A
6.	C	13.	B	20.	D		
7.	A	14.	B	21.	B		

Unit 20: Transfer of Title

Key Terms Review

1.	M	5.	I	9.	D	13.	A
2.	J	6.	G	10.	C		
3.	B	7.	L	11.	E		
4.	H	8.	K	12.	F		

Review Questions

1.	C	5.	B	9.	C	13.	D
2.	D	6.	D	10.	D	14.	D
3.	B	7.	A	11.	C	15.	D
4.	D	8.	D	12.	B		

Unit 21: Public Records, Titles, and Closings

Key Terms Review

1.	E	7.	M	13.	A	19.	O
2.	F	8.	B	14.	S	20.	P
3.	L	9.	G	15.	T	21.	U
4.	C	10.	J	16.	N		
5.	H	11.	K	17.	Q		
6.	I	12.	D	18.	R		

Review Questions

1.	**A**	8.	**C**	15.	**C**	22.	**C**
2.	**A**	9.	**C**	16.	**B**	23.	**A**
3.	**B**	10.	**D**	17.	**B**	24.	**B**
4.	**D**	11.	**C**	18.	**B**	25.	**C**
5.	**A**	12.	**C**	19.	**C**	26.	**C**
6.	**D**	13.	**B**	20.	**D**		
7.	**D**	14.	**D**	21.	**A**		

Unit 22: Real Estate Mathematics

1. **D** $4,320

   $144,000 × 0.06 = $8,640 total commission

   $8,640 × 0.50 = $4,320 Sally's share

2. **A** $235,000

   $14,100 commission ÷ 6% commission rate
   = $14,100 ÷ 0.06 = $235,000 sales price

3. **B** $1,550.25

   $79,500 sales price × 6½% commission = $79,500
   × 0.065 = $5,167.50 Happy Valley's commission

   $5,167.50 × 30% or $5,167.50 × 0.30 = $1,550.25
   listing salespersons commission

4. **B** $127,000

   $3,675 – $500 salary = $3,175 commission on sales

   $3,175 ÷ 2.5% = $3,175 ÷ 0.025 = $127,000, value
   of property sold

5. **D** $135.38

   $95,000 × 60% = $95,000 × 0.60 = $57,000,
   assessed value

   divide by 100 because tax rate is stated per hundred
   dollars

   $57,000 ÷ 100 = 570

   570 × $2.85 = $1,624.50, annual taxes divide by 12
   to get monthly taxes

   $1,624.50 ÷ 12 = $135.375

6. **A** $470.40

   $98,000 × 80% = $98,000 × 0.80 = $78,400 insured
   value

   $78,400 ÷ 100 = 784 hundreds

   784 × $0.60/hundred = $470.40

7. **A** 20%

   $30,000 Hal + $35,000 Olive + $35,000 Ron
   = $100,000

   $125,000 – $100,000 = $25,000 Marvin's
   contribution

   part ÷ whole = percent

   $25,000 ÷ $125,000 = 0.20, or 20%

8. **A** $51,750

   $45,000 + 15% of $45,000 = $51,750 (or $45,000
   × 1.15 = $51,750)

9. **A** $1,039.64

   $235,000 purchase price × 80% or .80 (portion
   borrowed) = $188,000 mortgage amount

   188 (thousands borrowed) × $5.53 (monthly
   payment per thousand) = $1,039.64 (see Figure 14.4)

10. **A** $675,000

    $4,500 × 12 = $54,000 annual rental

    $54,000 ÷ 8% or $54,000 ÷ 0.08 = $675,000
    original cost of property

11. **A** $180,000

    $168,000 + $1,200 = $169,200 sales price less
    commission

    $169,200 = 94% of sales price

    $169,200 ÷ 0.94 = $180,000 sales price

12. **A** $2,600 more at closing

    $80,000 × 3% = $80,000 × 0.03 = $2,400 payment
    for points

    $100,000 – $95,000 = $5,000 received with the
    higher offer

    $5,000 – $2,400 payment for points = $2,600
    realized with the higher offer after payment of points

13. **B** $2,128

    100% price – 97.76% loan = 2.24% down payment

    $95,000 × 2.24% = $95,000 × 0.0224 = $2,128

14. **B** $770.83

    $37,000 ÷ 12 = $3,083.33 monthly income

    $3,083.33 × 0.25 = $770.83 permissible mortgage
    payment

15. **A** $808.54

$1,800 ÷ 12 = $150 monthly property taxes

$365 ÷ 12 = $30.42 monthly insurance premium

$150 + $30.42 + $628.12 = $808.54 total monthly payment

16. **C** $28,722

$129,500 × 0.80 = $103,600 mortgage loan × 0.02 = $2,072 in points + $129,500 × 0.20 = $25,900 down payment + $750 closing costs = $28,722

17. **C** four years, nine months

Two points on a $90,000 loan = $90,000 × 2% = $90,000 × 0.02 = $1,800 paid in points

$817.85 − $786.35 = $31.50 saved each month with lower payment

$1,800 ÷ $31.50 = 57.14 months to recoup the payment of points

57.14 months = 4 years, 9 months

18. **B** $67,100.57

91.42 × 12 months = $4,697.04 annual interest part ÷ percent = whole

$4,697.04 ÷ 0.07 or $67,100.57

19. **A** $139,508

30 years × 12 months = 360 payments

360 payments × $665.30 = $239,508 total payments for principal and interest

$239,508 total payments − $100,000 principal repayment = $139,508 interest

20. **A** $173.33

$975 ÷ 12 months = $81.25/month property tax

$81.25 ÷ 30 days = $2.708/day property tax

$81.25 × 2 months = $162.50

$2.708 × 4 days = $10.832

$162.50 + $10.832 = $173.332 rounded to $173.33, prepaid unused tax

21. **B** $493.64

$161,550 mortgage balance × .05 interest rate = $8,077.50 annual interest

$8,077.50 divided 12 months = $673.13 this month's interest

$673.13 divided by 30 days = $22.44 one day's interest

$22.44 × 22 days = $493.64. That interest will be paid in the next month's payment, so seller owes it to the buyer.

22. **C** 290 feet

43,560 ÷ 2 = 21,780 square feet in the lot

21,780 ÷ 75 (width) = 290 feet deep

23. **B** 180 feet

1,200 square yards × 9 = 10,800 square feet

area = length × width

10,800 = length × 60

10,800 ÷ 60 = 180 feet

24. **B** 726 feet

43,560 feet per acre × 5 = 217,800 square feet

217,800 ÷ 300 = 726 feet long

25. **C** $277.16

12' × 9.5' = 114 square feet, area of rectangle

½ (3' × 9.5') = ½ (28.5) = 14.25 square feet, area of triangle

114 + 14.25 = 128.25 square feet

To convert square feet to square yards, divide by 9:

128.25 ÷ 9 = 14.25 square yards

$16.95 carpet + $2.50 installation = $19.45/square yard

$19.45 × 14.25 square yards = $277.1625, rounds to $277.16

26. **C** $36,000

120 front feet × $300 = $36,000 sale price

27. **C** 27,225

100 acres × 43,560 square feet per acre = 4,356,000 total square feet

4,356,000 × ⅞ available for lots = 3,811,500 square feet

3,811,500 ÷ 140 lots = 27,225 square feet per lot

28. **C** 20,800

150' frontage − 20' for the side yards = 130' width

200' depth − 25' setback = 175' − 15' rear yard = 160' depth

width × depth = buildable area

130' × 160' = 20,800 square feet

29. **C** 21

120 feet ÷ 6 feet per section = 20 sections

One fence post must be added to anchor the other end

20 + 1 = 21 fence posts

30. **C** $1,615.88

two sides of 95' plus one side of 42'6"

95' × 2 = 190 feet

42'6" = 42.5 feet

190 + 42.5 = 232.5 linear feet

232.5 × $6.95 = $1,615.875

31. **B** $10,000

$200,000 × 0.05 = $10,000 earnest money + $20,000 = $30,000 total escrow

$200,000 × 0.80 = $160,000 mortgage

$200,000 purchase price – $160,000 mortgage

$30,000 escrow = $10,000 balance due at closing

32. **C** $488

$775 taxes ÷ 360 days/year = $2.15 daily tax amount

June 6 to December 30 = 204 days × $2.15 = $438.60

$86 ÷ 360 = $.24/day × 204 = $48.73

33. **B** $150,222

Base annual rent = $460 × 12 = $5,520

Total rent of $7,780 – $5,520 = $2,260

$2,260 ÷ 0.045 = $50,222, which represents the gross sales over $100,000 that rent was based on; total sales were $150,222

34. **B** $8,727.27

100% value – 20% land = 80% building value

$300,000 × 0.80 = $240,000

$240,000 ÷ $27.5 years = $8,727.27 depreciation per year

Cumulative Review Quizzes

Units 1 through 8

1.	D	14.	B	27.	B	40.	C
2.	D	15.	B	28.	C	41.	C
3.	B	16.	D	29.	D	42.	D
4.	D	17.	A	30.	D	43.	C
5.	B	18.	B	31.	A	44.	C
6.	D	19.	A	32.	D	45.	A
7.	C	20.	A	33.	C	46.	D
8.	B	21.	B	34.	C	47.	B
9.	A	22.	C	35.	C	48.	D
10.	D	23.	D	36.	A	49.	A
11.	B	24.	D	37.	C	50.	C
12.	A	25.	B	38.	D		
13.	D	26.	A	39.	C		

Units 9 through 15

1.	D	14.	A	27.	D	40.	D
2.	D	15.	D	28.	B	41.	D
3.	B	16.	A	29.	A	42.	A
4.	D	17.	C	30.	C	43.	C
5.	A	18.	B	31.	C	44.	D
6.	C	19.	D	32.	C	45.	A
7.	B	20.	B	33.	B	46.	C
8.	C	21.	B	34.	D	47.	A
9.	C	22.	B	35.	C	48.	D
10.	B	23.	B	36.	B	49.	C
11.	A	24.	D	37.	A	50.	D
12.	B	25.	A	38.	B		
13.	C	26.	B	39.	C		

Units 16 through 22

1. C	14. A	27. C	40. B
2. B	15. A	28. D	41. D
3. B	16. B	29. A	42. A
4. C	17. D	30. B	43. C
5. A	18. B	31. D	44. B
6. C	19. D	32. A	45. A
7. D	20. B	33. D	46. C
8. D	21. A	34. B	47. C
9. C	22. D	35. C	48. B
10. D	23. B	36. A	49. A
11. B	24. D	37. D	50. C
12. C	25. A	38. D	
13. B	26. D	39. C	

Practice Test A

1. D	29. C	57. D	85. A
2. B	30. A	58. B	86. A
3. A	31. A	59. A	87. C
4. D	32. A	60. A	88. D
5. D	33. C	61. A	89. B
6. D	34. B	62. B	90. C
7. B	35. B	63. D	91. D
8. A	36. A	64. A	92. D
9. B	37. B	65. A	93. D
10. B	38. C	66. B	94. A
11. A	39. B	67. D	95. C
12. B	40. A	68. A	96. C
13. C	41. A	69. B	97. D
14. A	42. D	70. B	98. C
15. C	43. B	71. D	99. B
16. D	44. C	72. B	100. C
17. A	45. B	73. C	101. A
18. A	46. D	74. D	102. D
19. D	47. D	75. C	103. D
20. A	48. A	76. B	104. D
21. C	49. A	77. B	105. C
22. B	50. D	78. B	106. B
23. D	51. C	79. A	107. C
24. A	52. C	80. D	108. B
25. D	53. D	81. A	109. B
26. B	54. C	82. C	110. B
27. A	55. D	83. C	
28. B	56. B	84. B	

Practice Test B

1. D	29. D	57. D	85. B
2. C	30. D	58. B	86. C
3. C	31. B	59. D	87. B
4. A	32. C	60. B	88. C
5. A	33. D	61. B	89. B
6. D	34. C	62. A	90. D
7. B	35. D	63. A	91. C
8. D	36. D	64. A	92. C
9. B	37. D	65. B	93. D
10. B	38. A	66. C	94. C
11. C	39. B	67. B	95. C
12. A	40. D	68. D	96. A
13. B	41. B	69. C	97. D
14. C	42. B	70. C	98. C
15. C	43. A	71. C	99. A
16. D	44. C	72. C	100. B
17. A	45. D	73. C	101. A
18. A	46. B	74. B	102. D
19. C	47. B	75. B	103. A
20. B	48. D	76. B	104. D
21. B	49. C	77. C	105. D
22. D	50. A	78. C	106. C
23. B	51. A	79. B	107. C
24. C	52. C	80. B	108. A
25. D	53. B	81. A	109. D
26. B	54. C	82. B	110. C
27. A	55. D	83. C	
28. C	56. D	84. B	

GLOSSARY

abandonment   The voluntary surrender or relinquishment of possession of real property without the vesting of this interest in any other person.

abstract of title   The condensed history of a title to a particular parcel of real estate.

abstract of title with lawyer's opinion   An abstract of title that a lawyer has examined and has certified to be, in his or her opinion, an accurate statement of fact.

acceleration clause   The clause in a note or mortgage that can be enforced to make the entire debt due immediately if the mortgagor defaults.

accretion   The increase or addition of land by the deposit of sand or soil washed up naturally from a river, lake, or sea.

accrued items   On a closing statement, items of expense that have been incurred but are not yet payable, such as interest on a mortgage loan.

acknowledgment   A formal declaration made before a duly authorized officer, usually a notary public, by a person who has signed a document.

acre   A measure of land equal to 43,560 square feet; 4,840 square yards; 4,047 square meters; or 160 square rods.

actual eviction   Action whereby a defaulted tenant is physically ousted from rented property pursuant to a court order. *See also* eviction.

actual notice   Express information or fact; that which is known; actual knowledge.

addendum   A document separate from the contract altering the terms of the original contract; must be signed by all parties to the contract to be legally binding.

adjustable-rate mortgage   A mortgage loan in which the interest rate may increase or decrease at specific intervals, following an economic indicator.

adjusted basis   Original cost plus improvements, minus depreciation.

administrator   A person appointed by the court to administer the estate of a deceased person who left no will; i.e., who died intestate.

ad valorem tax   A tax levied according to value; generally used to refer to real estate tax. Also called *general tax.*

adverse possession   The actual, visible, hostile, notorious, exclusive, and continuous possession of another's land under a claim of title.

affidavit   A written statement sworn to before an officer who is authorized to administer an oath or affirmation.

agency   That relationship wherein an agent is employed by a principal to do certain acts on the principal's behalf.

agent   One who undertakes to transact some business or to manage some affair for another by authority of the latter.

air rights   The right to use the open space above a property, generally allowing the surface to be used for another purpose.

alienation   The act of transferring property to another.

alienation clause   The clause in a mortgage stating that the balance of the secured debt becomes immediately due and payable at the mortgagee's option if the property is sold or title is otherwise transferred.

ALIENS   An acronym to remember the six items that the lender must obtain before issuing a Loan Estimate (LE): address of the subject property, loan amount, income, estimate of property value, name of borrower(s), social security number(s).

amendment   A change used by the signing parties to correct or clarify something in the original contract.

amenity   Some extra that contributes to owner satisfaction: clean air, view, etc.

Americans with Disabilities Act (ADA)   Mandates certain adaptations of real estate to accommodate various disabilities.

amortization schedule   Written listing of each payment, broken down into interest, principal, and remaining debt.

amortized loan   A loan in which the principal as well as the interest is payable in monthly or other periodic installments over the term of the loan, resulting in a zero balance due at the end of the term.

annual percentage rate   Rate of interest charged on a loan, calculated to take into account upfront loan fees and points. Usually higher than the *contract interest rate*.

antitrust laws   Laws designed to preserve the free enterprise of the open marketplace by making illegal certain private conspiracies and combinations formed to minimize competition.

appraisal   An estimate of a property's value by someone who has specific training as an appraiser.

appraiser   Independent person trained to estimate value.

appreciation   An increase in the worth or value of a property.

appurtenance   A right, privilege, or improvement belonging to, and passing with, the land.

APR   *See* annual percentage rate.

arm's-length transaction   A transaction between relative strangers, each trying to do the best for himself or herself.

arrears   The opposite of "in advance;" payment after the service has been rendered.

asbestos   A mineral once used in insulation and other materials that has been linked to respiratory diseases.

assessed valuation   The valuation placed upon property as a basis for taxation.

assessment   The imposition of a tax, charge, or levy, usually according to established rates.

assignment   The transfer in writing of interest in a contract, mortgage, lease, or other instrument.

assumable   Of a mortgage, able to be transferred to another owner of the property.

assumption of mortgage   Acquiring title of property on which there is an existing mortgage and agreeing to be personally liable for the terms and conditions of the mortgage, including payments.

Attorney General's memorandum   Written statement about Fair Housing Laws to be presented to buyers and sellers.

avulsion   The sudden changing of course of a stream.

balloon payment   The final payment of a mortgage loan that is considerably larger than the required periodic payments because the loan amount was not fully amortized.

bargain and sale deed   A deed that carries with it no warranties against liens or other encumbrances but that does imply that the grantor has the right to convey title.

bargain and sale deed with covenant   A deed in which the grantor warrants or guarantees the title against defects arising during the period of his or her tenure and ownership of the property but not against defects existing before that time.

basis   The cost of a property that the Internal Revenue Service uses to determine annual depreciation and gain or loss on the sale of the asset.

benchmark   A permanent reference mark or point established for use by surveyors in measuring differences in elevation. *See also* datum.

beneficiary   The person who receives or is to receive benefits resulting from certain acts.

bequeath   To give or hand down personal property by will; to leave by will.

bequest   Personal property that is given by the terms of a will.

bilateral contract   An agreement entered into by two or more legally competent parties that is binding on all parties.

bill of sale   A written instrument given to transfer title of personal property.

binder   An agreement that may accompany an earnest money deposit for the purchase of real property as evidence of the purchaser's good faith and intent to complete the transaction.

biweekly mortgage   Repayment plan in which half a monthly payment is made every two weeks, the equivalent of 13 full payments a year.

blanket mortgage   A mortgage covering more than one parcel of real estate.

blockbusting   Also known as *panic peddling*, the illegal practice of inducing homeowners to sell their property by making representations regarding the entry or prospective entry of minority persons into the neighborhood.

blue-sky laws   Common name for laws that regulate the registration and sale of investment securities.

board of directors Elected managing body of a corporation, specifically of a cooperative apartment building.

board of managers Elected managing body of a condominium.

bond The instrument that creates a personal obligation for a debt that is secured by a mortgage or other lien on real estate.

boot Money or property given to make up any difference in value or equity between two properties in an exchange.

broker's price opinion (BPO) Licensee's written estimate of market value, used by lenders and mortgage companies where they believe the expense and delay of an appraisal is not needed.

branch office A secondary place of business apart from the principal or main office from which real estate business is conducted.

breach of contract Violation of any terms or conditions in a contract without legal excuse; for example, failure to make a payment when it is due.

broker One who buys and sells for another for a fee. See also real estate broker, transaction broker.

brokerage The business of buying and selling for another for a fee.

broker of record *See* supervising broker.

broker-salesperson A qualified broker who practices real estate in the position of a salesperson in another broker's office.

building codes Regulations established by state and local governments setting forth the structural requirements for building.

building line A line fixed at a certain distance from the front and/or sides of a lot, beyond which no building can project.

Bureau of Subdivided Land Sales Controls State agency that approves and registers sales of some out-of-state property.

buydown Payment of extra upfront points in return for lower interest rate.

buyer's broker A real estate broker retained by a prospective purchaser, who becomes the broker's principal or client and to whom fiduciary duties are owed.

bylaws Rules and regulations adopted by an association.

CAFRA New Jerseys Coastal Area Facilities Review Act, which sharply limits development in environmentally sensitive areas.

cap With an adjustable-rate mortgage, a limit, usually in percentage points, on how much the interest rate or payment might be raised in each adjustment period. For *lifetime cap, see* ceiling.

capital gains Profits realized from the sale of assets like real estate.

capitalization The conversion of future income to be derived from an investment property into an estimate of the present value.

capitalization rate The rate of return a property produces on the owner's investment.

carbon monoxide A colorless, odorless gas that occurs as a by-product of fuel burning. Carbon monoxide (CO) poisoning been linked to dizziness, nausea, and death.

cash flow The net spendable income from an investment after deducting expenses.

caveat emptor A Latin phrase meaning "Let the buyer beware."

CC&Rs Covenants, conditions, and restrictions of a condominium or cooperative development.

ceiling With an adjustable-rate mortgage, a limit, usually in percentage points, beyond which the interest rates or monthly payment on a loan may never rise. Sometimes known as a *lifetime cap*.

CERCLA The Comprehensive Environmental Response, Compensation, and Liability Act. A federal law administered by the Environmental Protection Agency that establishes a process for identifying parties responsible for creating hazardous waste sites, forcing liable parties to clean up toxic sites, bringing legal action against responsible parties, and funding the abatement of toxic sites. *See* Superfund.

certificate of compliance Inspector's statement that property is fit for human habitation.

certificate of occupancy (C of O) Document issued by a municipal authority stating that a building complies with building, health, and safety codes and may be occupied.

Certificate of Reasonable Value (CRV) VA appraisal statement.

certificate of title   A statement of opinion of title status on a parcel of real property based on an examination of specified public records.

chain of title   The conveyance of real property to one owner from another, reaching back to the original grantor.

chattel   Movable personal property.

chattel mortgage   A mortgage on personal property.

checkers   *See* testers.

client   The one by whom a broker is employed in an agency relationship.

closing date   The date upon which the buyer takes title to the property.

Closing Disclosure (CD)   The statement of final loan terms and closing costs; is compared to the Loan Estimate (LE).

closing statement   A detailed cash accounting of a real estate transaction showing all cash received, all charges and credits made, and all cash paid out in the transaction.

cloud on title   An outstanding claim or encumbrance that, if valid, affects or impairs the owner's title.

clustering   The grouping of homesites within a subdivision on smaller lots than normal with the remaining land used as common areas.

CMA   *See* comparative market analysis.

Code of Ethics   Standards of conduct adopted by the National Association of REALTORS®.

C of O   *See* certificate of occupancy.

color of title   That which appears to be a good title but which is not.

commission   Payment to a broker for services rendered, such as in the sale or purchase of real property.

common elements   Parts of a property that are necessary or convenient to the existence, maintenance, and safety of a condominium or are normally in common use by all of the condominium residents.

comparables   Properties listed in an appraisal report or a CMA that are substantially equivalent to the subject property. Also called *comps*.

comparative market analysis (CMA)   A study intended to assist an owner in establishing a listing price for a property.

competent parties   Those recognized by law as being able to contract with others; usually those of legal age and sound mind.

condemnation   Court action by which government takes private property, exercising the right of eminent domain.

condemnation suit   A judicial or administrative proceeding to exercise the power of eminent domain through which a government agency takes private property for public use and compensates the owner.

condominium   The absolute ownership of an apartment or a unit (generally in a multi-unit building) plus an undivided interest in the ownership of the common elements, which are owned jointly with the other condominium unit owners.

consideration   1. That received by the grantor in exchange for a deed. 2. Something of value that induces a person to enter into a contract. Consideration may be *valuable* (e.g., money) or *good* (love and affection).

construction lien   Claim placed against property by a worker who has not been paid.

constructive eviction   Landlord actions that so materially disturb or impair the tenant's enjoyment of the leased premises that the tenant is effectively forced to move out and terminate the lease without liability for any further rent.

constructive notice   Notice given to the world by recorded documents. Occupation of property is also considered as giving constructive notice.

Consumer Information Statement (CIS)   Written explanation of agency relationships presented to buyers and sellers.

contingency   Certain happening without which a contract will not be valid.

continuing education   12 hours of study required for license renewal.

contract   An agreement entered into by two or more legally competent parties by the terms of which one or more of the parties, for a consideration, undertakes to do or refrain from doing some legal act or acts.

contract for deed   A contract for the sale of real estate wherein the purchase price is paid in periodic installments by the purchaser, who is in possession of the property even though title is retained by the seller until final payment. Also called an *installment contract* or a *land contract*.

conventional loan   A loan not insured or guaranteed by a government agency.

convey   To transfer ownership by sale or gift.

conveyance   The transfer of title of land from one to another. The means or medium by which title to real estate is transferred.

cooperative   A residential multi-unit building whose title is held by a corporation owned by and operated for the benefit of persons living within the building, who are the stockholders of the corporation, each possessing a proprietary lease.

corporation   An entity or organization created by operation of law whose rights of doing business are essentially the same as those of an individual.

cost approach   The process of estimating the value of property by adding to the estimated land value the appraiser's estimate of the reproduction or replacement cost of the building, less depreciation.

cost basis   *See* basis.

counteroffer   A new offer made as a reply to an offer received.

covenant   Agreement written into deeds and other instruments promising performance or nonperformance of certain acts or stipulating certain uses or nonuses of the property.

CPM   Certified Property Manager, a designation awarded by the Institute of Real Estate Management.

credit   On a closing statement, an amount entered in a person's favor.

credit history   A list of open financial accounts, such as credit cards and mortgage loans, and closed accounts, usually from the preceding seven years, as well as issues including bankruptcy, foreclosure, and repossession. It will not include gender, income, or receipt of public assistance.

credit union   Cooperative organization for savers and borrowers.

cubic-foot method   A technique for estimating building costs per cubic foot.

customer   Third party in a transaction owed honest treatment but not owed fiduciary duties.

damages   The indemnity recoverable by a person who has sustained an injury, either to person, property, or rights, through the act or default of another.

datum   Point from which elevations are measured. Mean sea level in New York harbor, or local datum.

decedent   A person who has died.

dedication   The voluntary transfer of private property by its owner to the public for some public use such as for streets or schools.

deed   A written instrument that, when executed and delivered, conveys title to or an interest in real estate.

deed restriction   An imposed restriction in a deed for the purpose of limiting the use of the land by future owners.

default   The nonperformance of a duty whether arising under a contract or otherwise; failure to meet an obligation when due.

deficiency judgment   A personal judgment levied against the mortgagor when a foreclosure sale does not produce sufficient funds to pay the mortgage debt in full.

delinquent taxes   Unpaid past-due taxes.

delivery   The transfer of the possession of a thing from one person to another.

delivery and acceptance   Final action with a deed that transfers title.

demise   The transfer of property by lease.

demising clause   A clause in a lease whereby the landlord (lessor) leases and the tenant (lessee) takes the property depreciation.

Department of Environmental Protection (DEP) New Jersey agency overseeing natural resources.

depreciation   In appraisal, a loss of value in property due to any cause including physical deterioration, functional obsolescence, and locational obsolescence. For income tax purposes, yearly write-off of a percentage of the cost of a building as an expense.

developer   One who improves land with buildings, usually on a large scale, and sells to homeowners and/or investors.

devise   A gift of real property by will; the act of leaving real property by will.

devisor   One who leaves real estate by will.

discount points   An added loan fee charged by a lender to make the yield on a lower-than-market-value loan competitive with higher interest loans.

Do Not Call Registry   A registry established by the Federal Trade Commission that permits consumers to register their phone numbers to avoid sales calls.

dominant estate   A property that includes in its ownership the right to use an easement over another person's property for a specific purpose.

dominant tenement   *See* dominant estate.

dual agency   Representing both parties to a transaction.

due-on-sale clause   *See* alienation clause.

duress   Unlawful constraint or action exercised upon a person who is forced to perform an act against his or her will.

earnest money   Money deposited by a buyer that is applied to the purchase price if the sale is closed.

easement   A right to use the land of another for a specific purpose, as for a right-of-way or utilities; an incorporeal interest in land.

easement appurtenant   An easement that passes with the land when conveyed.

easement by necessity   An easement allowed by law as necessary for the full enjoyment of a parcel of real estate; for example, a right of ingress and egress over a grantor's land.

easement by prescription   An easement acquired by continuous, open, uninterrupted, exclusive, and adverse use of the property for the period of time prescribed by state law.

easement in gross   An easement that is not created for the benefit of any land owned by the owner of the easement but that attaches personally to the easement owner.

economic obsolescence   *See* external obsolescence.

electromagnetic fields   Energy fields generated by the movement of electrical currents.

electronic signature   A digital process used in place of manually signing a document that indicates acceptance (or rejection) of an agreement or record.

emblements   Growing crops, such as wheat and corn, that are produced annually through labor and industry; also called fructus industriales. Emblements are considered to be the personal property of a tenant.

eminent domain   The right of a government or quasi-public body to acquire property for public use through a court action called condemnation.

encroachment   The extension of an improvement beyond the land of the owner, illegally intruding on land of an adjoining owner.

encumbrance   Any claim by another—such as a mortgage, tax or judgment lien, an easement, encroachment, or a deed restriction on the use of the land—that may diminish the value of a property.

enforceable   Able to be enforced in a court of law through a suit for specific performance.

environmental impact study   Engineer's report often required before a building permit is issued.

equalization factor   Figure that adjusts assessments for varying community standards.

equitable title   The interest held by a vendee under a land contract or an installment contract; the equitable right to obtain absolute ownership to property when legal title is held in another's name.

equity   The interest or value that an owner has in property over and above any mortgage indebtedness and other liens.

equity of redemption   The right of an owner to reclaim property before it is sold through foreclosure by the payment of the debt, interest, and costs.

erosion   The gradual wearing away of land by water, wind, and general weather conditions; the diminishing of property caused by the elements.

errors and omissions (E&O) insurance   A form of malpractice insurance for real estate licensees.

escape clause   Protection for seller with a contract is subject to the sale of buyer's present home.

escheat   The reversion of property to the state or county, as provided by state law, in cases where a decedent dies intestate without heirs capable of inheriting or when the property is abandoned.

escrow closing The closing of a transaction through a third party called an escrow agent. Also can refer to earnest money deposits or to mortgagees trust account for insurance and tax payments.

estate The degree, quantity, nature, and extent of interest that a person has in real property.

estate at will *See* tenancy at will.

estate for years An interest for a certain, exact period of time in property leased for a specified consideration.

estoppel certificate A document in which a borrower certifies the amount he or she owes on a mortgage loan and the rate of interest.

eviction A legal process to oust a person from possession of real estate.

evidence of title Proof of ownership of property; commonly a certificate of title, a title insurance policy, an abstract of title with lawyers opinion, or a Torrens registration certificate.

exchange A transaction in which all or part of the consideration for the purchase of real property is the transfer of *like kind* property (for example, real estate for real estate).

exclusionary zoning Local regulations that discriminate, usually against low-income housing.

exclusive-agency listing A listing contract under which the owners appoint a real estate broker as their exclusive agent for a designated period of time to sell the property, on their stated terms, for a commission. The owners reserve the right to sell on their own without paying anyone a commission.

exclusive-right-to-sell listing A listing contract under which the owner appoints a real estate broker as his or her exclusive agent for a designated period of time, to sell the property on the owner's stated terms, and agrees to pay the broker a commission when the property is sold, whether by the broker, the owner, or another broker.

executed contract 1. A contract in which all parties have fulfilled their promises and thus performed the contract. 2. A signed contract.

execution The signing and delivery of an instrument. Also, a legal order directing an official to enforce a judgment against the property of a debtor.

executor A male person, corporate entity, or any other type of organization designated in a will to carry out its provisions.

executory contract A contract under which something remains to be done by one or more of the parties.

executrix A woman appointed to perform the duties of an executor.

express contract An oral or written contract in which the parties state the contract's terms and express their intentions in words.

external obsolescence Reduction in a property's value caused by factors outside the subject property such as social or environmental forces or objectionable neighboring property. Also called *locational obsolescence* or *economic obsolescence.*

facilitator *See* transaction broker.

Fair Housing Partnership An agreement between HUD and the National Association of REALTORS® to promote principles of fair housing to the public and within individual firms.

Fannie Mae (formerly Federal Home Loan Mortgage Corporation) Sets standards and buys mortgages.

Federal Housing Administration (FHA) Insures low-down-payment mortgages.

fee simple The maximum possible estate or right of ownership of real property, continuing forever. Sometimes called a *fee* or *fee simple absolute.*

FHA 203(b) The most popular FHA mortgage plan, with 3% or less as required down payment.

FHA loan A loan insured by the Federal Housing Administration and made by an approved lender in accordance with the FHAs regulations.

fiduciary One legally placed in a position of trust and confidence.

fiduciary relationship A relationship of trust and confidence as between trustee and beneficiary, attorney and client, or principal and agent.

fixture An item of personal property that has been converted to real property.

foreclosure A procedure whereby property pledged as security for a debt is sold to pay the debt in the event of default in payments or terms.

franchise An organization that leases a standardized trade name, operating procedures, supplies, and referral service to member real estate brokerages.

fraud   Intentional deception that harms another.

fraudulent misrepresentation   Intentional fraud and/or deliberate lying.

Freddie Mac (Federal Home Loan Mortgage Corporation)   Warehouses packages of mortgages.

freehold estate   An estate in land in which ownership is for an indeterminate length of time.

front foot   A standard measurement, one foot wide, of the width of land, applied at the frontage on its street line. Each front foot extends the depth of the lot.

functional obsolescence   A loss of value to an improvement to real estate due to becoming outdated, often caused by age or poor design.

future interest   A person's present right to an interest in real property that does not result in possession or enjoyment until some time in the future.

gap   A defect in the chain of title of a particular parcel of real estate; a missing document or conveyance that raises doubt as to the present ownership of the land.

general agent   One authorized to act for his or her principal in a wide range of matters.

general lien   Financial claim placed against all property owned by the debtor.

general partnership   Group in which each partner shares complete liability.

Ginnie Mae (Government National Mortgage Association)   Pools mortgages for investors.

Graduate, REALTOR® Institute (GRI)   Designation awarded by the National Association of REALTORS® after specific study.

graduated lease   A lease that provides for a graduated change at stated intervals in the amount of the rent to be paid; used largely in long-term leases.

grantee   A person who receives a conveyance of real property from the grantor.

granting clause   Words in a deed of conveyance that state grantor's intention to convey the property. This clause is generally worded as "convey and warrant," "grant," "grant, bargain, and sell," or the like.

grantor   The person transferring title to or an interest in real property to a grantee.

gross income   Total income from property before any expenses are deducted.

gross lease   A lease of property under which a landlord pays all property charges regularly incurred through ownership, such as repairs, taxes, and insurance.

gross rent multiplier   A figure used as a multiplier of the gross rental income of a property to produce an estimate of the property's value.

ground lease   A lease of land only, on which the tenant usually owns a building or constructs a building as specified in the lease.

Guaranty Fund   Money set aside to reimburse persons defrauded or badly served by real estate licensees.

guilty knowledge   Awareness of wrongdoing without any attempt to stop it.

habendum clause   That part of a deed beginning with the words "to have and to hold," following the granting clause, and defining the extent of ownership the grantor is conveying.

heir   One who inherits property under a will; one who will inherit under the state law of descent when someone dies intestate.

highest and best use   That possible use of land that would produce the greatest net income and thereby develop the highest land value.

holdover tenancy   A tenancy whereby a lessee retains possession of leased property after his or her lease has expired and the landlord, by continuing to accept rent, agrees to the tenant's continued occupancy.

holographic will   A will that is written, dated, and signed in the testator's handwriting but is not witnessed.

home equity loan   Additional financing for homeowner; type of second mortgage.

homeowners' association   A nonprofit group of homeowners in a condominium, cooperative, or PUD that administers common elements and enforces covenants, conditions, and restrictions.

Horizontal Properties Act   Law regulating the creation of condominiums.

hypothecation   A pledge of property as security for a loan without giving up possession of it.

impact fees   Charges to developers for extra roads, expanded schools, etc.

implied contract   A contract under which the agreement of the parties is demonstrated by their acts and conduct.

implied warranty of habitability   Landlord's responsibility for decent living conditions.

improvement   Any structure erected on a site to enhance the value of the property—buildings, fences, driveways, curbs, sidewalks, or sewers.

income capitalization approach   The process of estimating the value of an income-producing property by capitalization of the annual net income expected to be produced by the property during its remaining useful life.

independent contractor   Salesperson who sets his or her own hours and who is not covered by income tax withholding; contrasted with an employee.

innocent misrepresentation   Unintentional misleading of a buyer committed in ignorance.

in rem   A proceeding against realty directly as distinguished from a proceeding against a person.

installment contract   *See* contract for deed.

installment sale   A method of reporting income received from the sale of real estate when the sales price is paid in two or more installments over two or more years.

instrument   A written legal document.

interim financing   Bridge or swing loan to cover the gap between purchase of a new home and sale of the old one.

intestate   The condition of a property owner who dies without leaving a valid will.

inverse condemnation suit   The action taken by a property owner when a government action severely limits how the property may be used.

involuntary lien   A lien imposed against property without consent of the owners; e.g., taxes, special assessments.

ISRA   The Industrial Site Recovery Act, a New Jersey statute that provides for mandatory cleanup of industrial and some commercial sites when they are closed, sold, or otherwise change ownership.

joint tenancy   Ownership of real estate between two or more parties who have been named in one conveyance specifically as joint tenants. Upon the death of a joint tenant, his or her interest passes to the surviving joint tenant or tenants.

joint venture   The joining of two or more people to conduct a specific business enterprise.

judgment   The formal decision of a court regarding the respective claims of the parties to an action. After a judgment has been recorded, it usually becomes a general lien on the property of the defendant.

jumbo loan   Loan for a higher amount than those generally bought by the secondary market.

junior lien   An obligation such as a second mortgage that is subordinate in priority to an existing lien on the same realty.

laches   Loss of a legal right through undue delay in asserting it.

land   The earth's surface, extending downward to the center of the earth and upward infinitely into space.

land contract   *See* contract for deed.

landlord   One who rents property to another.

latent defect   Problem with property not discoverable by ordinary prudent inspection.

Law Against Discrimination   New Jersey's law listing protected classes for fair housing practice.

law of agency   *See* agent.

lead   Once used as a pigment and drying agent in alkyd oil-based paint, exposure to lead has been linked to serious brain, kidney, nervous system, and blood damage. Lead-based paint has been banned since 1978. Other sources of lead exposure include plumbing, incinerators, and lead-based gasoline. Federal law requires the disclosure of known lead-based paint in a property.

lease   A written or oral contract between a landlord (the lessor) and a tenant (the lessee) that transfers the right to exclusive possession and use of the landlord's real property to the lessee for a specified period of time and for a stated consideration (rent).

leasehold estate   A tenant's right to occupy real estate during the term of a lease; generally considered to be personal property.

legacy   A disposition of money or personal property by will.

legal description   A description of a specific parcel of real estate complete enough for an independent surveyor to locate and identify it.

letter of intent A nonbinding (usually) recitation of what the parties intend to do, preceding entering into a contract.

leverage The use of borrowed money to finance investments.

license 1. A privilege or right granted to a person by a state to operate as a real estate broker or salesperson. 2. The revocable permission for a temporary use of land.

lien A right given by law to certain creditors to have their debt paid out of the property of a defaulting debtor, usually by means of a court sale.

life estate An interest in real or personal property that is limited in duration to the lifetime of its owner or some other designated person.

life tenant A person in possession of a life estate.

like-kind property *See* exchange.

limited liability company (LLC) Organization that combines the simplicity and tax treatment of a partnership with the protection from liability offered by a corporation.

liquidated damages Sum agreed upon to serve as compensation if one party defaults.

liquidity The ability to sell an asset and convert it into cash at a price close to its true value in a short period of time.

lis pendens A recorded legal document giving constructive notice that court action affecting a particular property is pending.

listing agreement A contract between a property owner (as principal) and a licensed real estate broker (as agent) by which the broker is employed as agent to sell real estate on the owner's terms within a given time, for which service the landowner agrees to pay a commission or fee.

listing broker The broker in a multiple listing situation, from whose office a listing agreement is initiated, as opposed to the selling broker, from whose office negotiations leading up to a sale are initiated.

littoral rights 1. A landowner's claim to use water in large navigable lakes and oceans adjacent to his or her property. 2. The ownership rights to land bordering these bodies of water up to the mean high-water mark.

Loan Estimate A three-page, TRID-required document that itemizes important details of the mortgage loan; lender must provide the borrower within three business days after receiving the borrower's Intent to Proceed.

loan-to-value (LTV) Ratio between property's value and the amount lent on it.

locational obsolescence *See* external obsolescence.

marginal tax rate The rate at which the investor's top dollar is taxed.

marketable title Good or clear title reasonably free from the risk of litigation over possible defects.

market data approach *See* sales comparison approach.

market value The probable price a ready, willing, able, and informed buyer would pay and a ready, willing, able, and informed seller would accept, neither being under any pressure to act, and after allowing for a reasonable exposure on the market.

master plan A comprehensive plan to guide the long-term physical development of a particular area.

mechanic's lien *See* construction lien.

Megan's Law A New Jersey law requiring that communities be alerted to the presence of convicted sex offenders. All contracts and leases must include a Megan's Law Statement advising purchasers and lessees that a list of any known sex offenders who live in the area may be obtained from the county prosecutor.

metes and bounds A legal description of a parcel of land that begins at a well-marked point and follows the boundaries, using direction and distances around the tract back to the place of beginning.

mill One-tenth of one cent. A tax rate of 52 mills would be $0.052 tax for each dollar of assessed valuation of a property.

mineral rights Subsurface rights, which can be sold or retained separately.

minor A person under 18 years of age.

MIP Mortgage insurance premium.

month-to-month tenancy A periodic tenancy; that is, the tenant rents for one period at a time. In the absence of a rental agreement (oral or written), a tenancy is generally considered to be month to month.

monument A fixed natural or artificial object used to establish real estate boundaries for a metes-and-bounds description.

moratorium A halt to development, often temporary.

mortgage A conditional transfer or pledge of real estate as security for the payment of a debt. Also, the document creating a mortgage lien.

mortgage banker Institution set up to make mortgage loans.

mortgagee A lender in a mortgage loan transaction.

mortgage lien Lender's claim against specific parcel of real estate pledged as security for a debt.

mortgage reduction certificate An instrument executed by the mortgagee, setting forth the present status and the balance due on the mortgage as of the date of the execution of the instrument.

mortgagor A borrower who conveys his or her property as security for a loan.

Mount Laurel I & II A judicial interpretation that requires local zoning boards to provide realistic opportunities for housing that low- to moderate-income households can afford.

multiple listing service (MLS) An organization in which brokers share listings with each other.

National Association of REALTORS® Private nationwide organization of salespersons and brokers.

negative amortization Gradual building up of a large mortgage debt when payments are not sufficient to cover interest due and reduce the principal.

negligent misrepresentation Fraud committed, not necessarily on purpose, by someone who should have known better.

net lease A lease requiring the tenant to pay not only rent but also some or all costs of maintaining the property, such as taxes, insurance, utilities, and repairs.

net listing A listing based on the net price the seller will receive if the property is sold. Under a net listing the broker is free to offer the property for sale at the highest price he or she can get to increase the commission. This type of listing is illegal in New Jersey.

New Jersey Association of REALTORS® Statewide group of real estate licensees who choose to join the organization.

New Jersey Housing and Mortgage Finance Agency Lender of low-interest mortgage money in certain target areas.

New Jersey Real Estate Commission Administrator of real estate licenses.

nonconforming use A use of property that is permitted to continue after a zoning ordinance prohibiting it has been established for the area.

note An instrument of credit given to attest a debt.

novation Substitution of a new contract for an existing one.

obsolescence *See* external obsolescence, locational obsolescence, functional obsolescence.

offer and acceptance Two essential components of a valid contract; a "meeting of the minds," when all parties agree to exact terms.

off-site conditions In New Jersey, licensees must disclose conditions beyond the limits of a property, such as a hazardous waste disposal site, that may be considered material facts by a prospective purchaser.

open-end mortgage A mortgage loan that is expandable back to its original amount after the principal has been reduced.

open listing A listing contract under which the broker's commission is contingent upon the broker's producing a ready, willing, and able buyer before the property is sold by the owner or another broker.

option An agreement to keep open for a set period an offer to sell or purchase property.

package loan A method of financing in which the loan that finances the purchase of a home also finances the purchase of certain items of personal property, such as a refrigerator, stove, and other specified appliances.

parcel A specific piece of real estate.

parol evidence rule Agreement that the written contract overrides spoken promises.

partition The division that is made of real property between those who own it in undivided shares.

partnership An association of two or more individuals who carry on a continuing business for profit as co-owners. A *general partnership* is a typical form of joint venture, in which each general partner shares in the administration, profits, and losses of the operations. A *limited partnership* is administered by one or more general partners and funded by limited or silent partners who are by law responsible for losses only to the extent of their investments.

party wall A building wall that is located on or at a boundary line between two adjoining parcels of land and is used by the owners of both properties.

percentage lease   A lease commonly used in malls; rent is based on the tenant's gross sales.

percolation test   Investigation of soil absorption and drainage.

periodic estate   An interest in leased property that continues from period to period—week to week, month to month or year to year.

personal property   All property that is not real property.

physical deterioration   Loss of value due to wear and tear or action of the elements.

PITI   Principal, interest, taxes, and insurance: components of a regular mortgage payment.

Planned Real Estate Development Act   Land requiring registration of certain developments in New Jersey.

planned unit development (PUD)   A planned combination of diverse land uses such as housing, recreation, and shopping, in one contained development or subdivision.

planning board   Municipal body overseeing orderly development of real estate.

plat   A map of a town, section, or subdivision indicating the location and boundaries of individual properties.

point   A unit of measurement used for various loan charges; one point equals 1% of the amount of the loan. *See also* discount points.

point of beginning (POB)   In a metes-and-bounds legal description, the starting point of the survey, situated in one corner of the parcel. Also called *place of beginning*.

police power   The government's right to impose laws, statutes, and ordinances, including zoning ordinances and building codes, to protect the public health, safety, and welfare.

portfolio loan   Loan not intended for sale in the secondary market.

power of attorney   A written instrument authorizing a person, the *attorney-in-fact*, to act as agent on behalf of another person.

premises   Lands and tenements; an estate; the subject matter of a conveyance.

prepayment clause   A clause in a mortgage that gives the mortgagor the privilege of paying the mortgage indebtedness before it becomes due.

prepayment penalty   A charge imposed on a borrower who pays off the loan principal early.

price-fixing   *See* antitrust laws.

primary mortgage market   Lenders who make individual loans directly to borrowers.

principal   1. A sum lent or employed as a fund or investment as distinguished from its income or profits. 2. The original amount (as in a loan) of the total due and payable at a certain date. 3. A main party of a transaction—the person for whom the agent works.

principal broker   *See* supervising broker.

private mortgage insurance (PMI)   Insurance that limits a lender's potential loss in a mortgage default, issued by a private company rather than by the FHA.

probate   The judicial proceeding to confirm the validity of a will.

probation   The least severe discipline available to the Real Estate Commission.

procuring cause   The broker responsible for bringing about a sale.

property manager   Someone who manages real estate for another person for compensation.

proprietary lease   A written lease in a cooperative apartment building, held by the tenant/shareholder, giving the right to occupy a particular unit.

prorations   Expenses, either prepaid or paid in arrears, that are divided or distributed between buyer and seller at the closing.

prospectus   A printed statement disclosing all material aspects of a real estate project.

protected class   Specific group that must receive equal treatment in housing.

public records   County's collection of documents relating to real estate.

puffing   Exaggerated or superlative comments or opinions made to induce buyers to buy, not as representations of fact and thus not grounds for misrepresentation.

pur autre vie   For the life of another. A life estate pur autre vie is a life estate that is measured by the life of a person other than the life tenant.

purchase-money mortgage A note secured by a mortgage given by a buyer, as mortgagor, to a seller, as mortgagee. Also any mortgage for purchase rather than refinancing.

qualifying ratio Percentage of income a borrower is allowed to spend on mortgage payments.

quiet enjoyment The right of an owner or a person legally in possession to the use of property without interference of possession.

quiet title suit *See* suit to quiet title.

quitclaim deed A conveyance by which the grantor transfers whatever interest he or she has in the real estate, if any, without warranties or obligations.

radon A naturally occurring radioactive gas that is suspected of causing lung cancer.

rate lock A guarantee by the lender to issue the loan at the quoted interest rate; under some conditions, the rate can still change.

ready, willing, and able buyer One who is prepared to buy property on the seller's terms and is ready to take positive steps to consummate the transaction.

real estate A portion of the earth's surface extending downward to the center of the earth and upward infinitely into space including all things permanently attached thereto, whether by nature or by a person.

real estate broker Any person, partnership, association, or corporation who sells (or offers to sell), buys (or offers to buy), or negotiates the purchase, sale, or exchange of real estate, or who leases (or offers to lease) or rents (or offers to rent) any real estate or the improvements thereon for others and for a compensation or valuable consideration.

real estate investment trust (REIT) Trust ownership of real estate by a group of at least 100 individuals who purchase certificates of ownership in the trust.

Real Estate License Act, Title 45, Chapter 15 The law governing real estate practice in New Jersey.

real estate referral company A real estate firm that only engages in listing rental units to find prospective tenants.

Real Estate Sales Full Disclosure Act Regulation covering the sales of out-of-state property in New Jersey.

Real Estate Settlement Procedures Act (RESPA) Federal law regulating real estate closings.

real property Real estate plus all the interests, benefits and rights inherent in ownership. Often referred to as *real estate*.

REALTOR® A registered trademark reserved for the sole use of members of the National Association of REALTORS®.

REALTOR-ASSOCIATE® Salesperson associated with a REALTOR® who joins the national and state associations of REALTORS®.

Realty Transfer Fee (RTF) A seller fee, a prerequisite for recording the deed. Funds are shared between state and county, generally used for neighborhood revitalization, shore protection, and the state's general fund.

reconciliation The final step in the appraisal process, in which the appraiser reconciles the estimates of value received from the direct sales comparison data, cost, and income approaches to arrive at a final estimate of value for the subject property.

recording The act of entering documents affecting or conveying interests in real estate in the recorder's office established in each county.

rectangular survey system A system established in 1785 by the federal government providing for surveying and describing land by reference to principal meridians and base lines, outside the 13 original colonies.

redemption period A period of time established by state law during which a property owner has the right to redeem his or her real estate from a tax sale by paying the sales price, interest, and costs.

redlining The illegal practice of a lending institution's denying loans or restricting their number for certain areas of a community.

referral fee Part of a commission or fee shared with a broker who sends a client or customer to an agent.

Regulation Z Implements the Truth in Lending Act.

release The act or writing by which some claim or interest is surrendered to another.

remainder interest The remnant of an estate that has been conveyed to take effect and be enjoyed after the termination of a prior estate, as when an owner conveys a life estate to one party and the remainder to another.

remainderman The person who is to receive the property after the death of a life tenant.

rent A fixed, periodic payment made by a tenant of a property to the owner for possession and use, usually by prior agreement of the parties.

REO (real estate-owned) Property acquired by banks and other lenders through foreclosures.

replacement cost The construction cost at current prices of a property that is not necessarily an exact duplicate of the subject property but serves the same purpose or function as the original.

reproduction cost The construction cost at current prices of an exact duplicate of the subject property.

restriction A limitation on the use of real property, generally originated by the owner or subdivider in a deed.

return The income from a real estate investment, calculated as a percentage of cash invested.

reverse discrimination Also called *benign discrimination*. Housing discrimination, usually based on quotas, designed by a municipality to achieve a racial balance perceived as desirable.

reverse mortgage Mortgage through which an elderly homeowner can draw against equity, building up a gradual debt with no repayments until moving out.

reversion The remnant of an estate that the grantor holds after he or she has granted a life estate to another person, if the estate will return, or revert, to the grantor; also called a reverter.

reversionary interest An owner's right to regain possession of leased property upon termination of the lease agreement.

revocation An act of recalling a power of authority conferred, as the revocation of a power of attorney, a license, or an agency.

right-of-way The right to pass over another's land.

riparian rights An owner's rights in land that borders on or includes a stream, river, or, in New Jersey, any tidal waters. These rights include access to and use of the water.

sale and leaseback A transaction in which an owner sells his or her improved property and, as part of the same transaction, signs a long-term lease to remain in possession of the premises.

sales comparison approach The process of estimating the value of a property by examining and comparing actual sales of comparable properties.

sales contract A contract containing the complete terms of the agreement between buyer and seller for the purchase of a particular parcel of real estate.

salesperson A person who performs real estate activities while employed by or associated with a licensed real estate broker.

salesperson licensed with a real estate referral company (SLWRERC) A person who is authorized to only make referrals and no other real estate activity. This person is not required to complete continuing education hours unless/until they wish to change to another New Jersey license type.

satisfaction of mortgage Lender's statement that the debt has been paid in full.

satisfaction piece A document acknowledging the payment of a debt.

secondary mortgage market A market for the purchase and sale of existing mortgages, designed to provide greater liquidity of mortgages and increase the amount of mortgage money available to purchasers.

section A portion of a township under the rectangular survey (government survey) system. A section is a square with mile-long sides and an area of one square mile, or 640 acres.

seisin The possession of land by one who claims to own at least an estate for life therein.

selling broker *See* listing broker.

servient estate Land on which an easement exists in favor of an adjacent property (called a dominant estate); also called *servient tenement*.

setback The amount of space local zoning regulations require between a lot line and a building line.

severalty Ownership of real property by one person only; also called *sole ownership*.

shared equity mortgage A mortgage loan in which the lender, in exchange for a loan with a favorable interest rate, participates in the profits (if any) the mortgagor receives when the property is eventually sold.

sheriff's sale Auction of foreclosed property.

short sale A sale in which the lender agrees to accept whatever the property brings on the open market and lift the mortgage lien so the sale can close.

sole proprietorship Ownership of a business by one person.

special agent One authorized by a principal to perform a single act or transaction.

special assessment A tax or levy customarily imposed against only those specific parcels of real estate that benefit from a public improvement like a street or sewer.

specific lien   A lien affecting or attaching only to a certain, specific parcel of land or piece of property.

specific performance   A legal remedy whereby one party seeks to force another party to perform the promises specifically made in the contract.

specific performance suit   A legal action brought in a court of equity in special cases to compel a party to carry out the terms of a contract.

standard of care   Degree of competence normally expected of a licensee.

statute of frauds   The part of state law requiring certain instruments such as deeds, real estate sales contracts, and certain leases to be in writing for them to be legally enforceable.

statute of limitations   That law pertaining to the period of time within which certain actions can be brought to court.

statutory lien   A lien imposed on property by statute—a tax lien, for example—in contrast to a voluntary lien such as a mortgage lien that an owner places on his or her own real estate.

steering   The illegal practice of channeling home seekers to particular areas for discriminatory ends.

straight-line method   A method of calculating cost recovery for tax purposes, computed by dividing the adjusted basis of a property by the number of years chosen.

straight (term) loan   Interest-only mortgage.

subagent   A broker's sales associate, or cooperating broker in a multiple listing system, in relationship to the principal who has designated the broker as an agent.

subdivision   The division of a parcel of land into two or more parcels; a tract of land divided by the owner, known as the *subdivider*, into blocks, building lots, and streets according to a recorded subdivision plat that must comply with local ordinances and regulations.

subletting   The leasing of premises by a tenant to a third party for part of the tenant's remaining term, or the leasing of a part of the premises for the entire term. *See also* assignment.

subordination   Relegation to a lesser position, usually in respect to a right or security.

subordination agreement   Lien holder's agreement to give up priority.

subrogation   The substitution of one creditor for another with the substituted person succeeding to the legal rights and claims of the original claimant.

substitution   An appraisal principle stating that the maximum value of a property tends to be set by the cost of purchasing an equally desirable and valuable substitute property.

subsurface rights   Ownership rights in a parcel of real estate of any water, minerals, gas, oil, and so forth that lie beneath the surface of the property.

suit for possession   Landlord's court action to evict tenant.

suit to quiet title   A court action intended to establish or settle the title to a particular property, especially when there is a cloud on the title.

Superfund   Popular name of the hazardous-waste cleanup fund established by CERCLA.

supervising broker   The one broker registered with the Department of State as in charge of a real estate office, responsible for the actions of salespersons and associate brokers.

surface rights   Ownership rights in a parcel of real estate that are limited to the surface of the property and do not include the air above it (air rights) or the minerals below the surface (subsurface rights).

surrender   The cancellation of a lease by mutual consent of the lessor and the lessee.

survey   The process by which a parcel of land is measured and its area ascertained; also, the map showing the measurements, boundaries, and area.

suspension   The temporary lifting of a real estate license by the commission.

syndicate   A combination of people or firms formed to accomplish a joint venture of mutual interest.

tacking   Adding or combining successive periods of continuous occupation of real property by several different adverse possessors.

target areas   Neighborhoods in which the state wishes to strengthen housing stock.

tax credit   Direct deduction from tax due.

tax deed   An instrument, similar to a certificate of sale, given to a purchaser at a tax sale.

tax foreclosure Seizing of property for unpaid taxes.

tax lien A charge against property created by operation of law. Tax liens and assessments take priority over all other liens.

tax rate The rate at which real property is taxed in a tax district or county. For example, real property may be taxed at a rate of 0.056 cents per dollar of assessed valuation (56 mills).

tax sale A court-ordered sale of real property to raise money to cover delinquent taxes.

tax shelter An investment yielding paper losses that may be used to shield other income from taxation. In real estate, often the result of *depreciation*.

tenancy at sufferance A situation in which a tenant comes into possession of land by lawful title and keeps it afterward without any right at all.

tenancy at will An estate that gives the lessee the right to possession until the estate is terminated by either party; the term of this estate is indefinite.

tenancy by the entirety The joint ownership of property acquired by husband and wife during marriage. Upon the death of one spouse, the survivor becomes the owner of the property.

tenancy in common A form of co-ownership by which each owner holds an undivided interest in real property as if he or she were sole owner. Each individual owner has the right to partition. Tenants in common have no right of survivorship.

tenancy in severalty Ownership of property by one person only.

tenant One who holds or possesses lands or tenements by any kind of right or title.

testator One who makes and signs a will.

testers Members of civil rights and neighborhood organizations, often volunteers, who observe real estate offices to assess compliance with fair housing laws.

time is of the essence A phrase in a contract that requires the performance of a certain act within a stated period of time.

time-sharing Ownership of real estate for only a portion of the year.

title Evidence that the owner of land is in lawful possession thereof; evidence of ownership.

title insurance policy A policy insuring the owner or mortgagee against loss by reason of defects in the title to a parcel of real estate, other than the encumbrances, defects, and matters specifically excluded by the policy.

title search An examination of the public records to determine the ownership and encumbrances affecting real property.

Title VIII Section of federal Civil Rights Act covering housing.

Torrens system A method of evidencing title by registration with the proper public authority, generally called the registrar.

township The principal unit of the rectangular survey (government survey) system, a square with six-mile sides and an area of 36 square miles.

trade fixtures Articles installed by a tenant under the terms of a lease and removable by the tenant before the lease expires.

transaction broker A licensee who works with a buyer, seller, or both, without representing either one in an agency relationship.

transfer tax Tax required to be paid on a deed by state and/or local law.

trespass An unlawful intrusion upon another's property.

TRID An acronym for the rule that combines the disclosures required by the Truth in Lending Act (TILA) and the Real Estate Settlement Procedures Act (RESPA).

triggering terms Words in an advertisement that require disclosure of all financing conditions.

trust A fiduciary arrangement whereby property is conveyed to a person or institution, called a trustee, to be held and administered on behalf of another person, called a *beneficiary*.

trust account Escrow account for money belonging to another.

trust deed An instrument used to create a mortgage lien by which the mortgagor conveys his or her title to a trustee, who holds it as security for the benefit of the note holder (the lender); also called a *deed of trust*.

trustee *See* trust.

Truth in Lending Act A federal law that obligates a lender to fully disclose in writing all fees, terms, and conditions associated with obtaining credit.

Truth-in-Renting   New Jersey requirement that tenants be informed of their rights; the notice must be available in English and Spanish.

UFFI   Urea-formaldehyde foam insulation has been linked to cancer in animals, although its effect on humans is uncertain.

underwriting   Process of deciding whether to make a specific loan.

undivided interest   *See* tenancy in common.

unenforceable contract   A contract that seems on the surface to be valid, yet neither party can sue the other to force performance of it.

Uniform Commercial Code (UCC)   A codification of commercial law, adopted in most states, that attempts to make uniform all laws relating to commercial transactions, including chattel mortgages and bulk transfers.

Uniform Construction Code   New Jersey's standards for building.

Uniform Settlement Statement   Standard HUD-1, required to be furnished to buyer and seller.

unilateral contract   An agreement that is binding on only one of the parties.

unity of ownership   The four unities traditionally needed to create a joint tenancy—unity of time, title, interest, and possession.

useful life   In real estate investment, the number of years a property is useful to the investors.

usury   Charging interest at a rate higher than the maximum established by law.

valid contract   A contract that complies with all the essentials of a contract and is binding and enforceable on all parties to it.

valuation   Estimated worth or price. The act of valuing by appraisal.

value   The power of a good or service to command other goods in exchange for the present worth of future rights to its income or amenities.

VA mortgage   A mortgage loan on approved property made to a qualified veteran by an authorized lender and guaranteed by the Department of Veterans Affairs.

variance   Permission obtained from zoning authorities to build a structure or conduct a use that is expressly prohibited by the current zoning laws; an exception from the zoning ordinances.

vendee   A buyer under a land contract or contract of sale.

vendor   A seller under a land contract or contract of sale.

voidable contract   A contract that seems to be valid on the surface but may be rejected or disaffirmed by one of the parties.

void contract   A contract that has no legal force or effect because it does not meet the essential elements of a contract.

voluntary lien   Financial claim placed against property by the owner.

waiver   The renunciation, abandonment, or surrender of some claim, right, or privilege.

Waiver of Broker Cooperation   Seller's statement that only one office will be marketing the property.

warranty deed (full covenant and warranty deed)   A deed in which the grantor fully warrants good clear title to the premises.

waste   An improper use or an abuse of a property by a possessor who holds less-than-fee ownership, such as a tenant, life tenant, mortgagor, or vendee.

will   A written document, properly witnessed, providing for the transfer of title to property owned by the deceased, called the *testator*.

wraparound mortgage   An additional mortgage in which another lender refinances a borrower by lending an amount including the existing first mortgage amount without disturbing the existence of the first mortgage.

Your Home Loan Toolkit: A Step-by-Step Guide   A 28-page booklet issued by the Consumer Financial Protection Bureau that discusses the process of obtaining the best mortgage, understanding closing costs, and ways to be a successful homeowner.

zone   An area set off by the proper authorities for specific use subject to certain restrictions or restraints.

zoning ordinance   An exercise of police power by a municipality to regulate and control the character and use of property.

INDEX